Jasmine, it was an honor ·
tell your story

Best Wishes,

Ron Eaton

Local Legends II

BY RON EATON

THE STORIES CONTINUE

Vincennes

Washington

Mt. Carmel, IL   Jasper

Princeton

Mt. Vernon   Evansville   Rockpo

Gracie Lachowecki

Alisa Raymond

Castle Knights

Shannon Emmons

Deke Cooper

North High S

Clint Keown

BRYCE BROWN

John Schmitt

The Winsett Sisters

Volleyball   Boonville High Schoo

The Zeller Family

The McIntosh Brothers

pions Reitz High School

Golf   Jerry Schreiber

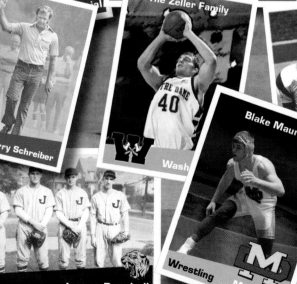

Wash

Blake Maurer

Evansville College Football

Jasper Baseball

Wrestling   Mater Dei

Gibson Southern Softball

FOREWORD

Even before he published *Local Legends: The Stories Behind the Headlines* in 2008, Ron Eaton realized there were far too many outstanding athletes and great teams from Southern Indiana – past and present – to capture in one book.

In *Local Legends II: The Stories Continue*, Eaton does much of the catching up.

The first "Legends" book provided outstanding details about some of the area's sports celebrities – people like legendary University of Evansville basketball coach Arad McCutchan, New York Yankees great Don Mattingly (now manager of the Los Angeles Dodgers) and quarterback Bob Griese, who won two Super Bowls in the '70s with the Miami Dolphins.

While working for Florida newspapers, I had the opportunity to first meet two of those legends – Griese, while covering the 1978 Pro Bowl in Tampa, and Mattingly during spring training in the mid-'80s.

Neither interview lasted long enough to get around to asking about high school heroics and hometown memories, though. So it wasn't until I decided to relocate to Evansville in 2007 that it dawned on me that Mattingly and Griese were both from here.

Of course, that was back when everything I knew about Evansville came from reading chamber of commerce brochures and Wikipedia.

The first "Legends" book filled me in on more of the area's rich athletic history, providing insight into dozens of other hometown heroes from Southern Indiana and the rest of the Tri-state region. The chapters on Aces basketball greats Jerry Sloan, Larry Humes and Don Buse gave me a greater appreciation for my new hometown.

The book also helped me realize that Southern Indiana's athletic roots run deep in basketball, football, baseball, tennis, golf and soccer and compare favorably with any other place I've lived in Florida and South Carolina.

Legends II brings that rich history to the present.

You will read about local golfing legends Jerry Schreiber and Kevin Wassmer, football standouts Deke Cooper and Curtis Painter, as well as basketball brothers Luke, Tyler and Cody Zeller.

Eaton even tackles the still developing stories of many of this generation's outstanding high school and college athletes.

By the time their stories are complete, Eaton may even have to consider compiling a third "Legends" book.

Randy Beard

(Randy Beard is the sports editor of the Evansville Courier & Press and has covered sports for 36 years in Florida, South Carolina and southwestern Indiana.)

Front Cover Photo Credits:

Bryce Brown – Texas Tech Athletics Communications
Gracie Lachowecki – Bill Vieth Sr.
Deke Cooper – Evansville Courier
The Emmons Sisters – Janet Metzger
John Schmitt – Purdue University, Sports Information

Evansville College Football – University of Evansville, Sports Information
Blake Maurer – Evansville Courier
Jerry Schreiber – Evansville Courier
Luke Zeller – Notre Dame, Media Relations

M.T. Publishing Company, Inc.™

P.O. Box 6802, Evansville, Indiana 47719-6802
www.mtpublishing.com

No part of this publication may be translated, reproduced or transmitted in any form or by any means, electronic or mechanical, including photocopying and recording, or by any information storage and retrieval system, without expressed written permission of the copyright owner and M.T. Publishing Company, Inc.

The materials for this book were compiled and produced using available information. Although every reasonable effort has been made to be as accurate as possible about descriptions of events and photos, discrepancies in recorded history and human error are always possible; therefore, neither M.T. Publishing Company, Inc. nor anyone involved with the creation of this book shall be held responsible for any inaccuracies in the content.

Printed in the United States of America.

Out of the first 500 books printed, this book is number 305 .

Copyright © 2012
Ron Eaton
All rights reserved.

Library of Congress Control Number:
2012947841

ISBN: 978-1-934729-98-4

Graphic Design by:
Alena Kiefer,
M.T. Publishing Company, Inc.

TABLE OF CONTENTS

TEST YOUR LOCAL SPORTS IQ

Before you dig into *Local Legends II*, try this quiz and see how your knowledge of local sports history stacks up with your friends'. There are 50 questions worth 200 points. Unless otherwise noted, they are current as of 2012 and pertain to a geographic area roughly inside a perimeter from Mt. Vernon north to Vincennes then east to Jasper and south to Tell City, with a short detour into Mt. Carmel, Illinois. Get out a piece of paper, number to 50 and then give yourself 15 minutes. Good luck!

1-POINT QUESTIONS

1. In 2012, who became the only athlete in Evansville history to be named the All-Metro Player of the Year in both football and basketball in the same year?
2. What area girl was on pace in 2012 to become the all-time career scoring leader in Illinois girls basketball history?
3. What area high school basketball team started three brothers in 2011-'12?
4. What basketball team of the 1950s also started three brothers?
5. What track coach holds the record for the most sectional wins?
6-9. (1 point each) Name the four female basketball players from Memorial to make the Indiana All-Stars.
10. What Huntingburg native played on the 1971 national championship Aces basketball team?
11. In 2011, what was the last name of the three local brothers who qualified for the State wrestling meet?

3-POINT QUESTIONS

12. What was the first Evansville school to capture an IHSAA football State championship?
13. What school's golf team was the first to win an IHSAA boys State title?
14-17. (3 points each) Give the four years that at least one Zeller brother won a State title.
18. What area pitcher did Scott Rolen face in his second major league game?
19. Who is the only local wrestler to win four individual State wrestling titles?
20. What area golfer played on the PGA tour in the '80s and early '90s?
21. What area school won both the boys and girls State championship in the same sport in the same year?
22. Hurdler Bryce Brown attended two colleges in what state?
23. What local golfer played in the 2009 U.S. Open?
24. In 2009, what local basketball team became only the 12th Indiana team to finish a season undefeated?

25-27. (3 points each) Name the three men who have won the most City golf titles.
28. What area school was the last in Indiana to win the State baseball title in the 1-class system
29. Who was the pitching ace for Castle's 2001 State championship softball team?

5-POINT QUESTIONS

30-33. (5 points each) Name four of the five area basketball players to play in the NCAA Division I Final Four for schools other than IU or Kentucky.
34. What area school was the first Catholic school to reach the IHSAA Final Four in basketball?
35. What local running back ran for 2,203 yards in 2010?
36. Who is the only area athlete to win a cross country State championship?
37-43. (5 points each) Name the seven area high school quarterbacks to be ranked in Indiana's top 25 in career passing yardage.
44. What athlete for Bud Garland at Bosse could high jump nearly 7-feet and was a State champ in the 200-meter run?

10 POINTS QUESTIONS

45. What is the smallest area school to win a State basketball championship?
46. What local sportscaster worked at Channel 7 with Marcia Yockey for seven years?
47. What female swimmer held Harrison school records at every distance as of 2012?
48. What area man threw one of the most historic pitches in history after taking the mound in the 1954 World Series?
49. What boys basketball coach with at least ten years experience has the highest winning percentage?
50. What young lady from Washington High School is the only area female to score 40 or more points in the IHSAA tournament?

Now turn to page 6 to find out how well you know your local sports.

STATE CHAMP UPDATE

Since the release of the first book, more of our local athletes have distinguished themselves by earning the state's ultimate prize, a State championship. To honor these achievements, these area athletes and teams will appear throughout the pages of *Local Legends II*.

INTRODUCTION & DEDICATION

Here we go again!! After a brief period of sanity following the two-year effort to complete my first book, *Local Legends: The Stories behind the Headlines*, I began to feel the need to tell some of the stories that were left untold. So with the blessing of my wife, I embarked once again on a second journey.

This sequel travels back in time to honor more heroes from as far back as the 1950s, but it also pays tribute to athletes who are just beginning to shape their legacies. The geographic area covered is still southwestern Indiana with a slight detour into Mt. Carmel, Illinois for three stories I just had to tell.

As always, the book is dedicated to my wife of over thirty years, Suzy, and our three children, Kelly, Chase and Casey, who have always been there for support and encouragement. *Local Legends II* was written for true fans of local sports who dedicate parts of their lives to learning as much as they can about athletes and coaches from our little corner of the world.

As one might expect, more women are included in the sequel compared to the first because more of their stories have emerged since Title IX took effect in 1972, and sports like golf and softball are more prominent, as well. I was also pleased to reunite with MT Publishing, a local company that uses the talents of Alena Kiefer to produce such a beautiful finished product. As an added bonus, we were fortunate to feature the stylings of local artist Jon Siau, a legend himself whose drawings, like the one shown here of yours truly, add another dimension to the book. This book could not have been completed without the help of literally hundreds of folks whose time and effort produced crucial material to complete each story. As with the first book, I was continually grateful for the unselfish, gracious efforts of those who offered their support of my endeavor.

As I mentioned in the first book, a project like this is a challenge because there will always be subjects who were omitted but deserved to be included. Without a doubt, there were excellent athletes, coaches and teams that were left out for myriad reasons, and it should not be inferred that those included are necessarily more deserving. I do believe, however, that those who are in these pages are a good cross-section of the athletic culture and history of southwestern Indiana and Mt. Carmel. To those who feel snubbed, let me say that I totally understand, and as I said in the introduction to the first book, I sincerely apologize to anyone who feels they were overlooked.

Local Legends II is meant for those die-hard fans who appreciate fine performances and have deep emotions about local sports history. What makes sports so appealing are the underlying motivations behind each achievement, and I hope the book will bring a greater appreciation for these events that have meant so much to local fans. As the stories continue in these pages, my wish is that the book will help to bridge generations by using a love of sports as a means of preserving those memories that have meant so much to all of us.

Ron Eaton

Artwork by Jon Siau

SPECIAL THANKS...

A special thank you goes out to the local newspapers, including the *Princeton Clarion* and *Vincennes Sun Commercial*, for their assistance with information and photos. Many of the uncredited photos in the pages of this book were likely taken from the *Evansville Courier/Press/Sunday Courier & Press*, and the *Courier* was gracious once again in granting permission for the photos to be used.

Special thanks should also be offered to Mr. Jon Siau, a mega-talented artist who was the first person to be commissioned by the U.S. Olympic Committee to be a contributor to *The Olympian*, a publication that is distributed worldwide. Jon enhanced *Local Legends II* by offering his creative opinions and by allowing us to use a few of his works of art throughout this book.

LOCAL SPORTS QUIZ ANSWERS

1 POINT EACH

1. Jalen Pendleton
2. Tyra Buss
3. Harrison (Duncans)
4. Central (Claytons)
5. Charlie Siesky
6-9. Jill Hartman, Kate Endress, FahKara Malone, Mallory Ladd
10. John Wellemeyer
11. Welch (Doug, Chad & Luke)

3 POINTS EACH

12. Mater Dei (2000)
13. North (2000)
14-17. '05, '08, '10, '11
18. Andy Benes
19. Blake Maurer (Mater Dei)
20. Brian Tennyson
21. Memorial (soccer, '08)
22. Texas
23. David Erdy
24 Princeton
25-27. Jerry Schreiber, Kevin Wassmer, Ed Wolf
28. Jasper ('97)
29. Beth Harmon

5 POINTS EACH

30-33. Larry Weatherford (Purdue, 1969), Vaughn Wedeking & Greg Nelson (Jacksonville, 1970), Tyler Zeller (North Carolina, 2009), Kyle Kuric (Louisville, 2012)
34. Rex Mundi ('64)
35. Logan Hayford (Castle)
36. Jim Kaiser (Mater Dei, '87)
37-43. Jake Schiff (#1), Adam Schiff (#7), Grant Gribbons (#8), Dustin Slaton (#9), Chris Owen (#13), Joey Elliott (#18), Eric Goebel (#23)
44. Mack Jacobs

10 POINTS EACH

45. Vincennes Rivet girls ('11)
46. Jerry Birge
47. Leslie VanWinkle
48. Don Liddle
49. Joe Mullan (Bosse)
50. Gretchen Miles

Good-bye, old friend.
(Roberts Stadium photo courtesy of the University of Evansville, Sports Information)

LOCAL LEGENDS UPDATES

Life Goes on. Not surprisingly, since *Local Legends: The Stories behind the Headlines* first came out in 2009, the local sports landscape has changed. Some of the icons featured in the book are no longer with us, like Reitz football coach **Bob Padgett** and Bosse basketball great **Broc Jerrel**. Others who passed are **Eileen Volkman**, the mother of Ron, Mike and Dean, and **Gene Morgan**, a die-hard Huntingburg fan who helped tremendously with the Dubois County stories.

Calbert Cheaney came back 'home' when he joined Tom Crean's coaching staff at IU, and **Jamey Carroll** signed a well-deserved $6.25 million contract with the Twins. Memorial basketballer **FahKara Malone** also joined the coaching ranks when she accepted an assistant position at U of E, and Memorial baseball legend **Don Mattingly** is now the manager of the Los Angeles Dodgers. **Quentin Merkel**, Don's high school baseball coach, is still going strong and recently passed the 900-win mark, while popular Aces player **Steve Welmer** was forced to retire from officiating in 2011 because of a knee injury. Another significant retirement was that of iconic Heritage Hills football coach **Bob Clayton** who dominated the local football scene for 34 seasons.

Several subjects of *Local Legends* received additional accolades since the book's release. Two-time tennis State champ **Elissa Kim** will be inducted into the Indiana Tennis Hall of Fame in 2013, and **Woodie Sublett Walker** was inducted into the Midwest Tennis Hall of Fame. Two U of E athletes were also recognized when pitching sensation **Andy Benes**' #30 jersey was retired at U of E in April of 2010 and Reitz and UE basketball star **Shelly Brand** was inducted into the Indiana Basketball Hall of Fame in 2012. Memorial High School opened its brand new athletic hall of fame in January of 2012 with an inaugural class straight from the *Local Legends* pages. Committee chairman Robbie Kent and other members honored the following seven Memorial greats into the hall's first class: **Don Ping, Billy Hillenbrand, Bob Hargrave, Bill Vieth Sr., Larry Stallings, Gene Logel and Don Mattingly.**

The physical environs of the Evansville sports scene changed as well. Central Stadium, Reitz Bowl and Enlow Field were all adorned with new state-of-the-art scoreboards and artificial turf, and Harrison High School showed off its long over-due football facility for the 2011 season. North High grads said good-bye to the nostalgic building on Diamond Avenue as the brand new school with phenomenal athletic facilities greeted the student body in January of 2012.

Most significant among the changes was the abandonment of Roberts Stadium and the arrival of its replacement. On February 26, 2011, the final Aces men's game was played with a huge crowd looking on. In front of over 100 former players and thousands of emotional fans, Marty Simmons' team withstood the pressure and took care of business by defeating Illinois State 73-67 behind Colt Ryan's 32 points. In June of 2012, Mayor Lloyd Winnecke proposed the razing of the beloved building to make room for a green space and recreational area.

In the fall of 2011, a new era began as the Ford Center opened downtown. So as the wheels of time continue to roll and the old is replaced by the new, the world of local sports will continue to create new memories as well. And as these stories unfold, a whole new generation of local legends will be born.

Broc Jerrel

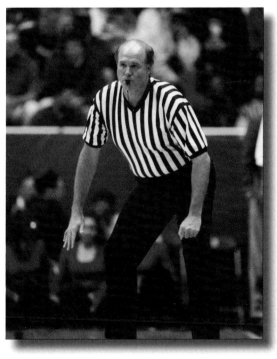

Steve Welmer

Jamey Carroll

Evansville College football star Ray Bawel of Boonville was part of a play that will live forever in the annals of Canadian Football League history. During the 1957 Grey Cup game, Bawel intercepted a pass and was streaking down the sideline for a score when Dave Humphrey, in front of the opponents' bench, tripped Bawel. Fortunately the play didn't affect the outcome as Bawel's Hamilton Tiger-Cats won 32-7.

IHSAA STATE CHAMPIONS UPDATE

FOOTBALL

Team	Year	Record	Coach
Reitz (4A)	2008	15-0	Tony Lewis
Reitz (4A)	2010	15-0	Tony Lewis

In the Company of Greatness
Former Boonville star Travis Williams once played in the same backfield as the legendary Jim Thorpe when they played for the Pine Village professional team in 1916.

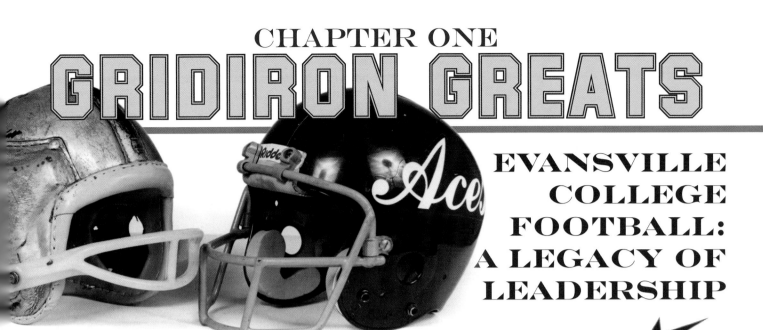

CHAPTER ONE
GRIDIRON GREATS

EVANSVILLE COLLEGE FOOTBALL: A LEGACY OF LEADERSHIP

A special thank you to Bob Boxell, former U of E sports information director, current director Bob Pristash and their staffs for much of the background information and to the LinC, the University of Evansville yearbook, for the photos for this story.

From a start in 1923 on a shoestring budget of $1,000 until the winter of 1996, hundreds of young men represented Evansville College/U of E on the gridiron, but the days of Purple Aces football are all but forgotten in the minds of most local sports fans. As everyone knows, football is a very expensive sport to maintain, and because of the number of players necessary, it is often difficult to compete with larger schools from larger cities. There is no question that Aces basketball has been the financial sugar daddy for all U of E sports over the years, but no sports program at the small private college has had a more dramatic impact on the local sports scene than football.

Evansville College itself was founded in 1854 as Moore's Hill College in Dearborn County Indiana. The college was moved to Evansville in 1919 and renamed. The college's first building was downtown before the liberal arts school was moved to its current location on the city's near east side.

In 1921, a group of students petitioned the school's business manager to fund a football program, and EC's first team took the field in 1923 under head coach John Harmon. Scraping together a team from only 160 male students, most of whom had never played the sport, Coach Harmon led the Aces to a 3-3-1 record.

The first local intercollegiate game was contested at Bosse Field on the Friday afternoon of October 18, 1921 against Union Christian College (no longer in existence) from Meron, Indiana. The game ended with Coach Harmon's boys winning 19-0, giving the program its first shutout.

The first football field was built on campus in the spring of 1924 at Walnut and Weinbach where Hughes Residence Hall now stands, but it was used primarily for practice. In 1926, lumber salvaged from a tabernacle that had been dismantled was used to build seating for 2,000. The first lights were 1500-watt bulbs inside old four-inch boiler tubes welded together on 28 poles, and it was not unusual for cold weather or snow to cause eight to ten lights to blow during a game.

In 1930, highly successful Reitz High School coach William V. Slyker took the helm for the Aces. Slyker could never duplicate his success at Reitz, winning only one-third of his games during a 13-year run that featured a dozen consecutive games where the Aces never scored.

World War II shortened the 1942 season to five games, and no football was played from '43 to '45 as many our boys left to serve our country. With returning vets forming the nucleus under new coach Don Ping, who had left his dominant program at Evansville Memorial, the program flourished and produced some of the best years in its history.

The 1949 team, still affectionately known as the 49ers, set a standard that stood for 25 years when they finished the season 8-2-1. Ping's years at the school were significant in many ways for the football program. Not only would he finish his 9-year term with a winning record (38-35-5), but the school would host some historic games and Ping would become an influence on young men who would serve the area for decades to come.

Throughout the late '40s and early '50s, the excitement for post-war football at Evansville College created a culture all its own, and students and the community showed their support. Some of the greatest memories of that era related to a window of time that saw the Pocket City in the spotlight for a good portion of the country from 1948 to 1956.

Before television placed its stranglehold on the football bowl scene each year, it was possible for a town the size of Evansville to host a bowl of its own. Because of the city's reputation as a producer of kitchen appliances, the game was christened the Refrigerator Bowl, and the inaugural game was possibly the most significant in EC/U of E football history.

In the winter of 1946, Reitz Bowl was rocking when Evansville College and Missouri Valley squared off in front of 7,500 fans. The Aces were given little chance against the powerful Vikings who hadn't tasted defeated in seven years, a streak of 41

First Lighted Field

INTERESTING TIDBIT

Former Aces coach Randy Rodgers had three sons in Austin, Texas. Jay Rodgers, the oldest, was All-State and played at Indiana, and middle son Jeff did well in Texas. Johnny, the youngest, was on his way to being the best of the bunch when he blew out a knee and was replaced by a little guy named Drew Brees. And the rest, as they say, is history.

straight games, but Don Ping's boys came through in a big way.

"Oh, that was a beautiful game," Jack Crouch told *Courier & Press* reporter Dave Johnson in the January 3 edition. "But we beat them and they were shocked."

On a cold but sunny afternoon, the Aces struck swiftly. In the first period, Aces halfback Gene Logel took a Tim Wright punt and returned it 85 yards for a score. The Aces then drove 94 yards in the second quarter for another touchdown, with Frank Endress plunging the final two yards, and then held on for a 13-7 win with Logel earning MVP honors.

A year later, Evansville College returned to the Bowl for a matchup with Hillsdale College out of Michigan, and the Aces made it two for two with a 22-7 win. Gene Logel, Mason Working and Johnny McDougal scored TDs with Ray Bawel (pronounced BAW•ble) taking home the W.A. Carson Most Valuable Player trophy. As a side note, Norma Jean Winternheimer, representing Seeger, was named Miss Refriger-adorable after defeating Jo Ritzert (International Harvester) and Doris Bradford (Servel).

Evansville College coaches Don Ping (seated), Paul Beck and Arad McCutchan (standing L-R) give instruction to an unknown player.

Though the Refrigerator Bowl was played for another seven years, the Aces never made the Bowl again, but the Ping era at EC left its mark on the program and the community. "The mentor, as we called him, was ahead of his time," said Ed Wessel to Dave Johnson in Dave's *Courier & Press* story. "We used the T (formation), the split-T, the Notre Dame box."

"Coach Ping used the spread offense before almost anybody else," added ex-fullback Morris Riley in the *Courier & Press* story. "We had the single wing, the double wing… It was wide open football. We were fun to watch."

Most would agree that the program at Evansville College/U of E always played a very ambitious schedule that made it tough to compete year after year. In fact, in the 50-plus years of football, the Aces finished with a winning record only 18 times. The first was in 1925 under John Harmon, and the next was 15 years later in 1940 under W.V. Slyker. Don Ping accomplished the feat in '46 (7-1-2), '48 (6-3) and '49 (8-2-1), and he was followed by Paul Beck who had assisted Ping for eight seasons. With the exception of 1957, when Forrest Page took over for a year, Beck led the program to winning seasons more than any coach, doing it six times during his 11 seasons, in 1954 (5-4), '55 (6-3), '59 (6-3), '60 (5-3), '64 (5-4) and '65 (5-4).

Coach Jim Byers followed Beck with winning seasons in 1970 (6-3), '74 (8-2) and '75 (7-3), and his 8-2 mark in '74 is on record as the best in the school's history. John Moses followed Byers from '77 to '79, and Randy Rodgers followed Moses for five years and had a winning season in 1982. Rodgers was succeeded by Dave Moore from '85-'90 with one winning season (5-3 in '88), and finally Robin Cooper took charge from '91-'96 with winning seasons in '92 (7-2) and '93 (6-4).

As the Aces program experienced moderate success in terms of wins and losses over the years, its evolution provided a culture that local fans could identify with, and the caliber of play was exciting to watch. Over the course of 46 seasons, Evansville competed in four conferences: the Indiana Collegiate

Bill Harrawood

Powder Puff Football

Bob Hawkins (#73) takes a breather.

Randy Mattingly, #18, led the nation in passing and later became a professional in the Canadian Football League.

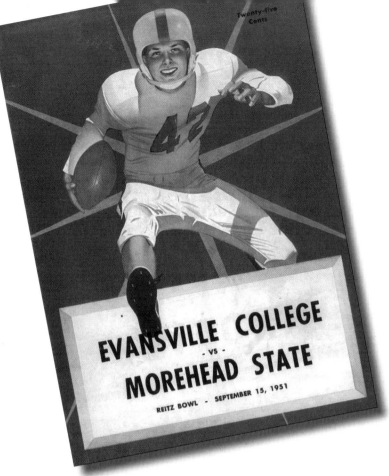

EVANSVILLE COLLEGE
- vs -
MOREHEAD STATE
REITZ BOWL - SEPTEMBER 15, 1951

Conference ('52-'77); the Heartland Conference ('78-'87); the Mid-South ('87-'90); and the Pioneer Football League ('93-'97).

Among the competitors they faced were some impressive names. Though better known as a basketball coach, Tony Hinkle led the Butler Bulldogs on the gridiron for almost 30 years from the '30s through the '60s against the Aces, and Bear Bryant roamed the sideline for the University of Kentucky. The local boys also faced hall of fame quarterback John Unitas when he played for Louisville in the early '50s. In addition, the Aces banged helmets with two of the best offensive linemen in NFL history: Sam Ball, a Henderson, Kentucky native who played for the Colts in Super Bowls III and V; and Fred 'Fuzzy' Thurston, who teamed with Jerry Kramer under Vince Lombardi in the early '60s to form one of the greatest guard tandems in history.

The Aces could boast some phenomenal players of their own over the years. Five Aces were named first team All-Americans in their divisions through the years: Bob Hawkins as a tackle in 1946; Bob Scott, a center in 1954; Larry Gates, an end who was named in both '58 and '59; Hanz Hoag, a three-time honoree at tight end in '91, '93 and '94; and Evansville Harrison's Sean Bennett as a running back in 1996.

Many other Aces were honored on All-Conference teams, and in two separate seasons, eight players made the team. In 1969, the All-ICC team included Richard Dick (end), Tony Hargrove (tackle), Steve Ierardi (guard), 'Spike' Bell (linebacker), Pete Rupp (DB & end), Paul Gerhardt (tackle), Craig Blackford (quarterback) and Doug Atherton (halfback). In '71, the All-ICC team included Ben Karasiak (end), Dave Weimer (middle guard), Mike Forche (linebacker), Bill Sharpe (DB), Dave Scheu (end), Keith Reiter (center), Fernando Villarruel (guard) and Randy Mattingly (quarterback).

The program also featured players that local fans would recognize because of their local connections as high school players.

In fact, four Aces played professionally. Boonville's Ray 'Bibbles' Bawel made catches for the Aces in 1949 that reporters described as "breathtaking in their magnificence and spine-tingling in their brilliance" and played in 1952 for the Philadelphia Eagles and for the Hamilton Tiger-Cats when they won the CFL's Grey Cup in 1957.

Randy Mattingly was a 1973 grad who led the nation in passing at Evansville and was drafted by the Cleveland Browns. After short stints in the camps of Chicago, Buffalo and Cincinnati, Randy spent three seasons in the Canadian Football League.

Marty Amsler was a Bosse grad who eventually grew to a very speedy 6'5, 250-pound defensive end. He was drafted in 1965 by Dallas but eventually landed in Chicago during the Gayle Sayers era. After a 21-sack first season, he nearly won the league's Defensive Rookie of the Year award, but his bright future was darkened by an Achilles tendon injury that ended his career after three seasons.

Sean Bennett was the star on U of E's last team in 1996. After starring at Harrison, Sean attended the University of Illinois to play football and baseball. After a year, he transferred to UE where he re-wrote the record book as a running back. When the program shut down in Evansville, he then finished his college career at Northwestern. Called "the fastest player I ever coached" by Harrison coach Mitch Marsch (another Evansville College football alum). Sean surprised many when he was selected in the fourth round of the 1999 NFL draft by the New York Giants after running a jaw-dropping 4.45 forty-yard dash. Before injuries took their toll, Bennett spent three seasons in New York before finishing his pro career in the CFL and, eventually, the Evansville Blue Cats.

Other local boys made headlines while representing the Aces, and some are still listed in the record books. Notable quarterbacks for the Aces included Mattingly (Rex Mundi), Talmadge Vick (Lincoln), Kim Devault (Memorial), Thom Endress (Rex Mundi) and Craig Blackford (Tell City). Memorial's Pete Rupp holds the record for TD passes in a game with 4 against St. Josephs in 1969, while Sean Bennett set records for rushing in a game (313 yards) and touchdowns in a season (19 in 1996) during his only season with the Aces.

All these men plus many others left their blood and sweat on the field of battle, and their memories are still vivid. Some played their home games at Reitz Bowl, while others played at Enlow or Bosse Field. Bob Glaser recalled a game against Murray State near the end of a season when a crew dragged the dirt surface like a baseball field before the game.

Marty Amsler remembers how 13 guys played virtually every minute of a game with nine acting as "60-minute men". He also remembers his teammates, many who became household names locally, like Mike Madriaga; QB Kim Devault; Charlie Zausch, the brother of basketballer Ed Zausch; John Lidy; and Paul Bullard, another hoopster who played tight end only in his senior year and made All-Conference.

Others reminisce about the atmosphere, the camaraderie and special bonds that formed. In the early years, basketball coaches like Wayne Boultinghouse and the legend himself, Arad McCutchan, served as assistant football coaches. "The wives (of the coaches) all knew each other," recalled Jim Beck, a former player and son of legendary coach Paul Beck. "They would rotate houses for the parties."

The travel was done by bus with business manager Bob Hudson carrying a wad of cash to pay bills. Bob Glaser remembered the huge win over the Southern Illinois Salukis, who were led by

EVANSVILLE COLLEGE/U OF E FOOTBALL
A LEGACY OF LEADERSHIP

Many feel that the greatest legacy the Aces football program created is the very long list of coaches who affected the lives of young men locally and elsewhere. Below is the list of those football alumni who became head coaches and the schools at which they served. Also singled out are those who coached State champions (*) and those who are in the Indiana Hall of Fame (•). Others in the Hall who did not play at Evansville College/U of E but have ties to the Aces program are Paul Beck, Jim Byers and Don Ping. The list was compiled by a group of ex-Aces, and it is possible that someone may have been omitted. We sincerely apologize for any errors or omissions.

Phil Aramowicz (Castle)
David Austill (Castle)
Jerry Bland (Edgewood)
Joe Brent (Boonville)
Dave Coudret (Indianapolis)
• Ken Coudret (Rex Mundi, Southport)
Don Crane (Haubstadt)
Jerry David (Mt. Vernon)
David Davies
• Jerry Denstorff (South Spencer, Mitchell)
Nick Eckert (Union County)
Charlie Fisher (Mississinewa)
Bud George (North Knox, Tell City)
Jim Giovanetti (Dale)
• Joe Gengelbach (North Posey)
Paul Hamilton (Kokomo)
Brad Hanner (Southridge)
• Bill Harrawood (Boonville)

Charles Harr (North Vernon)
Bob Hawkins (Southridge)
Norm Heard (Boonville)
Rob Hons (Lawrenceburg)
Bill Huff (Mt. Vernon, Red Hill)
John Hurley (Memorial)
J.O. Jackson (LaGrange IL)
Bill Krietemeyer (Princeton)
Don Leduc (Central)
• * John Lidy (Castle)
• Gene Logel (Memorial)
Mike Madriaga (North, Bosse)
• Mitch Marsch (Harrison)
John McDougal (Illinois)
Tim McIntosh (South Spencer)
John Obermeier (Gibson Southern)
• Archie Owen (Bosse)
Dan Phillips (Union County)

Cecil Raymond (Washington)
• Morris Riley (North)
Ron Rogier (Boonville)
Bill Russler (Bosse)
Bob Scott (Mt. Prospect IL)
•* Bill Sharpe (Jimtown)
• Paul Tevault (Boonville)
Charlie Uhde (North)
Talmadge Vick (Lincoln)
• Don Watson (Harrison)
Andy Weinzapfel (Bosse)
• Ralph Weinzapfel (Memorial)
• Ed Wessel (North)
• Frank Will (Mater Dei)
Lemois Wires (Washington)
Jim Wright (Tecumseh)

• Indiana Football Hall of fame
* Coached a State champion

---

future NFL quarterback Jim Hart. To win, the Aces faked an extra point with Glaser as the holder. Instead of placing the ball, he flipped it to Mike Madriaga, the kicker, and the speedy halfback scampered in for the 14-13 victory.

Joe Genglebach, the long-time coach at North Posey who played guard at Evansville College, remembers his teammates, like fellow guard Bob Banwart and quarterback Craig Blackford. He remembers Ryan LaGrange, who coached at Southridge, and Larry Merritt, a Reitz grad who coached at Bosse, and the great receiver Pete Rupp. Joe also understands the impact the football program has had on him and others, mentioning iconic Aces coach Jim Byers and how Coach Byers still sends him notes about the job he's doing at North Posey. "When they decided to drop football, I really thought it was going to hurt the area. When you look back, in just the years I remember, almost all the coaches in Evansville and surrounding areas were ex-players at U of E," Genglebach pointed out. "I student taught under Joe Unfried and Archie Owen (at Bosse). That's where I learned how to handle kids and treat people."

To a man, the alumni I spoke with treasured the time they spent in their Aces football uniform, and there is no doubt about the passion they feel about the program's contributions. "The important thing is the impact Evansville College/U of E football had on southern Indiana, Illinois and western Kentucky," said Mitch Marsch. "Think about how many people they impacted as coaches. You can't measure the importance of football in words. It's fascinating that that many people went on to become coaches."

"That's one of the legacies of Evansville College football," said Jim Beck, "that most of the Evansville coaches at that time played football there."

"What did they lose?" answered Joe Neidig, a North Posey and U of E football alum when asked about the decision to terminate the program in 1996. "It's reasonably simple. I think football at that level continues a commitment, a very deep commitment to something larger than yourself. I look at Coach Gengelbach and Bill Harrawood (who played and coached at U of E). Having that program brought it all back to the community. I think of names I played with – Scott Marsch, Mitch's son, Andy Benes and Randy Hobson – and every one of these guys are making significant contributions back to the community."

One of the officials for the 1949 Refrigerator Bowl was Jay Berwanger, the very first Heisman Trophy winner in 1935 from the University of Chicago.

Coach Jim Byers on the Aces sideline.

On May 14, 2011, a reunion was held for all the players who wore the uniform, and hundreds came from all over the country. With ages ranging from the mid-30s to well into their 80s, the men shared a common bond. They love the game of football, and they understand what Aces football meant to them and others.

The graphic on this page lists all the ex-Aces who became head football coaches, and it would be interesting to see how many other college programs produced such prolific numbers. The list shows that 52 alumni became head coaches, which means that, on average, one man from every season of Aces football chose to follow his mentors' leads in affecting the lives of future generations.

My own life was greatly influenced by such coaches as Morris Riley, Ed Wessel and Talmadge Vick at North, and I am certain that many who read this book have had similar experiences. The men who came together in May of 2011 are determined to bring football back to U of E, and perhaps they'll succeed. But even if they don't, they can be proud of themselves and their program, because the ultimate criteria for a sports program isn't wins and losses; it is the quality of the individuals it produces. Based on this guideline, the Evansville College/U of E football program passes the test because of its legacy of leadership that will continue to affect lives for generations to come.

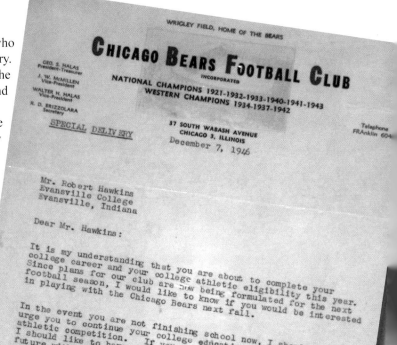

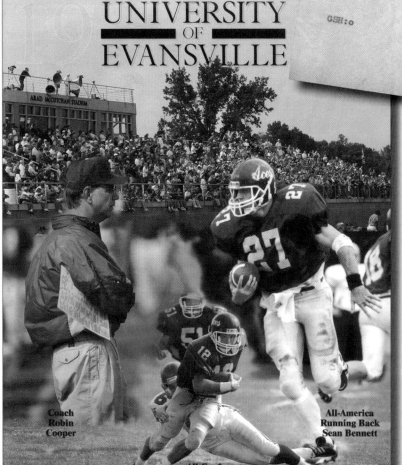

Sean Bennett, #27 on the cover of this program, starred on the last University of Evansville team before transferring to Northwestern and then building a career in the NFL.

In 1946, Bob Hawkins became Evansville College's first football All-American, and he was good enough to receive several letters like the one shown here from 'Papa Bear' Paul Halas himself. Hawkins had returned from the service in the mid-'40s to play ball for the Aces, and as he neared graduation, he planned on following in his father's footsteps and becoming an Evansville Police officer. The letters were intriguing, but at the time, a cop was paid better than a pro football player, so Bob said thanks but no thanks and began a 33-year career as a police officer. His sons, Bob Jr. and Brent, followed in his footsteps as Aces players.

In 1966, hall of fame Bears linebacker Dick Butkus came to Evansville for Marty Amsler's wedding and spent some time with former Aces players at the Forget-Me-Not Inn.

LEVRON WILLIAMS: HE BEAT THE ODDS

For several years in the mid-1990s, local sports fans witnessed one of the finest all-around athletes in Evansville history. But what they were probably unaware of were the obstacles he had to overcome to earn his place among the area's elite.

Levron Williams was born on January 12, 1979, the only son of Brenda Douglas and Tim Williams. During his formative years, he learned his football skills in the Lakeview Optimist program, but because of weight restrictions, fans never got to see him run the ball until he was much older.

Although Levron's parents were around, they were in and out of his life, so the responsibility of raising the young man fell on the shoulders of his grandparents, Shirley and James Owsley. As the boy approached his teens, Shirley Owsley saw signs that began to worry her. She saw that Levron was falling prey to some negative influences and contacted his mother immediately.

Levron's mother had moved between Evansville and Indianapolis several times as she tried to find her own way, and when Shirley informed her of the situation, she made arrangements for the move to Indy. For the next year and a half, Levron became a multi-sport standout at Guion Creek Middle School, and during his stay in the Circle City, Williams met a family who would provide a positive influence and re-direct him down the road to success.

Charles and Shirley Robinson were the parents of Levron's best friend, Tyrone Robinson, and Levron is very aware of how blessed he was to have had them in his life during that crucial period. "I grew as a person," Williams reflected. "It was a learning experience. It was rough at first. Tyron's parents embraced me while I was up there. It changed my mindframe. I was learning how to hunker down and be a student athlete. It was good to get around people where the family was structured."

During Levron's eighth grade year, he exhibited his athletic talents, and his potential was clear to everyone. Although the coaches at Pike were excited about his arrival, Williams missed his grandparents and seized the opportunity to return to Evansville. He arrived as a 6'2, 180-pound freshman and briefly fell into old habits and got into some trouble. As a consequence, Levron only played two football games as a freshman, but when basketball season rolled around, he was ready to focus. Williams earned a starting spot for Coach Gene Ballard as a freshman and had four successful seasons with teammates like Bryan Elkins, Idris Mitchell, Norman Jones, Ontario Jackson and Jimmy Reeves. As a junior, Levron led the city in scoring at 23.4 (13th in the state) while averaging 10.1 rebounds. He was a member of the *Courier* All-Metro Team as a junior and was the All-Metro Team's MVP as a senior, joining teammates Clint Keown and Dan Schnur of Memorial, LaMarco Norman of Central, Harrison's John Risinger and Brian Merriweather of North.

Even more impressive were Levron's accomplishments on the football field under coach Jeff May. Amazingly, in spite of playing running back for barely two years, Williams amassed 4,269 rushing yards, third on Evansville's all-time list behind Ricky Crider at Reitz (6,356) and Memorial's Ken Mills (4,841). He was one of four Evansville players to be named first team All-State, joining Central's Kurt Davies and Deke Cooper and Bart Blalock of North, and was the runner-up to Israel Thompson of Martinsville for Indiana's Mr. Football. To cap off his high school career, Levron was one of eleven running backs in the country to be named a *Parade* All-American, and to the best of our knowledge, he is the first and still only Evansville player to be honored as such since *Parade* began naming All-Americans since 1963.

(As an impressive side note, Levron also was a fine track athlete who qualified for the State meet as a 6'8 high jumper.)

Because of his prowess on the gridiron, Williams was courted by many of the best programs in the country, visiting schools like Ohio State, Michigan State and Southern Cal, coached at the time by John Robinson. Levron chose to play under Cam Cameron at IU and was told he could also play basketball under Coach

Levron Williams
(photo courtesy Indiana University, Media Relations)

Knight, but the hoops dream never materialized. As a freshman, his 6'4, 200-pound frame made it tough to compete with Dwyane Hogan (out of Ben Davis), Marcus Floyd and others at running back. So Levron earned playing time as a wide receiver with some occasional carries out of the backfield.

Levron was told that to play running back he needed to put on 15 pounds before his sophomore season began, so he dedicated himself to hitting the weight room, taking in more calories and getting plenty of rest. By the time the 1998 season rolled around, he had filled out to 215 and could still run a 4.43 forty-yard dash. By the third game, he had become the team's starter at running back, but Cameron still found ways to line him up wide to get the ball to him as a receiver.

Levron distinguished himself with the Hoosiers and was a standout during his four years there. Wearing his familiar #5 jersey, he teamed with close friend and four-year roommate Antwaan Randle El to form one of the country's top tandems. When he was through, Williams was second in IU history in all-purpose yards (4,700), third in career touchdowns (38 total – 31 rushing, 7 receiving) and fifth in career rushing with 3,095 yards (6.8/attempt). He also set a record for TDs in a game (6 vs. Wisconsin in 2001), rushed for over 100 yards in 14 games and became the first player in IU history to rush for over 3,000 yards and receive for over

1,000 in a single year (2001), finishing first in the nation in all-purpose yards while earning first team All-Big Ten honors as a senior.

As the season came to an end, Levron was pleased with his accomplishments and looked forward to the future, but the elation would suddenly be erased when fate dealt him a devastating blow only hours after he left the IU locker room for the last time. With thoughts of the NFL on his mind, word reached Levron that his mother, Brenda Douglas, had been murdered in Evansville.

As he tried to focus on the process of pursuing a career in professional football, Williams found it difficult to concentrate on the task at hand. He held his 'pro-day' at IU with representatives from twenty teams watching as he went through the physical challenges required (like bench pressing 225 pounds 16 times, for example). He signed with San Diego as a free agent, joining Coach Cameron, who had joined the Chargers as an offensive coordinator, but found it tough to make the squad with LaDainian Tomlinson and others ahead of him.

Williams returned to Evansville and received some calls from NFL teams but admitted that his heart just wasn't in it. He eventually joined the Evansville Blue Cats under Coach John Hart and had successful seasons there in 2003, '06 and '07.

In 2004, Williams completed his schooling by earning a degree in General Studies with a minor in Criminal Justice. He has spent the last few years as an assistant football coach in Evansville, most recently at Bosse under head coach Andre Thomas. As of January 2011, Williams was hoping to join the new arena football league team, the Evansville Rage, as a player/coach.

Levron overcame more than most to achieve success in the world of athletics, and he is to be respected for his accomplishments. He is quick to credit those who have helped him along the way, like his grandparents, coaches and the Robinsons in Indianapolis. He also mentioned his Aunt Leonilla, his Uncle David and a lady from his days at Bosse, Ms. Mary Lou Keating, saying, "She was a teacher and mentor. She was like a second mom to me. She was big in my life, her daughter Rachel, too. They were big influences on my life."

During his developmental years, Levron had several legit excuses for giving up or taking the wrong path, but he beat the odds. With the help of several family members and friends, Williams persevered, got an education and built a life, and most true local sports fans would agree that very few in our history used their God-given gifts better than Bosse's Levron Williams.

DYNAMIC DUO

In 2000, IU became only the second school in Big Ten history to have two 3,000-yard career rushers on the same team when the feat was accomplished by best friends and roommates Antwaan Randle El and Evansville's Levron Williams.

THE VERY FIRST

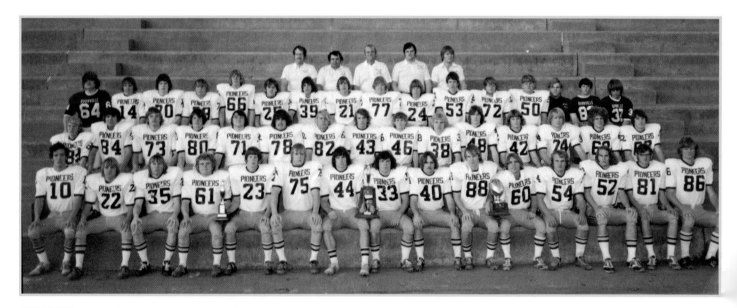

The very first area team to play for a State football championship was this 1974 Boonville team coached by Bill Harrawood. First row: (L-R): J. Kaposta, M. Baxter, J. Stevens, D. Crow, O. Holder, R. Goings, D. Ensor, S. Barnhill, T. Rice, K. Dimmett, J. VanWinkle, B. Bolten, K. King, P. Decker, M. Rhodes. Second row: M. Wilson, D. Wire, T. Kaiser, J. Cheshire, S. McKinney, M. Wilson, M. Adams, D. Payne, A. Bawel, M. Holder, K. Girdley, J. Gore, M. Kroeger, A. Lee, M. Beyers. Third row: B. Morrow, R. Medcalf, J. Branson, E. Ashby, K. Byers, D. Meyer, D. Newton, K. Grundhoefer,, J. Greer, D. Byers, T. Plassmeier, D. Harrawood, G. Kroeger, G. Betz, D. Bufkin, G. Sparks. Fourth row: Coach L. Riggs, Coach J. Amiano, Head Coach B. Harrawood, Coach K. McKinney, Coach B. Proctor.

MT. CARMEL FOOTBALL: A WAY OF LIFE

A special thank you is due Mike Mandrell, whose book, a labor of love called The Golden Dynasty: The History of Mt. Carmel Football, is the source of all the photos and much of the information in the following story.

As I took my detour into Illinois to research stories on Tyra Buss and Don Liddle, I discovered another subject that merited inclusion into the 'Local Legends' club. Our local football scene has featured periods of dominance by powerhouse programs like Reitz, Mater Dei, Heritage Hills, and Jasper and enjoyed the successes of legendary coaches like Herman Byers, Mike Goebel, Jerry Brewer, Bob Clayton, and many others, and the program at Mt. Carmel deserves mention with some of the area's best. Not only does its success merit recognition, but the Golden Aces are truly part of our sports scene because they are covered by our local media and actually play in a conference with our Indiana schools.

For decades, stories have been written about the mania experienced by fans from the tradition-rich local schools, and Mt. Carmel High School has developed a culture every bit as rich. The first reported news about Aces football was recorded in *The Daily Republican Register* in September of 1920. A schedule was announced that included two games each with Grayville and Albion and one with Princeton. It was announced in the article that 17 boys had reported for practice and that each had to pay $10 to help pay for uniforms.

Although Coach Loren Hill and his boys were 15 to 20 years behind other schools in the area, they traveled by automobile with nearly 100 fans to Grayville and trounced the Bison 32-0 in their brand new maroon and gold uniforms. Mt. Carmel finished the season 3 and 2 and improved in 1921 under new coach Clarence Jordan with a 5-1 record, with their five wins coming by a combined score of 216-0.

The Golden Aces continued their winning ways, and in 1924, under popular football and basketball coach Clifford Garrett, Mt. Carmel won its first championship and received the Silver Football trophy from *The Evansville Press* for winning the Tri-State League championship.

In 1927, Riverview Stadium was completed, and the quirky venue has been a source of pride and exhilaration for Aces fans ever since. In many ways, it can be likened to historic Reitz Bowl in Evansville. Like the Bowl, the home bleachers were built into the side of a steep hill. The seats spread between the 40-yard lines and seem to climb forever to provide seating for 3000 rowdy fans.

The field, now known as Legends Field, was originally built as a racetrack for autos, but when the track failed after the first year, it was sold to the school for $1. Across Golden Aces Way is a parking area that is not on school property, making it ideal for tailgaters to congregate before games.

The program's first losing season occurred in 1928 when the team went 0-8 in Coach Olin Driver's third and final year, and for the next 26 years, the program wallowed in mediocrity. But in 1957, a man came to town who would transform Mt. Carmel football from an also-ran to a perennial contender. Jim John took the helm in 1957 and in three years delivered the school's first undefeated season in 27 years, finishing 8-0-1 in 1960. The '60 team featured one of the best quarterbacks in Golden Aces history in Sharon Miller, who ended his career with four TD passes in a 45-14 win over Princeton. Behind a strong line that included Bob Alva, Don Williams, Richard Tenbarge and Gary Childers, Miller became a high school All-American and later earned All-American honors at Western Kentucky.

Some Aces fans may argue that the 1963 team was the best in the school's history as Coach John's boys steamrolled its way to a 9-0 record by outscoring opponents 317-38. The '63 team had plenty of firepower with Dick Miller under center and three speedsters, Doyle Bradley, Steve Wiggins, and Tom Wirth, taking Miller's handoffs.

After three more excellent seasons (8-1, 7-2, and 6-1-2), Jim John finished his 11-year career with a lackluster 3-6 season. Coach John was a great football coach but was also exceptional as an assistant in basketball and as the school's head track coach. Although the fans hated to say farewell to the man dubbed "The Father of Mt. Carmel Football," a new man would take his place who would also make his mark on the program, the conference, and the community by leading the Golden Aces into uncharted waters.

Larry Davis arrived in 1968 with some big shoes to fill, and it wouldn't take long for the Mt. Carmel faithful to realize that he was not the stereotypical football coach. "Larry Davis has to be the most interesting, complex, and unique

Sharon Miller quarterbacked the 1960 team.

Mt. Carmel's first team in 1920.

Coach Jim John transformed the program.

*Quirky Riverview Stadium,
now known as Legends Field, was completed in 1927.*

*John Rafferty quarterbacked
perhaps the greatest game in
Mt. Carmel football history.*

*Larry Lockhart
ran a tight ship.*

*Coach Larry Davis was a
unique character.*

character to ever grace the sidelines at MCHS," wrote Mike Mandrell in his book *The Golden Dynasty.*

Mandrell went on to explain that "LD", as Davis was affectionately known, was very recognizable by the "crumbled, old baseball cap, worn windbreaker and a cigarette…constantly on his lips." The ex-Marine was also known for playing dumb although he was well-read and, according to Mike Mandrell, a "renaissance man."

Davis proved himself to be an excellent coach who was always prepared. He was famous for his sophisticated blocking schemes and for his ability to get into the heads of his players. Throughout his tenure, LD had a knack for portraying a contest as being an "us against the world" situation, often referring to his players as "River Rats" to work them into a lather.

Although Coach Davis' reputation as a coach was solid, the same could not be said about his personal life. According to reports, Davis loved the night life and was prone to finding himself in situations that made their way into the gossip mill. As is usually the case, serious personal shortcomings often lead to demise, but Coach Davis would make quite a name for himself during his stay in Mt. Carmel.

After two solid seasons (5-4 in '68 and 6-3 in '69), LD fashioned a great 8-1 season in 1970, losing only to Carmi by a touchdown. The Aces were solid offensively but outstanding on defense, holding opponents to 40 total points while registering five shutouts.

One of the most successful seasons was 1974, and the season also produced one of the most memorable games in Aces history. The season marked the first time in Illinois history that a playoff system would be implemented, and several talented players returned from the 8-1 team in '73. Leading the list were quarterback Kent Kirkman, running backs Jeff Young, Randy Rigg, and Greg Keepes, and linemen Mike Gibbons and Jeff Stouse.

The team set a school record for wins in a season with 11 against 2 losses. The only regular season loss was to archival Lawrenceville, forcing a conference tie and requiring the principals and AD's to select the representative to the tournament. Mt.

Carmel was chosen, and they didn't disappoint. In the school's first playoff game, the Aces came back to defeat Mt. Zion in the 3A contest. After a win over Sparta, the Golden Aces were primed for the semi-finals, and the game would be one that fans would remember for a long time.

The stage was set in a quagmire at Q Stadium in Quincy, and the Raiders were loaded. The small Catholic school had amassed a sensational lineup from the pool of talent in Hancock and surrounding counties, not the least of which were QB Jeff Johnson and his favorite target Rollie Thomas. But on this night, the slick playing surface and the boys in maroon and gold would keep the game close to set up some late heroics. The Aces' Ted Kramer made the first crucial play with a touchdown-saving tackle of Thomas. The second do-or-die situation saw the Mt. Carmel defense stage a dramatic goal line stand with Jeff Young getting a fingernail on a fourth down pass to turn back the Raiders.

The game ended 0-0, and Coach Davis elected to go on defense to start the overtime period. After a five-yard run on first down, Quincy running back Mike Hummert fumbled the handoff and Mt. Carmel's Kyle Ernest recovered.

According to overtime rules, the Aces then started their series on the ten-yard line and moved the ball six yards in three downs. The decision was made to trust the team's kicker, and Doug 'The Toe' Peterson sloshed onto the field to make some history. After a perfect snap from Paul Casaleggi to holder Kent Kirkman, Peterson split the uprights to give Mt. Carmel its first shot at a State championship.

Peterson's "Kick heard 'round the world" sent Aces fans into a frenzy, and the scene would have made Hollywood proud as the sun burst through the clouds just as the referee threw up his arms to signal the kick good.

Although Mt. Carmel lost the final game to a strong West Chicago team, fans were experiencing a transformation. As Mike Mandrell said in his book, "Football was becoming so addicting in Wabash County, and the finalist team of '74 was the one that started it all. Winning is like building a Frankenstein monster; the bigger it gets, the more you have to feed it to keep it going."

Aces fans have nurtured that monster for years, and along the way have been treated to countless thrills. Two of them took place in 1981, the campaign that many refer to as "the Magic Season." After a 9-2 campaign the previous year that ended in disappointment after a second round loss to Harrisburg, Coach Davis was optimistic. Back from 1980 were record-breaking quarterback John Rafferty, running backs Steve Priest and Jeff Slater, and wide receiver Steve Singer. The line would be anchored by the massive Brad Jenkins alongside tight end Bruce Linson and others.

The Aces battled through some close games during the season as well as cakewalks over Red Hill (74-7) and Olney (65-12) to win their third North Egypt Conference championship in a row. As they attempted to make a long tournament run, they found themselves in a quarter-final matchup with Nashville, and the contest at the Hornets' field will forever be known to Aces fans as 'The Miracle'.

For the most part, Nashville outplayed Mt. Carmel and led 24-10 after three quarters. In fact, as the clock wound down to the six-minute mark, many of the Aces' faithful had made their way to the exits for the drive home. But those who stayed were witnesses to perhaps the greatest game in Mt. Carmel football history.

With the clock ticking, the Aces drove to the Hornets' 11-yard line. On the following play, Rafferty scrambled out of the pocket and into the end zone. On the next play, Rafferty found a wide open Bruce Linson for the two-point conversion to narrow the margin to 24-18.

After the kickoff, the Aces' defense held and forced a punt, and the next play set the stage for 'The Miracle'. After the snap, Leon Raber pierced the Hornet's line and blocked the punt. As the ball bounced away, John Kramer then gathered the pigskin and raced 12 yards for the TD to even the score. Kicker Kelly Johnson then delivered to give Mt. Carmel a 25-24 lead.

After four futile heaves by Nashville's QB and a drive by Mt. Carmel ending in a 5-yard TD run by Steve Priest, the Aces fans who still remained celebrated the team's unlikely victory.

With one miracle behind them, the Wabash County squad was feeling the fever of the elusive State title run. In the semi-final the Aces took care of Pittsfield 20-6 in a bloody battle marred by penalties and questionable hits. Behind stellar offensive play by Rafferty, Linson, Kelly Johnson, and Marvin Matchett, Mt. Carmel was headed for Hancock Stadium in Bloomington-Normal to face off with McNamara for the 3A title.

The 1981 Aces had shown their grit many times throughout the season, and they would need everything they had against the Bishop McNamara Fighting Irish. But on this day, the dominance of Catholic schools throughout Illinois history would not prevail.

Mt. Carmel took control from the outset, racking up 332 yards of offense while holding McNamara to a mere 57. The Aces controlled the ball for 31 of the 48 minutes, and the defense had two interceptions and 11 tackles for losses in the 22-8 win.

In the program's 61st year and the high school's 100th year, Coach Davis' boys of 1981 delivered the school's first football State championship, and they did so in style. Out of the eight classes that competed that year, Mt. Carmel was the only public school to defeat a Catholic school for the trophy, and November 28, 1981 will go down as one of the greatest days in Aces football history.

If 1981 was "the best of times" for the Mt. Carmel football program, 1982 would qualify as the program's "worst of times." For the first time ever, Mt. Carmel was rated #1 in the state's AP poll, but the joy would not last long. After the third week of the season, the community was stunned when Mark Treadway and Marvin Matchett were taken in a tragic automobile accident. In addition, the local economy was suffering and folks were growing tired of Larry Davis' style.

The team did manage six wins to start the campaign before falling to Olney for their only loss of the season. That loss kept the Aces out of the playoffs, and after the season, Coach Davis and Mt. Carmel parted ways.

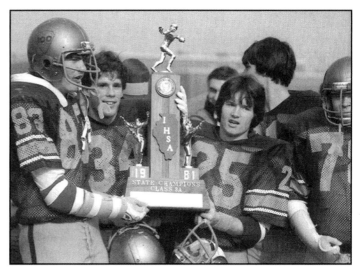

Celebrating the 1981 State championship.

In 1983, the reins were turned over to Larry Lockhart, a no-nonsense guy who ran a tight ship, and his teams reflected his style. During his seven-year run at Mt. Carmel, Lockhart took the Aces to the playoffs all seven years and won the conference six of the seven. After the '86 season, beloved assistant John Gates stepped down as the defensive coordinator and line coach, and his brilliant mind would be missed. Lockhart finished his stint at Mt. Carmel with a 61-16 record and left after the '89 season to coach at Lawrenceville, his alma mater.

As the program entered its eighth decade, a new coach was named that Mike Mandrell proclaimed in his book to be "one of the most interesting characters to ever grace the sidelines of Mt. Carmel High School." John Hart had played at Newton in Jasper County and was offered a great opportunity as a 24-year-old to head up the program at Albion Edwards County. It was there that he began to fashion a remarkable career that he is still building today. When he left to take the job at Anna Jonesboro, he left as the only E.C. coach to leave with a winning record.

While preparing for his new job, Hart faced an unusual situation when he received a call from Mt. Carmel. Many of the Mt. Carmel powers-that-be opposed the deal, thinking it would leave a bad impression if they "stole" a coach from another school. They also weren't fond of the fact that Hart was an Edwards County boy, an area that was looked down upon by some of the Aces faithful.

The deal was made, however, and Hart took charge, but not without some resistance. Not only was Hart an unknown from outside the system but his offense ran from the wishbone formation. For die-hard Aces fans, this was blasphemy, and they lobbied for the familiar I-formation they had used for years. The community wasn't known for its tolerance of change, and the scenes probably resembled the reception Norman Dale (Gene Hackman) received in the movie *Hoosiers*.

Hart faced a huge challenge, but his conviction got him through. He ushered the program into a new era, coordinating the Junior League program and building the weightlifting regimen into almost a religion.

John Hart left the program in 2000 as the coach with the best winning percentage in Mt. Carmel history (101-21, 83%), and his dominance of the North Egypt Conference played a role in the conference's demise, as Hart's teams captured nine titles in his eleven years and were part of a 31-game conference win streak.

John Hart led a 31-game winning streak.

From Mt. Carmel, Hart went to Evansville Reitz where he won 81% of his games in seven seasons with a State championship in 2007. From there, Coach Hart headed north to Warren Central where he won 80% of his games with a State title in 2009 before leaving in 2012 for Huntley High School in northern Illinois.

After the dissolution of the NEC, Mt. Carmel looked to Indiana for a new affiliation and joined Boonville, Jasper, Mt. Vernon, Princeton, Vincennes Lincoln, and Washington in the Big 8 Conference. In 2001, a favorite son took charge when defensive coordinator Darren Peach was named Mt. Carmel's new head football coach. Peach, an all-conference player for the '84 and '85 Aces, quickly led the program back to the 'carpet' at Memorial Stadium on the campus of the University of Illinois in Champagne.

Darren Peach was a stark contrast to John Hart. Hart was a high-profile man who declared each team as "the best he ever coached," while Peach was quiet and unassuming. In a program teeming with history, no one could represent the system better than Peach. He played for the legendary Larry Davis and then ended his playing career under another legend in Larry Lockhart. In addition, he served under a probable future hall of famer in John Hart.

Prior to Peach's debut season, another tragedy struck the program when highly touted freshman Jason Ile was killed in another horrible auto accident in June. Three other team members were also in the car but escaped with minor injuries. Under Coach Peach's leadership, the team rallied and bonded to forge another outstanding season.

Coach Hart had not left Darren Peach empty-handed, as captain Mark Crummley returned along with "the big redhead" Mike Conrad who would earn All-State honors as a linebacker. Other returners of note were Bryan Grant, Jake Howard, Bryan Straw, and Jason Ile's brother, Steven. The line was anchored by Chris Horton, Ryan Peach, Tyler Haycraft, and Charley Adams.

Coach Peach's premier was not a ho-hum affair as he began his head coaching career with a barn-burner, winning 15-12 at home in Riverview Stadium in two overtimes. The team also ended the regular season with another double overtime thriller by beating Robinson 26-20 heading into the playoffs.

After downing the Massac County Patriots (35-14) and the Nashville Hornets (25-8), Mt. Carmel was primed for a quarterfinal game that would place it among the greatest matchups in the annals of Aces football. As Mike Mandrell described in *The Golden Dynasty*, "The Mt. Carmel Golden Aces went in a blink of an eye from the worst moment in our football history to probably one of our greatest moments" to snatch victory from defeat in the historic contest.

Aces fans packed the stadium in Macon County to watch their boys battle Mt. Zion in a matchup of two 10-1 teams. Mt. Carmel was led by arguably the greatest quarterback in school history, Luke Drone, who showed his talent early and often. In the first period, he tucked the ball on the mid-line option and scampered 65 yards for the touchdown. The extra point try sailed wide, leaving Mt. Carmel with a 6-0 lead.

Darren Peach (right) with long-time assistant Kevin Smith.

Another huge play occurred late in the second period when Bryan Straw penetrated the Braves' backfield and literally swiped the ball from Mt. Zion QB Blake Hendrikson and recovered at the 19. Six plays later Clayton Storckman scored, and after a failed two-point conversion, the Aces had a 12-0 lead to take into halftime.

Early in the third, Drone struck again with a 38-yard strike to Storckman. The extra point kick was blocked, but the fans were breathing easy with an 18-0 lead. But fortunes can change quickly in the game of football, and Mt. Carmel was about to be slapped back to reality in a flash.

The awakening began late in the third when Mt. Zion traveled 70 yards in 7 plays for their first points, closing the gap to 18-7. The Golden Aces responded with a six-minute drive of their own but came up inches short on a crucial 4th and 3 play to turn the ball over at their own 33. The Braves then converted two key fourth down plays before a one-yard plunge to pull within five at 18-13.

With 1:28 on the clock, a perfectly executed onside kick allowed Mt. Zion one more opportunity. The key play on the drive was a 30-yard run by Donnie Remley for a score that saw him clearly out of bounds with no call being made. The Aces faithful sat in stunned silence while Braves supporters went wild. But the game was not over, and Coach Peach and his boys went to work.

With less than a minute left, the Aces found themselves 80 yards from paydirt with Luke Drone in control. Several quick outs and bubble screens to receivers chewed up yardage and saved clock. With 33 seconds left, Drone looked to Jake Howard for another bubble screen and the Braves closed in on the gutsy receiver. But Drone's eyes shifted right and found Michael Brewer on a slant that Brewer took into the end zone untouched.

Mt. Carmel's defense then did its job, and the 25-19 victory allowed Coach Peach's boys to advance. The 11-1 Aces would then knock off Benton 35-22 to send them once again to Champagne, where past crowds had witnessed the likes of Red Grange and Dick Butkus as well as local legends like Don Hansen (Reitz), Kevin Hardy (Harrison), Dean Volkman (North) and several others.

Mike Mandrell, who witnessed the game from the press box above Memorial Stadium, described the November 23rd State championship game as "the greatest game I have ever witnessed, and it was the most awesome thing to happen to me in my sports life." He went on to say that the contest had to be one of the most exciting in Illinois championship history and that the statewide media seemed "awestruck" by what they had witnessed.

Once again, Mt. Carmel was to face a powerful Catholic school, Addison Driscoll, who averaged over 27 points per game. The Highlanders drew players from the entire Chicago-land area, and the nearly 9,000 spectators would see a battle to the finish.

Mt. Carmel held their opponent on the first series and then drew first blood on a 12-play, 62-yard drive with Drone finding Bryan Gant on a 7-yard touchdown pass. Drone then split the uprights to put the Aces on top 7-0.

After a Driscoll field goal, Drone capped off another drive with a 2-yard scamper to put the Golden Aces up 14-3. The Highlanders answered with a TD, but Drone gave his own response with a 34-yard toss to Jake Howard. The high-scoring half ended with another Addison-Driscoll touchdown, and the teams headed for their locker rooms with Mt. Carmel holding a 21-18 lead.

Drone struck again with a touchdown on a 4th-and-3 pass play to Clayton Storckman to put the Maroon and Gold up 28-18. The Highlanders answered again to end the third period down 28-25.

The defenses stiffened in the final period. As the clock wound down, Coach Peach, with a reputation as a gambler, went for it on fourth down, but the strategy backfired as Drone was intercepted. With a few ticks over two minutes left, the Highlanders' powerful runner Victor Arliss led the charge as Driscoll reached the two-yard line with four seconds remaining. It was only fitting that such a well-played game not end in regulation, and a field goal sent the contest into overtime.

The Aces faithful were relieved that the Highlanders' coach didn't allow Arliss another chance to end the game in regulation, but they knew the victory they were feeling earlier was now in jeopardy.

Mt. Carmel started the overtime with another Drone TD toss to tight end Wayne Hammel for a 35-28 lead, but Driscoll answered two plays later. Once again, Aces fans feared that Coach Tim Racki would let Arliss run for two, but he took the conservative approach and tied the game at 35.

Addison Driscoll then took possession to start the second OT, and Arliss bulled over as the exhausted boys in maroon and gold tried to stop him. Down 42-35, it was now the Aces' turn, and Drone lived up to his billing with yet another scoring pass to Bryan Gant. With the anxious crowd looking on, Coach Peach and his staff pondered their options.

Peach wanted deeply to deliver another State title to the fans of his alma mater, and when he conferred with his boys, they wanted to put the game on the line. Like a riverboat gambler, Peach never flinched and decided that his Aces were good enough to win it.

Mt. Carmel came to the line in the Hogs Formation, with extra linemen in to protect Drone. There were three options available on the pass play, and the crowd was on its feet as the drama unfolded. After the snap, Drone rolled right, but a defender had slipped past one of the 'Hogs'. Drone was forced to pass too soon, and his throw to Steven Ile, wearing the number five in honor of his brother, fell short and the Aces fans' dreams were shattered.

Players and fans alike were drained from the emotional battle they had experienced. After the initial gasp of disbelief, the Mt. Carmel nation reacted in a way that surprised some. They not only clapped but they roared with pride for the boys who had left it all on the field.

Luke Drone finished the game with 196 yards of passing and 4 touchdowns on 14 of 24 throws to six different receivers, and the boys in maroon and gold had done themselves proud.

Coach Peach followed up his storybook debut season with another fantastic run behind great players like Drone, receivers Michael Wayne Hammel, and Lee Anderson, running back Jake Summers, hard-hitting Jacob Butler and linemen Michael Cheesman

and Chris Johnston. In the final season of the North Egypt Conference, the Aces dominated once again, as they skipped through the regular season with a 9-0 record outscoring opponents 372-66 (an average score of 41-7). But after three wins in the tournament, the Aces fell once against to Addison Driscoll in the State Finals.

Darren Peach is the fifth in a line of outstanding coaches who have molded Mt. Carmel football into a model of consistency. In the last 53 years, Jim John, Larry Davis, Larry Lockhart, John Hart, and Coach Peach have collectively won 429 games with 125 losses and 6 ties for a winning percentage of 77%, with only five losing campaigns. Because of their success, these five individuals with various quirks and styles have created a culture that has become a constant in the small community.

"Everybody thinks that as the schools get bigger, the football gets more important," said Coach John Hart when asked about his days at Mt. Carmel. "At Mt. Carmel, I thought the coolest thing was that there wasn't anybody in the community that wasn't involved in high school football. I remember a time in the middle of winter and we had graduated three linemen. A middle-aged woman came up to me and said, 'Hi, Coach Hart' and she asked me what we were going to do with our offensive line. When people in a grocery store understand the intricacies of the sport, you know you're in a football community. For people in Mt. Carmel, it's their life."

Author Mike Mandrell echoes that sentiment, saying, "I would say that Mt. Carmel football is a phenomenon. By 10:30 at night, everyone knows if we won or lost. Probably 75% of the people have lived here their whole lives. People here just don't understand average."

Mandrell cites examples like Lois Epler, an art teacher who retired in the '80s, whose brother played on the first team in 1920 and whose grandson played on the 2000 team. Ms. Epler has only missed four games (home and away) over the years, and she is just one of many examples.

Mt. Carmel has made the football playoffs in 32 of 36 years and held the state record of 22 straight appearances (from '83 to '87) until it was broken recently. In addition, they have won a State title ('81), been runner-up three times ('74, '04, '02) and dominated the North Egypt Conference, going 151-6 since 1980.

But the program is much more than numbers. "Football has been the one constant in everyone's lives and especially in the last 50 years," says Mike Mandrell in his book. "The dedication of those great coaches can be summed up by saying that they poured their hearts and souls into the program, and everyone in town has reaped what they sowed. Mt. Carmel Golden Aces football is a family."

The Mt. Carmel football program's excellence has endured the test of time and has produced men who have gone on to serve their community and their country. So when discussions about football dynasties in our area take place, Mt. Carmel should be given strong consideration. Like any great traditional sports program, the sport of football in Mt. Carmel transcends the game itself. It becomes a passion for fans and an obsession for players and coaches. Quite simply, in the words of Mike Mandrell, Aces football is a love affair for the Mt. Carmel community.

BOB STEPHENSON:
GRAY & BLUE – THROUGH & THROUGH

Like many young boys growing up on Evansville's west side, Bob Stephenson was well aware of the distinguished history of the Reitz High School football program, and to one day don the blue and gray on the gridiron was a lofty goal indeed. But as he grew into a young man, those dreams became a reality, and Stephenson not only played for the Panthers but became one of the school's superstars under the tutelage of one of the greatest coaches in the program's history.

Bob learned the value of hard work from his parents, Albert and Shirley. Albert was born in 1930 and lost his father in a coal mining accident when Albert was young, making him the man of the house. "Sometimes we think we work hard," Bob told me, "but it's nothing compared to what our folks did."

With his parents in the stands at every game, Stephenson fell in love with the sport, and there was no shortage of heroes to observe. His older brother, Tom Stephenson, was a fine athlete who excelled in football and baseball, but his potential was never reached due to a separated shoulder. Bob was also inspired by those who played before him, and he watched from the bleachers with awe as he wondered if he would ever be worthy.

"Tom Buck, Chip Schrode and Bob Nelson, who were on the mythical State championship team of '71, those were our idols," Bob recalled. "We looked up to those guys. I can remember in junior league football people would ask, 'Are you going to play football for Reitz?' I thought, 'are you crazy?! Those guys are GOOD!' I thought I would never be good enough to play for Reitz High School."

How wrong he was.

Bob was a three-sport athlete for the Panthers as the sixth man on the basketball team under Coach Jim Barnett and as a catcher for Coach Jack Schaffer in baseball, but his greatest thrills were under the lights at Reitz Bowl. He grew to 6'4, 210 pounds as a senior and starred as a tight end/wide receiver and kicker for iconic coach Bob Padgett.

Stephenson's class showed a lot of promise, going undefeated in cub football and losing only one as a freshman team, and after a 9-1 sophomore season, the Panthers were perfect Bob's junior year until a 7-0 loss in the semi-state to Indianapolis Cathedral. Stephenson's senior year was even more special. The biggest local game of the year was the matchup with undefeated North, a team

that featured the talented Stoner Gray (DB), John King (QB) and Steve Pence (WR). Reitz downed the Huskies 17-10. The '77 Panthers advanced all the way to the State championship game, and the 33-14 loss to Portage was the only defeat of the year. The team finished the season 12-1 and outscored their opponents 413-121, an average winning margin of 32.5 to 9.3.

Stephenson was also fortunate to be surrounded by two very talented back-to-back classes at Reitz, and under Coach Padgett's leadership, the group cemented their place in Reitz football history. The class behind Bob's featured talented running back Mick Schnell and Tom Conkling on the line. Six players from the 1977 Reitz team were named All-State: Bob (TE), Wayne Wargel (LB), Mike Morrow (QB), Mark Rippelmeier (LB), Dave Johann (LB) and Mick Schnell.

During Bob's three seasons on the varsity, his teams went 32-3 and earned a permanent spot in the Reitz record books by becoming the first Evansville team to make the playoffs (1976) and to advance to the State championship game (3A-1977). In the title

This Evansville contingent played significant roles on the 1979 IU team that played in the Holiday Bowl. Front row (L-R): Kevin Speer (Harrison), Jeff Phipps (Central), Marlon Flemming (Reitz). Back row (L-R): Bob Stephenson (Reitz), Brett Devault (Mater Dei), George Milligan (Reitz), Stoner Gray (North).

game, Bob set a championship game record that stood for 25 years with 7 catches. In addition, he was the recipient of the Phil N. Eskew Mental Attitude Award and was named the Most Valuable Lineman in the North/South All-Star game.

As a 4.0 student and the valedictorian of his class, Bob had numerous options to consider before continuing his education. College programs were not as aggressive in the late '70s, and the responsibility for contact was often on the player. "The first time I even saw a college recruiter was when we'd beaten Ben Davis (14-13) in the semi-state," Bob revealed. "It was a guy from Wisconsin."

Stephenson's first recruiting trip was to IU, where he got to sit at floor level and watch Bob Knight prowl the sidelines only a year after winning the national championship. He was impressed by the atmosphere in Bloomington but still open to other ideas – but not for long.

The following week, Bob traveled to Wisconsin, who just happened to be hosting Coach Knight and his boys, and when the same coincidence happened again a week later at Purdue, Stephenson decided that enough was enough. Bob's academic plan was to pursue a medical or business degree, two of IU's strongest areas, and with super-salesman Lee Corso making the pitch, Stephenson just couldn't say no to donning the cream and crimson.

Halfway through his freshman season, Bob was getting discouraged and contemplated asking to be red-shirted, but then fate stepped in. Starting tight end Dave Harangody (the father of Notre Dame and NBA star Luke Harangody) was injured and Bob became the starter against Michigan State.

After his freshman year, Stephenson was determined to make the most of his college football experience. "I worked my butt off," Bob told me. "Brett Devault (a teammate at IU and former star at Mater Dei) and I got up at 6:00 every day, then worked road construction for nine hours, then went to The Pit Barbell Club Monday, Wednesday and Friday to lift, then to Mater Dei to throw until dark, then we would run and then get up again at 6:00 and do it all over again."

The hard work paid off for Bob, as he experienced his best year with the Hoosiers. IU finished the season at 8-4, fourth in the Big Ten, and was selected for a rare appearance in a bowl game. Their opponent for the Holiday Bowl was Brigham Young, a team that, at 11-0 with a #9 ranking, made it known that they were insulted to have to play the lowly Hoosiers.

The Cougars' overconfidence proved to be their downfall, however, as Bob and his buddies took the insults personally. In a game the experts dubbed one of the most exciting of the '79-'80 season, IU slew might BYU. The game featured seven lead changes, and with Brigham Young leading 37-31 early in the fourth quarter, Indiana's Tim Wilber returned a punt 62 yards to put IU ahead 38-37. BYU had two more chances to take the lead but couldn't deliver, and after they missed a field goal as time expired, the Hoosiers left the field with a victory and a #16 national ranking. The Holiday Bowl was particularly sweet because Bob got to celebrate with teammates who had local ties, including Marlon Flemming (OT – Reitz), Jeff Phipps (G – Central), Kevin Speer (C – Harrison), Brett Devault (QB/TE – Mater Dei), Stoner Gray (DB – North), Steve Moorman (DL – Owensboro Catholic) and Tony Ahrens (RB – Jasper).

Still riding high from his bowl win, Bob had high expectations for his junior season, and the Hoosiers were 6-4 heading into the Old Oaken Bucket game. With 18 seconds left and the Hoosiers down one after scoring a TD, Coach Corso made a gutsy decision. Rather than kicking to tie, he chose to go for the win. But the win was not to be. The players heard rumors that if IU would have tied, they would have played in the Peach Bowl, but instead their 6-5 record kept them at home.

By the time Bob's senior year arrived, he had grown to 6'4, 238 pounds, and after a 3-8 finish to the season, he assessed his situation. He had started the pre-med program but realized it would involve ten years of school to become an orthopedist as he had planned. So while he prepared to explore extending his football life, he completed his degree in Business Management and Administration.

Stephenson started in both the Hula Bowl and Japan Bowl, and he was disappointed when he wasn't drafted. He was offered six free agent deals and chose Denver. At the time, the Broncos had four veterans, including Pro Bowler Riley Odoms, plus six rookies vying for three tight end positions on the roster.

Bob spent twelve weeks in the summer with the Broncos in camp and then another three in the fall before being released. He entertained the thought of trying out for the Baltimore Colts, who had called him in the fall of 1983, but instead started looking at business opportunities. He did find himself missing football, though, and attended a mini-camp for the Jacksonville Bulls of the USFL in the winter of '83, but when that didn't pan out, it was back to business.

Upon his return home, Bob called *Courier* writer Dave Johnson because he felt the local press had always been good to him. Johnson wrote a story telling the public that Stephenson was back. As a result, Gary West, an ex-player at Reitz, contacted Bob and helped him secure a job at Citizens Bank.

Later, Bob sold signage for Negele Signs as he constantly absorbed as much as he could about the business world. He started a dry cleaning business with Bob Geier when he was still with Negele, and eventually he was contacted by Mike Morrow. Bob had caught many a pass during Morrow's days as an All-State quarterback, and Stephenson had known him since kindergarten. In 1986, the seed was planted to start a computer business, and, shortly thereafter, The Computery was born.

A PATTERN OF SUCCESS

Bob Stephenson's three-year record, from 1975 to 1977, was the seventh best in Reitz football history. In fact, in the 92 years that the Panthers have played football, there have been 9 back-to-back-to-back classes to win over 90% of their games, and Stephenson was part of three of those 3-year runs. Below is a list of those classes and their head coaches.

1.	1960-'62	26-0	100%	Herman Byers
2.	1955-'57	29-1-1	96.7%	Herman Byers
3.	1946-'48	25-1-2	96.2%	Herman Byers
4.	2007-'09	39-2	95.1%	John Hart ('07)
				Tony Lewis ('08,'09)
5.	2008-'10	37-3	92.5%	Tony Lewis
6.	1945-'47	23-2-2	92.0%	Herman Byers
•7.	1975-'77	32-3	91.4%	Bob Padgett
•8.	1976-'78	31-3	91.4%	Bob Padgett ('76, '77)
				Bob Ashworth ('78)
•9.	1974-'76	29-3	90.6%	Bob Padgett

(•*Bob Stephenson*)

According to Bob, athletics paved the way for much of his business success, and he says that he learned valuable lessons as an athlete, like time management, getting up when you get knocked down and working with people. As he discussed the reasons for his success, he was also smart enough to not upset his mother. "Don't tell my mom this," he said, "but I got more out of playing football than I did in the classroom, as far as success in business."

When I asked why he was concerned about his mother's opinion, his answer was wise indeed: "Because I'm still scared of mom."

During his adult years in Evansville, Stephenson has had the opportunity to help as a coach at his alma mater, and he has become great friends with ex-coach Bob Gaddis and several others. His daughters actually competed at Central, Courtney as a standout in swimming and tennis and Kelsey as the *Courier*'s Metro Player of the Year in volleyball in 2006. When I expressed my surprise that the girls wore brown and gold rather than blue and gray, Bob's answer was short and very candid. "For the girls, it was OK to go to Central," he responded. "If I had had boys, they would have gone to Reitz."

Bob has enjoyed his Central ties and names Paul Neidig and his family among his closest friends, and he also enjoyed coaching his girls with Gary Holland, whose daughter Natalie starred at Central. As the girls got older, Bob said they stopped listening to him, so he looked into returning to help at Reitz. He thought he missed an opportunity when the Panthers won State in '07, but he lucked out when he joined the staff and they won again in '09.

Stephenson had a remarkable career in one of the premier football programs in the state, and he truly appreciates and understands what the tradition means to Reitz loyalists. "You know, way back then when the bands played football music, not orchestra music, we loved it," he stated. "Busting through the doors of the fieldhouse, there's nothing like it – the packed houses. My sophomore year, my dad had an offer to move to a Whirlpool (factory) down in Arkansas, and I cried like a baby. I did not want to leave Reitz football. We ended up staying, and I'm sure glad we did."

Bob played on some of the finest Panther teams in history and went on to a solid career at IU. He left Bloomington third on the all-time Hoosier list in career receptions (115) and led his team in receiving each of his final three seasons. He was All-Big Ten Academic three times. In 1993, Stephenson was named to the All-Time IU team as a tight end by the *Chicago Tribune* and received the same recognition in 2001 by *Inside Indiana Magazine*. Bob Stephenson has represented his school and his city well, and he received the ultimate recognition of his skill as an athlete when he joined many other Reitz alumni as a member of the Indiana Football Hall of Fame in 2007.

LOGAN HAYFORD: THE HEART OF A CHAMPION

The Castle High School football program has a long and storied history, including two State championships (1982 & '94) in the state's strongest class. For many years, hall of fame coach John Lidy led the troops, and in the new millennium, Coach Doug Hurt is keeping the tradition alive. Over the years, the program has produced some fine running backs, including the Brosmer brothers (Dave and Chris) and Tony Salpietra, but no Castle runner produced more from less than Logan Hayford.

Those who saw Logan as a youngster witnessed a boy who was a coach's dream as a steady performer with average physical skills. But what he lacked he made up for with his mind and his instincts. As a junior league player, he learned his craft playing for the Saints of Brian Cooper and scored 30 touchdowns in 9 games as a fifth grader.

As a junior high runner, he earned the position of feature back over athletes with superior speed and size, and each year he seemed to surprise everyone with his knack for gaining yards. Entering high school in 2007, he would compete during a generation of talented local backs like K'Andre Vaughn of Reitz, Tyreece Strong of Central and Mater Dei's Cody Hess, and each year the 5'9, 160-pounder would emerge at or near the top of his class.

Without the physique or speed of other runners, Logan churned out yardage in bunches and ran for over two miles in his career by learning his craft and studying the offensive system. An excellent student (3.62 GPA), Hayford maximized his production by understanding the intricacies of the game.

According to his coaches, Logan was always attentive in practice, whether he was running or watching. He observed the linemen as they blocked, knew every person's assignment on every play and listened to the audibles called by the linemen at the line of scrimmage. By processing all the data, Hayford could anticipate how the play would develop and use his explosion to create angles of opportunity.

Of course it also helped to be surrounded by talented teammates. Like any intelligent back, Logan is quick to praise his line, and the experienced crew his senior year was worthy of the praise. He began with center Chris Ford. "Chris is amazing," Logan said. "He started as a sophomore, which is unheard of at Castle, and he made the blocking calls." The guards were juniors Max Nicholson and Aaron Howard. Senior right tackle Evan Goebel "manhandled people," and sophomore left tackle Jake McCandless (6'3, 270) "went against some great defensive ends." The tight ends were Joe Williams and Hunter Renschler, and Logan's fullback was Morgan Lemond, "an animal on both sides of the ball." Hayford also mentioned Elijah Stone, who backed up all the line positions, Kyle Pitlick, who spelled Logan and Lemond in the backfield, and Jeff Bell, a strong tight end during Logan's junior season.

As is the case with any good running game, Castle's quarterback was a passing threat as well. Schuyler Cooper, a teammate of Logan's since junior football, was a running threat himself who also threw for 3,256 yards, placing him behind only Graham Saiko in the school record book.

In addition to his excellent vision, Hayford developed other qualities that enhanced his performance, and he soaked up coaching tips like a sponge. "Coach (Geoff) Bennett always talked about attacking half of the tackler instead of going head-to-head," Logan revealed. "That way you can get more yards after contact and you don't get blown up."

This technique was probably instrumental in one of Hayford's most amazing attributes. For his size, he accumulated massive yardage after contact was made and stayed relatively injury-free throughout his career. He was also rarely caught from behind despite his 4.8 speed in the 40 (- yard dash), thanks to his taking proper angles as he followed the blocking of wide receivers like Jon-Marc Anderson, Cameron Parus and Joe Redburn, all sophomores in 2010.

Perhaps more amazing than the numbers Logan put up was his durability, and his mother cringed more than a few times during her son's career. "That (injuries) was my biggest concern all year," said Laura Hayford. "Every game he finished without an injury I breathed a sigh of relief."

Logan knows that he was fortunate to avoid injury, but he also worked hard to prepare himself for the pounding. Josh Wildeman, a Mater Dei grad, joined the Knights' staff as a strength coach, and after a year with him, Logan increased his squat from 255 to 375 and his bench from 175 to 215. This extra power and muscle allowed Logan to navigate the season without serious injury with only one exception, a minor concussion late in the North game when he was "a little goofy" and didn't remember the last six plays.

With an impeccable work ethic and the heart of a lion, Logan fashioned a remarkable career at Castle. His senior year alone, he rushed for an amazing 2,203 yards, shattering the school record.

He also set records for career yards (3,826), touchdowns in a season (53) and TDs in a game (6) on his way to a berth on the All-SIAC first team and the 2010 IFCA 5-A All-State team.

At the time of our interview, Logan was entertaining offers from several small prestigious colleges so that he could follow in the footsteps of his father, Tracy Hayford, and earn an Engineering degree. He also wanted to find a school where he could contribute on the field as well.

He eventually enrolled at the University of Indianapolis to play for the Greyhounds and was red-shirted his freshman year to focus on his grades. But the following summer he made a discovery. After helping Doug Hurt coach the Castle Knights at summer workouts, he realized that playing the game wasn't as rewarding as developing young talent. Consequently, Logan opted to transfer to USI and continue his work as an assistant at his alma mater.

Though his days on the field are over, he made his mark on the local football scene. Knowing Logan personally, I have seen that there was no limit to what he could do, and his ability was only exceeded by his character. There have been many great players in southwestern Indiana through the years, and in most cases, they were physically superior athletes. Logan Hayford is the perfect example of what can be done with a strong mind and a relentless will to succeed, and through sheer determination, he set records at Castle that will likely stand for years to come.

SINGLE SEASON SCORING LEADERS

The state's single season scoring leader in football is Sheridan's Brett Law with 453 points.
Below are the area's leaders, their rank in the state and their totals.

6th – Cole Seifrig (Heritage Hills) – 308
7th – Billy Morton (South Spencer) – 302

11th – Cole Seifrig – 290
24th – Luke Schmidt (Jasper) – 252
(Source: IHSAA Website)

RUSHING LEADERS

Otis Shannon of Indianapolis Cathedral holds the state record for career rushing with 7,560. Below are the area leaders with their state ranks and totals.

4th – Luke Schmidt (Jasper) – 7,275
14th – Ricky Crider (Reitz) – 6,356
15th – Kevin Cartwright (Jasper) – 6,355
(Source: IHSAA Website)

RUNNING WILD

The single season rushing leader in Indiana history is Cory Jacquay of New Haven with 3,366 yards. Below are the area leaders with their state rank and total.

14th – Derenzo Bushrod (North) – 2,767
18th – Mike Burger (Jasper) – 2,643
19th – Luke Schmidt (Jasper) – 2,613)
(Source: IHSAA Website)

CURTIS PAINTER:
COURAGE UNDER FIRE

The life of an NFL quarterback can be tumultuous indeed, and only a handful of athletes from our area have experienced the intense highs and lows that come with that unique position. Evansville Rex Mundi's Bob Griese spent 14 years at the helm of the Miami Dolphins and was first greeted with an abysmal situation before becoming a two-time Super Bowl champion and the pilot of a team that after 40 years is still the only NFL team to finish a season undefeated (the 1972, 17-0 Super Bowl champs).

Another Rex Mundi Monarch, Randy Mattingly, spent some time under center in the NFL and in the Canadian Football League after a stellar career at U of E. Jasper's Matt Mauck took an unlikely path to a very short career in pro ball after leading LSU to a national championship as a 25-year-old who had spent several years pursuing a professional baseball career.

Today, in 2012, two local players are currently navigating the fickle world of pro football as they strive to build a career. Jay Cutler, a 2002 Heritage Hills grad, made a name for himself at Vanderbilt, a school not known for its football prowess, and has withstood the rigors and public scrutiny of the NFL as he now guides the Chicago Bears. But the man with perhaps the most intriguing NFL challenge is Curtis Painter of Vincennes Lincoln High School.

In just three seasons, Painter has walked the sidelines as he learned from one of the greatest QBs of all-time, has been inserted into one of the most pressure-packed situations in NFL history, and has felt the pain as he parted ways with his team and watched as his home-state franchise ended one of the greatest eras in its history.

Though some sources say Painter was born in Louisiana, he was actually born in Watseka, Illinois but spent most of his childhood in Ohio with his parents, Jeff and Cathy. Like many youngsters, Curtis tried several sports, including roller hockey, but as he reached middle school, he focused on the mainstream activities, football, basketball, baseball and track.

As he grew, his talents became obvious early on. "Being much younger than his brother (Scott LaGuire, Cathy's son from a previous marriage), he was always competing with him," Jeff Painter recalled. "He had to perform to try to keep up. You could tell he was athletic."

Others noticed, as well, and Curtis earned respect as a student (nearly straight A's) and as an athlete. "One sixth grade coach told me that the thing that impressed him most was that he was the best guy out there but he worked harder than anybody else," Jeff told me. "He said that he showed leadership even at that young age and that he wasn't above doing the work."

Cathy Painter received similar feedback. "I worked part-time for the school system when we lived in Ohio," she said, "and I remember a principal who also coached, and he said, 'I just want you to know that he's probably the best we've seen come through here.' He excelled in sports but was always very humble and never thought he was better than anyone else. He never felt like he deserved any special treatment."

Curtis was so well thought of, in fact, that when the family moved to Vincennes after his eighth grade year, his coaches in Ohio called the coaches in Vincennes to let them know that they had a special player coming their way.

And they were correct in their assessment. As a freshman, Painter played football, basketball and baseball but focused on football and basketball after that. Regardless of the sport in season, Curtis set an example with his work ethic by going in before school to either shoot baskets or throw to receivers in the gym. Though his basketball skills didn't match those he had in football, he was good enough to be a three-year starter and to earn All-Conference honors while averaging double figures in points and rebounds.

On the gridiron, he teamed with players like Jeff Cunningham, Levi Salters and Brandon Street and led the Alices to a three-year record of 28-7. At an eventual 6'3 and 200 pounds, Curtis threw for 4,946 yards with 49 TD passes and scored another 17 touchdowns on the ground. His breakout game was a performance against archrival Jasper on a rainy, nasty night his junior year. It was his first 300-yard game and sparked serious interest from college coaches.

As a finalist for Indiana's Mr. Football and a PrepStar All-American, Painter had some choices to consider. "After my junior year, we took visits to Ball State, Indiana, Michigan State and Purdue," Curtis explained. "I had a history at Purdue; my father went there, my uncle (Jay Venzin who played football at Purdue), and my grandfather (Don Beck) played basketball there. I had always grown up around it. I can remember having Purdue T-shirts when I was little. So when I got an offer from them, I pretty much jumped on it."

Curtis red-shirted his freshman year (2004) and then backed up Brandon Kersch for six games before starting the last five in 2005. For the season, he completed 89 of 170 (52.3%) for 932 yards, 3 touchdowns and 5 interceptions. With a season under his belt, Painter's sophomore season was a huge improvement as he threw for 22 TDs and ran for 6 more in 14 games. His 285 yards

(Photo courtesy Purdue University, Communications)

per game were 7th in the nation, and he set a new Big Ten season record with 3,985 yards, besting fellow Boilermaker Drew Brees by just two yards.

His junior year, Curtis again started every game, accounting for 32 touchdowns, 29 through the air. His 296 yards per game were 12th nationally, and to cap off another fine year, he completed 35 of 54 passes for a Motor City Bowl record 546 yards in a victory over Central Michigan.

As a fifth-year senior in 2008, Curtis struggled on a team that offered little run support and injured his throwing shoulder during the campaign. He did make nine starts during the 4-8 season, and in his final outing, he completed 34 of 54 for 448 yards and 5 TDs to secure the Old Oaken Bucket with a win over Indiana.

For his career, the 6'3, 225-pound Painter did himself proud in 'The Cradle of Quarterbacks', a place that has seen the likes of Len Dawson, Gary Danielson, Mark Herrmann, Bob Griese, Jim Everett, Kyle Orton, Drew Brees and many others don the black and gold. Brees still holds the Big Ten record for career yards with 11,792, but Painter is ranked second with 11,163, and had he not been injured his senior year, he might have been the conference's all-time leader.

Curtis also ranks second, fourth and eleventh for completions in a season with 356 (2007), 315 ('06) and 227 ('08). He left Purdue as the program's leader in yards in a game (546), TD passes in a game (6 vs. Eastern Illinois) and total offense in a game (540). For his career, Painter completed 987 passes out of 1,648 attempts (60%) for 67 touchdowns in 46 games.

With a degree in Computer Graphics Technology in his pocket, Curtis headed home from West Lafayette with an impressive resumé, and the waiting game began for the process known as the NFL draft.

The system that most professional athletes experience is unique among professions. Their fates are literally determined by the needs and desires of the participants as each team takes it turn in the rotation, and draft day can be agonizing for the hundreds of men who await the outcome. Knowing himself and the process, Curtis and his parents took a practical approach.

"The first day we were on the golf course," Jeff Painter revealed, insinuating that they figured his son would go on day two. "We didn't watch TV because Curtis didn't want to. Sunday was a little more anxious for everybody. Curtis got a call and looked at the phone and saw 'Indianapolis Colts' and said 'That'd be cool.'"

By all accounts, Curtis was pretty laid back during draft day and appreciated the low-key atmosphere as he socialized and played cards with his friends at the kitchen table. "We had a lot of family over," Curtis explained. "There were a few April birthdays, which made it a fun weekend. I really had no idea what to expect. Through my pro day and combines, I talked to about every team. The Colts were one of the only teams I never spoke to (prior to draft day)."

Painter joined the Colts in 2009, and to say that his brief career has been 'challenging' would not do the situation justice. In '09, he appeared in only two games as he observed and learned from one of the greatest quarterbacks in NFL history, and in 2010, he never touched the field. These circumstances set up a perfect storm for what would follow in 2011.

The Colts were cruising in 2009, and the media latched on to the scenario like a crazed pit bull. At 14-0, comparisons were being drawn to the 1972 Dolphins. Once again, Mercury Morris and Evansville native and Miami quarterback Bob Griese were providing sound bites almost daily on ESPN. As is always the case, speculation was rampant about whether the Colts, who were already a lock for home field advantage, would rest players or chase history, and the decision made was not a popular one.

Arguably, Curtis made the toughest debut for a quarterback in NFL history when he entered with 5:36 left in the third period with the Colts leading 15-10. Not only were the Colts within reach of a benchmark that hadn't been equaled in 37 years (the '72 Dolphins) but only two teams in NFL history had entered the post-season undefeated, the Dolphins and the 2007 Patriots. As Painter entered, the Colts crowd made it very clear that they did not like the decision, and the perfect storm enveloped Lucas Oil Stadium

Curtis was taking the field against a team, the New York Jets, with the ultimate motivation, surviving to play in the post-season. He was preparing to step under center after taking virtually no meaningful reps in the last six months in front of fans, teammates and a national television audience that did not want to see him out there. To add to the pressure, he was expected to pull out a victory with several key starters watching from the sideline.

After losing 29-15 to Coach Rex Ryan and his boys, it shouldn't be surprising that both Jim Caldwell, the Colts' head coach and Curtis were vilified by the media, and the final regular season game in early 2010 just added fuel to the fire. Once again, with nothing on the line, Painter replaced Peyton Manning and had an abysmal game as Caldwell pulled many of the starters early. The Colts advanced to the championship game and capped off their 59th season (the 28th in Indianapolis) with a 31-17 loss in Super Bowl XLIV to New Orleans.

The following season, 2010, Curtis was again relegated to clipboard patrol and never touched the field all season. The Colts finished the year at 10-6 and then lost a wild card game to the Jets. What no one knew at the time, however, was that the 17-16 loss would be the final game for Peyton Manning as a Colt and the beginning of a downward spiral that would rock the world for Curtis and the entire Colts organization.

In the off-season before the 2011 campaign, Manning underwent two surgeries in 15 months to alleviate complications from a pinched nerve. Recovery that was supposed to last six to eight weeks dragged on, and Manning's streak of 208 consecutive regular season starts came to an end. In a drastic move that had to affect Painter's confidence, the Colts' management brought Kerry Collins out of retirement to take control of the offense.

Many questioned the move, and it appeared that the majority of the Colts players wanted Curtis to get his shot. But Painter did what he had always done and continued to exhibit loyalty to the organization and his teammates. With Collins at the helm, the Colts were beaten in their opener by Houston 34-7 before falling at home to Cleveland 27-19. In the third game, Collins sustained a concussion and Curtis was brought in to finish a 23-20 loss to Pittsburgh.

As the season played out, Collins would never take another snap as a Colt and Painter would finally begin to take meaningful snaps in practice and work with the starters. In hindsight, it is

Curtis' parents thought he might one day play for the Chicago Bears. He only missed it by about a hundred miles.

interesting to speculate how the season and Curtis' career may have developed if only Lady Luck had stepped in for the next three games.

In week 4, Painter got his first career start, and in the second quarter, he hooked up with Pierre Garcon for an 87-yard touchdown that was the fifth longest in Colts history. Later, he connected again with Garcon for a 59-yard touchdown, but the Colts fell 24-17 to Tampa Bay.

On the opening drive in game 5, Curtis again hit Garcon for a TD at Lucas Oil Stadium, and Indianapolis led 24-14 at the half. But the defense couldn't deliver, and Kansas City came away with a 28-24 victory.

Week 6 was another nail-biter. The Colts cut the Cincinnati lead to 20-17 on a TD pass to Dallas Clark and were driving late in the game for a tie when Garcon was forced into a fumble that was returned for a score to seal a 27-17 Bengals win.

Had some or all of those games ended differently, who knows how the team's mentality may have changed and the attitude of the Colts' brass may have improved Painter's confidence. But it was not meant to be, and Curtis and his teammates struggled to a disheartening 2-14 season.

With Manning's future still in doubt, the Colts opted to release him, and shortly thereafter, the axe fell on vice-chairman Bill Polian, VP and GM Chris Polian, Bill's son, and head coach Jim Caldwell. In an all-out fire sale mode, key players were then shown the door, including Joseph Addai, Dallas Clark, Gary Brackett and Curtis, with several other blockbuster moves to come.

As he awaited his fate in March of 2011, Curtis handled his situation as he always had, with dignity and class. When asked what it was like to be the scapegoat for thousands of frustrated fans, he revealed a simple philosophy that seems to have served him well. "I've been the kind of guy that takes my criticism and praise from the people around me," he explained. "I don't read newspapers or the internet or watch much TV. I hang around my friends and family and coaches and team. I stay focused and don't get caught up too much in what anybody thinks."

Regardless what Curtis' future may hold, he feels fortunate to have seen first-hand what made Peyton Manning the great player he was, saying, "What I saw was how hard he works, in the weight room, on the practice field and the studying he does and attention to detail. As a young guy coming in, it was important for me to see what it takes to be a player at his level."

With all the scrutiny, the 2011 season had to be difficult for friends and family, and his parents aren't immune to 'experts' who criticize their son. "He coped with it the way he's coped with everything," Cathy Painter revealed. "His philosophy is, 'I'm in there to do a job, and I'm going to do it the best I can.' That's the only thing you can control. You can't control when you go in the game. The only thing you can control is the way you've prepared to do your best. He's done that forever. I think this year it was displayed for the public. He told me, 'Mom, it's making me stronger.' He handles it better than we do, I can tell you that."

Pro football can be a cruel world because so much is dictated by circumstance, and when his organization's confidence in him wavered and they brought in a retiree, he took it like a man and did his job. For the time being (in April of 2012), he will play the waiting game as the dominoes fall across the league. Through all the turmoil, Curtis Painter has never complained or caused a scene, and in the process, he has gained the respect of those who know him best.

Few people know that Curtis has a talent for art, as is shown by these two examples he shared with us.

JOE GENGELBACH: A CAREER OF SERVICE

Southwestern Indiana has been blessed with many fine football coaches over the years, but few have earned the respect and admiration of players and fans like North Posey's Joe Gengelbach (pronounced JING • uhl • baw). Carl Joe Gengelbach grew up in Tell City and played for some pretty good coaches himself. He learned his football from two hall of famers, head coach Joe Talley and Robert 'Bud' George, who assisted Talley then headed up the programs at Bicknell, Southridge and Tell City.

Joe played basketball at Tell City his freshman year but admits that he was not much of a hotshot on the court. In fact, with players like Tom Kron, who starred at Kentucky, and John Arnold (Georgia Tech), head coach 'Gunner' Wyman (also a hall of famer) politely suggested that Joe stick with football. And that is what he did.

Gengelbach was a three-year starter for the Marksmen as a lineman and earned All-Conference honors as a junior and senior. Joe showed leadership skills throughout his high school career, both on the field and as president of his senior class, and after his graduation in 1965, he signed on to play for Evansville College and Coach Paul Beck, who was replaced a year later by Jim Byers.

After four years at E.C., Gengelbach found a coaching opening at North Posey, a school that was a consolidation of five smaller schools: the Poseyville Posies, Cynthiana Annas, Wadesville Red Devils, Griffin Tornadoes and Stewartsville Owls. For one season, Joe assisted head coach Byron Brenton, and when Mr. Brenton became an administrator the next year, Gengelbach was handed the keys to the program as a 22-year old with no head coaching experience.

So as a biology teacher, Joe began his on-the-job training to build a career, and 43 years later he's still at the helm of the Vikings' program. He is quick to credit his success and his longevity to his coaches, several of whom he coached against when they were high school players. The two assistants with the longest tenure both played at county rival Mt. Vernon. Mike Kuhn has been on the staff for 29 years and handles the defensive backs and receivers. Paul Rynkiewich (30 years) is the offensive coordinator and the line coach. "I think Paul is as good as you'll find in the state," Coach Gengelbach told me. "He takes kids that are sometimes limited in ability and gets them playing like there's no tomorrow. I have tremendous respect for him. We've been friends a long time."

Competing every year in the Pocket Athletic Conference against teams like Forest Park, Southridge and perennial powerhouse Heritage Hills, Joe knows the importance of a loyal, knowledgeable staff and feels fortunate to have his other two assistants, as well. Patrick Rose (14 years) handles the line and linebackers, and Joe's nephew, Kevin Gengelbach, is the defensive coordinator and coaches linebackers and running backs.

As Joe's hair has grayed through the years, he has watched as the game he loves has changed as well. In the early '70s, most teams used double tight end formations and churned up yardage on the ground. Today, it seems that every offense is spreading the field with multiple formations and defensive schemes have become more sophisticated to enable them to compete.

But the one constant over the years has been Joe's love and respect for his players. He has had some very talented teams during his four decades at North Posey, including his semi-state teams in '95 and '96 and his '05 team that made it to the State Finals. Though the program from a school with less than 500 students hasn't had many Division I athletes, there have been some great ones over the years. Joe Neidig played at Purdue and then U of E, and his son Nick is now (2012) a wide receiver and DB for the Vikings.

Chris Sapp was a four-year starter at Indiana State, and Jared O'Risky played in the Las Vegas Bowl for Ball State. Joe also mentioned players like Corey Little (Indiana State), and Seth Morris (Purdue) and said there are too many to name who have played at smaller schools like Hanover and Wabash.

As an experienced coach, Gengelbach has also seen that the most enjoyable years aren't always the seasons with the best records. He mentioned how much he appreciated those teams that over achieved, like a team in the early or mid-'90s that was "a good bunch of kids who played above their ability level."

"Some of the teams that were the most enjoyable were kids that were very limited in ability but worked their tail ends off and played every game like it was their last one," Joe added. "I looked at it more as what those kids have to give and what they give you and how they react to the program."

Through the 2012 season, Gengelbach had amassed a 246-192-1 record in 42 seasons, with six PAC titles ('69, '81, '84, '96, '08 and '11). His teams have won 4 sectionals and regionals and

1 semi-state, but his value to his school goes much deeper than numbers, and nothing reveals his worth more than the words of those who know him well.

"I fondly remember our first game together on the varsity staff," recalled long-time assistant Mike Kuhn. "We were playing county rival Mt. Vernon, and during the game, a train came roaring through on a nearby track blowing its whistle. We won the game 16-14 with Layne Motz as our quarterback. I remember Joe's explosive temper during practice if the team was being sluggish. One time he even yelled at Rynk (assistant Paul Rynkiewich) and me. His face was beat red, and it seemed steam was rolling out of his ears.

"Joe has been an incredible force in all that North Posey football has accomplished, and he has evolved over the years. When I first got here, he was taping all the players before each practice and game, calling both offense and defense, and all the while he was our athletic director and a teacher."

Current AD Virgil Ferguson also has great respect for Coach 'G', saying "I always remind Coach Gengelbach that I played my last football game (for the Owensville Kickapoos) on the same night that he coached his last game as an assistant coach. Joe is a true professional. Quoting John Evers, Castle High School's retired AD, 'All Coach Gengelbach needs is a pen and a couple napkins and he can put together a game plan.'"

And summing up Joe's values perhaps best of all is *Courier* journalist Steve Ford: "Gengelbach is a fine coach and an even better man. If I was going to pick a man for my kid to play for, and there are a lot good choices, Joe would be it."

After 43 years, Coach Gengelbach has developed a keen sense of his role as a coach of young men. "You glean a little bit from everybody you've been associated with," Joe answered when asked to comment on his coaching philosophy and why he still coaches today. "The thing I've always tried to instill is to treat those kids like you'd want to be treated. That doesn't mean be soft on them, but we have a standing rule: If I chew a kid out, before he leaves the dressing room, we go talk to him to let him know that 'I don't like what you're doing' is not the same as 'I don't like you.'

"I think working with kids keeps you young, and I've never done anything else. I still get excited every time the season comes around. I like giving direction to kids and letting them know that somebody really cares about them."

As one could imagine, a man doesn't coach for four decades without an extraordinary woman by his side, and Joe lights up when asked about his wife of 43 years, Shannon. "Oh, my goodness," Joe replied. "Our anniversary is August 24, which is

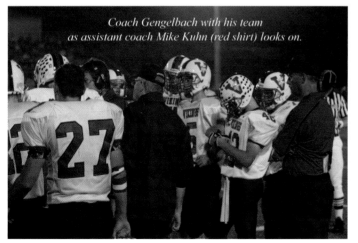

Coach Gengelbach with his team as assistant coach Mike Kuhn (red shirt) looks on.

Joe with assistant coaches Kevin Gengelbach (left) and Paul Rynkiewich.

probably the worst time in the world (during 2-a-day practices each season). Coach (Arad) McCutchan once told us in a coaching class (at Evansville College) when asked what the most important thing was to be successful in coaching, and he grinned and said, 'Boys, if you're going to get married, you'd better get a wife who can be second because you're going to be in situations where she won't always be first.'

"She's (Shannon) spent more time in the stands and in the emergency room on her birthday and anniversary than you can imagine. She's fixed meals (for the coaches) after every ballgame for 43 years, home or away. I can't say enough about her."

When asked what it is like to be a coach's wife, Shannon's answer was simple. "Well, you're busy!" And when asked about the hundreds of post-game meals? "I cook ahead of time. I have crock-pots galore – and dutch ovens and warmers and microwaves. Coaches are easy to cook for; they're not picky."

Joe has a wealth of experience, and when I asked what he might say to a young coach, he thought for a moment and then responded. "Coach hard and learn the game as much as you can," he said. "The key is enjoying what you're doing. Enjoy the kids, and don't forget that this is just a part of their lives."

And why does Coach keep coming back? "It's the people," he responded. "I've been blessed with some great people to work with – the kids, the coaches, the administration. Everyone gives up a tremendous amount of family time to work with our kids."

On my visit with Coach Gengelbach, it didn't take long to understand why folks view him with such affection, and perhaps the most telling sign during my trip to the small rural school off Highway 165 near Poseyville occurred after our interview was over. On that cold October day, as I was pulling out of the parking lot, I was waved down by Joe himself. He was concerned that he hadn't fully conveyed how much the people in his life mean to him.

That gesture is a symbol of what Joe Gengelbach is all about. To a person, the consensus is that Joe is a selfless man who cherishes those around him, and for 43 years and counting, the North Posey community has cherished him as well.

SUPER FAN – SUPER FAMILY

There are times when the world of high school sports transcends the performances of the athletes and coaches and serves a much higher purpose. Such was the case when the North High School football program and an enthusiastic student formed a bond that will last a lifetime.

Ben Grimm was born with an affliction that affects thousands of Americans and their families, and the disorder known as Asperger Syndrome (AS) makes it very difficult for the person to interact with others. AS affects social skills and is in the autism spectrum. It typically causes a pre-occupation with a narrow subject and a tendency to engage in one-sided and long-winded speech, often without context for the comments.

Fortunately for Ben, he had parents who dedicated themselves to finding solutions and educators who refused to let Ben drop through the cracks of the system. "He had mentors like coaches Mike Horn at Scott School and Steve Dedmond at Oak Hill," explained Tim Grimm, Ben's father. "It takes a village to raise a child, and in Benny's case, it took the entire town, people like Mike Horn, Steve Dedmond and Mr. Roberts at North. Those men wouldn't let Ben's eccentricities go."

When asked what he meant by that, Tim referred to autism and popular portrayals like in the movie *Rain Man*. "Benny obsesses on facts, and he gets involved in a conversation with you," Tim said. "He'll begin reciting facts that are germane to the conversation but won't be relevant to it. When most people would just walk away, his coaches had a way of channeling it. They would say, 'That's enough, Ben. Now you need to do this.' They would keep him focused."

By learning to direct his focus, Ben became (to Tim's knowledge) the first kid with that diagnosis to go into the mainstream classroom. But the classroom wasn't the only place where Ben became accepted. He found another passion when football coaches Mike Wilson and Marty Ohlsen greeted Ben with open arms.

Ben's parents, Tim and Kim, thought getting Ben involved in sports would help him deal with time issues and anxiety issues. They debated whether or not to let him play freshman football because the experts thought he should ease his way in before being confronted with a special environment.

Ben tried to play, but grasping the concepts were frustrating him, so when he was introduced to Mr. Harold Roberts, the team's equipment manager, Mr. Roberts declared, "We'll take him." Ben lost fifteen pounds as he toiled in the equipment room and on the field, and when Mr. Roberts stepped down the following year, Ben was placed in charge of the equipment. The new job enabled Ben to blossom, and he learned to set standards and the consequences of not reaching those standards. He developed a degree of self-worth. He also experienced friendships and became a regular at the senior table at lunch.

In fact, Ben became so proficient in his duties that Keith Kohlmeyer asked him to help out with the basketball program also. All this acceptance touched the Grimm family deeply, and at one point he approached Mike Wilson and said, "I don't know how I could ever re-pay you."

Mike thought for a moment and then made a proposal. Because the 50th anniversary of the school was approaching, he thought it might be a good time to organize the history of the football program. Because of Tim's background, he was the perfect candidate. So Tim committed a summer to completing the task. To start, he

Ben Grimm (right) with his dad Tim.

perused items from a cardboard box full of hand-written sheets of game stats given to him by Coach Wilson. After completing that task, he found that he had about 60% of what he needed for the 17 years during Wilson's tenure at the school.

Tim then recruited Ben's help, and the two spent three nights a week at the library examining microfilm to complete the stats and to settle discrepancies. After gathering numbers for such greats as Deke Cooper, Steven Jackson, Matt Hawkins, Derenzo Bushrod, Kendall O'Donnell and many others, Tim pondered his next move.

Even though he had sacrificed many of the hobbies he loved, he felt that if he was going to do the job, he should do it right. So with Ben by his side once again, he launched an effort to compile all the stats from fifty years of North football. The result is a beautiful website (NHSrecords.com), and Tim has done the same for the school's basketball program.

Tim has embarked on this labor of love to demonstrate his gratitude to those who showed compassion and respect for his son. Ben earned five varsity letters in football and basketball during his years at North, and today he serves as a varsity assistant in football. At Ben's senior football banquet, Coach Wilson stated, "There's only one guy around here that if you cut him, bleeds green." He then pointed at Ben and the crowd responded with a standing ovation.

Ben took great pride in doing his job at North, and he wrote about his emotions for a promo sheet saluting him. "It doesn't get any better than Friday nights in the fall," he wrote. "I put on my #10 jersey, stuff a towel in my pocket to wipe the football off, and I get zoned in on what's about to take place on the field. After a touchdown, I catch the extra point kick, run back to the sideline with the ball held high and I strike my pose in front of the stands – it's my trademark."

Tim Grimm is amazed at what Ben has accomplished, and the metamorphosis is not lost on him. "Here was a kid who didn't have a friend when I gave him to Mike Wilson and Marty Ohlsen," Tim Grimm recalled. "Benny graduated cum laude (3.0) in 2008. This was a child diagnosed at four with autism severe enough that they told us he'd never learn to read or write, he'd never be able to live or work outside the home. I could not have bought for my son the type of peer acceptance and growth he got from the football and basketball programs."

The Grimms truly appreciate the educators who were willing to take the time to make an impact on a young man's life, and because of the inspiration he provided others, the annual award given to the most outstanding student manager is called the Ben Grimm Manager Award.

Ben's impact on the program is unquestioned, and Tim Grimm realizes how fortunate his family was to be a part of the story, saying, "In large part to the skills he learned through his association with the football and basketball programs, taking care of equipment, maintaining a schedule, developing those skills, Ben went to Vincennes University, lived by himself in a dorm, graduated in two years with an Associates Degree in Graphic Arts and is now employed in his field here in town.

"He had teachers who taught him English and math, but the life skills that were essential for Ben were taught to him by a handful of men who cared."

IMPACT PLAYER

For those who believe that support staff like student managers can't make a tangible difference in a game, Ben Grimm might sway your thinking. It seems that Ben had a knack for keeping the ball dry during a game. In 2006, Ben's junior year, a good North team led by Dion Pendleton, Larry Merriweather and linemen Matt Hawkins, Justin Turner and Jordan Lewis played Bedford North Lawrence in a sectional game during a torrential rain.

Ben had been diagnosed with mono and had to miss the game. Trailing 13-12, North was three yards away from taking the lead late in the game. Dion Pendleton rolled out and tried to pass a slippery ball, but the pass in the corner of the end-zone to an open Damien Odom fell tantalizingly short. It is pure conjecture, but based on Ben's reputation, that game may have turned out differently, and if North had continued in the tournament – who knows?

DEKE COOPER:
THIS DOG COULD BITE

Art by Jon Siau

The story of Deke Cooper is more than a story of a phenomenal athlete who hit like a sledgehammer on the football field. It is also a tale about a young boy's journey into manhood under the tutelage of a father who had conquered demons of his own.

John Delvecchio Dennis Cooper was born in Georgia, and as he grew, 'Delvecchio' morphed into 'Deke'. The name was later changed legally, and the athlete we all knew has been 'Deke' Cooper ever since. Deke's father, John Dennis, was a fine athlete himself, but some bad decisions as a young man created a long separation from his son.

John Dennis is very open about his shortcomings and is thankful that Deke had some good people in his life who saw his potential and took action. John played some basketball and was a wide receiver in high school but admits that he wasn't nearly as fond of contact as his son was. His best sport was track, and he was talented enough to earn a track scholarship and to be ranked second in the nation as a triple jumper at 49'6". He was also a 6'6 high jumper at a time when Dwight Stone held the world record at 7'0.

Because of his athletic success, John confesses that he let it go to his head, and as a result, plunged into a world from which many never escape. "I tried crack cocaine, and there was an instant addiction," John Dennis confided. "I used for a couple years, and in 1990, I left Augusta (where he was teaching) and started driving."

With cocaine in his car, John headed for Newburgh, Indiana with $10, a tank of gas and a change of clothes to visit his brother Alfonso. "I wanted to get out of the rut I was in," he said. "I used alcohol to bring me down from the cocaine. I believe God used all that to get me here." Now a practicing minister at a church on Oak Grove Road near Burkhardt in Evansville, John experienced what he believes is a miracle on the trip to visit Alfonso. "All of a sudden, the addiction wasn't there anymore," he revealed. "The Lord miraculously delivered me. It just wasn't there."

While John was facing his tribulations, young Deke's mother faced challenges of her own, but fortunately Deke found a home with his paternal grandparents, John and Jeanette Dennis. When Deke was in the eighth grade, Jeanette Dennis saw patterns developing that she had seen before and took immediate action. She was afraid Deke was being influenced by the wrong crowd and made a phone call.

"I can't teach him to be a man," Ms. Dennis told her son. "He needs a role model." John Dennis, who had since cleaned up his life, married his wife Pam and was teaching school, welcomed Deke with open arms, but the young man had his doubts.

"I didn't want to come to Evansville," Deke told me. "I fought it, but looking back, it was the best thing that ever happened to me."

John Dennis had kept track of his son and knew he had athletic skills. He lived across from Bosse High School, but when the 6'2, 165-pound freshman arrived at football practice, he felt that the coaches didn't show much interest. John later found out that his home on Bayard Park Drive was in the North district, so he contacted coach Mike Wilson and North principal Jim Sharp to establish a plan to give Deke proper guidance and to lay out an academic schedule that would prepare him for college.

Coach Wilson admitted that he was skeptical of a father who had such high hopes for his son, but when he saw John's physique, his mind opened up to the potential of the scrawny freshman. According to Deke, on registration day at North, the coach introduced him to a young man who would create some thrills of his own for the Huskies. "This is Kareem (Neighbors), our quarterback," Wilson said, "and this is Deke Cooper. He's going to be a receiver."

With obvious concern, John Dennis went about the business of developing a young man. He recalls his anxiety on the first day of football practice when he watched secretly from the door of North's gym and how his concerns were relieved when he observed his son's talent.

John Dennis also kept a close eye on Deke and admits that he probably made some mistakes with such a regimented schedule. But there is one instance that was a defining moment for both, and it took a while for Deke to understand the value of the lesson learned.

"He always had to do his chores," John Dennis explained from his office at Faith Temple Church of God in Christ. "Football practice was on a Saturday morning, and he did not straighten up his bed. That was one of his responsibilities. I went to practice and went on the field and told Mike Wilson, 'Deke has not done what he was supposed to do.'

"Mike asked, 'Do you have to get him now?' and I said, 'Mike, if we don't keep this kid on the straight and narrow, we're going to lose him. He didn't make his bed; he didn't do what I asked him to do, so he has to miss practice.'"

Coach Wilson relented, but his sophomore star was not happy. "On the way home, I was furious," Deke reflected. "I was embarrassed. I was kind of quiet and mad, but I always respected my dad. He knew I was furious. He told me, 'When you make your bed, it creates a habit of never giving up. It's character building. What you do when nobody's looking carries way more weight than what you do when people are watching. What you do behind closed doors exposes a man's true character.'

"That lesson is part of why I never give up," Deke continued. "No matter what comes my way, I'm going to keep trying. I'm going to keep making my bed. It created a tenacity. It sounds simple, but for me it resonated. I can't really explain it, but it did."

Deke's arrival at North could not have been more timely, and he meshed with some of the best football talent North fans had ever seen on one of the strongest teams in school history. "1995 was a very, very nice year," Deke recalled. "Going through that season there was kind of a momentum build-up. From even before I got there, I think our class was City champs in eighth grade and our freshman year. There was a buzz in the air."

The 'buzz' Deke mentioned related to a special group of players featured in 1995. When the team blew out Bosse in the '95

The 1995 State champion North Huskies

opener, the *Courier* touted the team as possibly the best North team since the 1966 team that featured star running back Doug Atherton and All-State tackle Ron Jesop, and the '95 Huskies seemed to have all the necessary ingredients for a fine season. The offensive line had great size with center Andre Wright (6'1, 220), Aaron Holman (6'1, 232) and Erik Ernspiger (6'1, 270 at the guard positions and tackles Jason DuBose (6'0, 228) and Bart Blalock (6'5, 254). Brian Bennett (TE), Tom Bailey (WR) and William Beverly (WR) were targets for quarterback Kareem

Deke during his days at North.

Neighbors, and when Deke was switched from receiver to tailback after four games, he became a perfect running mate for bruising fullback Casey Sellers.

In the second game, North survived a tough Harrison squad led by running backs Jeremy Redd and Ricky Coleman as North's sophomore kicker Jason McCutchan split the uprights from 22 yards for a 10-7 win. The Huskies then downed Mater Dei (14-0), Castle (8-3) and Memorial (56-28), setting up a showdown with Reitz.

In anticipation of the matchup between the two undefeated teams, the press was comparing the game to the famous 1960 game when legendary coach Herman Byers led the Panthers to a 34-0 massacre in front of an estimated 14,000 fans at Reitz Bowl. The '95 Panthers of Coach Bob Gaddis were led by quarterback Duce Reeder, and unlike 35 years before, this game didn't disappoint the fans. In a game that North coach Mike Wilson calls "the most memorable game I ever coached," North clung to a 35-29 lead as Reitz mounted a drive with the clock running down.

Extra bleachers were set up for the event, and with the fans creating a college-like atmosphere at Central Stadium, Reeder dropped back to pass but was flushed from the pocket by Bart Blalock. As he sprinted for the goalline, he was met first by William Beverly and then brought to the turf by Casey Sellers and Nathan Brooks. As the pile was dismantled, the official declared that Reeder was an inch short and tempers flared as the crowd went crazy.

North had endured another thriller and left the game with a 6-0 record and a #6 statewide ranking. As they had in the Reitz game, North's defense was solid all season with their bend-but-not-break style. The defensive line consisted of tackles Brian Schmitt and Blalock and ends Myron Rucker and DuBose. Behind them were four strong linebackers, Joe Patterson, David Branch, Nathan Brooks and Derrick Garrett, with support from cornerbacks William Beverly and Michael Cooper and Deke roaming the field at safety.

After an easy evening at Mt. Vernon with a 49-14 win in week six, the Huskies squared off with a Central team that featured outstanding QB Andy Owen, powerful tailback James Brimm, fullback Kurt Davies and All-City receiver Jim Klusmeier. In another barnburner, North again prevailed 25-22 and captured the school's first SIAC title since the 1966 season.

After the 8-0 regular season, the green and white faithful had high hopes, and the Huskies opened the 5A tournament with Hoosier Hills Conference champs Bedford-North Lawrence. Deke gained 144 yards on 14 carries and scored twice in a 36-22 win to set up a rematch with the powerful Panthers of Reitz. In front of an announced crowd of 8,105 at the Bowl, North trailed 14-7 at halftime, and Coach Wilson decided to re-emphasize the triple option in the second half. The result was 172 rushing yards with the O-line dominating the line of scrimmage as 6'3, 233-pound Casey Sellers scored on a two-yard run to seal a 21-17 victory.

North then beat Harrison 28-7 to capture the sectional and looked ahead to Martinsville, a dangerous team piloted by hall of fame coach Bill Siderwicz. The 9-2 Artesians featured Mr. Football candidate Israel Thompson and the state's all-time career passing leader Earl Haniford (10,957 yards), and on a windy night, North came out on top in a 34-25 track meet of a game. Deke made an impact on both sides of the ball with 116 yards on 17 carries and a slobber-knocker hit on Thompson, and Neighbors made the highlight reel, as well, with a 78-yard scramble after a key block from tight end Brian Bennett.

North's road wouldn't get any easier as another hall of fame coach awaited them. Ben Davis' Dick Dullaghan had won five State titles, one at Carmel ('78) and four at Ben Davis ('87, '88, '90, '91), but on this night, the Giants were slain by the Huskies 21-14. William Beverly made a critical tackle late to preserve the win, and Deke ran for 165 yards on 19 carries and even threw a 28-yard option pass for a TD, prompting Coach Dullaghan to sing his praises. "He's the best player in Indiana," Dullaghan proclaimed. "The only guy close to him is Ron Mason, a wide receiver at Warren Central."

With the stage set, Coach Wilson's boys prepared for the biggest game of their lives against the Penn Kingsmen. Both teams were 13-0, and although the North crowd hoped that their dream season would end with the ultimate prize, it was not to be. Whether the RCA Dome environs were too distracting or Penn was just too talented, North couldn't overcome five turnovers and fell 35-13.

In the days following, the sting wore off and the North team and fans chose to focus on their successes during the remarkable season. The run made the boys the first North team to finish a regular season unbeaten as they captured the program's third sectional in four years. They were also the first Evansville school to play for a 5A State championship, and two of the players, Deke and Bart Blalock, were named first team All-State.

Without question, Deke made his mark at North High School and has since been honored in its athletic hall of fame. But there was much more to Mr. Cooper than his explosiveness in the arena. "Besides being a fierce competitor, the thing I remember is how he always made sure he talked to everybody," said long-time assistant football coach Marty Ohlsen. "It didn't matter if you were third string, and he was that way in the hallway too. He always talked to everyone."

Coach Wilson had similar feelings, saying, "What I always admired about him was that he had time for everybody. He was a hero around here. It didn't matter if it was a Special Ed kid or the prettiest girl in school. He was so genuinely good to everybody."

Surprisingly, even though Cooper was recognized locally, he was not a highly sought after college recruit, which confused Mike Wilson somewhat. In his long career, Wilson had seen only a handful of players who could run the 40-yard dash in 4.5 seconds, and Deke could do it at 6'2, 190. Wilson also feels that Cooper flew under the radar until the State championship game because extensive internet scouting connections weren't in place then.

Although the quantity of interested schools may not have been impressive, the quality certainly was. IU was one of the few schools that were on Deke early, but after his stellar play at the RCA Dome, some of the big boys entered the picture. According to John Dennis, Deke had previously scheduled five visits to other schools when Notre Dame came calling, and John responded by saying, "Deke is a resident of Indiana. You guys had the first opportunity. It wouldn't be fair. We are committed to five visits."

In response, Lou Holtz said, "Reverend Dennis, you are exactly right. We should have been on top of things, and I promise you that once Deke makes his five visits, if he decides to come to Notre Dame, we'll hold his scholarship for him." Although Reverend Dennis held a hard line with Notre Dame, Coach Wilson enjoyed the recruiting process as much as anyone. "When Lou Holtz walked down the hall here, he was like a movie star," Wilson said. "I was surprised how many kids knew him. He was mobbed. We came in here (the coaches' office), and he wrote some formations on the board. We left it there for a long time."

Deke at Notre Dame. (Photo courtesy of the University of Notre Dame, Media Relations)

Wilson was equally impressed with another notable visitor who came to town on a snowy December evening. "(Nebraska's) Tom Osborne called. We were going to meet at my house," Mike revealed. "He drove (from Illinois) and got down here at 9:00 at night. That was another legend. He was like Frank Sinatra as far as I was concerned. Kathie (Mike's wife) made dinner, and we found out Osborne was a vegetarian. We were lucky she had a plate of fruit."

Deke looks back on the recruiting process and realizes that his father's philosophy of 'process over product' played a role in his decision. "I'm a vision-oriented person," Deke explained, "and every school I would visit, I would close my eyes and ask 'Can I see myself on this campus, in this uniform?' At different schools, there was no connection. When I went to Notre Dame, it was as clear as day. It was almost eerie. And the crazy thing is, the week before, I was telling people I was probably going back down south and go to Georgia. Then three days later I visited Notre Dame and I committed before I left. As my dad taught me, it was the 'process'. You pay attention to everything and to the people around you."

At Notre Dame, Deke went to work, and his skills caught the attention of more than one of his coaches. According to the *Ft. Wayne Journal Gazette*, Coach Holtz was using him on offense when defensive coordinator Bob Davie requested his services. "You can take him," Holtz responded, "but he has to start."

Davie accepted the condition, and after Jarvis Edison was injured, Cooper became a starter at free safety. He finished the '96 season with three interceptions, second on the team, with big games against Navy (10 tackles) and Boston College (6 tackles, fumble recovery and interception).

His sophomore year turned out to be a defining season in his college career, as frustration set in and he faced his first true challenge. With the return of Edison as the starter, Deke's grades suffered, and he found himself in unfamiliar territory. "I started getting down on myself," Deke told the *Notre Dame Observer*. "I stopped going to class, and I was just down. My grades fell."

Although Cooper was technically eligible, Coach Davie called Deke into his office and informed him that he would be suspended from spring practice, prompting Cooper to consider transferring. As a result, Deke had to do some serious soul searching. "I thought about it," Deke confessed to the *Observer*. "I could've gone somewhere else where academics weren't as hard, but then I had to think about it graduation-wise." Cooper knew that a degree from Notre Dame could open doors, so he decided to tough it out.

With a new attitude, Deke re-dedicated himself, prompting Coach Davie to say, "I'm proud of the way he responded. He took the suspension, and he's a better person because of it." Playing primarily a backup role on defense and contributing on special teams, Deke earned a 3.08 GPA in his fall semester and received academic accolades with a 3.6 in the summer session.

As a junior, Deke was the third-leading tackler for the Irish with 78, including 45 solo tackles. Two of his games produced plays that defined his career at Notre Dame. Against Michigan State, he led the team with 16 tackles and made the play of the game when he ripped the ball from Spartan tailback Lloyd Clemons and raced 96 yards for a TD, a play that earned him MVP honors.

Against Boston College, Cooper experienced the single-most memorable moment in his career, and the play became one of the greatest highlights in Notre Dame history. With BC trailing ND 31-26, the Eagles had driven to the Irish 4-yard line with 1:07 remaining. The first three stops were made by linebackers Bobbie Howard and Jimmy Friday, setting up Deke's heroics. With time running out and a half-yard from paydirt, BC running back Mike Cloud took a handoff on the left side and was crushed by Cooper for a loss. Wearing his familiar #1 jersey, Deke sprang from the ground and was mobbed by teammates after a play that is a You-Tube sensation even today.

The play was dubbed the "multi-million dollar tackle" by the *Elkhart Truth* because of the ramifications for the team and for Deke personally, but Cooper responded with humility, telling the reporter, "The hole was so big, even Rudy (from the famous movie) would have made a play on that one."

Although Evansville fans always knew Cooper could hit, the play cemented the legacy for the 6'3, 220-pound bone crusher. In an article in the *South Bend Tribune*, Notre Dame coach Grey Mattison explained an award system the Irish used at the time. Mattison had a saying, "Do we have any dogs that will bite," so when an Irish player put a licking on an opponent, he received a T-shirt saying 'This Dog Will Bite'. Deke earned three such trophies that year.

Cooper's reputation grew as his senior year progressed. As a full-time starter, he became known as a hitting machine. Joe Tiller, Purdue's head coach, espoused his virtues to the *Journal Gazette* in 1999, saying, "I can't imagine playing against a more physical safety than Deke Cooper. He'll have something to say about people coming over the middle and catching the football."

In 1999, Cooper led the team as a senior in fumbles caused (3) and recorded his 200th tackle against Stanford, and after his appearance in the Blue Gray Classic, the NFL scouts showed some interest. After going undrafted in 2000, Deke began the grueling process of finding a place in the NFL as a free agent and soon found that pro football was a different world.

"That was when I ran into my most difficult times," Deke told me. "When I reached the pro level, it wasn't about athletic ability and being able to make plays; it was more about being in the right place at the right time under the right coach. You can get put on a team and have a coaching change and the whole dynamic changes."

Cooper learned this lesson immediately when he was courted by the Arizona Cardinals and then axed when Vince Tobin was replaced by Dave McGinnis. "It was like a ton of bricks. I can't explain the feeling when I walked out of that office," Deke recalled. "I'd never been told I'm not good enough. So I had to figure out how to deal with that and keep going. I knew I could play, and I knew the person I was, and I knew I had value. That's where the character building came into play."

As he gathered his thoughts, Deke got a call from the XFL and drove to Vegas for a tryout. By rule, the XFL team in Chicago had the rights to him because of its proximity to Notre Dame, but the Las Vegas execs said they would trade for him, so Cooper took them at their word and moved to Sin City. Deke had always been a cerebral person and needed to know how the defense worked, and

when he questioned the defensive coordinator's methods, he found himself in the doghouse and was later told that he wasn't a good fit. He admits that being cut from an XFL team was a low point, and he was quickly learning that pro football was "cold and dry and impersonal" and was quite a change from the warm, fuzzy feeling he got during his days at Notre Dame and North High School.

"I could say it crossed my mind," Deke responded when asked if he ever thought about quitting, "but it never stuck. I just looked at it as the Lord had something better for me." As is often true in life, when one door closes, another opens, and a week later the Arizona Cardinals called and sent Deke to the NFL Europe.

Cooper spent a successful season overseas and made the All-League team, and upon his return, he had a good training camp with the Cardinals. But on the last day, he got caught up in another numbers game and was cut after the team drafted two safeties. He then caught on with the Carolina Panthers, but when head coach George Seifert was replaced by John Fox, he heard a familiar tune.

Deke was sent back to Europe, and again he was named All-League and was repeatedly told that he was too good for the competition. After being named the league's MVP after recording 51 tackles and 5 interceptions in the 10-game season for the Dusseldorf Rhein Fire, Cooper again took the long journey home.

Deke led the Panthers in interceptions during training camp with 9, but on the final day, they called him in for another song and dance and said, "You're a good player…"

"Coach," Deke interrupted, "you don't know how many times I've heard this." Deke was then placed on the practice squad for three weeks as the coaches observed him. After three weeks, he was activated and saw his first NFL action on special teams. He finished 2002 with no starts but had another solid training camp. With two Pro Bowl safeties on the roster and two more selected in the draft, things looked bleak for Cooper. Once again, he was called in by Coach Fox to hear the verdict, but before Fox could finish, Deke looked him dead in the eye and said, "Coach, I appreciate it, but I'm about to make somebody look very good – whoever gives me a shot."

The next day, he was in Jacksonville for a workout and signed to a contract. (Deke later found out that Carolina had called earlier and wanted him back.) Deke started the first game and began a fantastic 2003 season. After the season, he received a very classy call from Dion Grant, a former Carolina teammate who had been a Pro Bowl safety. He told Deke that his contract was up and Jack Del Rio, Jacksonville's coach, wanted him in Jacksonville. He knew the tough road Deke had traveled and didn't want to get in the way of Deke's success. Grant was a class act and wanted Cooper's blessing, and Deke's answer was just as classy. "You know what?" Deke told Grant. "I can't get in your way."

In 2004, Deke served as Grant's backup, contributing 37 tackles, and in 2005, he was moved from free safety to strong safety and started 12 games with 58 tackles and an interception.

With his contract up, Deke was excited by his good season, and he decided to have surgery on a torn labrum, a painful injury that he played through for 13 games. He was all smiles when the Dolphins showed interest in using their defensive system to free up Deke's athleticism, but by the time mini-camp rolled around, he had gone from the slotted starter to fifth on the depth chart, prompting Deke to think "here we go again."

Deke was released and spent most of the 2006 season at home watching. He was picked up late by the 49ers and played in a game but began to question whether or not he should continue. "The NFL took me places," he thought at the time, "but maybe now I need to start thinking about transition. I still wanted to play, but I was trying to prepare myself mentally."

Although he was content with his decision, he couldn't resist one last chance, and the offer came from an unlikely source. "We've been trying to get you back for the past two years," Deke was told by Carolina coach John Fox, and for a season, Cooper was as comfortable as he had been for a long time.

After what was arguably his finest season, with 15 starts, 59 tackles and 3 picks, Deke walked off an NFL field for the last time. Though he had some inquiries from teams, the situations were long shots at best, and Deke faced his fate like a man. "I would still have liked to play," he explained, "but I'm not defined by football."

Thanks to the guidance of loving grandparents and a father who learned how to be a role model and accept his responsibilities, Deke became more than a football player. And when asked if he has used those lessons as a blueprint for raising his six children, his answer was swift. "My pops (John Dennis) had a lot to do with it, the way he raised me," he answered. "Everything was character building. He was getting me prepared to handle things in the real world. I tell my kids the same stories, and if I get the opportunity to pull them out of practice, I'm going to do it – because it works."

Just as there were moments in his life that shaped the man he became, there are memories that local fans will cherish about Deke as an athlete. Long-time North assistant coach Marty Ohlsen remembers the monstrous hits Deke delivered that were the result of the power generated from the explosive hips from the player who could power clean 270 pounds. "Against Martinsville in the ('95) regional championship, he laid the wood on Israel Thompson, who was Mr. Football the following year," Ohlsen said. "People still talk about that hit. When he made that hit, it was like slow motion. It was like the old 8-millimeter film. In one frame, he made the hit, and in the next, Thompson was on the ground. The whole crowd gasped in unison. The impact was incredible. It was bone-chilling.

"There were a lot of 'WOW' moments," Ohlsen continued. "He had a rivalry with Levron Williams. In one game, Levron came over the middle and Deke knocked him out of the game." Cooper was a true impact player, and he left his mark on the North High record book as a rusher, receiver and defender among such North greats as Ken Bargo, Jim Thomas, Mike Madriaga, John Mominee, Kendall O'Donnell and Derenzo Bushrod. Against Mt. Vernon, he averaged 22 rushing yards in 8 attempts, second only to Dion Pendleton, who averaged 44 in a game in '07, and Deke holds the school record with 3 receiving touchdowns against Harrison in '94.

Cooper also ranks #5 and #8 in interception return yardage at 80 yds (vs. Mater Dei in '93) and 68 (Mt. Vernon in '94), trailing #1 Jim Thomas who had a 102-yarder against Reitz in 1963. Deke's 92-yard kickoff return versus Bosse in '95 placed him fourth at North behind Cornell Garrett (96 and 93 yards) and Mark Garrett's 93.

As a career scorer, Cooper is #6 at North with 168 points (28 TDs), and in career rushing yardage, he is eighth (2,907) behind two of his '95 teammates, Kareem Neighbors (#5 with 4,109) and Casey Sellers (#7 with 3,060), among others.

But those who knew him also had special memories beyond those seen on the field. "Over the years, it seems the Lord giveth and the Lord taketh away," said coach Mike Wilson. "Sometimes you get the great physical attributes but you don't get the physical toughness. He was one of those rare individuals who had the whole package. He was like a rock star around the school; everybody loved and admired him. He was the most physically-gifted player I've ever had, and he had great leadership. But he was very humble, and Christianity was very important to him."

Even though Deke spent over five seasons in the NFL and four great years in the shadow of Touchdown Jesus and the Golden Dome, his fondest memories may surprise some fans. "When we beat Reitz, emotionally, that was the biggest game I ever played in," Deke recalled. "Just the energy I felt pulling up to the stadium (at Central). Coming down First Avenue and seeing the cars lined up to get in. It made a lasting impression. Even running out of the tunnel for the first time at Notre Dame or my first game in the NFL, it doesn't compare to the feeling I had that night."

During his four years at North, Cooper grew from a stringbean to a physical dynamo and led one of the greatest teams in North's football history. We watched him grow into a man before our very eyes, and today he is teaching the principles he learned to his children. He still spends time with his father as they sit together occasionally at Notre Dame games, and when he lays his head down at night he is content with what life has given him. He learned his lessons well, and one thing is certain: when he rises each morning, you can rest assured, his bed will be made.

FIRST TEAMERS

The 1995 North Huskies featured two players who made first team All-State. Below are all the area players who earned that honor in 1995.

5A
Bart Blalock – North tackle
Deke Cooper – North defensive back
Kurt Davies – Central linebacker

4A
Levron Williams – Bosse running back
Chris Cannon – Vincennes Lincoln wide receiver

3A
Kevin Cartwright – Jasper running back
Nick Mayer – Mater Dei tight end
Greg Nolan – Memorial linebacker
Jonathan Hulsman – Jasper linebacker
Sean Malone – Princeton defensive back

2A
Neil Laughbaum – North Posey guard

1A
Shelby Hess – Tecumseh running back
Justin Hess – Tecumseh linebacker

INDIANA BASEBALL
HALL OF FAME MEMBERS

The following are the 19 men who represent our area in the Indiana Baseball Hall of Fame and the years of their inductions.

(P – Player, C – Coach, CT – Contributor)

1979 – Edd Roush (Oakland City – P)
1979 – Gil Hodges (Princeton/Petersburg – P)
1979 – Roman Pfeffer (Jasper – P)
1980 – Bob Coleman (Huntingburg – P)
1980 – Pete Fox (Evansville – P)
1982 – Don Noblitt (Jasper – C)
1983 – Alvin Ruxer (Jasper – CT)
1990 – Ray Howard (Jasper – C)
1990 – Quentin Merkel (Evansville – C)
1994 – Bill Evans (Rockport – C)
1994 – Tim Nonte (Princeton – C)
1995 – Charles Harmon (Washington – P)
2001 – Buddy Blemker (Jasper – P)
2001 – Don Mattingly (Evansville – P)
2002 – Paul Gries (Evansville – C)
2003 – David Pursley (Evansville – CT)
2007 – Terry Gobert (Jasper – C)
2009 – Andy Benes (Evansville – P)
2012 – Jim Haaff (South Spencer – C)

IHSAA STATE CHAMPIONS UPDATE

SOFTBALL

School	Year	Record	Coach
Tecumseh (A)	2009	29-4-1	Gordon Wood
Tecumseh (A)	2011	24-7	Gordon Wood

BASEBALL

School	Year	Record	Coach
South Spencer (2A)	2007	27-6	Brian Kuester
South Spencer (2A)	2011	24-6	Brian Kuester

CASTLE SOFTBALL:
A MODEL OF EXCELLENCE

After 400 victories, it seems that Castle softball coach Pat Lockyear may have figured out the keys to success, but his drive to improve is still going strong. Like many local head softball coaches, Pat was around for the sport's early years, and he's seen it evolve from a curiosity played on makeshift fields to a sophisticated game on display for hundreds of fans at manicured ballparks.

For the Castle program's first five seasons, it was in the hands of Lisa Lewis and then Sherie Jenkins (Forston), but the schedule was thin and records are unclear. But in 1990, the program was turned over to the gentleman who would build it into a model of consistency and excellence.

Pat Lockyear was a Castle alum who had experienced the ultimate thrill as an athlete in Indiana. As a baseball player, he caught and played first for the Knights, and his football team captured the IHSAA's 3A crown. Led by quarterback Mike Davis, the versatile Joe Huff, receivers Kenny Brown and Deon Chester, and running backs Dave and Chris Brosmer, Castle knocked off Hobart 27-23 for the title, and Lockyear gained experience that would pay off in the future.

Pat entered IU to pursue school's the pre-med program but eventually opted for a teaching degree, and after graduation, he returned home to check out the job prospects. He was engaged to Tammy Fischer, whose sister Andrea was a future Castle Athletic Hall of Famer and a phenomenal all-around athlete as a star in volleyball, basketball and softball. When principal Cecil Raymond interviewed Pat, he assumed that Lockyear would want to help with the football program but was also aware of Pat's connection with Andrea Fischer. When Mr. Raymond asked Pat about the head softball position, Lockyear was intrigued and decided to accept.

Most young girls at the time were playing slow pitch softball until they reached high school, and Lockyear knew that a change was necessary. The program also lacked quality facilities and played games in the early years at John H. Castle Elementary on a field with only a backstop and an outfield fence.

The need for a new facility was evident, and with the weight of Title IX behind him, Pat didn't have to raise a ruckus to demand equality with the boys. The baseball team already had a nice field, and there was a great piece of land just south of the school. As a mental blueprint for the project, Pat used the facilities at Boonville and South Spencer. The field at Castle consisted of a clay-based soil that was extremely hard, and Lockyear recalls the early days when they would drag the field with a steel I-beam and huge spikes with Pat standing on it to break up the soil.

To solve the dirt problem, Pat once again looked locally for an answer. He knew that most schools north of here used brick dust on their fields, which is like "playing on fine rock as hard as an asphalt parking lot." Pat preferred the surface on the fields at Boonville and South Spencer and requested the same Sandridge dirt, a composition from the company near Rockport that offers a softer field. The project also included drain tiles and an in-ground sprinkling system.

Lockyear takes great pride in the facility and credits numerous parents and fans for making it the gem it is today. Many contributors provided the financial backing necessary, and the school corporation provided a double-wide trailer that serves as a concession stand and on-site locker room that inspired other schools, like Central and Pike Central, to do the same. Pat also sought the help of long-time Castle backer Bill Englebrecht, whose daughter Ande was a freshman during Lockyear's first season. Englebrecht supervised much of the project, like the dugouts and lights, and Dave Gossman, the father of the multi-talented Kaleigh Gossman, used his plumbing skills to oversee the bathrooms.

"There are always resources to get things done because of the people who are involved," Coach Lockyear explained. "If a dad

Castle's 2001 State champs. 1st Row (L-R): Mallory Craddock, Kacie Stone, Krista Keener, Sarah Ford, Beth Harmon, Stephanie Newton, Tina Wolfe. 2nd Row: Ashley Harwell, Katrina Sumrall, Mendy Martin, Tiffany Sollars, Sarah Hurley, Amanda Nelson. 3rd Row: Natalie Windell, Lauren Egierski, Kaleigh Gossman, Jessica Perry, Kendra Genet, Keli Kinney. 4th Row: John Evers (athletic director), Cecil Raymond (principal), Scott Fischer (assistant coach), Pat Lockyear (head coach), Sue Laughbaum (trainer). Not Pictured: Brande Tyler, Travis Snyder (trainer).

Coach Pat Lockyear talks with Andrea Fischer at third base. Pat was engaged to Andrea's sister, Tammy, when he accepted the job at Castle and having Andrea as one of his first stars was one of the reasons he took the job. (Photo from the Castle yearbook)

is an electrician, he is on call or on-staff." Pat's father, Harold Lockyear, is a jack of all trades and takes great pride in maintaining the outfield, a feature that always draws compliments from opposing fans.

As the new field was rounding into shape, Lockyear faced his next challenge, bringing the girls softball community together. For a while, there were two leagues for girls, slow pitch and fast pitch, and Pat worked to get everyone on the same page. The future of the sport was definitely the fast pitch variety, and after many discussions, virtually every youth softball league is now playing it.

When Lockyear accepted the softball position, he knew very little about the nuances of the sport, and looking back, there's a bit of humor in the approach he took. "The winter before I started my first season, I threw in the south gym in the dark," Lockyear revealed, "because I didn't want anyone to see me and I really think a coach should be able to throw batting practice. I was trying to learn how to pitch, and I realized pretty quickly that it's not easy. We went to several clinics. It was a tough transition for everybody in this area except Boonville. They had the pitching since day one."

Like all area schools, Castle had a long way to go to reach the status of Mike Wilson's program at Boonville, and Lockyear admits that his outlook as a 25-year-old was somewhat unrealistic. "Early, that's all I heard (Boonville)," Pat recalled. "There's always been a rivalry. We were in the same class in football for a long time. But there really wasn't a (softball) rivalry to start with because our program wasn't on their level. We were an easy game for them.

"The first year I coached, we beat them. We also went to Pike Central, the defending (State) runner-ups, and we beat them. As a first year coach, I thought 'What's the big deal?!' And I'm sure I thought I was the greatest thing since sliced bread. Our record

against Boonville, although we won the first one, is not terribly good. So the rivalry didn't really become serious for me until we beat them again. They had Wendy Wood, who was a great pitcher in her day, Mindy Bacon, the Emmons sisters (Rachel and Shannon) and (pitcher) Erica Taylor."

The Evansville schools had an even later start, and for Pat's first

Becky Lis still holds Castle records for doubles and career batting average. She was also the first Castle softball player to receive a Division I scholarship. This photo was taken during her days as an SIU Saluki.

four seasons, 1991-1994, Castle captured the SIAC crown followed then by an eight-year dry spell. They were also sectional champions in '93 and '94 and compiled a record of 63-20 for Pat's first four seasons.

Looking back through the years, Lockyear remembers several players who were very special athletes. The first was Becky Lis, the program's "first superstar," who was the daughter of legendary hitting coach Joe Lis and a slow pitch legend in the area before converting to fast pitch. Pat recalled a game in Carmi where Carmi was leading and Lis led off the seventh inning and was walked intentionally. She was so powerful, in fact, that the hitter behind her, Rhiannon Brock, set the school's RBI record because no one wanted to pitch to Becky. Lis earned first team All-State honors in 1993 and is still in the top five in many hitting categories in the Castle record book.

Trisha Poling was a star for the Knights from '93 to '96 who was "about five-foot-nothin'" when she was a freshman," according to Coach Lockyear. "She couldn't hit a ball out of the dirt (infield)," Pat told me. Poling was a right-handed second baseman with tremendous speed, and Lockyear decided to make her a left-handed slap hitter. The practice is common among coaches when a hitter has trouble as a right-handed hitter.

"I had some experience with it and learned how to teach it," Pat explained. "Trisha was full-steam in two steps, and she had a great touch from her volleyball experience and could deaden the ball." Although Trisha was an excellent fielder with a great arm, Lockyear used a designated hitter for her when she was a freshman, but after the switch to the left side, she became a .460 hitter.

"She was also one of the first players I had who would dive for a ball," Lockyear pointed out. "Even if she didn't get it, she would dive for a ball." Poling went on to become a Division II All-American at USI, and as a junior, led the team in slugging percentage as a slapper/bunter with lots of doubles, triples and inside-the-park home runs. Lockyear says that as a great athlete who was never satisfied with mediocrity, Poling kept working to become more than just a slapper and learned to take whatever the defense gave her.

While reminiscing about special players, Coach Lockyear also mentioned Autumn Byrd, another left-handed slapper from 1996 who led the state in hitting at .632. Another convert to left-handed slapper was Kelsey Maurer, a lifetime .416 hitter who followed the local pipeline to Wabash Valley College.

Emerald Graham could do it all.

But of all the position players Pat has coached during his 22 seasons, the one he describes as the most talented all-around is Emerald Graham. "She is the most physically-gifted athlete I've seen – PERIOD," Lockyear said. "She had unbelievable strength, speed, competitiveness and work ethic. She was just a great all-around kid. I toyed with switching her to a left-handed hitter when she was a freshman. That would have been a colossal mistake, because she ended up being a great power hitter."

Graham was another of the handful of Pat's players who would dive for balls, and she amazed fans with her glove as a center fielder. As a freshman, Lockyear batted her ninth ("that was some great coaching, wasn't it," Pat said with a grin), and placing her last in the order was the source of a story that Pat still smiles about today concerning the program's first black player.

Pat explained that before each game, the batting order is announced and each player runs onto the field. With Emerald waiting her turn while the eighth hitter was announced, she turned to Pat and said, "I know why you're batting me last." After Lockyear's inquiry about what she meant, Graham answered, "because I'm black" as she ran onto the field.

Through the first half-inning, with Castle in the field, Pat's mind was racing as to how to deal with the allegation. As Lockyear greeted her near the dugout, he noticed a huge grin. "Were you serious?" he asked.

"No, I do that to all my coaches," Graham replied.

"She got me," Lockyear said as he smiled with thoughts of his star of stars.

Pat also spoke of the incredible strength of Emerald and the strong bond they still have today. "She bumped into me once, and I don't know if I've ever been hit as hard," said the coach who played football for John Lidy. "She knocked me off the ground. And she was scary to pitch to (in practice), even if you had a protective net. But she was a great kid who would do anything you asked. She's one who always calls when she's home."

The 5'9 Graham left Castle as the career leader in home runs (14) and was second in runs scored (91) and third with 82 RBIs. She also played at Wabash and Division I Elon University, setting records at both.

Coach Lockyear is also extremely aware of the importance of good pitching in the world of fast pitch softball, and though he feels he has had several fine hurlers, there are two who were a cut above. Both girls were fierce competitors who flourished under pressure, and both lifted their teams on their shoulders and led the Castle program to new heights.

The first elite pitcher was Beth Harmon in the late '90s and early 2000s, and according to Coach Lockyear, she was the one "who raised the bar." Like many of the accomplished hurlers in our area, Beth spent long hours working with dear old dad, but by normal standards, she took up pitching later than most. She played the middle infield for many years on travel teams put together by Bill Englebrecht, Dave Brock and her father, Bob Harmon. Beth was also an "active kid," according to her father, who enjoyed many activities.

The Harmon family's life revolved around sports, and all the kids excelled as athletes. The girls, Beth and Katie, both starred in volleyball and softball and are now coaches, and Zeke Harmon wrestled, played quarterback and played center field for South Spencer.

Beth was an excellent back row player on the volleyball court but always considered softball her main focus. It wasn't

IMAGE IS EVERYTHING

Castle's first dominant pitcher, Beth Harmon, created quite a persona during her years in the circle for the Knights. One of her trademarks was her ever-present sunglasses, prompting opposing players and fans to characterize her as cocky. When asked if the opposing fan's perception was accurate, Castle coach Pat Lockyear didn't hesitate with his answer. "They were right," he said, "but she backed it up quite well."

Harmon's numbers support Lockyear's assessment, as she compiled a 66-16 four-year record and earned first team All-State honors twice ('01 and '02). Beth still holds the school record for wins in a season (25) and left the program with a 0.93 ERA for her four years.

Beth then spent four seasons with the IPFW Mastadons and met her husband while there. Ironically, her husband, Dave Zachary, was a pitcher for Penn High School when they won the State championship in 2001 while Beth's Castle team won the softball title. Beth is now the head softball coach at Penn High School and was named the state's Coach of the Year in 2010. As an interesting side-note, Madeline Brink, who took lessons from Harmon, was named the MVP of the Indiana All-Star game that same year. .

Beth Harmon, at right in her familiar sunglasses, with Madeline Brink and Coach Lockyear.

until the fall of her eighth grade year that she decided to take up pitching, and at 5'3, she wasn't the prototypical softball pitcher. But what she lacked in size she more than made up for with tenacity, and when I asked Bob why she was attracted to the idea of being in the circle, he referred to her competitive nature. "I think she saw that the pitcher was the focal point," Bob Harmon answered, "and I think she liked the idea of being out there and being in control."

Because of his job as a teacher and wrestling coach at Castle, Bob and Beth took advantage of the free time in the summer. "When she was little, we would go out beside the house 10 to 15 times a day," Bob recalled. "We'd come in and take breaks and then go back out and throw." Beth and Bob also studied videotapes from clinics and worked with private pitching coaches, like Tom Rupert and John Feld.

Feld was a highly successful coach in Indianapolis who had coached two of the three pitchers who won State championships that year. When Feld first met Beth, he couldn't help but notice her stature, saying, "You're not as big as I thought you might be, but you look like an athlete."

Beth had heard similar comments many times and learned to use them as motivation, and beginning in the winter of her junior year, long rides to Indy were part of her routine. Many a weekend were spent with Bob coaching all day Saturday at wrestling meets followed by a 3 ½-hour drive, a 2-hour lesson and a long return trip home. But the sacrifices were worth it as Beth became stronger and developed into a force to be reckoned with for Coach Lockyear.

Pat has stated many times that Beth Harmon was an example of the amount of work it takes to be really good, and the feisty hurler was the catalyst Lockyear needed to lead the Knights to the next level. With Harmon on the mound as a junior in 2001, Pat surrounded her with a very talented group of young players who were oblivious to the pressure and loved to play the game.

The only senior starter for the Lady Knights was left fielder Sarah Ford, who shared the outfield with sophomores Lauren Egierski (CF) and Ashley Lawyer (RF). The infield consisted of freshman Kaleigh Gossman (1B), sophomore Krista Keener (2B), junior Stephanie Newton (3B) and sophomore Mendy Martin (SS), with sophomore Kacie Stone behind the plate and freshman Tina Wolfe as the designated hitter ('designated player' in today's game).

Castle finished the regular season at 23-6, and after a 9-0 win over Central in the sectional opener faced Mike Wilson and his always tough Boonville Lady Pioneers. The Pioneers were led by seniors Brandi Bates, Morgan Metzger and Devon Guthrie, but Castle came from one run down to win on a two-run single by freshman sensation Kaleigh Gossman. In the final, Beth Harmon battled Harrison for nine innings for a 2-1 win, sending Castle to the regional for the third time.

The regional opener exemplified the grit of the 2001 Knights, with Harmon pitching out of tight spots and her teammates doing what they do best. Castle's only run came on two infield singles and two sacrifice bunts, and twice Castle gunned down runners at the plate, Sarah Ford from left field and shortstop Mendy Martin in the 7th to help secure the victory over Center Grove and legendary coach Russ Milligan. The regional final was another barnburner as the Knights broke a 0-0 tie scoring three in the final inning, with the big blow a two-run double off the fence by Gossman.

The State Finals paired Castle with the powerful Indians of Lake Central, who featured Brooke Baker, the best pitcher in the state who earned a full-ride to Purdue. The Knights clawed and scratched against Baker, scoring a run on a wild pitch and two others. One of the runs was an earned run, only the second of the year against the Lake Central standout. One of the subplots of the game involved Castle catcher Kacie Stone, and the drama is one that Coach Lockyear says he will never forget. During the game, Stone had taken a foul tip off her hand. The pain was so agonizing that she couldn't even throw the ball back to the pitcher, but Lockyear couldn't replace her because he had used his backup catcher as a pinch runner. With two outs and Castle ahead by a run, Lake Central laid down a bunt in front of the plate. Stone pounced and threw a rocket to first in a demonstration of what Pat called "unbelievable guts" to preserve the 3-2 victory.

Between games, Kacie iced her injury and was fine for the nightcap. The championship game in '01 was a little less intense as Beth Harmon fanned seven hitters in a 4-1 win over Pendleton Heights to deliver the program's first State title, making the Knights (along with Forest Park, who also won a class A title in '01) the first area school to win a State softball championship.

The 2001 Lady Knights set a new set of standards for future players, and they did so with a youthful exuberance that Coach

Lockyear looks back on as the key to their success. "Nobody knew what the heck was going on," Pat said with a smile. "They were babies, and I think that may have helped them. Ignorance is bliss. They were great and very mature for their age."

Needless to say, expectations were high with loads of talent returning in 2002, but as everyone knows, talent is not the only ingredient in the formula for success. One decision made for the new season concerned the team's pitching ace, a player for whom Pat Lockyear has the deepest respect. As the team's most valuable commodity, Lockyear had kept Beth Harmon out of the hitting lineup to minimize the risk of injury as much as possible. But knowing the type of competitor she was, he decided that the senior had earned the right to hit, saying, "After winning State, I figured she deserved that."

As the season played out, Harmon's bat was needed, as key injuries obliterated a very promising campaign. The team started the year strong with a 5-0 record against stiff competition, but in the Boonville Southern Slam tournament, junior stars Krista Keener and Mendy Martin sustained serious injuries. Both were out for about 17 games, and even though the team won 15 of the 17, they were victims of a major upset in the tournament.

It is rare for a Boonville win in the sectional to be considered an upset, but in '02 the Pioneers had a down year by their standards. In the sectional opener, Mike Wilson's girls shocked the 27-2 Knights to end Castle's season when Boonville pitcher Heather Metzger pitched the game of her life. As devastating as the loss was for the Lady Knights, the game is considered even today as one of the biggest wins in Boonville softball history.

In '03, with Beth Harmon gone and all the super sophs from the '01 team now seniors, Castle's main need was a replacement in the circle. The position was filled by a reluctant Abby Hornbeck, who preferred to be behind the plate as a catcher. But with Kacie Stone firmly entrenched there, Hornbeck accepted the challenge. The talented rookie responded well and became "an unbelievable pitcher," according to Coach Lockyear. "She had the best changeup I've ever seen – bar none," Pat said.

The '03 team finished 27-7 and ended the season with an extra inning loss in the regional to eventual State champion Center Grove. The '04 team suffered a similar fate with a 1-0 loss in eleven innings to eventual State champ Martinsville in the regional final, ending their season at 22-1.

In 2005, Castle won their third consecutive sectional and finished 17-13-1, and in '06, the Knights finished 21-10. But after three years of relative mediocrity, a team was on the horizon that would feature a young star who would become the program's second dominant pitcher and a lineup that could knock the cover off the ball.

Coming into the season, Lockyear was confident the team would be able to produce runs, but pitching was a glaring question mark. He began with two rookie pitchers, but halfway into the season it became obvious that one of them could be something special. The rotation of Madeline Brink and Samantha Meyer eventually became the Madeline Brink Show, and she thrived in her new role. "She was able to do things that freshmen normally can't do," Lockyear told me, "and one was to handle the pressure."

Pat was able to surround Madeline with an experienced crew that was anchored by six senior starters: Sarah Hart (C), Amber Chapman (1B), Amanda Pravdica (3B), outfielders Laura Helm and Emerald Graham and DH Casey Zahn. Other starters were freshman Jean Ann Scarafia (2B), juniors Catie Cozart (SS) and

In 2007, the three Warrick County schools accomplished a rare feat when all three (Castle – 3A, Boonville – 2A, and Tecumseh – A) played in the final game of the State softball tournament. Despite a rousing pep session in Boonville for all three teams, each fell in the finals, however, but the achievement is still exceptional. In case you're curious, it has happened at least once before when three schools from Delaware County played for a State title in the same sport in the same year. In 2002-03, Muncie Central (4A), Muncie Burris (2A) and Wapahani (A) all won State volleyball championships.

Castle's 2007 State runner-up team. 1st Row (L-R): Jacklyn Pate, Taylor Thompson, Amanda Pravdica, Sarah Hart, Amber Chapman, Laura Helms, Casey Zahn, Emerald Graham, Amanda Helms, Megan Darr. 2nd Row: Kourtney Schroeder, Jean Ann Scarafia, Carly Rentsch, Madeline Brink, Jenna Powers, Jessica Ryan, Bailey Brown, Mallory Wood, Natasha Seitz. 3rd Row: Sarah Kothe (asst. coach), Andrea Seavers, Alexis Reed, Leah Braun, Melanie Brown, Catie Cozart, Katie Nutt, Amy Watson, Courtney Eberhard, Amy Watson, Pat Lockyear (head coach).

seasoned competitor. As the sectional approached, fans had high hopes for Coach Lockyear's veteran squad, and the girls didn't disappoint. Castle made easy work of the sectional with a 5-0 win over North and a 7-5 victory over Harrison that featured long balls by Pravdica and Graham, and the duo delivered again in the 8-1 final over Central.

The regional presented bigger challenges, but the Knights continued their pattern of winning games in dramatic fashion with their bats. In the opener, Catie Cozart provided the game winner in the top of the 7th with a solo shot for a 3-2 win over Floyd Central, and Pravdica went deep against Mooresville in the final inning of the second game with a two-run dinger to deliver a 5-4 victory that sent Castle to the State Finals for the second time.

The Finals at Ben Davis proved to be a daunting task for the Lady Knights as Brink faced two hurlers who would go on to pitch at the Division I level. In the opener, the team faced Tori Collins of McCutcheon, who would later pitch at Louisville, and seven innings were not enough to decide the outcome. With the game tied at 3-3, more heroics were in store for the Castle faithful. Jessica Ryan had homered earlier in the contest, but it was Amber Chapman's two-run blast in the top of the ninth that provided the winning 5-3 victory.

The final game pitted Brink against one of the better players in Indiana history, and to add to the drama, Castle encountered an unexpected obstacle before the game even began. During the pre-game, third baseman Amanda Pravdica was warming up when a rock from the tightly packed infield flew up and caught her below the eye. Lockyear could see that Pravdica wasn't right and believes even today that she suffered a concussion that made her disoriented. But the Knights still had a game to play.

During the season, Megan Darr had earned the nickname 'Captain Clutch' because of her ability to answer the call wherever she was needed, and Lockyear didn't hesitate to insert her at third base. Darr lived up to her moniker, making every play and even driving in the team's only run as Castle battled Hamilton

Jessica Ryan (LF) with junior Jenna Powers as the DH.

The lineup proved potent throughout the year, and the team finished the regular season 23-6 as Brink became a

Southeastern. Brink matched the Royals' megastar, Morgan Melloh, pitch for pitch for ten innings. But Melloh, the future Miss Softball and star at Fresno State and IU, drove in the winning run herself for a 2-1 win, sending the Lady Knights home with a hard-to-swallow runner-up finish. As is often the case, Coach Lockyear looks at the 10th inning in retrospect and wonders what might have been: "I thought about walking Melloh, but we had gotten her out in her previous at-bats, and the batter after her had a couple of hits already. I called several rise balls to get her to chase some bad pitches, and unfortunately she chased one into left-center field. I will always wonder. I didn't follow my rule: don't let their best player beat you."

Though the 2007 Knights fell just shy of the ultimate prize, Coach Lockyear still believes it may have been his finest team, and their accomplishments justify his feelings. The team finished the year with 20 home runs, placing them in the top ten in Indiana history, and remarkably, at least a dozen went on to play college ball, including the entire starting lineup plus Melanie Brown, who was injured during the year.

Following the '07 season, Brink continued her fabulous career, leading the program to three more excellent seasons (24-7 in '08, 21-5 in '09 and 27-3 in '10), but the program could not reach the Finals again before she left for USI. After Brink's exit, Coach Lockyear put together a nice season in 2011 that he called "one of the most enjoyable years I ever had."

The 2011 team wasn't as talented as previous years but "always found a way to win," according to Lockyear, and behind two inexperienced pitchers, Devon Rutherford and Conci Nall, they captured the school's third regional. The team featured starters Taylor Abney (C), Danielle Saylor (1B), Brittany Casson (2B), Kayla Katterhenry (SS), and Casey Eaton (3B) with outfielders Hayley Snyder (LF), Kelsey Maurer (CF) and Shannon Mitchem (RF), and the overachievers advanced to the semi-state before falling to perennial powerhouse Pendleton Heights.

In 2012, Coach Lockyear suffered through an injury-plagued 19-13 season that every coach faces from time to time, but his girls rose to the occasion when it counted, finally falling in the semi-state to Roncalli. Through the years, Coach Lockyear's complete body of work has been stellar. As of 2011, his record stood at 417-158-2 (72%), and his win total places him in Indiana's top ten with legends like Boonville's Mike Wilson and Center Grove's

Russ Milligan. Unlike his Warrick County contemporaries, Wilson and Tecumseh's Gordon Wood, he never got to coach a daughter because he and his wife Tammy had two sons, Zachary and Conner. But Pat is thrilled with the choice he made to accept a new challenge coaching the girls and appreciates how far the sport has come.

"It's a little different now, 21 years later," Lockyear revealed. "In the early days, they (the girls) thought I knew more than they did, which wasn't necessarily true. The kids coming to me now have been coached so much more before I get them. It's amazing how good these athletes are."

Those who know Lockyear have watched him evolve along with the sport and appreciate him for how he handles himself and for the job he's done. "He's the same guy as back when I played," said Kacie Stone, who now serves as Pat's assistant.

"Well, he's won 400 games – enough said," stated Tecumseh coach Gordon Wood. "He's a great coach, year-in and year-out."

Through his first 21 seasons, Pat Lockyear's teams have never suffered a losing season, and Castle captured 12 conference titles, 10 sectionals and 3 regionals to go with the runner-up finish ('07) and the 2001 State championship.

When all is said and done, who knows where the coach will finish in the annals of Indiana high school softball history? But regardless of his final place in the record books, one accomplishment will last until the end of time. As the IHSAA records will always show, Pat Lockyear and his Lady Knights were the first southwestern Indiana team to capture the coveted title of State champion.

MAKING HISTORY

In 2001, Castle senior Sarah Ford won the mental attitude award. Head coach Pat Lockyear was a member of Castle's 1982 State champion football team and also won the mental attitude award, making them very possibly the only coach and player to win both a State championship and the award.

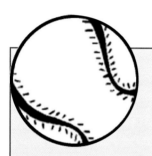

MADELINE BRINK: THE MAD DOG

According to Castle coach Pat Lockyear, Madeline Brink was one of those rare pitchers who could dominate opponents with power and intimidation, and her talents enabled her to re-write the school's record books. Lockyear places Madeline and Beth Harmon at the top of his list of Castle pitchers and credits their fathers for fostering their development. Like Bob Harmon (Beth's father), Tim Brink spent countless hours sitting on a bucket catching fastballs from his daughter.

"There were probably a lot of bruised shins," Coach Lockyear surmised. "I'm sure there were a few times that Madeline didn't feel like practicing and Tim had to encourage her. It's pretty common for pitchers and their dads to have that kind of connection. They spend a lot of time together."

Lockyear is also aware of the traits needed to become a star pitcher. "She had a tremendous mental toughness," Lockyear said. "When Madeline would strike people out, the dugout would cheer 'MAD DOG' like she was some kind of crazy animal out there. But she was very emotion-less. She had tremendous confidence in what she could do, and she performed well under pressure. You don't get that from drills or from a pitching instructor. It's just who you are, and not many players have that."

Obviously Coach Lockyear was sad to see Madeline leave after the 2010 season, not only because she would be virtually impossible to replace, but also because of what she offered on several levels. "Madeline was one of the nicest players I've ever coached," Lockyear said. "She was also very knowledgeable about every facet of the game. Once she stepped in the circle, she became a different person, very focused and determined, and she was also a great fielding pitcher.

"The only weakness Madeline had was that she couldn't see," Pat continued as he grinned at the memory. "She would squint to see the catcher's sign on every pitch. I often wondered if that made the batters nervous, that the pitcher was throwing 60 miles per hour at them and couldn't see where she was throwing it."

Madeline spent the 2011 season as one of two primary pitchers for USI as she worked to make the adjustment to the 43-feet distance to home plate in college (compared to 40 feet in high school), but her name will forever be written in the legacy of Castle softball as one of its finest superstars. Her four-year record at Castle was 71-12 (85.5%), and her ERA never exceeded 1.0, with a low of 0.16 her sophomore year. She also ranks (as of 2012) #1 in wins (71) and career strikeouts (769). And she wasn't too bad at the plate either, ranking third in home runs in a season with 7.

Madeline Brink (Photo courtesy of the Evansville Courier)

JIM HAAFF:
ROCKPORT'S MR. BASEBALL

When it's all over, Rockport fans will have a hard time adjusting to watching Legion baseball without seeing Jim Haaff in uniform. The reason? Because for nearly 50 years, Haaff has BEEN Rockport baseball.

Jim was born in Evansville on July 3, 1942 and then raised on a 170-acre farm northeast of Chrisney. He played basketball and baseball for the Wildcats before graduating in 1960, several years before the school was absorbed into Heritage Hills. Though Jim was good on the basketball court, averaging an estimated 12 points per game for his career, the spring and summer was when his true talent showed itself.

Remarkably, the sport that would consume his life for over 50 years was new to him as a freshman because the area had no little league baseball until Jim was 13. But it quickly became evident that the young man had a knack for the game.

With a fastball estimated in the mid-80s (mph) with great movement and a nice curve, Jim threw four no-hitters for Chrisney, and in the summer of his freshman year, the Rockport American Legion program was started with players like "Wayne Boultinghouse, the Vincent boys and Jimmy Boyd," according to Jim. The team was managed by Bill Evans, an eventual Indiana Baseball Hall of Famer who would become Haaff's mentor for many years. Jim says that he was "discovered" by Coach Evans when Haaff squared off in a pitching duel with Rockport ace Damon Vincent and Jim came out on top 3-1 in nine innings.

After high school, Haaff and Boultinghouse worked at the Show Me Baseball Camp in Branson, Missouri, back before the town became the tourist destination it is today. Goldie Howard ran the camp, and the boys would supervise and teach youngsters baseball during the day and then play games at night at places like Joplin, Missouri and Little Rock, Arkansas. Jim says that the league, based in Springfield, Missouri, had some nice talent and that he played against players like Lance Alworth, the great NFL receiver, two of Ken Boyer's brothers, and future Cardinals pitcher Ray Sadecki.

When Jim returned home in late July, he started school at Oakland City College and began a great baseball career there that would earn him a spot in the school's athletic hall of fame. Typically, Newburgh's Bill Stone would pitch the first game of doubleheaders and Jim would pitch game two, and the Oaks were good enough to beat teams like Indiana State, who featured the great Joe Don Decker from Princeton.

During the summers, Haaff pitched for semi-pro teams from Washington, Holland or Rockport. Jim admits that times were different in the early '60s and that Holland Dairy gave him $1,000 and a job to play one summer. "I made $2,600 that summer," Haaff told me in his thick southern drawl. "I don't know if it was totally legal or not, but nobody really cared. That was a bunch of money

for a kid going to school, and I was able to help my folks out. It's not like it is today where you can't even buy a kid a pizza."

Jim also mentioned that the Holland team from that season is still very close and had a reunion in 2009. The boys lost only one game with a strong lineup that included Joe Todrank, Roger Kaiser, Junior Buse (Don's older brother), Bob Peach and Jeep Kahle.

Haaff graduated from OCC in 1964 and set several records while he was there, including the record for strikeouts in a game with 20. In the spring of '64, a Boonville man asked Jim if he wanted to teach and coach and told him that there was a rare combination available, coaching and teaching English. Jim was the perfect candidate and began his 33-year career as an English teacher as he coached basketball, football and track at Clark Junior High.

In 1965, Paul Dunker, who had coached at Rockport for many years, called and asked Haaff if he would be interested in coming to South Spencer. Consolidation had just started in the area, and the school had an excellent coaching staff with head coaches John Jolly (football), Bill Evans (baseball), Al Ellison (basketball) and P.M. Sanders (track). Jim joined the staff, and when Evans moved into the counseling department in 1967, Haaff joined the teaching staff at the high school and took over the Legion baseball program before becoming the head baseball coach at South Spencer a year later.

In his first season, Jim had outstanding talent, including right-handed pitcher Jim Harris, who later played in the Detroit Tigers organization, and southpaw Randy Ayer. Haaff recalls the '69 team and how they won the Jasper Semi-state in what Jim called "one of the finest games I've ever coached in." Before beating Jasper 7-0 in the final, South Spencer beat Jeffersonville 2-1 in 15 innings, and the one run they gave up (a home run) was the only run that Harris, Ayer and the staff allowed in the sectional, regional and semi-state.

At one point, from 1971-1989, Jim had 19 straight winnings seasons, and his team in '05 won 30 straight before losing in the state tournament. Sitting at his kitchen table, Haaff spoke about Evansville North pitcher Jim Schmidt who played Legion for him and went 8-1 in 1974 and 7-0 in '75, including a four-hit win over Cedar Rapids in the World Series. Jim also mentioned South Spencer's Josh Garrett in '96 who signed with the Red Sox and Michael Mosby who played on the Legion team and was with the Orioles organization in 2011. To wrap up his recollections, Jim spoke of Kevin Davis who recently replaced the retired Bernie Meyer as the AD at Boonville, third baseman Mark Talbott and a shortstop he had for three years named Jay Cutler.

As of 2011, Haaff had coached the Legion team for 45 years with a record of 1,010-590 with 33 sectional and 15 regional titles. He was a part of six state championships, 1959 as a player and five others as the manager in 1974, '79, '83, '05 and '07. Jim is also proud to say that only eight Indiana teams have made it to the

World Series, with five of them only going once, and Rockport has been three times ('74, '84 and '07).

Haaff does regret that he never won the IHSAA State championship at South Spencer, but he did finish his 30-year career with a record of 488-330 with 10 Pocket Athletic Conference titles, 12 sectionals, 4 regionals and a semi-state. Along the way, Jim has had several loyal assistants with both programs, like Bob Snyder, who has been with him his entire career, and Larry Snyder, who does the scheduling, and Legion program organizer Owen Wells. Haaff also gives props to the new blood in the program, like Andy Ward and Shawn Kuester, whose son Brian is now the coach at South Spencer.

Jim is proud of what his program has accomplished and has kept the process simple from day one. "We've had good fortune through the years and established ourselves in the state," Coach Haaff confided. "People know us. When the kids come in, they know what to expect. I basically have two rules: show up and play hard. They know the other stuff. They're good kids. I've been blessed to be able to do it over such a long time. We're not that difficult to play for, but we have high expectations."

Jim Haaff knows that the time will come for him to step down, and it is obvious that he's thought about it and is taking a philosophical approach. In recent years, he has turned over most of the physical work, like hitting ground balls, to the younger coaches, but he isn't ready for the pasture just yet.

"I'd like to stay in it a little longer," said the 70-year-old Haaff. "I have grandsons that look like they're going to be able to play a little bit. I can't imagine (not coaching). I enjoy it more today than I ever did because I'm retired (from teaching) and all I have to do is get ready for the ballgame."

By all accounts, Jim Haaff still has a youthful exuberance for the game he loves. The man who once stood as a boy at a packed Bosse Field to watch a young Henry Aaron and his Braves play Al Kaline and his Tigers in an exhibition game has no immediate plans to call it quits. For his 45+ years of service to the game, Haaff was inducted into the Indiana Baseball Hall of Fame in 2012, and when asked to pose for his etching, he wore a South Spencer cap and a Rockport Legion jersey, the programs that were two of the loves of his life.

DID YOU KNOW?

Until 2011, Jim Haaff was the only man in the state to win a Legion state championship as a player and as a coach. Jim Lynch won as a player for Newburgh in the early '90s when he played with Jamey Carroll and others, and in 2011, Lynch's Newburgh team won with Jim as the manager.

TECUMSEH SOFTBALL CAN PLAY WITH THE BEST

In addition to 4A Castle and 3A Boonville, 1A Tecumseh gives Warrick County a trifecta of successful softball programs. Prior to the year 2000, the tiny Lynnville school with less than 250 total students had experienced some success on the diamond, but when new coach Gordon Wood took over in 2007, he led them to a whole new level.

Gordon grew up in Monon, Indiana, just north of Lafayette. His father coached legion ball and umpired for 25 years, and his mother ran the concession stand at the only field in the town for every level of ball. This meant that Gordon spent nearly every day at the ballpark.

At Vincennes University, he was one of only two walk-ons out of 40 to make the school's baseball team, and after playing for two years, he joined the workforce as a conservation officer. He coached little league baseball, but after he and his wife Susan had three daughters, Gordon realized he'd better learn the game of fast pitch softball.

The Tecumseh softball program was one of the first in the area to take up the sport, and the Lady Braves had held their own for many years under Leslie Oxley and Jenny Herrenbruck. Herrenbruck led Tecumseh to the State Finals in 2000 and 2003, and when Coach Wood took over in 2007, the program was poised for a breakthrough.

Tecumseh came very close to grabbing the brass ring with State runner-up finishes in 2007 and '08 when they were led by Katie Kruse, a .505 hitter who went on to play at Kentucky Wesleyan. After two years of frustration, Gordon finally felt that his

The 2009 State champs from Tecumseh. Front row (L-R): Ali Nora, Emily Tuley, Keshia Bryant, Audra Sanders, Megan Froman, Jaylen Buse. Second row (L-R): Torie Pace, Kara Snow, Chelsie Nuhring, Julie Roeder, Kayley Pemberton, Alishia Sexson-Lyle, Teri Newmaster. Third row (L-R): Mindy Rasche, Kim Wornica, Ashleigh Goff, Cherish Lamborn, Kimber Hunt, Rachel Morris, Gordon Wood (head coach), Sarah Stuart (asst coach). Fourth row (L-R): Assistant coaches Mike Sanders, George Julian, Mark Newmaster.

2009 girls had a real shot. His senior pitcher, Audra Sanders, had improved steadily over her 3 ½ years as the ace of the staff and had developed into a rare talent. "There's no doubt that she's a way better pitcher," Coach Wood answered in a *Courier* article when asked about Audra's growth from her sophomore season. "I called her a thrower back then, but she's a pitcher now; she's really developed."

Sanders faced an odd series of physical woes that slowed her down to begin the 2009 season. "Early in the season, she got sick for four or five days," Coach Wood told the *Courier,* "and I mean real sick. And then she pulled a quadriceps muscle and couldn't throw for another week. And then she came up with a bad blister. She just wasn't getting enough innings." But the girls persevered, and in Gordon Wood's mind, the potential of the '09 team showed itself in the team's 16th game. "We knew we were special when we beat Boonville 7-1," he confided. "Boonville is a major power; you don't beat Boonville 7-1, at least we don't."

Wood also sees other factors as keys to the team's success. Year in and year out, he makes an effort to schedule the best competition he can. In the 2009 Southern Slam tournament in Boonville, the Lady Braves lost 2-1 to Center Grove, a 5-time State champion. In addition, Tecumseh's conference is solid from top to bottom. "I believe the PAC (conference) is the best softball conference from Indianapolis down," Coach Wood said. "They're all 2A and 3A schools; we're the only 1A. Forest Park, Gibson Southern and North Posey, all three have been to State before. Forest Park won it; Gibson Southern's won twice; North Posey's been there; South Spencer's been there twice. Out of the nine teams this year (2011), eight of them were ranked in different classes."

Wood also gives props to his assistant coaches over the years, like Brian Beard, Lance Summers, Mike Sanders, George Julian, Mark Newmaster and Sarah Stuart. Stuart especially has been a mainstay on the staff and offers exceptional expertise. Sarah played at Boonville under Mike Wilson, one of the state's best, and a man Gordon considers the best assistant around, Mike Metzger.

"Sarah brings a lot to the game. I always say I'm not a very smart coach, but I'm smart enough to get good people under me," Coach Wood stated. "She is the hitting coach and calls pitches. If she leaves, I'm going to have to learn how to coach again."

The '09 season began with five easy wins, the first four by the ten-run rule. But the next nine games were a challenge as Audra Sanders dealt with her ailments and the Lady Braves lost four games to tough teams, 2-1 to Center Grove, 5-2 to Carmel, 4-3 to Carmi and 1-0 to Gibson Southern. By midseason, Tecumseh had developed a consistent lineup with Sanders in the circle and freshman Kara Snow behind the plate along with Megan Froman (1B), Cherish Lamborn (2B), Julie Roeder (SS), Ali Nord (3B), Chelsie Nuhring (LF), Teri Newmaster (CF), and Emily Tuley (RF). Kayley Pemberton also logged a lot of playing time and made several starts.

But as Sanders healed, Tecumseh went on a tear and ran the table. After finishing the regular season with 11 straight wins by a combined score of 86-7, Coach Wood and his girls prepared for the tournament. The players were determined to do what it took, and Coach Wood wanted desperately to get the gorilla off his back.

After easy wins in the sectional over Wood Memorial (6-0) and Northeast Dubois (5-0), Tecumseh survived two 1-0 thrillers in the regional over Henryville in 11 innings and North Daviess.

JESSICA MILLER

Jessica Miller is considered Tecumseh's first true superstar, and many place her among the finest of all the players in local history. A truly superb athlete, Jessica was a four-year letter winner in volleyball as well.

On the diamond, she led Tecumseh to the 2003 State Finals as the team's best pitcher and hitter and was voted the team's MVP and All-Conference all four years. As a pitcher, she compiled a career record of 67-20 while averaging .441 at the plate with 9 home runs. After earning first team All-State honors for three years, she chose Northwestern over Kansas, North Carolina State and U of E and launched a great college career.

As a Lady Wildcat, Jessica hit .328 in each of her freshman, sophomore and senior years, finishing her career with 6 home runs. Her senior year, she started 62 games in right field and led the team to a #2 regional seed in the NCAA tournament. Along the way, Jessica fashioned some memorable moments for Northwestern fans. Against # 1 Arizona, she went 2-4 with a double, and facing then- #1 Cal, she went 4-4 with a double, a home run, three RBIs and three runs scored. In another game, Jessica launched a two-run homer, the longest in the Sharon J. Drysdale Field history, onto the roof of Welsh-Ryan Arena against #10 Michigan.

With a flare for the dramatic, Jessica also drove in the game-tying run in the championship game of the NCAA regional against Illinois State. According to Tecumseh coach Gordon Wood, Jessica Miller is among the school's greatest pitchers, but she is definitely, in his mind, the finest "player" in Tecumseh softball history.

For the third consecutive year, the Lady Braves were in the final four and would settle for nothing less than a blue ring.

But accomplishing the feat would require that the girls handle a challenge like no team before or since has had to endure.

As the girls began their semi-final at 9:00 p.m. on Friday night, little did they know what was in store. What they did know was that they had a daunting task in front of them as they faced a strong Whiting team led by a young lady that Coach Wood believed was the best player in the state. Mel Dumezich was an Under Armour All-American who had pitched her team to State championships in '06 and '08 and had been named the Gatorade Indiana Player of the Year. The 5'8" star recorded 350 strikeouts in 2009 and was hitting .561 with tremendous power. After high school, she would go on to play major college ball at Texas A&M, finishing 19-3 as a pitcher in 2011.

But on this Friday evening, she would face a hurler who would match her pitch for pitch and a talented group of young ladies with destiny on their side.

Against a dominant pitcher like Dumezich, the last thing an opponent wants is to fall behind. Unfortunately, Tecumseh did just that by giving away a run on two miscues in the first inning. But Audra Sanders continued to battle to keep the game close. Admitting later that her eyes were beginning to tear up as the game reached the seventh inning, Sanders and her teammates prayed for a miracle.

Kayley Pemberton was the 2011 Mental Attitude Award winner.

Ali Nord was a rock at third base and a great all-around athlete at Tecumseh who continued her career at USI.

Shortstop Julie Roeder

Ali Nord ended Dumezich's no-hitter in the seventh with a single to left, and Julie Roeder sacrificed her to second. Sanders followed with a ground out that advanced Nord to third, and then the drama began.

With his team teetering on the precipice between victory and defeat, Coach Wood took some advice and reached into his bag of tricks. It seems that Mike Sanders, Audra's father and Gordon's assistant, approached Gordon and uttered the words "You do desperate things in desperate times. Get her in a rundown."

The proposed plan referred to a situation that Coach Wood's team practiced frequently. Typically, when girls are in a rundown situation, fielders sometimes have trouble staying out of the runner's way on the base path. So Gordon's strategy was to have Ali go half-way home, draw a throw and then try to run into a player to cause an interference call.

When Gordon whispered the plan to Nord, he wasn't surprised at her response to the risky venture. "I don't want to make the last out like that," she proclaimed.

Coach Gordon Wood has stated that one of the keys to the 2009 season was the play of freshman Kara Snow (left). After the graduation of Courtney Hillborn in 2008, Wood needed someone to step behind the plate to handle the powerful arm of Audra Sanders, and Snow was magnificent. She and freshman teammates Emily Tuley (center) and Cherish Lamborn (right) have two blue rings (championships) and one red (runner-up), making them arguably the most successful class in Tecumseh softball history.

"I don't want you to either," Coach Wood responded. "I won't sleep for three days."

So with each pitch, Ali prepared to draw the throw. But the opportunity never came. As Dumezich fired home, the hitter, Chelsea Nuhring, kept fouling pitches off. On the fourth pitch, the ball sailed low and wide, and after the wild pitch hit the backstop, Nord slid home to tie the game.

On the next pitch, Chelsea Nuhring struck out. With Whiting only one pitch away from crushing Tecumseh's hopes and winning their third State title in four years, Chelsea Nuhring had dug in and delivered, prompting Coach Wood to declare, "It was the greatest strikeout I'd ever seen in my life, because she fought and fought and fought."

The Lady Braves' prayers for a miracle had been answered, but no one could have expected what the rest of the night would bring.

For nine long innings, Mel Dumezich and Audra Sanders traded punches while the summer air cooled. Every time Audra would leave for the circle, she would look at her father, Mike, and say, "Dad, she can't outlast me," and Mike would reply, "I know she can't, babe. You can beat her."

As Friday night turned into Saturday morning, the Lady Braves came to bat in the top of the 17th inning. The number nine hitter, freshman Emily Tuley, laid down a perfect bunt and

Teri Newmaster earned second team All-State honors and batted over .400 while at Tecumseh as a center fielder and also started in center as a freshman at USI.

The 2011 State champion Lady Braves. First Row (L-R): Kara Snow, Katie Burkett, Kayley Pemberton, Jaylen Buse, Chelsie Nuhring, Laura Chase, Allie Beard, Emily Bailey, Katie Feldmeier. Second Row (L-R): Courtney Rudolph, Tiera Rush, Cherish Lamborn, Rachel Morris, Madison Oxley, Stefanie Gresham. Third Row (L-R): Brian Beard (asst. coach), Kim Wornica (equip. mgr.), Tiffany Summers, Brenna Floyd, Torie Pace, Ashley Westerman, Laura McKinley, Abby Jagelewski (equip. mgr.), Mindy Rasche (trainer), Sarah Stuart (asst. coach), Gordon Wood (head coach). Fourth Row (L-R): Dirk Buck (asst. ath. dir.), Bill Fritz (ath. dir.), Russ Newman (asst. princ.), Richard Lance (princ.), Lance Summers (asst. coach).

BACK TO THE DUGOUT, COACH!

To show how brutal the 2009, 17-inning semi-final game was, in the 13th inning, the home plate umpire went down with heat exhaustion. The crowd was concerned, but the Lady Braves were undaunted by the distraction. While the EMTs were tending to the fallen ump, the Tecumseh girls danced on the mound to tunes from the PA system at the park. As the girls and half the crowd danced to tunes like "Shout" and "YMCA", Coach Wood strolled to the mound to convince them to sit and save their legs. But the girls would have none of it, and Gordon escaped to the dugout, vowing never to try that again.

beat it out. Teri Newmaster then failed on two bunt attempts and drew the evil eye from Coach Wood, who gave her the bunt sign once again. Newmaster then delivered with a sacrifice to advance Tuley. Julie Roeder then came up big once again with a double to bring Tuley across for a one-run lead.

Coach Wood immediately started to look ahead to the bottom half of the inning and checked to see when Dumezich would be hitting. She was scheduled to bat fourth, so if a player got on, Whiting's star could end the game with one swing.

Shifting his attention back to the task at hand, Wood watched as a passed ball moved Roeder to third. Just prior, Coach Wood had noticed that the catcher had gotten upset after the tying run scored and was throwing the ball back to the pitcher without checking the runner. As a result, Gordon opted for "desperate measure" number two. He instructed Julie to pull off a delayed steal, something he had only tried maybe three times since he started coaching.

Her instructions were to take some steps toward home and then, just as the catcher was ready to throw, dash for home. As the catcher ignored her and cocked her arm to throw, Julie sprinted and tagged home plate with her hand, creating what Coach Wood called "probably one of the most exciting plays I can recall."

With a two-run cushion, Audra Sanders took care of the rest, shutting down Whiting 1-2-3 with Mel Dumezich on deck as the game ended. The marathon battle had set several IHSAA records as the teams left the field at 12:30 a.m. The 17 innings were a record, as were the 70 combined strikeouts and the 38 strikeouts by Sanders.

The game was dubbed a "fairy tale" by Coach Wood, but now the question became: "How will the team handle the emotions and get ready for the finals that were only a few hours away?"

As the girls climbed on the bus, they were drained, and the coaches were wondering, "How are we going to have anything left for tomorrow?" Coach Wood pondered the situation and decided to stroll to the back to prepare the girls for what could be a big disappointment.

"You know what," he said to the girls, "I got two red (runner-up) rings from the last two years, and they're all pretty doggone special. If we don't have anything left, this is going to be my most precious red ring." What was supposed to console and prepare the girls was met with silence at first, and then a response Coach Wood wasn't expecting.

Many times during the year, Gordon had challenged the girls and gotten in their faces. Now it was his turn.

Three girls began to slap him with their gloves and said, "If you don't have any better attitude than that, get back to the front of the bus. We didn't come up here to get another red ring."

Ali Nord then added matter-of-factly: "We're 16, 17 and 18 years old, and we've played a lot of times with four hours sleep! Just get back to the front of the bus!"

Coach Woods' verdict as he reached the coaches up front: "I think we're going to be all right."

It would stand to reason that the Braves' opponent in the finals, a well-rested Indianapolis Lutheran, probably figured that a victory was assured. But Tecumseh would have plenty to say about that, and they would leave nothing to chance. A highly superstitious bunch, the girls decided not to change into one of the two clean sets of uniforms they had brought. Instead, they would wear the same dark blue uniforms from the Friday night's game. And strict orders were given that no one was to wash them.

By game time, coaches and players alike showed up in soiled uniforms ready to go to work. "It was like they never went to bed," Coach Wood recalled. "They were ready to go. Megan Froman was high-fiving everybody. They didn't look tired at all."

For the second game in a row, Tecumseh was facing a quality pitcher in Morgan Lewis, who would be named Indiana's Miss Softball the following year. But with Sanders in charge, Tecumseh was not to be denied and Lutheran, who had banged heads with the

Cherish Lamborn had pitched in 2010 but became # 2 behind Tiffany Summers in 2011 and moved to shortstop.

Chelsie Nuhring hit .383 for the Lady Braves in 2011 and took her skills to Hanover College.

Tiffany Summers has the potential to be Tecumseh's best pitcher yet.

Lady Braves four of the last five years, were no match for the Warrick County girls. Unlike the semis, Tecumseh jumped out early, taking a 3-0 lead in the first on a two-run double by Sanders and an RBI single by Megan Froman. Those runs were the first scored by Tecumseh in their four State championship games ('03, '07, '08 & '09), and they would be more than enough, as the Lady Braves prevailed 4-1. Audra Sanders breezed through the seven-inning game with eight strikeouts and no walks while giving up only four hits.

With a determined bunch of young ladies who refused to back down and a coach who was not afraid to take chances, the Lady Braves of Tecumseh finished the season 29-4-1, survived the longest softball game in State tournament history, and brought home the proud program's first State title.

A TOUGH ACT TO FOLLOW

With Audra Sanders gone but a solid nucleus back, the Lady Braves made another great run in 2010 by advancing to the State's final four for the fourth consecutive year. As any softball aficionado knows, the teams that dominate are those with outstanding pitching, and Gordon Wood had such a pitcher coming up through the ranks.

As the 2011 season approached, Coach Wood knew the ultimate success would rest on the shoulders (and arm) of freshman Tiffany Summers. At 5'11" and 135 pounds, Summers had shown great athleticism for several years, making her attractive to coaches in several sports. Coach Wood encouraged Tiffany to play other sports to help the small school be more competitive, but Tiffany opted to focus on softball. So Gordon Wood required that she pitch three times a week in the winter and lift weights, and Summers followed orders.

Coach Wood also tweaked the proposed lineup early in the season. Cherish Lamborn, who was the ace of the pitching staff in 2010, became the #2 pitcher, which freed her up to move to shortstop. That move allowed Coach Wood to move previous shortstop Emily Tuley to center field, and the changes made a huge difference for the Lady Braves.

As the season began, close attention was paid to the development of Tecumseh's young pitcher. According to Coach Wood, Summers started the year trying to overpower hitters, as she had been able to do as a youngster. She also had control problems and got behind in the count against good high school hitters. As a result, the Lady Braves began the year 3-3.

The decision was made to take Tiffany back to the basic fundamentals of pitching by breaking down her motion in her arm circle. "We kept using her in the tougher games hoping that she would be ready for the post-season," said Coach Wood. The strategy may have cost the team some early wins, but it paid off big-time when it really mattered.

In addition, Tiffany developed her rise ball and change-up, a strategy that had also aided the development of the great Erica Taylor of Boonville just a few years earlier. In both cases, their coaches felt that the young ladies had progressed from a 'thrower' to a 'pitcher'.

After the 3-3- start and Tiffany's improvements, Tecumseh won 10 of their next 11 by a combined score of 85-17. That streak was followed by three horrible losses, and one of those was a turning point in the season, according to Coach Wood. After being thrashed by Gibson Southern (8-0) and Southridge (8-1), Tecumseh was spanked 20-6 by county rival Boonville in the Warrick County Classic at Tecumseh's field. For the first time in Coach Wood's career, his team had been 10-run ruled, and it was gut check time for his girls.

"I told them they could pout and tuck their tails between their legs or they could get better," Gordon said.

And his team responded.

Tecumseh followed the Boonville fiasco with five wins to end the regular season at 23-7, and they started the tournament with two easy wins over Cannelton (11-0) and Wood Memorial (4-1) and then won the regional with a 3-0 shutout of Springs Valley. After a 2-0 victory over Rising Sun, the Lady Braves were about to receive a monumental scare.

In the State semi-finals against Edinburgh, Tecumseh was on cruise control to the final when the motor starting knocking and the wheels nearly fell off. Tiffany Summers was five outs from the finish line when the fans, clad in their red, white and blue, were suddenly gasping in disbelief.

Tecumseh had amassed a nice lead after Summers doubled home a run in the first followed by Kara Snow laying down a squeeze bunt for an RBI and a 2-0 lead. The Lady Braves then scored four more in the fifth on Chelsie Nuhring and Kara Snow RBI singles and a Katie Burkett RBI double for a 6-0 lead.

But with one out in the sixth, Edinburgh mounted a comeback. They loaded the bases with two singles and a walk and Lancers Pitcher Nisha Brown singled home a run. After a strikeout, Tiffany Summers then threw a wild pitch to plate another run. Then two inexplicable dropped pop flies in the infield allowed two more runs to score. What seemed to be a smooth ride to the final was suddenly a 6-6 race to the finish.

In the seventh, Summers pitched her way out of a bases-loaded jam, and in the top of the eighth, Edinburgh's Brown retired the first two hitters. But Emily Tuley then singled, followed by walks to Cherish Lamborn and Chelsie Nuhring. Tiffany Summers then delivered the fatal blow with a bloop single down the left field line for a 7-6 lead.

With a large bruise on her throwing arm from being hit by a pitch earlier, Summers shut down the Lancers in the bottom of the inning, and the Tecumseh fans let out a collective sigh of relief.

After the semi-state thriller, Tecumseh capped off its great 2011 season with a relatively easy 5-1 win over Lakewood Park Christian. What had proven to be a very bumpy ride turned out to be a trip to victory lane as Coach Wood, his staff and his team celebrated the program's second State championship.

In their six post-season games, Tecumseh had outscored their opponents 32-8, with six of those coming from Edinburgh. Of those runs, only two were earned, marking the amazing improvement of the team's young pitcher. Tiffany Summers finished her freshman season with a 19-6 record, a 1.86 ERA and 210 strikeouts while walking or hitting 59 batters. In addition, she was the team's second-leading hitter at .400. Coach Wood knows that Tiffany is not in the same class as Audra Sanders, but he truly believes she "has that same kind of potential."

Summers was supported well by regulars Kara Snow (C - .290), Kayley Pemberton (1B -.328), Allie Beard (2B - .222), Katie Burkett (3B - .255), Cherish Lamborn (SS - .397), Chelsie Nuhring (LF -.383), Emily Tuley (CF - .402) and Courtney Rudolph (RF - .182), with significant innings by Rachel Morris, Brenna Floyd and Jayden Buse.

When characterizing his two State champs, Coach Wood quickly states that his most talented team was the 2009 group led by Audra Sanders. But he also states proudly that the 2011 team, a group with no true superstar, was by far the scrappiest and most competitive.

Tecumseh's softball program is running smoothly in the capable hands of its head coach. Coach Wood has developed a system and discovered methods that work, and he's smart enough to stick with them. Among those methods is a contract that each player signs each year stating three team goals and two personal goals for the season. Coach Wood and his staff also try their best to practice the motto: praise loudly and criticize softly. The players and fans also seem to love Wood's quirky superstitions, like taking the same bus to every game with the same driver, Kathy Patterson, and making sure everyone sits in the exact same seats so as not to tempt fate.

The program takes pride in its fitness as well, and the coaching staff makes the girls run ten minutes every day after stretching, believing that the running makes the girls tougher and prepares them for extra-inning games or bad weather. In addition, if any Tecumseh girl (JV or varsity) looks at a third strike without swinging, EVERYONE in the program makes a torturous run called "the clover."

Whatever the methods, the system is definitely working. In 2012, the Lady Braves made another nice run, finishing one game shy of the Final Four. Tecumseh has won 12 of the last 13 sectionals, and Coach Wood is 31-4 in the post-season. He gives a lot of credit to players like Jessica Miller, Kathy Wood and Andra Bailey (Lasher) from the 2003 team, whose runner-up State finish inspired local youngsters to emulate that success. In fact, he was recently (2011) informed that an 8-and-under team finished their season 16-0 and that the girls could not wait to play for an IHSAA State championship.

After leading Tecumseh to another semi-state in 2012, Gordon Wood was named the Indiana Coaches of Girls Sports Association Coach of the Year. Although he couldn't make the game because of a prior family commitment, he was honored to be selected for the same game where former Braves players like Audra Sanders, Jessica Miller and his daughter, Kathy Wood, had played in years past. After the 2012 season, Gordon went back to working with his young players, and the immediate future looks rosy. With a pipeline of players waiting to play for him and parents who believe in his system, Coach Wood has built a powerhouse program.

"If Gordon hadn't come in to coach, Audra (Sanders) may have just played travel ball," says Mike Sanders. "Gordon made this program what it is today. He works the girls hard, but he's fair. The kids work hard for him. After practice, if girls wanted to hit more or field more, we'd turn on the lights. Gordon has a philosophy that as long as they want to practice to get better, he'll stay until the last one says 'I'm done.' Then he'd go home."

But more than anything, Coach Wood has built a solid reputation: "Gordon Wood is a class act," says Dan Egierski, a popular radio personality for ESPN Radio. "He takes very little credit, and everything in the program is about the girls."

Great things can be accomplished even in the smallest of schools, and the parents and fans at Tecumseh should consider themselves lucky. Thanks to the guidance of Coach Gordon Wood and his staff, the young women at Tecumseh High School are getting the opportunity to turn their dreams into reality.

Tecumseh coach Gordon Woods

SUPERSTITIOUS, ANYONE?

Tecumseh softball coach Gordon Wood admits to being a little superstitious. It seems that he has been obsessed with using the same ink pen as long as the team is winning. If they lose, he starts over again with a new one. In fact, Gordon gets so antsy about using the correct pen that when his daughter Julie confiscated it and headed to Owensboro, he made her drive to Boonville to drop it off so that he could use it for a game that day.

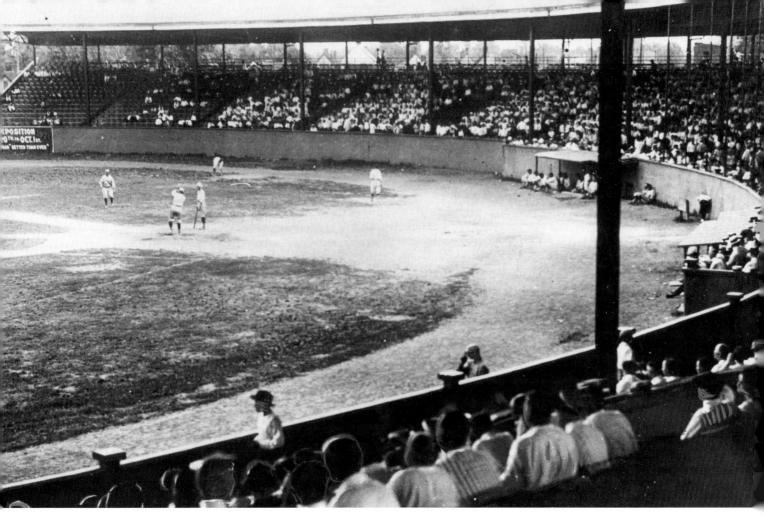

HALL OF FAMERS AT BOSSE FIELD

Bosse Field is the third oldest professional ballpark in continuous use in the country. Thanks to retired journalist Dave Johnson, we can appreciate the grand old field's history by examining the myriad Baseball Hall of Famers who played within its confines.

Early Wynn	Chuck Klein	Edd Roush	Johnny Bench	Bob Feller
Al Kaline	Bob Lemon	Ryne Sandberg	Lou Boudreau	Rollie Fingers
George Kell	Eddie Mathews	Billy Southworth	George Brett	Charlie Gehringer
Bob Gibson	Joe Morgan	Warren Spahn	Jim Bunning	Hank Greenburg
Lou Brock	Hal Newhouser	Bruce Sutter	Roy Campanella	Whitey Herzog
Stan Musial	Satchel Paige	Duke Snider	Andre Dawson	Monte Irvin
Red Schoendienst	Tony Perez	Hank Aaron	Larry Doby	Bert Blyleven
Reggie Jackson	Jackie Robinson	Sparky Anderson		

Special thanks to Rodger Beard and to Richard and Helen Lankford for the photos and much of the information contained in the Don Liddle story.

DON LIDDLE:
A PIECE OF WORLD SERIES HISTORY

The tri-state area has several ties to World Series history, like Pete Fox, a star for Detroit in the '30s; Gil Hodges, as a player in eight Series and as a manager in 1969; and Edd Roush, the hero in the notorious 'Black Sox' Series in 1919. But one of the least known tri-state connections came from our neighbor to the west, Mt. Carmel, Illinois.

Donald Eugene Liddle was taught the fundamentals of baseball by his father, who pitched every Sunday in a league for the railroadmen of the area. But as Don developed as a left-handed hurler in the 1970s, little did he know that he would one day play on the sport's biggest stage and be a part of perhaps the most memorable play in World Series history.

Don's baseball ambitions were put on hold for a while as he served in the Navy during World War II, and he admitted in a radio interview with Rodger Beard that it set him behind "probably four years." When he returned in 1946, he joined a Mt. Carmel independent team and began to make a name for himself. During his first season, Don beat two good Princeton teams, including one that featured Jim Pegram (Mike Pegram's father) as the catcher.

Liddle was so impressive, in fact, that he was asked to join his archrivals down the road in Princeton to compete in the Independent National Tournament. One of his fellow pitchers was Bob Hodges, the talented brother of local legend Gil Hodges. With teammates like the Coomer boys from Princeton and Bob and Chuck Harmon, Don pitched the team to the Final Four of the state tournament in Franklin. Liddle had won four games in a row, but the manager decided to go with Hodges in the semi-finals to save Don for the final game. Princeton didn't give Hodges enough run support, however, and Princeton fell 2-1.

During the tournament, Don was seen by several scouts, some of whom inquired about him. A problem some players faced at the time was risking losing a job as they pursued a baseball career, and Liddle experienced the same dilemma. Fortunately, he was employed at a time by a man named Walter Roner to learn the tool and die business on the GI Bill. Roner offered Don a 40-day leave of absence, and Liddle took full advantage of the opportunity.

He went 6-3 in independent Class C ball and caught the eye of the Brooklyn Dodgers, who invited Don to spring training. Although he was offered a contract, he wasn't happy with the salary offered and declined. He then tried out with iconic Evansville Braves coach Bob Coleman and made the team in the 3-I League with the Boston Braves affiliate.

Coleman made a reliever out of Don, and Liddle would often head to the bullpen in the sixth or seventh inning as the team's closer. Although he had some success, relief pitchers during Liddle's era were perceived as second-class citizens and he wasn't thrilled with the role.

The next season, in 1949, he was sent to Pawtuckett, Rhode Island to pitch for a team in the Class B New England League. Even after finishing the year 11-2, Don was on the verge of quitting because he was still a reliever and wasn't making much money. Unlike the relievers of today who make millions for only a few minutes work each week, starting pitchers in the '40s and '50s were expected to go the distance and were paid handsomely. Liddle offered an explanation of the relievers' predicament when he spoke with Rodger Beard late in his life. Put simply, a closer rarely got a 'win' because he was only used when the team was ahead. But if he had a bad night, he could record a 'loss', so accumulating a good win-loss record was virtually impossible.

The following year, Rip Collins, the old first baseman for the Gashouse Gang, was named Pawtuckett's manager. He sent Don a contract three times, but each was returned unsigned. With his future in the balance, Don discussed the matter with his wife, Marge, who wisely told him, "Don, you'll never forgive yourself if you quit too soon."

Liddle accepted the terms, and by mid-season was 11-2. Collins was then promoted to Class A and decided to take Don with him. Liddle continued his solid performance by going 14-6 in Atlanta, and in 1952, he experienced his best season as a minor leaguer. Just one step shy of the majors, Don finished 1952 with a 17-3 record at Triple A Milwaukee, leading the league in every important stat and earning *Looks* All American honors as a left-handed pitcher.

The next season, 1953, the franchise was moved from Boston to Milwaukee and Liddle was promoted to the parent club. Don finished his minor league career with a 50-20 record

AMAZING BUT TRUE

There is an interesting story behind these two photos. The first was taken in Don Liddle's driveway in Mt. Carmel after the town had presented him with this 1954 Olds Super 88 to commemorate his World Series victory. Anyone would have assumed that the car had passed on to the great highway in the sky, but incredibly Mt. Carmel native Phil Fischer did some research and found it. Today, Phil is the proud owner of the fully restored beauty that once belonged to Mt. Carmel legend Don Liddle.

and distinguished himself as one of the few players in history to play minor league ball one year and major league ball the next in the same city. In fact, although he was joined by several future hall-of-famers, to the Milwaukee fans, Don was the best known player on the 1953 Braves.

With the support of position players like Joe Adcock (1B), Johnny Logan (SS), and the great Eddie Matthews (3B), Liddle joined a pitching staff that featured the likes of Warren Spahn, Lew Burdette and Johnny Antonelli. Don relieved early in 1953, but when Spahn pulled a rib muscle while running in the outfield before a game, Liddle was surprised to find himself on the mound as a major league starter for the first time.

Don finished the season 7-6 with a 3.08 ERA, and the Braves finished second behind Brooklyn. Despite his solid performance, however, Liddle was shocked to learn that he was part of a block-buster trade with the New York Giants and would be joining the Giants for spring training in Arizona. As spring training began, Don admitted that he was not optimistic. "We thought we'd be lucky to finish third, maybe fourth," he told Rodger Beard. "Then we got hot and said, 'Hey, we're right in the middle of this thing.'"

The reason for Liddle's pre-season pessimism was based on the previous year, when New York finished fifth. What Liddle had not factored in, however, was the return of a young player named Willie Mays. Mays had made his debut in 1951 but had spent 1952 and '53 in the service, and with his incredible talent in the field, at the plate and on the base path, the Giants' stock rose sharply.

Don started the season as a long reliever, leaving the closing duties to Hoyt Wilhelm and Marv Grissom. This meant that Don would leave the bullpen after the seventh inning to head for the dugout. He would also serve as the team's fifth starter, pitching almost every second game of doubleheaders. He also appeared at times as a short reliever against left-handed hitters.

During the last six weeks, Don was moved up to be the team's fourth starter, and with six games to play, the Giants led Brooklyn by five games. To clinch the pennant, Giants manager Leo Durocher threw Sal 'The Barber' Maglie at Brooklyn and Maglie mowed them down. The victory allowed Durocher to rest his boys and to limit the pitchers' innings to keep them fresh.

Liddle thought he was in line to start the third game of the World Series, but late in the season Don was part of a 0-0 pitchers' duel in a game with Philadelphia. Don won the game 1-0, but the effort changed the rotation for the Series.

Entering the '54 Series, the Giants were heavy underdogs to the powerful Cleveland Indians. Cleveland's best hitters were Bobby Avila (.341), Al Rosen (.300), Al Smith (.281) and Vic Wertz (.275), and their experienced pitching staff was led by Early Wynn (23-11), Bob Lemon (23-7), Mike Garcia (19-8), Art Houtteman (15-7) and 35-year-old Bob Feller (13-3). Very few felt that New York could compete, and Don Liddle admitted late in his life that he and his teammates felt the same way, saying, "We didn't stand a chance against Cleveland. They had just set a record with 111 victories out of 154 ballgames. And here we eked out 94 or 95."

Most fans felt the Series would end quickly with a 4-0 sweep, and as the '54 Series played out, that's exactly what happened. But to everyone's surprise, it wasn't the mighty Indians that would dominate; it was the lowly New York Giants that would control the fall classic from start to finish.

No one could have imagined the outcome, and, looking back, many baseball aficionados feel that one play in the first game set the tone for the entire series, and Mt. Carmel's own Don Liddle was right in the thick of it.

Prior to the game, Leo Durocher informed Don that he needed him as a left-handed reliever throughout the Series, and since there were no travel days between games, he would pitch three relievers in Game 4 if he had to. So Game 1 began with Sal Maglie on the mound for New York and Bob Lemon throwing for Cleveland.

Twice during the game Don had warmed up, but Maglie had pitched himself out of the jams. In the eighth inning, the situation again became dicey and pitching coach Frank Schellenbach told Don to get ready again. Maglie had battled Lemon to a 2-2 tie but seemed to be losing his stuff as he allowed the first two hitters to reach with Vic Wertz coming to the plate.

The situation was perfect for Liddle, as a southpaw, to face the left-handed hitter, so Schellenbach glanced toward Liddle and said, "They're asking for you, Don." As Don strode to the mound with warm-up jacket in hand, the magic of the moment was not lost on the 29-year-old pitcher from Mt. Carmel. "There's a lot that goes through your mind when you walk from the right field line to the mound," Liddle said in his 1992 interview with Rodger Beard. "You know that TV sets are on all over the United States and a lot overseas and better than 55,000 at the Polo Grounds are watching you walk out.

"I popped the glove pretty good" (during his warm-ups on the mound), Don continued. "They thought Wertz was a low ball hitter. I was strictly a low ball pitcher. I threw a sinking fast ball. I threw a short, snappy curve ball. They wanted Vic Wertz pitched 'up', and I was very uncomfortable. I didn't want him to pull it into the short right field stands."

What soon followed was a moment in World Series history that fans have re-lived thousands of times through the magic of television.

Liddle's first pitch to Wertz was a belt-high fast ball down the middle for a called strike. With two on and no outs, catcher Wes Westrum had a hunch and headed for the mound. "Don, he'll bunt," Westrum said. Knowing that a hard one up and in is the toughest pitch to bunt, Liddle delivered. Westrum proved to be prophetic, as Wertz squared to bunt. He attempted to pull his bat away, but instead the ball caught the bat and squirted into the Indians' dugout.

At 0-2, Don teased Wertz with a curve outside, but Wertz didn't bite. The next pitch was a fast ball up and away and is the one that millions of fans remember. Until his dying day, Don swore he could not have thrown a better pitch based on the instructions given, but Wertz connected with a mighty swing.

The glove with which Willie Mays made 'The Catch' in the 1954 World Series was given to Don Liddle's son Craig. Today it is on display in the Baseball Hall of Fame.

During the pitch, Willie Mays was playing shallow, but at the crack of the bat, he spun and sprinted toward the wall in center field. In most parks and against any other team, the shot would have cleared the bases and Wertz would have ended up on second or third. But on this day in the Polo Grounds and with the 'Say Hey Kid' in center, the result was a play that has been replayed thousands of times.

As Willie sprinted, he followed the ball by looking over his left shoulder, and as the ball descended, he circled slightly to his right with his chin facing the wall. With the palm of his glove up, he cradled the ball as he reached the warning track 480 feet from home plate, and the crowd watched in awe as if they had just witnessed an optical illusion. Many, including Willie himself, believe that as great as 'The Catch' was, what followed was even more miraculous.

With the ball secured, Mays spun immediately and fired a strike to second base. Because Larry Doby had started for third and had to hustle back to second to tag, he was only able to reach third and the Giants escaped the inning unscathed.

Perhaps the only person at the park who didn't witness the play was Don Liddle himself. "I didn't see the catch," Liddle revealed later. "My job on a ball hit that deep is to back up home plate or third base. When I turned around, I seen the man on second going back (to tag up) and I knew Willie had caught it."

After the play, Leo Durocher followed standard protocol by bringing in right-handed reliever Marv Grissom to face the right-handed batter who was on deck. Liddle's first World Series appearance was the shortest of his career, but those two or three minutes in 1954 defined his career. As Durocher told the press after the game, Don "got his man," and the effort set the tone for the Series.

The score remained tied at 2-2 until New York's Dusty Rhodes smacked a three-run homer in the bottom of the tenth to send the Polo Grounds crowd home exhausted but ecstatic. In Game 2, Johnny Antonelli out-dueled Early Wynn 3-1, and in the third game, the Giants bested the Indians 6-2 with Ruben Gomez starting and Hoyt Wilhelm finishing.

After his appearance in Game 1, Don was told by Durocher that he would get the start in Game 4, and as game time approached on October 2, Durocher gave specific instructions to Liddle, saying, "Don't pace yourself, Don. Go as far as you can go." Since there were no travel days in '54, the start meant Don was throwing on two days rest, but he threw every pitch like it was the ninth inning. He lasted for an impressive 6 ⅔ innings before handing the ball to Wilhelm in the seventh, and the Giants jumped on Indians starter Bob Lemon early in a 7-4 win. As a side note, Vic Wertz finished the series 8 for 16 and popped out for the final out in game 4.

For the sixth straight year, a New York team had won the World Series, but the previous five had belonged to the Yankees. Liddle and his teammates came home to a ticker tape parade down Fifth Avenue and looked forward to the next season. Although the team couldn't match their dream season in 1954, Don had his best season as a professional in '55, going 10-4 with four complete games.

Despite his great season, Don was shocked when he became part of a blockbuster trade in 1956. Bill Wrigley was brought in as the Giants' new manager and promptly traded Don, Al Dark and two other Giants for five players from the Cardinals. During his final season with the Giants and Cards, Don's innings were diminished drastically and he could see the writing on the wall as his four-year major league career came to an end.

RARE INDEED

Don Liddle (left) is seen here with Helen and Richard Lankford. Don and Helen are double cousins. What's a double cousin? Well, Helen was a Frick; her mother was Elva Frick. Don's mother was a Frick and his dad was a Liddle. Helen's dad and Don's mother were brother and sister. Helen's mother and Don's dad were brother and sister. A Frick married a Liddle and a Liddle married a Frick, resulting in the very unusual double cousin scenario.

Liddle finished his career with a 28-18 record and a .375 ERA. He appeared in 117 games (427 innings) and started 54. He threw 13 complete games and compiled a 9-3 record as a reliever. Although Don will always be the answer to a trivia question about one of the most memorable moments in baseball history, 'The Catch' was only part of a remarkable career. He played in a golden era of baseball in New York City, with iconic parks like the Polo Grounds, Ebbetts Field/Sportsman's Park and Yankee Stadium. The city also boasted three center fielders who are among the greatest of all-time: Duke Snyder (Brooklyn Dodgers), Mickey Mantle (Yankees) and, of course, Willie Mays, a man that Don described as "the greatest ballplayer that ever played."

Don was amazed at Willie's abilities and recalled how Mays would play 'bottlecaps' daily, a game where someone would throw bottlecaps and Willie would hit them with a broomstick as they curved and darted in all directions. Don has similar memories of contemporaries like Jackie Robinson toward the end of his career and players who became friends, like Carl Furillo, Roy Campanella, Pee Wee Reese and Gil Hodges.

With the Cardinals, Don was able to influence a young pitcher with control problems named Bob Gibson. He also lockered next to Stan Musial and remembers when he shook hands with Musial after the trade. Apparently, Don had handled "Stan the Man' pretty well in the past, prompting Musial to greet him with the words "Good. Now I don't have to face that curveball of yours again."

After his retirement, Liddle returned to his roots in Mt. Carmel to raise his four sons (Craig, Donald, Kevin and Kim) with his wife Marge. During his years in Mt. Carmel, he worked at the Elks Lodge, owned a service station, sold insurance and worked at Snap-On Tools.

When Don and Marge returned home, they brought some fond memories, but they also found themselves with a memento that is on display today in the Baseball Hall of Fame in Cooperstown. As the story goes, the Giants were flying to New York from spring training, and Willie Mays overheard Don's son Craig saying that he needed a glove for little league. In the clubhouse the next day, Mays approached Craig and said, "I understand you need a glove to play baseball." Mays handed The Glove to the youngster, and the boy had no clue about the magnitude of the gift. In fact, Craig admitted later that he used it to play little league and even left the glove out in the sun and rain a few times.

It wasn't until years later that Craig realized the treasure he had been given, and when the curator of the Hall of Fame discovered the whereabouts of the legendary leather, the request was made. Today, the glove is displayed in the Hall and is explained with these words: "when Willie Mays made his astounding catch of a Vic Wertz blast in game 1 of the 1954 World Series, he used this glove. 'The Catch' was a turning point in the game, and according to many observers, the Series. Loan courtesy of the Liddle family."

Don Liddle passed away on June 5, 2000, and the funeral procession was packed with Mt. Carmel baseball players of all ages. In his honor, the ball field where young men now play is named Don Liddle Park. The little man with his big talent made his hometown proud with his ability and tenacity. Although, this part of the country can boast of a Super Bowl quarterback (Bob Griese) and others who have World Series rings, only one can lay claim to being the winning pitcher in a World Series game. Though small in stature, Don Liddle mastered his craft and left little to chance. In the words of Giants manager Leo Durocher, "He knew how to pitch. That was his secret."

> ### DID YOU KNOW?
> Legendary radio sportscaster Richard Lankford of Princeton has a rare distinction that few can match. He has worn a World Series ring (Don Liddle's) and a Super Bowl ring (good friend Duke Neff's who played end for the Kansas City Chiefs in the first Super Bowl). Richard has also held in his hand an Olympic gold medal from 1936. The Games were hosted by Adolph Hitler's Germany, and the medal belonged to Richard's friend Francis Johnson, a captain on the gold medal-winning U.S. basketball team.

LARRY COLLINS:
A LITTLE LEAGUE LEGEND

Millions of boys across America have gotten their first taste of organized sports by donning a little league baseball uniform, and that initial exposure to competition often made a lasting impression. Over the years, much has been written about the impact youth sports can have on youngsters, both good and bad, and we have all seen how the experience can sometimes bring out the best and the worst of kids and parents alike.

Many who choose to serve as youth baseball managers and coaches are there because their sons are involved, while a select few see the experience as a higher calling and choose to coach merely for their love of the sport and the boys who play it. Such was the case of a unique local leader who spent decades shaping the lives of his players, and he used his quirky style and individuality to make a lasting impression on those fortunate enough to play for him.

Larry Lee Collins played his youth baseball in the late '40s and early '50s, and was a good enough basketball player at Bosse to earn a scholarship to Florida Southern University. He finished his education at Evansville College, where he met his wife Donna and prepared for his career as a teacher.

While he taught physical education at Delaware and Caze, Larry stayed involved with sports as a basketball and football official, and his football crew that included Temme Patterson, Jack Behme and others even qualified to referee the State Finals a time or two. When the official little league program was taking shape under commissioner Arad McCutchan, Larry volunteered to coach, and for 45 years, his presence was a constant at the Evansville Youth Baseball complex at Vann Park.

Those who witnessed Larry's style in his later years probably did a double-take when they saw him for the first time. With his long hair and laid-back dress and demeanor, he didn't seem to be the stereotypical little league coach. "Early on, he looked just like the rest of them," Donna Collins explained. "After he retired (from teaching), he let his hair grow."

As for his style as a coach, Collins believed in keeping things simple and stressing fundamentals. In a special to the *Courier*, Mark McMurty spoke of his days as one of Larry's players and how Collins would have the boys field groundballs with no glove to emphasize the importance of using both hands. Mark also mentioned the simple signals used by Collins as the third base coach, a swipe across the chest for a bunt and a simple head nod for the steal sign. And every player was encouraged at one time or another by Larry's favorite phrase, "Go hard!"

But Larry's most distinct idiosyncrasy was his penchant for christening each of his players with a nickname. In another *Courier* story about Collins by Gavin Lesnick, the writer described a reunion in 2009 to honor Larry. At the gathering, the players' name tags displayed the monikers given to them many years prior by their beloved coach. Michael 'Smoke' Butts had driven 300 miles for the event, and Kris 'Shot' Gunn couldn't make it but was represented by his parents. Others mentioned in the story were 'Frog', 'Bronco', 'Legs' and 'Band-Aid'.

No one really knows how or why the tradition began, but those close to Larry are amazed at the sheer number of nicknames created by Collins. Steve Hopkins, a childhood friend of Larry's, was always impressed by the process. "I joined Larry as a coach for Wesselman's and coached with him for 13 years," Hopkins explained. "Each new Wesselman's player would get a nickname from Larry when he called them to tell them they were on the team. Sometimes there was a logical reason for the name and sometimes not. A kid who smiled a lot became 'Sunshine'; a kid named Bitter became 'Sug' (for 'Sugar'); a kid named Stein became 'Mug'; a fast runner became 'Speed' or 'Legs'.

"One of our better players was Brad Brownell ('Gun')," Hopkins continued. "He has since become the head (basketball coach at Clemson. To the best of my knowledge, none of the nicknames was ever duplicated, even though (local TV anchor) Randy

('Red') Moore's little brother became 'Little Red'. Around the East Little League Park, you were a 'made man' once Larry gave you a nickname. Larry told me after the reunion that there were several former players whose real names he did not know, but he remembered every nickname."

The reunion in 2009 served a dual purpose. The first was to pay tribute to Collins' 45 years of service to youth baseball by naming the field at Vann Park after him. The second purpose was to offer folks a final opportunity to be with Larry, who was in the final stages of his battle with lung cancer. Larry passed away three weeks later.

When Collins died on July 20, 2009, he left behind a wonderful family and a soul mate who was at his side for 47 years as he mentored the boys. "Little league baseball was what we did in the summers," Donna Collins told me. "He loved teaching the kids how to play and enjoy the game. He loved being at the ballpark and being around people who shared all those things."

Larry and Donna raised four wonderful children who in turn gave them nine grandkids, and as one might expect, Larry was given a nickname by them ('Pops') and each of them had a nickname. The Collins' sons, James Patrick ('Jock') and Matthew Ryan ('Rip'), both played basketball and baseball at Memorial. 'Jock' and Jill (what a coincidence!) have two sons, Nicholas ('Saint') and Joey ('Nails'), while 'Rip' and Shelby Collins have Leo ('Cleat'), Walton ('Colt') and Clara Kate ('Filly').

The two Collins girls played soccer at Memorial during the early years of the sport. Laurie ('Punkin') and husband Chuck Spagnoli have a daughter, Haley ('Bessie'), while Lainie ('Bird') and husband Mike Campbell have a boy and two girls, Robert ('Mick'), Evelyn ('Chick') and Mary Louise ('Sis').

As for Donna Collins, she jokingly says that Larry's nicknames for her are probably unprintable, and she still spends a lot of time in the familiar environs of Vann Park as her sons coach and her grandsons play on Larry Collins Field. Larry never got to coach his grandsons, but the legacy of his work is present in every man who played for him as a young boy. "Every kid who played for Mr. Collins knew how lucky they were to be on the field with him," said Mark McMurty in his *Courier* story.

Steve Hopkins was a close friend of Larry's all his life and was there when Larry coached both Steve's son Scott ('Ned') and his grandson Ben ('Bounce'), who was on Larry's very last team. Besides family, no one was closer to Collins than Steve, who spearheaded the effort to name the field after Larry and helped organize the reunion, and Steve's affection and respect for the man is obvious.

"The most striking thing about Larry's appearance was his shoulder-length hair," Hopkins said, "and when he coached third base, he typically had a long blade of grass dangling from the corner of his mouth. Playing your best was more important than winning to Larry, and players were never permitted to question an umpire's call; that was the coach's responsibility. When a kid walked onto the field, he became a baseball player. He was no longer subject to comments or yelling from his parents; he was the responsibility of the coaches until he walked off the field. I only remember one parent who had any problem with that approach."

In another *Courier* story shortly after Larry's death, Mike Jacobs wrote about Collins' contributions over the years and explained how he was shown a letter by Larry's daughter. The letter was from little league commissioner Arad McCutchan and was addressed to the players. McCutchan's commentary was a poignant message about youth sports and read as follows:

"All of us must be aware that with each honor or privilege that comes our way, comes also some responsibilities. The purpose of this letter is to invite your attention to the part you are expected to play.

"The objective of Evansville Little League Baseball, Inc. is to provide baseball for boys. Friendly competition is very desirable, however this may be carried to such lengths that many evils are associated with it. Competition at this age is undesirable when the wish to win is the chief consideration and the banner of superiority over opponents is held high. More important are the ideals: The determination to play one's best, to put forth every effort, to cooperate with fellow teammates, to play always with absolute honesty, to be tolerant of the errors of teammates, and to be friendly toward and appreciative of opponents.

"Good play, even without victory, is one satisfaction of a game. If victory comes today, defeat may come tomorrow. If these ideals are held high in our esteem, we can have a situation where sportsmanship is observed by all players, managers, coaches, and spectators. This means that, as parents, we will not tolerate the razzing of any team or boy and we will remember that these are only boys."

Mr. McCutchan's words are as pertinent today as they were decades ago, and Larry Collins was a living example of the values mentioned in the letter. Collins was a success in every sense of the word, and local baseball fans will be reminded of his impact every time they watch a son or grandson run onto Larry Collins Field. In this day and age, true heroes are few and far between, and although Larry may not be known for the lives he has saved, he will be forever remembered for all those lives he touched in such a positive way.

Larry 'Pops' Collins
(Art by Jon Siau)

GIBSON SOUTHERN SOFTBALL: A WINNING MACHINE

Like most fledgling high school athletic programs, Gibson Southern softball was launched with a grassroots effort by local parents and fans. The Lady Titans played their first game ten years after the IHSAA held its first softball State championship, and the 1995 team finished 7-12 under head coach Jason Blackard. The '96 and '97 teams quickly established milestones for the program behind the solid pitching of Allison Maurer. In '96 the Titans posted the school's first winning record, 10-9, and the 1997 girls (17-7) were the first to win the Pocket Athletic Conference title.

From 1998 through 2000, Gibson Southern continued to post winning records behind the play of such stars as April Foster, Amy Kamuf, Tina Anslinger, Courtney Woolston and Amanda Mayer and the pitching of Anslinger and a young Vicky Hale. In only five seasons after converting from slow pitch to fast pitch softball, Coach Blackard had fashioned a record of 88-58, and when the 2001 season rolled around, a new ingredient was added to the mix that would quickly boost the program to new heights.

When Blackard started the program in 1995, moms and dads saw a new opportunity for their young athletic daughters and began to get involved in the sport. One of these was a man named Gary May, and with his athletic background as a guide, he developed a plan. "I had three girls," Gary told me from his office on Evansville's east side. "I played college baseball and knew that you always need a pitcher, so I started to develop my daughter (Allie). We went to Casey, Illinois to work with Denny Throneberg, who gave pitching lessons."

Another local parent, Don Rhodes, had a daughter, Valerie, who was a year younger than Allie, and Gary and Don organized a travel team. With that effort came the development of a softball feeder system, and while Blackard was coaching the high school girls, the parents were molding young players who would enter the program as battle-tested veterans.

As the 2001 season approached, the first wave of feeder girls donned the maroon and gold, and the impact was felt immediately. With senior Vicky Hale in the circle, the Lady Titans went from 17-9 in 2000 to 28-6 and made their first trip to Carmel for the State Finals. But getting there wasn't easy, and the championship game was a definite reality check.

The Titans opened the tournament with their standard lineup: Nicole Will (1B), Allie May (2B), Tara Clevenger (3B), Kristy Scherer (SS), Lyndsi Dollison (LF), Kim Zimmerman (CF) and Ashley Maurer (RF) with Vicky Hale on the mound and Valerie Hale as the DH. The girls made easy work of Bosse (12-0) and Princeton (14-1) before prevailing in a 1-0 thriller over Memorial to capture the sectional title. They then took care of business in the regional with wins over Sullivan (2-0) and Corydon (7-1) and

were excited to reach the Big Dance for the first time. After a 3-2 win over Woodlan in the semi-finals, the Lady Titans had visions of a State championship, but reality quickly set in.

As the girls prepared to take on Roncalli in the final, their inexperience at the State level quickly showed, and Gary May noticed that the girls were "like deer in headlights." The game quickly got out of hand and revealed that the team and even the coaches weren't prepared as Gibson Southern fell 13-0, a record margin of victory that still stands today (2012).

In 2002, the Lady Titans finished 22-7 but couldn't get out of the regional, but the '03 team showed lots of promise and was poised to make another run. The primary lineup for the season featured infielders Jennifer Ziliak (1B), Valerie Rhodes (2B), Kristin King (3B) and Valen Eberhard (SS), outfielders Claire Will (LF), Kim Zimmerman (CF) and Jamie Lindauer (RF) with Jessica Ralph as the designated player and Allie May in the circle.

The Titans finished the regular season at 22-4 and entered the sectional as one of the favorites. Gibson Southern blistered North Knox 14-0 in Game 1, but in Game 2, Washington took Gibson Southern to the limit. With the score tied 1-1 in the sixth, the Hatches loaded the bases with no outs, but two strikeouts by May and a groundout to Valerie Hale eliminated the threat and allowed the Titans to win in the seventh.

In the regional opener, May was one out away from a no-hitter in a 2-0 victory over Corydon Central, and in the nightcap, Memorial stretched the Lady Titans to eleven innings before Valerie Hale blasted a walk-off homer for a 2-1 win. As the fans celebrated, the tired bunch of girls set their sights on another Final Four appearance, and this time they would not be denied.

After a relatively routine 4-1 win in the semi-finals over Norwell, the girls were sent to the hotel to rest. Meanwhile, the coaches stayed around to check out the other semi-final. As Gary May looked on, his mind began to race, and what followed was very serious at the time but is the source of some humorous reflection years later.

As the team's pitching coach, Gary made it a practice to meet with the pitcher before each game for mental preparation. Often he would say things like "Don't give them more respect than they deserve" or "Have no fear" or "Make your pitches and live with the results." But this occasion was different, and based on what he had observed in the other semi-final, he was at a loss.

"I'm watching New Palestine and I thought 'there's no way we can beat them; they're just so much better than us,'" Gary explained. To make matters worse, Gary would not only be speaking to the team's pitcher, but his own daughter.

"Before the game, I told Allie, 'Your margin for error is so slim, you can't make a mistake' Gary continued. 'You gotta pitch the game of your life.' I scared her to death."

The 2003 State champion Lady Titans. First row (L-R): Jessica Ralph, Jennifer Sollman, Darcy Hyneman, Kim Zimmerman, Allie May, Valen Eberhard, Claire Will, Jamie Lindauer. Second row: Amanda Maurer, Carrie Wilderman, Jessica Adamson, Janelle Johnson, Valerie Rhodes, Rachel Tenbarge, Kristin King. Back row: Pat Seib, Kristen Schmitt, Janessa Miller, Gary May, Jason Blackard, Bryon Will, Valerie Hale, Jennifer Ziliak, Glover Priar.

Allie May, who now works for her father, recalls the pre-game 'pep talk' and has similar reflections. "He usually told me that no matter who it is, you go after everybody as hard as you can," Allie said with a smile. "Play hard and don't worry about it. But when he called me into the room and said 'You're going to have to pitch the game of your life,' I thought 'Oh, my gosh! This is far beyond anything I've ever done.' So going in, I was really nervous. He scared me to death."

It should come as no surprise that Allie's nerves showed early, and as Gary watched his daughter walk the first hitter on four pitches, he must have wondered "What have I done?" But daddy's little girl quickly gained control and made papa proud as she mowed down the next 18 in a row. In the fourth inning, Gibson Southern took the lead with back-to-back doubles by Valerie Hale and Jennifer Ziliak.

In the seventh, New Palestine's leadoff hitter went to a 1-2 count batting left-handed but then switched sides and bounced a single off the bag at third. (Pete Swanson, the sports editor at the *Princeton Clarion* at the time, believes the runner could have easily stretched it to a double and that the conservative base running was a factor in the outcome.) The next hitter then stroked a one-hop single to right, leaving runners at first and second. After a sacrifice to move the runners, shortstop Valen Eberhard fielded a grounder and fired home for the out, leaving runners at first and second with the game on the line.

With the anxious crowd looking on, the next hitter lined a bullet that looked like the game winner, but the screamer down the first baseline was snagged by the webbing of leaping first baseman Jennifer Ziliak's glove. Allie May had persevered to 'pitch the game of her life' and the Titans had slain mighty New Palestine to deliver the program's first State championship.

In '04, the Lady Titans were strong as well, finishing 23-5 and advancing to the Final Four again before losing another close 1-0 battle to New Palestine. With the program on a roll and several players returning, who could blame Gibson Southern fans for having high hopes for the next season.

The 2005 team didn't have the explosive bats of some previous teams, but the girls could manufacture runs and pitcher Carrie Wilderman was talented enough to graduate as the program's strikeout leader with 298. Only Amanda Maurer surpassed .300 as a hitter (.319) with a starting lineup that featured Jennifer Ziliak (1B), Claire Will (2B), Kristin King (3B), Valen Eberhard (SS), Jessica Adamson (LF), Erin Wade (CF) and Jamie Lindauer (RF).

The team finished the regular season at 22-3-1 and was dominant in the sectional with easy wins over Pike Central (10-0) and Jasper (5-0). With the tournament now expanded to four classes, Gibson Southern downed Edgewood in the 3A regional before a dramatic win in the final over Heritage Hills when Valen Eberhard led off the 7th with a double and then scored on a single by Kristin King for a 1-0 victory.

After the Titans eliminated Gary Andrean in the semi-finals with a 2-1 win at Indianapolis Pike, the girls faced Pendleton Heights in the championship game. Even though their opponents had only lost one game all season, Gibson Southern hung tough and entered the bottom of the seventh tied 0-0. Down to their final out, Amanda Maurer singled and was replaced by pinch-runner Kristen Staback, who promptly stole second. With the game in the balance, Kristin King delivered a single to right-center to set off a raucous celebration for the second time in three years.

In 2006, Jason Blackard coached his final season and ended his career at 237-92, and a very popular decision was made when he was replaced by Gary May. Since the coaching change, the 'winning machine' has continued to roll, and in 2009 and 2011, the girls again made trips to the Final Four. Ironically, during the stretch from 2007-2010, the program featured its most dominant pitcher but could not win the school's third State title.

From her sophomore season on, Lauren Edwards led her teams to records of 20-8, 28-3 and 26-3 and completely re-wrote

59

Allie May, Gary May's daughter, was extremely tough mentally and was a great fielding pitcher.

Third baseman Kristin King delivered a walk-off RBI to give Gibson Southern the 2005 State championship.

Gibson Southern head coach Gary May

2005
State Softball Champions

Gibson Southern's 2005 State champs. Front row (L-R): Gretchen Michel, Jordan Maurer, Jamie Lindauer, Jennifer Ziliak, Valen Eberhard, Jennifer Sollman, Claire Will, Erin Wade. Second row: Kayla Becht, Kristen Schmitt, Kristin King, Katy Wanninger, Amanda Maurer, Carrie Wilderman, Jessica Adamson, Kristen Staback. Back Row: Terri Palmer, Jim Isaacs, Bryon Will, Jason Blackard, Gary May, Glover Priar, Pat Seib.

the school's record book. Her marks for career wins (65) and strikeouts (643) place her in a category with other local greats like Boonville's Erica Taylor and Castle's Madeline Brink, as all three reached meteoric levels.

Coach May has seen the program grow from its infancy and is well aware of the succession of fine pitchers at Gibson Southern. "Vicky Hale came along ('99-'01), and she was the very best at the time," Coach May recalled, "and then Allie (May) came along ('01-'03) and shattered Vicky's records. Then Carrie Wilderman came along ('03-'06) and broke Allie's, and then Lauren (Edwards) came along ('07-'10), and some of her numbers won't be touched."

May is also confident that the well is not dry. "I've got a freshman (in 2011), Bree Wilzbacher, who won 20 games and we went to State again," Gary informed me. "And for what it's worth, I have a couple grade schoolers who could really be something, too."

When asked to single out a few players who stood out over the years, Gary rolled his eyes and mentioned that there were just so many. Among the ones he named were the versatile Claire Will and Jamie Lindauer, who both played for the '03 and '05 State champs. Another member of both teams was Jennifer Ziliak, "the 'stud' in our lineup who could hit with power and for average." Gary also mentioned Valerie Rhodes from the '03 team who had sure hands at second base and was a great gap hitter and Kim Zimmerman ('03), who was "a great center fielder who caught every ball hit her way." Gary also mentioned Darla Dewig (2000-'02), a first team All-Stater who holds several school records, and Haley Taylor, another first team All-Stater from 2011.

Admittedly, there are far too many to try to remember, and May is very proud that 23 girls have gone on to play college ball (as of 2011). He has seen many players go off to school with varying results and feels that some of the girls don't realize how special their high school days are. "I wish I could explain to these parents and kids how different college is compared to high school," Gary explained. "Not that college is bad; it's just different. Pete Swanson (the beloved sportswriter for Gibson County) does a heck of a job covering us, and we even got covered on TV. Then you'll go to college and be lucky if there are a dozen people in the stands. If they realized the difference, they would appreciate high school more and not look ahead too much."

May is also quick to credit the assistants who have spent thousands of hours with the girls, like Bryon Will in the early years and current assistants Don Rhodes, Greg Wilson, D.G. Asay, Jeff Matse and Bernie Jordan. Like any smart coach, Gary also mentioned his wife Mary, saying, "She is a very valuable part of the Gibson Southern program. She does all the behind-the-scenes work that most people don't see. If I had to do what she does, I probably would have quit coaching a long time ago."

And when asked about the girls over the years and their work ethic, Gary didn't hesitate to give credit where it is due. "I think a lot of that is the values instilled in them by their parents," he mentioned. "We hardly ever have problems, and that comes from home." *(continued on page 62)*

LAUREN EDWARDS: QUEEN OF THE TITANS

Every program has one, and the 'one' at Gibson Southern is Lauren Edwards. Now that the sport has been around a while, we can analyze the truly successful local softball programs to see what they have in common. In every case, the consistent winners have a coach who is very involved with the school's feeder program and they also have one pitcher who has been influenced by those before her and has emerged as a truly dominant presence in the circle. Such is the case with Lauren Edwards. She began as most did with hours spent with dad learning the fundamentals, but Lauren will be the first to admit that when she first started, she was anything but a prodigy. "I was eleven when I started," Lauren told me, "and he (dad) thought he was wasting his time, because I was TERRIBLE." Then her father, Ken Edwards, hooked her up with Brent Hawkins at Extra Innings near Fulton Avenue.

Hawkins learned his craft from the true roots of local fast pitch softball when he played in the highly-popular men's leagues that were prominent in the area. In fact, he learned from one of the very best pitchers in local history, Gene Knapp. After spending time as U of E's women's pitching coach, he began to teach youngsters, and he remembers Lauren very well. "She was one of my first students," Hawkins recalled. "She must have been around eleven because she was moving up to 'big ball' (progressing from an 11-inch ball to a 12-inch). I thought she had a lot of talent. She may not have been the most athletic, but she out-worked everybody."

Hawkins works with around 80 girls a week, including the 2012 pitchers for Mater Dei, Harrison, Memorial and several from Kentucky and Illinois. He stresses to the girls that it takes more than time spent with him and their teams. The secret is the effort they're willing to put out at home. Lauren was a prime example of the dedication Brent stressed because of her long hours spent in the family's barn throwing thousands of balls on the indoor pitching area built by her parents.

Although Lauren wasn't big, maybe 5'6 and 120 pounds by Hawkins' estimation, her diligence in the weight room produced a very strong upper body, a physique Brent described as similar to that of a gymnast with powerful shoulders. That strength resulted in a scorching fastball that was timed at up to 63 miles per hour (the equivalent of a major leaguer throwing in the low 90s), and as she worked, her repertoire grew. "By the time she was a junior, she was throwing a riseball that hitters were having fits over," Hawkins revealed. "It's a tough pitch to hit. She threw six pitches, a fastball, changeup, curve, drop, screwball and riseball, and she had great command of them all."

Ken Edwards has been by his daughter's side very step of the way and also recalls the long hours spent catching Lauren. "Some of them weren't in the glove," he said with a laugh, "and I've still got a few scars to prove it. We tried to make every opportunity available that we could. Starting out, we never thought it would end up the way it did. The first six months, we thought we were throwing money away at those pitching lessons. She just kept working; she never quit."

Lauren's first actual lesson was from the program's first pitching star, Vicky Hale, and as she yearned for the days when she would don a Gibson Southern uniform, she built her strength with a tireless work ethic in the weight room. "My life centered around pitching and softball," Lauren said. "I used to play soccer and be a cheerleader. I gave up all that to put my energy into becoming a better pitcher. I didn't do things other kids did, like going ice skating, because I couldn't afford to get hurt and let the team down. I felt that I was a role model for the little kids, and that's how I conducted myself."

As Lauren developed, Ken noticed a trait that is rare in most high school hurlers. "It didn't matter what the situation was in the game, her expression never changed," he explained. "A lot of pitchers huff and puff and show frustration, but when she came off the rubber, you couldn't tell if we were ahead 10-0 or if a girl just hit one out of the park on her. She never showed emotion until the game was over. That always amazed me."

In 2009, Lauren led Gibson Southern to the IHSAA Final Four with a strong senior class that featured Lexie Holzmeyer, Angel Duran, Brittany Elpers, Lauren Atchison and others. Along the way, Edwards accomplished a rare feat, two no-hitters in one day, with a 3-0 win over Corydon Central and a 4-0 win over second-ranked Edgewood in the 3A regional. Although the team lost a heartbreaker to Andrean in the State semi-finals, the girls finished 28-3.

Lauren's senior season ended much too soon when her powerful 26-2 team lost in the 2010 sectional to an equally powerful Boonville team. Although she earned all the accolades that came with her talent, including first team All-State honors, she still considers the Final Four trip her most special memory, saying, "I remember the fans following us all the way to Indianapolis, and that was the best time I've ever had with the girls at Gibson Southern."

As Lauren contemplated college, she realized that her knees were wearing down and that trying to continue to play would likely result in injury, so she stepped away from the game to pursue a degree in Occupational Therapy at USI. When she left Gary May's program in 2010, she owned the record book, posting marks for career wins (65), strikeouts (643) and innings pitched (515) among many others.

Edwards made herself into a star with a relentless work ethic and the willingness to make sacrifices, and she earned every honor that came her way. It may be a while before another Gibson Southern pitcher comes along who can challenge her records, but for now she stands alone as the program's most dominant pitcher. So until another prodigy emerges to take her place in Gibson Southern history, we can christen Lauren Edwards the Queen of the Titans.

Through the leadership of Jason Blackard and Gary May, the softball program at Gibson Southern has been to the State Finals six times and brought the trophy home twice ('03 & '05), and from 2001-2011, their record stands at 264-64 (80%). In fact, after the inaugural season in 1995, the Titans have never suffered a losing season, and in their last 12 campaigns, they have won at least 20 games 10 times.

The Gibson Southern softball program has proven to be a juggernaut, and much of that success can be attributed to the hard work and dedication of its current coach, Gary May. Long-time assistant Don Rhodes worked with Gary when their daughters were very young and watched as Gary's influence took hold. "Gary had been a pitcher in high school and college," Don revealed. "We went to a lot of clinics to get an understanding of the game itself, but Gary studied the pitching side of it. When he started calling pitches in 2000-'01, he brought it to the next level. Gary's a key ingredient to that whole program."

Ken Edwards, the father of Lauren Edwards, the program's most decorated pitcher, has seen first-hand what Coach May has meant to the program, saying, "People always talk about how dominant your pitcher is, but a lot of the records Lauren has are because of the team Gary put behind her. He worked with that group since they were ten years old hitting ground balls for hours and practicing the basics. There wasn't a lot of thinking. The kids knew what to do."

It would be difficult to find too many people in Gibson County who aren't thoroughly impressed with the status of the softball program at Gibson Southern, and the ladies' presence has helped to establish southwestern Indiana as a stronghold of the sport. Don Rhodes is one who has lived through the highs and lows of the program, and his feelings are likely echoed by Gary May and everyone else associated with Gibson Southern softball.

"These kids are dedicated," Rhodes said. "They're willing to work, and success feeds downward and kids want to get to that level. The State championship is something that's going to be with me until the day I die. We've always been looked at as one of the better programs in the state, and it's fun to be a part of it."

JASPER BASEBALL: FIRST CLASS ALL THE WAY

One look at the complex that is the home of Jasper High School baseball is all it takes to understand why the program is one of the strongest in the state. And one discussion with either of Jasper's most recent coaches is all it takes to see that the program is so much more than that.

The first Jasper High School hitter stepped to the plate in 1931 under head coach Tom Rea, who piloted the program for five seasons before Wood Weir took over in 1936. Weir led the Wildcats to a 31-10 record for four seasons before legendary basketball coach Cabby O'Neill was hired in 1940. O'Neill won two-thirds of his baseball games from '40 to '48, and was succeeded by three men, Joe Rowekamp, Bob Fell and Wes Settle, who had limited success for the next sixteen years.

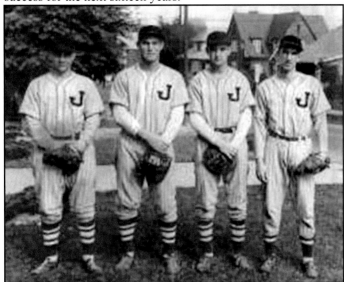

In 1965, Don Noblitt assumed control and guided Jasper baseball into the IHSAA tournament era before stepping down and eventually becoming the school's principal. Noblitt's 1967 team won the inaugural sectional and followed that win with the school's first regional and semi-state crowns. He left with a 114-53 record (67.4%) that included four sectional and regional crowns and two trips to the State Finals.

After a four-year run by Rex May (62-44-1) and a season under Dan Doyle (15-13), a man came to town who would offer stability, guide the program into the state's upper echelon and earn himself a spot in the Indiana Baseball Hall of Fame. Ray Howard was a talented hurler for Indianapolis Ben Davis High School in the '50s and was good enough to be offered a professional contract out of high school. He chose, however, to attend Indiana Central (now the University of Indianapolis) and led the Greyhounds to three conference championships.

Ray admits that he wasn't thrilled about coaching when he began his career at small schools in southeastern Indiana, then came back to a small Catholic school in Indy before testing the waters in the world of sales for several years. In 1973, he left the business world and accepted a coaching job at Decatur Central while he substitute taught, worked another job at night and finished his Masters.

He ended up in Jasper by what he calls a fluke. Things were going well at DC in 1977, and he had just finished building a new field at the school. In his past, he had attended clinics held by Don Noblitt and Jasper broadcaster Bob Simmers, so he was familiar with the town. While visiting friends in the area, he spoke with Don Poole, a good friend and college buddy who knew that Ray and his wife, Janet, were going to be staying at the Jasper Holiday

Inn. Don informed Ray that the Jasper baseball job was open and suggested he look into it. Ray decided to call Noblitt and they spent a Sunday afternoon together touring the town.

Coach Howard left Jasper extremely impressed, noting that the lighted field was something that even Indianapolis didn't offer, except for Victory Field where the Indians played. Ray knew it was a great opportunity but didn't want to leave his athletic director high and dry, with school starting in two weeks. To Ray's surprise, when he saw his AD on Monday about another matter, the AD asked, "Are you going to take the Jasper job?"

As it turned out, Devere Fair, the AD, knew Don Noblitt, and when Ray expressed his concerns, Fair would have none of it. "You go or I'll fire you," Fair told him, realizing the potential of the opportunity. So, thanks to an understanding friend, Ray Howard found a new home.

Howard inherited a program that had finished 15-13 the previous season, and he was anxious to see how the boys would respond to his coaching style. "We got off to a good start," Coach Howard revealed, "and I think that helped things develop. The first three years we lost seven games, so people around here thought I was pretty smart."

Ray's first three teams went 27-4, 29-2 and 28-1, won three sectionals and two regionals from 1977 through 1979, and may have gone all the way if not for the ultra-talented Memorial teams that won 59 straight games and starred Don Mattingly, Jeff Schulz and many others at the time. During Howard's eleven seasons at the controls, the Wildcats never had a losing season, and Ray finished his term one win shy of the 80% mark (265-68). He had always said that he didn't want to keep coaching if he couldn't devote 110% to the job, and with other interests he enjoyed, primarily hunting and golf, he opted to turn over the reigns in 1987.

With some huge shoes to fill, the administration considered seeking out a big name coach from outside the area, but when they consulted Coach Howard, he suggested they look in their own backyard. Terry Gobert had been a three-sport athlete (football, basketball and baseball) at Greencastle before attending IU to get his degree in Education. He then went to DePauw for his Masters and served as a grad assistant for Mike Steele. Terry then returned to his high school alma mater and coached football under hall of fame coach John Fallis, who had coached in the North-South All-Star Game with Jasper's Jerry Brewer. When Brewer contacted Fallis and told him that Jasper was looking for a Social Studies teacher and football coach, he recommended Gobert.

In 1985, Terry was hired, and when a position opened up on Ray Howard's baseball staff, Gobert added that to his workload. When the time came, Terry was thrilled to accept the head baseball position when Coach Howard departed, and for six years, he coached both baseball and the offensive line in football. He also found love and "married an Eckerle" (a very common Jasper surname). So as Terry worked to build the baseball program, he and Caroline started a family, and as the years passed, the program and the family became forever entwined. One of Terry's greatest sources of pride is the varsity baseball complex on 10th Street that is truly a magnificent sight to behold. The land on which it sits was leased from the Catholic diocese for many years, but in the early '90s, the school purchased the land and the renovations began. Today Alvin C. Ruxer Field sprawls majestically with its 2500-seat concrete stadium, manicured field and 55-foot sunken dugouts. The area is brightened by lights that extend 100 feet high (the standard used by AAA teams), and the media enjoys the comforts

Ruxer Field sets the standard in the Midwest.

of a 36'x10' pressbox while fans enjoy a complete menu at the concession stand.

"We try to make every ballgame feel like a big league experience," Coach Gobert explained from his office in the complex. "Every game is an event. We try to make it special." The office where we met was part of a facility that would be the pride and joy of many college programs. The idea was conceived when Jasper baseball alum Scott Rolen suggested that players, including himself, could use a nice place to hit in the off-season. From that seed grew a project, and contrary to what some folks believe, it wasn't funded by someone with deep pockets writing a huge check. Instead, Rolen offered signed memorabilia as an incentive for many smaller investors to have their names on the plaque at the entrance.

Gobert went on to explain that what would have been a $300,000 building was completed for under $100,000 due to donations of labor and materials by local contributors. The spacious fieldhouse features a locker room, lounge, coaches' suite, video room, laundry area and storage for heavy equipment in addition to a 60' by 80' Astroturf workout area complete with four full-length hitting tunnels. Beside the fieldhouse is another area that is very special to Coach Gobert, and the space is a constant reminder of what Jasper's baseball program means to Terry and his family.

In 1997, Sarah Gobert, the infant daughter of Terry and Caroline, was diagnosed with leukemia, and for the next year, the entire baseball community shared the horrible ordeal with the Goberts. When Sara's little body finally gave out in 1998, the outpouring of support was immense, and as a result, a small park was built where families can gather. Today, every time Terry pulls into the complex, he sees Sarah's Place, the small park that stands as a monument to the spirit of his little girl.

Terry is not shy about sharing what Jasper baseball means to him, and he takes great pride in everyone who has been a part of its success. He has had several assistants in his 27 seasons, and most of them are home-grown. The staff in 2012 included varsity assistant Jason Ahlbrand, who was an excellent three-sport athlete at Jasper and played baseball with his younger brother Brad during the transition from Ray Howard to Terry.

Phil Kendall, another varsity assistant, has been at Jasper for nine years and was a standout at Jasper in the mid-'90s, leading the Cats to their first State championship in 1996 before spending

Mike Ballenger was a phenomenal all-around athlete for Jasper in the early '80s.

four years in the Milwaukee Brewers organization. Jeremy Wolf is a 1995 Jasper grad who has coached several sports at Jasper and serves as the head JV coach with assistant Jeff Zink, who graduated from Forest Park. Eric Dall, the youngest of the staff, was a member of the 2006 State championship team and serves as the program's freshman coach.

Terry is also quick to mention all the volunteers over the years who help enhance the experience for players and fans. He singled out team doctor Jared Brosmer, P.A. announcer Carey Schneider, scoreboard operator Dave Eckert and groundskeepers Shane Werner and Luke Hopf, whose efforts beautify Ruxer Field and the outstanding junior varsity field, respectively. Another special group provides an atmosphere that is very rare in the world of Indiana high school baseball. Paul Knies, who owns radio and TV stations in Jasper, has made sure that Jasper baseball gets unprecedented media coverage. With Walt Ferber doing play-by-play and Coach Howard doing commentary, WITZ covers all games, home and away, and local cable station WJTS broadcasts games on tape delay with Karl Gutgsell calling the action. In addition, the *Jasper Herald* newspaper also provides thorough print coverage through sports journalist Brandon Perkins.

From concession workers to ticket takers to bat girls, the Jasper baseball program is a well-oiled machine, but the true stars over the years are the players. Like any coach asked to choose players from decades of teams, Ray and Terry did their best but knew they would forget some. But both tried to name a few who were special.

Coach Howard started with Dan Fuhs, an outfielder who played at Butler, and the Seger brothers, Ted and Scott, who were both excellent fielders. He also mentioned the Ahlbrands, Todd Krapf, a pitcher from the '86 and '87 teams who pitched for USI, and two catchers who also played for the Screaming Eagles, Jason Stamm and Blake Kruger.

Ray also singled out Andy Noblitt, who graduated in '92 and then played at UE and in the Frontier League. He then acknowledged an entire team that he said he would have liked to coach every year, the 1977 group that went 27-4 in Ray's first season after a very ordinary season the year before. Among those players were catcher Ken Brelage and left-handed pitcher/outfielder Keith Leinenbach, who both played at Bellarmine. Coach Howard also mentioned "big knockers" Mark Kunkel (OF) and Mike Meyer (1B).

Last but not least on Ray's list was Mike Ballenger, one of the finest all-around athletes in Jasper history. At 6'3, Ballenger had all the skills, including a powerful arm at quarterback that Terry Gobert heard was good enough to draw the attention of the Dallas Cowboys, who asked to see footage. Ballenger was also good enough in basketball to earn a spot on the Indiana All-Stars, and on the diamond, he left his name all over the record book.

One of Coach Ray's favorite memories of Ballenger was the 1981 baseball semi-state at Huntingburg. The Wildcats were scheduled to play Mooresville at 1:30, and Mike had to take his ACT exam at 11:00 in Bloomington. So Coach Howard came up with a solution. Local supporter Bob Ruckriegel owned BR Associates, a company that owned many Wendy's and Long John Silver's restaurants. Because of this, Bob had access to the company helicopter, which picked Ballenger up in Bloomington. One can only imagine the sight as the Mooresville players stood leaning on the right field fence as the chopper landed behind the centerfield fence. As Ray tells it, Mike emerged with his uniform on a hanger and then proceeded to mow down the Pioneers with a two-hit shutout. Ballenger was good enough to be offered a contract with Kansas City but opted to play basketball for Joe B. Hall at Kentucky because of his father's allegiance as a Big Blue fan.

When Coach Gobert was asked to single out a few players, he mentioned Ballenger again as one of the program's best. Ballenger was a great hitter and position player, but he was truly outstanding on the mound, holding career records for wins (28-4), ERA (1.07) and strikeouts (304) from 1979 through 1981. Scott Rolen was a fine pitcher as well and holds the record for the lowest ERA in a season (0.64 in '93), and Kendall holds the season strikeout record with 157. Brian Persohn had the most wins in a season with his 14-1 record in 1979, and three pitchers, Kevin Werner ('92), Jared Brosmer ('93) and Michael Boehman ('02) recorded perfect games.

When asked about hitters and position players, Terry Gobert recognized the Burger brothers, Jim and Mike, who played in the '80s. Three obvious choices were the three whose names are displayed on the Hall of Champions: Matt Mauck ('94-'97) who was named Indiana's Mr. Baseball for 1997 and was drafted in the sixth round by the Cubs; Phil Kendall ('93-'96), All-State in '96 and drafted in the fifth round by the Brewers; and Scott Rolen ('91-'93), an All-American in '92 and '93 who was drafted in the second round by Philadelphia and was playing in his seventeenth major league season in 2012. Those three are the only Jasper players to have their numbers retired, Mauck (#22), Kendall (#17) and Rolen (#21), and Neil Giesler was the only other Wildcat player to be drafted when he was selected in the 29th and 37th rounds in 2002 and 2003, respectively.

Other players worthy of mention are those who appear with distinction in the school's program and record book. Sam Linnette was the only player to earn MVP honors three times ('04-'06) and Rolen and Mauck are the only two to be named Mr. Baseball. Heath Uppencamp ('96-'98) was an excellent pitcher who also holds the career record for batting average at .454, while Chris Schmidt ('00-'03) holds the school record with 76 career stolen bases. Rolen and Neil Giesler's names are at or near the top of every hitting category, but the man that Terry Gobert considers the best hitter during his tenure holds school season records for home runs (15), total bases (122) and RBIs (64) and career records for home runs (28) and RBIs (14).

"I'd have a hard time not naming (1998 grad) Scott Kluesner as the best high school hitter I've ever coached," Gobert told me, "including Scott Rolen." Gobert

Scott Rolen, right, was an excellent multi-sport athlete and set the single-game basketball scoring record at Jasper with 50 points.

then told of the Barr-Reeve game in 1998, the first year of the class system for the State tournament. The Barr-Reeve coach was saving his best pitcher for the sectional, but having Jasper down in the bottom of the sixth, he had to go for a win over the Wildcats. He brought in his stud, and while the kid warmed up, Terry called Kluesner over for a chat: "Scott, you're a good hitter. Some people like to look at a pitch first…"

"How about I just hit the first one out," Kluesner interrupted.

"Well, that's an option," Gobert responded.

Kluesner then tomahawked a chin-high fastball into orbit and greeted his coach at third base with a smiling "How's that?"

Gobert revealed that he had nearly cut Kluesner because he was very slow and somewhat lazy, but after one swing in tryouts, told his coaches, "We have to change our plan."

Gobert also told the story of the 'ranger bat,' a "little-bitty bat" that was the color used by the Forest Park Rangers. No one used it, but in one at-bat, Kluesner proclaimed, "Give me the ranger bat!" After a long home run, he returned to the dugout, and Gobert later heard that Scott had looked at his teammates and stated, "It ain't the bat, boys! It ain't the bat!"

Student manager Caleb Lehman had his senior photo taken with his radar gun.

Each season of Jasper baseball is a quest for excellence, and the program's two premier coaches have fond memories of the people and of the dedication it takes by so many to stay on top. "There is certainly commitment to detail," said Ray Howard when asked about his memories, "whether it's hitting or fielding, the nuances of the game. We were looking for new things to teach to make them better players. Also there was the German heritage, and the work ethic was evident with the very first group of kids I had."

Ray also mentioned how the fans packed the stadium and how so many of them volunteered when needed. About Terry Gobert, Coach Howard said, "He wants to make the kids as good as they can be. He studies and goes to clinics. He tells the kids they have to get better every day."

Coach Gobert was philosophical when asked about some of his favorite moments, and those he mentioned had very little to do with wins or losses. Instead, they exposed emotions that come from the relationships built through the years and the lifetime moments, both good and bad, that were shared with some very special people.

He first spoke of one of the saddest moments in the program's history when one of their own was lost in a car accident a year after graduation. "He was a great kid," Terry confided. "He hardly ever played, but he loved baseball. He probably didn't bat 15 times in two years, but he was on two State championship teams. It's on his tombstone. He would introduce himself as 'Doug Kruger, two-time State champion." The boy's parents, Steve and Debbie, were obviously distraught and were touched by a gesture made by Terry. "I promised his mom that no one else would wear #14 (Doug's number) while I'm here."

Doug Kruger's death inspired the annual Kruger Heart Award.

Debbie, in particular, has worked to keep her son's memory alive, and since the accident, one player each year receives the Kruger Heart Award honoring the athlete with the most heart and passion for the sport. In 2012, the plaque went to student manager Caleb Lehman, who charted every pitch, timed pitches with the radar gun, shot video during games and went on scouting trips with Coach Gobert when others didn't want to go. Caleb is so passionate, in fact, that he is holding his radar gun in his senior photo.

Student managers are important to Terry, and as a means of showing appreciation, one of the team's traditions is centered around them. Each year, the senior manager gets to dress and start a game, and Gobert says it is amazing how often they get at least one hit.

Another event was a kind of 'aha moment' for Terry, and it happened in 1996 when his team became the last one to win the State championship in the one-class system. Terry is always one to keep things on an even keel and not celebrate excessively, and when the boys were posing by the teepee in center field at Victory Field, they all raised their index finger to indicate '#1'. Terry's instinctive reaction was to instruct them to lower them, but then he realized, "Hey, we really are #1 out of 400+ schools." The team had won the school's first State title in any sport since Cabby O'Neill's boys won the basketball championship in 1949, and Gobert's club repeated in '97 making them the first 3A champ in history.

Another of Gobert's favorite moments is a mound visit to talk to Heath Uppencamp, the outstanding left-hander who went on to pitch at Purdue. Heath was struggling against Carmel and thought Terry was going to read him the riot act. In actuality, Terry didn't even know what he was going to say. Upon his arrival, Terry looked around and noticed the huge crowd, something he was unaware of because of his focus on the game. "Wow, there are a lot of people here," Gobert told Uppencamp. "I bet if you get these three guys out, you could have a date with any girl in Jasper."

"Yes, sir," Heath responded.

Nick (left) and Terry Gobert

The Gobert girls: Front (L-R): Julia and Laura.
Back: Maria and Caroline

"Well then, get them out and see what happens."

That is exactly what Heath did, and Terry chuckled when Heath was asked by a reporter about the discussion on the mound and responded by saying, "he told me I needed to bear down and follow through."

Yet another thrill for Gobert was a call he received in 1996. Terry was working with announcer Kurt Gutsgell editing video footage at 11:30 at night when the phone rang. On the other end was Scott Rolen, and he said, "Coach, I got the call. I'm going to the big leagues!" Gobert promptly called Cory Luebbehusen, Scott's good friend, and within an hour, Cory, his little brother, Gutsgell and Gobert were on their way to Philadelphia.

After the 13-hour drive, the men took their seats and watched Rolen's first at-bat and then his first hit, a double against the Cardinals. Terry watched and later asked Scott what was said in his verbal exchange with hall of fame Cardinal shortstop Ozzie Smith. Apparently Smith asked, "Was that your first hit, kid?" Rolen politely said, "Yes, sir," to which Ozzie said, "I'm sure there will be many more" and tossed the ball into the Philadelphia dugout for Scott to keep.

Terry has had many special memories, and some can spark emotion even after many years. One light-hearted moment occurred amidst one of the darker periods for Terry. In 1998, little Sarah was diagnosed and the family had made the decision to keep coaching. The situation was filled with obvious stress and countless nights with little sleep, and there were times when Terry wasn't exactly a ray of sunshine at practice. One such day was a practice before the '98 semi-state in sweltering heat.

Terry admits that the coaching staff was concerned how the team was handling the normal pressures of the State tournament as well as the heartbreaking ordeal of Sarah's condition. As Terry ran infield practice with a fungo bat (a thin bat used for practice), he wasn't happy with the performance of his catcher, Brad Eckerle, who happened to be his wife's cousin. As his already short fuse burned down, Terry went into a tirade, saying, "So help me, if you don't get your act together, I'm going to take this fungo bat and shove it up your (butt)." He then slammed the bat to the ground, shattering it to pieces, and told Brad to take a seat in the dugout.

After a few seconds, an assistant told Terry to turn around, and both were surprised by the sight. To provide some levity to a tense situation, Eckerle had stuck half the bat between his legs as he walked to the dugout to make it appear to be lodged where the sun don't shine. Needless to say, the tension was broken, and the assistant looked at Terry and said, "I think they're going to be alright."

Like a Hollywood script, the boys brought home the trophy, giving Jasper three straight, making them the only team in Indiana history to win even two in a row. The year was special to Terry for many reasons, and he appreciates how the boys handled a very tough situation. 'Sometimes kids are forced to grow up, and they really did that year," Terry reflected. "They were so helpful. When I got mad, they saw the big picture. They were great."

As one could imagine, 27 years of experiences would have to include a coach's family, and one that will last a lifetime is a proud papa moment when Nick Gobert, Terry's freshman son, drove in the only run in a 1-0 semi-state win over New Palestine. Terry admits that he always tried to treat his son like all the rest but couldn't help a brief second to himself to say, "That's my boy!"

Like any coach, Terry's career is very time-consuming, and he credits a very understanding family for his success. He mentioned that Nick attended his first game when he was four days old, and his daughters, Maria, Laura and Julia "have been bat girls since birth." But no one has been more supportive than Terry's wife. "I tell you what saved baseball for me was when Caroline got involved," Terry explained. "She's the sponsor of the bat girls; she runs the concessions. It became a family deal. We include them. It's a great life."

As proof that Gobert's favorite memories aren't always success stories in terms of wins and losses, Terry's favorite occurred after a loss. "My greatest moment was in 1992," Terry explained. "Scott Rolen was my #4 pitcher; we were loaded. We were 32-3, the best team I'll ever have as far as up and down the lineup."

As expected, Jasper and Memorial, #1 and #2 in the state, were to meet once again in the long-time regional rivalry. Jasper had gone to State the previous year, but on this day, the team was uncharacteristically error prone and lost the game. Afterward, Terry watched as no player threw a helmet or glove or threw a fit. Instead, they shook hands and behaved like gentlemen. "I felt more validated by that than I did in '96 when we were the last team standing," Gobert informed me. "If you asked me for one moment, that would be it, seeing that team in '92, the hurt, the devastation. I'm not sure I'm over it (the game) yet. I still get mad because they were that good a team and they were great kids. I

This rendering by artist Jon Siau represents a light-hearted moment during a very dark time in Jasper baseball history.

knew I was on the right track as a coach because of the way they handled that loss."

With any program comes devastating losses, but Jasper has had more than its share of success. After 75 years, the numbers speak for themselves. When the State tournament began in 1967, Jasper won the first four sectionals and regionals, and they won 14 straight sectionals from '84-'97 and 8 in a row from '75-'82. The program ranks #1 or #2 (with LaPorte) in virtually every category, with 13 State Finals appearances and 5 State championships, second to LaPorte's 7. Jasper has won 88.7% of its sectional games (95-12) with an overall tournament record of 173-40 (81.3%), including 33 sectionals, 22 regionals and 12 semi-states to go with the titles in '96, '97, '98, '00 and '06.

Gobert's record as of 2012 was 594 and 189 (76%), and since 1963, no Jasper team has had a losing season. Indiana Baseball Hall of Famers Ray Howard and Terry Gobert know the Jasper baseball program is special and that they are only a part of its legacy. Howard knew when it was time to step down, and Terry is relying on his best friend to help with the decision when the time comes.

"I don't think she wants me around the house," Terry joked when asked what Caroline thinks about his retiring. "I trust her a lot, like any happily married man. She says, 'You wouldn't be happy. You need goals.' I told her 'If you ever see I don't have a passion for it, tell me.' Everybody needs a friend to say, 'Hey, it's time.' I don't want to be one of these guys who stays around (to chase numbers)."

Terry knows the day will come, and until then, he will continue to strive for perfection with the help of his staff, his players and the community. Jasper High School has built a model of excellence that many schools would love to emulate. Through the efforts of men like Ray Howard and Terry Gobert, Jasper baseball has withstood the test of time to become one of the truly elite programs in the state of Indiana.

Little Sarah Gobert captured the hearts of all who knew her, and her memory lives on in this secluded park near the baseball field.

IHSAA STATE CHAMPIONS UPDATE

GOLF

School	Year	Score	Coach
Harrison	2012	611	Josh Dahmer

Individual	School	Year	Score
Sean Stone	Harrison	2012	140

CHAPTER THREE
FORE!

THE EVANSVILLE CITY GOLF TOURNAMENT

Perhaps it is fitting that the Evansville City Golf Championship was launched in 1930. With the nation in crisis after the infamous stock market crash in 1929, a new concept for local golfers would offer a positive distraction. So for an entry fee of one dollar plus a caddy fee of 75 cents with a dime tip, 52 area men donned their knickers and hit the links for what would become a lasting tradition in the River City.

At the time of the tourney's inception, Evansville had only two 18-hole courses, Helfrich and the Country Club. The competition would be ground-breaking in that it was conceived to be more than a social event, so the decision was made to require strict enforcement of the rules. According to a story by long-time *Courier* sports editor Dan Scism, the tone was set in the very first round when a club pro named Ritchie disqualified two of his members, Peck Coldwell and Walker Anderson, for teeing off early.

In that first tournament, Dr. Robert R. Acre became the event's first champion with a 320 score, followed by Harold Bootz, Sr. (323), Herb Henderson (330), and Bob Hamilton (330). Dr. Acre repeated the next year with a 5-stroke win over teenage phenom Bob Hamilton. In 1932, the 16-year-old Hamilton trounced the field with an 18-shot win over his nearest competitor, Harold Bootz. For the next four years, the City belonged to Hamilton, as no one got within nine shots of him in any given year. Hamilton's last victory before heading to the professional tour was in 1936, the first year the City format was changed to match play.

The tourney returned to stroke play in 1950 with back-to-back wins by Earl Greenwell followed by a dominating stretch by 6-time winner Jerry Schreiber. In fact, from 1953 until 1968, 14 of the 16 City tournaments went to either Ed Wolf or Schreiber. The City stayed wide open for the next 24 years until a new king was crowned in 1992 when Kevin Wassmer won the first of his nine titles over the next 15 years.

In 1965, an important decision was made that would add new meaning to the City Championship's purpose. It was decided that merchandise previously given to the first 20 finishers would be eliminated in lieu of plaques and trophies and the money that had been used for prizes would then be used to benefit a young golfer each year in the form of a scholarship. The award would eventually be named the Daniel W. Scism Scholarship to honor the tournament's founder, and over the years, it has helped to fund the educations of some of the area's finest young players.

With the support of the *Evansville Courier* and many dedicated men and women who love the sport, the Evansville City Championship has flourished for over eighty years.

CITY GOLF TOURNAMENT FACTS

Multiple Winners	Multiple Runners-up	Back-to-Back Winners
Kevin Wassmer – 10	Jerry Schreiber – 8	Dr. R.R. Acre ('30-'31)
Jerry Schreiber – 9	Ed Wolf – 5	Bob Hamilton ('32-'36)
Ed Wolf – 6	John Kaposta – 5	Dan Scism ('33-'34)
Bob Hamilton – 5	Keith Bratton – 5	Earl Greenwell ('50-'51)
Francis Fleming – 3	Dan Scism – 4	Ed Wolf ('53-'54, '57-'58)
Billie Martin – 3	Ralph Stevens – 3	Jerry Schreiber ('61-'65, '67-'68)
Dan Scism – 2	Mike Small – 3	Jeff Howerton ('82-'83)
Earl Greenwell – 2	Harold Bootz – 2	Jeff Sanders ('90-'91)
Richie Moore – 2	Doug Winsett – 2	Kevin Wassmer ('92-'93, '99-'02)
Jeff Sanders – 2	Sam Stucke – 2	

Youngest Winner –Bob Hamilton, 16 (1932)
Olderst Winner – Sam Stucke, 45 (1966)
Biggest Margin of Victory (Match Play)
10 & 9 (twice) Cliff McKelvey over Rush Jerrel (1937)
& Dan Scism over Dutch Rittenhouse (1944)
Father/Son Winners
Bob Hamilton ('32-'36) & Jim Hamilton ('71 & '73),
Jerry Schreiber (9 times) & Troy Schreiber ('98)
Tournament Scoring Record
Ed Wolf – 277 ('54) – teed up in fairways
Jerry Schreiber – 278 ('62) & Sam Stucke ('66) – played as ball lies

DID YOU KNOW?

Evansville's Keith Bagby holds the distinction of hitting the first ball ever in the Evansville Men's Senior City Golf Tournament. Keith became the answer to this local sports trivia question when he had the honors in the first group in 2002.

LOCAL GOLFER CELEBRATES THE PAST

Evansville's Max Hollon is a member of a unique group of golfers who play the sport in its purest form. Max always loved the game and looked forward to more time on the course when he retired a few years ago after teaching Chemistry and Physics at North high School. In the summer of 2010, he discovered an organization called the Society of Hickory Golfers, and his life hasn't been the same since.

Members travel all over the country, dressed in knickers, knee socks, long-sleeved shirts and ties, and tee it up using either original hickory clubs or replicas that meet strict guidelines. Hollon's first tournament was in April of 2011 in Birmingham, Alabama, and three months later he was the runner-up at the US. Hickory Open on the Donald Ross Golf Course in French Lick, Indiana.

A year later, in 2012, Max topped the field at the same event with a late charge to overcome a one-stroke deficit and defeat his playing partner, Terry Howarth, with a two day total of 158 (77, 81). "I was striking the ball better than I ever have," Max told *Evansville Courier* journalist Steve Ford. "It's pretty much all I play with. I rarely play with my modern clubs anymore."

Hollon is passionate about his new pastime and estimates that the clubs reduce distance by about 20%. He mentioned that Fendrich pro Dave English won the second net division in the same tournament with a score of 140. The courses are usually about 6,000 yards in length, and Max wishes more folks would get involved so that they, too, could appreciate the past by testing their skill with the same clubs that the true pioneers of the game used.

Max Hollon (Photo courtesy of the Evansville Courier.)

BOB WALTHER: GOLF'S GURU

Evansville's Bob Walther has been a fixture in the local golf community for 45 years, and his impact on the local golf landscape has had a far-reaching effect on countless area golfers. From his beginnings as a diminutive teenager, he learned the secrets of success from some of the all-time greats, and as a result, became an outstanding golfer and an even better teacher.

Walther entered Central High School as a 5'2, 90-pound freshman, so his athletic options were limited. His infatuation with golf began even earlier when his uncle gave him an old set of clubs and Bob constructed a makeshift five-hole course in his yard using Planters Peanut cans as holes. In the early '60s, he went with a friend who caddied at Helfrich and fell in love with the game on the spot. When his father noticed Bob's interest, he arranged for his son to take lessons from Jim Riele (pronounced Real), the Helfrich pro, and Bob began working in the pro shop.

A major turning point in young Bob's golf life was a chance encounter with the legend himself, Bob Hamilton, and the event would help mold Walther into the man he has become. On this day, Hamilton was playing with local characters Hubert Cokes and Tubby Bunge, the father of Phyllis Schreiber (Jerry's wife), and Walther remembers the occurrence like it was yesterday. As he told the story, the respect he had for the city's most celebrated golfer quickly became evident.

"My first encounter with Mr. Hamilton was on a hot summer day at Hamilton Golf Course," Bob told me on the *Local Legends* radio show. "I was playing by myself and I was on the 11th hole and sliced my ball into the 17th fairway. He came up in a cart, and I knew him, with his physical presence and his big cigar. He threw some balls on the ground and said, 'Lad, let me see you hit a few.'"

After Walther smacked some balls, Hamilton made a proposal that would change young Bob's life. "Come up to my golf range. I want to teach you to play golf."

At 5:00 that evening, Walther hit bucket after bucket for more than five hours, and with his father and Mr. Hamilton looking on, he saw blood dripping down the shaft from the blisters on his hands. Walther had an inkling that he was being tested, so when Hamilton posed the question, "Well, lad, what do you think," Walther responded by saying, "Mr. Hamilton, could we hit one more bucket before we call it a night?"

Bob had passed the test, and a life-long relationship began. "He treated me like a son for years," Walther recalled, "and John and Jim (Hamilton's sons) were like my brothers. His philosophy was, the easy way (to learn) is to hit a bunch of golf balls, and every other way is the hard way. If you weren't willing to work, he would show you the door in a hurry. Why he took an interest in me, I don't know. He mentored me over the next eight or nine years and taught me to play competitive golf."

While at Central, Bob admits that, as a sophomore, he was "terrible," but as a junior, he could shoot par on a good day. As he grew, he became consumed by the game and played "all day every day." By the time his senior year rolled around, Bob was 6 feet tall and 125 pounds and was physically strong with large hands for his size. At the time, he had no ambitions to be a pro golfer and, in fact, was considering being a doctor. The M.D. never materialized, but his years at Evansville College (now U of E) inspired new visions for him to pursue.

As a member of the school's golf team, he won some matches over the years, and by his senior season, he had learned how to win golf tournaments. He even captured the conference individual title, becoming the first golfer in school history to accomplish the feat. His success at E.C. changed his outlook, and at age 21, he won almost everything, including the City tournament in 1969 and a near win at the State Amateur in 1970.

Bob turned pro in 1972 at a time when the only tours were the PGA, Canadian and Asian tours. A move to Tampa provided him the chance to compete on a mini-tour, comparable to the Nationwide now, where he teed it up with contemporaries like Tom Kite, Andy North, Larry Nelson and Dr. Gil Morgan. He also got to know a young player from southern California named Gary McCord, the popular golf analyst today with the handlebar mustache. Walther described McCord as "tall and rangy and athletic with long arms who could dunk a basketball behind his head."

Walther spent three years on the mini-tour and tried to qualify for the PGA twice, but with a nagging neck injury constantly recurring, he ended his playing days in 1975. When he returned home, Bob noticed that there were no practice ranges in Evansville, so he approached the city about leasing property on what used to be a city dump. So by covering garbage with dirt, Walther found a new calling, and in 1978, his 18 ½ - acre facility opened on the city's north side.

At the time, the only real competition was Hamilton's facility on the south side next to the McDonald's on Kentucky Avenue. To put the timeframe in perspective, the McDonald's was one of the franchise's very early locations with a sign that read "Over 1 million sold." So from his new complex on First Avenue, Walther went to work building a new career.

"I had no idea where it would all lead," Bob explained, "but I found that I really enjoyed teaching golf. I particularly liked teaching beginners, especially adults who are beginners who think they can't do this."

Bob admits to being on the impatient side but has always been extremely patient with his students. "I know how hard you have to work to be good at it," he said. "It's a very practice-intensive, delayed gratification sport."

Walther has promoted the sport and developed golfers for nearly 35 years now, and he has mentored many of the city's finest players, including current PGA star Jeff Overton. He has plied his trade with the same passion he used to learn the game as a teenager, and sometimes his teaching techniques have an eerie resemblance to those of his own teacher, Bob Hamilton.

Perhaps the student that best exemplifies the influence Walther can have on a golfer is a young man who is best friends with Overton and a teammate of his on the 2000 State champion golf team at North. Alex Abbott doesn't profess to be in the same class as Overton, but he would match his love for the game with anyone, and it was that passion that brought him to Walther.

"When I was young, I was diagnosed with epilepsy," Alex told me by phone from Indianapolis, where he lives, "but by God's grace, I had the only kind you can grow out of. I was a scrawny kid and loved basketball, but I was too small, so I tried golf and I loved it. I had a total romance with the game. I couldn't NOT do it."

Abbott started playing the game, and as his parents, Dave and Kathy, saw the effort he was putting in, they suggested lessons. They knew Walther from being fellow members of Christian Fellowship Church and thought he would be perfect to help their son develop as a golfer and as a man.

When Alex was in the sixth grade, Kathy took him to Bob, but Bob and Alex didn't hit it off at first. "His mother brought him in here as a student, and we didn't like each other at first," Walther revealed. "He had trouble changing his grip; it didn't feel good to him, and he was resistant. I said, 'Son, you don't have to do it this way, but you don't have to play golf either. If you're going to learn how to play golf, you do it this way or go home.'

"After about a year, something clicked between that boy and me," Bob added. "He had such a good work ethic, and once he determined that I meant business, he became the most compliant student I think I ever had. When he found out that I cared enough about him to scold him, we started liking each other."

Alex remembers the conflict, as well, and looks at the relationship as a turning point in his life. "Bob was brutal on me," he admitted, "saying that I didn't have a good attitude, wasn't focused and that I really needed to apply myself and start working harder. When we left (the range), I told my mom I didn't want to go back, but she said, 'he is exactly what you need.' I took lessons once every three weeks and just grew to love him. He told me later that when he first met me, he thought I was a spoiled rich kid and a brat and needed to learn how to work, and he was absolutely right.

"Bob was very rigid, very methodical. He would challenge you and not back down. He called me 'Double' (a name that originated from 'Double A' and morphed into 'Double'), and if I had a bad attitude, he would say, 'C'mon, Double, you're wasting your time and my time.' And if you whined, he would grab you by the neck with one finger on each side and pull you in and look at you with those focused eyes. He'd say, 'You gotta be tougher than a

two-dollar steak to play this game. But he was also very motivating and challenging. He was a dichotomy. If you could handle it and understand that he wanted the best for you, he was very loving and positive. I love Bob; I'd do anything for that man. He has had a dramatic impact on my life. I probably couldn't overstate it if I wanted to."

Abbott worked under Walther's tutelage for over six years, and after three years on the golf team at the University of Indianapolis, he decided to focus his energies on a Business degree. Like many of Bob's students, he never had the talent of a Jeff Overton, but the lessons he learned at the range have contributed to his success.

There is no question that Walther loves what he does, and there are too many success stories to count. In addition to Overton, Walther worked with Jeff Sanders (the son of P.M. Sanders who starred for Arad McCutchan at Evansville College), who won the State Amateur twice. He also mentioned Wayne Patterson, a lefty like Alex, who would hit 500 balls a day. Patterson had never played the game, but after three years with Bob finished fifth in the City tournament and is Walther's best friend today. He also cited fellow local legend Jake Schiff, the record breaking quarterback at Mater Dei, who has used his natural ability and exceptional work ethic to become a very competitive golfer.

Just as he did in the summers of his youth with the great Bob Hamilton, Walther uses the same tireless energy to go the extra mile with his students, and his dedication to the game has made him one of the premier instructors in our part of the country. The 1969 City champion has also worked diligently to keep the tournament going strong. The man who once worked with golf legends like Tommy Bolt and Byron Nelson has devoted his life to the game he loves. By sharing his knowledge, Bob Walther has left his mark on our local golf culture, and he will always be remembered as one of the most influential ambassadors in our area's golf history.

STEADY ED WOLF

Steady Ed Wolf in the mid-1950s.

For the first 23 years of the City golf tournament, 14 different men took home the trophy, but that era of parity came to end in 1953 when Ed Wolf made his mark on the local golf scene. Wolf was a Reitz graduate who learned the game with wooden-shafted clubs. After his graduation in 1942, Ed left to serve his country in WWII, and as he told his story from the kitchen of his west side home, his emotions showed. "There's not a day goes by that I don't reminisce about those days," he explained as he wiped away tears. "I think about it – some good, some bad."

Ed fought in the famous Battle of the Bulge and stormed Omaha Beach, saying, "By the time I got there, there were 3,000 killed on that beach." Mr. Wolf then left the room for a second and returned to show me his dress greens, smiling as he proudly proclaimed, "It still fits." On his uniform were the two Bronze Stars he earned for bravery when he knocked out a German tank and German machine gun nest. He also showed me two collages of photos, one of himself and the other of his older brother, Harold. Ed's eyes teared up again as he explained how Harold had been an All-State fullback for Herman Byers but instead of accepting a scholarship to IU, had enlisted and then lost his life with his crew when their B-17 was shot down.

Part of Ed's time in the service was spent honing his golf skills, and he admits that he was lucky to play golf on his free time while in England. While there, he met several players who played in the British Open, including Dale Reis, who won the event.

On his return home, Wolf decided to enter the City tournament and drew well-known sports editor Dan Scism for the match play event at Helfrich. Ed smiled as he described how the wily Scism got the better of the young war veteran. Ed had Scism down two after nine holes when Scism gestured for a photographer to join them. "This kid's a comer," Scism proclaimed. "You'd better get some pictures of him."

The crafty veteran had climbed inside Ed's head. "He got me all pumped up," Ed confessed, " and he took me on the back nine and beat me."

Wolf got his revenge, however, when he took his first title in 1953, and he admits that there was some good fortune involved. In his 36-hole final match against Scism, Ed was 8 down with 18 holes to play. On the front nine of the second round, Ed picked up two, leaving him 6 down with nine to play. After 8 more holes, Ed had squared the match with the par 5 18th still to play. And this is where the luck came in.

Scism had hit his first two shots, leaving himself a nine iron to the green. As he looked into his bag, he pulled out what he thought was his 9 iron. To Ed's amazement, Scism's ball air mailed the green. Scism bogeyed and Ed birdied to give Wolf his first City title. Scism was not one to make excuses, and it wasn't until a year later that Ed found out from Dan's caddy that Scism had mistakenly pulled his six iron instead of the nine.

As Ed Wolf's reputation grew, he became known as "Steady Eddie" for his consistent play. Although he had decent distance for his size (5'10", 160 pounds), he was best known for his short game and his laser beam accuracy. In fact, Scism once said of Ed's short game, "Ed Wolf's so good, he could get it up and down out of a closet."

As for his driving accuracy, Ed tells the story that involved local pro and current organizer of the City tournament Bob Walther. It seems that Walther was going to place sprinkler systems in the center of a course's fairways, and instead of using equipment, he joked that he would just use Ed's drives to place the lines.

As Ed settled into his job at Mead Johnson, golf became one of his passions as he played three times a week and practiced twice a week. He feels fortunate to have played when he did, citing Billy Martin and the Greenwell brothers, Bob, Dick, and Earl, as his contemporaries. He also appreciates the interesting people he's met through the game of golf. A couple of special memories involved the common practice of wagering on the course. In one instance, Scism proposed a $100 Nassau match with he and Ed against Francis Fleming and Les Greenwell where Scism offered to back Ed. Another match took place between Ed and the famous gambler Titanic Thompson, where Ed played for $50 a hole and won some cash. He also played an exhibition with touring pro Bobby Nichols and another with future LPGA pro Patty Berg at Fendrich.

Another individual that Ed considers special is Don Moore. Don served as Wolf's caddy for 15 years and travelled with Ed when Don was a teenager and in his twenties. Ed was amazed at the gift Moore possessed. He tells how he would hit a drive and Don would pull the exact club Ed would need for the next shot and Ed rarely had to change it.

Ed acknowledges that the game of golf has been good to him, and he will go down in local history as one of the area's all-time best. In the '50s and '60s, he won over 80 tournaments, including the Helfrich and Fendrich Club Championships, the State Amateur and the Tri-State Amateur.

In the City tournament, Wolf is third on the all-time list in wins with six (1953, '54, '55, '57, '58, '60) and was runner-up five times (1956, '59, '61, '62, '67). In fact, his dominance in the 1950s puts him in elite company. Only three men have dominated a decade in the City tournament. Kevin Wassmer dominated the 1990s, Jerry Schreiber was unstoppable in the '60s, and the 1950's were the domain of the man known as 'Steady' Ed Wolf.

KEVIN WASSMER: CHASING THE LEGEND

The third man to establish himself as a dominating force in the City Tournament landscape is Posey County's Kevin Wassmer, and the end of his reign isn't over yet (as of 2012). Beneath Kevin's quiet demeanor lies a competitive fire that has fueled his rise to legendary status, and he credits his success to the many fine golfers he's gotten to know over the years.

Unlike many top golfers, Wassmer didn't pick up a club as a toddler. In fact, he didn't get good at the game until he was "way out of high school." As a baseball and basketball player at North Posey High School, Kevin was a decent athlete who admits that his only claim to fame was scoring 24 points in a sectional game.

After graduating in 1984, he attended USI for a year before leaving school to join the workforce, and he didn't play on an actual golf course until he was in his twenties, after quitting his job at Pirelli to work at GE Plastics in Mt. Vernon. With no formal training, he relied on his athletic skills as he learned the fundamentals and then honed his game by watching and listening.

"Even from the beginning I could hit the ball OK," Kevin explained from a booth at a popular Poseyville watering hole, "but I fell into a very good group of players that helped me a lot. We played at Helfrich every day. They were either shift workers like me or firemen, and we played during the day. Rick Hankins, John Kaposta, Brett Salmon, Steve Staubenfeldt, my brother Mike, Scott Hamilton, Troy Schreiber, Darret Brinker. It was a large group who played every day, and when you play with better players, you get better. You pay attention and ask questions."

Kevin and Kim Wassmer lift the championship trophy.

"My golf progressed pretty quickly through the first two years, and after that, I dedicated myself to getting better every year."

Wassmer played in his first City tournament in 1988, failing to make the cut at age 22. The following year, he made the cut and hasn't missed one since. His first win came in his fifth try in 1992, and over the next 15 years, he hoisted the champion's trophy nine times ('92, '93, '96, '99, '00, '01, '02, '05, '07).

As Kevin became involved in the City tournament atmosphere in the early years, he learned to cope with the challenges and stress that golfers face during competition. The year before his first win, he came tantalizingly close, missing a playoff by two shots. "Two shots is nothing," Wassmer pointed out. "You go over the round and you can find two shots in five holes. That gnaws at you, and being a competitive person, when you get in that position again, you vow not to let that happen again."

As Wassmer told his story, his eyes revealed that intangible something that enables an athlete to achieve greatness. It is interesting to observe, and I realized that although hundreds aspire to be a champion, only a few get to experience it. When asked to choose his most memorable, Kevin's response was predictable at first, but then enlightening.

"They're all very memorable," he answered. "The first one obviously, because you don't know if you can win if you haven't won. You're trying your guts out, and you just don't know if you can. And when you get the opportunity, you don't know how you're going to react. It's all brand new to you."

In addition to experiencing being a City champion numerous times, Wassmer also achieved another benchmark that very few golfers get to experience. The Holy Grail in the golf world is scoring a 59, and Kevin did it in the 2006 Fendrich Amateur.

"You get into something like that, they call it being in the zone," he explained when asked what it felt like to play the last few holes knowing it's within reach. "But I really didn't think of it like that. You get to the point where you're playing really well and you're under par, but you're just going to hit the next shot.

"There's times I've been 7 or 8 under par and then I screwed it up because I began to think what I could do. I did know (that day). I had a three-footer on the last hole to shoot 59. I definitely knew! And believe me, the knees were knocking. I shot 27 on the front (8 under), and I was ten under after 11. I shot 59 with two bogeys. The best part was I shot 61 the next day (Kevin's two-round score of 120 was a record)."

Through the years, Wassmer has worked tirelessly on his game and credits many people for helping him progress. "I took lessons from Bob Walther and Bryan Simmons (a local pro in the '80s and '90s). You take a little from everybody. John Kaposta (1984 City champion and 5-time runner-up) was a tremendous ball-striker. Rick (Hankins) was tremendous around the greens."

Kevin is also aware of the rich history of the game locally and is quick to comment when I asked him about some of the greats.

Brian Tennyson: "Brian was the best anybody knew back then. He was a very analytical golfer, where me and John (Kaposta) and Rick (Hankins) were feel-oriented, Brian took me to another level by getting the golf swing technically better. He didn't hit it very far. His nickname on tour was 'Pure' because he hit the ball so well."

David Erdy: "A physical specimen, very dedicated."

Bob Hamilton: "He wasn't a direct influence on me, but he was an influence through his sons (John and Jim). I would go and see him at Hamilton's (golf course), but I would never go up and bother him. I wasn't into the game yet; I didn't feel worthy."

Jeff Overton: "Jeff is tremendously talented. He can look at a golf shot and pull it off with pure talent. We battled five or six years in a row in the City Tournament, and that was some of the most fun golf I ever played because he pushed me so hard."

Kevin also had kind words to say about Jeff Sanders (winner of the State Amateur, State Open and two City championships), Joe Padfield (played in two U.S. Opens and won the State Amateur), Jeff Howerton ("probably one of the best ball-strikers I've ever seen."), Ed Wolf, David Mills and Tyler Merkel.

And when finally asked about the man with whom he will be compared for all eternity, Kevin didn't utter a word about the man's golf game. He chose instead to remark about the man as a human being and role model.

Jerry Schreiber: "I was a hothead at a young age because I thought I was better than I was. Jerry had watched me over time, and after a casual round, Jerry Schreiber basically grabbed me by my shirt. I wasn't even playing with him. He told me that I cannot conduct myself like that on a golf course. He had seen me acting like I was better than I really was. Maybe he saw me throw a club, I don't know.

"It helped me realize what I needed to do to get to the next level. He basically told me that if I didn't quit it, that I'll never become the player I could be. He thought enough of me, and he knew what it took. Jerry Schreiber is a gentlemen and a man's man. We're lucky to have him."

Kevin married his wife Kimberly in 1990 and has three children, a situation that greatly reduces the amount of time he can dedicate to his game. When asked if he had ever aspired to see how far his game could take him, his response was as quick as it was realistic.

"I have," he responded, "but by the time I got any good, I was already married with a family. When I shot 17 (under - a City Tournament record) and Jeff (Overton) shot 14, it really made me think about what I could possibly do. Even now (at age 45), I still think I could."

Since the early 2000s, Kevin's priorities gradually shifted as his kids grew. His oldest daughter, Jordan, is an excellent student and played four years of high school volleyball and softball. She is a big fan of her dad's and has walked every hole of the City tournament with him since she was a fifth grader. Taylor, the second daughter, is "a cheerleader at heart," according to Kim, but plans to play golf for North Posey in the fall of 2012. The youngest, Caleb, plays basketball and baseball but "loves golf" and has had a club in his hand since he started walking. With three active children, it is no wonder that Kevin's practice time suffered as he coached them in soccer, softball, basketball and baseball through the years and even served as a 'cheer dad' at a football game.

Kim Wassmer has witnessed Kevin's passion for golf and knows the sacrifice he made by not pursuing the sport professionally. In 2012, she revealed to me that the children never understood just how good their father was when they were younger, but as teenagers, they began to realize that he put his dreams aside to spend time coaching them and watching them grow.

Kevin still hits the ball over 300 yards, but he seems content to keep his competitive juices flowing at local and regional events. He has also found a new passion as the head golf coach at his alma mater. The seed was planted in 2007 when a young lady from North Posey wanted to play golf. Since then, the program has grown from two girls that first year to five in the second and six in the third. By the third year ('09), Wassmer's team won the conference, and in 2010, they won again and advanced to the regional, with Maggie Camp advancing to State and Allison Koester missing by a shot.

As Wassmer speaks of the pride he has as a coach, his love for the game is evident, and the resumé he has put together is impressive indeed. He has played in twelve USGA National Championships and seven Publinx Championships, once advancing to the round of 16. He has won two Mid-Ams and two team State Championships as well as playing in the 2000 U.S. Amateur.

Through it all, Wassmer has developed a deep appreciation for the game he loves and the effects it has on those who play. "Golf is a reflection of yourself," he stated. "It doesn't build character; it reveals it. It is just a microcosm of life. It really is."

Kevin Wassmer now lets his game do the talking, and he feels fortunate for the God-given talent that has enabled him to earn a place among the elite names in local golf history. As of 2011, he stood alongside his good friend and mentor Jerry Schreiber with nine City titles, and going into the 2012 City, he was riding a four-year dry spell. Knowing that he wasn't getting any younger and that the event was loaded with good, young talent, Kevin rededicated himself to the game, and according to a beautiful *Courier* story by Steve Ford, spent hour after hour alone in his basement working with a new putter.

As a result, Wassmer put together a sparkling final round in the 2012 City and fired a 69 at Evansville Country Club, fending off Nick Frazer, Sean Stone and Brad Niemann to capture his tenth title. As Steve Ford revealed, Kevin was inspired by his mother, or "the lady in the pink hat," who was fighting a serious illness. Kevin had proven to himself and the local golf community that he was still a force to be reckoned with, and as the awards ceremony unfolded, the tears flowed.

Kevin spoke in the *Courier* story about his emotions as he finished his round and realized what would soon follow. "I knew what I was going to say to Mom," he said, "but I didn't know what to say to Jerry (Schreiber). It's humbling."

After a family hug, the group settled in for the presentation, and dry eyes were hard to find as Jerry Schreiber handed the trophy to Wassmer and said, "Congratulations. I know how hard it is to win one of those." And with his mother and family watching through tears, Kevin accepted the cup for the tenth time and cemented his legacy as one of the City's all-time greats.

JERRY SCHREIBER:
THE UNDISPUTED KING

As I sit writing this story in August of 2011, the eighty-first edition of the Evansville City Golf Tournament is underway with a winner to be determined in a few days. As these men weather the grueling heat in a quest for the title, the man whose name is emblazoned on the champion's trophy will watch from the ropes. This man set the standard for excellence and will be known forever as a champion's champion. This man is Jerry Schreiber.

Like many players of his generation, Schreiber's first exposure to the game of golf was as a caddy, and he learned his lessons well as a looper for some of the area's best. Two who came to mind quickly for Jerry were Doctor R.R. Acre, the winner of the first two City tournaments in 1930 and '31, and Francis Fleming, a 3-time winner (1946, '48, and '52).

Jerry and his fellow loopers would "go chase it around" on Mondays (Caddies' Days), and he remembers that his first club had a wooden shaft. As he saved money from toting bags, he added to his set one club at a time. His first full set was purchased as a high schooler, where he competed with teammates Joe and Jerry Clayton and John R. Richards for the Central Bears.

As juniors, the boys suffered through a dismal 0-15 season before shocking everyone by winning the sectional, with Jerry earning medalist honors. While he was at Central, he also teamed with the Clayton brothers to form one of the best basketball teams in Central history, a fact he showed great pride in as he pointed to the team picture in his trophy room.

After graduation, Jerry joined the Navy and finished fourth in the San Diego City Championship as a 19-year-old. Upon his return, he met a lovely young lady named Phyllis Bunge and was smart enough to marry her in 1958. Phyllis' father owned N.M. Bunge, a masonry contractor business, and Jerry worked there as a bricklayer as he began a remarkable career in amateur golf. Throughout his developmental years, Jerry only took lessons from two men. One was legendary instructor Bob Toski, and Jerry says he still has notes from that lesson. The other lessons came from the greatest golfer in local history, touring pro and PGA champion Bob Hamilton. Hamilton only worked with golfers who were willing to pay the price, and he was able to mold Schreiber into a fierce competitor.

In addition to competing locally, Schreiber made a name for himself regionally and nationally, as well. He and his partner, Chick Hendrickson, were runners-up in an international 4-ball tournament in Hollywood, Florida where Jack Nicklaus and Deane Beman teamed up, and he was also the runner-up in the Dixie Amateur in Miami in 1966.

In 1965, Jerry was a qualifying medalist in the U.S. Amateur Championship in Chicago, one of four U.S. Amateurs for which he qualified. In '64, he made the final 16 at the Cantebury Golf Club in Cleveland, where he fell one win shy of playing in the Masters at Augusta.

On the state and regional level, Schreiber was runner-up in the Indiana State Amateur in 1970 and was a five-time winner of the Tri-State Open in an era when the tournament had amateur and pro divisions. More than once, Jerry's winning score was the best of both divisions, and he remembers such pros as Herman Keiser, who won a Masters, and Lee Elder competing at Fendrich and Helfrich.

Jerry's resumé also boasts numerous victories in the tri-state area and four Fendrich Open championships. But what separates Jerry Schreiber from mere mortals on the local scene is the legacy he built with his dominance in the Evansville City Golf Tournament. Jerry splashed onto the golf scene during a period of domination by Evansville's Ed Wolf, who owned the tournament in the '50s. After a runner-up finish to Wolf in 1958, Schreiber seized control and put together the greatest streak in the competition's history.

Following his runner-up finish in '58, Jerry won for the first time in 1959, and for a 15-year period would finish first or second a remarkable 14 times. The streak included five wins in a row (a record) from 1961 to 1965 with eight wins and six second place finishes. The men to beat him during the streak reads like a who's who of local golf: Ed Wolf ('58), Sam Stucke ('66), Bob Walther ('69), Jerry McRae ('70), Jim Hamilton ('71), and Richie Moore ('72).

Jerry won his final City tournament in 1975, and as of 2011 held records for wins (9 – tied with Kevin Wassmer) and runner-up finishes with 8. Very few would argue about his place in local golf history, and for over twenty years, no one demanded the respect and yet evoked affection like Jerry Schreiber.

"There was an intimidation factor," said fellow competitor and current director of the City Tourney Bob Walther, "but it wasn't intentional. He just played his game. But he was also a very gracious loser."

Walther showed some emotion as he spoke of Schreiber's qualities as a gentleman. His respect for the man was obvious when he told of the moment on the 18th green at the Evansville Country Club in 1969, saying, "When he shook my hand, he really meant it." Walther also teared up when telling about his first encounter with Schreiber. Apparently golfing legend Bob Hamilton arranged for Jerry to play a round with Bob to try to motivate Walther. When Bob first met Jerry at Fendrich, he was admittedly "shaking in my boots," and Walther was very touched by the reception he received. "He was so kind," Walther related. "He was…KIND. He wanted me to feel like I belonged in that group. He is one class act."

As a teacher, Bob Walther was also very aware of the mental toughness and talent displayed by Schreiber during his formative years. "His competitiveness stood out the most," Walther explained. "You would see it in his short game around the green, his putting and his ability to pull off shots when the pressure was on. Had he not had a hard job, laying bricks all his life, it's hard telling how far he could have gone."

Today, Jerry is still enjoying the sport he loves even though he has physical limitations. After six back surgeries, he doesn't crus

Jerry follows through at the 1967 City tournament.

his drives like he used to, but the passion is still there. He readily admits that he owes a lot to the game of golf, as evidenced by the photos on his wall of Jim Crews, Fuzzy Zoeller, Bob Knight and Arnold Palmer.

When asked which of his victories was the most memorable, he thought for an instant and then spoke. "They're all exciting because you're in the heat of battle," he revealed, "but the most exciting was when my son Troy won in 1998." He also reminded me that Troy was the runner-up in '97 and that brother Ken was a fine golfer also and a City winner in 1979.

Jerry still can move the ball around the course and has shot his age "four or five times," saying modestly, "I'm getting up in age where I can shoot it now." And the one constant throughout all his years has been his wife Phyllis. A Reitz graduate, Phyllis is not too bad herself as a past winner of the women's club championship at the Country Club and a past runner-up in the women's City.

For over fifty years, Phyllis has watched every competitive round Jerry has played and often served as a forecaddie to watch where balls land. After 53 years of marriage, one can see a sparkle in the couple's eyes as they finish each other's sentences, and the pride is obvious as Phyllis says, "Jerry has always had a drive for everything he's ever done, and he's the most fair person you'd ever want to meet."

Jerry Schreiber is loved and respected by everyone who knows him, and his accomplishments earned him induction into the Indiana Golf Hall of Fame in 1982. His passion and love for the game made him the undisputed king of local golf, and his place is forever etched in the history of the Evansville City Golf Tournament. No one has summed up Jerry Schreiber's impact on local golf better than long-time friend and competitor Bob Walther. "He is strong, handsome, charismatic, and fun to be with. He is the Arnold Palmer of local golf."

Jerry Schreiber with the 1963 Fendrich Open trophy.

VICTORIA NATIONAL:
A DIAMOND IN THE ROUGH

If one were traveling north on Anderson Road just a couple miles northeast of Castle High School, the last thing one would expect to see was a world-class golf course. But thanks to the imagination and persistence of one man, that's exactly what can be found in the outer regions of Paradise, Indiana.

Terry Friedman is a self-made success story who grew up in Jasper and married his wife Irma in 1958. Terry's first exposure to the game of golf was as a caddie at the Jasper Country Club where he earned ten cents a round, and according to his daughter Lisa, he would look at the golfers and say, "I'm going to do that someday." Irma grew up just down the road in Ireland, Indiana, and moved with Terry to Michigan when he took a job at the Southhaven Rubber Company. Seeing the company's potential, Terry bought into Southhaven Rubber and eventually purchased the company outright.

As the business flourished, Terry began to fantasize about an idea that had motivated him for years. He had developed a love for golf and was a single-digit handicapper himself when he realized that his financial success might enable him to do something special.

"He wanted to give southern Indiana a ranked golf course," Irma Friedman recalled from her beautiful home on Medinah Dr., near the course. "I told him he was out of his mind. He thought it would work getting national members; he knew there weren't enough local members."

During a trip to one of his plants in Morganfield, Kentucky in the mid 1990s, Terry spotted some land from an abandoned coal mine. Over the years, Terry had gotten to know Tom Fazio and asked the renowned course designer to take a look. The story goes that Fazio surveyed the landscape and proclaimed, "I see a hundred great holes," to which Terry responded, "I only want eighteen great holes."

And that is exactly what the entrepreneur got.

After selling his business, Terry and Irma moved to Paradise to oversee the project. The course sits on over 300 acres with finger lakes formed from the overflowing trenches dug during the mining process. The pristine greens and fairways consist of the bent grass used at Augusta National. The roughs are a blend of bluegrass varieties, and each hole has six tee boxes, allowing the par 72 course to span from 5,184 yards to 7,209 yards.

Fazio also designed the concrete cart paths to be hidden from view during a round, and other amenities like restrooms and water fountains dwell in tunnels. The 12-acre practice facility is second to none, with three levels of tee areas, six target greens, and practice bunkers and greens. In addition, an indoor practice facility sets Victoria National apart from most Midwest courses.

The club also features a 22,500-Square foot clubhouse designed by Terry's daughter, Sheri, and son-in-law, George, and the technology for maintenance is state-of-the-art. An in-ground vault system lies under each green to control moisture and temperature and to allow the release of carbon-dioxide to keep the greens healthy, and the fairways are irrigated and fertilized for maximum health.

Terry Friedman passed away unexpectedly from a heart attack in 2004, but his family is dedicated to continuing his legacy. Although Terry's dream was for the club to host a U.S. Open, most agree that an Open would be too ambitious due to the lack of hotel rooms in the area. But with the help of the Terry Friedman Memorial Endowment, established by the family, Victoria National Golf Club has hosted several events since 2000. The first major step toward national recognition occurred on June 25, 2012 when the Club hosted the United Leasing Championship on the Nationwide Tour in front of a national audience on the Golf Channel. Victoria is also scheduled to host the event in 2013 and 2014, attracting an estimated 20,000 spectators each weekend.

Terry's hope was to create a top 20 golf course, and he came oh, so close. At one time, the course, which opened in July of 1998, was ranked 21st among private courses nationally, and it has been consistently ranked in the top 40.

Terry Friedman (left) and Victoria National architect Tom Fazio.

Although the course was sold to an investment group in Florida, the family remains involved and is proud of Terry's creation, welcoming luminaries from near and far. Dan Quayle and singer Vince Gill are members, and stars like Scott Hoch, Chip Beck, Fred Funk, Larry Bird, Jan Stephenson and Michael Jordan have enjoyed the splendor of Victoria National.

So when people ask how a town like Paradise or an area like southwest Indiana came to be the home of one of the elite golf courses in America, the answer is simple. A visionary like Terry Friedman saw its potential and had the tenacity and imagination to make a life-long dream come true. Terry's passion made Victoria National possible, and nothing expresses the legacy of the project better than a stone at the exit of the complex. "In memory of Terry Friedman. May his spirit continue to flow."

BRIAN TENNYSON: THE DREAM CHASER

Of all the fine golfers who have roamed our area's courses, less than a handful have made it on the PGA Tour, and one of those elite athletes is Brian Tennyson. With a laser-like focus from a very young age, the boy from Evansville's west side set his sights on a destination that few dare to pursue, and with an unrelenting sense of purpose, he molded himself into a world-class golfer.

Brian Tennyson was born in 1962, the youngest of Richard and Sylvia Tennyson's nine children, and with the guidance of a father who loved the game of golf and the encouragement of a big brother, he discovered a passion that would affect his life forever. Like many young boys, Brian enjoyed several sports and showed some talent as a youngster. He played his baseball at West Side Little League and Pony League, and he played basketball through his freshman year at Mater Dei. When the school started its soccer program in the late '70s, he learned the sport and lettered for the Wildcats his junior and senior years.

Tennyson was very talented on the baseball diamond, but when he discovered that he wouldn't be allowed to play both baseball and golf in high school, he considered his option carefully. His assessment led to the realization that his best chance of earning a college scholarship and perhaps playing professionally was on the links, and from that moment on, he poured himself into learning everything he could about the game.

Brian first picked up a club at the age of seven when he smacked Wiffle Balls in the backyard with a sawed-off 4 iron. His closest brother in age, Roger, was twelve at the time and had just received his first set of clubs, and young Brian couldn't help sharing the sport with the brother he "emulated, idolized and followed around."

The boys grew up on Mesker Park Drive across from the 11th fairway of the Helfrich course, and they learned the etiquette and nuances of the game by caddying for their father. Amazingly, Brian never took lessons as a boy, but instead learned by reading, talking with Roger and blasting thousands of balls on his own. He was tireless in his efforts to improve, and part of the reason he chose golf over baseball as a 14-year-old was his desire to excel. "I could practice it on my own," Brian said. "I couldn't find people (in team sports) who wanted to practice as hard as I wanted to."

Even as Brian got older, most of his learning was done on his own. He does credit men like Ron Reiner, the pro at Helfrich and later the Henderson Country Club, Don Bisesi, and Jim Hamilton for some occasional help but says that he preferred to hone his skills himself.

Brian's talents as a teenager caught the eye of Ball State coaches, and with his excellent performance in the classroom, he secured a golf and academic scholarship to play for the Cardinals. Before his graduation in 1984, Tennyson fashioned a great career in Muncie as a Division I Academic All-American and an honorable mention All-American as a golfer. He also made the All-MAC team three times and won 8 Division I collegiate events, a school record that still stands.

While at Ball State, Brian experienced something that illustrates how a random event can have a major impact on one's life. One of his roommates was a gentleman named John Schnatter, and during an evening of pizza and beer in their dorm room, a seed was planted. John was dreaming big as well, and the two brainstormed about a company Schnatter wanted to build one day. As the two shared ideas, a brand was created that we all know today as Papa John's Pizza.

Tennyson and Schnatter stayed in touch as Brian contemplated his career, as well. At the time, the only path to the PGA was the tour's qualifying tournament, and as Brian kept trying to qualify, he played on a mini-tour in Florida. The circuit was different from those today and was played in one geographical area. As he toiled in 1984, Brian realized that he wasn't improving and sought the help of Mike Adams from Illinois. The relationship was a turning point in Tennyson's career, and he worked with Adams for seven years fine-tuning his game.

In 1985, Tennyson began the nomadic life of a professional golfer and lived out of a suitcase on the TPA (Tournament Players Association). The tour was a "glorified mini-tour," according

to Brian, that hosted 54-hole events across the country. The top earners on the circuit would earn $45,000 to $50,000 a year, and Brian got his first look at players like Tom Lehman and Brandel Chamblee while there.

Tennyson also learned valuable life lessons on the tour and is proud of how his unorthodox approach allowed him to be successful. As is true with many aspiring pro golfers, Brian found backers for his endeavor, asking family and close friends to come up with $1,000 to $1,500 each. His final tally was $16,000, and Brian deeply appreciates their confidence, saying, "I owe a debt of gratitude to those people for helping me."

Though the journey was sometimes tough, Tennyson cherishes those days and recalls the methods he used with fondness. "I built my life on $16,000," he said. "I made it go a long way. I slept in my car more nights than I can count. I ate one meal a day. I would go with my friends to the bar at happy hour and drink water and eat the free finger food. I lived three- or four-people-to-a-room a lot. I did whatever it took to pursue my dreams."

Brian also feels good about what his frugality and unconventional ways allowed him to achieve. "I'm proud to say that, even in those days, I made a profit every single year I played professional golf," he told me, "and not many people can say that."

In 1986, Brian experienced one of the lows in his quest when he played through the sixth and final stage of the PGA Qualifier and fell one stroke shy of securing his card. He admits that the near miss devastated him and sent him into mourning for a month. But after gathering his sanity, he decided to leave for a ten-week stint on the Asian Tour. While there, he regained some confidence with several high finishes, including two national tournament victories in the '87 India Open and Philippine Open that helped him to a second place finish in the Order of Merit.

With a new hop in his step, he returned to the U.S. and promptly experienced the ultimate high for a journeyman golfer. In the fall of '87, he qualified on his fourth attempt at Q-School, finishing a comfortable 16th of the 50 golfers who earned PGA cards.

His first experience on the tour was at the Bob Hope Desert Classic, one of the five biggest tournaments at the time. He was awakened in the middle of the night and told that there was a spot available and flew overnight, arriving at 5:00 a.m. for a 9:00 tee time. When he got there, he was thrilled to learn that his playing partner in the pro-am was none other than Cincinnati Reds hall of famer Johnny Bench, his childhood hero. Brian shot a 67 in his first round and finished 15th, an unexpected great start to a solid first season.

Tennyson became fully exempt and started his first full season in 1988, and from 1988 through 1992 enjoyed his life as a PGA pro playing with such greats as Curtis Strange, Tom Kite, Nick Price, Mark O'Meara and Greg Norman, who was ranked #1 at the time. In 2002, Brian began to experience some burnout from the grind that took him away from his wife, Jeanne, and their two young kids and contemplated his future.

Through the years, Tennyson had stayed in touch with his college roomie John Schnatter, and as a result, Brian and his brother Roger had opened some Papa John's restaurants in Akron, Ohio. In April of '92, Schnatter asked Brian to become the company's VP of Strategic Planning, and Tennyson walked away from golf to join the corporate world. The new job entailed substantial travel as well, and as the years flew by, Jeanne noticed that her husband still had an itch to re-connect with golf. Brian had been fiddling with his game and decided

to take another unorthodox path and try to re-qualify for the tour. Miraculously, he made it on his first attempt and competed on the '96 PGA Tour. During the season, another twist of fate occurred that would affect Brian's golf when Jeanne had some serious medical issues.

Jeanne had battled kidney disease all her life and was experiencing problems that eventually required dialysis and several surgeries. Obviously, Brian's priorities lay with Jeanne, and his golf suffered. Incredibly, when the illness progressed to the point of needing a transplant, Brian's childhood hero, his brother Roger, was found to be a perfect match. Through the miracles of science and the generosity of one special man, Jeanne pulled through and was healthier than she had been in years.

At the age of 34, Brian's PGA days were over, but he walked away knowing he had done all he could to reach his goal. He never won on the tour, but he did finish second twice, at the 1990 Bob Hope Desert Classic and the '89 Hardee's Classic, earning nearly $1,000,000 for his career. His best season was 1990, when he placed 29th on the money list with eight top 10 finishes, and he teed it up nine times in majors, five U.S. Opens, three PGAs and the 1991 Masters.

Tennyson has few regrets about his career in golf, and he is quick to point out that his vision for his future was crystal clear during his days spent in Evansville. "When I was a kid, at 12 or 13, I shagged my own balls on the side of the 13th hole (at Helfrich)," he recalled. "Anybody who was around back then will tell you that they saw me there all the time. At Helfrich and Fendrich, you're hitting driver and wedge all day long, but I knew I wanted to play on the PGA Tour. Guys would chew me out because I was in their way. They would tell me, 'You don't need to hit any 3-irons out here!' I was practicing 3-irons, 5-irons and 4-woods all day long. People just didn't understand what my mindset was."

Brian is also aware how local courses can't compare to those on tour and just how incredibly talented the PGA players are. "I love Victoria National; I'm a member," he revealed, "but the PGA players would tear it up. The course isn't nearly long enough for today's players, and the greens are too flat. The PGA Tour is very different than playing anywhere else on the planet. The courses are much firmer. The lies are tighter, grass cut down to practically dirt. The greens are extremely fast and get faster every day of the tournament. And the competition! People can't fathom how good the players really are!"

Today (2012), Brian runs successful businesses in California and resides just south of LA in Orange County. He admits that golf took a toll on his body over the years, but he appreciates what the game has allowed him to do. When asked what the storyline should be when chronicling his career, he never hesitated with his answer. "I was an extremely hard worker who always found a way," he answered. "People talk about Vijay Singh working hard, but I promise you, Vijay didn't work any harder than I did during my golf years."

Brian Tennyson has every right to be proud of what he's accomplished and the way he did it. His efforts have landed him in the Mater Dei and Ball State athletic halls of fame, and he is one of only three area golfers to make a living on the PGA Tour (Bob Hamilton and Jeff Overton are the others). Tennyson is living proof of what can be achieved with a singleness of purpose and pure dedication, and in the face of those who didn't understand, he teed it up and competed with the best players in the world.

NORTH HIGH GOLF:
A MODEL OF CONSISTENCY

When Larry Tindle contemplated retirement in the late '90s, he could look back at an impressive body of work during his brief stint as the boys and girls golf coach at Evansville North High School. But when he assessed the talent of the young stallions in the stable at North, he just had to give them three more years. Larry's decision not only enhanced his personal resumé, but it was instrumental in filling a void that had grown for over thirty years. Tindle was a North alumnus who played his sports during a magnificent era that featured some of the school's all-time greats. His class included Mike Volkman, who paired with a younger Dave Schellhase on some of the best basketball teams in North's history. On the gridiron, Larry played with greats like quarterback Volkman, speedsters Mike Madriaga and John Mominee and tough linemen like Stan Barren, Bill Barning and Bill Newmaster. He also mentioned Jerry Bruner, a player that Larry describes as "a beast," who went on to play for Bobby Bowden at Florida State. As a senior, Tindle played in one of the biggest games in local history when the Huskies lost to the powerful Reitz Panthers, led by All-American Don Hansen. With a crowd so big that fans sat in the trees to watch, Reitz prevailed and went on to complete a perfect season where they were unscored upon. North finished 9-1.

After graduating in 1961, Larry then secured a teaching degree from Evansville College and began his career at Howard Roosa. In 1975, he joined the staff at North and worked as a wrestling assistant to Lenny Carr and as Mickey Martin's assistant in baseball. He also served as assistant AD for six years and accepted his first head coaching position in 1983 when he was asked to take control of the girls golf program.

During his eight years at the helm of the girls program, Larry's teams won two sectionals, three City titles and two SIAC championships with several girls playing significant roles. His best team finish occurred in 1990 after two of his golfers drew inspiration from some local competitors. After watching the Harrison Lady Warriors capture the 1989 State championship, North's Meredith Ashby and Jeanne Bassett, who had qualified at State as individuals, raised their expectation levels. With fresh motivation, Meredith, Jeanne and teammates Susan Maurer, Melissa Blessing and Mindy Sturgeon won the City and SIAC and then finished sixth at State.

In 1994, Tindle was asked to coach both boys and girls and did so for a couple years. The boys program had been a consistent force locally for many years with talented golfers like Phil White, Jim Love and Benny Brinker in the early years and Brian Jones and Dave English in the '70s. Another standout in the '70s was Jeff Howerton, who was on a State qualifier at North, was a two-time City champ ('82 and '83) and has been a club pro at places like Hilton Head Island and Sultan's Run in Jasper. Two of the area's most successful families have ties to North golf, as well. The Brinker brothers, Darrett, Darren, Dirk and Dean, were standouts for the Huskies, and Dean's son, Kyle, played there also. Scott and Rhett Schreiber, the son of Ken and nephew of Jerry also played there.

But with all the great history, one group stands out, and Coach Tindle could see the potential. "I followed them in junior golf," Tindle explained from his home on the north side of Evansville. "I knew what I had coming. They all worked with pros. Jason Jones worked with Don Bisesi; Jeff (Overton) and Zach (Smith) and Mike Birkenfeld worked with Bob Walther; and, of course, (Kyle) Brinker worked with the Brinkers (grandfather Roland and father Dean)."

Overton entered North in 1997, a year after the other four, and the young freshman had to battle to make the lineup. During that first season, the boys finished 13-3 and advanced through the sectional and regional with third place finishes to advance to State. They finished eleventh in the 1998 State meet, but with two years of growth ahead of them, the expectations were very high.

Overton, who had only been playing the game seriously for a year or two, proved to be a phenom at the game, and the entire team fed off each other's efforts year-round. "They were all very focused," Tindle recalled, "and work ethic was the big thing. When practice was over, it was nothing for them to stay there until dark. They were a very close-knit group. They would root for each other."

In 1999, the team improved to 15-1 and dominated the City and conference. They were also much improved when the IHSAA tournament rolled around, winning the sectional and regional and taking sixth at State. Overton led the way at the State meet with a 147 total, good enough for a second place finish behind individual medalist Nathan Fritz of Greenwood. As the four juniors looked ahead to their final year, thoughts of the ultimate prize were on everyone's mind, and the team was determined to achieve something that North fans hadn't seen in over thirty years. "Until we won, that was the only State banner that was hanging in

Evansville North's 2000 State championship golf team. Front row (L-R): Brenda Weber (principal), Jeff Overton, Blair Hanni, Jason Jones, Mike Birkenfeld, Kyle Brinker, Zach Smith. Back row: Bob Cuprisin (athletic director), Nick Dus, Jon Scully, Dan Neumann, Alex Abbott, Adam Gann, Larry Tindle (coach).

the gym," said Alex Abbott about the display on the gym wall commemorating the 1967 Huskies State championship basketball team. Abbott was a fine golfer himself who cracked the lineup after the 'fab four' graduated. "We looked at that banner and pointed at it all the time," Alex added.

In preparation for the highly anticipated season, Coach Tindle did his best to make sure the boys were ready. "I tried to play a lot of weekend tournaments, where you could play 18 holes, like at Bedford and Bicknell," Tindle explained. "I wanted to play against some of the better teams in the state. I thought that would make them tougher."

As the boys competed, Tindle was well aware of a factor that played a key role in their eventual success, saying, "There was quite a rivalry between our own players. I remember Kyle Brinker coming up and asking, 'Hey, coach, did I beat Overton?' That's what made them so darned competitive."

So as the boys entered the 2000 season, they competed against each other and a strong schedule on their way to a dream season. They finished the regular season 16-0 and then captured the City and conference. After decisive wins in the sectional and regional, the boys were ready to stake their claim, and Coach Tindle used past experiences to make sure they were ready.

"The kids could play golf or they wouldn't be there (at State)," Tindle said. "But you have to keep the pressure off. I would tell jokes, maybe some were a little off-color, to loosen them up. They would just laugh, but it kept them focused and not too intense. That's what happened the year before. They got a little bit tight and didn't shoot what they were capable of. I said, 'Next year's going to be different. I'm going to keep them loose, and I don't mind if they're cocky,' and they were."

Tindle's strategy worked to perfection as the experienced Huskies were confident throughout. When the day was done at

the Golf Club of Prestwick, the Huskies had earned a banner to place on the gym wall as the 2000 IHSAA champions with a 36-hole total of 608, nine strokes better than second place Carmel. In descending order, the boys' totals were: Zach Smith 158 (81-77); Mike Birkenfeld 156 (75-81); Kyle Brinker 155 (74-73); Jeff Overton 154 (77-77); and Jason Jones 147 (74-73). Jones' spectacular score earned him a runner-up finish, just three strokes behind Mike Shumaker of Columbia City.

The 2000 Huskies had withstood the pressure and lived up to the hype, finishing the season unbeaten. In fact, according to Coach Tindle, the team never trailed in a match all year long. As proof of the talent of the 2000 team, the entire first five earned scholarships, Jones to Ball State, Birkenfeld, Overton and Brinker to IU and Zach Smith to USI.

In 2001, Overton was joined in the starting lineup by Alex Abbott, Blair Hanni, Adam Gann and Dan Newman, and although the 'rookies' lacked the experience, the team still finished the regular season 16-0 and won the sectional. Coach Tindle retired after the '01 season, and he certainly did his part to keep the North golf program strong. Many fine men have coached golf at North over the years, and with the 2000 team serving as a standard, the program continues to thrive. In 2009, David Mills finished second at State, and in 2011, Natalie Schmett captured the girls individual title.

In Larry Tindle's 8-year run with the boys program, his teams won 85% of their matches (97-19) and won 4 City titles, 2 sectionals, 2 regionals and a State championship. Though there have been many fine golfers and teams from area schools through the years, including State medalists Bob Hamilton (Reitz, 1939) and Jerry McRae (Mater Dei, 1959) and, more recently, medalist Sean Stone and his State champion Harrison team, when it comes to consistency over time, it is hard to match the golfing legacy of Evansville North High School.

Artwork by Jon Siau

ANGIE BLYTHE: NORTH'S ALL-TIME BEST

According to ex-North golf coach Larry Tindle, the most accomplished female golfer in the school's history was Angie Blythe. Although she was small in stature, Angie could play the game and did very well in the IHSAA State tournament. She finished third and fourth as an individual as a sophomore and junior, then finished as the runner-up her senior year, giving her the third best finish for a local female golfer behind only State champions Suzanne Noblett ('83&'85) of Castle and Natalie Schmett ('11) of North.

Although Angie hoped to attend IU, coach Sam Carmicahel had only limited money to offer. So Angie accepted a full-ride scholarship at Purdue and had a fine career, earning all-conference honors twice and winning medalist honors at two tournaments her senior year. She then spent some time on the Futures Tour, one step short of the LPGA, and today (2012), Angie (Blythe) Buffardi is the proud mother of a one-year-old daughter and resides in West Palm Beach, Florida.

JEFF OVERTON: "BOOM, BABY!"

In over a century of local golf history, only three players (as of 2012) have teed it up against the best players of their generations and made a living on the PGA tour. One was Brian Tennyson, who played for several seasons in the '80s and '90s against Curtis Strange, Tom Kite, Greg Norman and others. The second is the great Bob Hamilton, who held his own against greats like Ben Hogan, Sam Snead and Byron Nelson and captured several titles, including the 1944 PGA Championship. The third of the triumvirate is Jeff Overton, the gifted North High grad who is now (2012) matching strokes with the likes of Tiger Woods and Phil Mickelson. Overton's career has only just begun, and those who have seen him play can't wait to see his raw talent reach its peak.

Jeffrey Laurence Overton was born in May of 1983, and under the guidance of his parents, Sharon and Ron, he thrived at the family home on Evansville's north side. "Good old Aspen Drive," Jeff answered when asked about the street where he spent his childhood. "It was a kid's dream to grow up where everybody was always having fun and competing."

Jeff went on to explain that the neighborhood kids were constantly busy with sports and games, and the talent level wasn't bad either. In fact, within a few hundred feet were three athletes who played or could have played professional sports: Jeff; Kate Endress, the Memorial basketball star who could have played in the WNBA; and Josh Tudela, the soccer star from North who spent

some time with the LA Galaxy of the MLS. According to Jeff, there was always a game going on somewhere, especially during the summer, from baseball to football to soccer to street hockey and Capture the Flag at night.

Jeff also received encouragement from his parents, who challenged him mentally as well. He spent many hours learning the game of chess from his mother and shared a love of math with her. He was good enough to earn a decent ranking and competed from kindergarten through middle school. According to Sharon, Jeff memorized Monopoly when he was four; he couldn't read but knew what the values were. She also mentioned that his favorite book was a book about money (along with Curious George).

For those who know the family, it was no surprise that Jeff was naturally gifted as an athlete. Ron was an excellent multi-sport athlete at Harrison who was the school's first true superstar, and Sharon practiced golf with Ron by hitting balls on the State Hospital grounds and caught on well enough to win the City 9-hole division. In fact, the trophy she won is the biggest in the house, according to Ron.

Without question, the main athletic influence on young Jeff was his father, and the bond is apparent as the young man speaks about his dad. "We both shared a common interest, the desire to compete, and he showed me how to have that burning desire," Jeff explained. "When it's in the genes, it's in the genes. He taught me how to work at it and be smart and choose my battles. You don't expect to win without a strategy."

Ron could see Jeff's potential very early and, based on his own history, wanted his son to be well-rounded. "Here's the thing," Ron philosophized. "I coached and played a lot, and you can tell when someone's born for this. Some kids just have it. Jeff was just born for sports. When I grew up, sports was everything for me. It was all I did, and I just felt like I became one-dimensional. I wanted my kids to be exposed to a lot of things and then gravitate to areas they liked. So we had Jeff play the piano and play chess, all kinds of things. But you could see at an early age that he just lit up when there was a ball around. He loved soccer. Josh Tudela lived right around the corner, and they would kick the soccer ball morning, noon and night."

So as a highly successful athlete himself, Ron Overton kept a close eye on the development of his kids. His daughter Jennifer (Eikenberry) ran track for four years but was much more interested in cheerleading and academics and is now an ophthalmologist in Indianapolis. Jeff, on the other hand, showed the same potential his father did several decades earlier. "He was a natural all-around athlete, but I never pushed him," Ron told me.

Ron went on to explain how Jeff seemed to pick up sports easily as an all-star in baseball and as the quarterback on the Oak Hill Middle School flag football team. He also played soccer and loved basketball. Ron could see that Jeff's size wasn't right for football, pointing out that "if he turned sideways, you could hardly see him. He was just so thin."

But basketball was another story, and as high school approached, Ron offered some guidance that would change his son's life forever. Ron had noticed that his son had a natural golf swing at age 10 or so when he saw him hit the cut-off 7-iron made for him by Ken Fisher, a competitive local golfer. He had also

Photo courtesy of Indiana University, Media Relations.

Jeff had a great time growing up on Aspen Drive.

watched as Jeff competed on Ken Wempe's golf team at Oak Hill and at the group lessons he took from the Brinker family in the sixth grade. Ron knew that Jeff planned to play golf and basketball at North, and he shared his thoughts with his son to add some perspective. "That was the summer he started getting some golf lessons and taking it seriously," Ron informed me. "He knew the golf team was going to be great. He went out for basketball, and the 'suicides' (a series of back and forth sprints) were really hard on his knees and he was in a lot of pain. I told him, 'Maybe you should sit out (basketball) this year and come back next year. But you have to decide, because if they pick you for the team, you have to play the whole year. You can't quit because you'll be taking somebody else's spot.'"

Jeff considered his father's words carefully, and part of the decision was based on the influence of the man who was giving the golf lessons. Ron knew that if Jeff was going to take golf seriously, he needed to find the right teacher who could influence the boy on several levels, and Jeff remembers the very first time he and Ron met Bob Walther. "My dad told him (Walther), 'I want you to mentor my kid,' Jeff revealed. "Being the great Christian man he is, he did whatever he could to help me. He was such a great role model in my life."

Jeff went on to explain how Walther emphasized more than just the intricacies of the golf swing and offered perspective on the modern golfers like Tiger Woods who thrive in the highly commercial world of professional golf. "He taught me that it is sponsorship and image," Jeff continued. "You are selling a brand that people will want to come and watch. My hat is off to Bob Walther. He would be great for any young up-and-coming kid to get their game where they want it to be. It would be an honor to work with a guy like that. He told me, 'Look, you have to be the best. Here's 500 balls, and if you really want to be on North's team, hit them every day!' Any true golfer understands the passion. I'd be out there in the snow and rain."

Ron echoed Jeff's sentiments and then offered a brief story that illustrated Walther's efforts to be a mentor as well as an instructor. "Jeff showed up one day with his shoes unpolished and muddy," Ron said, "and Bob wouldn't give him a lesson. It wasn't mean; he was just teaching him about respect for his equipment and keeping it in good shape."

At any other school in town, Jeff may have stepped right in and become an immediate star, but at North, the competition was stiff. As a seventh grader, he was only 5'5" tall, and his body was still maturing as he entered North in 1997. He was also joining a very strong team put together by Coach Larry Tindle, a man for whom Ron Overton has a lot of respect. "He was the perfect coach for that group," Ron explained. "He had the right approach. He let them play their games. They were expected to be at practice, but if they had a lesson, they were excused. He also worked with the area pros, especially Dave English at Fendrich. Dave would allow them to play more kids in a match. It really helped develop players. Otherwise, if they play just five and count four scores, the rest of the team isn't getting to play. Dave English helped accommodate that."

With such talent as Jason Jones, Kyle Brinker, Zach Smith and Mike Birkenfeld, Jeff could see that making the lineup wouldn't be easy. "I wasn't expecting to play," Jeff told me. "I had to work myself into position. I had a passion for it, and I knew that if I worked my butt off, I could make the team."

Jeff played in every match as a freshman at #5 on a 13-3 team that won the City and placed 11th at State. His sophomore year, the Huskies were even better, finishing 15-1 while capturing the City, SIAC, sectional and regional titles on their way to a sixth place finish at State. Battling every day with the best golf team our area has ever seen made Overton a fierce competitor, and the 1999 State tournament was an eye-opener for Jeff.

In addition to the team's sixth place finish, Jeff finished in a tie for second individually with a 147 score (73,74) four strokes behind Nathan Fritz of Greenwood, and that performance turned out to be a catalyst and an omen of things to come. "That's when I knew that I was getting better at such a great speed that I felt I could be as good as anybody in the world at this game," Overton confided.

His junior season was a non-stop battle with Jason Jones for the #1 spot in the lineup, and Jeff played the top spot until late in the season. "He clicked, and it was awesome to see," Jeff said about Jason's late season performance. "It was great to see him play well. He kept beating me by a shot, and I said, 'He should be #1!'"

The healthy competition among all the players spawned amazing results and set the stage for the greatest season in local boys golf history. The 2000 team finished a perfect 16-0 and captured the first State team title in boys golf in area history. (The Harrison girls won the championship in 1989.)

As a senior, Overton won every tournament as an individual except one when he was under the weather, and once again, the Huskies qualified for State with a new group that included Alex Abbott, Blair Hanni, Adam Gann and Dan Newman. Jeff finished a disappointing ninth and admits that he got ahead of himself and "choked."

With a fantastic career behind him, Jeff pondered his future and set his sights on the PGA Tour. His most immediate challenge was selecting a college, and with his parents' help, he analyzed the circumstances carefully. "You know, you always dream about going to Stanford because of Tiger Woods," Jeff confided, "but at the end of the day, IU made sense. It was in our backyard; it was a big-time University. It was a fantastic place to go. I think it's the biggest hidden gem in America, and it did so much for me."

Ron Overton agrees and remembers the key factors in the decision. Because of Jeff's late start as a golfer, "his best opportunities were in the Midwest," Ron pointed out, "places like Kansas

State, Illinois and Louisville. Jeff had always wanted to go to IU to play basketball, so IU was always prominent. I just wanted him to go somewhere where he could flourish, because I knew he wanted to be a professional."

Ron revealed that two other instances were instrumental in the choice. One was a talk given by Jim Furyk at the U.S. Junior Amateur where he advised the young golfers to choose a school where they could play rather than a national champ where they may sit on the bench. The other was a gentleman at a junior golf tournament who convinced him that great golfers also come from cold weather schools, as well, and that Jeff should choose a school for the entire scope of the college experience and not just the golf.

Just as Ron had hoped, Jeff did flourish under IU coach Mike Mayer, and the long par threes on the University's course helped prepare him for the tour. The school also boasts a state-of-the-art short game facility with six USGA greens with irrigation and a heated outdoor hitting facility.

Jeff's career at IU was one of the greatest of all time, and the honors he received are too numerous to be mentioned in their entirety. In his first season, Jeff became only the fourth IU freshman to be named All-Big Ten, and his 74.45 scoring average was the lowest for a freshman in school history. In his second season at IU, Overton lowered his scoring average to 72.25, currently the third lowest in school history, and earned second team All-Big Ten honors while qualifying for the NCAA Tournament. The following summer, Jeff won the Indiana State Amateur by twelve shots with a final round 64, the lowest in the history of the championship.

As a junior, Jeff was named a second team All-American and the Big Ten Player of the Year. In addition, he won the Les Bolstad Award for the low season stroke average in the conference. In his thirteen events in 2003-'04, Overton averaged a school record 70.62, and by the end of his senior year, his name was all over the record book. In '04-'05, Jeff won the first four events and won five for the year. He was also named the Big Ten Golfer of the Week for the eighth time in his career. In addition, Jeff was ranked the #1 golfer in the country by Golfstat, and his 11 under par 61 in the final round of the Xavier Invitational, including 11 birdies and an eagle, was the second lowest round in NCAA history.

Overton won eight career tournaments during his time at IU and was the Big Ten medalist in 2005. When his career was over at IU, he held the school's lowest career stroke average (72.25) and he owned the top two 18-hole scores (64, 65), the top three 36-hole scores (130, 131, 134) and the top two 54-hole scores (199, 203) in the program's history.

After graduating in 2005 with a degree in Sports Management, Jeff was ready to test his game against the best players on the planet, but wishing for it and doing it are worlds apart. Many toil for years on mini-tours and never get there, and still others spend years living the gypsy's life before finally making it to The Show. As the summer approached, Jeff examined his options, and Ron was there as a sounding board. "When you graduate, you don't have anywhere to play," Ron explained. "There are a couple of ways to make it on the PGA Tour. One is to get a sponsor's exemption into an event and then win, but those are hard to come by. They also have Monday qualifiers where you have 150 guys playing for a handful of spots."

Jeff plotted out his strategy and then went to work, and the result was nothing short of amazing. First, he moved to Scottsdale, Arizona and shared an apartment with former college roomie Ryan Cassidy. He then played in a couple tournaments where each player puts up his own money. He played around the Phoenix area and entered qualifiers for the Nationwide Tour and successfully qualified each time, all in preparation for Qualifying School in November.

When Q School rolled around, Jeff began the agonizing grind of the experience, matching shots round after round with some of the most talented and hungry golfers in the world. After Level One tournaments around the country, those who advance join an even more skilled group for Level Two, and as the field thins, a few get the golden ticket, others earn an exempt place on the Nationwide Tour and hundreds endure their devastation as they decide whether they will continue the grind or call it a day.

Miraculously, Jeff navigated the huge field and prevailed. In May, he was in college, and by November, he was a member of the PGA Tour and one of possibly twenty who successfully qualified on their first attempt. The effort was amazing, and the rarity wasn't lost on Jeff's father. "I give him so much credit for getting on tour the way he did," Ron told me, "graduating in May and playing on the tour in Hawaii in January. He was very fortunate and deserving."

As Jeff began his career, he also realized that there is much more to tour life than tee times and interviews. Ron received regular reports from his son as the young man dealt with the nuances of his new profession. "You have to find the right caddie, and you're dealing with sponsors," Ron pointed out. "And when you're first out there, you don't know anybody. You're going from town to town, and you don't even know where the course is. At first, you're really impressed. A tournament lasts a whole week, Monday through Sunday. They have a pro-am on Monday. Tuesday is the official practice round, and then Wednesday is another pro-am, and then you play Thursday through Sunday.

"Then Sunday morning you get up and pack your bags and put everything in the car. Then after your round, you go directly to the airport and fly to the next city. Somewhere you have to get your clothes washed. It sounds exotic on the surface, but it gets old after a while. It's a big adjustment, and a lot of guys don't make it because of that. It really is a 'tour'. Eventually, you get to know the guys and it becomes a traveling community."

Jeff knows that he is fortunate to live the life of a PGA pro but agrees that many golf fans may not appreciate what it takes to thrive in the environment. When asked what might surprise the average fan, he quickly responded: "How disciplined we are. We're waking up at 5:00 a.m. for a tee time, so on Tuesday, we're up that early so that we can get adjusted for that time on Thursday. You're trying to treat your body as well as you can. It's a different kind of 'glamorous', like walking down those fairways. You've seen many of them, and you feel like you belong, and you're trying to do the little things. It really is work, but the work is fun."

An obvious perk is the chance to rub elbows with the best golfers in the world, and Jeff is close with players like Dustin Johnson and Phil Mickelson, a man that players call 'The Genius' because "he knows everything about everything." Jeff also mentioned veteran Peter Jacobsen, whom he describes as "the coolest of all time, so charismatic, the most genuine person I've met in the sport."

Overton has put together an impressive seven-year career as he hones his craft. As of mid-2012, he had 23 top ten finishes and 50 top 25s and was approaching $10 million in earnings. Like many, his first win has been elusive, however, but he has been tantalizingly close several times and has had his share of highlights. In his first season, the 6'4, 195-pound Overton crushed a fairway wood on the 18th hole at the Barclays Classic and holed it for a

Jeff broke several school records during his years at IU. (photo courtesy of Indiana University, Media Relations)

rare double eagle (albatross), and in 2008, he fought through the aftereffects of an appendectomy for a 21st place finish in the final tournament to maintain his exempt status.

As for the pursuit of his first win, he has actually been rather unfortunate. Four times he has finished second, and although he has played well as the leader going into the final round, the opponents who beat him have shot the lights out to do so. He estimates that those four averaged 64 in the final round, including the otherworldly 59 shot by Stuart Appleby in the 2010 Greenbriar Classic to obliterate the three-shot lead Jeff held after 54 holes.

Without question, the highlight of Overton's career was earning a spot on the 2010 Ryder Cup team, making him the first American ever to make the team without a win. Although the team fell to the Europeans on a rainy weekend in Wales, one of the most memorable moments in the event was created by Jeff.

After a stoppage of play because of rain, the Session 3 Fourball competition was resumed the following afternoon, and on the very first hole, number 8, Overton smacked a 300-yard drive and holed out from 142 yards for eagle. With the camera on him, he then pumped his fist and let out a shout of BOOM, BABY! with the whole world watching. The scene became a YouTube sensation, and although Jeff and partner Bubba Watson lost the match to Peter Hanson and Miguel Angel Jimenez, it will go down as one of the greatest highlights in Ryder Cup history.

Jeff has been asked about that shot, and when I brought it up, he tried to explain the feeling and revealed that his words were rooted in his days as a high school golfer at North. "That reaction I had at the time fully describes the (Ryder Cup) experience," he said. "It's such an emotional week. You have no idea what to expect going in, the pressure involved. When that shot holed out, the emotion just came out. 'Boom, baby' was one of those things back in high school with my buddies. Kyle Brinker (a teammate) would make a putt from 30 feet on the last hole for a Coke or whatever and would yell 'Boom, baby' and dance around the green.

Jeff's success can be attributed to a healthy work ethic, and one who saw it first-hand was Alex Abbott, a teammate at North who later asked Jeff to be the best man in his wedding. "Jeff was at Oak Meadows and I played with him," Abbott recalled. "We played nine holes and I beat him, and I still kid him about that. We became best friends because I was the only guy who was willing to practice as much as he was. We were both taught by Bob Walther and both practiced just as much, so evidently he had a lot more talent because he's playing on the PGA Tour and I'm working for Berry Plastics."

All the effort paid off big-time, as Jeff fashioned a fine high school and college career and distinguished himself as an amateur, as well, including wins in the Evansville City Tournament (2003) and the Indiana Amateur twice ('03 and '04) and as a member of winning teams in the Palmer Cup and Walker Cup.

Two men who have a keen interest in Overton's journey are men who watched him develop during his early years. As I visited with North coach Larry Tindle at his north side home, he had one eye on me and the other on his computer screen as he watched Jeff as he led the field early in the Justin Timberlake Shriners Hospital for Children's Open in Las Vegas. "His dad was a hell of an athlete," Tindle said, "and Jeff had that athletic ability. His eighth grade year was when I really noticed his talent.

"He was always a gambler," Tindle continued. "If he's laying out there on a par 5, it's very difficult for him to lay up. He's going to go for it. A lot of times, that will get him in trouble. He has that gambler's mentality."

Bob Walther has strong memories of July 21, 1997 when Jeff took his first lesson from Bob. "You could see, even by the way he placed his hands on the club with what we call 'soft hands,'" Walther said. "Like the old adage, you could have put an open tube of toothpaste on the grip and he could take a swing without losing any toothpaste. He had such incredible touch and fine motor skills. But he also had great gross motor skills with big moves and raw power, all in the same guy. When Jeff saw Tiger Woods bouncing a ball on the head of a club, by the end of the day, Jeff could do that – and bounce it and hit it out of the air, bounce behind his back or two at once. It was child's play for him."

As for Jeff, he realizes his good fortune, and when asked to capsulize the influence on his life, he referred once again to his childhood on "good old Aspen Drive" and how lucky he was to have a mother who opened doors for him on an intellectual level. But more than anything, he appreciates the guidance from Ron. "I am so fortunate to have had the childhood memories with my dad as a role model," he said. "Whenever I have kids, I want to be able to raise them to have that same opportunity that was provided for me."

Only time will tell how Jeff's career will stack up to the greats of his generation and those who preceded him, and for those of us from his neck of the woods, we will watch with anticipation. Bob Walther referred to him as "a once-in-a-lifetime talent" and "the most talented player I ever taught," but perhaps more importantly, when asked to comment on Jeff Overton's career, he deferred to the young man's potential by simply replying, "Jeff's book is not written yet."

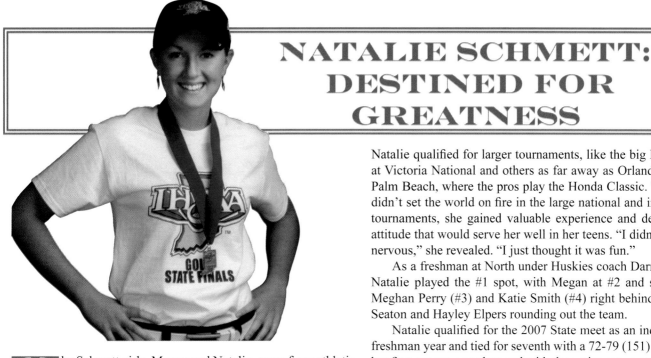

NATALIE SCHMETT: DESTINED FOR GREATNESS

T he Schmett girls, Megan and Natalie, came from athletic stock, and the athleticism paid off for the girls during their years at North High School. In fact, the youngest daughter took success to the extreme and became the first local lady to bring home the hardware as the individual IHSAA State golf champion.

The girls' parents, Brian and Ann (Chanley), grew up in Dubois County, where Brian played basketball and golf at Southridge and Ann represented the Northeast Dubois Jeeps in basketball and softball. In 2000, the family moved to Evansville and the girls were enrolled at Scott Middle School. From a very young age, both girls exhibited physical skills and did well in several sports, including basketball, tennis and soccer, and little Natalie often played up a level to compete on the same teams as Megan, who was two years older. They both continued with softball after the move, and Natalie stayed with basketball by playing in leagues at the Evansville Basketball Academy.

Both girls picked up a golf club for the first time shortly after coming to Evansville, smacking plastic balls in the backyard with Brian and taking to it like a duck to water. "I really liked it because it was different," Natalie said from the family home on the fourth fairway at the Eagle Valley Golf Course on the city's north side. "I had played action sports before I started lessons with Jeff Greenwell at Eagle Valley (at age ten)."

Brian Schmett knew the game well and could see Natalie's potential even at a young age. "I knew she had talent," Brian said, "but I didn't know she had this much. I knew she was athletic; I could see that."

The girls began competing before they were teens as they became involved with Evansville Junior Golf and Indiana Golf. Darren Brinker and his family were huge proponents of junior golf, and the girls began at the Wesselman course and then progressed to age group tournaments.

Natalie won several events locally from the 11-year-old to 14-year-old age groups and even played in some at the PGA Junior Series level. At about age 11, the family began to expand her range as

Natalie qualified for larger tournaments, like the big Rolex event at Victoria National and others as far away as Orlando and West Palm Beach, where the pros play the Honda Classic. Though she didn't set the world on fire in the large national and international tournaments, she gained valuable experience and developed an attitude that would serve her well in her teens. "I didn't really get nervous," she revealed. "I just thought it was fun."

As a freshman at North under Huskies coach Darren Brinker, Natalie played the #1 spot, with Megan at #2 and sophomores Meghan Perry (#3) and Katie Smith (#4) right behind and Molly Seaton and Hayley Elpers rounding out the team.

Natalie qualified for the 2007 State meet as an individual her freshman year and tied for seventh with a 72-79 (151) score. With her first season complete and with the entire group returning, it is safe to say that there were high expectations for Natalie and for the team, as well.

The 2008 season opened with a new man at the helm, as long-time local coach and sports advocate Jon Siau (pronounced SEE • oh) stepped in to replace Coach Brinker. Siau had tasted success before on the State level and handled the experienced group beautifully as the year progressed. The Schmett girls led the way to a fine season, as Natalie was consistent throughout and Megan showed inspirational leadership and was a steadying force at #2. The Lady Huskies competed against 97 teams in dual meets and tournaments during the season and finished the season 85-12, including an 11th place finish at State.

Megan Schmett finished her career in 2008 and would be sorely missed by Coach Siau. She always enjoyed the sport and had offers to continue playing, but she didn't love it like her sister. Though Megan had little interest in continuing to play in college, she did leave her mark on the local golf scene, however. Her senior year, she showed her character and initiative when she decided to honor a cherished family friend.

A neighbor of the family, Karen Pike, had passed away near the end of the season after a long fight with breast cancer, and Megan created Swing for the Cure. The scene was impressive at the Evansville Sectional at Helfrich when every player and coach

Natalie (center) with her parents, Brian and Ann.

Coach Jon Siau with Natalie (left) and Megan Schmett.

donned T-shirts designed by Megan to help raise over $2,000 for the project.

Coach Siau even nominated Megan for a state and national award (which she won) for volunteerism. "Megan was a leader," Mr. Siau told me. "She could set her sights on something, and she got results. She honored a dear friend in doing so and drew attention to the fight against breast cancer. Megan Schmett is an athlete I'll never forget."

Natalie Schmett missed the cut at State by one shot as a sophomore but soaked up even more knowledge that would prove beneficial in the future. As a junior, she had a new #2 for the first time, with senior Meghan Perry moving up, followed by senior Katie Smith (#3), freshman Olivia Price (#4) and senior Hayley Elpers (#5). The girls had a fine year, winning all four 'majors', the City, conference, sectional and regional, and the team only lost to one other team prior to the State meet, finishing 75-1 before another 11th place finish at State.

Again, Natalie shot an opening round 81 to miss the cut, and she entered her final high school season determined to get the job done. The teammates she competed with as a freshman were all gone now and she was surrounded by young Husky pups. Sophomore Olivia Price moved up to #2, but the last three spots were all rookies at the varsity level: sophomore Lauren Byers (#3) followed by freshmen Ashlyn Gomoll (#4) and Caroline Culley (#5). Although the ladies were competitive, Natalie's team failed to advance to State, and for the first time in three years, she could focus exclusively on her own game.

An omen of what was to come occurred earlier in the year at North's tournament, the Cambridge Classic. As fans looked on, Bob Brothers, the secretary-treasurer of the Indiana Golf Coaches Association, approached Coach Siau. "If there's a better golfer in Indiana, I'd like to see her," Brothers proclaimed. "That's your next State champ."

When Natalie teed it up for her fourth appearance at The Legends course in Franklin in the fall of 2010, she was all business, and had it not been for some nasty conditions, she may have eclipsed the all-time IHSAA scoring record. After an opening round 69, Schmett led the field by five shots, and she showed her maturity and mental toughness as she held steady while her competition succumbed to Mother Nature's torture.

"I went through a regular golf glove and two sets of rain gloves," Natalie revealed. "Everything was soaked." As cold rain pelted the course, Schmett showed her creativity and utilized her experience to improvise on the fly. The grips were so wet that she had to adjust the way she gripped the club, squeezing tighter than normal and opening the face to allow her to continue to swing hard.

The results were spectacular, as she recorded a 72 for a five-stroke win over East Noble's Katie Sharp and at least a ten stroke cushion over the rest of the field. Her 141 score was the second best 36-hole total in tournament history, trailing only Leigh Anne Hardin's 139 at Prestwick, and Natalie's was the best score during the twelve years of play at The Legends course. Because individual qualifiers tee off first at State, the Schmetts and Coach Siau spent three hours bundled up in wet clothing under a canopy glancing at the update board and waiting for the final results. And when the verdict was in, Natalie's name stood alone above the rest.

Needless to say, her performance impressed everyone, but those who knew her best were not surprised. "She was as cool as a cucumber," said Ann Schmett, Natalie's mom.

"It's one thing to go out with your buddies and have fun," Brian Schmett added, "but when it's tournament time, you have to be tournament tough. It's a whole different level. She had played in so many tournaments and in all conditions. The last day of State it was nasty, but it was really to Natalie's advantage."

Natalie confirmed her father's words and realized that experience breeds confidence. "I never really thought anything of it when I played in bad weather," she confided. "The conditions are the same for all the players, and I would just adjust to it."

Jon Siau marveled at his captain's showing at the State competition and put the effort in perspective. "There were a lot of girls playing in the State tournament," he said. "Not only did Natalie win the tournament – she owned the tournament. She played 14 holes in the rain. Other girls hit bad shots and it got to them; some cried. Natalie was psyched about it and used it as motivation. By the end of the second day, there were 80 people walking around watching her play. They kept coming up to me and her parents saying, 'What a great golfer!'"

Natalie finished her senior season where she belonged – on top, and her career was remarkable indeed. Her senior year, she defeated 667 other golfers and only lost twice, to Memorial's Dana Hayden, who went on to play at U of E. For the season, Schmett finished a collective 14 under par with a 9-hole scoring average of 35.36 (70.44 18 hole average). She was the City, conference and sectional individual champion and was named All-City, All-Conference, All-Sectional, All-Regional and All-State.

Natalie played #1 in every match of her high school career and was a three-time City individual champ, two-time conference

Cornell Garrett 1976 | Tad Grafton 1981 | David Williams 1981 | Elissa Kim 1991 | Elissa Kim 1992 | Natalie Schmett 2010

"Thanks for the Memories"

FABULOUS FEAT

Jon Siau is very likely the only coach in Indiana history to lead athletes to individual State championships in at least three unrelated sports. Those athletes are shown here in this composite put together by Eric Hassler. Jon was an assistant coach when Cornell Garrett won the 220-yard run in 1976, and he was the head coach for victories by Tad Grafton (pole vault) and David Williams (3200-meter run) in 1981. Jon was also the head coach when Elissa Kim won the tennis title back-to-back in '91 and '92 and when Natalie Schmett bested the field in the 2010 State golf tournament.

champ, four-time sectional champ, three-time regional champ and a four-time State qualifier. She was also honored all four years on the All-City, All-Conference, All-Sectional, All-Regional and All-State teams. In addition, she captured the *Courier & Press* Women's City Championship twice, at age 16 and 17 in 2009 and 2010, and won the Hoosier Junior Championship at Otter Creek Golf Club in Columbus.

With all her talent, it should come as no surprise that Ms. Schmett caught the eye of several college programs. At the time of our interview, no decision had been made and she was considering schools like Indiana, Illinois, Texas and Kansas, among others. When she finally decided a few weeks later, it was made known that her choice came from a tempting venue and a touch of fate. It seems that during her junior year, she was taking a private lesson from a pro in Florida. As they talked, he suggested she check out nearby Jacksonville University. The Schmetts decided to check it out, and as they toured the beautiful campus, they met a gentleman and struck up a conversation. When he learned where Natalie was from, he asked, "Do you know Jon Siau?" The Schmetts were blown away at the coincidence, and as things developed, Natalie decided that Jacksonville was the perfect fit.

In the fall of 2011, Natalie joined the Dolphin program and began to practice on one of the finest home courses in the nation, the famed Player's Stadium Course at TPC Sawgrass featuring its legendary signature hole, the par 3 17th with its familiar island green. With the beautiful Florida weather and outstanding facilities, it didn't take long for Natalie to prove that her full-ride scholarship was merited, and the local media began to notice Evansville's pride and joy.

In a story in March of 2012, the headline read "Nat the Great", and writer Allison Cornell raved about the young star. "In October, freshman Natalie Schmett became the first Dolphin in the women's golf program history to win an event," Cornell wrote. The journalist was referring to the Wendy's Invitational in Charleston, South Carolina, and she continued with an assessment that wouldn't surprise folks back home: "With thousands of successful women golfers in the U.S., what sets Schmett apart from the field is that she has a fiery competitive attitude and the unique ability to outright win a golf tournament."

In the *Atlantic Sun Insider*, under the headline "And a Child Shall Lead Them", Natalie was featured for her immediate impact on the program. "In a tune-up for the upcoming A-Sun Championship, JU defeated three-time defending champion Stetson 295-297 at Venetian Bay Golf Club," the story said. "Schmett joined teammate Morgan Jackson with a one-under-par 71. Natalie Schmett has six top-25 finishes, three top-10 finishes and an individual title (the Wendy's Invitational)."

In her first year with the Dolphins, Natalie lived up to her billing, playing the #1 position and tying the school record with a 69 in the final round of the conference championship in April. During the season, she averaged 75.5 per round and garnered two top five finishes and six top tens. In February, she and teammate Jessica Welch were rated 17th in the country as a freshman duo, giving Jacksonville a solid nucleus for the future.

Natalie is pursuing a degree in Sports Management as a backup plan for her aspirations of playing professionally, and with her dogged determination, she has a fighting chance to reach her lofty goal. One man who would never doubt her is Jon Siau, and he cites her intangibles as a basis for his belief.

One example of Schmett's makeup occurred during a State tournament appearance. "Natalie pushed her drive right," Siau described, "and the ball was on dry dirt with a pine tree behind. According to the rules of golf, if she knocks any part of the tree off with her backswing, it's a penalty. She went up on her toes and whiffed, and she could have easily gotten away with it. When she finished the hole, I said, 'Natalie, you made par, didn't you?' She said, 'No, I bogeyed. You missed my second shot.'

"Natalie has everything it takes to be a champion," Siau continued. "She has intelligence; she's athletic; she has the ability to concentrate. She has so much talent, so much knowledge and so much respect for the game."

Natalie Schmett may go on to play professional golf or she may become successful in the front office of a professional sports franchise, but regardless what her future brings, her place in local sports history is firmly entrenched. With her State title in 2010, she became the first local female to win the individual State golf championship and only the third athlete, male or female, to do so, joining Bob Hamilton of Reitz (1933) and Mater Dei's Jerry McRae in 1959. In addition, she became only the second athlete in North's 55-year history to earn All-State honors all four years, joining tennis player Elissa Kim.

As local girls sports continue to produce team and individual State champs in the years to come, young lady golfers may duplicate or surpass Ms. Schmett's feats. But for all eternity, the area's 'first' female State golf champion will always be North High School's Natalie Schmett.

DAVID ERDY: THE NATURAL

O f all the athletes who have graced the pages of the *Local Legends* books, it would be difficult to find many who had more natural talent for their sports than David Erdy. As a youngster, David excelled at several sports, but it was during an outing with his father that his natural talent for golf was discovered.

When I asked David's parents how early they saw his potential, his mother, Mary, responded with no hesitation. "The first time he picked up a club," she answered.

"We were at Tee time," added Gary Erdy, David's father, to explain Mary's reference concerning the afternoon they spent with their son. "He started hitting balls at the driving range and he was pelting the Volkswagen (an old car many aim at in the center of the range) time after time."

Nine-year-old David had never hit a ball or taken a lesson, and yet he was so smooth with his swing that Tee Time pro Mike Wolfe approached Gary and Mary and said "Don't change a thing." When he was told that this was David's first time ever with a club in his hand, his eyes rolled in amazement.

David used a baseball grip that day in 1999 and continued using it for a couple years as he began to work on his game. "I would take him there (Tee Time) at six in the morning at least five days a week," Mary recalled from the family's home near Quail Crossing, "and I'd pick him up at 10:00 p.m."

Although David eventually played regularly at the Boonville Country Club, Rolling Hills and Victoria National, it was at the small course on Morgan Avenue where he developed a love for the game. According to his parents, he would do odd jobs around the course in exchange for buckets of balls to hit. He also met young Logan Harper at Tee Time. Logan was a year older and was the son of pro shop manager Mike Harper. Because of the long hours Logan spent at Tee Time with his father, the two boys became friends and rivals as they practiced together and then competed against each other.

For a long time, Logan beat David, and once David bested his young nemesis, his confidence soared. David won his first tournament at age 9 at Wesselman's and then absorbed as much knowledge as he could playing junior golf. From 1999 to 2007, Erdy won 21 local tournaments on eight different courses, and

he was named the Evansville Junior Golf Player of the year in '03 and '05. In addition, David was the junior medalist in the Fendrich Amateur and McDonald Amateur and the Men's City champion, all in 2007.

Looking back, Gary and Mary agree that they probably should have done things differently. "Had we known then what we know now, we would have started him in national tourneys as soon as he started golfing," Mary admitted. "That's what college coaches rely on. They don't look at anybody who has just accomplished things locally."

At age 14, David was preparing for a huge international tournament at Deer Creek in Indianapolis when he made a decision that would have a major impact on his career. Always an outgoing kid, David took it upon himself to call local pro Jim Hamilton. "I hear you have the best short game in the region. Can you help me?" David asked Mr. Hamilton. Jim worked with the boy's grip and tweaked a few things and helped David win the qualifier at Deer Creek.

The bond between teacher and student grew over the years, and Jim appreciated the boy's approach to the game. "He listened," Gary Erdy explained when asked about why David continued to improve. "He listened to Jim Hamilton. They spent a lot of time talking and very little time hitting golf balls."

David's cerebral approach to the game didn't end with his sessions with Coach Hamilton. "From the time he was twelve, he bought all of Bob Rotella's books," Mary informed me. Rotella is a famous sports psychologist who deals with professional athletes. "He has them all and reads them over and over," Mary continued. "He saw that at a very young age, the importance of psychology in golf."

As a high school golfer, Erdy recorded wins as an individual four times in multi-team tournaments and was the team's MVP in '05, '06 and '07. In 2008, David was named Castle's Most Valuable Athlete and received the prestigious Castle Crest Award. In addition, he won five Indiana Junior Golf tournaments from '04 to '07 and was named All-State in '07 and '08. David also led the 2008 Castle team, including Chris Gregory, Tom Sutherlin and Ben Waits, to the SIAC title.

As David's high school career wound down, he zeroed in on the next phase of his education. He had made it clear early on that he wanted to play in the Big Ten, and he was courted by Ohio State, Wisconsin, Ball State, North Carolina-Charlotte, IU and, of course, Jim Hamilton at U of E. Although IU coach Mike Mayer had always wanted David, at one point, there was some confusion. It seems that Mary inadvertently stated to the Ball State coach that David had made up his mind. That information then spread to IU and Wisconsin, who were both working hard to recruit Erdy, and they ceased communication thinking he had committed to UE. When he learned of the mix-up, David then took the initiative and called Mike Mayer at IU to set the record straight. He wanted to be a Hoosier.

Following in the footsteps of Evansville legend Jeff Overton and joined a year later by outstanding North golfer David Mills,

Photo courtesy of Indiana University, Media Relations

*David spent long hours at Tee Time and,
even at age ten, had a natural swing.*

*David was also a fine basketball
player as a youngster.*

Erdy looked forward to working with Coach Mayer at the school's state-of-the-art practice facilities. As a collegiate athlete, David worked out in the weight room two hours every day, shaping his body into a 6'2, 190-pound machine that could withstand the rigors of hauling a forty-pound golf bag 36 holes a day, often in bad weather.

In 2010, David led his IU team to victory and earned co-medalist honors at the Firestone Invitational. He ended his junior campaign with a season scoring average of 72.83, earning a spot on the Ping All-Midwest Region Team. In the 2011 North & South Amateur, David advanced to the finals before falling in the championship match. He also won the 2009 Calloway Collegiate Match Play Championship-Stroke Play Qualifier by beating very strong competition with scores of 72-65.

But with all the success David has experienced through college golf, there is no doubt about what event stands as the crowning achievement in Erdy's golf career. It all began on May 11th, 2009. David and his IU teammates had just completed a disappointing outing in the Big Ten Tournament and had driven to French Lick for a qualifier to the U.S. Open. Imagine mom and dad's shock when David called with the news that he had won the qualifier.

As is the custom, when a player enters a qualifier, they also designate the sectional site (the next level) they will attend if they qualify. David had chosen Columbus, Ohio so that he could stay with his Aunt Claire and Uncle Ted. But those plans never materialized. Because many professionals who had played in Dublin, Ohio the week before had chosen Columbus, David was bumped to Dayton, a blessing in disguise according to Gary and Mary Erdy.

At the NCR (National Cash Register, the sponsor) qualifier it was evident from the beginning that David was on his game. He maintained his focus for 36 holes and shot 4 under in the first round and 1 under in the second. All that was left was to wait anxiously with his parents as the others finished. As they settled in, David was in second, but as others finished, his position dropped. When the dust cleared, he was part of a five-player logjam tied for the first and second alternate spots.

David's first tee shot against the two pros and two amateurs was straight and OHHH so long, according to Mary Erdy, and he survived the hole after one pro and one amateur were eliminated. On the second hole, a par three with a front pin placement just barely over a bunker, David launched a beautiful shot that left him a three-foot uphill putt. One firm stroke later and David was a first alternate for the U.S. Open.

As the group celebrated at Skyline Chili, David beat himself up for missing qualifying by one shot, and he couldn't imagine why anyone who was eligible would not play in the Open. After returning home, David prepared to play in the Rolling Hills Invitational on June 13th. He was one of several alternates from various qualifiers in line for the Open, and by the 13th, two pros from the field had already dropped out. David was told that there were two players ahead of him, so he and Gary decided to gamble and leave for the Open just in case.

But before the time came for them to leave, David got the call. He was in! After an hour of screaming and celebration at home, reality set in that Gary and Mary and David were on their way to Long Island, New York for the U.S. Open at the famous Bethpage Black golf course.

As Gary, Mary and I sat in the living room in their home two and a half years after the event, it was easy to see that the memories were still fresh and that they will be cherished forever. In a packet Mary gave me, with photos and stats and such, she included a journal of sorts. The journal chronicled the experience and was beautifully written, and I decided that I could never tell it like Mary did. Thus, much of the following comes from Mary Erdy.

Needless to say, the entire family, including David's siblings, Jason and Megan, were ecstatic about the news. Gary was assigned caddie duties for the event, and tickets were already reserved for their Tuesday flight. When David's news arrived on Monday that he had made the field, the phone call set off a series of tasks that would challenge even the most anal of organizers.

Mary: The first thing I did was run to the computer to see if I could get a plane ticket. How lucky could I be? Same flight as Gary's and David's (which had been booked on Friday). Wow! Was this meant to be or what?

I had to be ultra-organized. I had only one day to prepare for the trip of a lifetime. I became a focused machine. Umbrellas, rain-proof pants and shirts, extra shoes in case of sloshy mud, sweaters and jackets, as well as 95-degree heat advisory apparel – all in multiples of three.

It gets quite challenging to keep the suitcases at 50 pounds or less (to prevent an extra charge). Golf Plus gave us their biggest golf travel case to rent, and it was stuffed to the gills. Thank God they allow 60 or more pounds for those.

Mary also spoke in her journal about Gary's excitement and how he handled it at his office where he is a family physician.

Mary: Every patient who came in that day knew before they left the office that their doctor was going to caddie in the U.S. Open. Gary's ear-to-ear grin never left his face. Doctoring one day, caddying in the U.S. Open the next. Go figure!

Before they departed, the Erdys also experienced their first bit of celebrity at the airport, and Mary wasn't sure how they felt about it.

Mary: I had no clue that David and his picture had made front page news (in the Courier). The longer we sat, the more I felt that people were staring at us. I tried to inconspicuously glance at Gary and David to make sure their zippers were indeed zipped.

(Upon their arrival at JFK)

Mary: My primary and immediate concern (as always) was David's clubs. Every revolution of the baggage conveyor causes an increase in blood pressure and heart rate. It's not like a toothbrush or disposable razor. I mean, it isn't called the U.S. Open GOLF Championship because its played with toothpicks from Wal-Mart, right? God must have decided He shouldn't mess with us. The clubs came out first.

(And in the rental car)

Mary: I looked up and saw the big green sign for exit 32: Bethpage-Farmingdale. Seeing the word "Bethpage" on the freeway sign brought the whole turn of events into my reality. 'Holy Jesus, our son's playing in the U.S. Open.' This was just the beginning of a week packed with goose bumps and tear-filled eyes.

After collecting their credentials, the Erdys entered the Marriott and Mary noticed the crowd in the lobby area.

Mary: As soon as they spotted David with Gary behind him carrying his clubs, you could have heard a pin drop. This was my introduction to the reverence that the fans hold for anyone who even plays in the U.S. Open, whether famous or not.

A Little later, David returned after practicing chipping at the course.

Mary: With each ball, David kept getting closer and closer to the hole. One New Yorker finally challenged the crowd with bets on David holing a chip. When David obliged, he passed through the crowd giving out high fives and then autographs. All I could say was, 'Wow!' They'd barely been there three hours and already he was having a blast!

(And the perks!!)

Mary: They handed David the keys to an LS 460 Lexus, fully loaded. They also programmed the GPS with the coordinates of the player parking lot so that he could press 'Home' and never get lost on the way to the course. They also gave him a gift bag of cool stuff – expensive colognes, shirts, a bottle of wine, gift certificates. There was a sharp-looking black and gold magnetic plaque with the 2009 U.S. Open logo on it. It impressed me that they took the time to inscribe 'David Erdy' on each of the special

pieces of memorabilia, even though he had been an alternate and was the youngest player in the field. It was clear to Gary and me that he had legitimately played his way in.

(At Bethpage)

Mary: A vast array of buffet-style dishes were in the clubhouse from morning until evening – for free. During a rain delay, David and I actually planted ourselves next to the dessert table and feasted on pound cake for three hours.

On Wednesday, David left for the course several hours before his practice round to soak up the atmosphere while Mary waited for IU coach Mike Mayer, who had been in Texas scouting recruits. As the tournament neared, Mary reflected on what was about to take place and what it meant to them.

Mary: If there's one thing I've learned in this life, it's to enjoy the 'firsts'. They only come along once, and they're always the most special. This was the first time David Erdy would play in the U.S. Open and the only time he would play at the age of nineteen as a sophomore in college. I planned to milk it for all it was worth.

On Thursday, the Erdys piled into the Lexus and headed for Bethpage. With the words "Official Vehicle of the 2009 U.S. Open" emblazoned on each side, heads turned as they passed and they were waved through all security checkpoints. As the family finally entered the hallowed grounds of Bethpage, Mary noticed that the players parking area resembled a Lexus dealership lot. Mary also noticed several players during the tournament but tried to be judicious with her camera so as not to embarrass David.

Mary became enamored with the New York crowd and their accents, calling their enthusiasm "palpable." She also felt the emotion that our country's tournament inspires, saying "I don't care how many times I came and went through those double doors (of the clubhouse), I still got goosebumps – EVERY SINGLE TIME."

Mary watched her son warm up at his tee box between Geoff Ogilvie and Stewart Cink and enjoyed watching Coach Mayer smile as he took in the experience. David seemed to handle it all with ease, even when he learned his locker was next to Tiger Woods.

At the practice round, the Erdys and Coach Mayer witnessed the challenge that Bethpage presented, with three par 4 holes over 500 yards and the course playing at 7,426 yards. Mary stated that hitting out of the Open rough was like hitting out of "a gigantic twisted Brillo Pad that swallows balls for breakfast." The weekend was also affected by torrential rains that played havoc with schedules and scores.

Through all of this, Gary Erdy was facing challenges of his own. People seldom think about the job of a caddie, and Gary will be the first to say how his experience was tough and, at times, intimidating.

Heavy rains the night before cast an ominous pall over Thursday's play, but nothing could dampen the Erdy's spirit as they prepared for the experience of a lifetime. As David warmed up on the tee box with playing partners Zach Johnson and Lee Westwood, Coach Mayer was like a child, saying to Mary, "OK, here we go, Mary" just before they heard something Mary had heard many times but NEVER like this… "David Erdy of Boonville, Indiana!"

David just had to shoot a photo of the famous sign at Bethpage.

David's first drive couldn't avoid the U.S. Open rough, and he finished number one with a bogey. With the round underway, Mary observed her son.

Mary: It all seemed so natural to him. It was obvious that he was in his element. I could see this was where he belonged, and he knew it. Even Coach said, 'This is it, Mom. He looks comfortable, natural.' I had to wipe away tears as I watched David live his dream.

David also bogeyed the next two holes to put him at 3 over, which was disappointing but only slightly worse than the +2 of Johnson and Westwood. The start was tough for Mary to watch, but she still enjoyed the experience and marveled at how her son consistently out-drove the two professionals. Mary also talked about the large crowd and how hard it was to fight through it while lugging her umbrella through the mud. As the round developed, she began to hear the New York crowd comment about David, and she realized that some began to recognize her as David's mother.

After a spectacular approach shot at #4, David lined up a four-foot birdie putt as the crowd looked on. When his ball plinked into the cup, the crowd went crazy and David drew from their energy and saluted them with his putter in appreciation. From that point on, Mary was known as "duh kid's muddah," and she was loving every minute of it.

While David had played #4, Mary also experienced one of several situations that I found amusing in her journal. This one came immediately after a brilliant sand shot.

Mary: The mother in me was mortified to realize that when he picked up his ball after marking it, David was just on the verge of spitting on it to clean it. 'Oh no, David. You don't spit on your ball at the U.S. Open. Please NO!' Just when I was about to go ballistic, Lee's caddie grabbed the ball out of David's hand, cleaned it and with a big grin on his face, handed it back to him.

David parred number 5 and drove long down the middle on 6 when the deluge came and Mary and Coach began a very long, muddy walk to the clubhouse. In the clubhouse, Mary marveled at the fact that they were actually having lunch with Zach and Lee. Meanwhile, David, being the social animal he is, mingled and introduced himself to the pros. Upon his return, Mary witnessed another "goosebump moment."

Mary: When he made his way back, who should be standing there but Bob Rotella! He politely asked David if he could have a seat. In my mind, I began picturing David's bookshelf back home, lined with Rotella's books. I inconspicuously glanced over at David, and when our eyes met, he gave me an eye-popping look that was worth a thousand words.

During the conversation with Rotella, David was also surprised when legendary instructor Bob Toski joined them to discuss the concepts of the golf game. Although the rain eventually stopped, play was called for the day and the Erdys crashed for the night.

On Friday morning, the weather was decent but the grounds were a quagmire for the spectators.

David finished #6 with a par and then had a less than stellar day. He bogeyed 7 and double bogeyed 8 before gaining back a shot with a birdie on 9. The highlight of the day was the 15th, and much of this highlight could be attributed to dear old dad.

Throughout all the excitement of the practice round and early tournament play, Gary Erdy was doing his best to remember all the caddie protocol he had been studying over the last few days. The last thing he wanted was to cause problems for David or his playing partners. On the 459-yard 15th, the toughest hole on the course, Gary had his own moment on Bethpage Black.

After a gorgeous tee shot, David asked for his five iron but looked a bit indecisive. Gary, looking the part in his blue caddie bib, analyzed the situation and offered his opinion. Realizing that they were hitting into the wind to a wet, elevated green, he handed his son a four iron. David nailed the shot and the crowd roared as he holed his short putt.

David finished with a 78 and enjoyed dinner with some friends who had flown out to surprise him.

On Saturday, David hit practice balls three tee boxes down from Tiger as he prepared for his 10:28 tee time. He began his round on the back nine, and twelve holes into the round, Mary experienced another 'mom moment'.

Mary: David had just teed off on hole three, and that's when I came close to panic. I saw Gary walking towards the green without David. I broke out in a cold sweat, especially when I saw the grove of trees lining hole three. It's a well known and accepted fact in high school and college golf that if you look up and see a player missing, he will eventually reappear, emerging from the woods pulling up his zipper. 'Please don't tell me you're doing this at the U.S. Open, David.' My luck, it will be the only thing they televise about David Erdy. "Nineteen-year-old rising sophomore from IU takes bathroom break in Bethpage woods." Sure enough, he emerged from the trees, but thank God he had already taken care of his zipper.

For the record, Mary soon realized that David had used one of the 30 ace toilets in the area, and she vowed to herself not to tell David for a very long while what she was thinking at the time.

David parred the last hole for a respectable 74, but his two-round total of 152 meant that his first U.S. Open was over after missing the cut by four. The Erdys returned to the hotel and packed for their return home. I'm certain that Gary, Mary and David have memories that will last a lifetime, and Mary shared some of her thoughts as she finished her journal.

Mary: The youngest player, the barely-sophomore from Indiana University, the young amateur that the New York crowd embraced. How special can it get. The way the story developed is special in itself; winning the local qualifier, being bumped to Dayton, winning the playoff, having four exempt players drop out.

Fifteen years ago if someone had asked me 'What's the U.S. Open,' I honestly would not have been able to answer the question definitively. In 2009, in the month of June, the U.S. Open at Bethpage left an indelible smile on my heart that will never fade.

NCAA rules prevented me from interviewing David for this story, but fortunately, Mary had a recording of David in an interview with an Indianapolis radio station. When asked how playing in the Open affected his pulse rate, David said, "…standing in the middle of the road with a semi driving straight at you. That's how nervous I felt." He also reflected on the experience by saying, "Once you're out there, you want it again and again. Maybe not next week or next month, but I hope I can qualify next year. I didn't play my best, but I beat some good players, I tied some good players, and I felt like I could definitely hang out there if I work on my game a little bit."

While David was making his ascent into the upper echelon of the golf world, his mom and dad were there every step of the way. Mary has seen every competitive round except two, while Gary has seen many but jokes that "I had to work to fund their travels." When I asked if David aspired to play on the PGA Tour, without hesitation, Mary answered "Oh, yes. He's confident."

That confidence will carry David a long way, and his maturity level and work ethic make those dreams very possible. He is majoring in General Studies at IU with a minor in Psychology, but his parents say he never speaks of a fall-back plan. His eyes are on the prize, and if David Erdy has anything to say about it, there will be many more U.S. Opens for him and his family to remember.

IHSAA STATE CHAMPIONS UPDATE

BOY'S BASKETBALL

School	Year	Record	Coach
Princeton (3A)	2009	29-0	Tom Weeks
Washington (3A)	2010	23-3	Gene Miiller
Washington (3A)	2011	24-4	Gene Miiller

GIRLS'S BASKETBALL

School	Year	Record	Coach
Memorial (3A)	2011	28-1	Bruce Dockery
Vincennes Rivet (A)	2011	28-0	Tim Young
Mater Dei (2A)	2012	27-1	Steve Goans

DID YOU KNOW?

The Indiana girls record for scoring in a single game is held by Seeger's Stephanie White with 66 points in 1995. The only area player to crack the 50 mark is Washington Catholic's Eileen Weber, who did it twice in 1993-'94 with 56 and 52.

RARE AIR

Damon Bailey is Indiana's career high school scoring leader with 3,134 points. The only area player to crack the top 25 (as of 2012) is Jasper's Michael Lewis with 2,138.

(Source: IHSAA Website)

MARCH MADNESS

Making the Final Four is the holy grail for all Division I basketball coaches and players. Below is the list of area athletes who have played in the Final Four.

Phil Byers (Reitz) – IU – 1953 – national champs
Dick Farley (Winslow) – IU – 1953 – national champs
Burke Scott (Tell City) – IU – 1953 – national champs
Tom Kron (Tell City) – Kentucky – 1966 – runner-up (Texas Western)
Vaughn Wedeking (Harrison) – 1970 – Jacksonville – runner-up (UCLA)
Greg Nelson (Harrison) – 1970 – Jacksonville – runner-up (UCLA)
Steve Bouchie (Washington) – 1981 – IU – national champs
Calbert Cheaney (Harrison) – 1992 – IU – Final Four (Duke)
Walter McCarty (Harrison) – 1996 – Kentucky – national champs
Tyler Zeller (Washington) – 2009 – North Carolina – national champs
Kyle Kuric (Memorial) – 2012 – Louisville – Final Four (Kentucky)

CHAPTER FOUR
HOOPS HEROES

TEX GRAHAM:
A LEADER OF MEN

In the illustrious history of Evansville basketball, many coaches were revered by their players and fans, and one of the earliest was Tex Graham at Central. The man was a leader who guided the school's basketball program during the golden years of Central basketball, and he left a lasting impression on those who knew him.

As I sat with him at his home on Evansville's northeast side in 2010, we were joined by two lovely ladies, Tex's wife Joan (pronounced Jo Ann) and his daughter Susie. Tex was in failing health as we sat at the kitchen table, but his exuberance returned when he took me back to his days as a young coach, with Joan and Susie smiling as memories flowed.

My first question was one I was anxious to ask: How did a guy from Princeton, Indiana come to be called 'Tex'? It seems that while he was at Princeton High School, he was in study hall reading a western comic book. The floors of the old building were squeaky and attracted the attention of the female principal. As she entered, she saw that Marion wasn't studying and grabbed the book and showed it to the class. From that moment on, he was known as Tex, and the name stuck for 70 years.

Marion Ulysses Graham was born in 1921 and starred for the Tigers in football, basketball and baseball before leaving for Indiana State, where he played football and baseball for the Sycamores. He would have graduated in 1944, but his education was interrupted by the call to serve his country. As a member of the Marine Corps, Tex became a captain and served in WWII and the Korean Conflict, earning a Bronze Star in the process.

He returned to ISU in 1946 and met Joan during his senior year. Upon his graduation in 1947, he brought Joan to Evansville and began his teaching career as he coached golf, assisted in football and coached freshman basketball. His love for basketball grew as he learned from head coach Walter Riggs, an Evansville College/U of E Basketball Hall of Famer.

Tex's first year at Central was a historic one. The team featured an outstanding lineup, led by three of the greatest in the school's history. Joe Schwitz was the team's primary ballhandler, and Gene Southwood, who went on to star at Vanderbilt, was a phenomenal scorer. The Bears' superstar was Lee Hamilton, who eventually became a U.S. Congressman, a career that lasted five decades.

With the 6'3 Hamilton in the middle, Central demolished the competition in the State tournament and advanced all the way to the final game in 1948. In the semi-final game, a 48-40 win over Muncie Central, Hamilton suffered a painful knee injury. Doctors tried everything to prepare the knee for just one more game, and Tex applied the tape just before game time. But the injury was too severe and the Bears fell 54-52 to Lafayette Jeff with Hamilton on the bench. The team finished the season 24-4 and is still, even 65 years later, the last Central team to make it to the Final Four.

That season was the first for Riggs as a head coach, and he stayed in that position through the 1953-'54 campaign. Tex learned the game and the system well as he served under Riggs and got to see some amazing talent as Riggs put together seven consecutive winning seasons.

In 1954, Tex assumed control of the program and began to leave his own mark at Central. Graham continued the program's winning ways with only one losing season during his ten years at the helm.

After the '63-'64 season, Tex was offered a great opportunity in the insurance business, and with kids in college, he couldn't pass it up. In 1969, he returned to teaching but noticed that kids

Tex Graham coaching his Central Bears.
(Photo courtesy of the Evansville Courier)

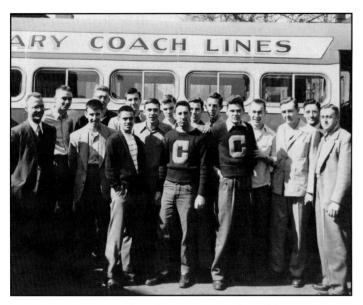

*Lee Hamilton (letter sweater to the right)
led his '48 team to the State Finals.*

This 1952-'53 team was one of the school's best. Head coach Walter Riggs is on the left, and Tex is on the right. Big Jerry Clayton stands tall in the middle of the back row.

had changed while he was gone and chose not to coach again. He retired from teaching in 1983, but he still looked back fondly at the days and nights spent at Central Gym during the remarkable era that he represented.

"It seemed like anywhere you would go they were familiar with the Central Golden Bears," he said as my guest on the radio show *Local Legends*. "When you have a gym that holds that many people and you have to have a drawing to get in (for the tournaments), it's one of those commodities. If it's hard to get, then people want to be part of it."

Graham also reflected fondly on the relationships that existed in the local coaching community. "They were very combative when the game was going on, but when the game was over, we were good friends," he said. "That was the spirit of the Coaches Association."

Tex was referring to the organization that would host parties that were held two or three times a year when coaches of all sports and their wives would congregate and socialize with a meal and dancing. The Graham's appreciated the bonds they formed with such icons as Jim Rausch (North), Hubert Scott (Central), Jim Myers (Bosse), Jim Barnett (Reitz) and Jerry Altstadt (Rex Mundi). They also mentioned John Wessel, who succeeded Tex at Central, Frank Schwitz (Harrison) and Tom Turner, who coached football and wrestling.

Those who knew and played for Tex are not shy about expressing themselves when it comes to their appreciation and respect. "First of all, they were good Christian men," said Harold Malicoat, who played for Riggs and Graham at Central. "No one used foul language, and if you had a bad attitude, you'd go in, and if you came back the next day and they saw it again, you don't play. They had discipline. They were very strict but very fair."

"We had some special coaches when I was at Central," Jerry Schreiber said. "He (Tex) was a role model. I looked up to and still look up to him."

While speaking with Tex and Joan and Susie, Joan related a very touching story that brought tears to her eyes as she spoke. She told me about Vaughn Wedeking, a local legend who was very possibly the greatest all-around athlete in area history. Vaughn, who passed away a few years ago from a devastating illness, had amazing success at Harrison but spent his freshman year at Central.

"Vaughn was in town with his twin boys (Drew and Graham)," Joan explained. "He made a special trip when he was in (from Oregon) and he came to the house and knocked on the door. He told Tex, 'I just wanted to tell you how much you meant to me.'"

Wedeking wasn't the only athlete who was impacted by Coach Graham, and many are still around to express their thoughts. "I'd like to pay tribute to Coach," said John Wessel on the *Local Legends* radio show. Wessel played for Central in the early '50s and coached at the school from '64 to '74, and as he looked at Tex sitting across from him, his voice quivered as he spoke into the microphone.

"In my mind's eye, I still see that young, strapping, good-looking Marine," he said. "I always maintained that I grew up during the very best time in the history of this country. During the Second World War, everybody was united and getting the job done. These guys came out of the service. I can still see Tex with his three-by-five card, and we never took the practice floor without him following everything on that card, and he stuck to that time schedule. To me, he is a true war hero."

Tex maintained great friendships all through his life, and he spent many days of his retirement on the golf course playing a game he truly loved. Over the years, he shot his age 25 times, and he finished second in the national Senior Games in Louisville in 2007. Tex played his last rounds at the age of 88.

Tex Graham passed away on February 24, 2011, leaving behind his wife of 62 years and three children, Susan, Steve and Mike. After his passing, Susie requested a copy of the radio show so that she would be able "to hear Daddy's voice."

Susie's daddy won 70% of his games during his tenure at Central, but his true legacy is the lives that he touched. Tex Graham stood as an example to all who knew him, as a soldier, as a coach and as a great man.

DID YOU KNOW?

When Tex Graham was in high school, he played American Legion baseball with local legend Gus Doerner and played against local legend Gil Hodges.

JERRY CLAYTON: THE BEST EVER?

Basketball has been a way of life in Indiana for well over 100 years, and high school basketball in particular has consumed myriad Hoosiers to the point of fanaticism. The topic has also been written about in depth by many, including the book *Hoosier Hysteria!* by Bob Williams, who could recall days when he would climb a ladder to retrieve a ball from a peach basket hung in his high school gym in Greensburg.

The sport has been around long enough now that the gaps between generations make it nearly impossible to draw comparisons between athletes who played several decades apart. There is also no question that the game itself has changed as the years passed and that athletes have certainly evolved physically. But despite the distorted views caused by generation gaps, one thing is certain: those who marveled as they watched Central's Jerry Clayton play in the 1950s do not even hesitate to place him at the top of the list of all-time local greats, regardless of how impressive younger players may be.

Clayton was born on the 14th of July, 1935 with his fraternal twin Joe Clayton, and while Joe eventually grew to 6'2, Jerry reached 6'7, an impressive size for a high school player in his day. Neither of Jerry's parents, Andy Joe and Neva, were particularly tall, but the grandfathers on each side stood 6'7, and the size Jerry inherited served him well on the local courts.

Jerry, Joe, younger brother Arbin and their sister Joan attended Henry Reis Grade School and then entered Central during its years downtown. In the early '50s, Central was one of six Evansville high schools, with Bosse, Reitz, Memorial, the brand new Mater Dei (1949) and Lincoln, the all black school on what was then the city's east side. At the time, Central drew from as far away as Newburgh, and the athletic landscape would change as the city opened new schools, North (1957), Rex Mundi ('58), and eventually Harrison ('62).

Central's basketball prowess was known statewide during the '40s and '50s, with Central Gym as the center of the local basketball universe. And no one thrived in that universe more than Jerry Clayton. As a freshman in 1950, Jerry played on the reserve team, and for the next three seasons, he was a permanent fixture on the varsity.

Clayton was surrounded by excellent teammates and coaches during the program's heyday, and the Bears enjoyed playing to the full houses at the gym that seemed to be built for Jerry. The atmosphere was electric as the fans stomped the wooden bleachers and the players felt the vibration in the locker rooms below. By all accounts, Central Gym was built for shooters, and no player was built for shooting more than Jerry Clayton. According to many

who played there, the ceiling was the perfect height and the lighting exactly right for area sharpshooters to fire at will.

Though everyone knew that Jerry was the star of the show, his co-stars at Central were very talented as well. As a sophomore, he teamed with John Harrawood, Bob Wessel, Bob Walker and Clarence Doninger to post a 19-8 regular season record. Though the season wasn't spectacular, the Bears seemed to always pick up their game when tournament time rolled around. In '52, the boys captured the huge sectional field with four easy wins and then defeated Boonville in the regional afternoon game before posting a 66-50 win over Princeton, a team that had defeated them twice during the season. The Bears then advanced to the championship game of the semi-finals (now known as the semi-state) with a 56-54 win over Terre Haute Garfield in four overtimes before a heartbreaking two-point loss to New Albany.

The '52-'53 season was Jerry's best, and many consider that team to be one of the finest in school history. Bob Walker graduated and moved on to a nice college career at Evansville College, but Clayton, Harrawood, Wessel and Doninger formed a strong nucleus. Walker's void was filled by four players, Joe Clayton, Charlie Martin, Harold Malicoat and Harold 'Rocket' Phelps, who added speed to an already strong player base.

The Bears won their first twelve games, averaging over 68 points per game, and only lost three regular season contests, to Bloomington, Reitz and Jasper. One of their most impressive wins was against Crispus Attucks in the Lafayette Holiday Tournament. Attucks was only two years from making basketball history. In 1955, led by a young phenom named Oscar Robertson, the Tigers would win their first of two back-to-back titles, making them the first Indianapolis school and the first all black team in the nation to win a state championship.

Led by future hall of fame coach Ray Crowe, the '52-'53 Tigers featured the dynamic tandem of Bailey Robertson, Oscar's older brother, and Hallie Bryant, who would be named Indiana's Mr. Basketball for 1954. The green and gold Tigers and brown and gold Bears traded blows the whole game, and Central had to hit 70% of their shots to finish off the 74-67 victory. The game attracted statewide attention because of the two superstars who were squaring off (Clayton and Bryant), and a legend was born as a result of the hype. As the story goes, an Attucks player looked at Jerry before the opening tip and said, "Big man, you've scored your last," and after Clayton lit up Attucks for 16 points in the first quarter, an Attucks player could be heard yelling at his teammates saying, "Somebody take that cat!"

Central dominated the '53 Evansville Sectional with easy wins over Memorial, Mt. Vernon, Reitz and Lincoln, and they were even more superior in the regional with wins over Owensville (80-37) and Tell City (82-54). After a 56-45 win in the afternoon game of the semi-finals over Washington, Central entered the final with a 23-3 record. Many fans felt that the Bears were on track for the school's first State title, but bad luck struck again like it had in 1948 when Lee Hamilton injured his knee late in the State semi-final game. In '53, Bob Wessel broke a finger prior to the tournament, and that very well may have been the difference when the Bears fell to Terre Haute Gerstmeyer one game shy of the Final Four.

As Coach Walter Riggs prepared for what would be his seventh and final year as Central's head coach, the media played up the unique makeup of the '53-'54 Bears. The starting lineup was "the three Claytons and two Harolds," and someone came up with the nickname "Clayton's Canyon" in reference to Jerry, Joe and Arbin. The brothers joined junior Harold Malicoat and Harold Phelps, who were supported by several others, including Jerry Schreiber, who would later become a local icon as a golfer, and Mel Lurker, a sophomore who would later start at center for the 1959 national champion Evansville College Aces.

The '53-'54 Bears finished the regular season a respectable 12-7, losing six of their last seven games, but, once again, they pulled it together for the tournament. In the sectional, Central escaped with a one-point win over Lincoln before knocking off Bosse (70-60) for the title. Ft. Branch nearly ended the Bears' season the following Saturday afternoon, but Coach Riggs' boys survived and then took out Rockport to advance for the third straight year to the semi-finals.

With only 16 teams still standing, Central was on course to advance to perhaps the most memorable Final Four in IHSAA history, and no one will ever know how Jerry Clayton may have affected the signature moment in the annals of Indiana basketball. After a 56-45 win over Winslow, the Bears again fell one game short with another loss to Gerstmeyer, keeping them from joining the famous Final Four that included Muncie Central and tiny Milan and their superstar, Bobby Plump.

With his final high school season complete, Jerry joined Milan's Plump and Ray Craft on the Indiana All-Star team, and Jerry's talent did not go unnoticed. He was contacted by several college coaches, including Adolph Rupp from Kentucky and others from West Point and many Midwestern schools, but Clayton chose to remain close to home and joined some of his former teammates at Evansville College.

Clayton never missed a beat with his transition to college ball, and he quickly became a starter for Coach Arad McCutchan. As a freshman, he scored 35 points in a game to break the record of the school's first All-American, Gus Doerner, and he was eventually named All-Conference and an All-American himself as a freshman.

Jerry continued his spectacular play as a sophomore, and one of the highlights was a game against the University of Louisville. The Cardinals featured Charlie 'Moose' Tyra, a 6'8 mountain of a man who would become Louisville's first superstar and the first to have his jersey retired at the U of L. He would also become the #2 overall pick in the 1957 NBA draft and spend five seasons there, mostly with the Knicks. By all accounts, Clayton made a mockery of the matchup and "made Tyra look silly," even blocking the star's famous hook shots.

As the season progressed, Clayton performed well but now admits that he was not as dedicated off the court as he should have been. Near the midway point of the season, he shocked everyone during a game with Beloit, Wisconsin. At halftime, the Aces went to the locker room at the Armory, and when the team returned, Jerry did not. When asked what happened, the quiet, unassuming Clayton's response was simple. "I just quit," he answered.

Jerry maintains that it wasn't a sudden decision, that he had thought about it before, and fans speculated for years as to the real cause of the split. Clayton explained that he was just "young and immature and made some dumb decisions."

"I can't tell the truth without hurting a lot of people, and there's no sense telling it 57 years later," he said. "I don't look back."

DID YOU KNOW?

Jerry Clayton was a very good golfer at Central and still is even today. One of his teammates, both on the course and the court, was fellow local legend Jerry Schreiber, a nine-time City golf champion.

In the blink of an eye, Clayton's basketball days were over, and one can only imagine what might have been had he completed his college years. Because of his abbreviated college career, he will never be listed as he probably should be in relation to other local greats, but it doesn't change the fact that he was a special talent. He was so good as a prepstar, in fact, that he was honored on the cover of *Life* magazine. Ironically, though the information was correct, the school mistakenly sent a photo of his twin, Joe, that actually appeared in the publication.

Today, Jerry spends a lot of time on the golf course and enjoys reminiscing occasionally about his days as a player. If he has regrets, he keeps them to himself, and he seems content with his place in local sports history.

As for the fans who were lucky enough to see him play, they will sing his praises for as long as folks will listen. "He truly had one of the best shots I ever saw for a big man," said Ed Cole, a local sports aficionado and past sportswriter for the *Courier.* "He is definitely one of our best of all time."

John Wessel, who played and later coached at Central, simply declared, "He was an offensive machine."

When asked to name Evansville's greatest player ever as part of a panel on the local radio show *Local Legends*, Harold Malicoat, a teammate and still close friend of Jerry's, never flinched and answered, "Without question, without a doubt, Jerry Clayton," to which Coach Wessel chimed in, "Amen!"

Malicoat also appreciates the good-natured ribbing he and Jerry have shared over the years, like his favorite "Jerry never met a shot he didn't like." He also revealed that Jerry would tell him "Harold, you get open and I'll fake it to you."

He says that Clayton would swear he was going to block Harold's shot because "I know you're going to miss it anyway." And when Harold would ask why Jerry would never pass him the ball, Clayton would respond, "I don't want to see you look bad."

As the ribbing will continue forever, so will the brotherhood between these two close friends. Jerry earned the respect of his teammates and fans, and his talent cannot be denied. As a high school player, he led his teams to three consecutive semi-state finals, and even during his short run at Evansville College, it can be said that his generation, players like Hugh Ahlering, John Harrawood, Harold Cox, Bob Walker, Bob Wessel, and Jerry stimulated the movement to build Roberts Stadium.

Out of respect for Jerry Clayton, the details of his departure from the Aces program shall not be disclosed and the mystery will live on. It is only fitting that the career of the man whose story continues to be told by fans over 50 years later ended in such dramatic fashion. We may never know all the details of the controversy, but the man's talent has never been a question.

Many feel that Clayton had NBA potential, and although we'll never know what may have been, we can be certain of what was. Without a doubt, Jerry Clayton must be counted among the very best to ever roam the courts of Evansville.

VINCENNES RIVET:
FROM JOKE TO JUGGERNAUT

Vincennes Rivet's 2011 State champs. Seated: Caroline Herman. Front row (L-R): Haley Potter (mgr.), Emily Montgomery, Mallory Niehaus, Amber Fowler, Sara Young, Lauren Tucker, Erin Wehrheim, Julia Finch, Casandra Brocksmith, Grace Waggoner. Back row: Charlie Waggoner (asst. coach), Brent Meeks (asst. coach), Sheila Herman (asst. coach), Tim Young (head coach), Bailey Dreiman, Lauren Herman, Elizabeth Keller, Allyson Wehrheim, Ellie Herman, Paula Westfall (asst. coach), Susan Brocksmith, Janice Jones (principal), Doug Ostendorf (AD), Jason Gries.

For many Indiana basketball purists, the game as it existed many years ago was what nature meant for it to be, but don't try to convince Tim Young and his Vincennes Rivet girls team of that. The tiny Catholic school with barely 100 students is one of the ten smallest of the 400 in Indiana, and pulling a 'Milan Miracle' would be next to impossible. But thanks to Title IX and the class system, schools like Rivet can offer young ladies the chance to be noticed by colleges and the opportunity to earn the title of State champion.

Even with the class system, it is no easy task to win a State title, and Rivet suffered through some hard times for many years. But thanks to the perseverance and dedication of some loyal supporters and the guidance of one man, the Patriots have become a powerhouse in Indiana Class A basketball.

Even with the limited population of athletes, Rivet has had some success in the past, like in boys tennis, where the team won several sectionals in a row before meeting stiff competition in the Terre Haute regional. The golf program is gaining respectability, as well, and the first girls team won their 2011 sectional by over 30 strokes with seven of the nine girls playing as freshmen. Rivet's baseball team has also prospered in recent years, making it to the State Final Four in 2009.

From a basketball standpoint, however, the efforts have been an exercise in futility for both the boys and girls, and the facilities and squad sizes sometimes resembled those from the movie *Hoosiers*. The senior class of the 2011-'12 school year included only thirteen males, and seven played basketball, and the girls program faces the same challenge each year.

The early years of Rivet girls basketball were uneventful, with the first seasons in the early '70s sponsored by the GAA (Girls Athletic Association) under Coach Pam Fry. After two years (1972-'74), Fay was followed by a long list of coaches who served from one to six years and experienced varying levels of success.

In the mid-to late '90s, Rivet lost by record margins, five of them to North Knox by deficits ranging from 67 to 83 points. In fact, from 1991 through 2003, the Patriots lost by 56 or more points 18 times and at one point they lost 42 straight games. With the program on the brink of collapse, the school's leaders were seeking a new coach in 2007, and the timing couldn't have been better.

As is often the case, turning a losing program into a winner is a combination of a class with exceptional talent and the right coach to lead them, and Rivet was no exception. The process began in 2001 when a man named Tim Young and some other parents decided to immerse themselves in the process of building a winning program. Tim began to coach a small group of third graders, and two years later, there were eight from that class with two girls, Elizabeth Keller and Ellie Herman, a grade behind.

When asked if he could see potential in the youngsters, Tim didn't hesitate to answer. "Yeah," he replied. "They all started preschool together. We got them together as quick as we could. We just wanted to develop a program where our kids could compete. We were tired of seeing our kids get beat to death. They (Rivet)

Chelsea Meeks was "a basketball junkie"
and one of the finest players in Rivet history.

of the program's existence – win a sectional. In the four previous seasons, Rivet had won 15 games and lost 95, and it took character just to stick with it. "When this group came in as freshmen, there were two seniors, Jenna Sievers and Chelsea Stafford," Coach Young said as we sat in his office in Vincennes. "They went through the tough times, and these girls vowed to win a sectional for the seniors."

The girls wasted no time establishing themselves as a force with two easy wins over Shakamak (56-41) and Eastern Greene (62-45) before dropping a close game to North Knox (50-47), the team that had bullied them for 25 years. They finished the regular season 16-3 after losses to Linton Stockton (52-50) and Northeast Dubois (65-59) and prepared to capture the sectional that had seemed out of reach for over three decades.

The sectional is one of the toughest in Class A with Barr-Reeve, Loogootee, North Davies, Washington Catholic and Shoals, but the Lady Patriots were well-prepared. After a 17-point win over Catholic, Rivet survived a nail-biter with Barr-Reeve (62-61) before knocking off Loogootee in the championship 51-38 to finally earn some hardware for their trophy case. Although their season ended in the regional with a 64-57 loss to Northeast Dubois, Coach Young's girls ignited a spark in Rivet fans that had all but died and sent the team's two seniors out with a well-deserved sectional title.

The '07-'08 team had shattered the losing stigma associated with the program, and the ultra talented freshman class had lived up to the hype under the leadership of sophomore Chelsea Meeks. Chelsea led the team with her 19.7 scoring average and was followed by four freshmen, Casandra Brocksmith (8.1 points), Sara Young (7.7), Mallory Niehaus (6.9) and Erin Wehrheim (6.2). Meeks also provided leadership, and with a strong contingent returning, a sectional in 2009 just wouldn't be enough.

With a new pep in their step, Coach Young's girls opened the next season with 11 straight wins, with only North Posey (56-53) and Bloomfield (38-37) coming within 11 points of the Lady Patriots. Early in the year, they were dealt a devastating blow when junior captain Chelsea Meeks went down with a season-ending ACL injury, but the youngsters stepped up to fill the void with Emily Montgomery starting and freshman Elizabeth Keller earning more minutes. After a 51-38 loss to White River Valley on January 12, Rivet then survived two barnburners against Loogootee (37-35) and Barr-Reeve (52-49) before two more wins to end the regular season.

At 17-1, the Patriots entered the sectional as one of the favorites, and after a 58-39 victory over North Daviess were faced once again with the task of facing Loogootee and Barr-Reeve. Rivet proved to be up to the task and squeaked by their nemeses to capture their second sectional in a row. In the North Daviess regional, the girls took care of Northeast Dubois 60-49 and South Central 55-49, and they downed University, a small private school in Carmel, for the Bedford Semi-state title.

In just two years, Tim Young's staff and the exceptional class of young athletes had turned a program that had been a perennial doormat with a record of 15-95 in the previous five seasons into one of the best Single-A programs in the state. The girls who entered Rivet only two years earlier were now on their way to Lucas Oil Stadium to play the biggest game of their lives.

With the program's first regional and semi-state trophies proudly displayed, the Lady Patriots prepared for a showdown with defending State champion Ft. Wayne Canterbury. With

couldn't compete. It wasn't any fun. You'd have maybe six or seven girls out for the team.

"We put that carrot out there real early," Tim continued, "that this is what we're striving for. We told their parents when they were fourth graders that we wanted to win a State championship. I think they thought we were crazy. There are a few who say to this day, 'We still think you were crazy.' But they were a dedicated bunch of young women who were not only good athletes but were also great individuals and super students."

Tim and his loyal staff went to work in 2007, and the improvements were immediate and drastic. Prior to his hiring, the school was lucky to have enough players to play a varsity schedule, much less a JV schedule, and in 2006-'07, 16 girls competed under the school's no-cut policy. The following year, 20 were out, and in 2009, the turnout was so large that Tim had to get permission to cut the number from 27 to 20.

In addition to the increase in quantity, the quality of Rivet's talent skyrocketed, as well, with the arrival of the fabulous freshman contingent in 2007. The strong class was eight ladies strong and included Erin Wehrheim, Mallory Niehaus, Casandra Brocksmith, Julia Finch, Lauren Tucker, Amber Fowler, Emily Montgomery, and Tim's daughter Sara Young. Returning from the previous season were seniors Jenna Sievers and Chelsea Stafford and three sophomores: Chelsea Meeks, Victoria Brocksmith and Macie McCoy.

The younger girls had been talking about winning a State championship for several years, but to reach that goal they had to first accomplish a feat that hadn't been done in the 36 years several thousand fans looking on, many clad in the school's familiar purple and gold, the ladies from Jean Frances Rivet appeared to be in control for most of the game, but elation quickly turned into heartbreak.

Trailing 53-44 with five minutes remaining, Canterbury mounted a comeback with Rivet struggling to hang on as the Cavaliers' Becky Pedro converted a three-point play with 13 seconds remaining to cut Rivet's lead to one. After a Sara Young free throw, Pedro delivered again at the four-second mark to tie the score at 62 and send the game into overtime.

In the extra period, Erin Wehrheim converted a bucket and two free throws, but Canterbury rode the momentum to a decisive 72-66 victory as the Patriots watched the celebration from the sideline. Wehrheim led the team with 18 points and 9 rebounds with Casandra Brocksmith contributing 12 and 7 and Sara Young scoring 11 points with 7 assists.

"I really thought we executed very well," Coach Young told the *Courier*. "The ball just rolled around and didn't go in at the end. We've hit some of those shots the last few weeks, but Canterbury hit them today."

With five sophomore starters and no seniors on the team, the girls from Rivet represented their school well and were left wondering what may have been had leading scorer Chelsea Meeks been healthy and in the starting lineup. The team did make some history, however, becoming the smallest school (92 students in '09) to play in the State Finals.

As Coach Young said to the *Courier*, "Sometimes close hurts," but with everyone returning and the Finals experience under their belts, the Lady Patriots were determined to return to Lucas Oil again.

When the sting of defeat wore off, the girls realized what they had accomplished and went to work. Coach Young greeted his entire squad at the first workouts in 2009 with seven players returning who had averaged six points or better the previous year: senior Chelsea Meeks (16.33) and juniors Sara Young (10.24), Casandra Brocksmith (9.12), Elizabeth Keller (8.16), Emily Montgomery (7.96), Erin Wehrheim (6.72) and Mallory Niehaus (5.96).

The girls seemed to play with a chip on their shoulder as they obliterated opponents in the early part of their 2009-'10 schedule, winning their first 13 games by an average winning margin of 29 points. After relatively close battles with rivals Loogootee (48-38) and Barr-Reeve (60-55), they continued the onslaught with huge wins over North Daviess (61-26), North Central (69-26), Northeast Dubois (64-47) and Princeton (69-44) to finish the regular season a perfect 20-0.

After easy sectional wins over North Daviess (65-28) and Shoals (69-51), the Patriots sweated out a triple overtime thriller for a 50-48 win over Barr-Reeve to capture their third consecutive sectional. They then waltzed through the regional and semi-state and made reservations once again for another date with powerful Ft. Wayne Canterbury.

In the final, the teams once again matched each other blow for blow, but as the duel played out, the Cavaliers' senior All-Stater Tabitha Gerardot's powerful inside presence was too much for Rivet. The 69-65 loss marked the end of the career of Chelsea Meeks, who once again led the team in scoring at 15.8 per game. "Chelsea's a basketball junkie," Tim Young said when asked about his lone senior starter. "It's hard to tell how many points she would have scored in her career if she hadn't had to sit out her junior year with an ACL tear."

Elizabeth Keller fights for the ball.
(Photo courtesy of the Vincennes Sun Commercial)

Meeks finished her career with 1,364 points, which might project to over 1,700 without the injury, according to Coach Young, a total that would have made her the top scorer in both the history of the school and the county. Her point total places her second on the Rivet's all-time scoring list behind Kelly Lane [Clauss], who had scored 1,663 and was named a member of the Indiana Basketball Hall of Fame's Silver Anniversary team in 2008. For her efforts, Chelsea was named All-Conference all four years, was Academic All-State, and was named the Southwest Indiana Player of the Year in 2010. In 2011, Meeks played in all 31 games for William Jewell College in Liberty, Missouri and averaged 9.8 points and 3.8 rebounds as a freshman.

Chelsea never got a State championship medal, but she was an integral part of the emergence of Rivet girls basketball. Her leadership would be sorely missed at Rivet, but the freshman phenoms of '07-'08 were approaching their final season together, and anything short of a State title just wouldn't do.

With the 2010-'11 season approaching, a senior-laden squad began their quest for the Holy Grail, and once again they flexed their muscles early by obliterating Shakamak 82-11 in the opener before comfortably winning their next 15 games. The only real test of the regular season was another dogfight with Barr-Reeve, which the Patriots won 49-48.

Rivet completed their second straight perfect regular season with a 44-26 win over Princeton and then easily dispatched Loogootee (66-29) and North Daviess (45-23) to set up the highly anticipated rematch with Barr-Reeve. Rivet's seniors had tangled with the Vikings seven times in their four years with six of the seven games decided by three points or less and Rivet winning all seven.

As the game unfolded, Rivet looked every bit the state's #1-ranked team as they led by 19 in the third quarter, but the Vikings would not go quietly. With a furious rally, Barr-Reeve pulled within four points, but some clutch free throws by freshman Bailey Dreiman secured the win to complete the four-year sweep over Barr-Reeve. With leading scorers Emily Montgomery and Sara Young in trouble much of the game, Dreiman had answered the call, and Rivet was led by junior Elizabeth Keller's 17 points.

In the regional, Rivet defeated Northeast Dubois 47-35 in workmanlike fashion and then downed Tecumseh 59-28 thanks to more steady play by Sara Young. A natural leader, Young had to step up her leadership a few weeks earlier when Erin Wehrheim went out with a torn ACL. Sara's job as the point was to run the offense, and in the regional final, she also heated up from long range with three of five three-pointers. "I just want to run my dad's basketball team," Sara explained to *Vincennes Sun-Commercial* journalist Tom Graham. "I want to make sure my teammates are scoring, and as long as we win, that's all that matters. I know they feed off me as a leader. If I can score, it creates openings for everybody else."

Early in the semi-state against Jac-Cen-Del, starter Emily Montgomery suffered damage to ligaments in her ankle, but her teammates pulled through to record a 53-38 win. With Emily on crutches the following week, the girls prepared for a third consecutive trip to the State Finals, and this time they wouldn't have to deal with Tabitha Gerardot and Ft. Wayne Canterbury.

For the first time, the finals were held in Ft. Wayne, and the Rivet fans made the long drive to hopefully witness a fairy tale ending to this Cinderella story. Even with Wehrheim and Montgomery still limited from their injuries, the Patriots competed hard from start to finish against Turkey Run. Rivet took a 21-16 lead to the locker room at halftime and led by as many as 11 in the third period, and as Turkey Run inched closer, the Lady Patriots closed out the game at the foul line with Bailey Dreiman connecting four times and Casandra Brocksmith sealing the win with 16 seconds remaining as Coach Young emptied the bench to set off the celebration. Behind Brocksmith's 11 points and a season-high 17 from Mallory Niehaus, the girls had lived up to their billing and delivered the happily-ever-after ending.

The Lady Patriots had finally slain the dragon and earned a centerpiece for the school's trophy case. With the talented seniors leading the way and support from underclassmen, Rivet had completed the perfect season with a 28-0 record with an average winning margin of over 26 per game. As one might expect, they did it with a balanced attack, with five seniors, Casandra Brocksmith, Sara Young, Emily Montgomery, Mallory Niehaus and Erin Wehrheim, averaging between 8.2 and 9.7 points per game and junior Elizabeth Keller right behind at 6.7.

With no one over six-feet tall, Rivet became adept at playing Coach Young's style, with eight to ten players in the rotation playing "up-tempo for 84 feet." Tim also isn't shy about explaining the keys to developing his system. "When they're young, we emphasize ball-handling, passing and catching," Young revealed, "and when they're big enough, we get into shooting. When they reach the fifth or sixth grade, we really stress defense, a man-to-man, get-in-your-face style where we press 84 feet." The offense is a 'dribble-drive' offense where the Patriots "keep the paint pretty clean" to allow for penetration.

In addition, Coach Young leaves no doubt about the importance put on conditioning and the somewhat unique philosophy the coaches use. "When I played, you paced yourself during practice because you knew at the end you were going to get on the line and run," Young explained. "Most of our drills encompass running the court and fast-paced movement. I'd rather condition them with the ball and do cardio on bikes and ellipticals."

Tim also offers praise for his devoted staff and points out that each puts in countless hours for a salary of $1. Paula Westfall has coached since 2001 and started the girls basketball clinics, and Sheila Herman serves as the JV coach. Brent Meeks (the father of Chelsea and little sister Peyton) and Charlie Waggoner assist as well and actually play an unusual role.

"Charlie Wagoner and Brent Meeks do all the substitutions," Coach Young told me. "That allows me to watch the game and I don't have to worry about how many minutes someone's been on the floor. It worked really well. After you get beat two years in a row at State, you start to analyze how you're doing things. They know what I'm thinking. I look at them and they know what to do."

By all accounts, Tim Young is a stickler for details and always strives for perfection, and he learned much of his basketball from one of the finest coaches our area has ever seen. Gene Miiller has compiled a magnificent career at Vincennes and currently at Washington, and Tim served as Gene's freshman coach at Vincennes Lincoln.

"He taught me a lot of things about the game. He's a great basketball mind," Young said. "With Gene, there were four seasons of the year – spring, summer, fall and basketball season. He taught me how to watch a game. Most people watch the ball, but the game happens away from the ball, what they did to get people open and how teams play defense off the ball. He taught me how to scout."

Under the guidance of Tim and his staff, the class of 2011 transformed the program at Rivet and lived up to the expectations of the fans. In a program that was wallowing in despair when they arrived, they won 93% of their games (96-7) in their four years, went unbeaten in the Blue Chip Conference three times and captured four sectionals, three regionals, three semi-states and a State championship.

During those years, they earned the affection of an entire community with their play and their quirky superstitions, like always standing in the same order during the National Anthem or when running onto the floor, playing the same music in the locker room, and insisting that the same bus driver (Nate from Auto Haus) take the wheel on trips to the State Finals. The girls also earned respect as students and citizens as they did volunteer work and compiled a team GPA of over 3.8, producing the class valedictorian (Amber Fowler) and two tied for salutatorian (Erin Wehrheim and Sara Young).

Five of the 2011 seniors finished their careers near the top of the school's all-time scoring list: Casandra Brocksmith (#5, 920 points), Sara Young (#6, 916), Erin Wehrheim (#8, 705), Emily Montgomery (#9, 702), and Mallory Niehaus (#14, 610). Of that group, three earned college scholarships, Casandra to DePauw, Emily to Danville Junior College and Sara to USI. The other two had opportunities but chose not to play for academic reasons.

The departure of the seniors of 2011 will obviously leave a void, but the program is still in good hands, and according to Brent Meeks, it has flourished for several reasons. "We have amazing support from the parents to do whatever is needed, whether it be driving buses, keeping scorebooks, providing food for trips. They all pitched in," Meeks explained. "Coach Young's five-year record speaks for itself. There are countless hours of watching game film, scouting, and planning."

Young's work hasn't gone unnoticed by the community either. "He has really taken that program places," said Hugh Schaefer, a retired teacher from Knox County. "Tim is so dedicated, and the money he makes, he gives back to the school. People say 'Well, he has good players,' but he has good players because he works with them twelve months a year. In fact, they almost dropped the program before he said he would take it."

With the 'super seniors' of 2011 leaving the nest, one would think that the cupboard might be bare, but the Rivet staff is creating a steady pipeline for the future. Tim said that there "are some good ones coming" from the grade school, and he understands what it takes to succeed. "It's just a lot of good people working together and teaching the fundamentals," he said. "We have great junior high coaches like Kevin Greenwood and John Anderson and Doug Halter and Don Altstadt from the past. Most of the kids have the athletic ability. It's just a matter of taking the time."

As proof that the system is truly in place, the 2011-2012 team, after losing 90% of the scoring from the previous year, fashioned an impressive season, finishing 18-4 and losing only to South Knox, Barr-Reeve twice and to 2A State champ Mater Dei by five points. Though they fell this time in a close game to Barr-Reeve in the sectional, the latest Lady Patriots played the system well with balanced scoring and suffocating defense.

The time Tim Young has given to the program has inspired a renaissance at the small Vincennes school, and it all began with a talented group of young ladies who dedicated themselves to one goal. The transformation in five short years has been truly remarkable, and the efforts of everyone involved have produced a rise from the ashes to one of the most consistent basketball programs in the state of Indiana.

AREA SCHOOLS WITH THE MOST IHSAA GIRLS SECTIONAL TITLES (AS OF 2011)

17 – Jasper
14 – Castle
13 – Memorial
13 – Vincennes Lincoln
10 – Boonville
10 - Bosse

AREA SCHOOLS WITH THE MOST IHSAA GIRLS REGIONAL TITLES (AS OF 2011)

Bosse – 7 ('82, '83, '84, '85, '88, '97, '07)
Memorial – 6 ('98, '00, '04, '06, '10, '11)
Washington – 5 ('93, '94, '95, '96, '97)
Jasper – 4 ('78, '79, '99, '01)
Vincennes Lincoln – 4 ('76, '78, '81, '08)
Castle – 3 ('01, '05, '06)
North Posey – 3 ('87, '02, '03)
Vincennes Rivet – 3 ('09, '10, '11)
Washington Catholic – 3 ('99, '01, '04)
Forest Park – 2 ('86, '00)
Southridge – 2 ('89, '98)

HISTORY MAKER

Emily Montgomery, a key cog in the Vincennes Rivet basketball State championship run in 2011, made some Indiana history two years earlier. It all began when Emily was a youngster and she played boys cub baseball instead of playing softball like the other girls. Because the boys' and girls' fields were far apart, Emily's parents, Mike and Laura, asked if their daughter could play on her brother's team to avoid transportation conflicts. Emily was accepted and held her own and even tried out for the all-star team and made it, and she continued in the boys league until age twelve.

As a high school freshman, Emily was content to focus on basketball in the spring, but at a tiny school like Rivet, the number of athletes is limited. A year later, she was an integral part of a basketball team that made it to the final game of the State tournament before losing to Ft. Wayne Canterbury, and in the spring, she was approached with an unusual request. Corey, Emily's brother, was a member of the school's baseball team, and the team had only nine players. When Logan Johnson, one of Corey's teammates, injured a leg, he was asked to stand at third base so the team wouldn't have to forfeit. Corey and Coach Billy Beard were aware of Emily's history and asked if she would consider playing. At first, she turned them down, but eventually she relented, and because Rivet had no girls softball team, she was eligible to play.

"Rivet is such a small school," said Laura Montgomery, Emily's mother. "It's like family and they needed players, and that's what you do at our school. People step up." Although Coach Beard usually used a designated hitter for Emily, she did become the starter in left field next to her brother in center.

In the spring of '09, the Patriots fought their way through the IHSAA tournament and into the State Finals. With the world watching, Emily started both games and even batted once, and although Rivet lost 14-1 to Lafayette Central Catholic in the final game, Emily got her moment in the sun at Victory Field in Indianapolis. On that day, Friday, June 19, Emily Montgomery made Indiana history by becoming what is believed to be the only female to play in an IHSAA State championship game in both a boys and girls team sport in the same year, a feat that will likely never be accomplished again.

Emily Montgomery in the dugout with her brother Corey

JOE MULLAN: THE WHITE SHADOW

Joe Mullan with his Bosse team in 1995. (Photo courtesy of the Evansville Courier)

Of the thousands of men who have coached Indiana high school basketball over the last 100 years, only a special few approach a winning percentage of 80%, and the man who may hold the best record in Indiana history is Evansville's own Joe Mullan.

Joe not only witnessed some of the finest players in local history, but he played his high school ball during possibly the most talent-rich era our part of the state has ever seen. Joe spent his first eleven years in Washington, Indiana and admits that his dream was to be a Washington Hatchet. While there, he looked up to a superstar athlete named Bud Garland, who coincidentally became a local legend himself as a track coach at Bosse.

When Mullan moved to Evansville in 1954, his considerable athletic talent immediately meshed with a strong group from North Side Little League #7. At the time, there were eight leagues at four Evansville parks: East Side at Rotherwood and Division, where the Aces play today; West Side near Helfrich; South Side, downtown at Sunset Park; and the North Side at Garvin Park. Joe's team, Finke Furniture, who wore black, were coached by Bill 'Dee' Mattingly, the father of the Mattingly boys, Jerry, Randy, Michael and Donnie, and Joe's father, Elbert Mullan, was Dee's assistant.

With teammates like future local legends Jerry Mattingly (Rex Mundi High School) and Paul Gries (Mater Dei), it is no surprise that Joe's team won the league. But the other teams could boast future stars as well, such as pitching great Mickey Martin (Coca Cola, the red team), Mike Volkman (Police, the blue team)

and Dave Schellhase (Optimist, the green team), who all later played at North High School with Joe.

In pony league, Mullan made the league's all-star team as a pitcher/second baseman and won a state championship with teammates like Martin, Schellhase, Gary Grieger, Gerard Buente, Ron Mills, Don Engbers, and others. The team fell at the regional level, however, to a team from Hamtramck, Michigan.

Joe played his pony and colt league ball (15- and 16-year-olds) at iconic Bosse Field, and his all-star teams advanced to World Series play both years. Once again joining players like Schellhase, Bob Griese (Rex Mundi), Steve Schroer (North) and others, the boys beat Hamtramck, a community surrounded by Detroit, two games out of three in Springfield, Illinois. As 16-year-olds, the team, which featured many of the same boys plus Mike Madriaga (North), Jim Meyers (Bosse), Tom Unger (Mater Dei), Larry Zimmer (Memorial) and Gerald Brizius (Central) won the regional in Lafayette, Indiana and advanced to the World Series in Ontario, California, a trip that offered Joe his first airplane experience.

Joe also competed and stood out as an athlete at North, and many of his coaches were among the finest in Evansville history. As a cub football player, he quarterbacked an undefeated team coached by Jim Rausch and Frank Schwitz, who both became very successful basketball coaches. As a freshman, his undefeated football team was coached by Don Watson, who later headed up the football program at Harrison. Mullan even saw some varsity action as a freshman when he ran onto the field at 5 feet tall and 87 pounds to join classmates Larry Lindenschmidt (fullback) and

John Mominee (halfback) as they ran out the clock in a win over Boonville.

Although Joe eventually grew to 5'7, 155 pounds, he knew that football was not his future, so he focused on baseball and basketball and was good enough in cross country to qualify for the State meet his senior year. On the basketball court, Joe was a fiery competitor under head coach Jim Rausch, and he played alongside one of the finest duos in Evansville history. Mike Volkman was a sweet-shooting guard (with a two-handed set shot) who played at Evansville College before transferring to the University of Miami to join NBA Hall of Famer Rick Barry. The second member of the dynamic duo was Dave Schellhase, the scoring machine who starred at Purdue and led the nation in scoring in 1966 with his 32.5 average.

In the spring, Mullan was a standout on the diamond, and the teams he was a part of were possibly the greatest in the city's history. The Huskies were led by one of the most potent pitching duos ever, Steve Schroer (8-0) and Mickey Martin (8-0, 0.0 ERA). The team was named Indiana's mythical state champion, and an example of their prowess were the post-season honors. In 1962, the *Courier* named its All-City team, and of the 11 players so honored, 6 were Huskies: Joe at second base and named the "captain", Gerard Buente (1B), Steve Fritz (LF), Herb Harrington (CF), Dave Schellhase (C) and Mickey Martin (P). Joining them were Tom Hunger (3B, Mater Dei), Mark Clark (SS, Reitz), Gerald Brizius (RF, Central) and pitchers Steve Barton (Memorial) and Paul Gries (Mater Dei).

With a great athletic career behind him, Mullan knew that his best sport was baseball and considered a half-scholarship to Murray State, but when coach Rausch's alma mater, George Washington University, offered a full basketball scholarship, the choice was a no-brainer. So Joe spent his college years just four blocks from the White House, and when he graduated in 1966, he was ready to go to work.

For the first four years after leaving GW, he taught and coached at a junior high in Arlington, Virginia, but in the fall of 1970, he received a call from Mr. Rausch telling him that Clarence Riggs was stepping down as North's AD and that a position was available. Equipment manager Jack Weatherholt replaced Mr. Riggs and Joe was brought in to handle the equipment and to teach Health, P.E. and Driver's Ed. In addition, Joe was asked to be the head wrestling coach, a position for which he wasn't particularly qualified. He had learned the basics in Arlington, but he found himself handling discipline and conditioning while two knowledgeable wrestlers taught the techniques while he sometimes sat on the top row of bleachers watching Mr. Rausch coach basketball.

By his third year at North, he was in his element as the freshman basketball coach, replacing Dick Hoagland with Keith Kohlmeyer as his unpaid assistant. In 1977, Coach Rausch retired and long-time assistant Bob Walker took over the program and named Joe as his assistant. The two worked well together, winning three straight sectionals with players like Mike Pendleton, Robert Farmer, Coach Walker's son Kent, John Miles, Don Patton and a young freshman named Brian Miles.

During his early years at North, Mullan applied for head coaching jobs as they came available, and he admits that he was close to giving up. But when jobs opened up in 1980, he decided to give it one more try. When City AD Jim Graham asked if he would prefer the position at Reitz or Bosse, Joe was quick to answer. "I'll take Bosse," he replied. "Reitz is a football school."

Mullan had also watched Bosse's young players when they competed against North and saw the potential. So as Bix Branson replaced popular Jim Barnett at Reitz, Joe inherited the Bosse program from legendary Bulldog coach Jim Myers. Coming into the situation, Joe believed that the boys needed to be free to show their skills, saying, "I knew from day one that we were going to press full court and run the floor."

Mullan was also very cognizant of a factor that was present but was seldom discussed publicly, and it had nothing to do with basketball. There was no doubt that race was an issue, and it needed to be dealt with. Joe was fortunate that he had coached black athletes in Arlington, and his approach was simple and to the point.

"My success at Bosse started the summer I got the job," Joe confided. "I went to Paul Schmidt (Bosse's principal) and he gave me a list of who had played before, and I went to each individual's home and talked to the family and told them how proud I was to be their son's coach. I wanted them to feel like they were a part of Bosse basketball. Being a white person, I think this was something they had never experienced, a white coach coming into their homes and sitting down to talk to them."

So Joe Mullan went to work building his legacy. In the summer of 1980, he showed his boys he was interested in them by stopping by the park near Lincoln Elementary to watch pickup games. Often, there were no words spoken, just a coach who cared enough to spend time with them. He also swapped sweat with them during open gym, demonstrating that even as a 36-year-old man, he was a competitor.

Mullan also surprised them by saying there were no written rules but that they shouldn't mistake that for leniency, and folks who know Joe were aware of his firm control. "I was a disciplinarian," Joe explained. "I always told the kids, it's 'yes, sir' and 'no, sir' and you hand the ball to the referee, and if there's anybody who's going to complain, it's me. I said, 'If you complain, you'll be sitting on the bench.'"

DID YOU KNOW?

The manager of Joe Mullan's pony league all-star team was Gene Whitehead, who played on the 1944 Bosse State champion basketball team.

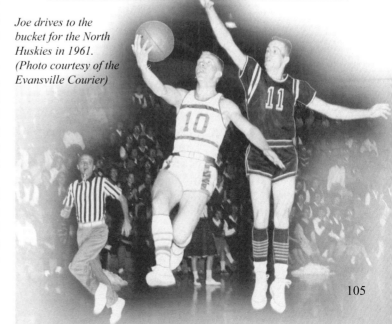

Joe drives to the bucket for the North Huskies in 1961. (Photo courtesy of the Evansville Courier)

Because of Joe's initial approach, the racial tensions lessened and the basketball culture at Bosse vastly improved. "My first couple teams were all black players, and I think we just developed such a rapport with the families," Mullan explained. "They used to call me the White Shadow (after the popular television show), and Macon Dowell, the father of superstar Derrick Dowell, was 'Boss Dawg', and he used to sit in the front row."

With everyone on the same page, Joe began his run at Bosse, and the immediate results reflected the abundant talent that was ripe to be harvested at the near east side school. During his first season in 1980-'81, Joe and his assistants worked with the varsity and JV while Harold Malicoat continued his masterful work with the freshmen. Malicoat had earned a reputation as a teacher of fundamentals, and Mullan could see the fruits of Harold's labor and the abundant skills of the young Bulldogs. "There was no doubt that Bosse was where I wanted to be," Mullan said. "I could see the talent; it was unbelievable for this area."

Joe's first team finished 16-4, led by junior Myron Christian and sophomore Derrick Dowell, and with youngsters like freshmen Mark Freels and Evie Waddell coming up the pipeline, groundbreaking success was just around the corner. After a slow-down close game win over Heritage Hills (a tactic Bosse would see several times), the '81-'82 team breezed through their early schedule setting up a showdown with the powerful North Huskies, led by Robbie Jones, Todd Erwin and eventual North hall of famer Brian Miles.

U of E coach Dick Walters was the color man for the Channel 14 telecast of the game with a packed house at North's gym looking on. For over 30 of the 32 minutes, it looked like Bosse had met their match, but some late game heroics produced a miraculous finish. Trailing by 11 with 1:08 to go, the Bulldogs swarmed North with their trademark man-to-man full-court press and closed within 2 (all without the benefit of the 3-point line). As time wound down, the ultra-confident Myron Christian launched a midcourt missile that found its target, and the Huskies could never recover, losing in overtime.

When the sectional rolled around, Bosse stood at 20-0, including another overtime win over North, and fans looked forward to a third dogfight between the Huskies and Bulldogs. But the rematch was not to be when a strong Harrison team, led by Reggie Hayes, Defferon Jones and Mike Newman, upset the mighty Huskies. The Bulldogs then downed the tired Warriors 60-27 to capture the Evansville Sectional.

Bosse continued to dominate in the regional with cakewalks over Vincennes and Heritage Hills and then survived two close games over Bedford North Lawrence and Terre Haute South to capture the semi-state. In the Final Four, the Bulldogs fell to Gary Roosevelt in the afternoon and Plymouth, led by Scott Skiles, captured the coveted State title.

Joe and his boys finished the year 27-1 behind the talented tandem of Dowell and Christian, who accounted for two-thirds of the team's points and over half of its rebounds. The staff had done a beautiful job of developing a winning formula with five supporting players who knew their roles and averaged between 3 and 6 points: seniors Monty King (5.5), Doug Bell (5.1) and Ken Claybourne (3.6) and sophomores Evie Waddell (4.5) and Mark Freels (3.5). But even with Indiana All-Star Christian and his two classmates leaving, the cupboard was anything but bare for Coach Mullan.

Joe filled the voids with Jeff Chestnut, Chris Johnson, Dave Kendrick and Robert Calhoun, and with Dowell, Waddell and Freels leading the way, the team began a season that would elevate Bosse into rarefied air among all who have played Indiana basketball.

The Bulldogs dominated their '82-'83 schedule and made some history by becoming one of only a few Indiana schools to complete two consecutive regular seasons with unblemished records. They also received national recognition when they were ranked #4 in the final *USA Today* poll in 1983, but the dream run ended with a heartbreaking four overtime loss to Princeton in the Evansville Regional.

Following the departure of superstar Derrick Dowell, Joe continued his winning ways, finishing 23-6 in '83-'84 for a four-year record of 91-12 (88%), and his fifth season was impressive, as well. With perhaps the smallest lineup of his career, 6'2 Junie Jordan, 6'0 Jerome Merriweather, 6'0 Jeff Thomas, 5'11 Robert Calhoun and 6'0 Tim Merriweather, the overachievers knocked off undefeated Princeton in the regional and advanced to the semi-state before falling to State favorite L&M, who then fell to Gary Duncan's Southridge Raiders.

Joe's early years at Bosse set the stage for a very successful career, and the culture that was created was the cornerstone. "They weren't just good basketball players; they were great human beings," Joe explained. "It was a blue collar community with very strong values. The parents were very supportive of their sons and of me, and they knew I cared about their sons."

Mullan also credits his assistants, Marshall Mason, Harold Malicoat, Brad Frasier and Mark Schwitz, and he deeply appreciated the opportunity to coach at Bosse given by principal Paul Schmidt. He feels fortunate for the chance to have guided the young gentlemen over the years, and a handful of players and teams stand out to him.

When asked to name a few who were a cut above, the list of memorable players began with Dowell and Christian, two Indiana All-Stars who went on to excellent college careers, at Southern Cal and Indiana State/Kentucky Wesleyan, respectively. Joe then mentioned his third Indiana All-Star, Andy Elkins. Joe recalled when Andy entered Bosse as a 5'11 point guard who grew to 6'6 as a sophomore. Andy began his sophomore basketball season on the bench with headaches from a concussion suffered on the gridiron as the school's quarterback, but by February, he was starting for Joe at center.

"He was such a great shooter, and he had a nasty streak," Joe revealed. "When he posted up, he would use his elbows and get by with it. He was smart. He was respected by the other players because of his toughness. He was meek-looking, but they realized he was pretty tough."

Mullan also placed Elkins' team his junior year right up there with the '82 and '83 teams. The 1989-'90 team finished one game short of the Finals in a game that many feel they should have won. Elkins and Ron Darrett led a strong team that included starters Rohi Fentress, Mike Cheaney (Calbert's cousin) and point guard Chris Clayton, and the boys advanced to the Terre Haute Semi-state to take on the Bedford North Lawrence Stars and their much ballyhooed star Damon Bailey.

As everyone knows, IU's Bob Knight had publicly proclaimed in *Sports Illustrated* that Bailey could have started for the Hoosiers as an eighth grader, and most fans across the state wanted to see him win a championship. According to fans who saw the game, a drastic turn in the game occurred when Coach Knight appeared in the tunnel of the Hulman Center to watch the game.

Bosse's 1981-'82 State Final Four team. Front Row (L-R): head coach Joe Mullan, Milt Stirsman (equip. mgr.), E. Douglas (student mgr.), Ryan Gray (student mgr.), Marshall Mason (asst. coach), Harold Malicoat (asst. coach). Back Row (L-R): Doug Bell, Jeff Chestnut, Monty King, Myron Christian, Derrick Dowell, Ken Claybourne, Randy Fintress, Evie Waddell, Mark Freels, David Kendrick, Tim Lander, Mike Rogers.

We will never know what might have been, but from that point on, Bosse's 9-point lead evaporated and the Bosse team that Coach Mullan described as "a machine" could only sit back and watch as Bedford went on to capture the State title.

The 6'4 Darrett was another of the special players Joe mentioned, along with Evie Waddell and Mark Freels from the back-to-back undefeated teams from '81-'82 and '82-'83. He also cited a player that he declared "one of the best athletes to ever play in Evansville," Dirkk Surles. Surles was a 6'2 ½" leaper who could high jump 6'9 and was a slashing guard who could penetrate and dunk with ease. "He was very intelligent," Mullan said. "He was in all the accelerated classes and had a great personality as a team leader." Surles used his intelligence to secure a scholarship to George Washington University and led the Colonials to two wins in the 1993 NCAA tournament before falling 72-64 to Michigan.

When Joe Mullan stepped down in 1991, he left a legacy of success, and many of his players truly appreciate what he did for them and for the school. "We all came together; we were a big family," Evie Waddell said on the *Local Legends* radio show honoring Joe. "My father wasn't always around," Waddell continued, "and Coach Mullan always made sure I did the right thing. He's always been more than a coach to me."

Mullan stayed out of coaching for three years before coming back as an assistant for his successor Gene Ballard and then retired from teaching and coaching in 1999. He says that he doesn't miss coaching and that he's proud that over half of his athletes went to college and that several still stay in touch. As was his style on the sidelines, he has preferred to keep things simple in retirement as he and his wife Judy enjoy life on Kentucky Lake. He also hasn't fallen victim to our high-tech society, saying that he will be one of the few who can say they never even turned on a computer.

Mullan finished his 11-year run at Bosse with 7 City and SIAC titles, 5 sectionals, 4 regionals and 1 semi-state championship, and two of his teams ('82 and '83) finished the regular season ranked #1 in the state. During one stretch from 1981 to 1985, his teams won 25 straight city games and 35 straight in the SIAC. But his greatest feat was his entire body of work.

Although he admits that he will likely never make the Indiana Basketball Hall of Fame because of his short career as a head coach, his numbers are among the greatest of all time. Complete records are hard to find for many coaches, but enough were found to put Joe's career in perspective. For example, of the 140 winningest coaches still active in 2012 who have at least ten years of head coaching experience, only 14 have topped the 70% mark in winning percentage. Only three are better than 75%: Mike Hackett at .802 (Munster, 13 seasons); Scott Hicks at .765 (Indianapolis Broad Ripple, 13); and Steve Bennett at .765 (New Castle, 23).

Records could not be found for greats like Jack Butcher, Howard Sharpe and Bill Stearman, but Joe Mullan's 79% career percentage places him at or near the top of Indiana's all-time list with his career record of 209-55. However you want to slice it, Joe Mullan's record speaks for itself, but his impact reached deeper than wins and losses. Joe was a living example of how barriers can be torn down and how trust and leadership can produce amazing results. His back-to-back undefeated seasons place him in rare company, and his 79% win percentage might very well place him at the top of the list of Indiana's greatest coaches.

DID YOU KNOW?
Bosse's Evie Waddell and Mark Freels are very likely the only basketball players in Evansville history to play three seasons without losing a game to a city school.

MARTY SIMMONS:
THE MAN FOR THE JOB

As Marty Simmons goes about his business of building a basketball program at the University of Evansville, he understands the challenges he faces every day as the head coach of a small private school trying to compete at the Division I level. He knows that the upper tier of recruits each year are beyond his grasp, requiring him and others like him to work even harder to build a team. Simmons has toiled tirelessly to find student-athletes who can help the program, and to find a model for the type of player he needs, all he has to do is look in the mirror.

Marty is a native of Lawrenceville, Illinois, and the town's small high school, enrollment 600-plus, has a very impressive basketball history. As a boy, Marty was well aware of the school's legacy, and his greatest role model was his older brother Walt, who led Lawrenceville to its first State championship in 1972, the first year of class basketball in Illinois. Walt played for legendary coach Ron Felling, who later gained national fame as Bob Knight's assistant at IU.

Lawrenceville also won a State title in 1974 and featured the state's leading scorer in 1976, Jay Shidler, 'The Blond Bomber' who went on to be a part of the national champion Kentucky team under Joe B. Hall that defeated Duke 94-88. Dave Brooks, a '79 grad, took his talents to Navy, where he earned MVP honors and was the Middies' scoring leader until 'The Admiral', David Robinson, came along.

Marty was an early bloomer, and with a strong supporting cast, his presence only added to the legacy of Lawrenceville basketball. As an eighth grader, his middle school team finished second in the state, and as he entered high school, the 6'1 freshman practiced with the varsity immediately. "I didn't start him the first game," said Coach Felling. "I told him, 'You've never played a game and it's not right to play you before I've seen you play at the varsity level.' He played and got 8 or 9 points and 6 or 7 rebounds, and I started him the next game and he started every game after that.

"You could tell right then he had the maturity, the IQ for the game. He wasn't the fastest, but I'll tell you what, he had a big heart and played very, very hard. He was on a mission every time he went out on the floor. He had a terrific set of hands, and he could score inside and out."

Marty's team finished 27-4 his freshman year before losing in the Sweet 16, and the following year the Indians lost again in the Sweet 16 to end a 28-3 season. One of the losses his sophomore year was a 47-46 loss in the holiday tournament to Effingham, a team led by future IU starter Uwe Blab. But that loss in the 1981 State tournament would be Marty's last.

Growing to an eventual 6'5, Marty was a four-year letter winner in golf, baseball and basketball, and his prowess on the hardwood placed him among the greatest in Illinois history. As a freshman, he averaged 13.6 points and 6.5 rebounds, and as a sophomore, his numbers improved to 20.7 and 11.0, enough to merit a position on the AP All-State team and first team status on the *Decatur Herald*'s All-Area and Evansville *Courier*'s All-Southern Illinois teams.

Nicknamed 'The Mule' because of his ability to carry the load, Simmons led the Indians to two consecutive Class A State titles, in 1982 with a 67-53 win over Monmouth and in '83 with a 44-39 win over Flanagan. During each year, Marty and his teammates navigated the schedule unblemished, finishing each season with a 34-0 record.

Marty finished his junior year with a 24.5 average with 10.7 rebounds per game and earned too many honors to list, including a spot on several All-State teams and recognition as the *Chicago Sun-Times* Player of the Year.

As a senior, Simmons' honors continued to flow, duplicating those from the previous year in addition to being named the state's Mr. Basketball after a season where he averaged 32 points and over 11 rebounds per game. Marty left Lawrenceville as the school's most decorated athlete after obliterating the school's scoring record with 2,986 points, a remarkable total for the pre-3-point era. His teams combined for a 123-7 record (95%) and won four conference titles, and his last two teams are the only ones in Illinois history to complete consecutive undefeated seasons.

Marty also set a state record with 128 points in four IHSA tournament games and was (and still is) the only player in Illinois history to score all his team's points in a half during the tournament. In addition, he holds Class A State tournament records for career free throws made (63 from 1980-'83) and rebounds in a career (136) and title game (19).

As one would expect, Simmons had many college options, but he chose IU over Illinois his junior year because Coach Felling and Coach Knight were a lot alike and IU's proximity to his hometown made Indiana a better fit. Marty joined a class that included Steve Alford, Darrell Thomas and Todd Meyer, and Marty saw substantial playing time as a freshman. The team even upset North Carolina in a game where Dan Dakich shut down Michael Jordan in his final year with the Tarheels.

IU went on to win a national championship in what would have been Marty's senior year, but circumstances prompted Simmons to rethink his future. According to Marty, he "was basically getting beat out and wanted to play more," so when assistant coach Jim Crews, who had recruited Marty, took the job at UE, Simmons followed him to Evansville.

Although he had to sit out a year, Marty's impact was immediate, and Coach Crews knew what Simmons would bring to the table as an athlete and as a role model. "To see how good a player he was, I don't think that took too much because of how productive he is," said Jim Crews from his home in Indianapolis. "He had great instincts for the game and made other people better, and I think that's carried over to his coaching.

"The best illustration of his leadership was the first year he came to U of E and sat out," Crews continued. "He changed the whole culture of my program, how you approach practices and games, how you listen to scouting reports, what you're doing off the floor with academics, holding people accountable. That's just leadership ability. Leaders lead. Marty and I had been together through the recruiting and at Indiana. He knew what was expected. Marty just took it and ran with it and has done a tremendous job in everything he has touched throughout his life."

Simmons came in the same year that Scott Haffner transferred to UE, and Dan Godfread red-shirted while Simmons sat out. Shortly after his arrival, Marty was introduced to a lovely lady by teammate Curtis Jackson at a soccer game, and he and Angie were married in 1986. When Simmons finally took the court, he didn't disappoint, averaging 22.4 points in 1986-'87 and leading the Aces as the team captain to the MCC title. His senior year, he finished sixth in the nation with his 25.9 average and finished ninth in the balloting for the AP College Player of the Year while leading the Aces to a 21-8 record.

Despite playing only two seasons, Marty left the program 22nd on U of E's all-time scoring list, and as he began to build a career, little did he know that he would one day sit in the same seat as coaches like Jim Crews and the beloved Arad McCutchan. After attempting to crack an NBA roster at camps for the Celtics, Pacers and Jazz, Marty spent a year with the LaCrosse (Wisconsin) Catbirds of the CBA and then two seasons in the World Basketball League for players 6'5 and under.

As his interest in pro ball diminished, Simmons actually interviewed for the freshman coaching job at Evansville North, and with Jim Crews mentoring him during the process, he decided to finish his Masters and accept a position as a non-paid assistant at U of E while Angie worked at Old National Bank.

In 1996, Marty took his first head coaching position at Wartburg College, a small school in Waverly, Iowa. After a 10-14 season, he was pleased to return 'home' to become a full assistant to Crews, and in '02, he was named head coach at SIU-Edwardsville. Simmons did well in Edwardsville, going 88-59 in five seasons, and when Jim Crews left to coach at West Point, Marty was the logical choice to replace him.

His first team in 2007-'08 finished 9-21, and the next year saw some drastic improvement as the Aces finished 17-14, winning 9 of 13 conference games. The team was led by Jason Holsinger, Shy Ely, Nate Garner and Pieter van Tongeren, and the boys enjoyed solid fan support with attendance of 111,400 for 19 home games.

The '08-'09 season was the last year with over 100,000 attendance, but Marty and his staff still continue to fight the uphill battles that small private schools face each year. By all reports, Marty is a tireless worker, and sometimes the coaching lifestyle can take its toll. As the years passed, fans couldn't help but notice that Simmons was putting on weight, and for someone in the public eye, the scrutiny can be hard to deal with. As his weight ballooned, Marty's friends and family were concerned, and after several interactions, he finally faced the situation and went to work.

"Angie was on me all the time," Marty confessed. "I heard that from a lot of people, and that's what got the ball rolling is that a lot of my family, my coaches, boosters, they all expressed their feelings. I took it as they cared about me."

Simmons admits that he was defensive about the topic but that he really didn't feel that bad — until he took a long hard look in the mirror, that is. "I don't know if I tricked myself, because I obviously had a problem," Marty explained. "I love to eat and I was stubborn. I didn't get the nickname 'The Mule' for nothing."

One of the catalysts for taking action was an exchange with Kirk Sarff, one of Marty's assistants. After a game in 2009, Sarff saw Simmons' intensity in the locker room and called Marty the next day. When he said, "Marty, I'm concerned," Simmons could tell by the tone of his voice that he was worried that he was putting their friendship on the line. "You need some help," he told Marty. "You need to get somebody who can coach you like you do those players."

Marty admits being angry and actually didn't speak to Sarff for a while, but the conversation as well as many before prompted him to reach the conclusion that "it was time." Sarff had previously contacted Pat Wempe, a local physical therapist, who introduced him to Jan Schenk, the owner of Perfect Plan.

Photo courtesy of the University of Evansville, Sports Information

Marty was a star at Lawrenceville High School.

"Listening to Jan's presentation gave me the belief that this was do-able," Marty said. "She made it sound like not only could we do it, but I could do it fast and still be able to eat." Marty went on to describe how there was no talk of calories or portion control or exercise, that she wanted him to be full. Meeting with Jan three times a week, Marty and Angie changed their lifestyle by eating lots of fruit and a baked potato every day and by following prescribed recipes. After a few weeks, the couple found themselves wanting to exercise, something they had missed, and as the plan progressed, the pounds melted away.

When I asked his maximum weight before the reduction, Marty smiled and politely declined, saying he would have to shoot me if he told. Out of respect, I pressed no further and simply congratulated him and Angie for their success.

In 2011, Colt Ryan, Kenny Harris, Denver Holmes, Ned Cox, Clint Hopf and Pieter van Tongeren reflected their coach's

tenacity when they faced a nearly impossible challenge. The local community had experienced a 55-year love affair with Roberts Stadium on the city's east side, and on February 26, 2011, a farewell celebration was planned for the final U of E men's game at the historic arena.

Thousands of fans took a final walk around the stadium's concourse to re-live the memories as they examined the displays of legendary high school and college players and teams who entertained basketball lovers through the years. Over 100 players, coaches and dignitaries from the past attended and were honored at halftime, including Evansville College/U of E greats like Jerry Sloan and Larry Humes and past coaches like Jim Crews and Dick Walters, the man who helped revitalize the program after the tragic plane crash in 1977.

With the retired jerseys of Aces legends Gus Doerner, Don Buse, Sloan and Humes peering down from the rafters, the young Aces were faced with a monumental task, delivering one final win for the emotional crowd. How they could focus and perform under such pressure is anyone's guess, but perform they did. Under the guidance of their fiery coach, the team sent the fans home with a final fond memory and gave Roberts Stadium the sendoff she deserved.

Colt Ryan was spectacular with 32 points and 13 of 14 free throws as the Aces defeated Illinois State 73-67. Evansville trailed 37-32 at halftime but came through when it counted as the final seconds ticked away. For the record, the final points at Roberts were scored by Illinois State's Kenyon Smith with four seconds remaining. The final Aces points were four free throws by Colt Ryan, and the final Aces field goal was scored by Forest Park's Clint Hopf with 2:09 remaining.

One of the highlights of the post-game celebration involved Coach Simmons. As Jim Crews addressed the audience, he sang the praises of his long-time assistant and then asked Marty to pull up his pants leg. To the crowd's delight, he flashed some red socks, a tribute to iconic Aces coach Arad McCutchan and the fashion statement he was known for during the heyday of Aces basketball.

During the celebration, several players also spoke, and the seniors were generous with their praise of Simmons. One after another spoke of his dedication and loyalty, and the tears flowed as they conveyed what his leadership meant to them. As fans sat and enjoyed the final moments in the treasured arena, few could argue that the program was not in some very capable hands.

Simmons fights the daily battles that come with the 'mid-major' label and searches for the formula that enables a school like Butler to compete for a national title against the big boys. "Duke can go to any player in the country with their name," Marty said. "We have to work 100 times harder to find guys who are also good enough academically. I think U of E was pretty darn close to where Butler is when Crews was here. (Scott) Haffner's team knocked out Gary Payton and Oregon State. Butler went a long time before they ever won a game in their conference tournament. We're getting there; we're moving into a state-of-the-art arena in one of the top ten conferences in the country."

Jim Crews isn't sold on the fact that Butler's success is due to a methodology by head coach Brad Stevens. He believes the process involves an element of luck as well, and proof that Evansville may not be that far away was the game in November of 2010 when Simmons' Aces knocked off the Bulldogs to end a 14-game winning streak at Hinkle Fieldhouse. Crews firmly believes that Marty is doing what is needed but that one key element is missing.

When he was in Evansville, Crews said that he could tell a potential recruit that he would get a quality individualized education at a small school and still play in front of 10,000 loyal fans. Crews described the town's support as "very, very, very crucial," and today that factor is missing. Jim Crews summed up the scenario best by saying, "People talk about the cart coming before the horse. Well, at U of E, the fans are the horse."

So as he tries to attract supporters to the new downtown Ford Center, Simmons will continue to scour the country for talent. In 2012, he was thrilled to find his first recruit for the high school class of 2013 literally in his own backyard when his son Blake signed with U of E. Blake is a 6'5 swing player who averaged nearly 20 points and 7 rebounds a game while leading Coach Brian Gibson's Castle Knights to a 20-5 record and a trip to the semi-state in 2012.

Although many fans miss the days of overflow crowds at Roberts Stadium, Marty and his staff are hoping to re-ignite the fans' passion as Aces basketball progresses into a new era. The fact is that Simmons bleeds purple, and many who work with him on a regular basis are amazed at what he has done.

"I've never met anyone who has the impact that Marty has," said Lance Wilkerson, U of E's Director of Development for Athletics, "and I know for a fact that Marty isn't even aware of it. He has no idea of the impact he has on people. I've never heard anyone say a bad word about him. I mean, everybody loves the guy. He is genuine. What you see is what you get. He has no ego; he doesn't like the spotlight.

"When I was a reporter (for Channel 25), I could go to his office in May and leave his office fired up for the season. You could bring up any topic and he could transition it into Aces basketball because that was always on his mind."

There is no question about Simmons' loyalty to Aces basketball, and if the community can increase its support, maybe 'The Mule' can carry the program to elite status again. Though his childhood was spent in Illinois, he and Angie have raised their kids, Brittany, Kelsey, Blake and Cole, as part of our community. For his incredible talent on the court, he has been inducted into the Illinois Basketball Coaches Association and the U of E Athletics Halls of Fame, and as a coach, he has earned the respect of all who have played for him.

Perhaps the best example of the emotion Marty Simmons can evoke were the words spoken by his high school coach, Ron Felling. As our conversation drew to a close, I asked for his final thoughts about the man who was one of the finest players in Illinois history, and as he spoke through his tears, he simply said, "You just tell Marty I love him."

Marty (left) battles future IU center Uwe Blab of Effingham High School.

TOP IHSAA ALL-TIME CAREER SCORING LEADERS

Damon Bailey is Indiana's all-time career scoring leader. Below are the players with area ties that are listed in the state's top 100.

1 – Damon Bailey – 3,134
#19 – Michael Lewis, Jasper – 2,138
#44 – Buster Briley, E.C. Aces – 1,985
#57 – Kent Ayer, South Spencer – 1,929
#64 – Jeremy Willis, Day School – 1,899
#74 – Parrish Casebier, South Spencer – 1,882
#79 – Larry Humes, E.C. Aces – 1,864
#96 – Bob Ford, North – 1,815

ONLY THREE INDIANA PLAYERS TO SCORE 1,000 POINTS IN A SEASON

Dave Shepherd, Carmel ('69-'70) – 1,079 (37.2/game)
Steve Alford, New Castle ('82-'83) – 1,078 (37.2)
George McGinnis, Indpls. Washington ('68-'69) – 1,019 (32.8)

STRANGE BUT TRUE

This amazing story is set in 1957 Gibson County during an era that young folks today just can't appreciate. According to native Gibson Countians Wini Brown and Hugh Schaefer, at least ten small towns in the county boasted tiny schools and were crazy about their basketball teams. And the gyms were as unique as the boys who played in them. Many were so confined that a line was drawn three feet from the wall to keep defenders back on throw-ins from out of bounds. The center jump circle was close to the circle near each free throw line, and it wasn't unusual for the ball to hit the low ceilings.

One of the most anticipated events each year was the Gibson County Holiday Tournament where four of the smaller schools would alternate as the host of the annual affair. As I asked around about this special contest, details seemed a bit fuzzy and varied with each version, but the gist of the story is fact and is truly remarkable.

To set the stage, a week prior to the tournament, some Hazleton fans had apparently harassed two officials (I'll call them Smith and Jones). When the 1957 tournament rolled around, Mackey and Hazleton squared off at the Mt. Olympus gym, and who should walk in wearing striped shirts? You guessed it. In walked Smith and Jones as the crowd let out a collective groan.

By all accounts, the game was never in doubt as the zebras whistled Hazleton for 46 fouls, but what made the game so interesting was the way the coaches handled a very touchy situation. With the referees nearly passing out from blowing their whistles, it should come as no surprise that the Lions began to get in foul trouble, and eventually five of Hazleton's ten players were on the bench, never to return. And then the inevitable moment came.

With the game totally out of reach, a sixth Lion was called for his fifth foul and meandered to the sideline, leaving Hazleton coach Max Cain with only four players on the floor and setting the stage for a gesture that displayed the true spirit of competition. When Hazleton was left with four players, the Mackey coach, Jim Skelton, took out a player of his own to even things out. In fact, he did the same thing again — and again — and again, which meant that with only ten seconds left, the stunned crowd stared down at Hazelton's John Hyneman and Mackey's Dwain Kramer, the only players left on the floor.

According to Hyneman, the last dead ball was a foul on him — imagine that! After Kramer sank his two free throws, John was faced with a dilemma — if he takes the ball out, to whom would he throw the ball? He thought about tossing it to Kramer for a return pass as he would in a neighborhood game, but he opted not to. As he stood there befuddled, the official waved to him to walk it in bounds and dropped his hand to start the clock. According to Hyneman, Kramer was still competing and swarmed all over John until "the buzzer mercifully sounded" before John reached the ten-second line.

Not only was the game the hot topic in Gibson County, but it even made the *New York Times*. Who would have thought that when they walked through the gym doors on that winter night in Mt. Olympus that the scoreboard would read 110-26 when the night was over, and certainly no one could have imagined that such a fiasco would play out. But what they witnessed was the magic and unpredictably of high school sports and the class and dignity of a man who understood the importance of respecting each opponent.

The vintage gym at Mt. Olympus High School.
(Photo courtesy of the Indiana Basketball Hall of Fame)

BIG NIGHTS

The highest single game scoring record was set by Herman 'Sug' Sayger from Culver with 113 points in 1913. According to IHSAA records, there are three area players to score at least 50 points in a game: Jasper's Scott Rolen who scored 50, Castle's Luke Sprague, who scored 52 against Bowling Green (OH) on December 28, 2007 and the biggest night in area history was recorded by Don Falls of Oakland City when he tallied 55 in '55.

MEMORIAL'S BRUCE DOCKERY:
"I COULD SEE IT IN THEIR EYES"

For 25 years, Evansville Memorial High School's Bruce Dockery has been prowling the sidelines for the Tigers, and the success he has brought to the small parochial school on Evansville's east side has not gone unnoticed. "I don't think there's anybody who loves basketball more than Bruce," said Janet Hartman, the mother of Jill Hartman, the most prolific scorer (boy or girl) in Evansville history. His true love in life is coaching girls basketball, and I think it shows."

Dockery was a self-professed mediocre athlete during his years at Bosse, and the '68 grad remembers some of the great Bulldog players of his generation, naming John and Wayne Hoover, Gene Ballard and Jerry Dennis among them. He entered college at Charleston Southern and played basketball for a year before finally finishing at USI in 1978.

Bruce admits that he had no real intentions of becoming a coach, but he is thankful he seized the chance when given the opportunity. While working at Keller-Crescent, Bruce was approached by Connie Laib, a friend of his brother, who talked Bruce into coaching 7th and 8th grade girls. Dockery piloted the girls team at St. Boniface (later named Westside Consolidated Catholic Schools) from 1979 until 1987 and coached future Mater Dei star Julie Goedde. While at St. Boniface, Bruce compiled a 124-18 record with two undefeated seasons and back-to-back Diocesan Tournament titles before accepting the job at Memorial.

During his 25 years at the helm of the Memorial's program, Dockery has crystallized his thinking when it comes to his role as a male coach in a female athletic environment, and he appreciates the differences between the genders. "You've got thirty wives in training," Bruce said from his AD office, "and you're their guinea pig. They're young women. They're four or five years away from being married, and they're starting to develop into the young women they're going to be for the rest of their lives.

"You have to deal with them almost the same as you do your wife. They're going to have ups and downs, and you're better off to ignore some and, for others, let them know that if they need to talk, you're there. I try not to get too involved."

Coach Dockery also sees other differences between the girls and the boys. "Another thing is that girls show their appreciation on a daily basis," he revealed. "The guys, sometimes in their early 20s they might come back (to express their gratitude), but girls do it every day. It's not uncommon for girls to thank you. They'll come right up and give you a hug and say, 'We had a good practice today. Thank you.' It helps motivate you on a daily basis."

Bruce also notices the difference when dealing with the girls' emotions. "Some female coaches I know, if a girl rolls her eyes at them, it drives them nuts. I don't even notice it."

In addition, Dockery recognizes how the girls react differently to losing compared to their male counterparts. "With girls, they're just as devastated as a guy," he explained, "but they get over it quicker. Girls will be heartbroken for 30 or 40 minutes and then they'll move on." He pointed out as an example a semi-state loss to Rushville in 2010 when Memorial had the game in hand and let it slip away. "The kids were crying in the locker room," Dockery recalled, "then we got on the bus and a half-hour out of town they're laughing and joking and ready to get something to eat. And that's kind of my makeup too. After a while, I'm ready to move on."

When discussing the comparisons of coaching girls versus boys, Bruce really doesn't understand the stance taken by some in the basketball community. "I got to know coaches who coached girls and they would say, 'Girls can't do this. You can't be hard on girls; they cry!' From my perspective, it's just basketball. I think they're just as capable of doing anything. Girls are like guys; some guys you can just jump all over, and other guys you have to handle a little different.

"The great thing about girls is they are a lot more coachable. I could go up to Mallory Ladd (the team's superstar in 2010-'11), one of the best players in the state, and I could tell her I'm going to change her shot and she would let me do it. She would work at it. A boy will listen to what you're saying, but he won't do it.

"I think it's an advantage that I never coached boys," Dockery continued. "You see very few girls teams play man-to-man because they (coaches) feel it's too hard to teach them. My team now can run four different defenses and can change on each possession. We can also run variations of offenses and two or three different presses." Bruce also feels that the state's premier coaches have views similar to his, mentioning Tom May, a three-time State champion coach at Crown Point and Stan Benge, another State title winner, saying, "He could switch over and coach a boys team and never miss a beat."

For the first nine seasons of Memorial girls basketball, the program was in the capable hands of Jan Millay, who led the very first team ('76-'77) to the school's first sectional title. During Millay's tenure, Memorial had seven winning seasons in nine years with a record of 101-50.

After Coach Millay stepped down, Dan Edwards filled in for a season and won the sectional despite a 9-11 record. The following year, 1987, Dockery took over and the journey began for the young coach and his young ladies.

For the first five years of Bruce's tenure, the program was respectable, posting an overall record of 43-42 due to such players as Kelli Simpkins, an '89 grad who was recruited by IU and Kentucky but chose to study drama, and Krista VanMeter, who was "ahead of her time" as a passer, according to Coach Dockery.

Photo courtesy of the Hackert family.

MEMORIAL TIGERS

Memorial's 2011 State champs: Front Row (L-R): Grace Shymanski, Jena Lutz, Maggie Minnette, Nicci Bland, Rachel Davidson, Ruth Hedrick, Kelsey Falls, Emily Purdue. Second row: Rachel DeWig, Meghan Gallagher, Natalie Cohlmeyer, Emily Nesbitt, Marie Hackert, Anna Hackert, Mallory Ladd, Sarah Stone, Coach Joan Miller, Coach Monica Auker, Jessica Durcholz. Back row: Head Coach Bruce Dockery, Coach Thom Endress, Coach Whitney Jenkins.

But thanks to a talented group in 1992-'93, the program took a dramatic upswing. Led by junior Mollie Darke and guard Missy Cummins, the Tigers finished 17-4, winning the City, conference and sectional titles before falling to Pike Central in the regional.

Five years later, the program turned another corner and began its ascent into the company of the elite programs statewide. This rise was due to several factors, the first of which was the feeder system that was developed over the years. Dockery is very involved and credits the hard work of volunteer coaches for much of the success. "The first thing you can say about Bruce is that he bleeds (Memorial) Blue," says Thom Endress, a recent addition to Coach Dockery's coaching staff and father of former star Kate Endress. "Nobody works harder during the development stage than he does. It's not by accident that Memorial's the best every year. He instills in them a pride in playing for Memorial High School."

Bruce also quickly points out that he has had some fine assistants over the years, like Endress, who works with the girls individually during practice. Dockery continued by praising Monica Auker, his JV coach whom he describes as "a tremendous asset" and freshman coach Whitney Jenkins, who played for Bruce.

But more than anything, the advancement to elite status is due to a steady flow of blue chip athletes. Most coaches are lucky to mentor one or two superstars in a career, but Dockery seems to have an assembly line with a steady supply of top-of-the-line athletes. The first came off the line in 1995, and by the time she was finished, she was the most prolific scorer in Evansville history. Jill Hartman led the Lady Tigers to their first regional title in 1998 and played her final two years with the school's second superstar.

Kate Endress entered the program in 1997 and teamed with senior Hartman her sophomore year on what many consider to be the best team in the program's history. Endress finished her career with four 20-win seasons and a record of 85-15 (85%).

By far the quickest player in Memorial girls basketball history, FahKara Malone began her career in 2002 and led the program to new heights in 2006 when the Lady Tigers captured the semi-state for the first time and finished as the runner-up in the State tournament. FahKara also contributed to four 20-win seasons and had a career record of 85-18 (82.5%).

One year after Malone left for Purdue, the school's fourth blue chipper took center stage and shared another incredible run with her teammates as they fashioned a record of 86-14 for her four years. Not only did Mallory Ladd set school records for career wins (86) and career winning percentage (86%) but she delivered the program to the Promised Land by leading Memorial to its first basketball State title in 2011.

Coach Dockery is smart enough to know that players like the four mentioned above are rare indeed, especially when they arrive so close together. "I've been blessed with a whole lot of great athletes," Bruce admitted. "In your coaching career, if you get one blue chip player, you're very fortunate. In my 24 years (as of 2011), I bet there have only been four or five years that I didn't have a blue chip player."

Whether that statement is totally accurate or not, the point is understood, and the numbers over the last 14 years support Dockery's view to a degree. From 1997, when Jill Hartman made her debut, until Mallory Ladd's exit in 2011, there were two seasons when the team had no blue chippers. Those seasons, '01-'02 and '06-'07 were completed with a combined record of 25-19, a 57% result. Conversely, during the twelve seasons with at least one of the four superstars, Memorial won at least 20 games ten times with a 12-year record of 256-47 (84.4%).

Dockery proved what kind of coach he had become with his team's run to the State championship in 2011, and many feel that the journey to the title really began in 2009. Bruce first saw the potential when four girls from St. Ben's, Ladd, Emily

Nesbitt and the Hackert twins, Anna and Marie, were joined by Natalie Cohlmeyer (Plaza Park), Sarah Stone (Christ the King) and Ruth Hedrick, who had moved in from California.

Dockery also made sure that the 2011 champions were mentally and physically ready when tournament time rolled around. The mental toughness was enhanced the year prior in the Rushville game. Memorial controlled the game for all but two minutes, and the gut-wrenching loss cut deeply. But ultimately, the defeat could well have been the catalyst for great things to come. Or as Mike Ladd, Mallory's father, put it, "That game hurt, but it was a motivation (for next season)."

The 2010-'11 Tigers were also toughened up by a brutal schedule put together by Dockery as the school's AD. The schedule was rated as the second toughest in Class 3A and the sixth toughest of all the classes in the state, according to the Sagarin ratings and an IBCA poll. Dockery stated several times that he felt his team could compete with anybody, and he was proven right when his girls knocked off 4A #2 Carmel at the Hall of Fame Classic. In fact, the only team to beat the Tigers all season was Brownsburg in the afternoon game of that same Classic.

Memorial opened the season on November 20 with a 25-point win over Jasper and won six of their first eight easily, with only North (54-51) and Plainfield (68-66) providing a challenge. After the Hall of Fame Classic, they stood 9-1 and then breezed through the rest of the regular season with twelve more victories by an average margin of 26 points.

In the Boonville Sectional, the Lady Tigers continued to dominate, with easy wins over Princeton (63-26) and Bosse (69-31). In the sectional final, Coach Dockery was not surprised when overmatched Gibson Southern tried stall tactics in a very painful game to watch. As the restless crowd looked on, the Titans kept the game close before Memorial pulled away late for a 21-9 victory. Games like this one are always difficult to coach, but Bruce Dockery respected his opponent for choosing the only viable option to win the game.

"After we got out to a lead, it was obvious they weren't even looking at the basket," Dockery said. "I didn't like it, but I really admire Mark Monroe (Gibson Southern's coach) for sticking with his game plan."

At the regional, Memorial made easy work of Silver Creek (51-27) before surviving a test from Edgewood 50-44 for Memorial's sixth regional title. Coach Dockery's girls then captured the program's second semi-state with a 69-59 win over Indianapolis Roncalli.

As the players and fans looked ahead to the State Finals, they weren't thrilled about the long drive ahead of them, but before they would embark on their journey, they would face a predicament that no one saw coming.

The situation began to develop on the return trip from Ft. Wayne, where Bruce had attended a meeting about the upcoming championship game to be played there. "We were coming back, and somewhere around Vincennes my lower back started hurting," Bruce revealed. "I just thought it was from being on the road for five hours. I got home and we had practice, and I started feeling like I was coming down with the flu.

"I went home and laid down on the couch, and my wife (Kathy Dockery) said, 'You've never looked like this before.'

"I said, 'I'm fine, I'll sleep it off.'"

The following morning, Bruce's stomach was still hurting, and when Kathy came home from a meeting, she said, "You're going to the doctor."

Being the corporate business manager for Evansville Radiology at Deaconess, Kathy made arrangements for pictures to be taken. The results showed severe appendicitis, and Bruce headed straight to a hospital room while Kathy arranged for a surgeon to come in.

Bruce had gone in at 3:00, was in surgery at 5:00, was out by 7:00 and feels very fortunate that the problem was discovered in time. For the previous two years, he had thought that he just had lower back problems, but the surgeon said the appendix was dead and full of gangrene and was the worst appendix he had ever seen.

While Bruce and Kathy were dealing with the emergency, word began to spread to the school's basketball community. "I was surfing the internet," said Mike Ladd. "I was looking at 'Indiana girls basketball' and saw the headline 'Bruce Dockery.' I clicked on it and saw a report that said, 'Bruce Dockery has had an emergency appendectomy and will not coach this week.'"

Mallory Ladd and her teammates found out the details later. "We found out after school," Mallory informed me. "They announced for all the varsity girls basketball team to come to the small gym. We honestly thought he might have died or something. I was terrified. Then they said he had appendicitis and may not be able to coach."

Though everyone was relieved that the medical problem was not life-threatening, there was still the issue of Saturday's game. Being the team leader, Mallory felt the pressure as she assessed the situation and the roles she might have to assume in her coach's absence. The other seniors and assistant coaches also stepped up.

On Wednesday, Bruce tried to coach but could only tolerate about thirty minutes before the pain got to be too much. Over the next two days, he followed the doctor's orders, and as Friday approached, he was cleared to make the trip. While the drama was playing out, the fan base at Memorial was trying to focus on the business at hand. Although the IHSAA had decided to schedule the finals about as far away as they could be, the school still pre-sold 651 tickets for the event, and Bruce believes the number might have tripled if the game had been in Indy, as it had been for many years.

Memorial's loyal fans had supported the team all year, and through the course of the long 2010-'11 season, only five teams had played Memorial within ten points. But on Saturday, March 5, 2011, Coach Dockery and his girls would be tested to the max, and the fans who made the five-hour trip got their money's worth as the Lady Tigers took on Benton Central.

The game was a brutal battle, and the front line of Ladd and the Hackert twins banged with Benton's bigs for 32 minutes of regulation and then some. It was obvious from the jump that the game was going to be a challenge, and the Tigers controlled the game early like they had all year. "We started out playing very well," Coach Dockery explained, "and then, in a matter of four or five minutes, we got away from everything we'd done all year."

Memorial shot only 15% in the half, while the 23-3 Bison weren't much better at 32% (7-22). Memorial was fortunate to hold a 17-16 lead, but they only scored 4 points in the second quarter, something Coach Dockery was quick to point out. "At halftime, the first thing I did was write a big '3' on the board," he revealed. "I said, 'that's the most passes we made before we shot the ball in the first half.'"

The second half was just as physical as the coaches matched wits and the girls' resolve was fully tested. Memorial played only six girls until the final seconds, and each of those six had to reach deep inside to compete. Coach Dockery did his part by making a switch late in the game. With under five minutes to go, Memorial pulled out of their trademark 1-3-1 zone and shifted into a man-to-man. This seemed to baffle Benton Central, and the raucous crowd at Memorial Coliseum in Ft. Wayne grew hoarse as the seconds ticked away in regulation. Anna Hackert nailed an eight-footer to tie the score at 41 with less than a minute left, and Benton Central then called timeout with 9.1 seconds remaining to set up a final play. When Caitlyn Tolen weaved her way through Memorial's defense and came up short on an eight-footer of her own, the Lady Tigers were still alive, and they were not to be denied.

As the players sat and listened to Coach Dockery before the extra period, they were determined to avoid a similar fate to the one they experienced against Rushville a year earlier, and they caught a second wind in the extra period.

Sarah Stone opened the scoring in overtime with a monumental three-pointer from the right corner to give the Tigers a 44-41 lead at the 3:32 mark, and the Lady Tigers steadily pulled away and emptied the bench as the starters began to celebrate the 58-50 victory.

Still hurting and on medication from his emergency appendectomy, Coach Dockery was rather subdued compared to the hoard who surrounded him in Ft. Wayne, but his jubilation was strong nonetheless and his affection for the team was genuine. "I've never coached a team quite like this one," he told me. "You could just tell that they weren't going to lose. Against Roncalli (in the semi-state), they were down five with 4:30 to go. As a coach, I wasn't concerned because I could see it in their eyes. They won by ten.

"In the State championship game, when it went into overtime, the kids sprinted to the bench. They all sat on the edge of their seats and waved off water and towels and they were all looking straight at me. I could see it in their eyes."

Bruce knows that a team like the 2010-'11 Lady Tigers doesn't come around often, and he looked like a proud papa when he re-capped their performances. He began with his 2-guard, who finished the title game with 13 points to go with 2 assists and 2 steals. "I can't say enough about Sarah Stone," Bruce said. "She hit some key buckets throughout the game and none bigger than the three-pointer to start the OT."

Bruce also praised the two girls who subbed during regulation. "Emily Nesbitt (9 minutes) came off the bench and did a nice job with 3 or 4 rebounds," Bruce recalled, "and Ruth (Hedrick) came in to give Sarah a breather and pushed Benton Central out defensively."

Dockery smiled when asked about his point guard, Natalie Cohlmeyer, the only starter who was not a senior. "Natalie probably had one of her worst games from a fan standpoint (no field goals, but 6 for 6 free throws)," Bruce said, "but I left her in the whole game because she did an outstanding job handling their pressure. Her turnovers came in the half-court on travel calls. That's the thing I love about Natalie. A lot of ballplayers would have gotten down, but Natalie was in the game mentally. For every turnover she had, she made three great decisions, and fans don't see those all the time."

Bruce was especially proud of his big front line and the job they did against Benton Central. "Anna Hackert had a tremendous game," Dockery mentioned. "I think 10 points (actually 12) and 13 rebounds and I think 4 assists on top of it. And her sister Marie, who's 6'3, played an outstanding game for us (10 rebounds, 2 blocks, 3 steals to go with 1 point), creating all kinds of havoc."

And what about the team's superstar? "Mallory Ladd was Mallory the whole game," Dockery said. "She took over in the second half – 24 points, 13 boards, tied a State Finals record with 10 for 10 free throws (to go with 3 assists and 5 steals)."

Dockery loves to talk about his girls, and one story he told personified the type of competitors the 2011 champs were. Late in the final game, Bruce had told the team to keep the ball in the hands of Ladd, Cohlmeyer or Stone because "they have to foul us."

Benton Central soon fouled Anna Hackert, who immediately drained two free throws to help put the game away. Late in the contest, with the victory in hand, Anna looked down the bench at Bruce and indicated that she had taken his earlier remark personally. "Why didn't you want the ball in my hands?" she asked.

Dockery's response: "That's why I love you, kid."

When the Lady Tigers returned home, they took some time to enjoy the fruits of their labors as they climbed aboard a fire engine at Harrison High School and drove past fans lined up on both sides of the street to eventually be greeted by 500 fans at their gym. The girls shared their emotions and beamed as they addressed the crowd, and many expressed their feelings about the man who had shrugged off the aftereffects of surgery to lead them to the program's first State championship.

Dockery is a phenomenal coach, and his numbers put him on track to enter the Indiana Basketball Hall of Fame one day. During his 25 seasons (as of 2012), he has won over 70% of his games and is rapidly approaching 400 wins. He has been named the SIAC's Coach of the Year 8 times, the HBCA District 2 Coach of the Year 5 times and the ICGSA (Indiana Coaches of Girls Sports Association) Coach of the Year in 2010-'11.

As of 2012, 14 of Dockery's girls had played at the next level, and he takes each of his player's ambitions seriously. He knows that some players may want to put athletics behind them or focus on another sport. He is also aware that being overly ambitious can create huge disappointment, and he has a unique system he uses to convey his thoughts to the girls when they are ready to talk college ball.

He speaks with each girl about the different college divisions and what it takes as a high school player to compete at each level. He explains that a potential Division III player will dominate occasionally in high school, while a Division II player will stand out in most games and a Division I athlete will dominate virtually every game.

If a girl is good enough to be recruited, Dockery will sit down with them early to help them decide what might be right for them. He then explains that: "If you go D-I, you're going to play basketball 365 days a year. If you go D-II, you'll play 300 days, and D-III about 220 days. If you think that a level is too much, you want to go down."

Bruce references star players who made college choices, like Krista VanMeter, who chose Oakland City College, and Paige Rudolph, who was recruited Division I but wanted to go to a smaller school. He also mentioned FahKara Malone, who started every game while at Purdue.

It is easy to see that Dockery sincerely cares about his players and the feeling is mutual among players and parents. "Bruce is the best," said Mike Ladd. "He runs his program like a college team. If you play for Memorial, there's something about that place. The managers pack the bags, and when the girls step into the locker room, their stuff is ready. He takes care of those girls."

But no one can sing the praises of Coach Dockery better than his players. Jill Hartman, the school's all-time scoring leader, credits Dockery for much of her success. "He was always the coolest because he was the head coach of the team you wanted to play for someday," Jill explained. "He always pushed me to do things I would have never done. I would never have broken the scoring record without him. I told him the record book should say my name but his name should be next to it."

"He's so amazing," said FahKara Malone when asked about Bruce. "You just can't imagine how a man who is so soft-spoken can reach his players while everyone is screaming. He's like a dog whisperer. As a player, you hear his voice over everything. He makes basketball fun, but he makes you a better player at the same time."

"He is one of a kind," replied Mallory Ladd. "He is one of the greatest coaches I have ever been around. He knows so much about the game, it's ridiculous. He's not afraid to bench you if you're doing it wrong, and if he's told you multiple times, you're going to sit. And he never argued with the ref; he had a clever way of working refs."

Like his program, Dockery is first class, and he has handled the recognition he has received with humility. There is no doubt that Bruce has had some phenomenal talent over the years, and he downplays his role in the program's success, saying that "anybody could have won with those kids." Others may feel the same way, but that kind of thinking is an easy position for outsiders to take when discussing such talent. The fact is, there have been many boys and girls coaches over the years who have had phenomenal talent but couldn't get the job done.

Whether you look at his numbers or listen to players and parents pay tribute to Coach Dockery, there is no mistaking that the man is a winner. He has worked very hard and has dedicated himself to his profession. It is true that Bruce Dockery has been blessed with some marvelous blue chip athletes over the years, but there is so much more to the story. Dockery is a rare individual who understands what it takes for a team to excel. He has molded himself and his program into a winner, which makes him, in the opinion of those who know him, a blue chipper as well.

Over the years, one measure of individual basketball success has been recognition as an Indiana All-Star. From 1941 to 2011, there have been 89 area players (male & female) named to the teams. Here is the list of those honored and a breakdown by school and decade. *(Boys list on page 132)*

GIRLS
1977 – Janice McCracken (Vincennes Lincoln)
1979 – Cassandra Lander (Bosse)
1981 – Shelly Brand (Reitz)
1982 – Barb Dykstra (Reitz)
1984 – Marilyn Reckelhoff (Southridge)
1985 – Cheryl Dowell (Bosse)
1986 – Julie Goedde (Mater Dei)
1987 – Vicki Lander (Bosse)
1989 – Krista Blunk (Tell City)
1994 – Eileen Weber (Washington Catholic)
1995 – Julie Helm (Washington)
1995 – Haley Harris (Wood Memorial)
1996 – Nicole McDaniel (Princeton)
1997 – Stacie Mueller (Harrison)
1998 – Jill Fenneman (Southridge)
1999 – Jill Hartman (Memorial)
2001 – Kate Endress (Memorial)
2006 – FahKara Malone (Memorial)
2006 – Maria Olsthoorn (Castle)
2007 – Jasmine Ussery (Castle)
2010 – Khristian Hart (Harrison)
2011 – Mallory Ladd (Memorial)

Local Girls Indiana All-Stars by decade
1970s – 2
1980s – 7
1990s – 7
2000s – 4
2010s – 2

Local Girls Indiana All-Stars by school
Memorial – 4
Bosse – 3
Reitz – 2
Southridge – 2
Harrison – 2
Castle – 2
Vincennes Lincoln – 1
Mater Dei – 1
Tell City – 1
Washington Catholic – 1
Washington – 1
Wood Memorial – 1
Princeton - 1

TOP 100 IHSAA GIRLS CAREER SCORING LEADERS
#1 – Shannon Zolman, Wawasee – 3,085
#11 – Julie Helm, Washington – 2,236
#31 – Jill Hartman, Memorial – 1,926
#39 – Eileen Weber, Wash. Catholic – 1,879
#40 – Kate Endress, Memorial – 1,875
#44 – Vicki Lander, Bosse – 1,843
#55 – Mallory Ladd, Memorial – 1,803
#93 – Gretchen Miles, Washington – 1,588
#95 – Leslie Ricker, North Posey – 1,582

JILL HARTMAN: EVANSVILLE'S #1

Photo courtesy of the Evansville Courier.

During her years as a high school athlete, Jill Hartman (Early) was as focused on a single goal as any athlete I've ever spoken with. The irony is that fate stepped in to shatter her dream but also gave her the drive and passion for the game to make her arguably the greatest basketball player (male or female) in local history.

"You could pretty much tell right away," said Jill's father, Mike Hartman, when asked about his daughter's early potential. "She dominated in softball when she was very young." Jill played T-ball at age six and was an outstanding pitcher at eight. At age seven, she attended Carl Wade's basketball camp and won ribbons while competing against boys, and she was the only girl on her team in the 8-year-old Lakeview Optimist boys league as a six-year-old and started at center at age eight when her team won the title.

Jill's athletic ability came naturally. Mike played baseball in Edwardsville, Illinois and qualified for the State track meet in the 800-meter run. Jill's mother, Janet, was a cheerleader and sports fan when she was young, and Jill's siblings also benefited from the rich heritage. Her older brother, Matt, played soccer at Memorial for four years and basketball for only three after realizing he wasn't going to pass the great Clint Keown on the depth chart. He was also a standout in track, winning the sectional in the 800 in a time that still stands (as of 2012) as the sectional record. His talent earned him a track scholarship to Purdue, where he held the 600-meter record for a while.

Younger sister Laura, who was in the same class as and was a good friend of local legend Kate Endress, was a first teamer on the All-Conference basketball team, averaging 15 points per game. She had offers to play Division II ball but decided to attend IU after tearing her ACL.

Jill also displayed her talent on the diamond as a youngster and experienced great success with her teammates, winning two sectional championships in Pony Association softball and two state titles in ASA softball.

As she progressed through elementary and middle school, bonds were formed that would define Jill's high school career. As a youngster, she teamed with Kristin Sartore, Emily Markwell, Cathy Kipta, and Meredith Tappan on AAU teams, and all five girls played together at Memorial. In fact, they all started as sophomores before giving way in their last two years to Jill's sister Laura and Kate Endress as underclassmen.

Jill credits her parents for encouraging her and for the time they spent chauffeuring her and her siblings to various basketball, volleyball and softball camps, and she recalls the long hours spent with her father in the yard and driveway perfecting her skills. "She did a lot of shooting outside by herself also," said Jill's mom, Janet, "especially before school at 6:00 or so."

"I practiced all the time," Jill added when asked about those early years. "I would go outside and shoot free throws, and I had to make ten in a row before I would go in. We had practice at 5:30, so I'd come home for an hour and go outside and shoot. I would play in the rain or put gloves on that had grips on the fingers and shoot in the cold."

All the pounding of the ball in the driveway under the lights at night paid off for Jill, as she started as a fourth grader on her eighth grade team in preparation for Coach Bruce Dockery's program at Memorial. But nothing had a bigger influence on her success than a trip she took as an eighth grader in 1995. In March of that year, her Evansville Lutheran team won the Lutheran state championship, and while they were in central Indiana, she and her parents decided to take in the high school State Finals at Market Square Arena.

"To me, it was the most amazing thing I'd ever seen, seeing all these girls playing for the State championship," Jill recalled. "When I saw that, that's when I said 'I've got to do that someday.' It was a big inspiration for me to practice every day and get our team there someday. A lot of my motivation was ultimately from that game at Market Square. In the mornings, I would set my alarm for 5:30, and every time I would roll back over (to go back to sleep), I would say to myself, 'If your team's going to get to the State championship, you're going to have to be ready.'"

In the years prior to Jill's arrival at Memorial, the program was struggling. During her final year at Evansville Lutheran, Memorial went 4-16, and before she moved on to high school, she let her feelings be known. "I told Coach Dockery in the eighth grade 'We're going to the State championship someday,' Jill explained. "I remember I called Coach Dockery when I got back from Market Square and I said, 'We're going to do that

someday.' He didn't laugh. He just said 'You're right!' He always believed in me. That's why I practiced."

As Jill began her career at Memorial, she continued to develop as an all-around athlete. Growing to a solid 5'11", Jill never played a freshman or JV sport. In softball, she was an exceptional pitcher, perhaps one of the best in the state, leading the Lady Tigers to the school's first sectional softball title before giving up the sport after her sophomore year to concentrate on volleyball and basketball.

During her years with the Lady Tiger basketball program, Coach Dockery's teams improved dramatically, going 6-13 her freshman year, 11-9 the next and 21-4 when she was a junior against some stiff local competition. Archrival Bosse took the floor with stars Lashelle Porter, Schmeyko Bolden, Lashaun Easley and Jill's childhood friend Latoya Jagoe. Central boasted the outstanding Emily Hester, and Harrison's Stacie Mueller finished her senior year as the second-leading scorer in the state.

While the Lady Tigers were improving each year in the late '90s, so was Ms. Hartman, and she quickly learned to cherish her role as her team's go-to player. "I knew that at the end of a game, if it was close, that the pressure was going to be on me," she confided, "and I was OK with that. I knew I had to practice to be able to step up."

I think it came naturally. I loved that role. In softball, I was a pitcher. There wouldn't have been any other position I would have wanted. I was really passionate about that leadership role, and I wanted it in my hands."

Someone else who wanted the ball in Jill's hands was Bruce Dockery. "I'll tell you one thing about Jill," he said from his office at the school, "as soon as the game was in hand, she was all about the teammates."

Dockery knew his star was going to shatter records and would often leave her in during runaway games to help keep her numbers up. "But Jill would get mad at me," he said. "She's a sweet girl. You couldn't tell from the stands, but I know Jill. She wanted out of the game. But if a game was on the line, Jill was going to take it over."

As Jill continued to work, she never lost focus on her goal of playing for a State title. She and her teammates came close in 1998, making it to the Final Four in the first year of the class system before losing in the semi-finals. Jill had come within one game of fulfilling the prophecy she had shared with Coach Dockery as a skinny eighth grader only four years earlier. She had only one year left to play for a State championship, and her senior year would feature some of her greatest moments and, without question, her greatest disappointment.

The Lady Tigers roared through the regular season, finishing 23-1, and were poised to make a run at the program's first State title as Indiana's #1-ranked 3A team. Jill played with abandon and led the team to the sectional championship, but even her singleness of purpose could not prevail when the fickle finger of fate stepped in.

In the week prior to the regional, Jill was feeling lethargic and was diagnosed with mono. On Friday, she came to school for a half-day to meet the requirement to play Saturday, but she was not herself in the game and Memorial fell to Jasper. What had been a dream season suddenly ended, and Jill still feels the pain as she philosophizes about the hand she had been dealt.

"I think I cried for a long time, and people were so supportive," she explained, "but to me it was like, 'how could I ever dream and hope for something again,' for a while at least. With mono, you just lie around and sleep, and I think I was mad at my body for letting me down. Looking back, I know that I'm a Christian, and I believe everything happens for a reason. If that was God's plan, then that's how it was."

Despite the disappointing ending to her high school career, Jill's drive to reach her goal enabled her to fashion a remarkable season and career at Memorial. She had been named an AAU All-American and an Indiana Junior All-Star in 1998 and was first team All-State and an Indiana All-Star her senior year. But it took some time for Jill to snap back from the loss in the regional and to carry on with the business at hand.

"I left a little bit of passion and heart for playing on that court when I lost," she admitted. "For every birthday, every wish I ever made for like five years was for our team to win a State championship. That's what got me up every morning and got me motivated. I was devastated for a really long time."

But life continued for Jill and she went about her business of examining her college options. She wasn't always confident about her chance of playing at the next level, but that's when Bruce Dockery stepped in.

I was so focused on winning the State championship that Coach Dockery sat me down my sophomore year," Jill recalled. "He said, 'If you really pick it up, you could be a major Division I ballplayer.' It hit me because it wasn't something I'd thought about. He put the bug in my ear and then my competitiveness kicked in and I thought 'Hey, if it's possible, I might as well do it.'"

Jill as a 6-year-old on a Biddy Ball team that had several athletes who would make future headlines. Front row (L-R): Derek Grimm, Cory Meisel, Bart Browning, Jill Hartman, Brian Claybourn. Back row: J.P. Claybourn, Matt Hartman, Ty Browning, Brad McElya, Adam Mueller, Chad Schwartz. Coaches (L-R): Jim Claybourn, Dave Grimm.

And do it she did. Jill was pursued by numerous programs, and U of E coach Kathy Bennett had been after her since she was young. When she made the decision to take IU coach Jim Izzard up on his offer, she visited Coach Bennett to deliver the news personally as a show of respect.

At IU, Jill flourished in her first season, making the All-Big Ten Freshman Team as a starter for the Hoosiers. But after the season, bad luck struck again. Coach Izzard left and was replaced by U of E's Kathy Bennett. For whatever reason, Jill's playing time was reduced drastically, but she stuck with the program and finished her education. She did start half the games her senior year and was a captain and contributed to IU's Big Ten Tournament title her junior year. She also left the program as the school record holder for 3-point field goal percentage.

While coping with the challenges during her years at IU, she again relied on a valuable resource for perspective. After explaining her circumstances to Coach Dockery, her mentor responded with some simple advice: "Just go and play like you know how and do your thing."

Looking back, Jill is philosophical about her career, especially her years at Memorial. "I learned a very good lesson from that experience," she said. "After the heartbreak healed, I could look past the disappointment and take in all the amazing things I accomplished as an individual and, most importantly, with my team. What I learned is that if you set your goal higher than you ever thought possible, higher than anyone thinks you can reach, you stretch yourself to crazy limits and achieve things you never thought of. Junior year, we were one game from the championship game, and two years before we had won only six games. I think that is a lesson we can use as adults."

Jill Hartman learned her lessons well, and the legacy she left while pursuing her dream is amazing. As a senior, she averaged 23.2 points, 11.1 rebounds, 3.5 assists and 3.1 steals per game while shooting 58% from the floor. For her four-year career, she averaged nearly 22 points per game and finished her career with 1,926 points, making Jill Hartman the all-time scoring leader (male or female) in local history.

KATE ENDRESS: THE WHOLE PACKAGE

The second of Coach Dockery's superstars was a young lady named Katherine Marie Endress, and to say that Kate was driven to succeed would not do the statement justice. Kate and her sisters, Sarah and Ann, came from an impressive gene pool like many of our local legends, and they were destined for success at a young age.

Thom and Cindy Endress were both 1971 grads of Evansville Rex Mundi High School on the city's north side, and Thom was a part of the phenomenal sports programs during the short history of the school. Thom was an All-City performer in both football and basketball for the Monarchs and was the quarterback of the school's only undefeated football team in 1970.

When the girls were young, Thom and Cindy began to buy them balls and bats instead of dolls, and the girls showed a lot of natural ability. The oldest daughter, Sarah, eventually ran some cross country but enjoyed other interests more, and Ann had great talent but lacked Kate's drive and later chose to focus on her studies in college. But Kate was the daughter who developed a tenacity for learning, and whether it was in sports or the classroom, she never settled for mediocrity.

According to Thom and Cindy, Kate was self-motivated and spent hours watching a series of training tapes by LSU icon Pete Maravich, a series that Thom still recommends to young players today. As often as possible, the Endresses would place Kate in boys' leagues to toughen her up, and although the boys wouldn't pass her the ball much when she was five, she was good enough later to be drafted #1 in the boys 8-year-old league.

As the sisters grew, many hours were spent on developing skills, and Kate's parents could see that their daughter was something special. "Thom showed her different parts of the game in stages," Cindy explained. "They would play together for hours in the driveway. She was the one who would say, 'Dad, come out and play.' We never went on a vacation without a basketball. When the kids were little, we would walk together and Sarah had a book, Ann was on a Big Wheel and Kate had a basketball."

"Kate became very skilled both right-handed and left-handed," Thom added. "She was and still is the most driven individual I've ever met in anything."

As Kate developed, she showed promise in several sports and could have been a standout at Memorial in any of them. In track, she was one of the best half-milers in the state as a freshman and sophomore, once showing her toughness by taking a cast off her sprained ankle to run the 800. She even held the Evansville Sectional record for a while before giving up the sport to concentrate on playing AAU basketball with Indiana's Finest.

Many who watched Endress thought that softball was her best sport, but she chose to focus on volleyball and basketball at Memorial. As a great leaper, Kate was dominant on the volleyball court, and that same ability, along with off-the-chart skills, made her one of Evansville's best on the basketball court, as well.

One of Kate's high school highlights was playing on a team that many consider to be the best in school history, meaning no disrespect to the fabulous State champs of 2010-'11. Led by senior scoring phenom Jill Hartman, the team was ranked #1 all year and could very well have captured a State championship had fate not stepped in. With a starting lineup of Hartman, Endress and three Emilys, Markwell, Scheessele and Sartore, the girls were poised for a run in the 1998 tournament, but with Hartman suffering from mono and Kate recovering from injuries from a car wreck, the Tigers fell to Washington.

Thom and Cindy Endress look back at some of their favorite moments as those when Kate and Ann played together at Memorial. Ann, who was two years behind her sister, averaged close to 12 points a game and was good enough to earn second team All-Metro honors. She was talented enough to play college ball but opted instead to concentrate on being a student in college. Kate, on the other hand, wanted to go as far as her talent would take her.

As a junior, Endress was the city's scoring leader at 24.4 per game and joined Angie Rodgers (Castle), Amber Calhoun (Bosse), Maurita Farmer (Harrison) and Shauntay Oshodi (Central) on the *Courier*'s All-Metro first team. As the state's 7th-leading scorer, Endress shot 47 percent from the field and 80% from the line while also grabbing nearly 9 rebounds per contest.

The following year, 2001, Kate again earned All-Metro honors along with Rodgers of Castle, Erika Foster (Harrison), Chelsea Wessel (Reitz), and Memorial teammate Laura Hartman, Jill's younger sister. Once again, Coach Dockery's Lady Tigers finished another great season (20-4) but were bitten by bad luck in the tournament when fellow senior Laura Hartman tore an ACL in the sectional championship.

Despite stellar numbers and abundant talent, Kate's college recruitment hit some snags along the way, but with her outstanding grades and athletic resumé, she was confident she would find a home. During her junior season, Endress was being recruited heavily by big-time programs like Notre Dame, Wisconsin and Iowa, among others, but when Kate encountered a physical problem, the interest waned.

According to Coach Dockery, the 6-foot Endress suffered a common malady for tall, athletic girls — weak stomach muscles. The weakness then contributed to a stress fracture in Kate's lower back sustained while playing with boys at the Tri-State Athletic Club, requiring a brace from the belly button to the chest. Endress battled through the problem and tried to compete on the AAU circuit, but many coaches looked at her as "damaged goods," according to Coach Dockery.

But the circumstances turned out to be a blessing, and the snub by the large programs allowed mid-major Ball State to enter the picture. The Cardinal program was run by one of the top young coaches in the country, Brenda Oldfield, and the school was a perfect fit for a girl who wanted to be a true student-athlete. When Oldfield left for Minnesota (where she became the NCAA Coach of the Year), her assistant, Tracy Roller, became the beneficiary of Kate's talent.

Endress arrived in Muncie in 2001 and thrived in the school's atmosphere. The school didn't require that athletes live together, which allowed Kate to experience the true diversity of a college campus. She had originally planned to study Architecture but decided to switch to the Miller Business School's Entrepreneurial Program, one of the top five in the country.

As she flourished academically, Kate also blossomed on the court. In 2005, she capped off a remarkable career, and she left the school as one of the greatest players in the program's history. A 4-year letter winner, Endress became only the second player ever at Ball State to earn All-MAC first team honors more than once, and as a senior was named the Mid-America Conference Player of the Year.

Kate also led the league in scoring her final season with an 18.5 average and was #1 in 3-point percentage at .461. Endress also became only the second woman (and fourth male or female) from Ball State to surpass 1,800 career points, and her 1,843 place her second on the Cardinals' all-time list and #11 in MAC history. During her career, Kate hit double figures 93 times, including 36 times with 20 or more points and a high game of 30.

For all her efforts, Kate was twice chosen for the *ESPN the Magazine*'s All-American first team and was also the publication's Academic All-American Player of the Year. In addition, Endress was honored in 2005 as the NCAA Woman of the Year for the state of Indiana.

Kate graduated Summa cum Laude from BSU's Honors College with a 3.96 GPA and actually considered taking her basketball talents to the next level. In fact, she actually signed a free agent contract with the Connecticut Sun of the WNBA, but when they told her they wanted her to gain 25 pounds, she told her dad, "I'm not doing that for anyone."

Instead, Endress began a new life in the financial world. For two years, she worked with Citigroup on Wall Street and then for two years with an equity firm in Chicago. Never one to get complacent, Kate then attended Stanford and got her MBA in 2011.

There is no limit to what Kate Endress may achieve in her lifetime, and it all began with a loving family that nurtured the girls and encouraged them in whatever endeavors they chose. Coach Dockery knew how special Kate was early on and has great admiration for what she's accomplished. He also remembers her years at Memorial. "Kate Endress was the best communicator on the floor of any player I ever coached," he said. "I always had a habit on sectional final game day of going to the school at 11:00 and staying all day watching film. Kate showed up one Saturday and told me, 'Go home, coach. We'll win tonight.'"

Many local fans will remember Kate as a player, and some may recall her phenomenal sweeping hook shot, a very rare skill in today's game. But Endress was rare in so many ways. As an athlete, she was a two-time Metro Player of the Year in both volleyball and basketball, and her four basketball teams at Memorial finished 85-16. She finished her high school career as the city's #3 scorer (male or female) with 1,875 points, behind only Jill Hartman's 1,926 and Day School's Jeremy Willis' 1,899. She also represented our area as an Indiana All-Star and fashioned one of the greatest college careers ever by a local lady.

More importantly, Kate Endress was just as impressive off the court and always understood the value of education. On April 26th, 2012, Kate launched her new company, ditto.com, and one of her first strategic moves as the company's founder was to hire her dad to head up the Indiana branch. Wherever her life may take her, Kate is a sure bet for success, and the stringent standards she sets for herself and will to win will make her an asset wherever she goes.

Kate Endress at age 14.

FAHKARA MALONE: TINY LADY – BIG TALENT

One year removed from the departure of Kate Endress, some big shoes were again filled by a diminutive young lady who made heads spin in more ways than one. FahKara Malone was 5'3 in the 4th grade and even played the post as a youngster, but additional height was not in her future and, at the same 5'3", she not only enhanced the Memorial legacy but made a name for herself as an individual as well.

From her home in Evansville, the charming Ms. Malone flashed her easy smile as she spoke of her development as an athlete. She quickly revealed that her success was a by-product of her parents' genetics and their parenting styles. Her father, Floyd, was a stand-out athlete at Central in football and basketball, and her mother, Alzie, ran track at Bosse.

One of Alzie's earlier memories of her daughter's athleticism was watching FahKara dribbling a basketball at the bus stop when she was seven. "Floyd was in the military," Alzie recalled from her office at Berry Plastics. "I called Floyd and said, 'I think the girl has skills.' So when he got home, he started working with her, and then she just excelled. She just loved it."

Alzie was quick to point out that FahKara had a focus that made her successful off the court as well, and her parents made sure of that. "As our kids were growing, it was important for us to be their parents," Alzie explained, "especially up until age eleven or so. That was an important cycle because you have to grab hold of them and make them understand what you expect of them. Once they get older, they start developing their own train of thought. It was not acceptable to ever bring home anything lower than a 'B' in grades K through 8," Alzie continued, "because it only gets harder. FahKara and her sisters (Danika and Jacoba) always had that drive to excel."

FahKara's first organized ball was played at the YMCA as a ten-year-old, then at Impact Ministries on 7th Street, and then on an AAU team with a coach out of Boonville. During her formative years, she observed Coach Dockery working with his girls in developmental leagues, and the seed was planted in her mind.

As her game progressed, she became part of some very strong teams at Culver Elementary and Washington Middle school. In fact, she and Washington teammates like Latiffany Flemming, Amber Dickman, Britney Villines and Molly Wayne never lost a game, and as an eighth grader, FahKara's mother approached Coach Dockery and arranged for her daughter to play AAU ball for him.

With high school approaching, the young Ms. Malone enjoyed how Bruce Dockery had worked with the girls at the Evansville Basketball Academy, and when her mom weighed in that she thought Memorial would prepare FahKara for college, the decision was made. From a basketball standpoint, Malone also saw potential at Memorial after watching talented players like Jill Hartman, Kate Endress, Paige Rudolph and Andrea Fichter. She specifically remembers Hartman and how she was "blown away" at the talent she witnessed.

When FahKara entered Memorial in 2002, she realized the importance of earning respect, and she was fortunate to play on four very successful teams. "I was no superstar by any means,"

Photo courtesy of Purdue University, Sports Information.

she admitted. "It was just a bunch of girls who played really well together and knew their roles."

As a freshman, FahKara started for a team that won the sectional and went 21-5, and her sophomore year in '04, she led a 21-4 team to the school's third regional title. Competition at the time was stiff, and schools like Gibson Southern and Castle were making noise as well. Castle particularly had been consistently strong, and Malone and her cohorts had epic battles with the likes of Kaleigh Gossman, Leah Phillips, Maria Olsthoorn, Stephanie Gehlhausen and Jasmine Ussery.

But FahKara was surrounded by talent as well, with teammates like Courtney Reising, Jennifer Balbach, Ebony Ricketts, Karey Stieler, and Chelsea Falkenstein, to name a few. After a 20-4 junior season, Malone led the program to a new level her senior year as she used her magnificent quickness to befuddle opponents on the way to a runner-up finish in the 2006 State Tournament.

Malone left Memorial as the program's leader in steals and was a four-time all-conference selection, averaging 20 points and 4.5 steals per game as a senior. The three-time *Courier* Metro Player of the Year was named an Indiana All-Star and McDonald's All-American finalist, so she had no problem drawing interest from college programs.

FahKara and her parents scrutinized the candidates and proceeded with caution. When asked about the process, the young Ms. Malone didn't hesitate with her answer. "I had heard before," she began, "that you'll just know, and that's kind of how it happened." For months the Malones carefully examined each piece from the barrel of mail she had received. She wanted to go to IU, but it "didn't feel right."

After months of contemplation and deliberation, the petite Ms. Malone finally found her answer when a few minutes spent in West Lafayette made her decision crystal clear. While standing in the bowels of fabled Mackey Arena, FahKara had the epiphany after she saw the inflatable train that the Boilermakers run through before every game. "I walked down the tunnel and said, 'This is it,'" she stated. "I don't need to see anything else."

FahKara had committed during her sophomore year to play for Coach Kristy Curry, but when Curry was replaced by Sharon Versyp, the Malones were concerned. Coach Versyp understood the situation and how she had to handle it if she was going to reap the benefits of Malone's talent. "I had watched FahKara on the AAU circuit," Coach Versyp explained. "At that time (when FahKara committed), I was at IU. When I got the job at Purdue, I flew down with the two assistants to see FahKara and her family to put their minds at ease. I knew she was going to be our point guard as a freshman. I was a point guard and I played as a freshman at Purdue, so I understood her apprehension, and I knew I was the right person to coach her and guide her through the next four years.

"We only had nine players at the time," Versyp continued from her office. "We had Katie Gearlds and Erin Lawless, so there was an opportunity for a lot of young kids. FahKara was the only freshman. There were supposed to be three, but she was the only one who decided to stay; she really reaped the benefits from that."

One of the benefits about which Coach Versyp spoke was immediate playing time with experienced players, especially the great Katie Gearlds. Malone started 36 of 37 games as a freshman and was third on the team in minutes played as she scorched the floor in front of home crowds that averaged over 7,500. In her inaugural season, FahKara averaged 8.4 points and easily led the team in steals with 104 while earning Big Ten All-Freshman Team honors.

For the next three years under Coach Versyp's guidance, FahKara made her mark on the Purdue program as a player and as an individual. Not known for her scoring, she was proficient enough to become the 25th Boilermaker in the 1,000-point club. Her forte, however, was her leadership and, of course, her stifling defense. She led her teams to 111 victories during her four years there and finished her career with more than 1,000 points, 300 rebounds, 500 assists and 300 steals, joining two-time All-American Katie Douglas as the only players to reach all four milestones as a Boilermaker.

FahKara was a consistent performer in the classroom as well, earning Academic All-Big Ten honors three times. While majoring in Psychology and minoring in Child Development, FahKara quickly learned the importance of time management when dealing with the rigors of both academics and Division I athletics. "The weird part was that after the season was over, you're just a student," she described. "I felt like I should be doing so much more because I had time on my hands. Being busy all the time is normal for a student-athlete." But her stock-in-trade was her defense. She made the Big Ten All-Defensive Team as a freshman, and she passed Katie Douglas as the schools all-time leader in steals, finishing her career with 351.

No one knew FahKara as a defender and as a leader better than her last two head coaches. Bruce Dockery remembers the youngster's relentless defense, describing how Malone would suffocate a ballhandler with her quickness. He explained how the dribbler's body would be cocked to one side and how instead of making the player switch hands, she would circle the player like a dog chasing its tail. She was so quick that she would catch up to the ball and leave the dribbler dizzy as she made the steal.

Coach Versyp was just as amazed at Malone's ability, "FahKara was so competitive, coachable and hard-working," said

Verysp. "She also learned how to become a great leader, understanding that everybody around you isn't going to like your decisions, but they had so much respect for her. She was obviously one of the best defenders I've ever been around. She was our sparkplug, our Energizer Bunny that kept us going. She's low to the ground and extremely quick. She would study video and count dribbles. She knew if they had a two-dribble count before they were going to cross-over. She would time it and then pounce.

"As a person," Coach Versyp continued, "she had that contagious personality and lit up a room when she came in. She had a passion for the people around her and a passion for academics."

The passion of which the Purdue coach spoke made FahKara Malone a success both on and off the basketball court, and she has used the same qualities in life since graduating. Her first job was with Ireland Home Services where she showed her compassion as she transported kids who had been separated from their parents by Children's Services.

Beginning with the 2011-'12 school year, she accepted a new challenge as the Graduate Assistant Director of Women's Basketball Operations with the University of Evansville. Perhaps it is only fitting that the diminutive dynamo is positioned where she can use her considerable talents as a positive influence on student-athletes who aspire to be where she has been.

FahKara with Boilermakers head coach Sharon Versyp. (Photo courtesy of Purdue University, Sports Information)

DID YOU KNOW?
The only area girl to score at least 40 points in an IHSAA tournament game is Washington's Gretchen Miles, who scored 40 against Washington Catholic in 1997.

123

MALLORY LADD: THE DRIVE TO EXCEL

Last but not least in the long line of Lady Tigers is Mallory Ladd. Mallory's earliest influences came from her own family. Her mother, Kristie, starred at Harrison in the '80s as Kristie Blair and shared All-City honors with a very talented class. Joining her on the 1986 All-City team were Bosse's Vicki Lander, Memorial's Diane Starry, Mater Dei's Julie Goedde and Shannon McCullough of Reitz. Kristie also ran track and cross country at Harrison and then played her college basketball at USI.

Mallory's father, Mike, was a baseball and football standout at Dawson Springs (Kentucky) and then played football at UK under Frank Curci and the legendary Jerry Clayborne. Like many young men of his generation, Mike met Kristie at the popular local nightclub Funky's and admits that when he saw her, he said "Wow!" and knew from that moment he was going to marry the lovely young lady.

Sitting in the family's home near St. Ben's and Memorial with Mike, Kristie, Mallory, and younger brother Matt, the love and respect was evident as the story of Mallory's career unfolded. Before her athletic talents blossomed, Mallory was faced with a medical crisis. "We took her to the emergency room at least thirty times," Kristie revealed. "No one could figure out the problem."

By the age of three, the Ladds' little girl had gotten to know the medical staff all too well, and amazingly the diagnosis was revealed by little Mallory herself. It seems that in one visit, she was given permission to mess around with the ultra-sound equipment, and as she ran the device over the cold gel on her abdomen, the doctor made a discovery. The family believes that the discovery made Mallory the first child in Kentucky born with gallstones.

That realization led to the detection of a birth defect of the kidneys, resulting in corrective surgery as a three-year-old. For a full year after the surgery, Mallory had to avoid activity, but after that it was "FULL TILT," said Kristie, and Mallory hasn't slowed down since.

Mallory's early years were spent in Madisonville, Kentucky, where she pitched and played first base on a team that was runner-up in the state softball tournament. After moving to Evansville as a fourth grader, she continued with her softball until her seventh grade year. Although her natural athleticism would eventually be displayed on the volleyball and basketball courts, it was also visible on the diamond.

"You didn't want to get in the cage with her," Mike said. "I had bruises all over. If you did get in, you'd better be behind the (protective) fence. She had excellent hand-eye coordination and was a great hitter. The infield would back into the outfield when she came to the plate."

In Evansville, Mallory played softball for Pat Wempe, Mick Schnell and Steve Capan, whose daughter, Calista, went on to star at Harrison and then Georgetown. For two consecutive years, Mallory's teams were undefeated, and she won a state championship with Lakeview under the guidance of Duane Schmidt, Steve Hillenbrand and Dirk Hartman.

Although she enjoyed softball, Mallory admits that the hours and extensive travel wore on her and resulted in her 'retirement' after her seventh grade year. She does harbor some regret because she feels she could have helped Memorial's softball team during her years there.

At St. Ben's, Mallory excelled in volleyball and played her sixth grade basketball with her mother as the head coach, but Kristie stepped down to be an assistant when Angie Oliver came in as the head coach for Mallory's final two years. With future Memorial teammate Emily Nesbitt and the Hackert twins, Marie and Anna, St. Ben's captured the diocese championship and defeated Vincennes Rivet for the title, making St. Ben's the only school to beat the future state champs in elementary school.

Both Mike and Kristie agree that they saw their daughter's basketball potential early on. "I was working in the golf business and I saw Bruce (Dockery)," Mike explained. "I told him, 'I've got one coming for you.'"

And how right Mike was. The girl in question was a precocious little fourth grader named Mallory, and she would eventually place herself among the program's elite by lifting the Lady Tigers on her broad shoulders as she led them to the program's first State title.

With successful volleyball and basketball experiences behind her, Mallory entered Memorial in 2007, and her impact as an athlete was felt immediately. In volleyball, she started on a sectional champion that featured teammates Abby Greif, Chelsea Falkenstein, Heather Barnes, Helena Craig and Lindsey Will. She also started in basketball alongside Falkenstein, Melissa Nesbitt and Megan Balbach and earned All-Metro and All-SIAC first team honors.

The following year, Mallory helped Chrissy Stieler, Brie Kormelink and others complete an 18-4 season before losing to Gibson Southern in the sectional. One of the "others" was a young

Mallory with big dreams at age 2.

As if their athletic achievements weren't enough, Mallory and fellow local legend Max Lachowecki were voted the king and queen of Memorial's homecoming dance and senior prom.

freshman named Natalie Cohlmeyer, who would join Mallory as part of the nucleus of the record-setting team that was developing.

Mallory's junior season proved even more successful for her as an individual and as part of the team. The team reached the semi-state before falling to Rushville, and Mallory was named the *Courier's* Metro Player of the Year and was once again named to the All-Metro and All-SIAC first teams. In addition, she was selected first team All-State by *Hoosier Basketball Magazine*, was a Junior Indiana All-Star and was named an ESPN Player of the Week for the second year in a row.

Little did I know when I sat down with the family in late summer of 2010 that this talented young lady sitting across from me would soon embark on a journey that only a precious few get to experience. Her senior year was the culmination of years of sweat and dedication as the 6'2" Ladd flexed her muscle and dominated the competition. Mallory was spectacular throughout the State tournament, especially in the finals. In the 58-50 win over Benton Central, she led Memorial with 24 points and 13 rebounds and set a State Finals record for free throws without a miss, going 10 for 10.

Mallory was again named the Metro Player of the Year, joining teammates Anna Hackert and Natalie Cohlmeyer along with North's Georgia Stringer and Mater Dei's Maura Muensterman on the All-Metro first team. She was also a first team All-State honoree and a McDonald's All-American nominee. In addition, Mallory was named an Indiana All-Star and was very close to being named the first Miss Basketball from Southwestern Indiana.

By any measure, Mallory Ladd fashioned one of the most amazing careers in local history, and by all accounts, the results were the product of hours of hard work. "She was the first one in the gym and the last one out," said little brother Matt, prompting a rub on the head from his sister.

In fact, she was a common sight in the school gym, much to the dismay of the school's cleaning staff. "I think I've snuck in every window at Memorial," she admitted. "The janitors would see me and say, 'Hey, Mallory, how are you?' I would sneak in football doors, boys locker rooms. The scariest was at night. I've run across that gym floor with my eyes closed a lot (to turn the lights on)."

"I am very competitive at anything I do," Mallory added. "I like to sweat and work hard." Without question, Mallory's work ethic is one of her strengths, and she is also generous with praise for those who have helped her along the way.

She is aware of how fortunate she was to receive good coaching through her formative years, from her mother and Coach Oliver to Coach Dockery and Thom Endress. She also gives credit to a man who she believes was the missing ingredient in her formula to success.

"Bob Miller really heightened my game," Mallory explained, "because in order to have an all-around game, you have to be in the best shape of your life. I thought I was in shape, but a friend of mine, Elliott Nilssen, told me to call Bob Miller at Eastside Barbell on Morgan Avenue.

"In the first workout, I started crying. It was the hardest workout I'd ever done in my life. It wasn't your normal strength workout. Like, I'd be outside pulling a chain attached to a sled in the dirt that had nails in it so it would get stuck in the roots. A 75-pound chain plus the weight he put on it!"

Mr. Miller had apparently garnered quite a reputation after working with local athletes like Memorial football star Steven Scheu, Cuda Dimmett from Reitz and Bosse's Jalen Pendleton. "He is a master of getting them where they need to be," Kristie added. "He doesn't like the limelight, but he likes to see the kids progress."

Mallory became such a believer in Bob Miller that she followed some unorthodox advice that even those close to her had serious doubts about. "It was the week of the State Finals," Mike

IMPRESSIVE COMPANY

In the off-season one year, Mallory Ladd played for Lady Legit, a Ft. Wayne team that competed in national tournaments, and the entire 12-player roster are now playing Division I basketball.

Ladd explained in a later interview, "and he said, 'Mall, you need to go over to Burdette Park and run those hills.'"

While the other players on her team and the opposition were probably tapering off and resting, Mallory didn't hesitate and navigated the steep hill near the park's entrance five times on Wednesday and Thursday before the team left Friday for Ft. Wayne.

When asked why she blindly followed his instruction, Mike revealed that Mr. Miller's words inspired Mallory. "He said, 'It's going to help you win a State championship, I promise you," Mike explained. "He said, 'You will not be winded. You'll be ready for overtime, double overtime and a third one if you need that.'"

As the story played out, Bob's words proved prophetic, as Mallory dominated the overtime to deliver Memorial's girls program its first State title.

Though Bob Miller provided Mallory with the conditioning she needed, there is no doubt that her family is the source of her greatest inspiration. Countless hours were spent on neighborhood courts and gyms with Mom taking on Mallory one-on-one while Mike offered instruction, and although Mom is her biggest fan, it is Dad with whom she has a special bond.

"I call him the shooting guru," Mallory said as she glanced at Mike with her pale blue eyes. "He can see it and know exactly what's wrong." Mallory also spoke of the drills she would work on with her dad watching, like the alignment drill where Mike would recite the mantra "toe, knee, elbow, hole (basket)." Or the one-handed drill where she would place her very large palm face up with the ball in it then rotate the hand and stroke it with one hand as Mike would remind her "not out the windshield, but out the sun roof (high release)."

But most memorable of all were the rituals on game day, especially the pre-game walks with her father. "Every game she played at Memorial, volleyball, basketball, anything, she and I would walk from this house (two blocks) to the school," Mike proudly stated. "And that was the motivating time."

After Kristie added that "we knew how to start her engine," Mike continued as Mallory's eyes lit up while she listened to her dad explain. "We did it rain, sleet, snow, tornadoes; it didn't matter," Mike said.

When asked what was discussed on the strolls, Mallory responded. "We would set the goals of the day," she confided, "like staying out of foul trouble or digging or spiking if it was volleyball. Or rebounding or blocking out, being smart — and to have fun."

While discussing her game-day procedure, it was also revealed that Ms. Ladd is more than a little superstitious. Apparently she has a talent for braiding hair, and even though she didn't braid her own, superstition dictated that she braid all her teammates' hair before each game. She also wore the same socks, underwear and sports bra for every game (always cleaned, Kristie was quick to explain), and she would not switch tennis shoes even if they were totally worn through. In fact, her insistence to wear the same thread-bare socks actually caused serious problems during the season when it was revealed that, for the Rushville game, she had two blood blisters on both feet larger than quarters and her feet had to be taped before she could play.

In addition, Mallory also tied her hair with the same rubber band and had to use the same shampoo each day and had to listen to the same playlist on her ipod as she sat on her bed before a game. Songs included "The Warrior", "We Built This City", "The Feeling" and "I Want You Back", by Michael Jackson. Her final superstition involved her pre-game nourishment. She would start with a Supreme protein bar, but only after the first bite was taken by teammate Sarah Stone (Only Sarah will do). And then the bar was washed down with two (and only two) swigs of Mountain Dew.

As one might expect, Mallory's quirks came naturally. Mike and Kristie always wore the same clothing to games, and Mike always sat at the very top of the gym while Kristie sat closer to the floor with several of her thirteen brothers and sisters and their families.

It is apparent that Mallory Ladd left little to chance, and her efforts were certain to pay off with a college scholarship. UCLA was the first school to contact her, sending two hand-written letters her freshman year. She was also contacted by North Carolina, IU, Wisconsin, Butler and many others and played several games with Pat Summit watching at a national tournament. Mallory was very interested in the University of Indianapolis but was smart enough to realize that Coach Leann Freeland (a local legend who starred at USI) was too good and would probably move elsewhere, which she eventually did.

Later that November, Mallory signed with Valparaiso and was determined to lead the program to new heights. But several months into the school year, she made a decision that came as no surprise to those close to her. As hard as she tried, the time away from her family and friends was too painful and she returned home. The ultimate winner as a result of the move was Oties Epps, the coach who replaced Misty Murphy as the head coach at the University of Evansville. The Lady Aces desperately needed help, and Ms. Ladd could very well be the catalyst the program needs. And with Dad nearby to share pre-game thoughts, local fans can expect big things from Mallory.

So as Mallory begins a new chapter, she leaves behind a legacy that few before her could match. She played in 100 high school games and won 86, making her the winningest player in Evansville history. Had it not been for a last second shot by Bosse's Ashley Morehead, Mallory's four Memorial teams would have finished undefeated in the conference. She also showed amazing consistency, earning All-Metro and All-SIAC first team status all four years.

Her senior year, Mallory scored 650 points (second in the state) and shot 40% (44/110) on three-pointers, 58% on field goals and 81.6% at the line. She also ended her senior season as the state's #2 rebounder with 343 in 29 games. For her career, Mallory averaged a double-double and finished as the area's all-time rebound leader with 1,163 and as the third-leading scorer in Evansville history with 1,803 career points, behind only Jill Hartman's 1,926 and Bosse's Vicki Lander's 1,843.

It is no wonder that Bruce Dockery's program stands as the standard by which others are measured, and Mallory Ladd did her part. She pushed her body to the limit and by doing so, molded herself into one of the all-time greats in southwestern Indiana history.

DID YOU KNOW?

Mallory Ladd is known throughout the halls at Memorial for doing an excellent impersonation of Chewbacca, or 'Chewie', the loveable, hairy character from *Star Wars*.

'LITTLE DICKEY' KINDER:
LONG-RANGE SNIPER

Over the last 40 years, there have been many basketball pundits who have declared that the greatest single performance in NCAA Tournament history was the 1973 Finals when UCLA's Bill Walton connected on 21 of 22 shots against Memphis State. The 95% shooting effort set a record for the highest percentage made with over 20 attempts, but most fans from our area probably didn't realize that the incredible feat by the big redhead had some local ties.

Southwestern Indiana has had its fair share of spectacular shooters, and fans from different generations could espouse the virtues of such greats as Jerry Clayton (Central, mid-'50s), Steve Holland (North, mid-'60s), Michael Lewis (Jasper, mid-'90s) or Melvin Hall (Harrison, early 2000s). But the finest of all time might very well have been Dick Kinder. During the 1940s and '50s, the Winslow Eskimos were as respected as any team in the state as they roamed the floors of historic small-town gyms, including their own that was famous for its four pot-bellied stoves in the corners.

'Little Dickey', as Kinder was known, was a reed-thin, 5'6, 135-pounder who could dial it in from 25 feet or more with deadly accuracy with his smooth two-handed set shot. In addition, Kinder enhanced his game by developing a picture-perfect jump shot and a hook shot he could use from nearly anywhere on the court. The result was a great all-around game, and with sensational teammate Dick Farley, Winslow put together the finest seasons in the school's history.

The 1948-'49 team went undefeated during the regular season and then won two sectional games before falling to Cabby O'Neill's Jasper Wildcats, the eventual State champions. In '49-'50, Dickey's junior year, the Eskimos were just as impressive, finishing the regular season 19-1 and then avenging their loss from the previous year by beating Jasper to capture the sectional. They also won the Vincennes Regional before demolishing Evansville Bosse in the Sweet 16 and falling to New Albany in the semi-state final game. Kinder led the team in scoring both years and averaged 18 points and 4 assists as a junior, but his senior year would present an unexpected challenge.

During the summer of 1950, the gym in Winslow was condemned and the team was forced to find other accommodations. While playing their home games at places like Otwell, Washington, Petersburg and Oakland City College, Coach Kern McGlothlin's boys finished a remarkable 20-2 entering the tournament. Once again, the Eskimos won the sectional and regional but fell to New Albany in the Bloomington Semi-state, and Little Dickey's high school career was over. Kinder's teams at Winslow won 92% of their games (71-6), and Dickey averaged 21 points and 8 assists as a senior.

Kinder had originally committed to play for Arad McCutchan at Evansville College (now U of E) but withdrew before the season started. He then accepted a scholarship to Memphis State. Dickey averaged 6 points as a freshman but was slowed considerably with an injury. During a game against Seton Hall, seven-foot Pirates center Walt Dukes came down on Kinder, and even though Dickey had matured to 5'11 and 180 pounds, the incident did some serious damage. Kinder continued to play but had surgery after the season to remove half-dollar-sized pieces from each kneecap.

Although Dickey's legs weren't the same, the shooting touch never faltered, and in December of 1953, the Tigers beat #4-ranked Marshall College 104-85 with Kinder connecting on 22 of 26 field goals for a percentage of 85%, an NCAA record for 20 attempts or more. Six weeks later, Dickey was forced to call it quits because of pain from the injury.

After some rehab, Kinder transferred to Murray State in 1954 and started 26 games against several big-name programs, averaging over 15 points and 6 assists per contest. In '55-'56, Dickey started 25 games and averaged 19 points, and as a senior, he teamed with Kentucky icon Howie Crittendon to average 41 per game between them, an NCAA record for two guards on the same team.

Kinder was drafted by the St. Louis Hawks in an era when the NBA had only eight teams, but he knew he would soon be drafted into the military and declined. After his induction into the Army, Kinder was the player/coach for his team in Fort Meade, Maryland and was good enough to be named MVP. He was also selected to be one of the two men who would represent the U.S. Army at the 1960 Olympic trials.

When Bill Walton rocked the sports world in 1973, Dickey Kinder became an answer to a trivia question, and it is likely that even fans from this part of the country weren't aware of his place in NCAA history. In a story by blogger Ken Lindsay, the publisher of *guidetocoachingbasketball.com*, Lindsay revealed that Walton once introduced Kinder at an event in Evansville and made an apology. His reason was that he felt Dickey's 22 of 26 was more significant because Walton's shots were all close to the basket and virtually all of Kinder's were from long range.

Kinders's amazing record stood for 19 years, and along the way he drew some very high praise. IU coach Branch McCracken once said, "Whenever Kinder looks at the basket, the net flinches," and both Ken Lindsay and former Wisconsin coach John Powless have gone on record as saying that Kinder was "the best pure shooter" they had ever seen.

Dickey Kinder passed away in 2010 and was not around when he was given his greatest honor. Because of his phenomenal career, he joined his high school coach, Kern McGlothlin, and his high school teammate, Dick Farley, as members of the Indiana Basketball Hall of Fame. In that shrine, his name will forever be emblazoned as one of Indiana's all-time greatest sharpshooters.

> ## DID YOU KNOW?
> Washington is ranked #3 in Indiana for the longest period between basketball State championships at 63 years (1942-2005). Vincennes (Lincoln) is #4 at 58 years (1923-1981).
> *(Source: IHSAA Website)*

Photo courtesy of the Indiana Basketball Hall of Fame.

Special thanks to the Princeton Clarion for their generosity in sharing the photos used in this story.

THE 2009 PRINCETON TIGERS: PURE PERFECTION

The State champion Princeton Tigers. Front row (L-R): Leanna Myers (asst. cheer coach), Kelsey Brittingham, Alyssa Brittingham, Lacey Ainscough, Kat Bammer, Andrea Walton, Jewel Scott, Leslie Rogers, Dakota Schafer, Courtney Wallace, Jade Boner, Jordyn Jones, Katelynn Bryant, Katie Brink. Second row: Julie Koberstein (asst. cheer coach), Dale McQuiston (NGSC Supt.), Bill Niederhaus (asst. coach), Brian Douglas (asst. coach), Jalen Packer, Trevor George, Jordan Simmons, Brandt George, Keenan Johnson, Terrance Young, Rontray Chavis, Justin Simmons, Terri Myers (asst. cheer coach). Third row: Steve Hauger (asst. principal), Tom Weeks (head coach) and son Chandler, Collen Barrett (mgr.), Alex Holder, Dustin Duncan, R.J. Morris, Jake Thacker, Casey Deffendall, Matt Hughen, Paul Fulfer, Dontray Chavis, Alec Thompson, Andy Elkins (athletic director), Raleigh Brink (mgr.), Jon Abbey (principal).

When the 2008-'09 basketball season rolled around, it is safe to say that the small Gibson County town of Princeton was full of anticipation, and the excitement was long overdue. The school had experienced moderate success over the years, winning 33 sectionals and 7 regionals, and the Tigers had even made it to Indianapolis twice for the Final Four (in 1965 and 1983). But with the class system now in place and a talented group finally ready for varsity play, Tiger fans were dreaming big for the first time in years.

The program had seen its share of stars over the years, beginning with the Stoll brothers: Joe, a 1946 grad who played in the NCAA Finals for North Carolina State; Gary, a '57 grad who played for Tulane; and Roy, a '53 grad who also played for Tulane and was the only Princeton player inducted into the Indiana Basketball Hall of Fame. Another great was Larry Kidwell, a '65 grad who was the first Tiger to be named an Indiana All-Star and was a member of the 1990 Indiana Silver Anniversary team with Mr. Basketball Billy Keller and Evansville Rex Mundi's Earl Schneider.

In addition, Princeton fans saw such talent as Vaughn Chavis, the father of Dontray and Rontray Chavis from '09, and brothers Travis Trice and Justin Lynch, to name a few.

But no group of players had drawn such superlatives from local fans like the boys of the '08-'09 team. "When the boys were young, we always used to say 'We can't wait until you guys are in high school so you can play together,'" said W.W. George, the father of Trevor and Brandt George of the '09 Tigers.

"When they were in the 7th and 8th grade, they only lost one game," recalled radio legend Richard Lankford, the long-time voice of Gibson County sports. "Everyone knew they were good. They had three or four players who could score 25."

When asked to draw comparisons to other Gibson County teams, Richard Lankford reflected for a moment and then gave it his best shot. "The '09 team was the best team I'd seen in a long time," he responded. "The 1967 Oakland City team was outstanding, with Larry Harris, Rick Smith, Steve Nelson, Gary Duncan and that bunch. And the '65 team with Kidwell, Jimmy Peck, Alan Rogers, Ron Speedy and Glen Early. Speedy was awfully good."

Lankford also praised Princeton coach Tom Weeks, who had taken over the program a few years before the '08-'09 season. "Coach Weeks did a super job. That team had talent." Richard said. "Some teams may have one (extraordinary talent). Princeton had three, and sometimes that's hard to coach. You have to be coached if you're going to win."

The man hired on to guide the young stallions knew what he was facing when he took the reins in 2005, and as his teams suffered early on, he could feel the pressure as expectations rose. When Tom Weeks arrived, the George brothers, Trevor and Brandt, were freshmen and the others were still in middle school. The program was coming off back-to-back two-win seasons, but as he talked with new AD Andy Elkins and saw game film of the boys coming up, he thought to himself, "There's enough athleticism here that we could do something."

Weeks and his staff went to work, and in the first and second year, they still struggled in the win column, but they did defeat Gibson Southern the first year, a team they hadn't beaten in eight seasons. As the youngsters developed as competitors, their results improved, and in Weeks' third season, the Tigers won 17 games, losing a close game in the sectional final to a Memorial team led by Kyle Kuric. Though the Princeton program was losing A.J. Rogers and Wes Robinson, the 'dream team' everyone had raved about for years was ready to take the town on the journey of a lifetime.

Princeton had not won a sectional since 2002 when Tyler George, the brother of twins Brandt and Trevor, played for the Tigers. Tyler was quite a talent himself, eventually playing for Dan Sparks at Vincennes University and the University of Tennessee-Martin. Brandt and Trevor were entering the '08-'09 season as senior leaders, and when the season began on November 29, the Tigers were firing on all cylinders.

From the beginning, Princeton used a six-man rotation who piled up big minutes on the floor. Three of the starters were listed as guards: 6'2 sophomore Jalen Packer at the point with 6'4 sophomore Rontray Chavis and 6'1 junior Jordan Simmons. The front line starters were 6'3 senior Trevor George and his brother, 6'2

Brandt. The first man off the bench was 'sixth starter' Dontray Chavis, a 6'4 sophomore. Keenan Johnson, a 6'1 junior, also provided valuable minutes in 23 of the 29 games.

The Tigers began the season with blowouts over Wood Memorial (88-39) and Heritage Hills (85-57), and they survived their first real challenge with a 71-68 win over Bosse. They then rattled off seven more yawners with an average winning margin of nearly 30 points. After a three-point win over Southridge, the Tigers then faced the team that area fans thought might provide the first blemish on Princeton's spotless record.

The Washington Hatchets had dominated the series for years as the Zeller boys (Luke, Tyler and Cody) had led the school to State titles in 2005 and 2008, but the 13-0 Tigers whipped the 10-2 Black and Gold in the Hatchet House 57-50. The play of the game very possibly set an IHSAA record that may stand forever. Near the end of the first quarter, after a missed put-back by Cody Zeller, Dontray Chavis grabbed the rebound and flung the ball almost underhanded from 77 feet. As the buzzer went off, the ball tickled the twine, making it, in all likelihood, the longest shot ever made in a high school game. That win motivated Coach Weeks' boys, and they finished the regular season 23-0 with only two teams coming within nine points in the final eight games, Jasper (58-55) and Evansville Central (67-65).

Princeton had drubbed county rival Gibson Southern by 41 earlier in the season, and in the Princeton Sectional, the Titans fared only slightly better, losing by 24. The Tigers then made easy work of the rest of the field by downing Boonville (82-59) and Evansville Memorial (60-51).

At the regional, the Tigers were psyched for a rematch with the 21-2 Hatchets, but the dream matchup was not to be. Princeton did their part with a 75-66 win over the stubborn Edgewood Mustangs, but Washington was stunned by Salem 58-51. In the final, Princeton took care of business with a 74-61 victory over Salem and made plans for a semi-state date with Greensburg.

Trevor George saves a loose ball from going out of bounds as coach Tom Weeks dodges the action. (Photo courtesy of Daily Clarion/Jeff Stanton)

Coach Tom Weeks

Rontray Chavis in action in the Class 3A State Championship game. (Photo courtesy of Daily Clarion/Jeff Stanton)

Who knows how long it may be before the Princeton fans get another taste of playing for a State title, but until that day comes, they savor the fruits of 2009. Looking back, some see defining moments over the course of the year. "I would say when we beat Washington," Brandt George answered when asked when he realized the team's potential. "We knew if we could get past Washington, we had a good chance to win it."

Coach Weeks totally agreed, saying "The Washington game was huge. That set the tone and was a confidence builder. Another key game was the Harrison game. They had Kendall Brown, and we were able to pull that one out."

W.W. George, the father of the twins, drove a lot of miles to pick up tickets from whatever schools had them available and remembers the frenzy that ensued in the community. "It was exhausting," Mr. George explained. "People were wanting tickets. I drove to North Davies to pick up 50, and I drove to Bloomington and Salem. As the season went on, every place you went you'd see a sea of red. People came out who hadn't come to games for years."

Coach Weeks recalls the support he had and the pressure as the wins mounted. "I had great assistants," Coach Weeks said. "Brian Douglas and Bill Niederhaus were two great guys to work with and were a huge help all season long. And I had great support from all of the administrators and board and fans. I kind of dubbed them 'The Big Red Nation'. When it came to game day, I think the only guy left in town was Barney Fife because the stands were a sea of red." Weeks continued by discussing the pressure. "Everybody kept saying, 'You need to lose one,' and I said 'Why?!' It doesn't make sense. We set goals to do exactly what we did. You never expect it to be as hard as it was. I thought if we took care of the little things and played one possession at a time, a lot of good things could happen."

And happen they did – in a big way. Most fans will remember the boys themselves. Four players averaged double figures in scoring for the season. Rontray Chavis led the way at 16.7 followed by Trevor George (15.0), Jalen Packer (14.3) and Dontray Chavis (11.5), followed closely by Jordan Simmons at 8.6. Trevor and Rontray and Dontray shouldered most of the rebounding load at 8.1, 6.1 and 5.1, respectively.

But the '09 Tigers were much more than numbers. Each added his own ingredient to the recipe. "A lot of our offense came from defense," Coach Weeks explained, "and we would get burned occasionally when we pressed. But they had a mental toughness that helped us win close games, like Bosse and Harrison and Washington."

played great defense, and Brandt, he didn't score a to because he didn't have to; he did the little things for us Dontray (Chavis) could come in and explode; he coul score 6 or 8 real quick."

As the '09 season came to an end, several of th Tigers were recognized for their season. Jalen Packe was named to the *Courier*'s All-Southwestern Indian second team while Trevor George and Rontray Chavi made the first team. Coach Weeks was named the All SW Indiana Coach of the Year, and the team may hav also distinguished itself in another way. It is highly un likely that a basketball varsity team has ever filled hal of its roster with brothers, namely the Chavis boys, th Georges and Jordan and Justin Simmons.

When the Tigers brought home the trophy in 2009 they became only the third Gibson County team to wi a title in any sport (Gibson Southern won softball title in '03 and '05) and the first Princeton team to captur a championship. And they did it by putting together perfect season.

After the 2010 campaign, Coach Weeks accepte a new challenge when he left for Frankfort, Indian a school that hadn't won a sectional in 13 season When he left, he took with him some fond memories The journey he took with the boys in '09 was one onl eleven groups have experienced in Indiana history – th perfect basketball season.

The magnitude of the feat isn't lost on Tom Week as he put the '08-'09 season in perspective: "You g undefeated and everybody thinks you're having blast, but it's harder than anybody knows. You don' really get the time to enjoy it until it's all said and done And at that last moment, everything you've wanted t achieve in your professional life you've done. And t watch the kids and community come together at tha time, it was like our own stimulus package. It was very very special."

Below: Jordan Simmons (22) is airborne against Rocheste as teammates Jalen Packer (left) and Dontray Chavis. (Phot courtesy of the Daily Clarion/Jeff Stanton.)

Above: Tiger guard Jalen Packer in hot pursuit of a loose ball.(Photo courtesy of the Daily Clarion/Jeff Stanton.)

"Jalen (Packer) was a true point guard," Weeks continued. "He could have scored more but sacrificed himself for the team. Rontray was kind of under the radar that year. He had 24 points and 12 rebounds in the State championship game. Trevor and Brandt were solidifying factors. Trevor was a great high school basketball player. He could take you on the drive, post you inside or shoot the three. Jordan (Simmons) was very tough. He shot the ball well and

When Princeton's Larry Kidwell was named to the Indiana Basketball Hall of Fame's silver anniversary team in 1990, he joined 58 other players from our area to receive the honor. Here are the names of those so honored and the year they graduated.

Robert Menke (Huntingburg) – 1937
Jim Myers (Bosse) – 1939
Leo Kiler (Washington) – 1940
Leroy Mangin (Washington) – 1941
•Charles Harmon (Washington) – 1942
•James Riffey (Washington) – 1942
Paul Hoffman (Jasper) – 1943
Gene Schmidt (Bosse) – 1944
•Norris Caudell (Bosse) – 1945
•Julius 'Bud' Ritter (Bosse) – 1945
Orvis Burdsall (Vincennes) – 1946
Bob Kohlmeyer (Central) – 1946
J.P. Salb (Jasper) – 1946
Marvin Keener (Central) – 1947
Mike Sermersheim (Jasper) – 1947
•Lee Hamilton (Central) – 1948
•Gene Southwood (Central) – 1948
Jack Heldman (Jasper) – 1948
Dimp Stenftenagel (Jasper) – 1949
•Paul Rumbach (Jasper) – 1950
•Tom Schutz (Jasper) – 1950
Burke Scott (Tell City) – 1951
Jerry Whitsell (Reitz) – 1951
•John Harrawood (Central) – 1953
•Bob Wessel (Central) – 1953
Sam Gee (Washington) – 1954
Donald Bates (Jasper) – 1955
Carl Pitts (Vincennes) – 1955
Larry Pitts (Vincennes) – 1956
David Giesler (Jasper) – 1957

Roger Kaiser (Dale) – 1957
Sam Alford (Washington) – 1960
Bob Luegers (Jasper) – 1960
Bob Merder (Jasper) – 1961
Gary Grieger (Bosse) – 1962
Tom Kron (Tell City) – 1962
Mick Stenftenagel (Jasper) – 1962
Larry Kidwell (Princeton) – 1965
Earl Schneider (Rex Mundi) – 1965
Don Buse (Holland) – 1968
Bob Ford (North) – 1968
•Jerry Memering (Vincennes) – 1969
•Tom Turner (Vincennes) – 1969
Keith Huff (Reitz) – 1970
Steve Lochmueller (Tell City) – 1971
Ronald Thomas (Vincennes Lincoln) – 1973
John Thomas Brown (Washington) – 1978
Steve Bouchie (Washington) – 1979
Mike Ballenger (Jasper) – 1981
•Doug Crook (Vincennes Lincoln) – 1981
•Courtney Witte (Vincennes Lincoln) – 1981
Myron Christian (Bosse) – 1982
Derek Lindauer (Central) – 1982
Tim Vieke (Vincennes Lincoln) – 1982
Derrick Dowell (Bosse) – 1983
Brian Miles (North) – 1983
Craig Neal (Washington) – 1983
Chris Schafer (Princeton) – 1984

(•2 teammates in same year)

Over the years, one measure of individual basketball success has been recognition as an Indiana All-Star. From 1941 to 2011, there have been 89 area players (male & female) named to the teams. Here is the list of the boys honored and a breakdown by school and decade. *(Girls list on page 115.)*

BOYS (* Mr. Basketball)

1941 - Leroy Mangin (Washington)
1942 - Jim Riffey (Washington)
1942 – Charles Harmon (Washington)
1943 – Paul Hoffman (Jasper)
1944 – Gene Schmidt (Bosse)
1945 – Broc Jerrel (Bosse)
1945 – Norris Caudell (Bosse)
1945 – Tom Hoffman (Jasper)
1946 – Bill Butterfield (Bosse)
1946 – Bob Kohlmeyer (Central)
!947 – Joe Keener (Central)
1947 – Mickey Sermersheim (Jasper)
1948 – Gene Southwood (Bosse)
1949 – Bob White (Jasper)
1950 – Dick Farley (Winslow)
1951 – Jerry Whitsell (Reitz)
1953 – Bob Wessel (Central)
1954 – Jerry Clayton (Central)
1955 – Donnie Bates (Jasper)
1957 – Roger Kaiser (Dale)
1957 – David Geisler (Jasper)
1959 – Alan Nass (Huntingburg)
1961 – Bob Merder (Jasper)

1962 – Dave Schellhase (North)
1962 – Gary Grieger (Bosse)
1962 – Tom Kron (Tell City)
1963 – Tom Niemeier (Rex Mundi)
1963 – Jerry Southwood (Bosse)
1965 – Larry Kidwell (Princeton)
1965 – Earl Schneider (Rex Mundi)
1967 – John Wellemeyer (Huntingburg)
1967 – Larry Weatherford (Bosse)
1968 – Bob Ford (North)
1968 – Don Buse (Holland)
1969 – Jerry Memering (Vincennes)
1970 – Keith Huff (Reitz)
1979 – *Steve Bouchie (Washington)
1981 – Mike Ballenger (Jasper)
1981 – Doug Crook (Vincennes)
1982 – Myron Christian (Bosse)
1983 – Craig Neal (Washington)
1983 – Brian Miles (North)
1983 – Derrick Dowell (Bosse)
1989 – Calbert Cheaney (Harrison)
1990 – Travis Trice (Princeton)
1990 – Parrish Casebier (South Spencer)

1991 – Andy Elkins (Bosse)
1992 – Walter McCarty (Harrison)
1993 – Toby Madison (Washington Catholic)
1993 – Scott Rolen (Jasper)
1994 – Sean Daugherty (Vincennes Lincoln)
1995 – Kent Ayer (South Spencer)
1996 – Michael Lewis (Jasper)
1998 – Clint Keown (Memorial)
1999 – Frank Mujezinovic (Jasper)
2000 – Blake English (North)
2002 – Matt Kiefer (Mater Dei)
2002 – Dedrick Finn (Castle)
2005 – *Luke Zeller (Washington)
2005 – Darren Cloud (Reitz)
2006 – Brandon Hopf (Forest Park)
2007 – Bryan Bouchie (Washington)
2007 – Clint Hopf (Forest Park)
2008 – *Tyler Zeller (Washington)
2008 – Kyle Kuric (Memorial)
2009 – Kendall Brown (Harrison)
2011 – *Cody Zeller (Washington)
2011 – Eric Stutz (Castle)

Local Boys Indiana All-Stars by decade:
1940s – 14
1950s – 8
1960s – 13
1970s – 2
1980s – 7
1990s – 11
2000s – 11
2010s – 2

Same School – Same Year
1942 – Washington (Jim Riffey, Charles Harmon)
1945 – Bosse (Broc Jerrel, Norris Caudell)

Father/Son
Steve ('79) & Bryan ('07) Bouchie – Washington

Brothers
Gene ('48) & Jerry ('62) Southwood – Bosse
Luke ('05), Tyler ('08) & Cody ('11) Zeller – Washington

Local Boys All-Stars by schools:
Bosse – 11
Jasper – 11
Washington – 9
Central – 4
North – 4
Harrison – 3
Reitz – 3
Vincennes (Lincoln) – 3
Memorial – 2
Rex Mundi – 2
Huntingburg – 2
Princeton – 2
Castle – 2
South Spencer – 2
Forest Park – 2
Washington Catholic – 1
Mater Dei – 1
Winslow – 1
Dale – 1
Tell City – 1
Holland – 1

A special thank you to the University of Evansville Sports Information Department for the photos used in this story.

THE JIM CREWS ERA: THE DAWNING OF A NEW DAY

For those old enough to remember a school called Evansville College, memories of University of Evansville basketball are deep-rooted and very special, and the transformation to Division I was painful. But in 1985, a man was brought in who had strong ties with Hoosier basketball fans, and this man would lead U of E's program to new heights with players who developed into some of the best in the school's illustrious history.

The Evansville College basketball program tipped off in 1919 under Coach G.B. Schnurr, and the first five coaches did one-year stints before John Harmon took over for a 13-year run. The ninth coach at the college was a local boy who galvanized the community as he built a dynasty at the College Division (Division II) level. Arad McCutchan was loved by his players and coaches, and his 31-year reign produced nine 20-win seasons, 12 NCAA Tourney appearances and 5 national titles ('59, '60, '64, '65 and '71).

When the decision was made to take the program to the Division I level, Arad opted to step aside. His replacement was a fine young coach named Bobby Watson, who immediately won the hearts of U of E fans when he revived a popular mascot of the past, the riverboat gambler Ace Purple. With a growing fan base, the season looked promising, but after only four games, the unthinkable happened. On the evening of December 13, 1977, the entire team and coaching staff was lost in a plane crash just after takeoff from the Evansville airport.

Needless to say, the community was devastated, and after a long grieving period, the decision was made to rebuild with a new coach and staff. Dick Walters did his best under difficult circumstances but had little success, so after the 1984-85 season, Walters was replaced. The choice of a successor was a popular one, and the new kid in town brought with him an air of familiarity.

Jim Crews grew up in Normal, Illinois and was a three-sport star at University High School as a 6'5 quarterback and defensive back on the gridiron and as a standout in basketball and baseball, as well. Jim's college choice couldn't have been better, as he became part of what many fans believe to be the greatest team in Indiana University history. With a starting lineup that featured Kent Benson, Quinn Buckner, Scott May, Bobby Wilkerson and Tom Abernathy, Coach Bob Knight reached perfection. In 1976, they were crowned NCAA champions and to this day are still the last team to finish a season undefeated.

Crews was part of the rotation on the '75-'76 team but more importantly, his experiences prepared him well for his future. "It was a great choice for me," Jim Crews explained, "because Coach Knight believed in the same things my parents did, so that was easy — work hard, help other people, be team-oriented. He was tough to play for, no doubt, but it was not a shock to my system."

After graduation, Jim served as an assistant under Knight for eight years, and when I asked who had first contacted him from the University of Evansville, his voice perked up. "Jim Byers (UE athletic director) and I met up in Bloomington for about four hours one day," Crews told me. "You hit the nail on the head when you asked if he was part of my decision. The things he discussed and thought were important in college athletics coincided with what I believed. He explained how Evansville loved basketball and the fan support and what it meant. Jim Byers was the number one, two and three reasons I came there. There were a lot of reasons, but he was the top three. You know what, everything he said in those four hours and as long as I've known him, everything's been the truth."

Jim Byers remembers the meeting also and was impressed by Jim's methods and his results. "That evening (in Bloomington), we had dinner with Coach Knight," Byers recalled, "and Knight made the statement that Jim was ready for a head coaching position and that the job at UE was a perfect fit.

"One of the first things Jim did when he arrived in Evansville was meet Coach McCutchan and talk about the great tradition. He told Mac that he was going to have the players wear sleeved jerseys (like they did in the early years) in his honor. When Jim arrived, the program was in dire condition, and he was facing a major rebuilding job."

Coach Crews went to work immediately, and one of the first moves he made was to do some housecleaning. He dismissed some athletes whom he felt didn't mesh with his philosophy, and he was also very lucky to land two players who were open to a

No one has dedicated themselves more to U of E athletics than equipment manager Daryl Buente. Daryl bleeds purple and is so much a fan, in fact, that he owns over fifteen pairs of purple pants like the ones in this photo. This story about the Jim Crews era would not have been this thorough without the significant contributions made by Mr. Buente, and his efforts were greatly appreciated.

change of scenery. The first was Marty Simmons, whom Jim had recruited to IU. The second was Scott Haffner, a 6'3, 180-pound guard who had become disillusioned at the University of Illinois. So as the two ex-Big Ten players sat out, Crews began the building process.

At the peak of Dick Walters' term at UE, the Aces finished 23-6 in 1981-'82 under the leadership of seniors Brad Leaf and Theron Bullock. The team won the Midwestern Conference and made the program's first trip to the Division I NCAA Tournament, and most importantly, drew over 10,000 fans for their home games. But after three mediocre seasons (13-16, 15-14, 13-16), attendance had dropped to 6,245 in 1984-'85.

Using a pared down roster from his housecleaning and with Simmons and Haffner waiting in the wings to become eligible and 6'9 freshman Dan Godfread redshirted, Crews began to implement his system. With players like 6'6 Larry Brand from suburban Chicago and 6'5 Chris Bomba (the son of IU team doctor Brad Bomba), the Aces finished 8-19, but the momentum was escalating for a major re-vitalization and a return to the atmosphere of old at Roberts Stadium.

In 1986, the sensational Marty Simmons began a two-year U of E career that would land him in the school's hall of fame, and Haffner began the first of his three years of eligibility. Godfread also showed great promise as a redshirt freshman, as did true freshman Brian Hill, a recruit from Baltimore. The boys started slowly but fashioned an eight-game winning streak late in the season to finish 16-12. Amazingly, the so-so record was good enough

to tie for the conference title, and with the late season surge, home attendance rose 1,400 per game for an average of 7,923.

In 1987-'88, the value of the two Big Ten transfers became obvious to everyone as senior Marty Simmons averaged 25.9 points and junior Haffner tallied 750 points on the season. After a 20-7 regular season and second place finish in the MCC, Evansville hosted two games in the 1988 NIT, defeating Utah and then falling to Boston College.

Although Coach Crews would miss Marty Simmons' production and leadership the following year, the 1989-'90 Aces put together a fantastic season. During the 25-6 campaign, the highest win total since the amazing 29-0 season in 1965, Coach Crews surrounded Scott Haffner with some outstanding talent. Godfread, now a 6'10 junior, was a great defender and rebounder who was complemented well by junior Brian Hill, freshman Scott Shreffler from Marion, Illinois and guard Reed Crafton, who finished the season with 211 assists, a single season record.

Attendance at UE home games rose to 9,280 as the boys put together a streak of 21 wins in 22 games and captured another MCC title. The season was memorable in many ways, but two games in particular became part of Aces basketball lore. The first came on February 18, 1989 in a game at Roberts Stadium against the Dayton Flyers. On this night, Scott Haffner found himself in the zone and rocked the house as he caught fire, hitting 23 of 29 field goal attempts, 11 of 13 three-pointers and 8 free throws for 65 points. At one point during the game, Haffner looked at the bench, a la Michael Jordan, and shrugged his shoulders as if to say, "I can't miss!"

Scott's effort was the highest point total in the nation in the '80s and was the seventh best of all-time against Division I opponents. Coach Crews remembers the game well and was much more concerned about beating Dayton than sitting back and admiring Haffner's work. "We needed every one of those points," Crews pointed out. "I got lost in the game. At halftime, Scott had 30 and I said, 'This is not good. I mean, we're not up by 20 and he's not going to get 30 again.' He ended up getting 35 (in the 109-83 win)."

Scott Haffner finished the season with 760 points, the third highest total at the time in Aces history, and was named the MCC Player of the Year. He also set the UE record for three-pointers in a season (98) and finished third on the career list with 245 treys.

The second highlight of the '88-'89 season occurred in the post season when the Aces appeared on national television from Tucson, where they faced off with Oregon State. Like any good coach, Crews pounded home the point that every year a #11 seed takes down a #6, and as the game developed, the Aces became believers. UE dropped behind 21-10 early but came back in the second half to take the game to overtime. With eleven seconds on the clock, Reed Crafton buried a 25-footer to put the Aces up 92-90 and Evansville hung on for a 94-90 victory. Although Coach Crews' boys fell in the second round to eventual runner-up Seton Hall, the team became the first, and still only, U of E team to win a Division I NCAA Tournament game.

The following year saw home attendance rise once again (to 9,648), but the victory total fell as the Aces greeted freshmen Sascha Hupmann from Munich, Germany and Chaka Chandler from Columbus, Ohio, along with 6'10 Mark Jewell who transferred from Iowa. The Aces finished fifth in the conference and completed the year at 17-15 with Godfread setting the record for career blocks and then moving on to a short career in the NBA and the Continental Basketball Association. Fellow senior Brian Hill placed his name in the record book as well with a season field goad percentage of .648.

In 1990, Coach Crews added recruits Todd Cochenour (Mooresville), Mark Hisle (Terre Haute North) and Parrish Casebier (Rockport), but with Scott Shreffler injured, the team finished 15-15. The highlight of the season was a 136-128 overtime win over Butler in which ten players fouled out and Sascha Hupmann hit 13 of 14 filed goals for the best single game percentage (92.9%) in school history. Despite the mediocre record, Aces fans did show their support, however, with attendance topping the 10,000 level for the first time in many years.

The '91-'92 attendance dipped some but did stay above 10,000 as fans flocked to see the newly-remodeled Roberts Stadium. The team responded to the support with a 24-6 season, good enough to top the conference and send the Aces to the Big Dance once again, where they fell in the first round. Two outstanding freshmen joined the squad, Andy Elkins (Evansville Bosse) and Reed Jackson (Norris City, Illinois), and Parrish Casebier showed his potential with 41 points in a 74-56 win over Notre Dame in front of a sellout crowd of 12, 471.

Aces fans swarmed the stadium during the '92-93 season with an average home attendance of 11,740, a figure that placed UE 30th in the country and was the pinnacle for the Jim Crews era. The team responded with a 23-7 record and another MCC title before losing again in the opening round of the NCAA Tourney.

The season would prove to be Parrish Casebier's final one at UE as he finished #7 on the career points list and left school to turn professional. Scott Shreffler also completed a fantastic career, and although it ended with an emotional loss to #3 seed Florida State in the Southeast Regional, Scott's body of work was admirable.

Shreffler's career had been marred by injury, and those close to him knew the courage it took to battle through a shoulder injury from diving for a loose ball as a sophomore and an ACL tear as a junior. "Every coach thinks his kids are special," Jim

THE SLEEVES
BY SCOTT SHREFFLER
*(re-printed from the
UE basketball media guide)*

It is an honor indeed
To wear the sleeves.
An honor that only a
Select few achieve.

The sleeves stand for
Championships, attitude and desire,
A tradition that will raise
One's standards higher.

The respect they have earned
Is quite unique,
A commitment to excellence
That all programs seek.

Hard work, determination,
Success and pride
Are characteristics of the
Sleeves known nationwide.

Scott Shreffler

Crews said to journalist John Feinstein in the *Washington Post*. "But I doubt you'll ever find a kid who has put more into getting the chance to play the game than Scott. Coming back is remarkable. He did it twice."

Scott Shreffler left UE #10 on the school's scoring list and second in assists, and he was eventually named to the All-Time Aces Team. Though he admits that he was far from the most talented player, his place in UE history is solid. In 1993, he became the first Aces player to score over 1,000 points while also recording over 500 assists, and more importantly, he became the only Aces player to play in the NCAA Tourney three times

With Shreffler gone, the leadership roles fell on juniors Andy Elkins and Reed Jackson, and both came through with the help of a solid supporting cast. Seniors Mark Hisle and Todd Cochenour provided stability and experience, and freshmen Jeff Layden, a center from Lawrence North High School, and Chris Quinn from South Bend gave the program new blood. Coach Crews also welcomed two other transfers, Scott Sparks, the son of legendary Vincennes University coach Dan Sparks, and Evansville Harrison sharpshooter Brent Kell, who moved in from Niagara. The team finished a respectable 21-11 and lost to Tulane in the NIT, and those returning would face some new competition as they became the first Aces team to compete in the Missouri Valley Conference.

The '94-'95 Aces finished fifth in the MVC and won 18 on the season against 9 losses. One oddity that occurred during the year was due to a quirky schedule that equipment manager Daryl Buente recalls as a very unusual situation. After a Saturday night game in Tulsa in January, the Aces returned to their hotel. That Saturday afternoon, Bradley had played at Indiana State before driving to their Evansville hotel for a Monday night game with UE. When the Aces arrived home on Sunday, Coach Crews realized that it was the first time in his career that the visiting team was in town before the home team. (The Aces lost to Bradley by one point.)

Dan Godfread

Marcus Wilson

Reed Crafton

For the season, Aces junior college transfer Brian Jackson won the AT&T Long Distance Award as the nation's most accurate three-point shooter, and Andy Elkins became the only Aces player to be named first team All-Conference in both the MCC and MVC. Reed Jackson joined the Aces' 1,000-point club with 1,101, and Elkins finished fourth on the all-time scoring list (1,761) on his way to an eventual 2003 induction into the U of E Hall of Fame.

The 1995-'96 season saw an influx of more transfers as Chris Hollender (Lakeland), Stuart Sullivan and Kareem Richardson (East Carolina) joined Jackson, Kell, Sparks, Quinn and Layden on the Aces roster. In addition, a new freshman was brought in from South Bend Riley who would make his mark by becoming one of the program's all-time greats.

Marcus Wilson quickly became a starter for Coach Crews and finished the season as the team's leading scorer, and although the Aces were affected by Brian Jackson suffering a broken leg early in the year, Wilson showed signs of things to come. The team finished the season at 13-14, the first losing season for Crews since his first year, and the next couple years would be more of the same.

To open the '96-'97 season, Evansville hosted Drexell and Iowa in the pre-season NIT before losing to Indiana and Tulsa at Madison Square Garden. Against IU, Wilson canned a shot to put UE up with three seconds remaining only to have Andre Patterson hit a fluke shot for the win. After the game, Coach Knight told reporters, "That is the only time in my career that the team that player harder than us lost. They deserved to win that game."

Wilson finished the year with 486 points, sixth in the MVC, and Chris Hollender finished with 366, 17th best in the conference. Although the team finished 17-14, there were some impressive performances, like Wilson's 33 versus Indiana State and the team hitting 17 of 35 three-pointers against Southern Illinois. The '96-'97 season also saw the first of a heavy decline in attendance, and many attributed it to the opening of Casino Aztar. But regardless of the reason, the plummeting figures became a pattern in the coming years.

Four freshmen joined the team in 1997, and each of them would play significant roles over the coming years. Jeremy Stanton came on board from Coach Crews' hometown, Normal, Illinois, and Craig Snow came in from nearby Mt. Carmel. Two Hoosiers also enrolled, Kyle Runyon from Fairmont and Adam Seitz from Winslow. At one point, the Aces won nine consecutive

Andy Elkins

games from December 28 until January 24, but the team finished just 15-15 as attendance fell to 8,177.

With Marcus Wilson entering his senior season, hopes were high for the 1998-'99 Aces, and the season would feature many highlights before the program would begin a downturn that would bring the Jim Crews era to a close. Senior Curt Begle had another fine season off the bench, and the Aces capped off a solid year with a thrilling game at Roberts Stadium to end the regular season. In an overtime nail-biter, Wilson stroked a three to seal the victory and clinch the MVC championship by two games.

Though the Aces lost in the first round of the NCAA Tourney, there was some excellent play from several Aces. Craig Snow finished second on the team with a 13.4 average, followed by Kwame James, Begle, Seitz and a freshman named Clint Keown. Begle won the MVC Sixth Man of the Year Award, while Jeremy Stanton (All-Defensive Team) and Adam Seitz (All Freshman Team) won conference honors as well.

As for Marcus Wilson, he led his teams in scoring all four years and was named the MVC player of the Year in 1999. He ended his career with 2,053 points, second only to the great Larry Humes' 2,236, and he set a school record for free throw percentage (88.69%) and an NCAA record for three-pointers without a miss (9 for 9 against Bradley). Marcus once drew praise from Coach Roy Williams after Wilson torched the Kansas Jayhawks for 34 points, saying, "Marcus Wilson is the best shooter we faced all year." Wilson was eventually named one of the Top 50 All-Time players in MVC history, and he was close to making the NBA before spending twelve years playing pro ball overseas.

After the '98-'99 season, the program struggled, with the boys finishing 18-12 then 14-16 and 7-21 as attendance plummeted to a low of 5,822 in '01-'02. After the 2001-'02 season, Jim Crews

was replaced by Steve Merfeld, who led the program for five years before Marty Simmons was hired in 2007. Jim Crews went on to coach for seven years at Army before doing a year as a broadcaster and then returning to coaching.

By almost any standard, Coach Crews had a very impressive run at UE, and there are many who feel that we were fortunate to have him for 17 seasons. "He put us on the map," said Lance Wilkerson, who was the sports director at WEHT-TV Channel 25 for many years and is now the director of development for UE athletics and play-by-play man for Aces games on radio. "He spoiled us," Lance continued. "What he did was bring a lot of Indiana basketball traditions and instilled them in Evansville, like running the motion offense, putting the team first, building a fan base, and it really worked. And he brought in players, like Brian Hill from Dunbar (Ballimore). I still don't know how he landed Hill. He just kept re-loading. I just remember how we were so deep. Everybody could shoot.

"Coach Crews had that discipline," Wilkerson continued. "It was probably tough love at times. His number one asset was his influence on all the young men who graduated and to this day are leaders in their communities. He graduated virtually every senior. He did it the right way. He ran an extremely clean program.

"He really embraced the tradition of Evansville basketball then added to it. When Arad (McCutchan) passed away, he went to the all-orange sleeves for that year, and the fans loved it so much that they made orange a secondary color (the colors were purple and gold during the Crews era)."

Crews himself says that, overall, his years in Evansville were a great period of his life as he and his wife Kim watched their kids grow up. Many of the memories were moments on the floor, like Haffner's 65 points or the night Godfread had 40 and Haffner 30 against Loyola. He also mentioned the final game in 1999 when

Marty Simmons in Action

137

ALL-TIME GREATS

I thought it would be fun to compile a list of the all-time greatest U of E players from the Jim Crews era, so I enlisted the services of four gentlemen who know Aces basketball as well as anyone. With the help of former AD Jim Byers, former Sports Information Director Bob Boxell, and long-time fans Lance Wilkerson and Bill Bussing, these are the lists we came up with. The participants were asked to offer a first team, second team and MVP, but as you will see, these men had ideas of their own. Their passion for Aces basketball entitles them to their own perceptions, however, so here are their choices.

Lance Wilkerson
First Team
Scott Haffner (MVP)
Marty Simmons
Andy Elkins
Marcus Wilson
Dan Godfread

Second Team
Scott Shreffler
Reed Jackson
Sascha Hupmann
Parrish Casebier
Craig Snow
Chris Bomba (Mr. Intangible)
Jeremy Stanton
   (Best Defender & Assist Man)

Bill Bussing
C – Dan Godfread
C – Sascha Hupmann
F – Parrish Casebier
F – Andy Elkins
F – Reed Jackson
F – Craig Snow
F – Marcus Wilson
G – Scott Haffner
G – Scott Shreffler

Jim Byers
First Team
Marty Simmons (MVP)
Scott Haffner
Marcus Wilson
Andy Elkins
Parrish Casebier

Second Team
Scott Shreffler
Reed Jackson
Dan Godfread
Brian Hill
Chris Hollender

Bob Boxell
First Team
Marcus Wilson (MVP)
Marty Simmons (MVP)
Scott Shreffler (MVP)
Scott Haffner
Andy Elkins

Second Team
Parrish Casebier
Reed Jackson
Dan Godfread
Brian Hill
Sascha Hupmann

Curt Begle and Marcus Wilson led the team to a win over Southwest Missouri State to clinch the conference crown. But there was much more to Jim's tour in Evansville than wins and losses.

"We had so many good players and experiences," Crews explained, "and so many were off the floor." Jim went on to mention how proud he was when he heard the news about Kwame James' heroism in December of 2001, just three months after our lives were forever changed after the terrorist attacks. James, a dual citizen of Canada and Trinidad & Tobago who later became a U.S. citizen, was one of the brave men and women who subdued terrorist Richard Reid before he could detonate a shoe bomb on an American Airlines flight.

Crews also remembered another act of heroism and the effect it had on the entire program. In 1990, a player named Milt Donald had graduated and was doing his laundry when tragedy struck. While reaching into an old washing machine, his hand was caught and his arm was torn to shreds. Fortunately, teammates Scott Shreffler and Chaka Chandler were nearby and handled the pressure situation like pros. Donald was air-lifted to Louisville. Chandler and Shreffler had likely saved their teammate's life, but what really impressed Coach Crews were the events that followed.

Through the long treatment and rehab process, the Aces family set up a schedule so that someone was with Donald every day. For months, two people, a combination of players and coaches, would drive to Louisville to be by Milt's side. But what impressed Crews most was the fortitude of his fallen player. "What was really cool about the situation," said Coach Crews, "was that everyone was going over to make this kid feel better but it ended up being Milt Donald making everyone else feel better."

Coach Crews brought more to U of E than winning basketball, and those around him benefitted from his presence. Off the court, he initiated the Jim Crews Reading Aces Program, an initiative that drew critical acclaim from the NCAA where coaches and players visited schools to motivate young students. He also worked closely with the local Boys and Girls Clubs and encouraged his players to stay engaged and get involved.

Through his approach, he made an impact on the community, but he also produced some of the best basketball in school history. The four-time conference Coach of the Year is still the only Evansville College/U of E coach to put together nine consecutive non-losing seasons, and for six straight, 1991-1996, home attendance averaged over 10,000. Crews' teams also produced 15 straight seasons where they finished at least .500 in conference play, and when the streak ended in 2002, only six other schools could make the same claim: UCLA, Princeton, Syracuse, Xavier, Temple and Arizona.

Jim's players thrived as well, with seven of them making the program's top ten list of three-point shooters, with six among the top ten scorers and four in the top ten career rebounders. Five of Crews' players made the 15-player All-Time Aces Team, Simmons, Haffner, Elkins, Jackson and Wilson, and six players joined Jim in the U of E Athletic Hall of Fame: Haffner, Simmons, Godfread, Elkins, Schreffler and Wilson.

Leading a small school to success in a small market is a daunting task, and Coach Crews proved that it could be done. "He put us on the map, and he spoiled us," said Lance Wilkerson. "We were averaging 10,000 fans and were going to the NCAA Tournament. He WAS Evansville Division I basketball, and that's how he should be remembered, not how he didn't succeed the last couple years. He was vilified for just being .500. The fan base got spoiled."

DALE CAMPBELL: U OF E SUPER FAN

When I met Dale Campbell at Solar Bron Pointe where he lives on Evansville's west side, it was no surprise that he was dressed in his Purple Aces Sixth Man shirt. Even in his 90s, Dale is active with any group that supports Aces basketball, and his roots are deeply entrenched in the glory years of the program.

Dale is originally from McLeansboro, Illinois and went to school with Jerry Sloan's older siblings. Dale moved to Evansville at the age of 19 to work on the L & N Railroad, and his interest in Aces basketball piqued in the early '60s when Sloan came to town. Because of their hometown ties, Dale and Jerry became quick friends, and Sloan often spent the summers as a guest in Dale's home, and during the school year, Jerry and his wife Bobbye would stay in Dale's basement during storms.

Mr. Campbell has fond memories of Sloan, including the trips Jerry would make to St. Louis in his "old Ford coupe" to visit Bobbye. Dale was also a regular on Aces flights to away games and could often be seen playing gin rummy with business manager Bob Hudson. One of his darkest memories was the night of December 13, 1977. Campbell had a reserved seat on the flight for Murfreesboro but had to work. Hudson even called that morning to see if his gin partner would change his mind. When the tragic crash occurred at 7:21 p.m., Dale was the conductor on a train in East St. Louis and Sloan contacted Dale's wife to get the message to him that the entire team and several staff members and fans were gone.

But overall, the man who has had season tickets since 1961 has spent many happy days and nights dressed in purple. He smiles when asked about All-American Hugh Ahlering and the popular and talented Buster Briley, and he loved Marty Simmons and Chris Hollender during the Jim Crews era. Like most fans, Don Buse was a favorite, and it should come as no surprise that Sloan was his vote for 'the greatest'.

In May of 2011, Dale celebrated his 90th birthday and was made an honorary trustee at UE. Lance Wilkerson helped organize the two-day event that included Sloan, Simmons and Crews among those who traveled great distances to honor the Aces super fan. Though his memory isn't what it used to be, Dale Campbell looked spry for his age, and for as long as he can, he will be in the stands as the Evansville Aces' biggest fan.

At a celebration of Dale Campbell's 90th birthday, some of his friends got together for this photo. Front row (L-R): Wayne Boultinghouse, Robbie Kent, Dale, Ken Maikranz, Jack Barner. Second row: Jerry Sloan, Larry Meeks, Bob Clayton, Niel Ellerbrook, Marty Simmons, Lance Wilkerson.

"When I think of Coach Crews, I think of integrity," Wilkerson added. "I bet that word is used a lot when you ask about him. At one point, I think we were the third-smallest Division I school and we were going to the NCAA Tournament on a regular basis. Even with the high academic standards, he got some good players!"

Jim Byers totally agreed with Lance's assessment, citing admiration for Jim's "passion to do the job the right way" and describing Crews as "a man of great integrity, loyalty and a true role model."

Such praise is rare in the world of Division I basketball, and Jim Crews did the school and our city proud. He built the program on sound principles, and as Lance Wilkerson told me, "I think UE will always be in debt to Coach Crews, and now one of his players (Marty Simmons) is our head coach."

So as Coach Simmons guides the program, a piece of Jim Crews' legacy and philosophy is still present and can be seen on the wall every day. Though iconic Roberts Stadium has been replaced by the new downtown Ford Center, the goal of developing young men is still at the forefront, and as the sign in the locker room reads, "Those who stay will leave champions."

MATER DEI'S LADY WILDCATS: "DON'T STOP UNTIL YOU GET THERE."

Mater Dei's 2012 State champions. First row (kneeling L-R): Laura Greenwell, Ashlynn Spahn, Casey Jochem, Aubrey Goebel, Katelyn Bueltel and Jenae Gries. Second row: McKenzie Hartz, Brianna Dickerson, Maura Muensterman, Erin Wildeman, Tori Schickel, Beth Fischer, Hannah Ubelhor and Sister Mary Francis. Third row: Joe Herrmann, Allison Garrard, Gary Alles, Steve Goans, Terry Muensterman, Micah Konkler, Casey Wahl and Chris Tanner.

Sometimes you just know. That was the case when I first witnessed for myself what the 2011-'12 Lady Wildcats of Evansville Mater Dei were all about. It wasn't at a game in a crowded gym, but rather in the small practice gym at the west side school as the coaches put them through their paces.

As a typical sports fan who had the good fortune of playing on a State championship team (Evansville North 1967) and as an ex-coach who has observed many scenarios over the years, I was well aware of the potential pitfalls that can derail a season for even the finest of teams. But I also can sense when the pieces are in place for a very special season.

As I sat on the sidelines in the dark confines watching the girls work out, I observed the no-nonsense approach taken by a very high-caliber coaching staff, and I saw the respect shown by the players as sneakers screeched on the floor and perspiration soaked through their jerseys. I witnessed a nice blend of talented front line players with a tandem of quick guards who could run the floor or execute in the half-court. I also observed how the starters were challenged by a second unit who would become valuable contributors on game day.

Any fan would agree that it is rare to find a squad with both the tangibles and intangibles to navigate the gauntlet to an Indiana State basketball title, and after watching this team for an hour, I couldn't wait to climb on the bandwagon to watch these young ladies make some history.

The Lady Wildcats were preparing for the tournament and were entering the sectional as the top-ranked 2A team in Indiana. In addition, they were led by a young sophomore who was already among the all-time greats in local history. To say that expectations were high would have been an understatement, but the team did not have a strong tradition to look back on. They were to become

the trailblazers, the team that would set a new standard at Mater Dei, and they looked the part on this unseasonably warm day in February of 2012.

When Steve Goans assumed control in 2007, it was his second tour of duty with the Mater Dei girls program. He began at age 19 as the reserve coach under Carl Voegel, and after two seasons, he became the head coach when Voegel left in 1979. He inherited a young program that had never won a game on the varsity level, and after suffering through a one-win and then a two-win season, Goans built the system through the development of a feeder program for younger players and his girls finally started to see results.

Coaching became the driving force in his life, and fortunately he had an understanding wife who was an excellent athlete and coach herself. Becky Goans was a volleyball player at Central who later became a successful soccer coach, and the couple enjoyed the profession as their children grew.

In 1989, Steve made a tough choice and stepped down at Mater Dei to spend time coaching and watching his kids, Matt and Leslie, compete. But he always stayed in contact with the coaches at his alma mater, and when the position opened up again in '07, he was ready to step in.

One of Steve's first priorities was to enlist the services of a man whose knowledge and passion are second to none. Terry Muensterman is well known in the Mater Dei community for many reasons. As an athlete, he was outstanding, setting the school's scoring record in the early '70s, and as a coach, he was instrumental in building the schools' feeder program. In addition, he nurtured and developed the game of this team's superstar, Maura Muensterman, Terry's daughter.

For several years, Terry mentored many of the young women who would make up the 2011-'12 team and shaped several of the girls into a unit that became nearly unstoppable at the Feeder and AAU level. As these youngsters developed and learned to compete, Coach Goans could see the potential, and with his good friend at his side, Steve set lofty goals going into 2011.

The Lady Cats returned three seniors (Casey Jochem, Erin Wildeman and Brianna Dickerson) and four juniors (Beth Fischer, Aubrey Goebel, Jenae Gries and Laura Greenwell) to go with some very talented younger players who showed outstanding promise. Steve knew that to reach their potential, the girls would have to dedicate themselves and form bonds that would withstand the rigors of a grueling season, so plans were made for a busy summer. Several of the girls had played Biddy Ball and AAU together since second grade, and four of the underclassmen (Maura Muensterman, Ashlynn Spahn, Tori Schickel and Hannah Ubelhor) had played together recently under Phil Kessler, a respected AAU coach in the area. But the key was blending the talents and the egos of the juniors and seniors with the newcomers.

Coach Goans thought a strenuous summer schedule was necessary, and he was well aware of the sacrifices his girls and their families would have to make. Several girls let other sports they loved, like softball and volleyball, take a backseat, and every single member of the team attended every camp and tournament for the entire summer. The girls, and often their parents, attended team camps and competitions from Martinsville to Bloomington to Benton Central and dominated teams from across the state. When asked which event confirmed his suspicions that this team could be great, Coach Goans answered quickly: "Definitely the Plainfield Shootout. The only team we lost to was Ben Davis (1 point in OT). That's where we got the sense that we could play with these teams."

When the season began, the girls were tested immediately when they faced a tough Southridge team in Huntingburg to open the season. The Raiders were led by senior Cassie Wertman and the dynamic junior duo of Victoria Schaffer and Kendyl Dearing. The game lived up to the hype, and the Wildcats prevailed 50-48. For the next five weeks, Mater Dei steamrolled their next six opponents by an average of 25 points, setting up a matchup with Bosse.

Bosse, led by future All-Metro players Ashley Morehead, Kiawna Porter and Irina Perkins, proved to be too much for the Cats and defended their home turf in a 64-63. The overtime thriller was a game that would offer Mater Dei a reality check and enable Angie Oliver's Lady Bulldogs to capture the City and SIAC titles with an eventual spotless record.

With a new focus, Coach Goans' crew went back to work and ran the table with only Vincennes Rivet, Jasper and Bosse coming within six points of the Lady Wildcats. With high hopes, the girls worked hard before the tournament, but their journey almost

After Maura Muensterman (center) hit the game-winning shot to secure the State title, she was mobbed by her teammates: Ashlynn Spahn (front), Tori Schickel (left), Casey Jochem (right) and Brianna Dickerson (back). (Photo courtesy of the Evansville Courier & Press)

ended before it began. After a lopsided win over South Spencer (58-15) in the Forest Park Sectional, Mater Dei was on a collision course for a rematch with Southridge. Once again, the teams battled to the wire, and the Wildcats ended the Lady Raiders' season at 19-3. After a 61-40 win in the final, Mater Dei was headed to the regional for only the sixth time in school history.

As the raucous Mater Dei crowd converged on Paoli, the stage was set for the girls program to rise to new heights. As expected, Maura Muensterman ran the show as she stroked three-pointers and snapped beautiful passes inside to Tori Schickel. Casey Jochem was also a force inside, and Ashlynn Spahn showed glimpses of things to come with some threes of her own.

Entering the third period, Mater Dei led 26-23, and 5'11 Brianna Dickerson was doing great work on Sullivan's 6'2 junior star Rhagan Smith. In the fourth quarter, Erin Wildeman executed a beautiful blockout that drew an over the back call on Smith, and Spahn later hit two big free throws to put the girls up 41-25 with 5:23 left. For the last five minutes, Muensterman orchestrated things on both ends as the Wildcats hit their free throws for a 51-35 win.

In the final, Paoli was no match for Mater Dei's balance and size, and the Wildcats captured the school's first regional title with a 59-33 win. As the red and gold nation celebrated, Steve Goans and the team enjoyed every minute and then set their sights on the one team standing in the way of the State Finals, the Triton Central Tigers from Fairland.

As I sat with my wife Suzy and listened to the Bedford Semi-state game on February 25th, I vowed that if the girls could pull it off, we would make the trip to Terre Haute the following week to watch them finish off their dream season. Suzy had become a convert herself, and for the only time in our thirty-plus years together, we listened to an entire ballgame on the radio. Phil Kessler, who had coached many of the girls in AAU, served as the color man for ESPN's Dan Egierski, and the Wildcats asserted themselves early.

Muensterman was hot from the get-go, launching a 22-footer early that hit nothing but net, and on her second trip down the floor, she crossed-over her defender for a silky-smooth jumper. Triton Central's plan was obvious, as they jammed the cutters and man-handled freshman sensation Tori Schickel underneath. The first quarter saw each team record six fouls, and Mater Dei led 7-5 after a five-minute scoring drought for both teams.

Schickel picked up her second foul one minute into the second, and back-to-back threes by Muensterman and Spahn put the Cats up by 13 at the 2:30 mark. Maura had ten points in the quarter, and at halftime, she had 15 with three 3-pointers as Mater Dei led 24-15.

To begin the third, Bri Dickerson scored first on a putback, and Schickel swatted away a Tiger's shot at the other end. After another score by Dickerson and a layup by Muensterman, the Wildcats led by 15, and after a cold spell, Ashlynn Spahn delivered a huge three to restore order for an eight-point lead.

In the fourth, the stubborn Tigers kept it interesting, and at the 3:50 mark, Casey Jochem delivered when she boxed out, rebounded and then slipped a beautiful pass to Tori Schickel to put Mater Dei up by five. With a five-point lead, the Lady Wildcats spread the floor and nailed the coffin shut with free throws. Coach Goans emptied the bench with 25 seconds left, and after Katelyn Bueltel hit two free throws, Mater Dei was on its way to the Hulman Center for a date with powerful Bishop Luers.

It was only fitting that the state's two top-ranked teams would face off for the title, and experience definitely favored the Knights. Luers were the defending champs and had made the most finals appearances (8) among all schools in all classes. They were led by 6'1, powerfully-built senior Miracle Woods and 5'11 senior Brooke Ridley. Conversely, Mater Dei had never gotten out of a regional, and although they were ranked #1, many pundits across the state were projecting a seventh title for Bishop Luers.

As championship week began, the local press played up the fact that Mater Dei had already lost three State Finals during the school year. In the fall, the boys soccer team lost in the final to Ft. Wayne Canterbury and the football team fell to Bishop Luers 41-17, and just weeks earlier, the Mater Dei wrestlers were beaten by Perry Meridian in the semi-finals. These facts weren't lost on Coach Goans, and with no experience to guide him, some decisions had to be made.

Although the team had spent the night for the regional in Paoli because of the early game time, Goans chose not to do so for the State Finals. On Thursday, the girls took the floor at the Hulman Center for a shoot-around, and the coaches had some immediate concerns. Steve admitted that the open background behind each basket worried him, but when the girls shot the lights out at practice, he felt better. The floor at the arena was another concern. Being a college-length court, the baskets had to be moved in five feet at each end, and makeshift diagonal out of bounds markings made it confusing. "We were really worried about that," Goans disclosed. "When they shortened the floor, it messed up the (free-throw) lane markings that the post people use (for positioning)." (In fact, at one point during the game, Maura Muensterman was out of bounds with the ball by two feet and the referees didn't even notice.)

On game day, the bus left at 8:00 a.m. for the 11:45 tipoff. "We didn't want a whole lot of time," Coach Goans revealed. "We just wanted enough to get our feet under us and give the girls time for their rituals. That's their time." The "rituals" Steve mentioned referred to singing and other pre-game bonding the team had practiced all season.

With a caravan of a dozen cars or so trailing the bus, the team was met by a police escort at Stuckey's a few miles from Terre Haute. Upon their arrival, the girls spent a few minutes in the locker room and then watched some of the Class A final between Northeast Dubois and Ft. Wayne Canterbury.

As game time neared, one thing became very clear: Who would dominate the game itself was uncertain, but when it came to fan support, it was no contest. Red and gold blanketed several sections, and the Mater Dei faithful out-numbered all other schools two or three to one.

When the team took the floor, the atmosphere was electric, and after the starters were announced, the team hugged each other as if to say "This is our day."

From the opening tip, the tactics were obvious. Luers was focusing on stopping Muensterman, and the Knights' massive front line intended to wear down the long but lanky Lady Cats. Tori Schickel opened the scoring with a nice assist from Casey Jochem, and Mater Dei settled into their trademark 3-2 zone. Brianna Dickerson went right to work swapping sweat with Miracle Woods. After a late three by Ashlynn Spahn and a big bucket by Beth Fischer at the 12-second mark, Mater Dei led 15-14 at the first break.

In the second period, Erin Wildeman provided valuable minutes spelling Dickerson as she defended Miracle Woods. Before taking a break, Bri started the scoring with a beautiful spin move and layup and then a putback to put the Wildcats up by five. Meanwhile Maura was chipping in with occasional points but was showing her basketball IQ by taking what Luers was giving and feeding teammates. As the half wound down, Muensterman nailed a three sandwiched between two more threes by Spahn to earn the Wildcats a 28-25 lead at the break.

To open the second half, Schickel hit a pretty left-handed layup in traffic and Dickerson knocked away a pass to Woods at the other end. As the game wore on, a key difference between the teams became apparent. Despite the frenetic pace and the close score, Luers seemed almost indifferent and uninspired, while the Lady Cats seemed to be having fun and enjoying the competition. At every timeout, the bench would greet their teammates on the court, and the players seemed focused but relaxed.

This demeanor, which showed wisdom beyond the girls' years, would prove to be vital as the drama played out. At 5:22 of the third, Tori Schickel picked up her third foul and Brianna continued her battle against Woods with the heart of a warrior. As the game took its toll, valuable contributions were made by Beth Fischer and Erin Wildeman to keep the beefy Knights in check.

At 2:50, Dickerson converted a pretty shot from the free throw line, and Muensterman followed with a jumper. When the third period ended, Mater Dei clung to a 41-37 lead, and the game was developing like a classic chess match. As both coaches made preparations for the end game, the girls smiled and took the floor for the final chapter.

Luers opened the fourth quarter by cutting the lead to two, but Ashlynn Spahn answered with another huge three from the right side. As the teams fought like two Titans, the girls seemed to draw energy from the Mater Dei crowd, and it was anybody's game as the clock wound down. With the score tied at 49, Muensterman controlled the ball with 30 seconds left. Just as Coach Goans stood to tell his star to hold the ball for the last shot, Maura launched an ill-advised three that missed everything. The last 25 seconds were a series of timeouts as the chess match played out, and with time running out, Brooke Ridley's shot was swatted away by Tori Schickel. With zeroes on the clock, 32 minutes had not been enough, and #1 and #2 were going to overtime.

With four minutes placed on the clock, Bishop Luers won the tip, but Muensterman came up with a steal that led to Schickel getting fouled. Tori hit the second of two and then traded baskets with Woods to give Mater Dei a 52-51 lead. As the clock wound down, Brooke Ridley converted a free throw to knot the game at 52 and the score stayed there until a timeout at 9.1 seconds. Following the TO, Schickel's layup was blocked and Steve Goans called timeout at 5.1.

Throughout the season, Terry Muensterman had called the out of bounds plays, and this would be no exception. "The play we ran is one we've run since third grade," Maura revealed, "where Tori sets a screen for me and then I go to the corner. He told me to shoot a three or go baseline. I don't even know why I spun to be completely honest. I just did the opposite of what he said. You can hear it if you watch the game (on re-play). You hear my dad yell 'JUMP SHOT'."

The play she was describing was without doubt the greatest and most significant in Mater Dei history. After looking baseline (which was not available), Muensterman made a beautiful spin move to her left and elevated at the right side of the free throw line. As she rose, she finished with a text book one hand release that sailed perfectly through the net. After timeout was called by Luers, Maura stood at mid-court and was all smiles as her teammates rushed her in celebration.

With two-tenths of a second showing on the clock, Mater Dei's beloved scorekeeper, Sister Mary Francis, motioned to Steve that Luers had called an illegal timeout because they had none left. As a consequence, the ball was again placed in Maura's hands, and she delivered once again with two free throws for the 56-52 victory.

With the Mater Dei faithful looking on, the girls basked in the limelight and enjoyed the atmosphere. As a spectator, I couldn't help but respect the way the team conducted themselves in every situation. While the ladies laughed near the podium, Terry Wannemueller slipped on a gray T-shirt that was difficult to read from the stands. I later learned that the team had worn them all year and that they read "Set your goals high and don't stop until you get there." The phrase symbolized their season, and Maura told me a week later that when the phrase was chosen, "we had State in mind, to be honest."

Like any good story, this magical season had several subplots. Few people knew that in the week of the Finals, Beth Fischer, a junior who, with senior Erin Wildeman, serves as an inspirational team leader, was very ill. "Beth had the flu Wednesday and Thursday," Steve Goans told me. "We had to make her go home from practice, and she was in tears. She thought she was letting the team down. We called her every night, and by game day, she was able to make the trip."

Another obvious subplot was the effort put forth by senior Brianna Dickerson. Although inside help was provided by Casey Jochem, Tori Schickel and Erin Wildeman, the bulk of the battle against Luers superstar Miracle Woods was fought by Dickerson. Woods had the potential to take over a game, but there was no 'Miracle' on this day thanks to a beaten and bruised Brianna.

Yet another feel-good story was the breakout game by 5'3 sophomore guard Ashlynn Spahn. Spahn's performance added some irony to the weekend, because as things played out, the biggest impact came from the smallest player on the court, and it couldn't have been summed up better than by Bishop Luers coach Denny Renier. "We knew number 31 (Maura) was their star," Renier told the *Courier*'s Gordon Englehardt, "but number 12 (Ashlynn) killed us. Her confidence had to be overflowing. She hit five (threes)."

As Renier surmised, confidence was the key for Spahn, who had only hit five threes during the entire regular season, and after each huge three at State, her smile lit up the arena. "Terry and Coach Goans and my dad (Steve Spahn) worked with me," Ashlynn explained, "and during the season, Maura would always tell me to keep shooting. She said, 'Don't ever stop.' By the end of the season, I started hitting more. The reason I smiled so much was

because Maura always told me that and I was finally hitting shots that really counted."

And perhaps the best storyline of all involved the team's leader and the man who groomed her for greatness. No one knows his daughter's game better than Terry Muensterman, and the two have spent countless hours together leading up to their date with destiny. "It can be a love-hate (relationship) at times," Maura confided. "I know he knows what he's doing, and I trust everything he says, but I also have to live with him, so sometimes it's hard. He's usually right, even though I'm stubborn sometimes."

Steve Goans has witnessed the Muensterman dynamic for years as he watched his good friend mentor Maura. "Do they look at each other (during a game)? Yeah," Steve explained. "Is he harder on her than the rest? Yeah. But the hug on TV after the Finals, Terry had a tear in his eye, and that says it all. They love each other."

As the Luers game came to a climax, I watched as the huddle broke before the final play and noticed a moment between father and daughter. As she walked onto the floor she glanced back at Terry and giggled, and when I asked what was said, she revealed a moment that they will probably re-live a thousand times.

"He had been telling me all game to shoot a jumpshot," Maura said, "and I hadn't shot one all game. So when I walked away, he said, 'Now would be a good time for a jumpshot."

Any story worth telling usually has a defining moment, and in this case, it lasted 4.9 seconds. With the game on the line, the team looked to a special player and Maura Muensterman delivered (with a jumpshot). Steve Goans had the best view in the house and a deep appreciation of what 15-year-old Maura pulled off.

"We knew we wanted the ball in Maura's hands," Goans said a week after the game. "We (the coaches) were watching from a perfect angle, and we knew it was going in. She was just playing the game of basketball. You can't be a robot. She knew what was on the line, and she made the play. I'm still on Cloud Nine."

The 2011-'12 Lady Wildcats completed their season as State champs with a 27-1 record. During the regular season, they outscored opponents by 22 a game (1,289-820), and those numbers improved in the post-season. Their talent is unquestioned, but their success went far deeper than ability. Coach Steve Goans did a masterful job and knows that there is plenty of credit to go around. He had always looked up to his #1 assistant and watched as Terry Muensterman led the city and SIAC in high school. "He was somebody I wanted to be like," Steve said. "His attention to detail was amazing."

Steve also credits the rest of his staff. Gary Alles led the JV team to a perfect 21-0 record, and Allison Mesker, the reserve assistant, was valuable as a female leader who was a sounding board for the girls. Micah Konkler coached the school's prep team and served while also attending USI full-time.

But most of all, Goans appreciates the maturity and class of the young ladies who did the work, and those young ladies learned valuable lessons, as well. "In girls basketball, chemistry is everything," Coach Goans declared. "Our seniors did not have to accept a freshman and two sophomores coming in and leading us in scoring. They made this all possible for us."

"Every single person did something that we needed," added Maura Muensterman, "from the people on the bench to the starters. I mean, Erin Wildeman and Beth Fischer, you could sub them in and there wouldn't be any difference. Hannah Ubelhor came in for Casey Jochem and did a great job. Without all those people, it

STATE FINALS GREAT PERFORMANCES

Below are the individuals and teams who rank in the top 5 in their classes in the State Finals (Final Four) record book.

Scoring (1 game)
31 – Shelly Brand (#4) – Reitz 1981 (one class)
28 – Kara Meyer (#2) – Southridge 1998 (2A)
24 – Mallory Ladd (#5) – Memorial 2011 (3A)

Rebounds
16 – Jasmine Ussery (#2) – Castle 2006 (4A)
14 – Kelly Wilhite (#5) – Wood Memorial 2007 (A)
13 – Anna Hackert (#4) – Memorial 2011 (3A)
13 – Mallory Ladd (#4) – Memorial 2011 (3A)
13 – Jill Fenneman (#2) – Southridge 1998 (2A)
13 – Kara Meyer (#2) – Southridge 1998 (2A)

FG Made
12 – Kara Meyer (#1) – Southridge 1998 (2A)

3-Pointers Made
5 – Ashlynn Spahn (#1) – Mater Dei 2012 (2A)
5 – Sara Young (#1) – Vincennes Rivet 2010 (A)

FTs Made
10 – Mallory Ladd (#1) – Memorial 2011 (3A)

FT %
.1000 (10-10) – Mallory Ladd (#1) – Memorial 2011 (3A)
.917 (11-12) – Chelsea Meeks (#1) – Vincennes Rivet (A)

Blocked Shots
10 – Katie Cochren (#1) – Wood Memorial 2007 (A)
8 – Jill Fenneman (#1) – Southridge 1998 (2A)

Steals
7 – FahKara Malone (#1) – Memorial 2006 (3A)

TEAM

FTs made
31 – Castle (#1) 2006 (4A)
22 – Memorial (#1) 2011 (3A)

FT attempted
42 – Castle 2006 (4A)

FT %
.864 (19-22) (#1) – Vincennes Rivet 2009 (A)

Blocked Shots
10 (#1) – Southridge 1998 (2A)

Runner-up Finishes
2 (T #3) – Vincennes Rivet '09, '10 (A)

(Source: IHSAA)

wouldn't have been possible at all. We definitely got to share winning a State title with some of our best friends. I wouldn't have wanted to share it with anybody else."

Steve Goans is looking forward to next season even as he enjoys this one. He knows that it will be tough to replace Brianna's toughness and Casey's speed, but five of his top seven and the top three scorers in the Finals (Spahn – 15, Muensterman – 14 and Schickel – 13) all return. "We have a nucleus coming back, and our JV was 21-0," Goans reminded me. "Believe it or not, I already have our plans for the summer. We're going to do a lot of the same stuff we did last year."

As local fans looked on, Steve and his staff produced a storybook season, and the quality of his athletes as individuals didn't go unnoticed. One of the more prominent observers was Rick Stein, The USI head women's coach who actually helped Goans acquire a tape of Triton Central. "Steve, there are so many good coaches who never get the chance to do what you're doing," Stein told Coach Goans. "When I hear the girls being interviewed and read what they say in the paper, I know why you're where you are. Those girls are smart, level-headed and coachable."

With a wealth of talent returning and a cast of quality young ladies set to compete, the possibility of a repeat or perhaps a three-peat is a definite possibility. But tomorrow is another day and fate can be fickle. For now it is important that these twelve young ladies enjoy the moment. In a few years, it will all be a memory, but no matter where their separate paths may lead, they will be forever linked. Together they made school history, and any time their paths cross, the memories will flood back and the smiles will return.

In the 35-plus years that the IHSAA has sponsored girls basketball, area teams have advanced to the final game 15 times, with 6 teams hoisting the trophy. Below are those teams (as of 2012).

Southwestern Indiana's Elite

(• champions)
• 1981 – Reitz (one class)
• 1998 – Southridge (2A)
  2000 – Forest Park (2A)
  2002 – Gibson Southern (3A)
  2004 – Washington Catholic (A)
  2005 – Northeast Dubois (A)
• 2006 – Castle (4A)
  2006 – Memorial (3A)
  2007 – Wood Memorial (A)
  2009 – Vincennes Rivet (A)
  2010 – Vincennes Rivet (A)
• 2011 – Memorial (3A)
• 2011 – Vincennes Rivet (A)
  2012 – Northeast Dubois (A)
• 2012 – Mater Dei (2A)
(Source: IHSAA)

THE BEST OF THE BEST
(SOUTHWESTERN INDIANA'S TOP 20 BASKETBALL PLAYERS)

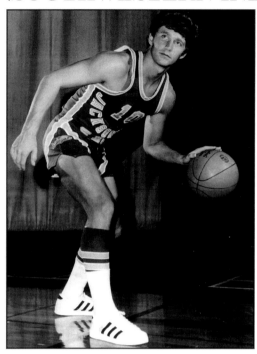

Vaughn Wedeking

When I was asked to write an article for *Indiana Basketball Magazine* naming southwestern Indiana's greatest male basketball players of all time, I was very aware of the difficulty inherent in such a task. Obviously, there is no definitive answer and the list would be highly subjective, so I approached the assignment with the goal of reaching a reasonable conclusion as rationally as possible.

To begin the process, I contacted a group of individuals whom I consider to be extremely savvy on the topic and capable of submitting impartial choices. As a result, nearly 100 players were nominated, and 65 of them from 25 different schools (11 of which no longer exist) received votes.

The 13 men (12 plus myself) who cast votes ranged in age from their mid-30s to over 70 and have literally hundreds of combined years of experience as players, coaches, referees and members of the media. Each was instructed to select 20 players (ranked 1-20). To determine the players' scores, a ranking of '1' was awarded 20 points, a '2' was worth 19 and so on down to a score of 1 for a ranking of '20'.

My thanks to the following for sharing their expertise in this Top 20 poll: Keith Bagby, Jerry Birge, Ed Cole, Steve Ford, Jim Hummel, Keith Kohlmeyer, Richard Lankford, Randy Mattingly, Bob Parker, Ben Shoulders, Jon Siau, and Terry West. Using their wisdom as my basis, I respectfully submit our Top 20 in reverse order with commentary and explanation.

20 – Porter Merriweather (39 points)

Merriweather was a superstar who graduated in 1958 from Evansville Lincoln High School, an all-black school that closed as a high school in 1962. Four fellow Lincoln Lions (John Barnhill, Ted Lander, Walter Miles and Jim Smallins) were nominated, but only Merriweather cracked the Top 20.

#19 – Paul Hoffman (40 ½ points)

Probably ranked lower than he should be due to his generation and distance from Evansville, Paul 'The Pulverizer' set the Jasper career scoring record with 780 points from 1940-'43 under legendary coach Cabby O'Neill. Hoffman then forged a great career at Purdue by making at least one All-American team in each of his four years there and leading his team in scoring every year.

Hoffman was the first draft pick of the Toronto Huskies of the Basketball Association of America (the forerunner of the NBA) and was then claimed by Baltimore. As a rookie in the NBA, Hoffman helped the Baltimore Bullets win the championship and became the league's very first Rookie of the Year.

17 – (tie) Dick Farley (42 points)

Another generational underdog in the poll, Farley led tiny Winslow to a record of 83-8 during his four years there. He also played on IU's 1953 national championship team and in the NBA.

17 – (tie) Tom Kron (42 points)

Kron was a phenomenal three-sport athlete at Tell City who started for three years under legendary basketball coach 'Gunner' Wyman. Tom then played the point for the famous 1965-'66 Kentucky Wildcats known as 'Rupp's Runts', who fell to Texas Western in the NCAA Finals, a game that inspired the movie *Glory Road*.

16 – John Harrawood (58 points)

Harrawood starred on perhaps the greatest Evansville Central team in history. After graduation, he attended Evansville College (now the University of Evansville) and blossomed under iconic coach Arad McCutchan. Harrawood was the ICC Player of the Year in '56 and '57 and left as the program's career scoring leader with 1,479 points.

Tom Kron
(Photo courtesy of Collegiate Images)

15 – Vaughn Wedeking (65 points)

Considered by many to be the greatest all-around athlete in Evansville history, Wedeking could do it all. The 5' 11", 165-pound guard led the Harrison Warriors to a three-year record of 58-7 (89%). As a collegian, Vaughn joined future NBA great Artis Gilmore at Jacksonville and led the Dolphins to the 1970 NCAA final game before losing to UCLA 80-69.

14 – Luke Zeller (78 points)

Luke 'Big Country' Zeller was the first of Steve and Lorri Zeller's three boys to make history for the Washington Hatchets. Luke put an exclamation point on a remarkable senior year when he tickled the twine from mid-court to secure a 3A State title for his team in 2005. The four-time All-State selection and Trester Award winner finished his career as Washington's career scoring leader with 1,727 points and was honored as a McDonald's All-American and Indiana's Mr. Basketball.

13 – Jerry Clayton (88 points)

"He truly had one of the best shots I ever saw for a big man," said poll participant Ed Cole. The 6'7 sharpshooter's ranking value probably suffered greatly because of his sudden exit from the Evansville College program, but before that, he was a superstar at Central, an Indiana All-Star and an All-American as a freshman in college.

12 – Gus Doerner (93 points)

The 'Mackey Marvel' was the first player to earn All-American honors at Evansville College, and in 1942, he shattered the Aces record with his 24.4-point average, the third best in the country. At 6'4, Doerner had a nose for scoring inside and a beautiful left-handed hook shot.

11 – Roger Kaiser (94 points)

Roger Kaiser led the Dale Golden Aces to two consecutive sectional titles in 1956 and '57, a rare feat for a school with barely 50 students. He left Dale as the school's scoring leader with 1,549 career points and headed south to the Georgia Institute of Technology (later Georgia Tech) and re-wrote the school's record book. Kaiser finished his three-year hardwood career with 1,628 points. He was a consensus All-American who owned 25 Georgia Tech records when he left.

10 – Bryan 'Broc' Jerrel (101 points)

"Broc Jerrel was ahead of his time," said pollster Keith Bagby. The fiery redhead was despised by opposing fans because of his brash demeanor and flashy style. Though the 5'8, 140-pounder infuriated many as he pounded the ball between his legs or snapped passes behind his back, his results speak for themselves. Alongside his best friend, Julius 'Bud' Ritter, Broc led Evansville Bosse to back-to-back State titles in 1944 and '45 as the team's leader in scoring and assists.

9 – Derrick Dowell (102 ½ points)

Derrick Dowell's ranking would likely be better had fate not cut his career short. In high school, Dowell was the undisputed leader of two amazing Evansville Bosse teams under coach Joe Mullan. In 1981-'82, Derrick and teammate Myron Christian led Bosse to two consecutive undefeated regular seasons. After averaging nearly 27 points his senior year, the 6'6" Dowell took

Derrick Dowell (Photo courtesy of the University of Southern California, Sports Information)

his considerable talents to USC where he became the PAC 10 Newcomer of the Year in 1984 and earned All-PAC 10 honors as a junior and senior, finishing his career third on USC's all-time scoring list with 1,484 points.

After being selected 37th overall in the 1987 NBA draft, Derrick tore his Achilles tendon, ending his pro career before it started.

8 – Larry Weatherford (106 points)

"Smooth as silk" is how Ed Cole describes our #8 selection, and Larry Weatherford was that and much more. Even 45 years after his graduation in 1967, Weatherford is still Bosse's all-time scoring leader with 1,559 points. After being named All-State and an Indiana All-Star, Weatherford then became part of one of the best teams in Purdue history, joining Rick Mount, Billy Keller and Herm Gilliam as Boilermakers.

7 – Walter McCarty (137 points)

McCarty blossomed at Evansville Harrison as his skills caught up with his body while he watched and learned from such greats as fellow Warriors Calbert Cheaney and Chris Lowery. Growing to 6'10, Walter is the tallest of our Top 20, and he finished

Walter McCarty (Photo by Mike Thomas)

his high school career as an Indiana All-Star and McDonald's All-American.

After his graduation, Walter chose to join Rick Pitino's Kentucky Wildcats and flourished because of his versatility and ability to run the floor and shoot from deep. He was a cornerstone of the 1996 national championship team, and after being selected in the first round, spent ten seasons in the NBA.

6 – Cody Zeller (143 points)

The youngest of our Top 20, Cody's body of work is still being played out. He and his brothers, Luke and Tyler, set a standard that is all but certain to stand forever, as all three were voted Indiana's Mr. Basketball. As a senior, Cody also added the family's fourth State championship in 2011 as he garnered MVP honors and tied a State Finals record with 26 rebounds in the Hatchets' 65-62 win over Gary Wallace to go with 20 points.

After averaging 20.5 points and 11.4 rebounds as a senior, the highly-touted, 6'11 phenom surprised many when he joined a talented class set on helping Coach Tom Crean return IU basketball to elite status.

5 – Tyler Zeller (171 points)

Tyler being ranked one step higher than his younger brother at this time is probably appropriate because of the head start he has on Cody as a collegian. Tyler was a factor in two 3A State titles for Washington ('05 & '08), and the 7'0, 225-pounder was named Mr. Basketball in 2008 and a McDonald's All-American after averaging 33.1 points and 11 rebounds as a senior.

As a North Carolina Tar Heel, Tyler was part of a 2009 national championship team as a freshman, and as a junior, he hit double figures in scoring in 32 of the team's 37 games and led the Tar Heels in scoring 15 times.

To sum things up for the Zeller brothers, during the nine seasons that a Zeller was on the floor for Washington, the Hatchets amassed the best record in the state, 182-36 (83.4%), and it is almost certain that Indiana will never see three brothers reach the level of Luke, Tyler and Cody, a fact that undoubtedly makes Steve and Lorri Zeller humble and very proud.

4 – Calbert Cheaney (202 points)

Of the four remaining players in our poll, most would agree that any of the four would make a legitimate #1.

Calbert Cheaney spent hours as a youngster perfecting his sweet left-handed stroke at neighborhood courts in Evansville. Growing to 6'7", Calbert averaged 21 points as a junior and 28 as a senior at Evansville Harrison by slashing to the hoop or stopping for a silky smooth jumper.

Cheaney joined a strong class at IU and proceeded to have one of the finest college careers in NCAA Division I history. His teams put together a 54-game home winning streak, and Calbert led the Hoosiers to the Final Four in 1992. During his college years, Cheaney won 105 games at Indiana, more than any other player, and was a three-time All-Big Ten player, a three-time All-American and a four-time MVP for the Hoosiers. He finished his career as the Big Ten's all-time scoring leader with 2,613 points. In 1993, Cheaney won all twelve national player of the year awards, including the prestigious Naismith and John R. Wooden Awards.

Calbert also spent 13 solid seasons in the NBA.

3 – Don Buse (205 points)

Don Buse overcame less than ideal personal circumstances to fashion a career that landed him in the Indiana Basketball Hall of Fame. Admittedly "very poor" as a youngster, Don lost his father at age three. He was fortunate to find a father figure in Holland coach 'Woody' Neel, and under Neel's tutelage, Buse led tiny Holland to two sectional titles. His senior year, the Dutchmen finished the regular season 23-0, led by Don's 22.5 scoring average and 14 rebounds per game.

As an Indiana All-Star in 1968, Don drew the attention of many colleges but chose to stay close to home at the University of Evansville. While there, Buse led the Aces to the school's fifth national championship in 1971 and was named the Division II Outstanding Player of the Year.

Don landed with the Indiana Pacers and used his 6'4, 190-pound frame to continue to develop into the prototypical blue collar, team-oriented player. He hung his hat on his tenacious defense and set several Pacers records. Deemed the "total package" by those who worked with him, Don Buse showed amazing consistency throughout his high school, college and professional careers.

2 – Dave Schellhase (208 points)

Considered by most as a "scoring machine," Dave Schellhase (pronounced SHELL-house) could flat put the ball in the hole. The son of a high school official, young Dave would often tag along with Dave Sr. and watch such Indiana legends as Terry Dischinger and fellow Top 20 member Roger Kaiser.

While at Evansville North, Dave set a city career scoring record with 1,325 points as he averaged over 30 his senior year. After his graduation, Dave became a Boilermaker and made his mark at Purdue as a scorer under Coach Ray Eddy. He was named his team's MVP three times and was also a three-time All-Big Ten player. A model of consistency, Schellhase averaged 24 points as a sophomore, 29 as a junior, and 32.5 to lead the nation as a senior, earning consensus All-American honors in 1966.

After a brief NBA career, Dave left his playing days behind and joined the college coaching ranks.

1 – Bob Ford (227 points)

Interestingly, our #1 selection followed our #2 selection at both Evansville North High School and Purdue and watched Schellhase roam the North gym while he was attracting attention as an elementary school player. Bob earned a starting role for Coach Jim Rausch midway through his freshman season, and he displayed intelligence and maturity beyond his years. At 6'7 and 220 pounds, Ford had a rare combination of cool under pressure and a competitive fire that made him virtually unstoppable.

His greatest achievement, without question, was his journey as a junior in 1967, and that exhibition is what influences fans to hold Ford in such high esteem compared to other local stand-outs. In 1967, Bob teamed with another star, Steve Holland, and a few role players to take the trip every Indiana player dreams of. Ford carried North through the tournament and set a record for four games (semi-state and State) with 128 points. After the win over Lafayette Jeff in the final game, Ford's place in Indiana history was cemented. He finished his career as Evansville's all-time scoring leader (1,816 points) averaging 24.2 for his four years.

Ford was named to several All-American teams and was touted as the #1 recruit in America by *Sports Illustrated*. He chose Purdue and put together a solid four years as a Boilermaker, earning first team All-Big Ten and Academic All-American honors. He finished his career with 1,233 points (a 17-point average) and 648 rebounds (8.9).

Obviously arguments could be made for many great players from our area, even some who finished out of the Top 20. But Bob Ford's finish at the top would not surprise most fans who were around to watch him. In the crazy world of Hoosier Hysteria, high school basketball is king, and although there are players who had better careers as collegians and professionals, Ford's light shone brightest at State tournament time, where Indiana basketball legends are made.

Bob Ford (Photo from the Jim Rausch collection)

IHSAA STATE CHAMPIONS UPDATE
WRESTLING

Individual	School	Year	Weight Class	Record
Drake Stein	Princeton	2010	171	44-2
Drake Stein	Princeton	2011	171	46-0
Doug Welch	Castle	2011	152	50-1
Chad Welch	Castle	2011	160	50-0

CHAPTER FIVE

MULTI-TALENTED

JOHN WELLEMEYER COULD DO IT ALL

As I sat with John Wellemeyer and his wife Elaine at their home not far from Roberts Stadium, I was immediately struck by the humility and laid-back demeanor of someone who had starred on a team that brought U of E its last national title. Our meeting took place a short time before the 1971 Aces were to unite for the 40th reunion of the championship. With good size at 6'4, 215 pounds, many believe Wellemeyer was one of the finest pure athletes southwestern Indiana has ever produced.

John displayed his talents as an all-around athlete for the Huntingburg Happy Hunters, earning 13 varsity letters, two in track as a freshman and senior, four each in basketball and baseball and three in football because of an illness one year. John played football for Bud George as a freshman and sophomore and later for Cecil Raymond. Raymond is one of those who was very impressed by Wellemeyer's abilities. "He was the best athlete I ever saw," Mr. Raymond revealed. "He was unbelievable. I threw batting practice to him and he could hit a ball out of the country. He could stand and jump and reach a foot over the basket. And he could literally punt a football farther than anybody I've ever seen. I told him he could punt at the professional level. I've seen him on a windy day punt from one end zone to the other."

Mr. Raymond recalled a particular incident while he was coaching Wellemeyer in baseball that stands out in his mind even today. "In a game at Bosse, I remember Joe Unfried (Bosse's coach) came out of the dugout to talk to his pitcher when John came to bat," Cecil explained. He told his pitcher, 'Get the ball in there; I want to see him hit. Don't be afraid of him.'" On a 3-0 count, Coach Unfried got his wish. "John hit the ball off the property between two houses," Cecil continued. "He got to see him hit!"

Although John played halfback and quarterback on the football team, he was forced to wear number 87 when he was a sophomore because there were no jerseys large enough with the appropriate numbers. Some of his notable teammates were quarterback Chuck Tabor; Bob Rehl, who played at the University of Louisville; and John Blemker, an All-State halfback who scored 202 points to break the scoring record of Terry Cole.

In baseball, John pitched when not playing first base, shortstop or the outfield, and he was so good as a .500 hitter that Wayne Boultinghouse once stated that John should have played pro ball. In track, John used the western roll in the high jump in the days when the jumpers would land in sand, and if that wasn't enough, John also spent three years in the choir and two playing baritone in the band at halftime of the football games.

As with many athletes of his generation, Wellemeyer credits much of his development to the hours spent in the sandlots and on the neighborhood goals in and around Huntingburg. "All the kids would get together and play," John recalled. "At night you didn't come home and sit around and watch TV. As soon as baseball was over, you'd play football, and when football was

John Wellemeyer (#53) starred for the Aces.

over, you'd play basketball. Whether it was muddy or rainy or snowing, you'd play. You don't see that today."

Despite John's many talents, it was on the basketball court that he truly distinguished himself. As a four-year starter, he played for coaches Hobby Gibbs (John's first two years) and Jack Davis. Playing a tough schedule that included Bedford, New Albany and the Evansville schools, the Hunters were competitive, and John experienced his best year as a junior with teammates Pat Gooch, Mike Ubelhor and others.

Wellemeyer finished his high school career with 1,623 points, averaging 25.2 points as a senior. As a result of his fine season, he was named first team All-State and served as an Indiana All-Star alongside such players as Ft. Wayne South's Willie Long, Gregg Northington of Indianapolis Wood and Evansville Bosse's Larry Weatherford.

*John carries the ball for
The Huntingburg Happy Hunters against Jasper.*

Looking back on his high school days, some of his best memories were created in the classic gym in downtown Huntingburg. The town's Memorial gymnasium was dedicated in 1951, and the cream-colored building with a gym floor 16 feet below ground level has welcomed some of the greatest talent in area history. "It was a wonderful place to play back in the '60s when basketball really meant something to small towns," Wellemeyer stated. "I know a lot of people would get season tickets just so they could get tickets to the sectional. We were exceptionally fortunate to have a gymnasium like that."

Wellemeyer himself was responsible for many highlights for area fans, including a 52-point performance against Rockport at a holiday tournament in Tell City to set the county record. After his successful senior season, the multi-talented star began to analyze his situation, and his options were many.

John had been contacted by over 100 schools and could have gone for any of the three sports. Purdue wanted him for both baseball and football, and he was also intrigued by Louisville. In fact, he made several trips to U of L and was visited by Butch Beard and Wes Unseld. He also received interest from schools like Georgia Tech, Jacksonville, Florida State and LSU.

In addition, the San Francisco Giants wanted him to attend Arizona State to prepare him for a life in professional baseball, and Elaine produced a letter John received from the Dallas Cowboys.

But throughout the entire process, the University of Evansville was in the back of Wellemeyer's mind. John's mother, brother (Mike) and sister (Marcia) had all attended UE, and Coach McCutchan took a low-key approach, telling John, "Take your time and make up your mind, and I will always have a scholarship for you down here."

John had followed the Aces during the heyday of the program when Jerry Sloan, Larry Humes and others dominated the NCAA college division, and when the dust cleared, he found himself wanting to be part of the program's legacy. He and his classmates didn't

experience great success in the early years, and as Wellemeyer and his teammates searched for a team identity, the seemingly distant memories of national titles in 1959, '60, '64 and '65 were making the Aces faithful antsy for another championship run.

When the '70-'71 season began, the team looked like anything but world beaters, as they struggled against the freshman team in an exhibition. The eventual starting lineup primarily used by Coach McCutchan was essentially five guards that averaged about 6'3 but played well as a unit. The guard positions were manned by Oakland City's Rick Smith and Holland's Don Buse with Wellemeyer and Rick Coffey at forward and rebound master Bob Clayton in the middle.

Wellemeyer was praised by Coach McCutchan for his pure shooting stroke and his ability to drive to the basket, even drawing comparisons to Aces All-American Hugh Ahlering. John was a steady force, with a 37-point game at Ball State and a 28-point night against Southwest Missouri State, and the team finished the season with a lukewarm 17-8 record.

Entering the NCAA tournament, the unranked Aces vowed that they would not lose again, and Wellemeyer teamed with Rick Coffey for 47 points in their opener against Ashland College. After a 78-60 win over Central Michigan, John torched Southwest Louisiana for 23 in another win to send the school to the NCAA Finals for the eighth time in 16 years. With surprisingly easy wins over Hartwick (105-69), Southwestern Louisiana (93-74) and Old Dominion (97-82), the Aces had pulled off the unexpected miracle in spectacular fashion.

The '71 Aces delivered the school's fifth title, and Wellemeyer made preparations for his life after basketball. John will be the first to tell you that one of his greatest achievements at U of E was meeting his wife Elaine, and it is evident that Elaine is John's biggest fan. During our visit, she read a newspaper story by Princeton's Pete Swanson that pointed out that John was the first Ace since Larry Humes in 1966 to average over 20 points a game. Pete also pointed out that the versatile Wellemeyer's 158 rebounds in the '70-'71 season was two more than starting center Bob Clayton, five more than Don Buse and nine more than 6'9 Steve Welmer.

At a 40-year anniversary celebration of the '71 championship in 2011, Wayne Boultinghouse, an assistant to Arad in 1971, mentioned all the players then praised two players at the end. About John and Don Buse, Boultinghouse said, "It was just natural. You couldn't teach them anything. They could already do it."

To put his career in perspective, only two Aces players bested his 37-point single game effort, All-Americans Ed Smallwood (47 points) and Larry Humes (48). Growing up an hour away from Evansville, John's name isn't always mentioned with other great athletes, but he was good enough to draw serious interest by both the NFL and major league baseball and was a mainstay on U of E's last national champion. When discussions about all-around athletes take place, without question, a name that always deserves consideration is Huntingburg's John Wellemeyer.

GET A GRIP

Cecil Raymond, who coached John Wellemeyer at Huntingburg, recalled the day that he discovered one of Wellemeyer's quirks. It seems that when Wellemeyer gripped the football, he did it with no fingers touching the laces. When asked why he didn't use the laces, Wellemeyer's answer was simple — "It makes the ball wobble."

JIM SCHMIDT:
A MAN FOR ALL SEASONS

Many local fans may not know the name Jim Schmidt, but those who knew him well recall the North High School athlete as an exceptional multi-sport talent. Jim grew up watching North basketball stars like Tommy Overfield, big Mike Smith, and super shot blocker Harold Miles, and when he entered North in 1971, he made the most of his time there.

Schmidt played his basketball under Coach Jim Rausch and averaged nearly 17 points as a junior. In baseball, he was the team's ace on the mound as well as Mickey Martin's shortstop, and in football, he starred as the quarterback for Coach Morris Riley and still holds the school record for the longest TD pass with an 83-yarder against Mater Dei.

In the '70s, North baseball players were assigned to the Rockport American Legion team, and Jim was a cornerstone for Coach Jim Haaff. With fellow Husky teammates Scott Doerner and Greg Tuley, he led Rockport to the 1974 World Series.

What set Schmidt apart from many high school athletes were his reputation as a leader and his exceptional ability as an all-around athlete. Rather than talk about his triumphs, Jim is quick with his self-deprecating humor, pointing out that although his North baseball team was 28-5 his senior year, 3 of the 5 losses were with him on the mound, one being a one-run loss to a Memorial team that featured Andy Rice and Jim Nally and the other to Castle. In the Castle game, Schmidt lost a 1-0 pitching duel to Dave Sensenbrenner. In that game, Sensenbrenner smashed a ball down the right field line at North where there were no fences, and Jim joked that the ball "is probably still going."

When his career was over, Jim had earned eleven letters, three in football and baseball, two in basketball and three in track. His letters in track are an example of his versatility, as he rarely practiced but was a consistent 6'4 high jumper doing the western roll. Jon Siau, the long-time coach at North, cites Schmidt as one of the best he's seen and remembers a case in point. After pitching a baseball game against Mater Dei, Schmidt rushed to the City track meet and arrived just in time to make his first jump with no warm-up while still wearing his baseball uniform. After changing clothes, he then proceeded to capture the City high jump title, setting the City record in the process.

Jim Schmidt against Northern Illinois.

Earning All-City honors in each sport, Schmidt then played the 1977-'78 season for Wayne Boultinghouse at ISUE before leaving for Morehead State to complete his degree in Education. Brent Hawkins, who played football with Jim, remembers the impact Schmidt had as a leader and speaks of the ease with which Jim could pick up sports like tennis and golf. In fact, Hawkins summed up Schmidt's talents by comparing him with one of the greatest multi-sport athletes in local history. "If you look at Clint Keown," Hawkins said, "to me, Keown is a modern-day Jim Schmidt."

An impressive comparison indeed.

Jim stiff-arms a Bosse player.

JALEN PENDLETON:
PLAYER OF THE YEAR

As Bosse coach Shane Burkhart was developing his three 'diaper dandies' (JaQuan Lyle, Perry Fairrow and Bo Burkhart) in 2011-'12, he was very fortunate to have a senior on the team who could set the ultimate example of what an athlete should be. Jalen Pendleton not only fashioned a fantastic season on the court but he also did the same on the gridiron, and in the process, achieved a feat that had never been accomplished by even the most talented athletes in Evansville history.

Jalen came by his talents naturally. His father, Dion Pendleton, starred at North as a fullback and linebacker, and his mother, Stacy (Parker) was All-City as a basketball player at Bosse. 'J-Bird' as Jalen became known (today, he's known as 'Bird') focused on football and basketball at Bosse, although he did score some points in track his junior year as a long jumper and shotputter. On the football field, Jalen started at quarterback for the JV as a freshman but played safety for the varsity as a sophomore.

As he grew into his eventual 6'2, 197-pound frame, Bird established himself as a rare talent in both sports as a junior. Under new head football coach Andre Thomas, who starred at Harrison, Pendleton showed remarkable leadership skills and was an explosive threat as both a runner and passer. On the court, he blossomed as well as a scorer and a force on the boards.

Jalen made the All-City basketball team as a junior, but the recognition of his abilities reached new heights during his senior year. When asked to comment on his senior quarterback, Coach Thomas smiled and rolled his eyes. "He's the total package," Thomas responded. "Jalen may be one of the most complete athletes I've seen in this area in a long time. I came up with guys like Levron Williams (Bosse) and Clint Keown (Memorial), who I consider to be in the upper level of athletes when it comes to all sports. Jalen's right up there with them. He averaged 315 total yards in football and 20 points in basketball. He threw for 4,100 yards in two years and ran for over 2,000 with 60 total TDs. If he would have played quarterback for three years, there's no telling…"

Jalen is quick to credit several men for helping him develop, as an athlete and as a man, including his father, his brothers, Josh and Dion Jr., Coach Thomas and Coach Burkhart, and his AAU coach (and Bosse assistant) Lamar Brown. He also takes his role as a leader seriously, saying, "I learned how to be a leader growing up. I try to make sure everybody stays focused and make sure they realize that the little things are important."

With solid academics (2.8 GPA) and good ACT scores, Jalen looked at opportunities from Houston (both sports), Morehead State (football), and several for basketball, like Indiana State, Tulane, and Middle Tennessee State. In May of 2012, he opted to play for Coach Barry Hinson at Southern Illinois, citing Hinson's similar no-nonsense approach to Bosse's Shane Burkhart as the main attraction. As he joins Harrison standout Kendall Brown in Carbondale, Jalen's versatility and leadership skills should serve him well as he works toward his college degree.

With Pendleton as a steadying force, Bosse's young basketball team in 2011-'12 nearly went all the way, and head coach Shane

Burkhart has a special place in his heart for his departing team captain. "The kid's such an amazing young man," said Burkhart from his office at Bosse. "He tries so cotton-pickin' hard, you just want what's best for him in every aspect."

Burkhart spoke of an evening when Jalen won the Kiwanis Award and how Shane was supposed to introduce him to the crowd. He explained that it took him two days to find just the right words to put Pendleton's qualities into perspective. In the speech, he began with numbers — 1,169 points in two years and 589 his senior year, placing him third on the school's all-time list behind Derrick Dowell's 669 and Myron Christian's 610. He mentioned that Jalen made Junior All-State and was the team's MVP in 2011 and 2012. Shane also expressed his disappointment when Pendleton was only recognized as honorable mention All-State as a senior and was left off the Indiana All-Stars.

Though Jalen's numbers and honors were impressive, the bulk of the coach's comments related to the young man as a person, and as he spoke, the emotions flowed. He spoke of Jalen's work with the feeder league kids and his volunteer work for the Arthritis Foundation. He mentioned a motivational speech Bird gave to the Glenwood Academy before the ISTEP tests about how the 'R' word (retard) should be replaced with 'Respect.'

Burkhart also related his feelings about Jalen as a member of Bosse's basketball team, referring to words like "warrior" and "passion". "These two words define the character and demeanor of Jalen on the floor," he said. "The strong hand-claps and loud screams are his battle cries to his teammates to jump on board and follow him to victory. Those totals for two years equal 42 wins, 1 City title, 2 sectionals, 1 regional and one of the gutsiest efforts I have ever witnessed."

The "effort" to which Shane alluded was perhaps the defining moment of Jalen's career. After a fairly smooth run through the tournament, the Bulldogs faced Guerin Catholic in the semi-state, one game shy of playing for the championship, and this final game represented what Pendleton is all about.

"We were horrible that night," Burkhart said matter-of-factly. "The bottom line is, our sophomores were like deer in headlights. It was their first time on a national stage (Fox Sports Midwest covered the game). We jumped to a 15-7 lead and then went stone cold. They all looked to Jalen. He ended up with 36 points, 12 rebounds and 4 assists.

"With three minutes to go in the game, there was a TV timeout and we're down 17 points. The game is basically out of reach. We're trying to decide when to take the kids out to give them their send-off for a great season (23-5). I couldn't talk; all of them were crying because they were devastated. They knew Bird's career was over and we had let each other down, but none of them could say that about Jalen."

During the tournament, when the games really counted and the team was firmly on his back, Jalen was at his best. In the sectional, he scored 28 (Gibson Southern), 26 (Boonville) and 29 (Memorial), and in the regional, it was 14 (Vincennes in a slow-down game) and 34 (Brownstown). And in his final game, with teammates imploding all around him, Pendleton poured in 36 points.

At one point during the Guerin Catholic game, Jalen approached Burkhart and said, "Coach, you need to take me out; I can't feel my legs," and when Burkhart said "no way," Pendleton smiled, shook his head and continued to compete.

He left the court that night exhausted, something Shane had seen time and time again. "He just gives you so much effort he completely wears himself out," Burkhart revealed. "We have had to stop our buses after games because of his cramps from pure exhaustion."

When Jalen's career ended in March of 2012, he left his heart and soul on the floor, and shortly thereafter, he was recognized in a way that had never occurred before, even with such athletes as Keown, Williams, Bob Griese and the Mattingly brothers. After his final game was played, he was honored as the only athlete in Evansville history to earn All-Metro Player of the Year honors in both football and basketball in the same season.

The distinction that Jalen Pendleton received was well-deserved, and both his high school football and basketball coaches are well aware of how rare a player of his caliber is, and nothing could sum up Jalen's value more than the words spoken by Coach Burkhart at the Kiwanis Awards Banquet.

"As a coach, there are certain kids you know you will never replace," Burkhart said. "Coach Thomas and I know that Jalen can never be duplicated. He will be unwillingly replaced, but for me, it will be the hardest replacement I ever made. The last word that describes Jalen is 'Bulldog'. Congrats, Jalen, there is no doubt you are a Bosse Bulldog and one that I am so proud to be affiliated with. The sky is your limit."

DAN EGIERSKI:
"IT'S ALL ABOUT THE KIDS"

In this modern age of global technology, the world of sports broadcasting has become a cacophony of sound bites and tweets that spew from every source imaginable. But in the midst of this universe is a small group of individuals who are striving to maintain some semblance of the pure values that true sports fans appreciate. One such man is Dan Egierski (pronounced ee • GUR • skee).

As a young man in South Bend, Dan's first foray into the world of entertainment was somewhat less than a success. "It was back in my second grade musical," he explained. "My voice was so bad that the teacher told me, 'just move your lips.'"

Dan had a deep voice, and as he reached high school age, he took a lot of English classes with plans of studying Communications. His first true inspiration occurred during a sunny afternoon spent watching Harry Caray doing a White Sox game. "He's sitting out there in center field in the bleachers," Egierski recalled. "He's out there with his shirt off drinking his Budweiser, and I thought, 'If that guy's getting paid to do that, that's what I want to do.'"

With excitement in his booming voice, he shared the ambition with his parents, but once again, he wasn't met with encouragement as they responded by saying, "You don't have the personality to do that! Do something else."

Egierski was an excellent athlete at LaSalle High School as a pitcher and shortstop in baseball and as the quarterback on the gridiron. After a year at Holy Cross Junior College, Dan came south to attend the University of Evansville, and that is where his pursuit of the dream began.

Having enjoyed his days as a player in high school, Dan felt that covering sports would be a great way to "stay in the game," so he majored in Interpersonal Communications. During his junior and senior years, he worked an internship at WEVC (now WUEV) where he covered some games and did some in-studio anchor work.

During his senior year, he experienced the tragedy of the U of E plane crash along with the rest of the community, but the event hit much closer to home for him. As plans were being made just before the Christmas break for the team's trip to Murfreesboro, Tennessee, the primary play-by-play man, Mark Moulton, had gotten sick. The next in line was a female, Laura Gottschling. As the WEVC brass contemplated, they decided not to allow Laura to go because they would have to spring for a separate room because she was a female. They also concluded that Dan, the next in line, did not have enough experience. So on the evening of the crash, Dan and Laura and Laura's friend Cindy were out shopping when they heard the devastating news. (As a side note, Cindy, Laura's friend, eventually became Dan's wife.)

During the fall semester of 1978, Dan went to work at WGBF, working 3 a.m. to 7 a.m. five days a week as the morning street reporter covering the police beat. After graduating in December of '78, he left for a full-time position in Tell City at WTCJ, where he worked sports, news and as a DJ until 1986. While there, he learned the ropes and cut his chops on the heavy equipment used in those days. His first games as a play-by-play man were football games for Cannelton and Hancock County, and as he gained experience, he covered the Tell City Marksmen.

In 1986, he was re-hired at WGBF to do news, but as fate would have it, the sports director left, leaving the position open for Dan. He began covering local high school and IU games, and over time, he picked up some games at USI, beginning during Mark Bial's final season. His USI gig really took off in 1992 when a brash young coach named Bruce Pearl burst onto the scene. Pearl had a vision, and part of that vision was having every game broadcast and doing a coach's show on radio.

Needless to say, the Pearl years were some of Dan's most exciting, and the coach made an instant impact on Egierski. "It didn't take me very long to notice (his potential) because of his attention to detail. In practice, I would see

Art by Jon Siau

him spend five minute on a jump ball, and nobody else did that," Egierski disclosed. "When I traveled with them, I saw how much time he spent watching film and preparing compared to previous coaches, and I figured this guy knows what he wants and how to get it."

Pearl and company provided tons of memories for Dan and the fans as they finished as the national runner-up in '94 and then pulled off a miracle in 1995. As Dan watched from press row, the Screaming Eagles stunk up the gym in the first half at the Commonwealth Center in Louisville and were lucky to be trailing UC-Riverside by only 18 at the half.

After the break, USI chipped away at the lead through the efforts of Marc Hostetter, Cortez Barnes, Stan Gouard, Brian Huebner, Chad Gilbert and others. When the game was on the line, Egierski watched as the Eagles pulled out the win, and the evening was one he'll never forget.

"The second half was unbelievable," Egierski recalled. "As aggressive as Pearl was, you would have thought in the locker room at halftime that the paint would have been peeling off the wall. But when I talked to the players, they said he was very calm and he told them, 'We can't play any worse. Let's go out and start chopping away at it.' They certainly did, and I was exhausted after that game."

Through the years, Egierski has been a fixture during many of the area's most memorable sports moments. In addition to three USI national championship games, he has been our eyes and ears

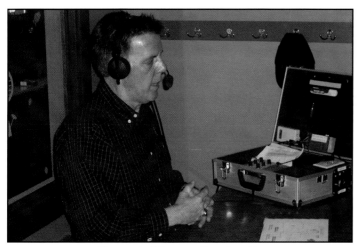

For most of the year, Dan does his live show, **All about Sports,** *five days a week.*

at several State championship games in basketball, baseball and football. In 1995, he was the very first Voice of the Evansville Otters with his partner Bob Buck (Jack Buck's brother). He covered U of E baseball for coach Jim Brownlee when the Carroll brothers (Jamey and Wes) were there, and he covered the Evansville Blue Cats for three years, as well.

Along the way, Dan also got to meet and work with many fine coaches, including Rick Herdes and Rodney Watson in the last few years with USI and countless high school coaches. "They've all been special in their own ways," he told me from behind the set at Gatti Town from where he broadcasts his daily show *All about Sports*. "Probably the coach I had the most fun with was Brent Chitty at Central. He always had a sense of humor about what was going on. And Quentin Merkel would set me straight on baseball terminology, like if I asked him about the hit and run, he would say, 'No, run and hit; you run first, then hit the ball.' They've all treated me with respect, and I try to do the best I can."

Dan is proud that he hasn't had the first run-in with a coach, although he came close once. In 2001, he was covering a football sectional in Tell City that featured the mega-talented quarterback duo of Mater Dei's Jake Schiff and Tell City's Phillip Johnson, who passed for nearly 1,000 yards between them. On Monday, Dan received a call from a rather irate Mike Goebel asking, "What in the world were you thinking Friday night?"

Perplexed, Dan asked, "What do you mean, coach?" It seems that Goebel had heard from fans that the broadcast talked incessantly about how Mater Dei recruits athletes.

After giving it some thought and realizing what had happened, Egierski set Mike's mind at ease. He explained that his frequency, 1280, could not reach Evansville and that Mike's fans must have been tuned to Tell City's broadcast, located at 1230. Needless to say, Mike Goebel apologized profusely and Dan's spotless record with coaches was still intact.

Dan's favorite sport to call is basketball because of the constant action, but he also enjoys being out in the elements on a crisp fall night at a high school football game. In fact, it was just such a night that was the setting for his favorite broadcasting moment.

"From a personal standpoint, my most memorable game was in September of 1999 against Memorial," he informed me, "when my son (Ryan) was a senior at Castle. During his time on varsity, I'd never called a Castle game. I wanted to watch and not worry about being on air.

"It was Ryan's final home game, and we invited my folks down. I invited my dad (Jerry) to do the game with me. You think of these fathers and sons, like Joe and Jack Buck, and I thought, 'how neat would that be?'

"I prefaced the evening (on air) by saying, 'I have a special color commentator tonight – my dad. It's special for all of us, so anything that goes out over the air tonight, if you're a Memorial fan, please disregard it because it's a grandfather cheering for his grandson."

Needless to say, the evening was not without its moments, like when Ryan caught a long pass behind the secondary for a TD ("Run, Ryan, Run!") or when Dan's son was chasing a runner from his safety position ("Get him, Ryan, Get him!") But despite the glitches, Dan will never forget the night, saying, "Nothing will ever top that game for me personally."

Dan truly believes he is a lucky man, and the blessings start with Cindy. "I have the most wonderful wife," he revealed, "and I told her when we were dating that there would be a lot of nights when I wouldn't be home. We talked about it when we were courting. I can't tell you how many birthdays and anniversaries I've missed."

Egierski was also lucky that his kids chose fall and spring sports. Ryan was an excellent football and baseball player, while Lauren, his daughter, played volleyball and started in center field for Castle's 2001 State champion softball team. Those days were important to him as he recalled how his dad had gone to his games, inspiring him to do the same for his kids.

After 35 years behind the mic, Dan looks back philosophically. He admits that larger markets like Indianapolis, Nashville and even Denver had offered opportunities, but he chose to keep things in perspective. "I had an uncle who worked in New York," he related, "and he said, 'This profession took my family away. I was never home, and it cost me my family.' I had opportunities, but I always kept my family first."

A few years ago, Dan joined forces with Gary Jossa to form ESPI, Evansville Sports Programming, Inc., and then found Mark Lang in Vincennes. Lang's station, WYFX based in Mt. Vernon, became our local ESPN affiliate, and Egierski works hard to supplement ESPN's national programming with as much local fare as possible. "It's all about the kids," Dan stated. "I try to promote the athletes and coaches, whether its play-by-play or my show. I think the athletes in this area are very special. It's been a wonderful experience for me, and I'm just trying to do my part."

Dan isn't fond of the high-tech methods used today, and he's the type who wouldn't use a cell phone if he didn't need to. He is a true sports fan who appreciates the mentalities of athletes who work for what they get without a sense of entitlement, and those characteristics also define his career. Without question, Dan Egierski has earned the respect of local sports fans, coaches and athletes for over thirty years, and that dedication has earned him a place in the Indiana Sportswriters and Sportscasters Hall of Fame.

JULIE GOEDDE:
VERSATILE AND TALENTED

High school athletics for girls have only been around in earnest for less than 35 years, and to paraphrase a popular ad slogan, they've come a long way, baby. Today's girls (c. 2012) are exposed to coaching and training methods that far exceed those of the early years, and their stats and accomplishments are transmitted instantly to college coaches across the country.

For these reasons and more, it is difficult to compare a female athlete of the '80s with one from the new millennium. But one thing does remain constant regardless of the generation: a competitor is still a competitor and talent is still talent.

Most local fans would agree that of all the girls who have competed for local schools since 1980, only a small number would stand out as truly elite multi-sport athletes, and one of the earliest of that ilk was Julie Goedde of Evansville Mater Dei.

Julie was the second-youngest of the eight children of Marvin and Annette Goedde, and virtually all the kids were athletic. After the oldest, Brenda, played in the band, came Deb (basketball), Steve (football, baseball and track), Mike (football, basketball and baseball), Don (football and basketball), Kathy (basketball), Julie, and Chris (football, basketball and baseball).

As a youngster, Julie practiced on the hoop in the backyard, often shoveling off snow to play ball, and she spent many hours dribbling in the family's concrete basement. Her work ethic paid big dividends as she developed, and Bruce Dockery, the current head girls coach at Memorial who coached Julie in middle school, remembers her scoring 34 points in a half as an eighth grader. "She was years ahead of her time," Dockery told me. "She was the best I have ever coached in bringing the ball the length of the court and going inside or pulling up off the dribble from any range."

By the time she entered Mater Dei in 1982, Goedde was a seasoned athlete, starting as a freshman in volleyball, basketball and track and eventually earning twelve varsity letters. Standing 6 feet tall throughout her entire high school career, Julie teamed with athletes like Lisa John, Tammy Bailey and Marie Anslinger in an era that featured Cheryl Dowell and Vicki Lander (Bosse) and Linda Christman (North) as area stars. In volleyball, Goedde earned first team All-State honors as a senior, and on the basketball floor, she shared All-City honors her senior year with Diane Starry (Memorial), Lander, Shannon McCulley (Reitz) and Kristie Blair (Harrison). Julie was the top vote-getter after averaging 18 points, 12 rebounds and 4 steals per game.

In the spring, Julie was a four-time State qualifier for the track team, throwing the shot over 42 feet and the discus over 133 feet. In fact, as of 2011, she still held the City Meet record with a 41'9" throw in the shot (1985) and 125'4" throw in the discus (1986). With her athletic skills and solid academics (3.76 GPA), Julie was pursued by Purdue, IU and Ohio State among others, and several schools, including those from the Big Ten, gave her the choice of volleyball or basketball. Her parents assumed she would take the more traditional route and play basketball at IU, but Julie decided to play volleyball for the Hoosiers.

Goedde lettered all four years at IU and led the team in total blocks and block assists for four consecutive seasons. She left the program as the record holder in career solo blocks (128) and career total blocks (521) and was named first team All-Big Ten as a senior. In 1986, she played on the East squad at the U.S. Olympic Festival and was a three-time Academic All-Big Ten honoree. In addition, she earned the coveted Big Ten Medal of Honor, which is presented each year to one girl from each Big Ten school.

As if her volleyball and academic load weren't enough, Julie satisfied her competitive urge by helping the IU track team during her fourth and fifth years in Bloomington. She scored enough points to letter both years, and to prove her natural abilities, she finished second in the Big Ten in the outdoor javelin. Her track coaches even thought enough of her athleticism to suggest that she stay with the sport and take up the heptathlon.

After her graduation in 1991, Goedde took a job at U of E as an assistant volleyball and basketball coach for a year before accepting a job at Evansville Harrison to teach math and assist Darla Edwards in volleyball. Edwards had coached Julie at Mater Dei, and upon her retirement, was more than happy to turn the program over to her protégé in 1995.

At Harrison, Julie, who had since married to become Julie Sellers, assisted John Chapman with the basketball program for seven years and served as the head track coach for eight years. As of 2011, she had piloted the school's volleyball program for sixteen years. During her years there, Julie has worked with some of the school's finest female athletes, like Christian Hart, an Indiana All-Star in basketball, the Lynch twins, Megan and Reagan, and the great Stacie Mueller, a volleyball standout and Indiana All-Star in basketball, as well.

Mater Dei's Julie Goedde

Julie witnessed many changes as the years passed, including the evolution of the game itself. "In volleyball, we had an eight-minute clock (while the ball was in play)," Julie explained. "Also, the serving team was the only team that could score a point. That's changed to rally scoring now (where either team can score). Now, it's three out of five (games), not two out of three, and you go to 25."

Julie has also observed the advancements in women's sports since she played. "When I went to college, that was about the time girls started lifting weights, and that was not a good idea," Ms. Sellers revealed. "We did a lot of jump training and weightlifting, and we weren't ready for it. Lisa (John, her teammate at Mater Dei) and I both went to IU and played volleyball, and we both have had knee surgeries since then.

"We're more knowledgeable now. Kids in middle school now start lifting, but you have to prepare your muscles. Some kids are lifting too much and pulling muscles off the bones. Kids are getting injured younger now."

Julie Sellers was one of the true pioneers of local girls' sports, and she was a star early on. In a *Courier* story by David Rutter, the journalist revealed Julie's talents as a 14-year-old. "She's very mature for a freshman," Rutter wrote. "After two weeks of practice, Julie Goedde stepped into Mater Dei's starting lineup and helped the Wildcats to a 5-0 record. She's averaging 13 points a game and, according to MD coach Steve Goans, may become the best female basketball player ever produced in Evansville."

The story went on to praise fellow Mater Dei starters Tammy Bailey, Darlene Rooney, Brooke Heathcotte and Barb Seib and stated that fans envisioned "Miss Goedde and 6-foot sophomore Cheryl Dowell of Bosse as the dominant city players for the foreseeable future."

Kristie (Blair) Ladd, the mother of local legend Mallory Ladd, witnessed Julie's skills up close and personal as a competitor at Harrison and had nothing but praise for Ms. Goedde. "Julie was a fabulous player. She was probably the best post player I played against. And she was an even better volleyball player."

Most pundits would say that today's athletes are more skilled than those years ago, and perhaps they are right. But an athlete is an athlete, and Julie Sellers was one of Evansville's first. During her four-year Mater Dei career, she was named All-City and All-Conference all four years in all three sports, something that has likely never happened before and may not happen again.

As debates arise about our area's greatest, the quiet Ms. Sellers' name may get lost in the discussion, but those who saw her compete know how good she was. The Mater Dei girls sports program made another surge in 2012 as the ladies won the school's first State championship in girls basketball, and with the young team, the talent is there to repeat. But no matter how things turn out, one thing is certain. The lady whose skills first put Mater Dei on the map is none other than Julie Goedde (Sellers).

The 1986 Courier All-City team (L-R): Diane Starry, Vicki Lander, Shannon McCully, Kristie Blair and Julie Geodde. (Photo courtesy of the Evansville Courier)

BRUCE LOMAX: HOMETOWN PROUD

Bruce Lomax will be the first to admit that he wasn't the greatest athlete in local history, but few loved sports or fought for their beliefs as he did over the years. At 96 years young in 2012, Bruce still perked up at the mention of the battles he fought, and though his memory isn't what it used to be, the emotion is still there. The man was a fine athlete in his day, but it was his willingness to get involved and to take a stand that set him apart, and it would be difficult to name many who championed the growth of the local sports culture more than Mr. Lomax.

Bruce was born in Bristow, Indiana, a small Dubois County town near St. Meinrad. His father, Russell, managed Piggly Wiggly supermarkets for years, and he and wife Carrie eventually settled in Evansville and owned their own grocery at 6th and Gum. As an athlete at Bosse, Bruce became a standout on the diamond and the hardwood, and although he was only 5'7, he packed a powerful punch as a hitter. He was so explosive, in fact, that the local sportswriters called him 'Home Run Lomax' and 'Bambino', the nickname given to Babe Ruth.

Bruce's younger brother Jack stood 6'4 and excelled on the gridiron, but Bruce made a name for himself on the basketball court. In high school, he helped Coach Harry King win the City championship at Bosse and then played for Bill Slyker at Evansville College. He left Bosse in 1935, and his '35-'36 Aces team was the first to take on IU.

Lomax served in the Navy during WWII, and upon his return, he entered the business world and remained active as an athlete. He played on a Hon. E. Krust Bakery team that featured his brother Jack, Walter Riggs and Arad McCutchan, and he was the player/coach for a Sunbeam Bakery team that once played the Harlem Globetrotters at the Armory.

Meanwhile, Bruce earned a living in the sporting goods business, first working for Tom McCain before launching out on his own. He worked with Joe Nicholson for a while at a store on Locust Street called Lomax & Nicholson, and for eight years, he teamed with local legend Gus Doerner as they ran the popular Lomax & Doerner store on 2nd Street.

The store was located across from the Lamplight Inn, and it was there that the seed was planted for an organization that is still going strong today. As the story goes, Bruce and some of his cronies spent many hours at the Lamplight for lunch, and their shared interest in sports inspired the group to form the Quarterback Club, a fraternity of hundreds of men who still meet weekly to promote local athletes and coaches. As a founding member, the club is Bruce's pride and joy, and its membership is a literal Who's Who of local sports history.

As the decades passed, the sports atmosphere in the area underwent many transformations, and Lomax did not shy away from controversy. As plans were proposed and disputed publicly, Bruce was always front and center, and he had no shortage of opinions.

As a member of the Roberts Stadium Board, he was largely responsible for much of the memorabilia that was displayed in the Corridor of Champions around the concourse, and at one point, he fought to have a domed arena constructed adjacent to Roberts. It was common for Lomax to display his witty repartee at public meetings, and the 'Mouth that Roared' wasn't shy about speaking his mind as the press covered the events.

One journalist referred to Bruce's two-handed set shot as a player when he wrote, "Doerner made some quick shots of the verbal variety that would please even Bob Knight." Another referred to Bruce's hearing aid business that he ran after leaving Lomax & Doerner, saying, "If you don't know where Lomax stands, you must be hard of hearing." Yet another writer even likened Lomax to Ollie North, the famous retired Marine who welcomed controversy when he challenged the status quo and blew the whistle about clandestine arms being sold to Iran.

As the public debate raged on, locals had varying points of view. *Press* sports editor Dick Anderson wrote, "If we built an arena that seated more than 6,000, it would be the biggest white elephant this city would ever know," while Dan Scism, the sports editor of the *Courier* disagreed, wanting to see the building hold at least 20,000.

In another instance, when the proposal was made to allow the city government to take over the running of the Stadium, Lomax responded as only he could. "It's ridiculous that the Parks Department has anything to do with Roberts Stadium," he said to the press. "They have a hard enough time keeping the grass cut."

Another prime example of Bruce's way with words concerned the facilities at Roberts at the time. "The restroom layouts are abominable," he stated. "I've been in there at times when it looked like first and goal at the Chicago Bears' one-yard line."

Bruce was a fixture in the local press and never hesitated to call or visit the *Courier*'s office, and when he came up with an idea, he always thought big. He was an advocate of re-designing Enlow Field to hold 12,000-16,000 fans at football games, proposing that it also be used for nighttime softball leagues.

Whether fans agreed or disagreed, there is no doubt that the man had a vision of what he thought Evansville's future should look like, and once again, he made his views public in a letter to the editor entitled "Lomax's post-war recreation plan": "In my opinion, Evansville needs a new combination golf course, lighted tennis court, football stadium, lighted softball field and huge swimming pool. Such a living recreation memorial could be established on the 80-acre site between Outer Lincoln (just west of Green River Road) and Washington Avenue." He also proposed "a dozen concrete tennis courts with lights for night playing. Those courts could also be designed so they could be used in winter as ice-skating courts, which can be accomplished by having an 8-inch concrete rim around the courts, making them water-tight."

As one can imagine, Bruce's comments were not always popular, and some took potshots at him in an attempt to challenge his credibility, but others defended him publicly. Pete Fisher, a magnificent athlete at Reitz and owner at the time of Pete Fisher Athletic Supply Company, knew Lomax well as a fellow member of the Roberts Stadium Board and spoke publicly in Bruce's defense, saying, "Those who question Bruce's motives don't really know him. He's the most civic minded person I've ever met."

Lomax was never afraid to take a stand, and as we sat in a room at Willow Park, he smiled each time I read a quote that conjured up memories about his days as an advocate. As the years passed, he remained a loyal fan of Aces basketball and was a close friend of legendary Aces coach Arad McCutchan his entire life. As we talked, his daughter Janet pulled out a chairback cover that designated Bruce as a member of the Tipoff Club, and though Bruce's memories were a bit fuzzy on details, he smiled when he was asked his opinion on a few Aces greats.

Buster Briley: "You didn't know what Buster was going to do next."

Jerry Sloan: "(Heck) yeah, I liked Jerry Sloan. He could have gone anywhere he wanted and played. He was just tough."

Larry Humes: "Humes was tough. It was hard to handle him. He could do things a lot of people just couldn't do."

Bruce's influences are still present though he is no longer in the public eye. Janet believes that he was one of the first to sign the first rafter in Roberts Stadium, and he recently repeated the gesture on the first rafter at the new Ford Center downtown. His name is also listed on a plaque at Roberts that honors him as a member of the Evansville Municipal Stadium Planning Commission, joining Mayor H.O. Roberts (chairman), Charles L. Oxley (co-chairman), Ronald Shively (secretary), Victor H. Goeke, Donald B. Engle and M. B. Wedge.

It could easily be argued that no one in the history of Evansville has dedicated himself more to building and inspiring the local sports landscape as vehemently and for as long as the Might Mite himself, Bruce Lomax. He spoke his mind and fought for what he believed. Perhaps his long eventful life can be summed up best by the words spoken by his loving daughter Janet. "My dad lived his passion," she said, "and not many men can say that."

First Row (Seated): Bruce Lomax, Walter Riggs, Loren Bailey, Otto Thuerbach. Second Row (Standing): Arad "Mac" McCutchan, Jack Lomax, Ox Harley, Bill Dunkin, Ed Moody, Bus. Manager.

Evansville College 1934-1935. Left to right, front row: Emerson O. Henke, Chris P. Maglaris, Joe Theby, Bruce Lomax, Robert Polk. Middle row: Fay V. Johnson, Otto P. Thuerbach, Loren Bailey, Colby Pallard, Constant Hartke, Walter R. Riggs. Standing: Hugh R. Thrasher, Ron Jacquess, Howard Selm, Coach William V. Slyker, Harold Selm, Melvin Seeger, Alfred Rose.

WAYNE BOULTINGHOUSE: FROM FARM TO FAME

From a tiny country schoolhouse to enshrinement in not one, but two halls of fame, Wayne Boultinghouse fashioned a career as a player, coach and athletic director that ranks among the finest of any in local history. With a quiet confidence and unquestioned integrity, he has earned the respect of everyone who has known him, and because of his successes, he has been uniquely honored among all those who preceded him.

"We had a rich family life, but we didn't have two shiny dimes to rub together," said Wayne Boultinghouse when asked about his upbringing. Wayne's parents, Oscar and Anna, were farmers, and he and his siblings learned the value of hard work early on. Along with older brother Bill, and younger sisters Jane and Ann, who died at the age of seven, Wayne and the other kids tended to the family's milk cows and chickens and were entertained by riding ponies.

The kids were educated at South Central Grade School, a four-room schoolhouse that held two grades in each room. Like many from his generation, Wayne rode the bus to school, but unlike many, outdoor privies were used until he was in the fifth grade. The athletic facilities consisted of a field outside and a makeshift gym fashioned from a converted auditorium under the classrooms. The gym was obviously cramped and had 12-foot ceilings and rims a few inches shorter than the standard ten feet. Consequently, Wayne and his teammates occasionally banked shots off the ceiling, which was not ruled out of bounds.

As an eighth grader, Wayne led his team to the Spencer County championship, no small feat against much larger schools like Rockport and Dale. For such a tiny school, the talent at South Central was really quite remarkable, and a few were very successful as collegians and even professionals. The Lillpop brothers, Garry and

Larry, were outstanding, along with Jim Boyd (baseball scholarship), Randy Miller, Bill Evans, Bob Zimmerman and sixth grader Gene Vincent (SIU and the Angels).

These same athletes joined others to form a strong nucleus at Rockport High School, where Boultinghouse starred in football, basketball, baseball and track. With Wayne as the team's quarterback for four years, his high school teams never lost a game while playing in the Pocket Athletic Conference's 8-man football league. In the 8-man game, teams typically lined up with a quarterback, fullback and halfback behind a center, two guards and two ends. Wayne did mention that the school played two 11-man exhibition games in 1959 against Castle and North. Although Rockport was at an obvious disadvantage, their talent was such that they simply flanked the three extra men out wide, ran their regular 8-man plays, and won both games.

Rockport didn't start a track program until his sophomore year, and Wayne was good enough to qualify for the State meet in the 440-yard dash. A vivid memory Boultinghouse still has today is his excursion to the big meet and his experience with the staggered start on the cinder track at IU. The race started with two runners in each lane, and Wayne drew lane 8. As they rounded the curve, he believed he was on his way to a gold medal but quickly discovered otherwise. As the stagger evened out, he was in eleventh, and though he finished sixth, his recollections are still vivid. "I'd never had cinders thrown in my face before," he confided, "and I can still describe that feeling today."

Although Wayne missed most of his junior basketball season, he ended his career with close to 1,200 points. With a few of his grade school teammates and others like Jerry Daniels and Connie Pounds, the Zebras were competitive but could "never crack the nut" of winning the sectional against the likes of Roger Kaiser and Bob Reinhart of Dale; Al Nass, who starred at Huntingburg and Georgia Tech; and Tommy Kron, who was coached by 'Gunner' Wyman at Tell City.

Wayne (#12) led his South Central Elementary School eighth grade team to an undefeated season. Behind Coach Raymond Taylor are (L-R): Randy Miller, Gene Vincent, Garry Lillpop, Larry Lillpop, Wayne, Jimmy Boyd, Ronnie Hart, Mickey Greene, Tommy Faye and Bobby Zimmerman.

Wayne lines up at quarterback for Evansville College with Central's Jim Greer (#32) in the backfield. His linemen are (L-R): Todd Clark, Chris Herdel and Jim Horstketter.

Looking back at all the greats he competed with and against, Wayne made an interesting observation when asked to name the best he'd seen in his playing career. "I think Jerry Sloan (his future teammate at Evansville College), Gene Vincent (grade school and high school) and my brother Bill were the greatest competitors I've ever been around," he answered. "Bill has been my mentor all my life, and he pretty much pinned my ears back all the time."

Most folks, including Boultinghouse himself, felt that baseball was Wayne's best sport, and his love for the game played a major role in his college plans. He was pursued by many schools, including Kentucky, Louisville, Evansville and Ole Miss, and he weighed his options carefully. "Playing professional baseball had been an ambition since the fourth grade," Wayne told me, and although he knew that basketball was his ticket to getting school paid for, baseball had to be a part of the deal.

After his senior year, Wayne played for the Rockport American Legion team and led the three-year-old program to its first state title in 1959. He also joined fellow local legend and teammate Jim Haaff while they worked as counselors at the Show Me Baseball Camp in Branson, Missouri. While there, they played against stiff semi-pro competition, which scratched his baseball itch for a while.

When the summer was over, Boultinghouse enrolled at Evansville College and joined some of the greatest talent in EC/U of E history to create some incredible memories for local fans. Wayne entered college brimming with enthusiasm and continued his high school routine by donning the football pads under coach Paul Beck. Beck's boys ran a little single wing in '59, and Wayne spent some time at halfback while also sharing quarterback duties with the very talented Kim Devault, a Memorial grad.

He continued his arduous schedule as a freshman under legendary Aces basketball coach Arad McCutchan before heading to the diamond under baseball coach Don Ping in the spring. After a full year that included spring football, Wayne knew that he couldn't serve three masters and made the decision to focus on baseball and basketball.

Boultinghouse continued his spectacular play on the diamond, earning MVP honors for the ICC playing shortstop and hitting .440 while teaming with Bob Glaser, Mike Madriaga, catcher Chris Herdel and Paul Bullard, among others. But it was during

the winters that Wayne's reputation grew with local fans, and the electric atmosphere of Aces basketball in its prime made quite an impact on the young athlete. "I'll never forget coming out of the tunnel at Roberts Stadium," Wayne recalled, "with 12 or 13,000 people. My legs were jelly."

Wayne's years at EC coincided with the career of all-time Aces great Jerry Sloan, one of Wayne's best friends to this day, and 'The Boulder' played a key role in the 1964 national championship. The team that Coach McCutchan christened "the greatest club we've ever had" defeated 24-6 Akron on Friday the 13th of March, and Wayne was a strong presence. The nearly 135,000 fans (sixth in the country) who saw the Aces at home that season grew accustomed to the platoon system used by McCutchan. The starters for most of the season were Sloan and Sam Watkins at guard with big Ed Zausch in the middle flanked by Buster Briley and Larry Humes. Providing valuable minutes were the "Fabulous Four": Wayne, Jim Smith, Russ Grieger and Paul Bullard. When the Fab Four would enter, Sloan would stay on the floor, something Wayne wryly described as "a real good move by Coach McCutchan."

Upon his graduation, Boultinghouse began the pursuit of his ultimate dream. Through his Legion and college career, he had caught the eye of pro scouts, with the Orioles and Cardinals showing the most interest. In those days, there was no draft, so Wayne had to sift through and compare offers. Although the Orioles offered twice as much, Wayne's heart had always been with the Cardinals, so he couldn't resist the opportunity.

When he arrived in Rockhill, South Carolina, the Rookie League team's offices were closed, so Wayne strode onto the field and struck up a conversation with the first person he saw. Amazingly, after seeing the gentleman up close, Wayne realized that the first person he was meeting as a professional player was none other than Cardinal hall of fame pitcher Steve Carlton.

The first contract Boultinghouse signed was for $500 a month, and he was only paid during the season. He played 60 games in '64 and was then sent to Cedar Rapids, Iowa in Class A. During his years there, he saw such greats as Reggie Jackson, Sal Bando, Vida Blue, Craig Nettles and Joe Rudy, and Wayne held his own as a .290 - .300 hitter.

In 1966, Wayne changed uniforms, but the change was drastic and totally unexpected. At the time, he was leading the team in hitting when the Cold War and Vietnam prompted a re-classification of his draft notice. Wayne had received a teaching exemption and had even earned his Masters, but the classes he was teaching in the off-season were no longer included in the exemption.

Boultinghouse admits to feeling some bitterness at the time but, in retrospect, appreciates the time spent in the Intelligence Corps in France and Germany. In the Spring of '68, Wayne was back in the Cardinals organization with improved power numbers ("thanks to military pushups"). He was teaching in Martinsville in 1968-'69 and intended to resign in the spring to return to baseball. But when he received a phone call and heard a familiar voice, his plans quickly changed.

Arad McCutchan had thought of Wayne and called to tell him that a position was open at the college. They were asking Boultinghouse to head up the baseball program, assist in basketball and football and teach physical education. Wayne's response?: "Coach, give me 48 hours to think about it and pray about it." And that's just what he did before moving to Evansville for the $7,500-a-year job.

Dan Labhart's signing in 1976 sparked a resurgence in the ISUE program under Coach Boultinghouse.

Wayne spent three years as Jim Byers' assistant in football before exchanging that duty with the assistant AD job. He was a basketball assistant until 1974 while also returning the baseball program to prominence.

In 1974, Boultinghouse became the AD and head basketball coach across town at Indiana State University-Evansville (now the University of Southern Indiana), replacing Jerry Altstadt as the school's coach. One of his first tasks was to oversee the renovation of the old Central Gym downtown that was to become the home of the Screaming Eagles.

The crowds during the early years were sparse, perhaps 250-400, and Wayne's teams finished 6-19 and 11-15 in his first two seasons. But in 1976, the program began its ascent. "In 1976, I signed Dan Labhart," Wayne informed me. "He was a local product (Boonville) and a model student-athlete. He started from his freshman year on and became the face of the program. Dan's leadership on the court was very much in evidence."

Labhart remembers the recruitment process and still smiles at the recollection. "Knowing that I liked brain sandwiches, Coach bought me two of the largest sandwiches I had ever seen from a west side restaurant during my official visit," Dan revealed. "The standing joke was that I told Coach that he had me at one, to which he replied, "You could have had three.""

With Labhart at the helm, the crowds came, as did post-season bids and GLVC banners. Wayne was in charge when ISUE made its first NCAA tourney appearance in 1978, and the program improved steadily with players like DeJuan 'Spider' Rowser, Lawrence Knight (who played one year before leading the nation in scoring in junior college and going in the first round to the Jazz), Kelly Williams of Poseyville and 'Big John' Hollinden from Central.

During his years at ISUE, Wayne had a reputation for deflecting credit from himself to others, but Dan Labhart observed the job Boultinghouse did first-hand. "The real truth was that Wayne Boultinghouse is the entire foundation of the success of the basketball program, and also the athletic department. I personally witnessed his tireless efforts and willingness to do anything to transform his dreams into reality."

Wayne was also an integral part of the university's progression from an NAIA school to NCAA Division II while working with Dr. Charles Bertram as he served in other positions after stepping down from coaching in 1981. He later joined the staff at Kentucky Wesleyan under Wayne Chapman before taking over the program in 1990. Wayne won three more GLVC titles at KWC (1991, '92 & '95), giving him a total of five.

From KWC, Wayne returned to his high school alma mater (now South Spencer) as an administrator and girls basketball coach before spending two years at Daviess County Middle School prior to his retirement.

Wayne and his wife Billie are enjoying retirement as they spend it with their three daughters, Alden, Gentry and Abigail, and seven grandchildren. The man who was raised in meager surroundings has built a remarkable life, and he is still active doing the color commentary for fellow 'legend' Jerry Birge as they cover games in the Owensboro area.

Whether he was born to succeed or molded by his environment, Wayne has excelled at every level. In high school, he was class president, sang in the chorus and was strong academically, and as an athlete, he earned 15 varsity letters, never lost a football game and earned a scholarship in basketball. He was good enough on the diamond to play professionally, and as a coach, he was named the GLVC Coach of the Year in 1980 and the District 4 Coach of the Year in '81.

With humility, Wayne credits his rural childhood and blue collar influences for molding his character and great coaches like Bill Evans (baseball), Paul Dunker (football) and Bob Gardner and Mr. Evans (basketball) for his growth as an athlete. If respect is the measure of prosperity, then Wayne Boultinghouse is wealthy indeed, because virtually every person who knows him loves him. He shared his talents with us as fans and had tremendous impact everywhere he coached, and as a result, he is the only person who has been honored in both the USI and U of E Athletic Halls of Fame.

It is hard to say how many young men's lives have been touched by Wayne, and the words by one of his early protégés reflect the deep emotions many of his players felt and the legacy 'The Boulder' has created. "I have been blessed by having fantastic men influence my life," said Dan Labhart. "I can say that next to my dad, Coach Boultinghouse has had as much to do with my development as anyone. One of my biggest sports thrills was when Coach asked me to present him into the USI Hall of fame. Wayne Boultinghouse is a man I deeply respect, a coach I greatly admire and a person I consider a friend."

THE NAME GAME

Most area fans know Wayne Boultinghouse as 'The Boulder', but those who know him very well are aware of the first nickname given to him by his beloved mother Anna. Anna likened him to the great Babe Ruth, thus the nickname 'Baby Wayne'.

JERRY BIRGE HAS DONE IT ALL

Southwestern Indiana has been blessed with many fine sportscasters over the years, but it is doubtful that any of them could match the career of Jerry Birge. Born and raised in Jasper, Jerry was the second oldest of Cyril and Antoinette Birge's nine children, and the fact that sports became his life should come as no surprise.

Jerry's father, Cyril Birge, was an exceptional basketball player who, with good friend and teammate Eddie Rottet, led the Jasper Wildcats to some of the greatest seasons in the school's history. Cyril's 1934 team is still the only Jasper team to win all of its scheduled games, winning 29 games and only losing in the holiday tournament and the 16-team State Finals. Cyril was robbed of a college career by a serious illness but went on to become one of the most respected officials in the Midwest.

Jerry was a member of Jasper's very first football team, and his basketball team played in the last semi-state in Bloomington and the first at Roberts Stadium. The starters his senior year were five teammates known as the "Five J's": Jerry, Jim Eckerle, Junie Schnarr, Indiana All-Star Jody Giesler and John Hoffman, who played four years at Georgia Tech. The team was good enough to defeat powerful Terre Haute Gerstmeyer their last two years. Gerstmeyer was coached by icon Howard Sharp and featured Charlie Hall, Howard Gardeen and Sam Smith. As seniors, the Five J's beat a fabulous Dale team led by local legends Roger Kaiser and Bob Reinhart and then upset possibly the best Evansville Lincoln team in history that starred such athletes as Ted Lander, Charlie Vance and Porter Merriweather.

At 6'4 and 160 pounds, Jerry was no physical specimen but was good enough to receive a scholarship to Indiana State. According to Jerry, two very important things occurred very early in his college experience. First of all, Jerry admits that he quickly found out how good he *wasn't*, and secondly, in his very first class on the very first day, he met Maggie, the lady who has been by his side for over fifty years.

In 1959, Birge took a news director position in his hometown at radio station WITZ, and he fondly recalls those days as a 22-year-old play-by-play man. "In those days, the sectional was at Huntingburg and it started on Wednesday," Jerry said as we sat in his home in Owensboro. "There was a big snowstorm and no one could get from Jasper to Huntingburg. There was a snow truck heading to Huntingburg and I asked for a ride. The announcers couldn't make it, and there were very few fans. I did all the games and got $5 a game. There were so many games that, for the first time, my take-home pay was over $100 for the two weeks. We thought we were in hog heaven."

In 1961, Jerry and Maggie moved to the big city (Evansville) to take a similar position at WJPS. Although the station was known for its rock & roll, Jerry convinced the brass to let him call some games. Birge had always idolized the great Dick Shively and, in fact, had emulated Shively's style when developing his own. One can only imagine Jerry's shock when he was contacted in 1962 by the man himself. Dick had heard Jerry doing a ballgame and as the

Jerry Birge, center, does a broadcast with Jim 'Tiger' Ritter (left) and Gus Doerner at the Jasper gym.

GM at Channel 7, had called to offer Birge the sports anchor job. Jerry accepted, and for five of the next seven years, WTVW was the top-rated sportscast in town.

Looking back, Jerry marvels at the timing of his move to Evansville. In '62, he got to cover the remarkable Bosse Bulldogs, coached by hall of famer Jim Myers. Led by the starting lineup of Gary Grieger, Jerry Southwood, Ken Rakow, Gene Lockyear and John Wilson, Bosse captured the State title, and two years later, Rex Mundi became the first Catholic school in Indiana history to make the Final Four. Jerry called the action in the '60s for such Rex Mundi Monarch greats as Jerry Mattingly, Tom Niemeier, Bob Griese, Mike Minton, Norm Heard and Rick Kingston, and his run of tournament luck was just beginning.

In 1967, I got to know Jerry when I was a member of the State champion North Huskies. Jerry was on hand during what many consider to be the most talent-laden basketball season in Evansville history. To illustrate the point, the AP poll in March ranked Oakland City at #1 in the state (Larry Harris, Rick Smith et al) with Harrison ranked #3 (Vaughn Wedeking, Terry Wedgewood, Greg Nelson, Greg Fenner, Bob Winchell and Mike Shoulders). North, featuring All-American Bob Ford, Steve Holland, Jim Hildebrandt, Ron Jesop, Preston Smith, Dave Senning and Mark Mason was #4 but finished only third in the city before making our run to the 1967 State title. Reitz was #6 (Curt John, Keith Jeffries, Bob Parkman, Steve McCullough and John Walters), and Bosse followed at #7 (Larry Weatherford, James Utley, Steve Wessel and others). As the North Huskies navigated through a tough sectional and regional on their way to the championship, Jerry was with the team every step of the way. His fondest memory is the late night hours after the nets were cut at Hinkle Fieldhouse. Our team stayed at the Holiday Inn on West Washington, and the team was lounging in the lobby as midnight approached. Coach Jim Rausch made a statement to Jerry and Gus Doerner, Jerry's color man, that the team was probably starving. Birge offered to spring for food and ran across the street to fetch over 100 White Castle burgers. He recalls a bevy of young men with constant smiles on their faces covering the lobby floor with empty boxes, and even today,

163

Jerry with good buddy Marcia Yockey.

he grins as he remembers the many encounters he had through the years with the late Jim Rausch. "I loved that guy," Jerry said. "Every time I saw Jimmy, the first thing he would say was, 'Let's go have a White Castle.'"

In addition to covering three teams in the Final Four in five years and two State champions, Birge and Doerner also basked in the glow of Aces basketball in its heyday. At the time, Channel 7 was very active in covering local sports, and the station owner, Ferris Traylor, used two company planes to transport his crew to away games. Jerry's first excursion was to Denver, and he also flew to Notre Dame, Arizona and New Mexico State, among others. As he reflects on the experience, he is amazed that as a 23-year-old, he was younger than two of the Aces, Jim Smith and Walt Henry, who had spent time in the service.

His most memorable trip took place in 1965 when the Aces, led by Jerry Sloan and Larry Humes, battled the Southern Illinois Salukis, led by All-Everything Walt Frazier, three times in Aces victories that were won by a total of five points. At times, the game would be taped and then aired by tape delay at 10:30 after the news. For the game at SIU, Jerry and Gus were joined by Maggie and local weather gal Marcia Yockey. To meet the deadline, when the first half was over, the pilot flew the two-inch tape reel back to Evansville so that the broadcast could begin at 10:30 and then returned to Carbondale. After the game, Jerry, Gus and the girls were whisked away and then met at the airport by a helicopter. They landed at the station, guided by floodlights, just in time for the second half reel to be loaded to continue the broadcast.

Without doubt, Birge enjoyed some of the finest years in local broadcasting history, and he covered much more than basketball. Jerry served as the voice of the City swim meet at Hartke Pool, the City track meet at Enlow Field and the Tri-State Open golf tournament, using three cameras to cover the final two holes at Helfrich.

Birge also covered ISUE (now USI) during Coach Wayne Boultinghouse's tenure when the Eagles played at the newly renovated Central Gym downtown. Even after he moved back to Jasper in 1967 to raise a family with Maggie, he continued to display his talents. For eight years, he co-hosted the IHSAA basketball tournament draw show, joining Evansville local legend Bob Ford (representing the Lafayette semi-state), Jerry Baker (Indianapolis) and Hilliard Gates (Ft. Wayne).

In the late '60s and early '70s, Birge appeared live on Channel 25 for his *Race of the Day* show at 5:00 live from Ellis Park. During the program, he would give results of prior races and then show video of the fifth race. After that, the "race of the day" would be broadcast live and guests would be interviewed. Because of his relationship with the Executive Inn, he scored big when he was able to snare The Four Aces, Jerry Van Dyke and various politicians who were appearing or staying at the hotel.

During Jerry's fifty years of broadcasting, he has amassed thousands of memories of his days behind the mic and has seen his industry make dramatic changes. In the early days, there were no teleprompters to rely on, and the on-air talent had to develop their own film. For many years, he appeared only in black and white, and the video machines could only be transported by converted bread trucks.

As one would expect, some recollections are sad ones, and two of them were eerily similar. The first was a call from Jerry Altstadt, a good friend who coached basketball at Rex Mundi High School and USI. Altstadt's first words to Jerry were, "Are you sitting down?" He proceeded to inform Birge that Jerry Mattingly had died in a construction accident at age 23. Birge had gotten to know Mattingly well after an Aces game when he had driven him home and sat in his car for an hour listening to Mattingly talk about life and his future.

Later in his career, Jerry received another call that began with the same words, "Are you sitting down?" The call was from *Courier* writer Tom Collins, and he told Jerry, "We lost Bernie," referring to beloved *Courier* journalist Don Bernhardt.

Though memories like those and others like the U of E plane crash in 1977 are inevitable, the vast majority of Birge's experiences were positive, and he is well aware of his good fortune. He and Maggie spent countless hours in arenas around the area, and throughout the years he has rubbed elbows with the likes of Ted Williams, Wilt Chamberlain, Stan Musial, Mario Andretti, Mickey Mantle and Wilma Rudolph, to name a few.

Today (2012), Jerry and Maggie are enjoying their seven children, thirteen grandchildren and six great-grandkids, and Jerry still goes to work every day to host his show on cable channel 8 in Owensboro called *Around Owensboro with Jerry Birge*. In 2004, Jerry received a lifetime achievement award from the Owensboro Parks & Recreation Department for his promotion of kids and athletics, and in 2010, he was inducted into the Indiana Sportswriters and Sportscasters Hall of Fame, an honor he truly cherishes.;

"Being a lifelong sports fan from a sports-minded family, I've been very fortunate," Jerry said. "I've seen hundreds – perhaps thousands – of games and many major events like the Kentucky Derby, Indy 500, World Series and ABA and NBA playoffs. And I've not only witnessed these events, but I was paid while doing so! Yes, I've been truly blessed."

While Jerry feels he was blessed, his fans were as well, and though his talent is undeniable, his career is also defined by the remarkable era in which he worked. For those of us who have enjoyed his passion and style, Jerry Birge will be remembered for his talent, but he will also be remembered as a man who did what he loved and loved what he did.

TIMING IS EVERYTHING

To emphasize the point that Jerry Birge couldn't have launched his career at a more opportune time, one need only consider two seasons that occurred during his early years as a broadcaster. His first year in Evansville was the 1961-'62 school year, when the Reitz Panthers, led by All-American Don Hansen, were undefeated and unscored upon as the mythical state football champs. After that, Bosse won the IHSAA State title in basketball followed by the North Husky baseball team, with Mickey Martin and Steve Schroer on the mound and Dave Schellhase behind the plate, being named mythical state champs in baseball.

Five years later, 1966-'67 the area saw a caliber of basketball talent the likes of which it hadn't seen and may never see again. The eventual State champion North Huskies did not win the City or the SIAC titles, with Harrison winning the conference and sharing the City with Reitz. Below are the *Courier*'s 1967 All-City team and the state rankings by the Associate Press in mid-February. Note that 5 of the top 7 are local teams, almost certainly the only time it has happened in Indiana history.

1967 Courier All-City Team
Curt John – Reitz – 6'3 jr. – F
Jim Hildebrandt – North – 6'4 sr. – F
Greg Nelson – Harrison – 6'5 sr. – C
Bob Ford – North – 6'5 jr. – C
Larry Weatherford – Bosse – 6'2 sr. – G
Vaughn Wedeking – Harrison – 6'0 sr. – G
Steve Holland – North – 6'0 sr. – G
Greg Fenner – Harrison – 6'3 sr. - F

1967 Associated Press Top Ten (Feb. 12)
1. Oakland City
2. Michigan City
3. Evansville Harrison
4. Evansville North
5. Cloverdale
6. Evansville Reitz
7. Evansville Bosse
8. Ft. Wayne South
9. Loogootee
10. Fountain Central

DID YOU KNOW?

When Jerry Birge's Jasper Wildcats defeated the Evansville Lincoln Lions in double overtime in 1957, the rules were different then. The first overtime was three minutes, but if the score was still tied, the winner in the second OT was the first team to score two points.

CLINT KEOWN:
VERSATILITY PERSONIFIED

It is very doubtful that anyone in local history bounced a basketball more times than Evansville's Clint Keown. From the time he could walk, he had a ball in his hand, and as he grew, it was obvious that his athletic skills stretched beyond the basketball court. In many ways, Keown was a coach's dream, respectful and coachable, but in other ways, he walked to the beat of a different drummer. His story is one of phenomenal successes and extraordinary feats, and his competitive approach to life has served him well in a profession that many people treat with disdain and in which very few can cut the mustard.

By all accounts, Clint had all the natural tools from the day he was born, and thanks to his obsession with athletics and self-imposed drive to excel, he experienced tremendous success even as a youngster. Much of his ability came from his father, Rick Keown. Rick rarely left the field when he played for Harrison football coach Mitch Marsch. Playing with fine athletes like quarterback Bob Meyer, Tony Suggs and Courtney Watt in the mid-'70s, Rick played running back and wide receiver while also handling the punting and kicking duties.

He also ran track and wrestled at Harrison, and it was on the wrestling mat that his dreams of playing ball in college were dashed. During his sophomore season, Rick had lost only one match thus far when disaster struck. Shortly before the sectional, a wrestler slipped and his body weight severely jammed Rick's shoulder out of its socket. After an 8 ½ - hour

surgery and eight months with his arm taped to his body, he still played football but admitted that he was never the same after the accident.

Julie Keown, Clint's mother, was a Memorial grad who became her son's biggest fan as Rick and others coached young Clint and his siblings. Clint's younger brother Cory played baseball, football and basketball for two years but found it hard to follow in Clint's footsteps, and the youngest, Katie Keown, was a four-year starter for soccer coach Joe Lattner and earned All-State honors twice.

When asked how early he could see Clint's potential, Rick Keown thought for a moment and then responded. "Probably at six," he said. "I was practicing basketball with him out back and I came in and told Julie that he was something special."

Rick credits Herb Hardy, the father of local legend football star Kevin Hardy, with much of Clint's early development. Hardy and Rick did a lot of the coaching when the boy played basketball and baseball in the late '80s and early '90s, and Clint and his teammates made some local news along the way. His baseball teams included such stars as Mike and Chris Mattingly and Marshall Raibley and Tim Long, who both eventually starred at Bosse. Clint's teams captured several state championships, and his pony league team won two games at the World Series.

In basketball, Clint's St. Ben's team won the eighth grade Catholic diocese tournament under coach Jeff Byrley, and his Biddy Ball team won the world championship, defeating Puerto Rico in the final in New Orleans after Clint stole the ball with eight seconds left and laid the ball in at the buzzer. That team, coached by Mike Hale, featured several outstanding players who became excellent high school players, including Matt Redd (Harrison), Patrick Kelly (Central), Jay Williams (Reitz), Tim Long (Bosse), Joey Kirkhoff (North) and Derek Grimm (Reitz), who was named America's 'Mr. Biddy'.

Rick Keown is well aware of his son's natural abilities, but he also credits the coaching his son received and Clint's tenacity for making Clint the athlete he became. Rick appreciated Herb Hardy and Mike Thomas, who coached Clint through AAU basketball. He also spoke highly of Mike Hale and Ron Barnett, a man who gave Clint a headstart at Lakeview Optimist. Ron ran the baseball program there and allowed Clint to join the league early as a six-year-old.

According to Rick, 'Clinton', as he often calls his son, got his first dose of reality during that first season, and after that, he always had a ball in his hand. After the first practice, Clint saw how skilled the older boys were and expressed some trepidation to his father. "If you want to be like them, you have to get out there and practice every day," Rick told him, and Clint took his father's advice to heart.

As Clint worked, he steadily improved, and according to Rick, after Clint's second season at LVO, the league had to change the rules. It seems young Clinton was making plays all over the infield and outfield, so the new rule stated that a player had to stay in his area to allow other boys to make plays.

Clint's work ethic was most evident in basketball. "If he was sent to his room, five minutes later you'd hear the ball bouncing off the wall," Julie Keown recalled.

MEMORIAL TIGERS

"When I would come home," Rick added, "Clint was either standing at the door or in the driveway waiting to show me another move he had practiced."

The Keowns lived directly across the street from the gymnasium at Memorial High School, and young Clint's frequent presence in the gym at all hours of the day and night was the source of some mystery around the school. Rick and Julie never worried about where their son might be because they knew they would find him in the gym. In fact, Rick recalled a particular evening that he still chuckles about today.

"It wasn't unusual for him to be in there at 8:00 at night, running and shooting," Rick revealed. "One night, I fell asleep and then woke up at about 3:00 a.m. I went to check on Clint and he wasn't in his room. I went to the gym and pounded on the wall. Clint walked over sweating with a ball under his arm." Clint had taken a break and laid down on the bleachers and fell asleep, and when he woke up, he decided to practice some more.

Several coaches have commented about seeing Clint in the gym and wondering how he was gaining access. Coaches and custodians alike caught him in the act, but apparently he wasn't causing trouble so they would just say "hi" and let him do his thing. The big mystery has always been – how was he getting in? After much speculation, I decided to go straight to the source, and the answer was very simple and extremely honest.

"I stole a gym key," Clint confessed while we had lunch at Rafferty's in Evansville. "They were in the door. On Sundays at Memorial, they would have their basketball league. They were the janitor's keys, like a hundred of them. I went home and hid them under my bed and waited like a week. I was scared. I made copies.

"Sometimes Mr. Wannemueller (who coached at Memorial) would see me in there, but he would never say anything. Friday and Saturday nights I'd go over around midnight. I'd turn on just one set of lights on one side of the court."

Clint didn't use the key often for fear of getting caught, but he had learned to keep a door ajar when he was younger by placing a piece of carpet in the door, and the long hours of practice resulted in quite a reputation. One of the most famous stories of the young phenom even made the newspapers. On a wintry afternoon in the late '80s, Rick Risemus was putting his Memorial team through its paces as the end of practice approached. Typically the team would end each workout with sprints, but on this day, the coach had a different plan. "He had this old ball that must've had 50,000 miles on it," Risemus told *Courier* reporter Michael Pointer. "I told the kids that we were going to run, but if the kid hits a free throw, we won't. The kid stepped up and stroked it."

When Clint entered Memorial in 1994, it didn't take long for him to make his presence known. In basketball, he became a starter with seven games remaining in the season, and he saw some time in the varsity outfield for Coach Quentin Merkel as well. Clint had tremendous respect for all his coaches, but has very high praise for Coach Merkel, an Indiana Baseball Hall of Famer.

"He was my favorite coach in any sport in any league," Clint informed me. "He's the real deal. He has so much passion for the game and his kids. He taught more than baseball; he taught you about life."

Coach Merkel had a great respect for Clint as well, recounting the remarkable senior season Keown had when he hit .506 and led the team to a city record of 11-1 during a 25-6 season. Clint torched the basepaths and center field, and according to Quentin Merkel "of his 41 hits, 10 to 15 were drag bunts. I don't care where he bunted it, he was a tough out."

Although he played football as a freshman, Clint sat out his sophomore year because his father worried about injury. He became a fixture in center field for Coach Merkel and began to dominate on the court, stealing the ball three times in one game from Harrison senior standout John Risinger while scoring 22 points in a 57-55 Memorial win.

In basketball, the 6'2 junior averaged over 27 points and hit 45% of his three-pointers while also starring in baseball and football. When he left Memorial in 1998, Keown had placed himself among the best all-around athletes in local history, earning All-City honors three times in basketball and baseball and twice in football.

On the gridiron, Clint had fantastic hands, and many, including Clint himself, believe it may have been his best sport. On the baseball field, Clint ran like a deer and was one of only five Memorial players to hit over .500 in a season (Don Mattingly being one of them).

Despite these accomplishments, it was on the basketball court where Clint made his greatest impact in this hoops-crazed state of Indiana. He was an Indiana All-Star with Mr. Basketball Tom Coverdale and was All-City, All-SIAC and All-State three years in a row. In addition, he was named a *Street & Smith* high school All-American and was

Young Clint was a star at whatever sport was in season.

rated the #1 senior in the state by *Hoop Scoop* Magazine. He also placed himself in some elite company historically. First, he joined Topcat Tyler (Central) and Damon Cobb (Memorial) as the only players to be named the *Courier*'s conference Player of the Year two years in a row, and he became the second-leading scorer in SIAC history with 1,766 points, 49 points behind North's Bob Ford and 19 points ahead of Bosse's Larry Weatherford.

To put those numbers in perspective, it is fair to say that if Keown's Memorial teams could have won just three more tournament games during his four years, he would have become the conference's all-time scoring leader. Another oddity is the fact that despite hitting over .500, he was not named All-State in baseball. Had

167

he been, he would have become one of the few players, and possibly the only player, in Indiana history to be named first team All-State in three sports.

With this amazing high school resumé, it should not be a surprise that Clint had several college options. Michigan sent someone to watch him catch passes on the football field, but most football schools lost interest when word got out that he was pursuing basketball offers. Just before getting run out of Bloomington, Bob Knight showed interest, and schools like Valparaiso, Butler and Central Florida were contacting him regularly, some seeking him for both basketball and baseball.

Clint's mind was practically made up when Mike Davis, who had taken over at IU, had promised that he would see Clint at the Wide World of Sports facility in Kissimme, Florida for an AAU tournament. But when Davis stood Clint up, IU lost out. When Rick and Julie returned from their long drive from Florida, they were shocked to see TV news trucks parked in front of their home. They soon discovered that Clint, who had flown home, was ready to make his announcement. Because Coach Crews had remained loyal and never wavered, Clint had chosen to play for the Evansville Aces.

At U of E, Clint was the team's sixth man as a freshman on a team that featured such players as Kwame James, Curt Begle, Craig Snow and conference Player of the Year Marcus Wilson. By his junior season, he was logging over 27 minutes a game and averaging nearly 10 points, but his comfort level just wasn't there anymore.

Having lost confidence in himself on the court, Clint transferred to the University of South Carolina-Aiken near Augusta, Georgia, where a high school friend, Sammy Garau, was playing baseball. While there, he used his final year of basketball eligibility to lead the nation in Division II scoring (26/game), once hitting ten 3-pointers in a conference game.

On the baseball field, Clint was just as impressive as he led the country in stolen bases, stealing 52 in 56 attempts. He was so good, in fact, that he caught the eye of major league scouts. At a scout day, the scouts were shocked when he ran a 6.4 60-yard dash and asked him to run again. Clint promptly repeated the feat and was subsequently picked up by the Reds organization and sent to the Class A Dayton Dragons.

As his minor league career progressed, he experienced the challenges that face a free agent in which the parent club has little invested. Although he loved the life, playing in front of 7,000 fans, he could see that it would take more than a .255 average to get to the Big Show.

During his minor league experience, Clint became fascinated with a segment of the lifestyle that would eventually lead to a highly unusual profession. With little else to keep them occupied while on the road, many of the players would play poker during their downtime, and as he had done with everything else in his life, he immersed himself fully in becoming the best. He discovered that he had a knack for the game, and with the poker boom in full force, he set his sights on a new world to conquer.

In the minds of many, poker was a game played in seedy back rooms by shady characters, but in 1998, a movie called *Rounders* sparked a movement the likes of which the gaming industry had never seen. The game (many call it a 'sport') had been televised semi-regularly since the '70s, but *Rounders* brought it to the forefront. Starring Matt Damon and Edward Norton, the movie showed the game's dark side but somehow regenerated the public's interest.

Poker received another boost when a 27-year-old accountant from Tennessee captured the World Series of Poker Main Event in 2003. Chris Moneymaker (his real name) played in a $39 satellite tournament and won, giving him an entry into yet another larger satellite and so on. His victories in satellites landed him a spot in the main event, where 838 players paid $10,000 to play poker's most popular game, Texas Hold 'em. One by one, players were eliminated until only Moneymaker and pro Samma Farha were left. Miraculously, Chris bested Farha in dramatic fashion to capture the $2.5 million first prize in front of a worldwide television audience.

The event resulted in what the industry calls the "Moneymaker Effect," and the following year, 2004, the WSOP Main Event saw the field triple with 2,576 players entered. Since that time, the field is consistently over 6,000 and the top prize is worth more than first place in the Masters, Wimbledon, the Daytona 500 and Indy 500 combined. Today, the WSOP is shown on a series of broadcasts on ESPN and names like Doyle 'Texas Dolly' Brunson, Johnny Chan, Phil 'Poker Brat' Helmuth and Mike 'The Mouth' Matusow are household names.

With the proliferation of the TV poker boom and internet poker sites, young men and women like Clint Keown began to look more seriously at poker as a profession, and Clint analyzed the game and planned his approach. Over the last few years, he has realized that he prefers to play in cash games rather than the big tournaments that get all the exposure. In a cash game, you can play for a set amount of time and then leave, whereas in a tournament, you can play for days and just miss the money and leave with nothing. Clint prefers the less dramatic life that exists outside the spotlight.

"It's a hard way to make an easy living," he stated. "I enjoy it because it's competition. I started with nothing. When I finished minor league ball, I had $2,800. I didn't have a job. I pay taxes. I do it the right way. I have health insurance and a Roth IRA. A lot of people just think, 'He's a gambler.' I'm not a gambler. It's all discipline.

"Poker is a game of skill. It's not like playing craps or blackjack or pulling a slot machine. In the long run, the best players are going to get the money. I enjoy the winning and losing. What people don't understand is that poker is a game of emotion. It takes a very disciplined person to be a professional poker player. You need money management. I look at it as one big long game. It's my job. It's a grind sitting there eight to ten hours a day and folding 80% to 90% of your hands."

Clint makes no excuses for the life he leads, and he has done very well in his chosen career. He admits that he currently enjoys the lifestyle, living out of a suitcase for six weeks at a time, and he also gets a kick out of another common practice in the poker culture.

During their off hours, many players engage in what they call prop (proposition) bets. These may include challenges such as losing so much weight before a deadline or other tasks, and Clint has found some unique ones of his own. The ones he is known most for are sports-related. For example, he has been known to bet that he can make 85 out of 100 free throws while sitting in a wheelchair or that he can beat someone in a footrace.

His most amazing challenge is to bet someone that he can hit 75 out of 100 3-pointers and that he will bank them all in within one hour while he gets his own rebounds. Amazingly, when I asked how many times he had lost that bet, his reply was "Never."

Keown realizes that some people would call this "hustling," but he doesn't agree. He takes pride in the fact that he doesn't pretend that he is less than he is to entice someone to bet. In fact, he says that he always tells them that he is a good shooter and has done it many times before. Apparently people are willing to risk good money just to see him do it.

Clint admits that his chosen profession wasn't terribly popular with his family, and his father confirmed that point. After flashing a smile at my question, Clint's father offered this answer: "I work hard and make a regular paycheck, and for someone to make more money in a day than I do in a month is hard to take. We back him, but it wouldn't have been our choice."

Clint is well aware of how some perceive him, but he has always been a little unconventional. He knows there might come a day when he may want to settle down and try something else. Regardless of what he chooses, the one part of his life that we as fans will remember is the time he spent as an athlete here in our midst.

A man who summed up Clint's talents beautifully was Dave Hayden, Keown's high school basketball coach. "Clint is the most gifted athlete I've had the privilege to coach," he wrote in an email. "On the basketball floor, Clint's talents blossomed over the years. As a sophomore, he averaged 20.8 points and was an instrumental leader in the 1996 sectional championship and regional finalist team.

"He was also an excellent passer and team player. For example, in one particular game during his senior year, we were winning quite handily and some of the down-the-line players were getting playing time. Clint wanted to stay in the game, not to score, but to get the ball to a teammate. Clint repeatedly passed up good shots and tried to get the ball to his teammates so they could feel the elation of scoring a basket in a high school game. Clint certainly has the cockiness that all gifted athletes possess, but this story of concern for a teammate's success shows another side of him."

There are many local fans who consider Keown the greatest all-around athlete in local history, and his stats and honors are strong support for the argument. From the kid who sneaked into the gym, to the young adult who earned a degree in Criminal Justice while leading the nation in scoring, to the man who makes his living in a world that most of us dare not enter, Keown has always done what it takes to succeed. By all accounts, Clint Keown was as blessed with talent as anyone our area has seen. He has been known to pick up a tennis racket and hold his own with highly skilled players, and one year after taking up golf, he was a scratch golfer. As a youngster, he played soccer for a year and led the league in scoring, and he can master with ease any game that requires eye-hand coordination.

There are many who have stated that Mr. Keown would make an excellent coach, and Clint has said that he believes he would enjoy working with young athletes. If this should come to pass, we can only hope that Clint can inspire others to devote themselves the way he did, and if only a few show the passion for competition that Clint had, his influence may spawn the next generation of athletes for local fans to enjoy.

ONLY IN CLINT'S WORLD

Clint Keown is known for his adventurous spirit, and that mentality paid big dividends for him in 2012. On a whim, he and some buddies went to Louisville to catch the U of L – UConn basketball game, and while there, Clint noticed a long line of fans and wondered what it was. When he asked, he was told that it was a Pop-a-Shot contest and that the person who scores the best at each home game is eligible for the finals at the end of the season. (Pop-a-Shot is the arcade game with a basket and balls surrounded by netting.)

Clint stood in line for 25 minutes to give it a try, and when all was said and done, he won with 24 baskets in 30 seconds. In the finals, the 31 winners competed in a game of knockout, a game where the person behind you in a single-file line can knock you out if you miss.

When Clint won the event, he had the option of $19,000 cash or a brand new 2012 Mitsubishi Outlander SUV. Clint's mother, Julie Keown, had never owned a new car, and Clint surprised her with the gift.

Many players looked up to Clint during his days at Memorial.

*Most of the photos seen with this story were taken from the
Scepter Review, the annual Rex Mundi yearbook.*

REX MUNDI HIGH SCHOOL: 13 YEARS OF EXCELLENCE

Rex Mundi
HS

"It was the best of times, it was the worst of times…" Although this famous opening line from *A Tale of Two Cities* by Charles Dickens may have referenced a far more dramatic era, it is somewhat pertinent to the brief 14-year history of a school that many from today's younger generation may not know even existed. The "worst" was the announcement of the school's closing in 1972, and the "best" were the glorious years when a few thousand students roamed the halls at 3501 First Avenue in Evansville.

Rex Mundi High School was built on a 15-acre parcel of land on the city's far north side (at the time) to accommodate a growing population created by the offspring of a generation known later as 'baby boomers'. With the '60s rapidly approaching, Evansville's two Catholic high schools, Memorial and Mater Dei, were already bursting at their seams, and the local diocese decided to take action.

It was estimated that by 1964, there would be 3,700 Catholic high school students in Evansville, and Memorial and Mater Dei were already housing nearly twice the students they were designed to hold. So a new school, nestled near the neighborhoods of Country Club Meadows and Country Club Manor, seemed to be the answer.

Rex Mundi, meaning "King of the World" in Latin, opened in 1958 with 280 students, 200 or so freshmen and the rest sophomores. Father Charles Meny was the superintendent who watched over the excited teenagers, and the Catholic school culture was quite structured when compared to a modern school environment. At the time, Memorial kept male and female students apart during the day, with the girls housed on the top floor. At the end of the day, the boys were dismissed first and instructed to "clear the grounds," and although the Rex Mundi students weren't separated to those extremes, most of the classes were gender separated.

From an athletic standpoint, the young 'Monarchs' were exposed only to football, basketball and baseball in the first year, with other sports added over time. In 1958-'59, Jerry Altstadt handled the coaching duties in all sports as the freshman and sophomores competed on the JV level. The following year, Rex Mundi played full varsity schedules.

Ray Trapp, who was in the first class to attend all four years at Rex Mundi, had signed up to attend Mater Dei but was told that his home on Wedeking Avenue near North High School was in Rex Mundi's district. Ray was a center on the 1959 football squad and was flanked by Frank Hertel and Bob Dezember at the guards, Bob Merrimee and Tom Baumgart at the tackle positions and Tom Akin and Ed Cheaney at the ends. The runners were fullback Ken Godsey and halfbacks Mike Minton and Walt Foley, and the team's starting quarterback was a freshman named Bob Griese. Other contributors on the defensive side were Ron Hess, twins Mike and Mac Blake, and Harold Ligget, who played at "5'8, 140 pounds, soaking wet," according to Trapp.

The Monarchs were 1-7 in their first varsity season in 1959, but under new coach Ed Labbe, the boys quickly became a force to be reckoned with. "We had a coach that was very demanding," Ray Trapp recalled. "When we'd get off the bus after losing, he would tell us what we did wrong and we would run around the track at 10:30 at night and then practice again Saturday morning."

Whether it was Coach Labbe's discipline or an abundance of talent, the turnaround of the program was amazing, and Griese, who went on to star at Purdue and then with the Miami Dolphins, had some rough games early. Because his grade school, Assumption, didn't have a team, he entered Rex Mundi with no organized football experience, but his learning curve was steep.

The following season, 1960, the Monarchs finished 8-2, and in '61, they were a perfect 9-0 before losing to a Memorial team led by Don Crane, Jim Buedel and the Mills brothers, Kenny and Ronnie, in the season finale at Enlow Field in front of 8,000 fans. The following year, Ken Coudret assumed the controls and guided Rex Mundi through another outstanding campaign. The team nearly ran the table if not for their first meeting with powerful Reitz, who had finished the season unbeaten and unscored on in 1961. Under senior QB Bob Griese, the 1962 Monarchs came close but lost 7-0 to a team that featured Steve Vessels and the speedy Fendrich twins Gary and Jerry.

One of the more memorable moments in Rex Mundi football history took place at a 'home' game at Bosse Field during Griese's final season. The play involved some deception on Coach Coudret's part and utilized the fact that speedy halfback Mike Minton had been injured the week before. Minton's leg was in a brace for the game and he was used sparingly. Late in the game, two subs ran onto the field while three, including Minton, headed for the sideline. The departing players were ignored by Tell City's defense, and as Minton approached the sideline, he stopped while still in the field of play. The ball was snapped, and as the play developed, Minton hobbled downfield all alone, thinking, "Oh gosh! Just don't drop the ball." He didn't, and according to Mike Minton, Tell City promptly dropped Rex Mundi from the schedule in all sports.

The early years at Rex Mundi were highly successful in several sports as the boys held their own in baseball and even made some statewide history on the basketball court. Under Coach Altstadt, Rex Mundi built a winning program that was competitive year in and year out, and the talented players of the early '60s set the standard for those to come later.

After a 7-8 season in 1959-'60, the program never had another losing record, and the crescendo began the following year. From 16-6 in '60-'61 through the seasons of '61-'62 (20-2) and '62-'63 (19-3), Rex Mundi was consistently among the area's best with players like Griese, Rick Kingston and big Tom Niemeier leading the way. In addition to being a superb baseball player and future NFL Hall of Famer, Griese was both smooth and rugged on the basketball floor, finishing as the school's third-leading scorer

Rex Mundi's first football team.

(1,041 points) and second-leading rebounder with 714. Kingston was a 6'1 shooter who went on to play at Evansville College, and the 6'9" Niemeier was the school's all-time leader in several categories and played at Purdue.

During the early '60s, Rex Mundi battled some of the most talented city-wide talent in Evansville's illustrious history, and Randy Mattingly has vivid memories of watching his brother Jerry play against some all-time greats. He remembers the '61-'62 season when the highly anticipated matchup against Bosse was moved to the Stadium on a Tuesday night to afford space for 10,000 fans. Bosse boasted a starting lineup of Gary Grieger and Jerry Southwood at guards with Ken Rakow, Gene Lockyear and John Wilson up front and eventually captured the 1962 State title. The game went down to the wire, and if not for another close loss to Bosse in the sectional, who knows what may have been for Rex Mundi's team in the '62 tournament?

North's lineup was dynamic as well, with future Purdue All-American Dave Schellhase, Ted Mattingly, Charlie Lawrence, Joe Mullan and Mickey Martin, among others. Randy watched many of the classic contests as a grade schooler and points out that the season ended in a three-way tie for the City title, a rare occurrence, after North beat Bosse, Bosse beat Rex Mundi and the Monarchs defeated North.

The '62-'63 team was excellent as well, with many of the same players leading a team that would average more points than any other in Rex Mundi history with 75.6 points per game. After the 19-3 season ended in 1963, some big voids were created when Niemeier and Griese left for West Lafayette, but with a nucleus

returning and a talented big man in the middle, the '63-'64 team were set to go where no Monarch team had gone before.

The newest version of the Monarchs had decent size and excellent team speed, and Coach Altstadt could see they were something special. Senior Jerry Mattingly was the heart and soul of the team as a 6'2 guard. His backcourt mate was the small but quick Al Heard, and the typical starting front line was Earl Schneider (6'4), Mike Owens (6'5) and Nick Adams (6'3).

"We had an outstanding fast break team" Coach Altstadt told me from his home in Huntingburg. "We got into transition quickly." The run-and-gun style made the team tough to deal with for opponents, and several players were utilized for the fast-paced style. Greg Hofmann was first off the bench on the front line, and Bruce Goodwin, Bill Schneider and Mike Minton logged valuable minutes as well.

The Monarchs finished the regular season 26-2 and then began the tournament in the large Evansville Sectional. They barely survived the opener with Mattingly out with the flu and Mt. Vernon in slow-down mode. After a 27-25 win, they made easy work of Reitz (75-59), North (68-56) and Memorial (87-53) to deliver the school's first sectional title. They then topped Tell City (69-66) and Princeton (85-61) to take the Evansville Regional.

The fans and students were ecstatic as they dreamed of winning the State tournament, and the atmosphere reached a fever pitch when the boys won the semi-state with surprisingly easy wins over Martinsville (78-53) and Seymour (76-53). Though the party ended in the afternoon game of the finals with a loss to the eventual champion Lafayette Jeff Broncos, the team provided plenty of thrills for the Rex Mundi faithful.

"The school was a utopia," Jerry Altstadt said on the *Local Legends* radio show. "Those guys made me a very good coach." The '63-'64 team put the school's basketball program on the map and made statewide history by becoming the first Catholic school to make it to the Final Four. Though the season ended with a loss, it was only fitting that a final thrill of the '64 tournament sent

DID YOU KNOW?

Rex Mundi's official school colors were royal gold and white, but when they realized that numbers were difficult to read with that combination, the familiar black was added as an 'unofficial' color.

171

Coaches Coudret (left), Altstadt (middle) and Will (right) spent many years at Rex Mundi coaching football, basketball and baseball, respectively.

the season out with a bang. With the game out of reach and only a few seconds remaining, sub Mike 'Titanic' Thompson took an inbounds pass and hurled the ball through the net from 65 feet to put a bow on a spectacular season.

From 1965 through 1968, the basketball program had some moderate success with a four-year record of 51-35, and during the same period, the football and baseball programs provided some highlights for Rex Mundi fans. On the gridiron, the Monarchs defeated Reitz for the first time as Coach Coudret reached into his bag of tricks once again. The play worked perfectly as Tim Minton fielded a kickoff and headed downfield to his right. With the Panthers converging on him, Minton stopped suddenly and fired a pass all the way across the field and slightly backward to Mike Nally who streaked down the deserted left side for the TD.

Nally and Minton were also mainstays on the 1967 baseball team that won the very first IHSAA sectional, and the following year, five Monarchs were selected for the *Courier*'s All-City baseball team: Nally, Minton (pitcher), Randy Mattingly (2B), Tom Gardner (1B) and honorary captain Doug Bell (RF) with Rex Mundi's Frank Will named Manager of the Year. Rounding out the powerful lineup were Randy Miller (SS), Dave Ford (C), Lee Ashby (LF), Spike Bell (CF) with Larry Woehler also on the mound.

The basketball program made a comeback during the '68-'69 season when a fully matured group of seniors produced one of the finest campaigns in school history. Led by five senior starters, Randy Mattingly, Bob Boyd, Doug Bell, Larry 'Bunny' Ross and Michael Young, the team finished the regular season 22-4 under coach Don Sheridan, and then the boys made a nice tourney run themselves. In the sectional, Rex Mundi defeated North, Bosse and a very good Reitz team that featured Keith Huff, Tim Fletcher and Charlie Farmer. They followed that with regional wins over Tell City and Chrisney and a semi-state win over Bedford before losing to a Vincennes team led by Jerry Memering, Tom Turner and Mac McCormick.

Though the '68-'69 team fell a game short of making the Final Four, evidence of its athletic talent showed when the five starters all received college scholarships: Doug Bell (Ball State – football); Bob Boyd (Ball State – basketball); Mike Young (ISUE

– basketball); Larry Ross (Central Missouri State – basketball); and Randy Mattingly (Florida State/U of E – football).

In 1970, more history was made when the school's football team made a run that was every bit as impressive as the '64 basketball team's run to the Final Four. With 18 lettermen returning from the previous year, expectations were very high, and Coach Coudret's boys lived up to the hype. The team had all the ingredients, with good size, phenomenal speed and talent on both sides of the ball. The O-line featured Bill Lampkins at center with guards Ron Miller and Mark Werner, tackles Wilbur Hackner and Joe Debes, and ends Ron Kane and Charlie Eckert. Starters in the backfield were halfbacks Bob Barnett and Don Jochem with Tim Werner at fullback and Thom Endress at quarterback.

The team started with lackluster wins over North (23-14), Bosse (17-7) and Jasper (21-14) and then found their stride as they steamrolled the competition for the next five weeks, beating Mater Dei, Reitz, Mt. Vernon, Boonville and Central by a combined score of 225-13. Reitz scored the 13 points, but the 41 points Rex Mundi tallied against the Panthers was the first time Reitz had 40 scored against them since Memorial beat them 45-7 in 1943. Remarkably, Rex Mundi racked up 40 without starting QB Endress for much of the game, as backup Chuck Schimmell filled in capably when Thom was injured with the Monarchs leading 19-7.

In the ninth week, Rex Mundi won 29-14 over a Harrison team led by linebacker Scott Studwell and scatback Fred Heseman. To finish the season, Rex Mundi faced a tough Memorial team on a cold, miserable night at Enlow Field, and Thom Endress gives credit where it was due for the 6-0 win. "We played Memorial in a mudfest," Endress said. "You couldn't throw the ball. I attribute that win to our offensive and defensive lines."

When the Monarchs took the field in 1970, it was safe to say that expectations were high, and Coach Coudret's boys validated that confidence with their performance. "It was a great time," recalled Thom Endress on the *Local Legends* radio show. "We followed some great teams. There was a benchmark that was set for high caliber football. It was an exciting time; we had a lot of talent."

As evidence of that talent, the senior-laden team had several who went on to play college ball, perhaps more than any team in local history. Tackles Wilbur Hackner and Joe Debes were both big and talented. Debes took his skills to the Air Force Academy, while Hackner passed on Notre Dame to play at the University of Evansville. Ends Charlie Eckert and Ron Kane played for Syracuse and Murray State, respectively, and the entire backfield, Endress, Werner, Jochem and Barnett all played at U of E.

When the 1970 football season was over, no one knew that the school would close a year and a half later, and although the 1971 team wasn't as successful, the '70 team had done its part to keep

This 1964 Rex Mundi team became the first from a Catholic school to make it to Indiana's Final Four. Front row (L-R): Earl Schneider, Mike Thompson, Mike Minton, Al Heard, Jerry Mattingly, Nick Adams. Back row: Bruce Goodwin, Bill Schneider, Tom Halbig, Mike Owens, Greg Hofmann, Tom Lampkins, Steve Reinhart, John Reinitz.

Tom Niemeier

Mike Owens

Randy Mattingly (left)   Earl Schneider

THE REX MUNDI ERA

The following is a list of the winners of the Evansville basketball sectional during the Rex Mundi era.

1959 – Bosse
1960 – Lincoln
1961 – Bosse
1962 – Bosse
1963 – Bosse
1964 – **Rex Mundi**
1965 – Central
1966 – Memorial
1967 – North
1968 – Reitz
1969 – **Rex Mundi**
1970 – Memorial
1971 – Reitz
1972 – Reitz

Jerry Mattingly

173

Mike Nally

This baseball team from 1967 won the very first IHSAA sectional. Front row (L-R): Shane Gerth (mgr.), Tim Minton, Lee Ashby, Jack Burgdorf, Eddie Singleton, Mike Nally. Second row: Larry Woehler, Cecil Poag, Doug Bell, Grady Winstead, Kent Todisco. Back Row: Frank Will (coach), Randy Mattingly, Spike Bell, Dave Ford, Randy Miller, Tom Gardner, Marty Smith (mgr.)

the Rex Mundi football legacy alive. From a program that compiled a record of 71-49-3 in 13 varsity seasons and featured two future pro quarterbacks (Bob Griese and Randy Mattingly), only the Monarchs of 1970 reached perfection with their 10-0 record.

The 1970 football squad is just one example of the success experienced at Rex Mundi, and the highlights created during the school's 14-year lifetime can be attributed to several excellent coaches and myriad fine athletes that wore the white, gold and black. Among those were several sets of brothers, like Jerry and Randy Mattingly. Jerry graduated and had a wonderful career at Evansville College (U of E), and Randy followed in his footsteps at U of E then played in the NFL and CFL.

Three Endress boys, Steve, John and Thom, played at Rex Mundi, as did four Millers, Randy, Rick, Ron and Rusty. Doug and Spike Bell were great all-around athletes, with Doug later becoming a Kodak All-American center at Ball State. Other talented brothers included the Mintons, Mike and Tim, and Mike and Pat Casalena.

Two Monarch basketball stars, Tom Niemeier and Earl Schneider, became Indiana All-Stars, and three huge linemen, Bob Merrimee, Dave Ford and Jim Wilson, were some of the best the city has seen. Mike McManaway could have dominated on the track during most eras but had the misfortune of being a contemporary of Harrison's ultra-talented Don Sellers. Other excellent runners at Rex Mundi included sprinters Bobbie Barnett, Kevin Hines and Vic Delacoma and hurdler Ron Shirk, and many others were fine multi-sport athletes, like Larry Lennon, Greg Hofmann, Cornell LaGrone, Dale Prevo, Ken Smith, Rick Kingston and Dan Dilegge, to name a few.

When the Catholic school enrollment fell from 2,530 to 1,900 between 1967 and 1971, the local diocese had some serious decisions to make. After a 12-4 vote, the Diocese Council chose Rex Mundi over Mater Dei as the sacrificial lamb, and the school's illustrious history was over. With the closing came hundreds of broken hearts, but whenever possible, the alumni gather to re-live the glory days.

Mike Minton chuckles as he recalls his days at Rex Mundi and speaks of his appreciation for the teachers, fans and atmosphere, including the dances when chaperones would swat a young man with a ruler if he got too close to his girlfriend.

Coach Altstadt spoke of another moment that players may recall. It seems that the basketball team had a dress code for away games, and on a specific evening, a couple of "star players" (he wouldn't reveal names) decided to test the system. When they arrived in their sport coat but without a tie, Altstadt instructed the bus driver to stop by his house. After returning to the bus, he presented his stars with the two ugliest ties he could find and made the boys wear them. Problem solved.

Memories like these are plentiful, and Rex Mundi grads are fortunate to have had great experiences in the classroom and in the athletic arena. For a school with such a short existence, the amount of success is impressive indeed. Although the details may fade slightly as the years pass, the loyalty of Rex Mundi's alumni is unquestioned. In only 14 years, the school's athletic program produced a Final Four basketball team, an undefeated football team and a sports history that could stand with any school in town.

AND BY THE WAY...

Ron Glass (center), best known for playing Detective Ron Harrison on TV's *Barney Miller*, attended Rex Mundi before transferring to North.

The undefeated Rex Mundi team of 1970. Front row (L-R): Charlie Eckert, Joe Debes, Mark Werner, Bill Lampkins, Ron Miller, Wilbur Hackner, Ron Kane. Second row: Frank Will (asst. coach), Bob Barnett, Thom Endress, Mike McManaway, Chuck Schimmell, Mark Todisco, Don Jochem, Ken Coudret (head coach). Third row: Tom Stofleth, Dale Prevo, Gary Bauer, Kim Byers, Ken Smith, Scott Ferderber, Shane Gerth (mgr). Fourth row: Tim Werner, John Endress, John Fiester, Kevin Hines.

Mike Minton

Bob Merrimee

Bob Griese

Vic Delacoma

Ray Trapp

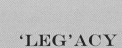

'LEG'ACY

For six straight seasons, the U of E football team's punter was a Rex Mundi alum: Greg Hofmann ('67, '68), Spike Bell ('69, '70) and Randy Mattingly ('71, '72).

Thom Endress

175

Varsity cheerleaders (L-R): Sandy Bender, Nicki Frey, Donna Holtz, Bev McManaway and Sandy McBride all agree it's worth it.

CHAPTER SIX

ALISA RAYMOND:
POWER PERSONIFIED

The fact that Castle's Alisa Raymond became the best thrower in local track and field history is quite understandable when one discovers her mental makeup and pedigree. The genetic influence came from her father, and her mental approach came from working with dad and developing a relationship with a kindred spirit who lived hundreds of miles away.

Alisa's father, Cecil Raymond, was a fine athlete himself, starring on Central's baseball team and as a 5'10", 170-pound lineman on the Bears' football squad. On the gridiron, he teamed with Ron Voight, a lineman who played at Vanderbilt, as well as quarterback Errol Yeager and fullback Jim Greer, one of the greatest runners in local history. As a team, Central tied for the 1959 City title with a strong Memorial team that featured quarterback Kim Devault and teammates John Titzer, Jack Boehme and Quentin Merkel.

Cecil was recruited as a catcher in baseball by Indiana State and SIU but pumped himself up to 215 pounds and chose to attend Evansville College to play football under head coach Paul Beck. Joining many football alumni from the Aces program, Cecil went into coaching. In 1964, he was the line coach at Evansville College, and in 1965, at age 22, he became Huntingburg's head coach in football and baseball and an assistant in basketball, all for $1,350 a year. After two years, he moved to Paoli to coach the Rams and met his wife, Patrice, while there. During Cecil's three-year term in Paoli, his teams finished 23-7 and he had the opportunity to coach Phil DeLong, who played in the North-South All-Star game and earned a full ride to Indiana State as a 275-pound tackle.

From Paoli, Cecil moved to Washington, Indiana in 1970 and took over a program that had won ten games in the previous ten years. The program was in such disarray that Cecil described the situation like this: "It was the worst football team in the history of football. I would literally come home nauseated." In fact, the year prior, Raymond's Paoli Rams had blistered the Hatchets 70-0.

Cecil and his staff went to work in 1970 and finished their first season 1-9. But after working hard to get the athletes out for football, Cecil and his family left after five years with a winning record.

In 1975, Cecil accepted a job at Castle as an assistant principal, and that is when he began to develop his daughters as athletes. Alisa (pronounced uh•LEE•suh) was a good athlete as a youngster who could clobber a softball when she played in the youth league with local star Becky Lis. She also swam for the Newburgh Sea Creatures.

As a sixth grader, the elementary schools didn't have girls basketball, so Alisa played on the boys team and then joined the girls teams in junior high, where she also took up the shot put and discus. As high school approached, Alisa said good-bye to softball and basketball but continued to swim, earning a letter each year as a self-described team contributor in the 200 IM. With the strength she had developed, she was told by fans that they could hear her legs churning in the pool from out in the gym. She also began to take her throwing events in track very seriously as a freshman.

When asked how early he could see his daughter's potential, Cecil could recall precisely. "In the 7th grade," he responded. "Our oldest daughter, Allison, swam at SIU, and the best shot putter in the world was at SIU. So I called over there and told them that I had a young daughter that I thought was going to be an outstanding thrower."

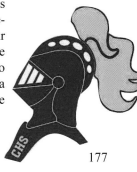

Cecil had worked with Alisa in the backyard, and she was throwing what high schoolers were throwing (mid 30s), so the decision was made to seek some first-class coaching. Connie Price-Smith lived in Hobart with her husband John Smith, the throws coach at Ohio State, and they welcomed the Raymonds with open arms. Connie was a four-time Olympian and 25-time national champion in the shot put, and she and John had a small gym at their home with throwing nets so that they could hold workouts year-round.

The Smiths grew fond of Alisa and Cecil and let them stay at their home when they came up. Connie, at 6'4 and 215, had actually come to SIU on a basketball scholarship and didn't throw the shot until her senior year, when she qualified for nationals.

With the Smith's help, Alisa flourished. "In high school, we really turned it on," Alisa explained from her home in Newburgh. "We worked out year-round. The weight room was a good environment, with football players and other guys."

With the boys pushing her, Ms. Raymond pushed herself to the limits, and the results soon followed. Thanks to her work on the snatch lift, her quickness across the circle improved, and as she grew to be able to bench press 315-pounds, her power increased. She revealed her height at 5'8, but would not disclose her weight in high school, absolutely a young lady's prerogative.

As a high school thrower, Alisa had little competition locally, and her goals were set early. "Dad had my workouts written out and tailored to peek for the State meet," Alisa told me. "If the girls (State) meet was on Friday, it was at night, so we practiced at night under the lights. We also intentionally practiced in the rain because I wanted to be prepared for any environment."

The techniques used by Cecil to train his daughter certainly paid off, as she won the sectional her freshman year and then began to dominate. For the next three seasons, Alisa captured the State shot put titles with tosses of 44-1, 46-5 and 44-10, respectively. She also won the championship in the discus her junior year (1993), as well, with a toss of 138-1.

In the '93 discus competition, her meet was almost over before it began when her first two throws during prelims were way out of bounds. At that point, Connie Price-Smith came out of the stands and approached the tearful thrower. "She gave me an earful," Alisa recalled. "She said, 'You are better than this. Get your butt in gear.'" Alisa then let loose with a huge throw and no one topped it, giving her the title.

As her high school career ended, Alisa was courted by nearly every college coach in America. According to Cecil, the North Carolina coach told him "Our two top recruits in America are your daughter and Marion Jones." Alisa had won the Tennessee Classic beating athletes from thirty states, so the University of Tennessee pursued her heavily. She also fielded offers from Texas, UCLA, Florida and Kansas. As a 3.6 student, she was very interested in Vanderbilt, but when push came to shove, she wanted to stay close to home.

Alisa opted for Purdue and had a fine career in West Lafayette, breaking the throwing records and earning All-Big Ten honors. At one time, she was ranked in the top 50 in the world, and she won a silver medal in the 1995 Pan American Games in Santiago, Chile.

With her desire to excel, Alisa became one of the strongest females in the world. At one point in her career, she could bench 315, power clean 250 (from knees to chest) and squat 500 pounds. Her goal was to compete in the 2000 Olympics, but four knee surgeries cut her dream short.

Alisa and Dad in a quiet moment.

As Alisa looks back, she is proud of what she accomplished. She was a 7-time National AAU Junior Olympic champion, a national record holder in the shot put, a State record holder, and a high school track and field All-American. As she reflected on what she had done, one fact was certain: she owed a great deal of her success to her dad.

"I consider my dad my best friend," she said through tears. "There were a lot of days I didn't like him because I didn't want to practice. But he stuck with me. When I need somebody to talk to, it is still my dad. That was one of the reasons I kept my last name (Alisa Raymond Knapp). I was proud to be a Raymond, and my first daughter is his namesake, Cecilia."

Today (2012), Alisa and her husband Randy (an ex-Mater Dei wrestler and soccer player) are raising two daughters, Cecilia and Callie, both of whom are showing great promise as athletes. As the young ladies grow, perhaps Mom will share her story with them someday, because they deserve to know what Mom accomplished. As a local athlete, Alisa Raymond has distinguished herself. Her four individual State titles place her in the company of other local legends like Bryce Brown (5 in the hurdles), Lanae Renschler (4 in tennis) and Blake Maurer (4 in wrestling) to make her one of our area's truly elite athletes.

JOHN SCHMITT: STAR GAZER

John in his Air Force dress blues.

In a sport that receives little attention locally and has only one facility available for the entire city of Evansville, only a handful of athletes have persevered to win a State title. The sport is swimming, and one of that handful is John Schmitt of Reitz, who not only accomplished a feat that hasn't been equaled before or since but did so in a very unique way.

John's parents weren't particularly athletic, Steve, a Castle grad, and Mary (Anslinger), who attended Rex Mundi until it closed in 1972 and then finished at Mater Dei, but their children did show some talent. Bryan Schmitt graduated from Mater Dei in 1998 and won the 400-meter run at the SIAC track meet, and sister Jamie played several sports at Mater Dei, including track, volleyball and soccer.

John came along six years after Jamie, and though he tried the 'ball sports' like most young boys, he quickly discovered his calling in the pool. "It was just obvious," said Mary Schmitt about her son's natural talent. "From the minute he got in the pool (at age six), he could just swim."

John's first competitive swimming was done at the Evansville Country Club where his team competed against other clubs. His first coach was Frances Enzler, who now coaches swimming at Memorial with her husband Dave. At age eleven, John's swimming became more competitive as he joined the Evansville Pepsi team, a very small group that competed together as a team. While there, the first true signs of his potential began to show as a coach proclaimed, "next year, he's going to be the 12-year-old

state champion." The words proved prophetic, as John not only won once but finished first in the 100 free, 200 free and 500 free with two seconds in backstroke events at the Natatorium in Indianapolis.

At age 13, John joined the Newburgh Sea Creatures to get more competition at practices and to learn from coach Andy Haas and, later, Donnie Brush. John continued to improve and again earned state championships in the 100 and 200 frees as a 14-year-old.

Although he was serious about his swimming, John wanted a more diverse life, and as high school approached, he was excited about the prospects. First of all, he decided to attend Reitz instead of Mater Dei like his older siblings because he wanted a larger school environment. He also chose a path that very few top-notch swimmers opt for – to become a multi-sport athlete, and part of his motivation came from reading the daily newspaper. "Reitz had a great track program" Schmitt said. "Coach (James) Brinkmyer had taken the team to State and almost won one year. I saw all the stories in the *Courier* about track and thought that was neat."

John was also mature enough to understand that the high school experience only happens once. "I'd been swimming USS (United States Swimming, similar to AAU in basketball) since I was eleven," John confided. "As a kid, that can burn you out. I didn't get to spend a lot of time with friends at school or in the neighborhood. When I was an eighth grader, I was ready for a break, with a whole new chapter of my life beginning. I had competed in cross country and track in the eighth grade, and I loved them."

So John spent the fall season running cross country, the winter in the pool and the spring on the track. Even with the trimmed down swimming regimen, he still had moderate success by making the consolation finals and finishing 12th in the 200 freestyle at State. The next year was much the same with the three sports, but at the State swim meet, the young sophomore had an 'aha moment'. After finishing fifth in both the 100 and 200 at State, Schmitt's desire to excel prompted action. "I saw that I was getting close, in the top five," John explained, "and I said, 'Let's go for it!'"

DID YOU KNOW?

Keanu Stevenson's winning time of 54.92 in the 100 breaststroke in 2011 was the fastest time ever swum in the 100 breast final. The record, however, is held by Tyler Lemert of Ft. Wayne Concordia who swam 54.82 in a prelim, making Lemert and Castle High School's Stevenson the only two swimmers to ever complete the event in under 55 seconds.

From that moment on, John's mindset changed and he re-dedicated himself to the sport. He immediately joined the YMCA and set up a schedule for workouts with Reitz coach Amy Peckinpaugh. Thanks to the dedication of Coach Peckinpaugh, Schmitt worked out downtown three or four days a week with a new purpose, and he admits that it wasn't an easy process. "I realized that I had to get in more practice, going back to my USS roots when I practiced twice a day," John said. "I remember setting my alarm at 4:30 and eating lots of Pop Tarts (breakfast of champions) in the truck on the way there."

John knew that more effort was needed to compete with the elite swimmers who focus solely on swimming, and the intensity of his training increased when he met Taz Greiner, who ran a new entity called Evansville Greater Aquatics, a small group of USS swimmers. "He made a definite impact on my swimming career," Schmitt revealed. "He revolutionized my training and my mentality and got me motivated."

With his team of Amy, Taz and Reitz assistant Dave Baumeyer (now Reitz's head coach), John worked tirelessly to reach his goal of becoming #1. For the first time since he entered Reitz, he swam during cross country season, and the cross-training made for some very long days. For two years, John worked out at the YMCA, then went to school, then ran several miles at cross country practice before driving from USI to the Lloyd Pool on the north side to swim some more. In addition, he would lift weights twice a week to build his strength. During swimming season, the routine continued with five miles of swimming in place of the cross country workouts.

With the system in place, Schmitt kept improving, and as a junior, he was oh, so close, finishing second in the 200 free and third in the 100. Following the State meet in 2004, John went back to work, and the long grueling hours finally paid off for the 5'11, 165-pound senior. In February of 2005, John bent over not once, but twice to have the gold medal placed around his neck. In the 200 free, he beat Drew Sease and Peter Jameson, two juniors from North Central, with a clocking of 1:39.25, and in the 100, he clocked at 45.76 just ahead of Jameson and Castle's Ryan Decker.

In addition to his two State titles, Schmitt also had some success on the track in the spring, clocking a 50-flat leg on a 4x400 relay team that included Randy Baize, Michael Weber and Darius Thomas and finished 9th at State. John also received the Outstanding Senior Male Athlete award at Reitz, an honor that typically goes to an athlete in one of the more mainstream sports.

John admits that the thought of swimming in college never really appealed to him, but the second he stepped off the award stand at State, he became a hot prospect. As a youngster, his thought of college did not include sports. Instead, he looked at college as a way to fulfill a dream he had nurtured since childhood. "I consider myself a Trekkie," John said with a little embarrassment in his voice. "I was a nerd about *Star Trek*, and I was fascinated by the space race and the exploration on the moon."

John was alluding to his dream of joining the Air Force and becoming an astronaut, and when college swimming coaches came calling, his ambition was part of the equation. "John wanted to be in the Air Force, so we looked at the ROTC (Reserve Officer Training Corps) at the schools," Mary Schmitt explained. "IU's coach was after him hot and heavy as soon as he won his two State medals." Though John and his parents visited Bloomington as a courtesy, they all knew the likely conclusion to the process.

"From the time he was a kid, Purdue just intrigued him," Mary said. "Ironically, Purdue wasn't after him at all, but once we visited Purdue, that was it. He fell in love with it."

The first step was getting the blessing of both the swimming coach and ROTC commander to allow him to pursue both. He was told that the schedule was possible but that it would take an incredible work ethic. As the past had shown, that was not an issue, and Schmitt began the taxing regimen of a full class schedule, 20 to 30 hours a week in the pool or weight room and 10 to 12 hours a week at ROTC events.

As he had always done, John thrived under the pressure and continued his success. As a four-year letter winner in swimming, he was a solid competitor for the Boilermakers, finishing third in the 100 free and fifth in the 200 at the Big Ten meet and barely missing the qualifying standard for the NCAAs. In '08, he even participated in the Olympic Trials in Omaha for the Beijing Olympics. As he had discovered in high school, the Olympic Trials were tough for a guy whose time wasn't totally devoted to the sport, and he was proud of his finish in the middle of the pack of 100 swimmers.

John has now begun a new challenge, and swimming helped him get there. As an athlete from southwestern Indiana, the odds were stacked against him, and it is only natural to wonder 'what if'. "I always wonder how much better he might have been had he been a Carmel swimmer," Mary Schmitt confessed, "with all the great facilities they have. Or I wonder what might have been if he had chosen to stay in USS (year-round) instead of swimming for Reitz."

Mary's thoughts are valid, but she is well aware of what her son has accomplished. Today, he is an active duty second lieutenant in the United States Air Force in Pensacola, Florida, and is still pursuing his dream using the same drive and ambition as he did at Reitz. "If I wasn't goal-oriented, I wouldn't be where I am now," John told me, "as a pilot in the Air Force and keeping that astronaut dream alive."

What John was able to accomplish under less than perfect circumstances as a high school swimmer set him apart from virtually all others in his sport. In 2005, he joined a very short list of local State champs in boys swimming: Castle's Bryce Hunt (2000, 100 backstroke); Mt. Vernon's 1998 200 free relay of Jonathan Wainman, David Franklin, Ryan McNally and Thomas Rueger; and since John, Castle's Keanu Stevenson (2011, 100 breaststroke). Schmitt did that while competing in two other sports during his entire high school career, something very few, if any, swimmers have ever done.

John Schmitt may not be one of Indiana's greatest swimmers, but because of his ability to focus and pursue well-defined goals, he distinguished himself locally by becoming the only area swimmer in history to capture two State titles. Only time will tell if John's ultimate dream will come true, but there is no doubt that he will do what is necessary as he continues his quest and reaches for the stars.

MARY COX:
A TRUE BOONVILLE PIONEER

While local legend Ginger Lutterman was building her volleyball dynasty at Castle, Mary Cox was creating a reasonable facsimile a few miles up the road in Boonville. Also like Ginger, Mary was a frustrated athlete with no place to develop her skills at Boonville High School. As a student at Indiana State, Mary played field hockey and competed on the badminton team, proclaiming "That was an experience!! It wasn't your backyard badminton."

After earning her BS degree in 1975 and her MS in '77, Ms. Cox filled in for teachers on maternity leave at Castle and then Boonville Junior High. She then accepted a position at BHS and headed up the track program and assisted Marlene Day in Volleyball. Four years later, Mary took Marlene's place and began her reign over the fledgling volleyball program.

As was the case with virtually every new coach in the early years of Title IX, Mary grabbed on to any morsel of knowledge she could find. "We went to a lot of clinics," she said from her home in Boonville. "I think what lit it up for all of us was when we went to Southern Illinois to watch the Olympic team."

Mary continued by describing the camaraderie with other young coaches, even divulging the potentially dangerous trip when she, Pat Zehr (Jasper) and Fred Bracher (an assistant at Castle) drove on black ice on the way to Indianapolis and ended up laughing as they slid onto a median.

"You learn from the people around you," Mary recalled. "I learned a ton from Ginger (Lutterman at Castle), Darla Edwards (Mater Dei), Annie Gunselman (Heritage Hills) and Pat Zehr. In the off-season while we drove to different meetings, we would compare notes."

Using all her resources, Mary became a quick study, and as her program blossomed, it became one of the elite in the area and across the state. For much of her career, Mary's Boonville girls shared dominance with perennial local powers Castle, Jasper and Mater Dei.

When asked to select her best players, the soft-spoken ex-coach perks up but admits that naming only a few is difficult. She does recognize Brittney Whitten, who went on to play at Ball State, and Julie Breivogel, who played at Jacksonville State. Mary also singled out Robyn Gebhard, currently (2012) in medical school, and Mindi Wilson, who Mary said "would run through a wall for you," in a *Courier* article. But without a doubt, the players that put the Lady Pioneer program on the map were the Winsett sisters, Becky, Beth, Barb, and Billie.

Through the '80s, the Winsetts elevated Boonville to the pinnacle of local volleyball and pushed the mighty Castle Knights to secondary status temporarily during what Castle coach Ginger Lutterman called "the dreaded Winsett years."

When Coach Cox retired after the 2010 season, the Boonville program lost a lady with legendary credentials, and her numbers speak for themselves. During her 29 seasons, she compiled a record of 714-253 (74%) while winning 12 Big Eight titles. In the State tournament, Mary's Lady Pioneers captured 17 sectionals, 8 regionals and progressed to five State Finals ('84, '89, '04, '05 & '08). In addition, the Boonville program leads all other area schools with two State runner-up finishes ('04 & '05), with only Jasper joining them with their lone second place finish in 1991.

But Mary's greatest pride lies in the girls she's coached and the kind of program she ran for nearly thirty years. Many of her girls have advanced to the next level, and Mary feels that her philosophy may have played a role. On the topic of athlete specialization, Coach Cox isn't a fan of the current trend. "I try to encourage the kids to do as much as they can," she explained. "However, it is evolving now where most of it is year-round. The kids feel pressured. I've had college coaches tell me that they would rather have a well-rounded athlete that they could train than one who has only played one sport."

The Lady Pioneers also had some fun during their tenure there, and Mary encouraged lighter moments by hosting an annual pig roast on her parents' farm. The events became so popular, apparently, that boys would seek out volleyball players as girlfriends to secure a seat at the table on Sunday afternoons.

As Mary sat in her living room trying to capsulize 29 years into a few minutes, she seemed content to leave her legacy behind. She has left the sport with the respect of her players and opposing coaches alike, as reflected in the words of Ginger Lutterman, Mary's archrival for many years: "We have been friends; we have been competitors; we have been supporters for the sport of volleyball and girls athletics in Warrick County," said Lutterman. "And I've enjoyed the competition (laughing) – most of the time. I respect her

This 2005 team was the last to finish the season as the state's runner-up.

as a person and as a coach. Her dedication to the sport has been tremendous."

As for her retirement, Mary says simply, "I just felt it was time for a change, a good time to go. I had a great run." Mary relishes the opportunity she had to touch the lives of her girls and to watch them become doctors or become successful in business or as mothers, and she humbly states, "Just this little bit that I've been able to be a part of is pretty neat."

She says that she will miss the fun, and it is certain that the Boonville program will miss her leadership. For 29 years, Mary Cox plied her craft in a very important era of women's athletics. Because of this dedication to her sport, she was honored in 2011 when she joined Ginger Lutterman and Pat Zehr as an inductee into the Indiana Coaches of Girls Sports Association Volleyball Hall of Fame.

Mary's teams knew how to have fun.

VOLLEYBALL STATE FINALS APPEARANCES BY AREA SCHOOLS

6 – Boonville ('80, '84, '89, '04, '05, '08)
5 – Castle ('74, '75, '76, '77, '81)
5 – Jasper ('82, '91, '93, '06, '07)
3 – Tecumseh ('02, '03, '04)
3 – Mater Dei ('78, '79, '85)
1 – Heritage Hills ('03)

BUD GARLAND: THE RELAY MASTER

In the world of local track and field, there have been many fine coaches over the years, but most would agree that two men have distinguished themselves above the rest as they developed a rivalry that lasted for years. One of these men is Bud Garland, a man whose innovative spirit made him a specialist of sorts and lifted the Bosse track program to levels that had never been reached and still haven't been to this day.

Richard 'Bud' Garland grew up in Washington, Indiana and was quite an athlete for the Hatchets. As a freshman, he joined three seniors and qualified an 880 relay team for the State meet. He was also solid on the basketball court and baseball field, but his most memorable moments took place on the gridiron. Not many 70-year-old men can lay claim to nearly every school rushing record 50 years after graduation, but Garland is one who could.

Until the versatile Joe McCormick came along in 2010, Bud was Washington's leader in points scored in a season (145) and career (258), touchdowns in a season (22) and career (39), and was second in career yardage to Derek Graber with 3,298 yards. After his graduation in 1958, Garland played football for three years at Evansville College and also played a year of baseball and a season of basketball with the Deuces.

Bud left with a degree in Education and found out immediately that local school officials took their sports very seriously. He recalls his interview at Vogel Grade School during the school's basketball heyday immediately after Bob Ford's departure for North High School. "I met with Principal David Royalty, and the only question he asked me was 'Can you coach,'" Bud explained from his home on Evansville's far north side. "When I said 'Yeah,' he asked, 'Can you coach basketball?' When I said 'Yeah,' he said, "You're hired. But you better win!'"

After eight years at Vogel, Garland was offered a job at Bosse as the head track coach, and for the next 23 years he would guide the Bulldogs to statewide prominence and create a dominating presence in a very important facet in the world of track and field.

Art by Jon Siau

Bud began his work at Bosse in 1975 and soaked up knowledge like a sponge by reading and attending conventions and seminars. Though there was talent at Bosse, he was never able to attract a huge enough turnout to be consistently competitive on a team level, especially against his archrival, Charlie Siesky of Harrison. So Bud played the hand he was dealt and worked with the individuals he had.

Listening to Garland recount his days as a coach, it seemed that there were two events that were turning points for the Bosse track program. The first involved a young man who moved in from Henderson and drastically change the mindset of the top tier runners at Bosse.

"Until 1991, your sprinters were 100-and 200-meter guys," Garland explained. "You couldn't get them to even think about the 400- or 1600-meters. That was out of the question. It was too far." Bud went on to explain how he heard about the move-in and how the newcomer would facilitate a change that Garland had been seeking for years.

"The principal (Bob Adams) loved track," Bud continued, "and he came (to the classroom) and got me and said, 'Hey, we just got a new track guy!' I asked him what he ran, and he said the 400. I said 'YESSS!' Word spread, and by noon every track guy had heard about the new kid on the block.

"Eugene Tremill (pronounced truh•MEEL) came to track practice with a big black bag like baseball players have, and he probably had six pairs of track shoes, and the guys couldn't believe it," Bud continued. "Then he went through this extensive warm-up routine. The other guys thought if you worked up a little sweat that you were warmed up. So, trust me, things changed at Bosse. Once they saw him do it, they did it. He was on the first team in 1991 that won the 1,600 relay (Bud's first state championship). From that time on, it became even more competitive, not only for the 400 relay but for the 1600 too."

Bosse's 1993 State champion 1600-meter relay team. Front (L-R): Anthony Thomas, Tracy Smith. Second Row: Mack Jacobs, George Madison. Standing: Terry Recker (asst. coach), Bud Garland (head coach).

The second 'aha moment' for Coach Garland occurred a year or two later. "We always took guys to State," he pointed out; "that was never a concern. After we were the team runner-up in '91, I got to thinking. It (the idea) probably happened during one of my frequent visits to the Haubstadt Inn with Terry Recker (a long-time assistant and friend). It's so true today also. The only concern, be it basketball or football, track or whatever, was beating the other local teams. Then the other teams would come into town and whip us. We were only focused on beating Harrison or Reitz or whoever.

"We thought 'we have to stop competing against the times here in Evansville and start competing with the times around the state.' A guy from Gary would send us their times every week. Another friend sent me times from Indy. So when our guys would run a 43.2 (in the 400 relay), I would tell them, 'they're running 42.8.' So we stopped worrying about competing locally. We focused on our times and how they stacked up statewide."

Bud always took pride in his relay teams, and that was what he hung his hat on as a coach. "My specialty was always the relays," he confided. "I never had the numbers to compete with Charlie (Siesky). Charlie would kill me in a dual meet, maybe (by a score of) 90-36, but we could beat them in the relays. We worked hard on them. I went to a lot of clinics."

Always looking for an edge, Garland confesses that one technique he gleaned from a coaching clinic caused quite a controversy. He had learned a method to maximize his team's exchanges. He researched the technique and found it to be legal. It involved cutting a tennis ball in half and placing it on a line on the track to use as a guide. When the incoming runner hit that mark, the next runner knew to take off at full speed.

Before the sectional, he was called to report to the starter, the legendary Harold Gourley, because a coach had protested. Gourley admitted to never seeing it used but ruled that Bosse couldn't use it. The Bulldogs won anyway, and according to Bud, "Mr. Gourley called the next day and apologized because he read the rules and even verified with the IHSAA that the technique was legal."

Looking back, Bud appreciates everyone who competed for him but has special admiration for a few individuals and teams. The '91 team holds a soft spot in his heart because they were the first area team to compete for a State, falling six points shy of Gary Mann.

A special athlete that he recalls is Mike Rogers. For four years, he rarely lost in the high jump, and he was a State qualifier every year. What made him so unique and special wasn't just that he was a consistent 6'9 jumper, but that he stood only 5'3" tall. Garland remembers throngs of fans crowding around the pit to watch the amazing freak of nature do his thing.

Bud also singled out the 1982 relay team of Bobby Lewis, Greg Ott, Jim Bennett, and Jim Kinsey, but there is little hesitation when asked to name his best team and finest competitors. He is quick to mention Tracy Smith, who holds school records for the 400, 800, 1600 and cross-country and was a State champ in the 400 in 1995.

But the best of the best, without question, was Mack Jacobs, and Garland thinks he may be the all-time greatest in local history, saying, "He was a 6'11 high jumper, the anchor on our relays (once running a 47.4 split in the 1600 relay), an excellent sprinter up to the 400 and a State champ in the 200-meters (1994). If I needed him in the long jump, he probably could have gone over and jumped 22-23 feet, but I had a guy who could do that (Prince Coleman)."

Also a sure thing, the best team ever at Bosse and very possibly in local history, was the '94 Bulldogs. "To my knowledge," Garland said, "it's the only team in Evansville history to rank #1 in the state. We had seven or eight #1 seeds at the State meet. We thought Tracy Smith and both relays were sure things."

Obviously, things didn't fall into place and the Bosse faithful were disappointed. Many factors were in play, but in one specific case, Bud felt responsible. "Tracy (Smith) had the best time in the state by far," Garland explained.

A reporter from the *Louisville Times* called Bud and wore him down until he finally predicted a Smith victory in the 400. The writer then used the quote to motivate a runner from New Albany (Jon Jones) who pulled the upset. "I should've kept my mouth shut," Bud confessed, "but I was pretty proud of him. He was a hell of a runner. I felt so bad about that."

If Garland was responsible, it was one of only a few mistakes for the Bosse legend. Throughout his 23 years, three of his relay teams captured State titles (see below) to go with those by Jacobs and Smith. In addition, Bud is still the only local coach to finish second at the State meet.

Bud Garland retired in 1995 to spend more time with his wife Ginger and to watch his sons, Benji and Brian, compete. He still has cinders in his knees from falls at the track at iconic Enlow Field. When asked if he missed it, he confessed that he was surprised when he went to a meet a year after he retired. With his buddy Terry Recker as the new head coach, he saw the 400-meter relay team doing something he didn't like during warm-ups. He couldn't stand it and proceeded onto the track to correct it. "After I did that, I felt so bad," he admitted. "I couldn't let it go. I just literally stayed away after that."

Bud Garland seems content in his retirement, and he appears happy as he and Ginger enjoy their grandchildren. Whether he truly misses the competition is somewhat irrelevant, but it is certain that the local track scene has missed Bud since his departure. Admittedly, his sport is not on the level of basketball and football in the hearts of many local fans, but for over two decades, Bud Garland put Evansville on the map in the world of track and field.

BUD GARLAND'S STATE CHAMPION RELAY TEAMS

400-meter: Darrell Bacon, Norman Jones, Prince Coleman, Mack Jacobs (42.15, 1994)

1600-meter: Marcus Ivy, Ronald Riffert, Anthony Thomas, Eugene Tramill (3:18.08, 1991)

1600-meter: Anthony Thomas, George Madison, Tracy Smith, Mack Jacobs (3:16.06, 1993)

184

JIM KAISER COULD 'DELIVER'

Athletic opportunities are limited for teenage boys who stand barely 5-feet tall and hardly push the weight scales into triple digits, but in the case of Jim Kaiser, he found his place on the lonely local landscape and prospered. Not only did young Jim become one of our areas most decorated distance runners but he has turned his passion for the sport into a career.

As a student at Corpus Christi School on Evansville's west side, Jim couldn't wait to be a fifth grader and try the various sports at the school. When the day finally arrived, he immersed himself in the flag football, basketball and baseball competitions between the city's Catholic schools. He had also watched his older sister Amy run track and decided to give that a try as well. "I thought of myself as a sprinter, like many young kids do," Jim told me from his home in Lexington, Kentucky.

At 4'9" and 90 pounds, competing in most sports was tough, and although Amy would eventually become an excellent soccer player at Mater Dei, little Jimmy stuck with track. In the sprints, he never finished better than fifth, but he found his calling by a fluke occurrence on a spring weekend in 1980. The Catholic schools held their track meets on Sunday afternoons, and on this particular weekend, Jim was on a camping trip with the Boy Scouts. He arrived home late and begged his parents to hurry to the meet. Upon his arrival, he found that the only event left was the 800-meter run and asked his coach if he could run. On that day at the Mater Dei track, he finished second, and according to Jim, "from that point on, I was a distance runner."

For the remainder of his grade school days, Jim's workouts were low-key and unsophisticated. Each practice, his coach would simply tell him to run two laps then rest and continue the process until he got tired. Reflecting on those early years, Jim realizes that another facet of his life may have had a huge influence on his success, and he likened the experience to a popular movie.

"When I look back, the actual secret to my success was a paper route I had," Jim told me. "I had a morning *Courier* route and had to get up at 5:30, and I had to be ready for school at 7:00 and was always late. I would jog my paper route with about 50 pounds on my back every week, three jogs a week of two miles. There's no doubt that it played a huge part in muscle development and strength training. I never even gave it a thought at the time; I never thought of it as extra training. It's like the old *Rocky* movies where he would use wheelbarrows and rocks instead of modern weight equipment."

Although he lacked Sylvester Stallone's physique, he did enter Mater Dei in 1983 at 5'2 and 100 pounds and eventually grew into his current frame at 5'5 and 110 pounds. Under the guidance of Coach Herb Neighbors, Jim dedicated himself to cross country and track and had moderate success at the City freshman meets. As a sophomore, he continued to mature and won some dual meet races but still could not advance past the sectional.

As a junior, he noticed that his workouts became more "directed" and believes that Coach Neighbors was learning more also through his affiliations with successful Memorial coach Del Schiavone. He began to appreciate the technique of pacing and the value of resting the body in order to peak at the right time.

He also discovered additional motivation during his junior year when he accepted a job at a running store called Sports Quarters on Franklin Street. The business was owned by some former USI runners who were devoted to distance running, and every Tuesday and

Thursday evening they would close the doors at 6:00 and run as a group around the city. The experience was invaluable to Jim as he matched strides with runners like James Nolan and Mike Orban, both All-Americans for the Screaming Eagles. Jim also mentioned Larry Ziegler, who, at 40 years old, was the "father figure" who took Jim under his wing as they traveled to road races in nearby cities like Nashville.

As a junior, Jim qualified for the State cross country meet and finished 65th, and although the finish doesn't sound too impressive, it was a revelation for the young runner and springboarded him to unprecedented success on the local front. "It opened my eyes," Jim explained. "It gave me confidence for track. I knew I could qualify, and I wanted to do something at State."

Jim continued to work, and at the State track meet in 1986, he finished sixth in the 3200-meter run, prompting him to believe, "there's no reason as a senior that I can't be up there with the leaders." With his motivation sky-high, Kaiser began to extend himself even harder, and running against strong local competitors like Boonville's Andy Vandiver and Larry Riggs and Memorial's Mark Schuler (who now coaches at Memorial), Jim toiled year-round to become a champion.

Kaiser admits that distance running can be a lonely activity, and although he often trained alone, he did develop a camaraderie with Memorial runners who met regularly at places like Wesselman Park to log miles. Distance runners are a different breed of cat, and many, including myself, can't fathom the dedication it takes to put down one foot after another for mile after painful mile. But Kaiser revels in the challenge and is passionate about the process.

"There are different levels," Jim pointed out. "There is the physical distance runner with natural ability where it feels very easy with a breathing rhythm and being efficient and light on your feet. And then there's the mental aspect that people don't realize, where running isn't about the clock anymore; it's solely about the contest, you versus another runner. That squint of the eyes where you're zoned in on winning and the mental will to cross the finish line first."

Jim even found himself playing mental games as he trained. "You come up with fake enemies," he said. "That Mesker Park hill, it was a killer. It almost took on a persona to me. I would imagine the hill speaking to me, saying, 'I'm going to make you slow down today,' and I would say, 'I'm going to defeat you,' even though the hill wanted me to slow down or stop or walk up it. And once I'd get to the top, I could look back and laugh at the hill."

Jim gives lots of credit to Herb Neighbors for helping him to prepare for his senior year and believes Neighbors helped him peek at the right time. His goal for the cross country season was a top ten finish, but he found himself in the thick of things as the run neared the finish on a rainy fall day. As the race reached its end, Jim had plenty left in the tank and conquered the field just as he had conquered the hill at Mesker Park, and with the first place medal around his neck, he looked ahead to the spring season.

Unlike today, the world of cyberspace and instant communication was nonexistent, and Kaiser had little knowledge of how he stacked up against statewide competition, but the knowledge he had developed left him fully prepared for what he would face at the State meet. "At the State level, everyone is talented," Jim explained. "You're not going to just run away from people. You have to utilize your strengths and run a smart, strategic race. Forget the clock! If you're strong, you have to push the pace, and you know it's going to come down to a kick at some point."

Just as he had done during his days as a paper boy, Kaiser delivered, and he captured his second State championship by blowing past Brett Polizotto of Valparaiso with a 9:04.2 clocking in the 1987 3200-meter run. The time was the second fastest time in Indiana history at the time and still is the sixth fastest in the 32 years of the event (as of 2012), and Jim joined Central's Adam Renfro and North's David Williams as the only area runners to win the event.

As the 1987 season ended, the late bloomer began to receive serious attention from colleges. In the pre-Internet age, it was difficult for coaches to hone in on prospects, so before his recognition as a State track champion, the interest had been sparse. USI coach Bill Stegemoller was very aware because of Jim's proximity and affiliation with the group from Sports Quarters and actively pursued Kaiser his junior year. Jim had also received interest from smaller schools like Hanover. Ball State was the first to contact him by phone and with personalized letters, making them and USI the frontrunners.

Coach Neighbors and Jim's parents wisely advised him to hold off on making a decision, and after his victory at State, his options increased. Kaiser had always dreamed of running at IU, and he was excited when iconic coach Sam Bell offered a half-scholarship. Notre Dame also offered serious money, and the decision became even tougher. With a full ride available at Ball State and other serious offers on the table, another player entered the picture that crystallized Kaiser's thinking.

While he was pondering, University of Kentucky coach Don Weber requested that Jim make a visit, and while Jim was there, the coaches saw traits they liked and offered the total package. The tiny runner from Mater Dei had found a home, and Jim flourished at UK and improved each year, earning All-American honors as a senior. He then set his sights on the future.

With his Business degree in hand in 1991, he decided to spend a year training for the 1992 Olympics in Barcelona. To make ends meet, he earned a little money at road races, and though he gave it all he had, he finished four seconds away from qualifying for the Olympic Trials in the 10,000-meter run. He now looks back and wonders what might have been had he chosen an even more meager existence and trained with future Olympians like IU's Bob Kennedy, who held the American record in the 5000 meters, and Todd Williams of Tennessee. But it was not to be, and Jim pursued other options.

Kaiser had always wanted to coach and quickly seized an opportunity at UK. He started out as a grad assistant and then became full-time. One of his duties as a newbie was learning to set up and operate the electronic timing equipment, an experience that would launch a whole new career. Being entrepreneurial in nature, he examined the potential and reflected on his childhood. Remembering the days of his paper route and how good it felt to be his own boss, he created his own company, AllTrax Timing, based in Lexington.

Today, Jim's business is thriving as he takes his equipment across the country for track meets. He even uses special high-tech equipment for cross country meets where chips are planted in the runners' shoes and the official times are recorded when the chips come in contact with a mat at the finish line.

Jim approaches his business as he did his running, with the individual drive and focus of a champion. In the process of learning to compete, he distinguished himself as a runner and stands alone in local history. Our area has produced many greats in several sports, but when it comes to distance running, only one has captured the cross country State title and also won the 3200-meter run State championship in track. And that distinction belongs to Mater Dei's Jim Kaiser.

GINGER LUTTERMAN:
THE QUEEN OF LOCAL VOLLEYBALL

A few minutes with Ginger Lutterman is all one needs to draw some conclusions about her as a competitor and as a person. My first conclusion was that there is no doubt that if she had been afforded the opportunity to compete in high school, she would have found a way to excel at whatever sports she chose. Second, as a coach, no one was better suited to tackle the challenges that came with the passing of the landmark legislation called Title IX.

Ginger was a member of the Englebrecht family, known locally for their apple orchards. As a high schooler at North, the only source of competition was GAA (Girls Athletic Association), which offered 'play days' where girls could get an occasional taste of competition by scheduling events with other schools. The contests were little more than casual affairs without coaches or referees, and Ginger yearned for more. She took sports seriously and spent countless hours shooting baskets at the hoop in the family barn or leaping over a makeshift high jump bar on the property.

As a student at St. Paul's Lutheran, Ginger did get to compete in a track meet and an occasional softball game, and while at North High School, she showed a glimpse of what her future would hold by challenging the status quo. As a "semi-serious" gesture, she and good friend Kathy Wilhite approached coach George Alvey about joining the boys track team. Although Mr. Alvey was gracious and open to the idea, the lovely lasses relented after only two practices. But that event may very well have been the last time Ginger ever backed down.

After graduating from North in 1967, Ginger completed her studies at IU in only three years and married Randy Lutterman, an excellent athlete from Harrison who also graduated from IU in 1970. The couple spent the summer in California and then returned to the Midwest when Randy was offered a job in Sandusky, Ohio. Meanwhile, Ginger student taught in Bowling Green and then joined Randy as a teacher in Sandusky.

Realizing that Ohio wasn't for them, Ginger applied for and secured a job at Castle and Randy took a position at Day

Ginger Lutterman coaching her Final Four team in 1981. In the background are Kathy [Brown] Huff (#2) and Kady Berger.

This team wore the very first uniforms purchased just for volleyball. Back row, left to right: Coach Lutterman, JoAnn Brumley, Donna Taylor, Julie Richardt, Lisa Stein, Sherry Timmons, student manager Anita Happel. Front row: Liz Veatch, Dawn Lands, Robin Owen, Cathy Ossenberg, Cindy Farrond, Jaynibeth Goodwin, Krista Mann.

School. While Randy spent five years at Evansville Day before moving to Castle also, Ginger was launching a career that would change the lives of young female athletes while also blazing a trail that would lead Ms. Lutterman to the Indiana Volleyball Hall of Fame.

With her competitive spirit aching for an outlet, Ginger's timing was perfect, and she also feels fortunate to have landed at Castle. "In my interview with Mr. (John) Wittenbraker, I was surprised to learn that they had the Warrick County track meet every year," she recalled. "I thought, 'Wow! The girls get to actually compete in something, and I was really excited about that.'"

Ginger would be the first to admit that none of her accomplishments would have been possible without the ground-breaking legislation in 1972 called Title IX. The bill changed the face of sports forever and was

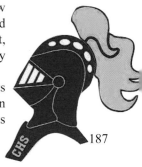

not readily accepted by many members of the establishment. In fact, there were several attempts to undermine the legislation by watering it down. In 1974, the Tower Amendment, authored by Senator John Tower, tried to make "revenue-producing sports" exempt, and late the same year Senator Jacob Javits proposed "reasonable provisions considering the nature of particular sports," an attempt to create loopholes in enforcement. The law was also opposed by the NCAA and challenged with the Civil Rights Restoration Act of 1988. But Title IX withstood the onslaught and has been bolstered several times to give it teeth and to allow proper monitoring.

With her path cleared in 1972, Ms. Lutterman was excited but was hardly prepared for the task ahead. "When I went to IU," she explained, "there were no coaching classes. It has now evolved into multi-faceted training areas, but I didn't have any of that." So Ginger just lowered her head and dove into the uncharted waters.

As one might imagine, the girls programs were not always met with open arms, and Ginger joined the River City Coalition to help coordinate the efforts of local advocates of girls sports. In the early stages, her teams were forced to wear hand-me-down uniforms of the freshmen and JV boys basketball teams and were relegated to 7:30 a.m. practice times. As is often the case, the inequality continued until someone stood up and protested. Roger Benson, the boys' basketball coach was able to enjoy open gym after school with his team, and that didn't sit right with a teacher, Mark Augsberger, who had a daughter on the volleyball team. With the power of Title IX behind him, Augsberger made his point and the atmosphere at Castle began to change.

At the beginning, Ginger coached several sports, and she has a warm spot in her heart for those early years, saying, "Some of my fondest memories are the cinder track and coming out on Saturdays and Sundays to roll it." She also recalls her first track meet at Reitz against legendary coach and athlete Louise Owen.

The schedules were limited in the early years as schools came on board with teams, but it was obvious from the beginning that the movement was long overdue. "My first year, we had a hundred girls try out," Ginger revealed, "and we had 40 girls who wanted to be managers."

Ginger dabbled in soccer, coaching two matches in 1971, and even coached gymnastics from '79-'83, but it was volleyball that lit her fire from the beginning. In the summer of '73, she immersed herself into learning the sport. She particularly recalls a camp she attended by Indiana legend Don Shondell, who made history as the coach at Ball State and whose sons have created a dynasty at Muncie Burris. "The place to go for volleyball in the country was Muncie," Ginger said. So she and Central coach Jan Wilson made the five-hour drive to the Mecca of volleyball. Ginger is quick to point out the virtues of the camp, but also recalls the pain that came with the experience by saying, "I had never been so sore in my life. We played and drilled and had night classes."

During the earliest years, no Evansville schools were on board yet, so Castle competed with the other Warrick County schools plus Vincennes and Jasper. In 1972, the first year with the Title IX in effect, there were 240 schools statewide with girls competing, and the vast majority were in central and northern Indiana. In fact,

Ginger learned volleyball primarily because it was the only sport besides gymnastics that was IHSAA-sanctioned in 1972.

If Lutterman was considered a trailblazer as a coach, then she offers props to those who laid the groundwork as players. Among them are Debbie Kopatich, Ginger Gilles, Lisa Stein (Finnick), Ginger Scott (Schaperjohn), Mary Lou Allen (Heisler) and Sherry Timmons (Eberhart), who coaches the sport at St. John's and whose daughter played at Castle as well. She also pointed out Kathy Huff (Brown), who coached the sport in the Castle system, and Cady Berger, who became an orthopedic surgeon.

When Coach Lutterman went to her first SIAC meeting in Jasper in the early '70s (when the conference included schools from Terre Haute, New Albany and in between), she rode up with Castle legend John Lidy and Rockport legend Wayne Boultinghouse. When she arrived, she discovered that the

---

TOTAL DOMINATION

Without question, the undisputed ruler of Indiana high school volleyball is Muncie Burris. Led by Steve Shondell for 34 years, the program has amassed over 1,200 wins, ranks in the top ten nationally and has lost less than 100 (92+%). Burris has won 22 State titles, and as of 2010 was riding a 14-year winning streak.

---

meeting would consist of 356 men and her. But when she joined the ICGSA (Indiana Coaches of Girls Sports Association) a bit later, the membership was all women. Since then, the makeup has changed again, and Ginger is well aware: "You look at Castle now (2011), volleyball is a man (as the coach), basketball's a man, and softball. At one time, I think Lynn (Zwilling) and Marcia Fisk (Lynn's assistant in track) were the only women."

Lutterman will willingly admit "I don't like to lose," and she makes no apologies for that. "I'm very organized," she states. "I always came into each practice with it planned down to the minute. I had goals for each day. Early on I wanted to develop a love of the game, and they always had fun."

Randy Lutterman nodded as Ginger explained and then spoke up to continue Ginger's point. "She really worked at motivating each player," he said. "As far as competitiveness, I could take you out on the golf course today and she'd just as soon beat you as look at you. She was able to get her players to play at a very high level. She's famous for 'the Lutterman Look'. She would sit on the bench and just stare; they knew they were in trouble. And after a bad game, they were known for their get-togethers behind the bleachers."

Archrival Mary Cox agreed, saying, "Ginger was the most competitive coach around and probably did more for the game than any coach in the area. We're (Boonville and Castle) in different classes now, but when we were in the same class, we could not get through them (in the tournament). It's like watching Pat Summitt (legendary Tennessee basketball coach). She'd shake your hand after a game and it was like 'Aargh! Someday she's going to have to congratulate me for the win.'"

Coach Lutterman did more than just win at Castle. She constructed a program that was the benchmark in southwestern Indiana. During her 23-year career, she fashioned a 381-124 record (75.4%), but she also left a solid foundation for her successors. Her loyal assistant, Fred Bracher, continued the tradition with a ten year 274-72 (79%) term followed by Jana Reiter's 134-41 (76.6%) five-year record.

Coach Lutterman was a dominant force for many years, winning 21 consecutive SIAC titles from 1975-1995. In addition, her resumé also included 13 sectional titles to go with seven regionals and five State Finals appearances, including one in 1976 when the

South Bend Adams team eliminated the Knights by using three boys in the lineup. (Adams was pushing an agenda to allow boys volleyball. A few years later, boys were banned from high school volleyball in Indiana.)

But Ginger is most proud of the lives she has touched over the years. In a *Courier* story, she reminisced about her program, stating, "We got the girls in the sixth grade and they stayed until they were seniors. Then they went to college (35 by scholarship) and became coaches, teachers, and outstanding citizens."

Ginger Lutterman fought the early battles and helped to engineer the emergence of girls sports in the area, and in 2010 she was recognized for her efforts, joining Jasper's Pat Zehr as inductees into the ICGSA Hall of Fame. There is little doubt that her players and competitors alike would agree about her status as a local legend, because for the first 35 years of local volleyball, the queen of the sport and its biggest ambassador was Castle's Ginger Lutterman.

CHARLIE SIESKY: THE MAESTRO

Ask any aficionado of local track whom they consider the most successful coach in area history, and Charlie Siesky's name will usually top the list. Siesky's records over his 33 years of coaching are staggering, but before he became a legendary coach, he made a name for himself as a local athlete.

Siesky was born in Pennsylvania but moved here as a young boy in 1947. In high school, he played two years of football and four seasons each of basketball, cross country and track. As a runner at Bosse, he set a City record in the mile in 1955 and another in '56 (4:31.6) that stood for twenty years. The man whose record he broke, the late Larry Higgins of Reitz, was in Korea when the record fell, and after hearing the news from his parents, showed his class by sending a letter of congratulations from Korea.

After winning several sectionals and conference and City titles, Siesky accepted a track scholarship to run at IU under coach Gordon Fisher. Although he admits to being "a small fish in a big pond," he thoroughly enjoyed his years in Bloomington.

To complete his degree in Education, Charlie split his student teaching days between Bosse, under football coach Phil Beverly, and Dexter Elementary under Jerry Canterbury. When Canterbury moved to Bosse the following year, Siesky was hired at Dexter and his coaching career began.

One of the school's rivals was Vogel, and Vogel had dominated the local basketball scene for several years. At the time, Bob Ford, who later went on to earn All-American status at North High School, was a seventh grader surrounded by a superior team. But Charlie's boys weren't too bad either. Dexter's team was loaded with future stars as well, featuring such players as Terry Wedgewood, Jim Giannini, Jim Campbell, Harold Henry and Chester Schmidt. With the game on the line, Schmidt finished a layup at the buzzer to give Vogel its only loss in three seasons, something in which Charlie still takes great pride.

Being the new kid, Charlie was saddled with a heavy load, including flag football, basketball, safety patrol and track. After three years, he was moved to Central High School downtown as the head track coach and freshman basketball coach under John Wessel. The following year, Ed Claybourne, who was an assistant at Harrison, was asked to take Dan Howard's place as Central's

head football coach. Claybourne expressed his desire to run the track program as well, so Charlie was sent to Harrison to take charge of the school's track team. Later, he took over the cross country program when Bob Gilham stepped down, and the rest, as they say, is history. For over three decades, Siesky led Harrison's track program like a virtuoso conductor and orchestrated one of the finest examples of domination of a sport in local history.

Charlie knew the diversity of the skills used in track and field and never professed to be an expert in every phase of the sport. "You can't know them all," he told me from his home. "We had some wonderful volunteers who helped, like Marlon Flemming (the State shot put champ from Reitz) and Bobby Madison (a greater sprinter from North).

To learn the key to Siesky's success, one only needs to examine the meticulous records he kept as a coach. The workout for every athlete was charted, and notations were made for each practice. He showed me one that read: "Monday, March 1 – first official day of track practice. Weather: 42 degrees, cool, 8" of snow on ground – track clear because David (the school's custodian) snow plowed it for us."

His charts showed hurdler workouts, where they would "stretch, 5 times 300 (meters), 200 (-yard) jog between, then 6 times 100 off curve at ¾ speed, then jogging." In the book, every runner was listed, including his son Brent, and there was a schedule for each set of athletes.

Charlie also had records of each meet with scores, the team's cumulative record and the results of each athlete. He showed me a page for the City meet where Bosse scored 144 points, Harrison 115, etc. and an SIAC meet showing Bosse with 128, Castle 106 and Harrison 84.

As a coach, Siesky had one rule: If you miss practice one day without a valid reason, you COULD BE gone. If you miss two, you ARE gone. To illustrate the weight of the rule, Charlie showed me a notation about one of his excellent athletes (he wouldn't mention the name) who failed to show up at a practice. "He told one of the team members his father had a heart attack. We called home Friday morning, and there was no truth to this at all. This is one of the biggest disappointments of my coaching career. I must get tougher on who I allow to come out for track. This will start next year."

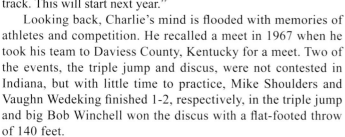

Looking back, Charlie's mind is flooded with memories of athletes and competition. He recalled a meet in 1967 when he took his team to Daviess County, Kentucky for a meet. Two of the events, the triple jump and discus, were not contested in Indiana, but with little time to practice, Mike Shoulders and Vaughn Wedeking finished 1-2, respectively, in the triple jump and big Bob Winchell won the discus with a flat-footed throw of 140 feet.

Siesky spoke of several who competed in college, like Winchell and Don Sellers, and others who could have. "Calbert Cheaney could have been a world class 400-meter hurdler," Charlie revealed. "He had excellent size and strength. Gary Shelton ran a 4:02 mile at IU, and Walter McCarty only ran his senior year and finished third at State in the 800 meters."

Charlie reflected on others, like Travis Johnson, one of the city's greatest sprinters who finished second in the 100, third in the 200, and second at State in the 400 relay, and Steve Markey who ran a 4:18 mile while at Harrison. He also recalled competitors and teams that impressed him, like North's David Williams, the State 3,200-meter champ in 1981, and Cornell Garrett, a phenomenal sprinter who almost qualified for the Olympics. He also recalled a Hammond Noll team that had three runners under 9 minutes in the 2-mile, including the amazing Rudy Chapa.

Locally, he cited Harrison runner Kevin Eastridge, a phenomenal runner who had the bad luck of having the fantastic Don Sellers a year behind him at Harrison. "Don came in and stole his thunder," Charlie recalled, "but Kevin kept running without one moment of jealousy."

One of the all-time local greats created a memory for Charlie that still gets a chuckle out of him and also illustrates the impression his coaching methods made on local runners. The great middle distance runner Tom Martin from Memorial called Siesky out of the blue one day. Charlie's first thought was that the young man was calling about transferring, but no such luck. Martin had called before his senior season to ask if he could see Siesky's workout books because he wanted to copy every workout used by Don Sellers.

Through the years, Charlie compiled a legacy that may never be seen again, and his arduous attention to detail will be remembered by his teams and competitors alike. "Charlie Siesky is a legend, obviously the best track coach this area's ever seen," said Jon Siau, a Harrison grad and opposing coach while at North. "It was always a pleasure to compete against Charlie. He was a character. Some asked why he was always upset at meets, and I always said, 'Charlie's not happy unless he's unhappy.'"

Through his career, Siesky had three individual State champs (Sellers, Winchell and Wedeking), won 37 City titles in track and cross country, 33 SIAC meets, 29 sectionals, 9 regionals and 3 top ten team finishes at State (fourth in '67, tenth in '72 and eighth in 1990). He won a remarkable 93% of his dual meets (198-14-2), including 51 straight from '70-'79 and 68 in a row from '79-'92.

With these numbers, it is no surprise that the synthetic track in the new Harrison Stadium will bear his name, and the reasons for his successes are as uncomplicated as the man himself. "First of all, I had really good athletes at Harrison," Charlie explained, "and really good assistants, like Mitch Marsch, Jim Giovanetti and Brent St. Clair. We tried to make it a point to say something to every athlete who was out there practicing. It's easy to feel alone when 50 athletes are spread out in 15 events.

"I received a lot of criticism for not spending more time with the elite athletes, but I disagree completely. I believe that each and every kid who comes out, if they do the workouts, they deserve the attention."

Today, Charlie and his wife Janice are enjoying retirement, and it won't surprise those who know him that Charlie isn't a fan of computers and other technology. He built a career by keeping it simple, and that formula enabled him to become the first and still only local member of the Indiana Track & Field Hall of Fame.

MEMORIAL SOCCER:
DOUBLE DOMINATION
MEMORIAL TIGERS

In the world of high school athletics, true dynasties are very rare, and in all the years the IHSAA has sanctioned sports, only a precious few could qualify. Carmel is far and away the most prolific school statewide with 103 team State championships in 14 different sports. They are also the most dominant in a single sport, with 27 titles in girls swimming. Others who have achieved or approached 'dynasty' status over the years include Bloomington/Bloomington South (wrestling, 24 titles), Muncie Burris (volleyball, 22), Gary Roosevelt (track, 20), North Central (29 combined in boys and girls tennis) and Evansville Mater Dei (12 total and nine consecutive in wrestling).

Other Indiana schools that don't make the grade as dynasties have established a winning 'tradition' in various sports that make them dominant in their region and highly respected statewide, like Reitz, Heritage Hills and Mater Dei in football, Memorial and Jasper in baseball and Washington in basketball, to name a few locally. In the world of soccer, the unquestioned leader in tradition in our area is Memorial, and in 2008, they displayed that strength by capturing both the boys and girls IHSAA State championships.

The boys program was initiated in the late '70s by Bill Vieth Sr. and Dick Shymanski. Vieth helped organize the city's youth leagues and high school leagues when Indiana schools played under the umbrella of the IHSSA (Indiana High School Soccer Association) before the IHSAA sanctioned the sport in 1994. Bill Vieth Jr., who starred for his father at Memorial and then at St. Louis University, took over Memorial's program in 1986 and led

the Tigers to four IHSSA state titles in '88, '89, '90 and '92, giving the school nine state championships in 14 years.

In 2007, Memorial won its first IHSAA title with a 1-0 win over Chesterton and were ranked as the #1 high school team in the country. The program already had seven All-Americans among the program's alumni, and in 2008, the Tigers had another very strong nucleus returning and were favorites to repeat. But while they prepared to launch a new season in the fall of 2008, their female counterparts had a few plans of their own.

Memorial's girls program began competition in 1979 under head coach Fred Williams and immediately set the tone with an 8-0-1 record and a City championship. Williams guided the program for eleven fantastic seasons and had a record of 153-17-11 (90%) while dominating area competition and winning four McGuire Cups (the trophy for the unsanctioned state tournament for four years before the IHSAA sanctioned girls soccer in '94). Like the boys, the Lady Tigers were one of the state's finest in the pre-IHSAA years, reaching nine Final Fours with four state championships during Coach Williams' tenure.

Dave Kassenbrock took charge for the 1990 season and finished as the state runner-up, and then Joe Lattner came on board to lead Memorial into the IHSAA era. In 1992, the girls finished 17-3-2 and won another state title, and in the first year with the IHSAA presiding (1994), Memorial made its first Final Four before finishing second in '95 and capturing their first State championship in 1996 with players like Beth Csukas, Elaine McAdams,

Memorial's 2008 girls State champs. Front row (L-R): Paige Popham, Brittany McCall, Susan Ellsperman, Celia Pauli, Ashley Short, Olivia Robinson, Lauren Lamb, Lindsey Phipps. Second row: Alex Kixmiller, Sarah Crowson, Lisha Murphy, Courtney Deem. Third row: Sara Logel, Meghan Day, Katie Milligan, Megan Koch, Katie Loehr, Emily Hayden, Mariah Phipps, Sarah Stone, Haley Meyer, Mary Ulrich, Skylar Werne, assistant coach Holly Happe, head coach Angie Lensing. Fourth row: assistant coach Scott Miller, Lauren Fuchs.

Holly Wimberg and Emily Markwell, to name a few. Coach Lattner left the Memorial program after the 1998 season to head up the program at Castle, and during his eight-year run at Memorial, his teams went 123-28-11 (81%) and became a steady presence at the State Finals.

Lattner was a hard act to follow, but the transition to head coach by Angie Lensing was seamless. Lensing played her high school soccer at North in the late '80s and witnessed Memorial's dominant local presence as an opponent. At the time, Memorial featured talented sisters Angie and Laura Gries and Leslie Wallender. Angie Werne (Lensing's maiden name) was a three-sport athlete in high school who graduated in 1990 and then played soccer and basketball at Missouri Valley College. She then returned to Evansville and played the first two seasons of women's soccer at UE under Coach Mick Lyons. In 1996, she was hired as an assistant under Lattner at Memorial and then became the head coach in 1999.

Lensing has won 75% of her games during her eleven seasons prior to 2012 and has made it to the Final Four five times, but without question, the highlight of her head coaching career began in the fall of 2008. Coming off of a respectable 11-4-3 season, the girls were itching to get back to the State Finals. The team had a nice mix of experience and youth, and as the season progressed, three seniors, Susan Ellsperman, Celia Pauli and Olivia Robinson, carried much of the scoring load. Memorial opened with a 2-1 loss to Ft. Wayne Bishop Dwenger and then won two before losing 1-0 to a strong Washington team led by All-District selection Shay Miller. From that point on, the Tigers took no prisoners, winning twelve in a row to finish the regular season. During the streak, Memorial scored at least four goals seven times, and nine of the twelve wins were shutouts thanks to the stellar play of sophomore goalkeeper Sarah Stone.

In the sectional, Stone was impenetrable in net as the Tigers rolled over Evansville Day School (6-0), Castle (4-0) and Harrison (4-0), and in the one-game regional, Reitz couldn't find an answer for Stone either as she came through again in a 1-0 victory with Ellsperman scoring off a pass from talented freshman Meghan Day. In the semi-state, Sarah Stone continued to befuddle opponents as she shut out Center Grove 6-0 and Bloomington North 2-0. Coach Lensing's girls had rattled off 18 wins in impressive fashion to punch their ticket for Indianapolis, and they would have plenty of company for their journey.

The 2008 season marked the 25th year with Bill Vieth Jr. at the helm of the boys soccer program at Memorial, and even after the prior season when the Tigers were the best in the country, the talent was plentiful once again. The typical starting lineup featured forwards Max Lachowecki, John Riedford and Jeff Stapleton with midfielders Austin King, Mitch McCord and Tyler Vieth and backs Matt Fehn, Jonathan Behrens, Emile Garcia and Justin Neville with Trev Wilgus in goal. Key subs throughout the season were Travis Latta, Andy Diehl, Jace Jarboe and Alex Peters.

Memorial opened on August 21 with a 4-0 win over Jasper and were not scored against until a 6-3 win in the sixth game.

They finished the regular season 15-0-2 and had an easy time in the sectional with wins over Harrison (3-0) and North (6-1). The regional was easier yet as senior goalkeeper Trev Wilgus recorded his fourteenth and fifteenth shutouts of the year in wins over Gibson Southern (7-0) and Heritage Hills (8-0) while the scoring onslaught was led by five goals from sophomore Max Lachowecki and four from senior John Riedford.

Lachowecki continued his scoring barrage in the semi-state with a goal in each game, wins over East Central (3-0) and Columbus North (1-0). The boys had navigated another perfect season, and although Coach Vieth expects a high level of success each year, he wasn't sure of this team's potential until they faced some outstanding teams from Missouri and Ohio. "The weekend we played in St. Louis at the Gateway City Classic," was Bill's answer when asked if there was a moment of truth for the season. "That tournament built the momentum going into the State tournament, to go on the road and win three games in 24 hours against quality teams that were all ranked in their states."

On October 25, 2008, the boys did their part and looked forward to returning to Indy as the defending champs, and this time the celebration would be twice as much fun.

As November 1 approached, the Memorial faithful were fired up, and fortunately for them, the boys and girls Final Four are played as part of the same event at the same venue. "The whole week leading up to the finals was an exciting atmosphere, to have so many kids who are touched in such a small community here," said Angie Lensing from her office at Memorial. "Friday, we had a great pep assembly with both of our buses lined up to leave immediately following. It was a fantastic sendoff. The parents were great."

With Kuntz Stadium inundated with blue and white, the girls took the field for the semi-finals against an undefeated Noblesville team that hadn't been scored on all season. Lensing believed that powerful Noblesville was trying to intimidate her girls when they showed up ten minutes late for the game and that Memorial's team had nothing to lose and everything to gain. With the largest crowd they'd ever played in front of looking on, the girls battled against the physical Millers, and when all was said and done, two periods would not be enough – nor would two seven-minute overtimes.

Throughout the contest, the Lady Tigers had not been able to penetrate past the reach of goalkeeper Ashley Szalwinski, who had pitched twenty shutouts in '08, and Memorial's Olivia Robinson was forced to leave with a head injury from constant warfare with Noblesville's star Chrissy Tchoula. As the officials prepared for penalty kicks and the crowd held its collective breath, Angie Lensing recalls the situation vividly. "I can remember seeing the boys warming up to my right and we went to PKs and the boys stopped and watched," Lensing recalled. Both teams had had scoring opportunities during regulation and overtime, but Sarah Stone and Szalwinski were airtight in goal. Most of the game had been played in the midfield, and when the time came for penalty kicks, the entire crowd was on its feet to see which team would break the 0-0 tie.

Memorial's 2008 boys State champs. Front row (L-R): Nick Bafunno, Tyler Vieth, Mitch McCord, Jace Jarboe, Andy Diehl, Justin Neville, Robert O'Bryan, Maxx Hagan, Jim Schopmeyer. Middle row: Max Lachowecki, Jeff Stapleton, John Riedford, Jackson Colavecchia, Austin King, Matt Fehn, Justin Mulherin, Alex Peters. Back row: Layne Miller (asst. coach), John Mudd, Jon Behrens, Matt Minnette, Adam Ulrich, Trev Wilgus, Emile Garcia, Travis Latta, Bill Vieth (head coach). (Not pictured: Sean Landry, assistant coaches Chad Perkins, Jon Rietman, Neil Peluchette and Rob Smith)

To open the action, the Millers' Ellen Duckwall fired and Stone extended to her right for the save. Memorial senior Brittany McCall then found the net for a 1-0 lead. After two more makes by Noblesville and one each by seniors Celia Pauli and Ashley Short, Memorial led 3-2, and after superstar Chrissy Tchoula missed, the game rested on the foot of Memorial freshman sensation Meghan Day and she found the net, sending Noblesville home and the Lady Tigers to the final game.

The girls had played free and loose and advanced to the championship match with a win over a very imposing opponent, and the win must have served as an inspiration to the boys as they took care of Ft. Wayne Homestead 1-0 on a goal by Max Lachowecki in their semi-final. The stage was set for a very special evening as both the boys and girls would do battle to bring home State championship trophies.

As the girls took the field for the final, the sea of blue and white dwarfed the crowd from Ft. Wayne Snider. The Lady Tigers took the field in their flat back 4 formation with their typical line-up: forwards Susan Ellsperman (sr.), Celia Pauli (sr.) and Meghan Day (fr.); midfielders Olivia Robinson (sr.), Courtney Deem (jr.) and Katie Loehr (jr.); and defenders Brittany McCall (sr.), Lauren Lamb (sr.), Emily Hayden (jr.) and Alex Kixmiller (fr.) with sophomore Sarah Stone in goal. Valuable minutes were also provided during the year by seniors Ashley Short and Paige Popham, junior Haley Meyer, sophomore Katie Milligan, and freshmen Lisa Murphy and Mary Ulrich.

From the outset, Memorial outclassed the Panthers as they outshot Snider 7-3 in the first period and took a 1-0 lead to the locker room after Alex Kixmiller assisted on a goal by Susan Ellsperman at the 23:38 mark. In the second period, Brittany McCall connected after a pass from Ellsperman inside the six yard box to put the game away. Sarah Stone was amazing once again with three saves, and the game gave her 15 shutouts in the final 16 games and her 18th shutout for the season. With the win, the ladies delivered the school's first girls State title since 1996 and, more importantly, came through with the first half of the daily double that Memorial fans had come to see.

The boys final would offer all the excitement the local fans could ask for and would also provide the perfect ending for the glorious day. Goals by Lachowecki and Jeff Stapleton were enough to force the game into overtime against Zionsville, and once again, two overtime periods weren't enough. The irony was not lost on Angie Lensing as she and her girls watched the boys fire penalty kicks just as the girls had done hours earlier.

As the PKs played out, both teams connected on three of the five kicks in the first round, with John Riedford, Max Lachowecki and Emile Garcia connecting for Memorial. In sudden death, Noblesville connected on the first kick as did the Tigers' Jeff Stapleton. Memorial's Travis Latta then found the net and the victory was secured when goalkeeper Trev Wilgus made the save on the final kick of the tournament.

The boys had done their part and finished their remarkable two-year run with consecutive 23-0-2 seasons and back-to-back State championships. Looking back on the '08 season, Coach Vieth assessed the accomplishment and offered credit to the special group. "That team was very mature; they had played through the previous year undefeated, and it never seemed to bother them," Vieth said. "It was a crew of kids who had been playing together for lots of years throughout our junior high program."

Vieth was also sure to mention the contributions of his assistants, Chad Perkins, Layne Miller, Jonathan Rietman, Neil Peluchette and Rob Smith, and the consistent excellence of senior goalkeeper Trev Wilgus, who finished the season with 18 shutouts in the 23 matches. Bill also mentioned what he called "the backbone of the team," four players who earned first team All-State honors: Wilgus, Lachowecki, Garcia and Tyler Vieth, Bill's son.

The boys outscored their competition 98-10 on the season with five players scoring at least 21 points (2 points for a goal and 1 for an assist): Lachowecki (27 goals, 11 assists, 65 points); Stapleton (13, 11, 37); Riedford (13, 7, 33); Vieth (7, 14, 28); and Latta (5, 11, 21). Lachowecki was the only player with a hat trick (three goals in a game), but six players had multi-goal games: Lachowecki (6), Stapleton (4), Garcia, Riedford, Alex Peters, and Andy Diehl.

The 2008 team gave Coach Vieth a very nice gift for his 25th anniversary, and he has every right to be very proud of the program he has fostered for the last quarter-century. One of his proudest achievements is the fact that over 100 of his athletes have played the sport in college, and if the past is any indication, that number will rise each year.

As for the girls program, the 2008 team finished the year 22-2 and outscored their opponents 92-7, and the great season was just one more achievement for a program that has dominated local play and is one of the best programs in the state, as well. Several players from '08, including Celia Pauli, Brittany 'B-Mac' McCall and Alex Kixmiller were honored locally, and three were named to the All-State team: Susan Ellsperman and Olivia Robinson on the first team and Sarah Stone on the second team. Like Coach Vieth, Angie Lensing knows that success to this degree is attributable to many, including her assistants, Polly Happe, who played for Memorial's 1996 State champs, and Scott Miller, who also played at Memorial. "They're all part of this beautiful puzzle we have now," Lensing explained, and although Angie is the only Memorial coach who is not an alum, she did marry Bill Lensing who was a teammate of Bill Vieth Jr.

As the 2008 season began, no one could have imagined what would happen a few months later, and dual championships were the farthest thing from the coaches' minds. "We don't ever talk about that," Bill Vieth responded when asked if the subject ever came up. "I mean, obviously it's always a goal. As we kept progressing through the tournament, certainly then the school started talking about it."

In November of '08, both teams were honored at the state senate, and the gathering marked the celebration of a feat that had never been accomplished before, boys and girls champions in the same year from the same school in the sport of soccer. In the grand scheme of things, Memorial soccer may not be as dominant as the Carmel swimming program, but the consistency of excellence over time does qualify the Memorial soccer program to be included among the finest programs in Indiana history.

DUAL DOMINANCE

When the Memorial boys and girls soccer teams both won State titles in 2008, Memorial became the first Indiana school to do so in that sport. But in all IHSAA sports, the feat is not as rare as one might imagine. In fact, boys and girls teams from the same school have won State championships in the same sport in the same year 35 times since the girls started competing in the 1970s. Below are the schools that accomplished this dual dominance.

Soccer (1)
  Evansville Memorial – '08
Basketball (1)
  Oregon-Davis – '07
Track & Field (4)
  Gary Roosevelt – '83
  Ft. Wayne Northrup – '04
  Warren Central (2) – '06, '07
Tennis (6)
  North Central (3) – '77-'78, '84-'85, '86-'87
  Park Tudor (2) – '97-'98, '06-'07
  Carmel – '10-'11
Cross Country (8)
  Carmel (5) – '82, '87, '88, '96, '08
  Floyd Central – '91
  Valparaiso – '00
  Columbus North - '09
Swimming (15)
  Munster (2) – '76, '77
  Carmel (13) – '90-'94, '96-'97, '01-'04, '10-'11

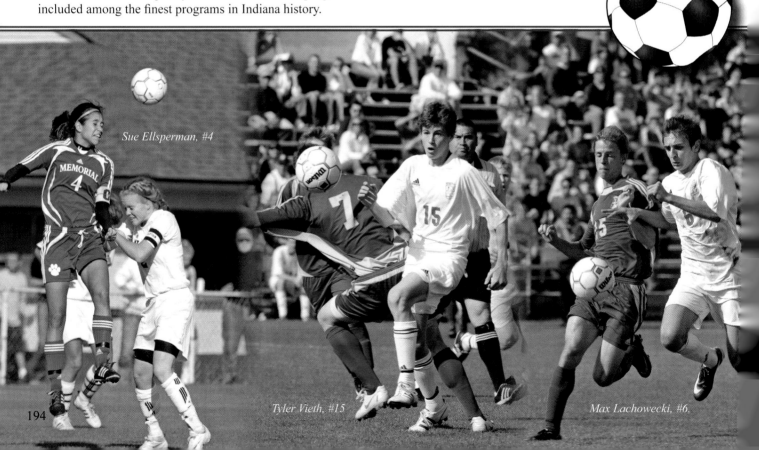

Sue Ellsperman, #4

Tyler Vieth, #15

Max Lachowecki, #6.

194

Olivia Robinson, #3

Mitch McCord, #4.

Celia Pauli, #17

Sarah Stone, #00

Emile Garcia, #8

QUITE A YEAR!

One might say that Sarah Stone had a pretty decent school year in 2008-2009. Not many athletes can claim to have been a part of two team State championships in one year, as Sarah did as the goalkeeper on the soccer team and the starting point guard on the basketball team.

Trev Wilgus' PK save was the game winner

BRYCE BROWN: SIMPLY THE BEST

Our area has had its share of quality track athletes, including 60 individuals and five relay teams that won State championships, but looking back over the 100 years of competition, one athlete stands out among all the rest. From his record-setting performances as a runner at Harrison to his sparkling career as a collegian, Bryce Yante Brown has set standards that may not be reached for a very long time, and those who were fortunate enough to see him run are still amazed at his pure talent.

Bryce played the usual sports as a youngster with moderate success in little league baseball and youth basketball and football at Lakeview, but he found his true calling at McGary Middle School. As a member of a very strong team, he wanted to run the sprints as a sixth grader, but with so much talent in the upper grades, he was delegated to the hurdles. Little did he know at the time that the coach's decision would change his life and create a vehicle for him to achieve legendary status and receive a college education.

When he entered Harrison in 2003 as a "skinny" freshman, he played basketball and football and ran track, but after realizing that his future in basketball wasn't promising and that he wasn't fond of the contact in football, he decided to focus on track. As spring approached, Harrison track coach Seth Bauer was anxious to see if the young hurdler could live up to expectations. "I knew about Bryce as a seventh grader," Bauer informed me. "They had a real talented class at McGary. His eighth grade year, their 4x100 team broke the City record, Bryce won the hurdles and they dominated the City meet."

Bryce had worked on the hurdles for three seasons and had even practiced on the 39-inch high hurdles used by the high schools. Bauer felt that this helped Bryce because he had seen many hurdlers have trouble with the nine-inch increase from middle school to high school. Bryce had basically been self-taught, and when he got to Harrison, he received some help from assistant coach Bruce Durden, who improved Brown's aggressiveness off the hurdles and his arm motion. Durden also worked on Bryce's body control, once telling *Courier* journalist Dave Johnson, "with improved body control comes speed."

As his freshman season progressed, Bauer watched as Bryce gained confidence, and he wasn't sure how good Brown could be. But it wouldn't be long before his questions would be answered. "I knew that he would be good locally," Seth explained, "but I didn't realize how good he was until the State meet. He was the only freshman to advance to the finals in both hurdle events. At that point, we thought 'this is pretty special.' And then he placed seventh in the 300 hurdles (in 38.5)."

After his freshman season, Bryce went to Indianapolis to work with an AAU team, and with that training and a year of maturity, the improvement was significant. Bauer was amazed as he observed what would become a remarkable year, and one instance revealed that his runner had character that would rival his abilities. "I think the only race he lost from his sophomore year on was to his teammate, Jeremy Stewart," Seth recalled. "Jeremy beat him by a hundredth of a second out at Central, and I remember the way he handled it. You could tell that he didn't like losing, but he went over with a smile, shook his hand and congratulated him. I could see that this was a special kid we were dealing with."

Bryce breezed through the sectional and regional, and at the 2005 State meet, the legend began to take shape. "The 110 hurdles came first and he advanced to the finals," Coach Bauer recalled. "We talked before the finals and I told him 'go out and run your race and try to feel the guys around you and see what happens.' He got out of the blocks real well, and at the end, he looked and saw that he was right there (in the lead). Then he had this explosion of speed and you could hear the whole stadium react.

"He won that and came back in the threes (300 hurdles) and that was an even better move. I don't remember ever seeing a kid look like he was going full speed and then go into a whole 'nother gear. He had the inside position on the favorite and again the crowd reacted. He ended up breaking the State record in the 300."

The 300-meter record Seth cited was 36.34, and Bryce's time in the 110 highs (13.83) was at least one-tenth of a second faster than any runner in the previous 11 years. The young star had indeed emerged as a true talent, and his coach was a little disappointed at some of the reactions to Brown's success. "Once he won those State titles (in '05), there was a lot of talk," Bauer told me. "There were a lot of positives but also some negatives that he'd never be able to repeat and that it was a fluke. But he just let it roll off his shoulders. He had just the right temperament to be a winner."

Though Bryce's work ethic was solid, he wasn't a big fan of the weight room, even confessing with a smile that he "used to run from the weight room," when asked about it. He did mature physically however, eventually filling out at 5'11, 170 pounds, and as each season passed, he became virtually invincible.

His junior year, he was untouchable locally and again turned heads on the big stage. He lost by an eyelash in the 110 highs and then turned in a 36.56 for his second State championship in the 300-meter intermediates. As he matured physically, he also displayed a willingness to sacrifice for the team, and during his final season, he and Coach Bauer made some decisions that carried some heavy risks.

"We had finished fourth as a team at State his sophomore year and sixth his junior year," Bauer revealed, "and he said, 'I think I can run the 100.' I knew that would be awfully tough to do with the 110s and the 100 being back to back and then to come back and run the finals. And then he ran the 4x100 as well, meaning he would run in five of the first six events.

"We tried it in the last meet of the season against Reitz. He was running against his cousin, Daylon Redding, and they both hit like 10.6 (seconds). We did it in the City and SIAC, and I told him that at the sectional we would probably pull him out of it. He had no problem winning the City and conference in the 10.7s and 10.8s, and he said, 'I want to go for it,'"

At the State meet, Bryce nearly pulled it off. More than once, he would finish a race then walk around the track and arrive just in time to begin the next event. He won the 110s in 13.69, tying the State record of Southport's Robert Kennedy in 1985. He then finished third in the hundred in what was nearly a three-way dead heat before breaking his own record in the 300 with a 36.26 clocking that hasn't been approached since.

In '07, Bryce scored 27 points as an individual plus 3 points as a member of the 4x100 relay with teammates Jeremy Stewart, Lucian Harris and Ryan Hayes, and because of his magnificent high school career, Bryce was courted by such schools as IU, Southern Cal, Baylor, LSU and Texas Tech. Because he wasn't fond of flying, he initially planned on going to Indiana, but as the process drew to a close, he realized that his grades weren't strong enough and that junior college was the best route. He chose South Plains

College in Levelland, Texas, a school that had a tradition of fine hurdlers and often beat Division I schools in meets.

Bryce started hitting the weights and the books in college and prospered in the environs of South Plains. With a stronger body and excellent coaching, Brown became a two-time national champion and earned a full ride to Texas Tech just down the road from South Plains.

Bryce continued to flourish in Lubbock, and with fellow standout hurdler Jamele Mason pushing him stride for stride, captured the Big 12 title in the 400-meter hurdles as both a junior and senior. Brown set a personal best at the Big 12 meet in 2011 with a 49.04, and went on to earn All-American status for the second time after a fourth place finish as a junior and a third as a senior at the NCAA National Championships in Eugene, Oregon.

Bryce's ultimate aspiration is to run in the Olympics, but his hopes were dashed for 2012 due to a nagging injury. His plans are to continue training for the World Championships and possibly the 2016 Olympics, but regardless of what his future holds, his place in local history is undeniable.

Brown made himself into a world-class hurdler, ranking as high as #8 nationally, and Seth Bauer believes he will be looked at for a long time as one of the greatest runners in Indiana history, alongside such greats as Rudy Chapa, Memorial's Tom Martin and outstanding distance man Austin Mudd from Center Grove. "There's no doubt Bryce is the best runner to ever come out of Evansville," Bauer said, "with five State titles and breaking the record twice. The things he did are mind-boggling to me. We have kids who do 300s in practice, and they think they're doing something special when they're running 36 and 37 (seconds). Then I'll tell them, 'now put eight hurdles in there and think about running that 36. It puts it in perspective how good he was."

Bryce Brown was good enough to be named Athlete of the Decade by *Indiana Runner* magazine, and as a high school runner, he had one of the fastest times in the nation. As of 2012, he was still the only Indiana runner to run the 300 hurdles in under 37 seconds, and his three State championship runs are the top three times in the 14-year history of the event. As a senior, Bryce narrowly missed winning three titles at State, and it is hard to deny that his five State championships make him the finest track athlete, male or female, in local track & field history.

DID YOU KNOW?

Only three individuals have won four State titles in the same event in boys track & field. They are:

Amos Abrams (Gary Froebel, '30-'33)
220-yard low hurdles

Eugene Yates (Anderson, '37-'40)
880-yard dash

Futsam Zeinasellassie (North Central, '09-'12)
3200-meter run

28 male athletes have won three consecutive State championships in the same event, including Bryce Brown of Harrison (300 hurdles - '05-'07) and Mark Buse of Southridge (pole vault - '89-'91).

BLAKE MAURER:
IN A CLASS OF HIS OWN

Though debates may rage about the greatest area athletes in various sports, the closest one could come to a sure thing is very possibly the argument for Mater Dei's Blake Maurer. But for an athlete who accomplished such greatness, the early days of his career might surprise you.

Like many youngsters, Blake's athletic influence came from his father, Kelly Maurer, who was born and raised in Haubstadt. Kelly's class was the third to spend all four years at the new Gibson Southern High School. As a 185-pound running back, Kelly played for hall of fame coach Jack Jewell and was good enough to have led southwest Indiana in rushing his junior year, narrowly edging local legend Bruce King of Heritage Hills.

Kelly hadn't considered wrestling until Joe Gossman came to town. Gossman had turned the Mater Dei program over to a young man named Mike Goebel so that Joe could assume control of the Trojan's wrestling program. During Kelly's senior year, Coach Gossman's heavyweight became ineligible and the coach turned to Maurer to fill the void.

Though Kelly's wrestling career was short, it was eventful, and Maurer jokingly confesses that he does have the dubious distinction of being pinned in seven seconds (a school record) by a 330-pounder from Tell City. He did prove to be a quick study, however, when he surprised everyone by avenging losses during the season to win the sectional.

Kelly admits that wrestling wasn't even on his radar before Coach Gossman arrived and appreciates how the events over thirty years ago influenced the lives of both his sons. "Joe was big on conditioning," Kelly said from the family's west side home. "I hated it while it was going on, and I probably never would have gotten involved in wrestling. I wouldn't have known anything about wrestling. It's kind of funny how things work out."

Blake's mother, Amy, moved from Indianapolis to Owensville her sophomore year and was crowned homecoming queen as she and Kelly became high school sweethearts. Even though he "was just a slow white kid," Kelly was offered a chance to be a walk-on at IU, and Amy joined him in Bloomington. Before long, though, the two made a decision to return home and marry, and both went to work at Mead Johnson.

In the late '80s and early '90s, Kelly was an assistant in Tim McIntosh's Gibson Southern football program while another assistant, Mike Woods, was also the wrestling coach. When the football season was over, Woods suggested that little Blake roll around on the mat, but Kelly was skeptical. Mike watched over him and kept it low-key, and Blake's first taste of competition was a memorable one. As it happened, the boy who would one day become an Indiana wrestling icon lost his first match to a red-headed girl named Heather Weiss, and Kelly says he will never forget her name.

In 1992, the Maurers moved to St. Joe, "Mater Dei country," when Blake was just six, and when he first tried out for the St. Joe wrestling team, he didn't make it. Although he weighed less than 60 pounds, the team had an opening at 77 and the coach chose Blake for the spot. He never won a match that season, but Kelly saw something that would serve Blake well for years to come. "The thing about Blake was, he was never concerned about losing," Kelly explained. "That never was a big deal. I always had him wrestling against older, bigger kids, and he always had a sense of wanting to get better."

Blake hung tough and took his medicine, and at age 11 or so, he started attending Jeff Jordon's wrestling camp in Ohio. Jordan was a four-time State champ in the Buckeye State with a career record of 159-1, the best in Ohio history. His Jeff Jordan State Champ Camp is one of the premier destinations in the county, and it was at this camp that Blake learned to work hard and dream big.

"The idea of being a four-timer (State champ) was given to me by Jeff Jordan," Blake informed me as we sat in Mater Dei's coaches' office. "I was in the eighth grade, and he sat me down and asked what my goals were for high school. I said I wanted to be a State champ some day, and he said, 'Why just one? How about four?' He gave me a disappointed look, like 'why haven't you thought about this sooner?' I respected him a lot, and I thought, 'Dang! If he thinks that, then I should be able to do it.'"

When Blake came home and did some research, he learned that there had been only four Indiana wrestlers to accomplish the feat, but when he set the goal, he had yet to even put on a Mater Dei singlet. In fact, when he informed a few friends about his new aspirations, they laughed and said, 'Hey, why don't you just make the varsity first?'

In 2000, Blake entered Mater Dei and began a brilliant two-sport career. In football, he led the team in tackles as a sophomore free safety on the Wildcat team that finished second at State to Bishop Luers. Because of his success, he was convinced that he should be 'the man' and was determined to make a switch, a decision that would cause problems in the future.

"He came to me and said, 'Dad, I'll do anything you tell me to do if you put twenty pounds on me,'" Kelly said. Kelly wanted to help and admits that he is not a certified trainer, but common sense told him that 20-rep squats and whole milk should do the trick.

"It did do it, but it hurt his hip," Kelly confessed. "I screwed his hip up." Kelly had asked Blake to load too much weight on his shoulders, and the strain became too much. By the time the damage was done, the doctor gave his order: "No more squats!"

Realizing that his son wasn't going to abandon his goals, Kelly sought the advice of Dick Connor, a highly respected trainer who owns The Pit. Connor is a proponent of 'super slows', a method where each rep of an exercise lasts ten seconds and takes all the pressure off the joints.

As Blake's junior year approached, the rapid weight gain had also caused severe shin splints, but Maurer continued to work with Connor. The workouts were only twelve minutes long but were so grueling that it would take a week to recover. To articulate the type of man Connor is, Kelly told of the time Blake and good friend Matt Coughlin were highly skeptical of Connor before he made them believers. Dick had coached numerous power-lifting champs over the years, and the 65-year-old was not afraid to demonstrate his methods.

As the story goes, Dick told the boys that "super slows are mental. You're never going to do anything harder."

According to Kelly, the boys were thinking, "Fine, old man, show us!"

Connor then approached the weight machine, did the super slow and his eyes rolled back in his head, terrifying Blake and Matt to do the point that they thought, "He's doing to die." When Connor came to, he looked at them and said, "Boys, that's what I'm talking about," and Maurer and Coughlin were instant converts.

Kelly says that Dick Connor was a major influence on Blake, with his methods and also with his motivation. Kelly believes that his son was too humble, downplaying his strengths, and that it was working against him. Connor took the opposite approach and was constantly telling Blake, "Hey, man, you're the best; act like it!"

When asked about Connor's contribution, Blake was concise and to the point, saying simply, "I can't thank Dick Connor enough." As a result of the sessions, Blake's confidence soared, and the workouts didn't put on weight but enabled his speed to go off the charts. Connor had told Kelly that Blake was the most focused kid he had ever worked with, and his focus paid off big time as he completed his career at Mater Dei.

During his final two seasons, he morphed into a 5'11, 185-pound running back/linebacker and placed himself among the finest defensive players in Mater Dei football history. He was a three-time All-Conference player, finishing #1 in the record book with 100 solo tackles and second in career tackles (397) to Jeff McDurmon, who finished his three-year career ('92-'94) with 419. Blake also set the school record for average yards per carry (7.2) and earned All-State honors three times, as a defensive back as a sophomore and as a linebacker his final two years.

Each year at Mater Dei, Blake would cut 20 pounds or so for the wrestling season, and he began his quest for perfection with a fantastic first year. He finished the campaign in 2001 a spotless 42-0, and when he stepped atop the podium for the 130-pound presentation, the freshman was joined by six seniors and a junior in his weight class.

The 2001 championship was special for another reason that most fans may not have been aware of. Three years earlier, Mater Dei senior Austin Van Ness was ranked #1 in the state but was

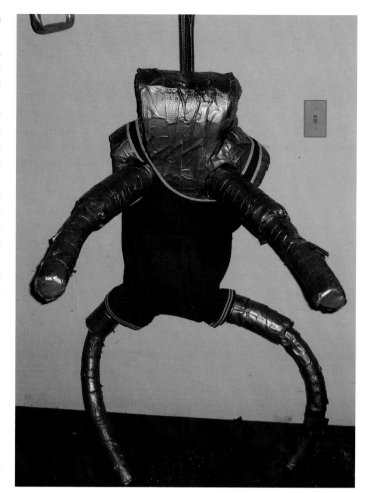

The contraption seen here was created by Kelly Maurer, Blake's father. Suspended by springs in the garage, the young wrestler practiced countless numbers of takedowns. Note the inscription: "Don't be outworked – Everyone is gunning for you – 4 times"

DID YOU KNOW?

During Blake's senior year, the track coach approached him and asked if he would be part of the 4x800 relay team. Blake had never run but knew that the others were strong. He joined Scott Koressel, Patrick McKinney and Andy Crock and proceeded to set a school record and qualify for the State meet.

upset by Bellmont freshman Nick Koons. Van Ness returned to Mater Dei to work with the younger wrestlers, and when the 1998 tournament draw found freshman Blake Maurer paired against senior Nick Koons, Van Ness used his embarrassing defeat as motivation. As the drama played out and the 15-year-old Maurer delivered the victory, he raised his arms and his eyes found his mentor in the stands to share the moment.

Maurer wrapped up his freshman season with a 3-2 decision over Nick Hobbs of Beech Grove to win his first State title in the 130-pound class, accomplishing the first stage of his lofty aspiration.

Fresh off a State title in football, Blake prepared for his sophomore wrestling season, and it didn't take long to bring him back to reality. Still carrying some weight from football, he wrestled at 152 for the first meet against Bloomington South. He faced a wrestler who had been a two-time state champ in Washington and lost in double overtime 4-4 on criteria. To illustrate the type of competitor he was, when the Wildcats were scheduled for a dual meet with Bloomington South later in the season, Blake was down to weight but had a request for his coach. "Do you care if I bump back up," he asked Coach Goebel. "I'd like to get a little revenge." And that's just what he did as he pulled out a 2-1 double OT victory.

IHSAA MAT FACTS

- *Four-time Champions*

  Estil Ritter – Bloomington – '24-'27 (175, 175, Hwt, Hwt)

  Willard Duffy – Muncie Central – '30-'33 (100, 108, 115, 115)

  Howard Fisher – South Bend Central – '49-'52 (95, 112, 127, 133)

  Lance Ellis – Indianapolis. Cathedral – '86-'89 (98, 112, 112, 119)

  Blake Maurer – Mater Dei – '01-'03 (130, 145, 171, 171)

  Alex Tsirtsis – Griffith – '01-'04 (119, 130, 135, 145)

  Angel Escobedo – Griffith – '02-'05 (112, 125, 130, 135)

- Although Mater Dei holds most of the IHSAA wrestling records, surprisingly, they do not have the most individual champs.

  66 – Bloomington (Bloomington South)
  27 – Hammond
  25 – Mater Dei
  25 – Southport
  (7 – Castle)
  (5 – Princeton)
  (4 – Central)
  (3 – Mt. Vernon)

- From 1944 – 1949, there was no IHSAA wrestling tournament due to lack of school participation

---

Returning to his new 145-pound weight class after the meet, Blake ran the table. He finished the year 43-1 and once again climbed to the top of the podium at Conseco Fieldhouse. What most fans didn't know, however, was the courage it took to complete the second leg of his journey. Maurer was not the type to toot his own horn, but the secret was revealed in a *Courier* article written by popular sportswriter Steve Ford. Ford had just witnessed Blake's 2-1 win over Nate Newport of Franklin Central. "I found him alone in the tunnel," Ford explained in his story. "He was bent over catching his breath, so I smacked him on the arm in congratulations and dropped him to his knees." Steve went on to tell how Blake had separated a shoulder and was "basically wrestling with one arm."

This tenacity served Blake well throughout his career, and his junior wrestling season was the setting for a feat that will likely never be accomplished again. Maurer finished the regular season with only one loss, to a wrestler in Ohio who took him down with two seconds left for a 3-1 win. Entering the State meet, Mater Dei had high hopes, but they couldn't have imagined what was about to take place.

In the eighth match under the lights, Mater Dei's Craig Weinzapfel scored a first period takedown and then hung on for a 4-1 decision over Lake Central's Justin Mora. At 152, Dustin Nosko then squeezed Yorktown's Brad Milius for a pin in 4:32. Next up was Sam Wildeman at 160, who felt some extra pressure. Not only had his two teammates just gone back-to-back, but his father, Chris Wildeman, had won a State title in 1981. But Sam came through with a pin at the 5:08 mark.

When Maurer stepped to the mat, the crowd was buzzing. He had dominated in earlier matches but was about to face undefeated Alex Dolly of Mishawaka. The match lived up to its billing as the two unbeatens battled, and when the horn blew, Blake had literally hung on by a shoelace to win 1-1 in overtime by criteria. With his win, Maurer and his three teammates pulled off the unthinkable, four consecutive State championships.

Blake finished his high school career with a 45-0 senior season, making his career record 187-2. With his credentials, he could have chosen one of many fine schools, but his mind had been made up long before. For years, Mike Goebel had tirelessly toiled to build his program into a juggernaut, and one of the steps he took was to host a camp for his wrestlers to learn from the staff at Ohio State. After several years at the camp, Blake's mind was made up and he became a Buckeye.

While wrestling at the high school nationals for free-style and Greco-Roman, Blake broke his neck after his senior season at Mater Dei and had to have surgery. Ohio State honored his scholarship, knowing the type of man he was, and red-shirted him for a year. The next year, he was in the starting lineup and was ranked 14th in the country, and the following year, he was 7-1 and ranked 8th when the neck problems re-surfaced, forcing him to retire.

Today, Blake has been a constant presence in Mater Dei's wrestling room, and his father has stated that he is becoming a better coach than he was a wrestler. Coach Goebel had recognized Maurer's potential years ago when he asked Blake to wrestle on and coach the 16-year-old freestyle team. "He was the head coach," Kelly Maurer revealed. "Mike Goebel gave him that responsibility. He's always taken a lead role."

Blake's coaching placed him in an unusual situation that his father found very interesting. Dane Maurer, Blake's brother who is eight years younger, had been a phenomenal football player for the Wildcats, quarterbacking them to the State Finals in 2011, and many assumed all along that he would wrestle like his brother. "When Dane was four years old, he was doing step-sliding (a common wrestling maneuver) before he was genuflecting (kneeling for prayer)," said Kelly Maurer with a smile on his face. "He went everywhere with Blake."

But Dane never had the same mindset as his older brother and perhaps felt the pressure of following one of Evansville's all-time greats. He chose instead to build a remarkable football career – until his senior year, that is. In a very unusual turn of events, Dane decided to return to the mat in 2011. Although he had pondered it before, he considered it in earnest after his final football game, telling his father, "Dad, if Blake will coach me, I'd like to wrestle."

Taking Dane at his word, Blake and good friend Matt Coughlin (a two-time State champ himself) went to work on Dane and "beat him up pretty good." Through the summer, Dane wrestled 29 matches with 28 first period pins and was ranked third in the state behind Mitch Sliga of Fishers and Courtney Berry of Merrillville.

As the season progressed, Kelly could see Dane develop under Blake's guidance. "Dane excels in the weight room more than Blake did," Kelly observed. "He was the strongest kid on the football team – even stronger than Cody Hess, who was an absolute animal. Dane made the 1,200 club (1,200 pounds on three lifts). He benched 300, squatted 475 and dead lifted 500 (for a 1,275). And Blake is in his corner and has him figured out. They work good together."

The combination was so good, in fact, that Dane finished the regular season a perfect 42-0 on his way to a third place finish at State.

Only time will tell where Blake's future will lead, and he and his father are quick to credit others for his success. As for Coach Goebel, Kelly Maurer says, "We owe him everything," and Kelly appreciates others as well. "Blake's been around so many good coaches," he said, "like Russ Hellickson from Ohio State."

And like any Mater Dei wrestler, Blake credits the culture Coach Goebel built. "It's a huge advantage, just having that 'MD' on your chest," he declared. "It intimidated a lot of kids. And when you hear that roar from the crowd, it's Mater Dei against the world out there."

More than anyone, Blake realizes how blessed he was to have parents who made sacrifices to help him and his brother. "My dad has been there every step, every place," Blake told Steve Ford for another *Courier* story. "He didn't have much wrestling experience but found those kids who did and put me in a position to succeed."

As for his mother, Blake gets emotional when speaking of her, not only because of her support, but for the courage she has shown over the years. "Mom's pretty sick," Blake told me. "She has Chronic Fatigue Syndrome. She's bed-ridden, very sick. The way she described it was, 'your worst flu times a hundred,' and that's how she feels every day. She's had it since she was 24, and she's 48 (in 2012). I just think she's very strong for getting up and being here every day. She always has a positive attitude."

Despite the fatigue and extreme migraines, Amy never let her afflictions prevent her from living life, and she admits that on trips she would have to find a bed to use between matches. "She always made it to the meets, but then she'd be out for a week," Blake confided. "We wouldn't see her all week at home because she'd be sleeping. She gave everything she had at the athletic events. For her to do that, it meant everything to me."

Blake raises his arms in victory as he looks into the stands at Curtis Van Ness. Van Ness had been upset as a senior by Bellmont freshman Nick Koons three years earlier, and Blake avenged the loss as a freshman when he upset Koons his senior year. (Photo courtesy of the Evansville Courier & Press)

Amy Maurer is a living example to her children, and when asked what keeps her going in the face of such pain, her answer is short and sweet: "You're there for your boys."

In an interesting twist of fate, Blake found a coaching opportunity at the place where it all began. In August of 2012, Chris Branam, the wrestling coach at Gibson Southern, was offered a job in his hometown and resigned. The first person called was Blake Maurer, and the administration was excited to name Blake as the head coach with long-time friend Matt Coughlin as his assistant. It will be intriguing to watch as Maurer, Coughlin and current Titan assistant Sean Whitten build the program and compete on the local scene, but regardless of the results, Blake's place in local history is secure.

In 2004, he was named an All-American by two governing bodies, and he secured 248 takedowns his senior year (a school record) while never being taken down himself. In 1995, he was the national Folkstyle champion at age 9 and finished third at the nationals in Freestyle. But what defined Blake Maurer's career the most is the distinction of being a four-time Indiana State champ. Unlike many local legends, he wasn't a phenom who used natural talent to dominate at a young age. Rather, he used a single-minded desire to surpass his wildest ambitions. Of the thousands who have toiled in wrestling rooms across the state, he achieved a feat that has been attained only seven times in the history of Indiana wrestling.

LESLIE VAN WINKLE:
BORN TO COMPETE

Leslie brought home the hardware at an early age.

Like any other teenage girl, Leslie VanWinkle spent her formative years learning to cope with the physical and emotional challenges that present themselves as young women grow into adulthood. And it was during those years at Benjamin Harrison High School in Evansville that she also learned that by channeling her emotions, she could elevate herself into elite status as an athlete and achieve goals she never thought possible.

Leslie's amazing story began when her maternal grandmother, Peg Poston, shared her aquatic knowledge with Leslie and her younger sister Jordan when they were mere tadpoles. It didn't take long for Peg to see Leslie's potential, and Peg quickly proclaimed, "She's got natural talent." In fact, by the time Leslie joined her hometown YMCA in Henderson and swam for Coach Jim Rogers, she was very skilled in all four strokes, (backstroke, breaststroke, butterfly and freestyle).

Jordan VanWinkle became an excellent swimmer in her own right, setting sectional and school records while at Castle and earning a full ride to the University of Toledo. But it was Leslie whose dedication and tenacity would propel her to stardom on a national level. After moving to Evansville, Leslie's parents, Bob and Debbie, witnessed their eldest daughter's ascension into the upper echelon of her sport and were there with her through every emotional moment.

"She always had a deep passion for swimming," Bob said from the family's current home on the west side of Newburgh. "She's always been a self-motivated, self-driven young lady." Bob and Debbie knew about the stellar reputation of the Newburgh Sea Creatures and were quick to enroll the girls. It was there that young Leslie met the third major influence on her swimming career. After some training from grandma and Jim Rogers, NSC coach Andy Haas stepped in and supervised workouts at the family's home near Plaza school.

Leslie began competing at age eight and was successful early on, even winning some statewide competitions, but it was a weekend in 2000 that changed the young swimmer's life. At the IU Natatorium in Indianapolis, 12-year-old Leslie dominated the meet by winning 4 of the 5 events she entered (she finished second in the other). After the same meet, her 200 freestyle relay team, featuring Megan Miller, Hadley May, Lauren Grimes and Leslie at anchor, was ranked #1 in the nation after setting a state record that stood for twelve years until it was broken by a team from Mt. Vernon in 2011.

Throughout the three-day event, skinny little Leslie VanWinkle climbed atop the medal stand, and each time her dreams became bigger. After the meet, she informed Bob and Debbie that she wanted to earn a college scholarship, and as she worked toward that goal, she let it be known that she would someday swim in the Olympic Trials.

Leslie's record-setting relay teammates dropped out of the sport at various levels, but Ms. VanWinkle had larger worlds to conquer when she walked through the doors at Harrison in 2001. Although she was a natural athlete, running track at Plaza and even showing promise as a golfer, Leslie entered high school totally focused on swimming.

As a freshman, she trained under Harrison coach Jody Fulkerson, sharing the Lloyd Pool facilities with athletes from the other Evansville schools. She also worked out privately at Tri-State Athletic Club, logging mile after mile with only her father looking on after the 5:00 a.m. drive. As the high school season began, no one in the VanWinkle camp knew what to expect, but by season's end, Leslie's long hours in the pool would pay off in a big way.

With perennial powerhouses like Carmel dominating Indiana swimming every year, local swimmers dare not dream of a State title, but 15-year-old Leslie VanWinkle shocked the world by finishing sixth in the 50-yard freestyle and then touching the wall ahead of all others in the 100-yard breaststroke. After a brief but well-deserved break, Evansville's newest State champion began her year-round training regimen with visions of bigger and better things, but what lay ahead for young Leslie were heartbreak and disappointment.

The following year, Erin Jankowski assumed the head coaching position at Harrison, and a valuable bond was forged between athlete and coach. Jankowski had been an excellent swimmer at Ball State and had swum in the 2000 Olympic Trials. As Leslie's drama played out during the spring and summer of 2002, the defending State champ found herself facing a challenge that neither she nor Coach Jankowski had seen coming. In all sports, especially at the high school level, there is often more to the story than what the casual fan reads in the paper or sees in the arena. We don't often think about the realities of life, that there are other forces at work during an athlete's quest for success. In Leslie's case, her sophomore challenges were biological, as Mother Nature worked her magic on the young adolescent. The wiry but reed-thin young lady suddenly found her body maturing, and the changes wreaked havoc in the pool. "She gained 20 pounds," said Debbie VanWinkle. "Her stroke was totally off."

"It was a bad year," Bob VanWinkle added. "The breaststroke is a stroke of technique, and with her body changes, her timing and technique were off."

Leslie looks back on the transformation realistically and with a philosophical approach. "It was especially tough because I was a breaststroker," she recalled. "It's a gliding stroke, and I went from no hips to hips, and it changes your buoyancy a lot. My timing was off; my rhythm was off. I felt very off in the water.

"Swimming was my passion. Girls become teenagers, and you go through personal things. Your body changes. I couldn't come home anymore and eat a whole row or Oreos because it was going to affect my body differently that it did before."

Needless to say, the '02-'03 season was an eye-opener for the VanWinkles as Leslie dropped from first to 18th at the State meet. For many young athletes, the situation would have been an excuse to quit, but Leslie would not only conquer her physical challenge, but another emotional one as well.

As her junior year approached, Leslie had begun to re-capture her stroke, but another aspect of high school life presented another obstacle. "I experienced my first love," Leslie lamented, "and I got my heart broken."

As is the case with any teenager trying to find the way, Leslie was fortunate to have a strong support system in place. In addition to the steady guidance of Bob and Debbie, Leslie sought help from Coach Jankowski. "We had the same passion for swimming," Leslie explained. "She worked and talked with me a lot."

With her heart aching, Leslie turned to one of the constants in her life, and the revelation provided the foundation for the rest of her life. She realized that her life had become too social and that she had become de-focused.

"I threw myself back into swimming," she said. "I started to push myself so hard because I was angry, to be honest. I was hurting, and swimming became my best friend. When things were going on in my life, I could always get in the water and swim. I

would push myself out of hurt. I liked feeling that pain, not being able to breathe and my muscles burning. It made me feel better."

Leslie's decision to re-dedicate herself enabled her to re-establish her status as one of Indiana's finest. With her new body, now packed with solid muscle, she finished third in the 100 free and second in the 200 IM (individual medley) in the 2004 and 2005 IHSAA meets. In both cases, she lost close races to strong swimmers: Carmel's Erin Sparks in '04 and eventual four-time champ Michelle McKeehan of Center Grove in '05. With her passion rejuvenated, it was now time for Ms. VanWinkle to push her body to the max at the next level.

After a tumultuous yet productive high school career, the VanWinkles carefully assessed Leslie's choices. They began with 30 potential schools from as far away as Florida and Michigan and quickly narrowed the choices to a manageable dozen or so. After eight visits, the choice became evident, and Bob VanWinkle feels that the stars aligned for his daughter as the process unfolded.

"It was hands down the University of Louisville," Bob revealed, "and one of the big reasons was Louisville was moving to the Big East the year Leslie was going to be a freshman. Also, two years before, they hired a coach, Arthur Albiero, and they connected. He has been her mentor in life and swimming. Leslie thought he could help her reach her goals better than any other coach."

Whether or not celestial factors were at play is debatable, but one aspect about which there is no doubt is that the recruiting process involved the most memorable moment in Coach Albiero's career. As the story goes, the coach came over to watch a meet and then planned to visit the VanWinkles for a home-cooked meal, but as the evening developed, plans changed rapidly. On the way from the event to the VanWinkles' home, one of southwestern Indiana's infamous storms blew in and locals were hunkering down in preparation.

As Coach Albiero pulled into the driveway, he was greeted with a handshake and the words "Hi, I'm Bob" and then rushed inside. The coach's first heart-to-heart with the VanWinkle family was in a dark house sitting in a closet by candlelight, and the irony of the moment wasn't lost on the coach.

"That was quite something," Coach Albiero stated after laughing quietly at my question. "It was definitely one of the most interesting recruiting trips I've had. We had pizza by candlelight as I showed them plans for our new facility. We certainly got to know each other on a different level that day."

The new facility about which the coach spoke was the Ralph R. Wright Natatorium, a 41,000-square foot arena that would play a role in Leslie VanWinkle's development into one of the most decorated swimmers in U of L history.

Although Leslie had always shown a fanatical approach to training, her college experience took her to new extremes. She spent six hours a day in the water, three in the morning and three in the afternoon, in addition to her classroom responsibilities and running and hitting the weight room on alternate days. Early in the year, she would log 9,000 yards per day, and as the season progressed, she would peak to 18,000, the equivalent of over ten miles per day.

Under the guidance of the coaching staff, Leslie's body was at a world-class level, and her results were immediate. As a freshman, she won the Big East 200 IM championship, setting a school record in the process . She also set a lifetime best on the first leg of the 800 free relay and scored team points with a fourth in the 200 free and a tenth in the 200 breast. During the year, she set lifetime bests in the 400 IM and the 50 free as well.

In '06-'07, Leslie made the Olympic Trials qualifying time in the 200 IM at the National Championships and set school records in the 200 IM and 400 IM as a sophomore. She also scored big points for the Cardinals as the runner-up in both IM races and was a U.S. Open participant also.

Leslie's junior season ('07-'08) was her breakout year. At the 2008 Olympic Trials, she attempted to qualify in three events, the 200 and 400 IM and the 100 free. She laid siege to the U of L record books during the Big East meet setting school records as she won the 200 back, 200 IM and 400 IM events. She also contributed as a member of the All-Conference and school record-setting 200 free and 400 free relays and 800 free relay team that won the Big East title. In addition, Leslie became the first female swimmer to make the NCAA championships, representing the U of L in three events, the 200 back, 200 free and 200 IM. To cap off her remarkable year, she was honored as U of L's finest female athlete and the 2008 Big East Conference Swimmer of the Year.

Leslie's years at Louisville were memorable for everyone involved. Her father recalls the butterflies in his stomach while watching his daughter as she swam in the Big East finals her freshman year. Bob was so distraught that he couldn't watch, and as he heard the race ending, he turned to a fan from Rutgers and said, "Please tell me she got third," only to have the man slap him on the back and proclaim, "Third hell. She just won it!"

Bob also recalls Leslie's senior year when a girl nearly broke 2:00 in the prelims of the 200 IM and the crowd erupted. Knowing that Leslie's record was 1:59, he looked down at Leslie, only to see her look back expressionless. He then remembers his daughter slicing through the water in her heat and hearing the crowd exploding even louder as the clock showed 1:57 as his daughter shot him a glance and a smiled.

Leslie looks back at her U of L years as some of the best of her life. First and foremost, she met her husband there in April of 2009. Ironically, she fell in love with another local athlete who made a name for himself as well. Neil Angermeier was an accomplished star in basketball and track at Gibson Southern who finished second at State in the high jump in 2007 and was the Big East indoor champion at 7'2 ½.

Leslie also feels fortunate to have competed under Coach Albiero. "He made me believe in myself," Leslie said. "He and his wife (Amy, who coached a club team that Leslie helped with) were not just coaches to me; they were like parents and mentors. Arthur genuinely cares about every kid on his teams as a person. His door was always open. They both (Arthur and his wife) taught me how to be a better person.

Perhaps as much as anyone, Coach Albiero appreciates what Leslie accomplished and the sacrifices she made along the way. "She had lofty goals, and she boldly went after them," he said from his office in the natatorium. "From a personality standpoint, at times, she was so driven that she even drove her friends out of the way. But she was the one you wanted on the end of a relay. She was clearly on a whole different level.

"She was one of our pioneers. She helped us put the program where it had never been before. She was one of the first NCAA qualifiers, and that's not something to be taken lightly. It's extremely difficult to qualify for the NCAAs. She was the first one. Now, it's expected; it's the new norm. She helped us create that."

Leslie herself appreciates the journey she's taken and realizes that to reach exceptional goals takes exceptional dedication. "I probably lost some friendships," Leslie admitted. "You get competitive in practice, and I'm sure some people got more mad at me than they wanted because I was always racing. The fact is, I hate to lose.

"When the other swimmers would go out on weekends, I would stay in and go to bed. If they went to get ice cream, I wasn't going with them because that's a big temptation and that wasn't something I wanted to put in my body. My mindset was 'swim-swim-swim' and not everybody wants to do that."

Leslie VanWinkle has come a long way from the day when she was a skinny little girl swimming laps alone at the Club in the wee hours of the morning. She admits that there were times when "the water was very cold and I would rather have played with my neighborhood friends." But Leslie values her mother's persistence and the constant support of her father.

As a junior swimmer, Leslie was a national qualifier in 2002, '04, '05 and '06 and was at one time ranked #12 in the nation. In high school, she was All-Conference 13 times, a three-time All-Stater, a five-time All-American and four-time MVP for the Lady Warriors. In addition to her State title in 2002, Leslie's name appears on the wall at Harrison gym (as of 2012) as the record holder for EVERY swimming event for the Harrison program.

As a collegian, Leslie was a Big East champ multiple times and, at one time, held seven school records. To say the young lady was merely a competitor would be a gross understatement. "I don't like to be bad at anything," Leslie confirms. "I think that's why I was an IM-er. I wanted to be better than everybody in everything."

Her coach goes even farther. "I consider her the greatest IM-er in the history of the Big East," Coach Albiero stated emphatically. "She was by far, in my career (almost 20 years), very possibly THE toughest female I've ever met in terms of mental toughness. You knew she was going to leave it in the pool and battle to the end."

One thing is certain; Leslie VanWinkle Angermeier will never just sit back and watch as life passes her by. Today she works as a fitness trainer (appropriately, she can be reached at *leslie@thenextlegend.com*) and has already achieved success in

As you can see from this photo, fitness is a passion of Leslie's, so much so, in fact, that she is contemplating becoming a professional triathlete.

triathlons. She has done so well, in fact, that she was been approached to turn professional. One aspiration still in her crosshairs is qualifying as a triathlete in the 2012 Olympic Trials, which she thinks would be "kind of cool" to do so in two different sports.

When asked why she continues to drive herself, Leslie answers simply, "I have to keep racing," and if her mind is set on the Olympic Trials, my money is on Leslie.

As of 2012, Leslie still owned the record at Harrison for every distance.

IHSAA STATE CHAMPIONS UPDATE

SWIMMING

Individual	School	Year	Event	Time
Keanu Stevenson	Castle	2011	100 breaststroke	54.92

IHSAA STATE CHAMPIONS UPDATE

BOY'S SOCCER

School	Year	Record	Coach
Memorial	2008	23-0-2	Bill Vieth Jr.

GIRL'S SOCCER

School	Year	Record	Coach
Memorial	2008	22-2	Angie Lensing

CHAPTER SEVEN
A FAMILY AFFAIR

THE WELCH BROTHERS: CASTLE'S TRIPLE THREAT

From the time they were very young, the sons of Curt and Dawn Welch loved to wrestle, and as they grew, the fun became a passion that has shaped their futures and placed the boys among the elite wrestlers in local history.

Curt and Dawn grew up in Boonville, and while Dawn displayed her musical talents in the band and choir, Curt competed for the school's baseball and wrestling teams. A 1983 Boonville grad, Curt grew up watching local stars like Don Mattingly at Memorial and Dan Labhart, who was a few years ahead at Boonville, but Curt never fulfilled his full potential because of a serious leg injury in high school. He was good enough on the mat, however, to defeat the #1-ranked wrestler in the nation in the regional but admits that he was not in the same class as his sons.

The oldest of the Welch children, Courtney, followed in her mother's footsteps as a member of Castle's show choir, and the boys became athletes like their father. They tried several sports and were still playing basketball and football as late as middle school, and although wrestling has been their primary focus, Curt has always encouraged them to stay diversified.

"I think if they concentrate twelve months a year (on one sport), they lose that drive," Curt told me as we sat with his youngest son at Curt's office as the head baseball coach near Castle's baseball field. "They need to play multiple sports and support the school, but it also gives them the drive for the sport they love. By taking a little time off (from their primary sport), you can see a little bounce in their step."

The older boys, twins Doug and Chad, were rolling around with each other since the age of three, and Curt "could just tell" that there was some serious potential there. For eleven years, Curt was Bob Harmon's assistant wrestling coach at Castle, and the twins began observing wrestling practices at age five or so. When the boys got really serious about the sport, Curt stepped down as Harmon's assistant so that he and Dawn could travel with the boys to tournaments.

As the boys progressed, they steadily improved in what many believe to be the most physically challenging of all high school sports. Wrestling is so demanding because each wrestler is not only challenged by other athletes but by other physical factors as well, not the least of which is maintaining or cutting weight, something Curt Welch kept a close eye on.

As a former high school and college wrestler (Indiana Central, now the University of Indianapolis), Curt has seen the extremes that wrestlers would go through to shed pounds, and he is not an advocate of losing weight at all costs. "I wouldn't let the boys cut weight until they got to high school," he revealed. "They ate three meals a day but they would cut down on portions and do extra workouts. Their senior year they didn't cut at all."

Trailing two years behind the twins is Luke Welch, and all three have thrived under the tutelage of long-time Castle coach Bob Harmon. In his 31-year career (as of 2011), including 28 at Castle, Bob has won over 76% of his dual meets and has coached 7 State champs and 4 high school All-Americans. He has built a proud program in Paradise and has put a significant dent in the armor of perennial powerhouse Mater Dei over the years. "Coach Harmon's a competitor, and in wrestling, that's what you need," said Curt Welch. "If you can't handle giving up a takedown or a guy getting ahead of you, you're going to have trouble wrestling. He's intense, and his philosophy really helped the boys get tougher mentally."

"I love Coach Harmon," Luke added, admitting that he was intimidated by Harmon early on. "He pushes me like my brothers did."

Like most younger brothers, Luke had to be tough to be accepted by his brothers, and he vividly remembers the influence they had on him many years ago. "When we were little, I remember in junior high, Mom and Dad would be gone and Doug and Chad would start wrestling and I would watch," Luke recalled. "I got to where if one got a certain grip, I knew they were going to shoot for a takedown."

Often the scuffles led to an argument over which of the two was better, and the verbal exchanges quietly affected little brother. "I would tell myself, 'I'm probably going to be in this argument one of these days.' I wanted to push myself to be better than them."

How the hierarchy will finally shake out is still up in the air, but one thing is certain: as high school wrestlers, the Welch boys have done themselves proud. Wrestling from 2008 until 2011, the twins battled local wrestlers each year as they set their sights on State. Their most consistent competitor was John Sims of Mater Dei, a wrestler they faced nearly twenty times between them. Doug wrestled Sims as a freshman and junior, while Chad faced

Chad, Doug and Luke 1998

Twins Chad and Doug Welch

Luke Welch is the youngest of the brothers.

him in his weight class as a sophomore and senior. Sims placed at State (top 8) all four years, and the Welch boys didn't do too badly themselves.

Doug was a three-time SIAC champ ('09, '10, '11), while Chad won the conference twice ('10, '11), and both boys won four sectionals ('08-'11). Chad was a three-time regional champ ('08, '10, '11), one better than Doug's two ('10, '11), and both won the semi-state in 2010 and 2011. Most impressive was their ability to qualify for the State competition, with Doug qualifying his last three years and Chad all four. In 2009, Doug placed 5th, and the following year he was the runner-up with Chad placing third in his weight class. 2010 also saw the twins honored as All-Americans when Chad finished 7-0 and Doug 6-1 at the Scholastic Duals.

The twins' final season, 2010-'11, was a special year indeed for the Welch family, as Luke joined his brothers as a State qualifier, finishing 5th at 120 while Doug and Chad climbed to the very top of the award platform as State champions, Doug at 152 and Chad at 160. Continuing after their high school season was over, Chad and Doug distinguished themselves even more, as they were both named high school All-Americans for the second time, with Doug finishing 8th nationally at 145 and Chad winning the national championship at 152. At the Senior Nationals, Chad finished first and ended the year ranked 16th in the country. Doug was not ranked but lost 4-3 to the second-ranked wrestler in America, Jason Green, an All-American as a true freshman at Nebraska. In the next match, he got choked out (nearly out cold) and also blew out an elbow (the type that requires Tommy John surgery). Down 5-0, the doctor let Doug resume and he came back and won with one arm and then won two more matches after that.

After the amazing 2011 season, Chad and Doug prepared for the next phase of their careers. Curt had told the boys to list the schools they might want to attend and had contacted those colleges, but when Chad and Doug visited Purdue, the decision was made.

It didn't take long for the boys to discover that the progression from high school to college can be very intimidating, and not everyone is able to withstand the challenge. "Everybody's a State champ," Curt Welch stated. "In high school, Doug and Chad had each other to push them, but most of the good ones never got taken down in practice or gave up points. In college, you're always getting taken down. It's tough on your ego when you start out."

As the college season started, Chad actually won the wrestle-off in his weight class and Doug was very close, but the coach chose to red-shirt the boys because of their potential. As red-shirts, Doug and Chad had to cover their own expenses and entry fees for meets, but the experiences prepared them for four good years at Purdue. For the 2011-'12 season, they both wrestled open tournaments all year, many times against varsity wrestlers or graduates. Chad wrestled University of Wisconsin All-American Ben Jordan at 165, and lost 3-2 at the Midlands tournament, one of the biggest of the year. Chad also lost a close one to a Purdue grad who had been an All-American.

Chad finished the year at 38-10, won two tournaments and placed (6th or better) in every tournament except one. Doug won one tournament and finished 21-7. In Doug's second match of the season, he was head-butted and lost a tooth, an injury that caused him to miss six weeks.

Curt and Dawn saw many of the boys' matches, often watching Luke at a Saturday high school meet then driving all night to watch Chad and Doug on Sunday before another long drive back Sunday night. Curt says that Dawn is the boys' biggest fan and has learned the sport over the years, and as he watched the two oldest compete as collegians, he has seen dramatic improvement. "Early in the year, they were frustrated in the wrestling room," Curt admitted. "It was good to get that first year under their belt. Late in the year, you could see the difference, because they were taking kids down, and they were beating kids who were beating them early in the year."

The boys plan to start as red-shirt freshman next year as they continue their schooling, Doug with a major in Education and Chad in Criminal Justice. Meanwhile, little brother will continue to build his legacy at Castle. Luke has finished 5th at State his first two years and has bigger plans for the future. Like his brothers, he has already shown toughness while dealing with some adversity of his own. "He has asthma," explained his father. "His lung capacity has been about 70%, and this year (2011-'12), he got up to almost 90%, though he is still vulnerable to weather and a high pollen count."

Luke loves working with his dad and has learned valuable lessons during his young career about the intricacies of his favorite sport. Chad and Doug couldn't be interviewed because of NCAA restrictions, but Luke's words and emotions probably speak for them as well. "I love wrestling," he said, "because it's just me out there. If I lose, I know it's on me and I can't blame anyone else."

Luke also knows the mental toughness it takes and has seen examples close up and personal. "You can have the greatest talent in the world, but if your head's not on straight, you can get beat. I remember when Doug passed out from training and I thought, 'If he can work that hard as a freshman, I can work that hard as a junior.'"

Coach Harmon and the Knights have had some excellent results during the Welch years, and Harmon gives some of the credit to several good wrestlers who challenged the twins in practice, like Preston Richards, Andrew Pettijohn, Cory Weikel and the Seitz cousins, Andrew and Phillip. Harmon also appreciates the work the boys put in, as well, saying, "I've known the twins since the day they were born. They're hard workers. They didn't win everything at the beginning, but they just kept working."

With all their similarities, their father can also see what makes them individuals. Interestingly, Chad was born one pound heavier than Doug and has always wrestled one class heavier. Curt also says that Chad is more outgoing while Doug is shyer and Luke is somewhere in between. There are also differences on the mat. The twins have always preferred to turn their opponents for the pin while Luke would rather wrestle on his feet, choosing to take his opponent down, let him up and take him down again to rack up points.

But one thing is certain for all the boys: they have emblazoned their names all over the Castle record book and earned their places among the program's finest. As of 2012, in their 11 combined seasons in high school, they have qualified for State 10 times (placing in 7 of the 10). Chad qualified 4 times, making him the only Castle wrestler to do so, and he and Doug join Matt Deters (103 in '94), Thad Oldham (142 in '95 and 145 in '96), Pat Mayes (215 in '95) and Caleb Schmitt (135 in '07) as Castle State champs.

Doug ranks first at Castle in career points scored for the team (1,105) with Chad second (1,090) and Luke 16th (654.5) with a year to go. The boys also rank #1 (Doug – 183-11), #2 (Chad – 177-14) and #6 (Luke – 130-14) in career wins. The twins trail only Pat Mayes (89) in career pins, with Doug producing 88 and Chad 78, and to cap things off, the boys hold 6 of the top 12 best records for a season, with Chad's 50-0 in 2010-'11 leading the way.

As Luke finishes his senior year in 2012-'13, he is already in touch with Purdue and IU, among others, but regardless of how he and his brothers fare in the world of college wrestling, their feats as a family will be recognized in the annals of IHSAA wrestling. In 2011, Doug and Chad joined only David and Daniel Mudd (1963, Hammond High) as the only twins to win State titles. In addition, the 2011 State Finals also gave the Welch family another distinction that will be re-lived by the family for years to come. To the best of anyone's knowledge, the only family in Indiana wrestling history to have three brothers qualify for the State tournament in the same year is Castle's Welch family, with brothers Doug, Chad and Luke.

MAX & GRACIE LACHOWECKI: SUPER SIBLINGS

When it comes to local soccer, few would argue that the Vieth family, Bill Sr. and his sons Bill Jr. and Tim have been major influences on the sport. But also near the top of that list would be the Lachoweckis (pronounced LACK•uh•WEHK•eez), father AJ and his two children, Max and Gracie.

Anthony John (AJ) Lachowecki grew up in Evansville and was a teenager when soccer was in its infancy on the local scene. Like most his age, he looked at soccer as a bit of a novelty, but he picked up the game quickly in the youth league started by Bill Vieth Sr. As a sophomore at Memorial, AJ played on the school's very first soccer team in 1977 under Vieth, but scheduling was limited to only a few games against opponents like New Albany (twice) and schools in St. Louis.

In 1978, the Evansville schools began soccer as a club sport, and in AJ's senior year, 1979, Memorial won its first state championship with players like Greg and Mark Riedford, Jim Short and Bill Vieth Jr. AJ played stopper for Coach Vieth at Memorial, but he had fooled around a few times as a goalkeeper, and when he walked on at U of E, he saw an opportunity.

UE coach Fred Schmalz had taken over the program when Vieth Sr. left to initiate the program at Memorial, and Fred had great respect for Bill. Unlike today's sophisticated soccer world where proposing such a change would be snickered at, local soccer was so young that Vieth was able to convince Schmalz to develop Lachowecki as a goalkeeper.

By his junior year, AJ was a starter and was good enough to help send UE to its first NCAA tournament, where they won their first round game before losing to Jerry Yeagley's IU squad. During his years at UE, AJ was named the team's MVP, earned All-Conference

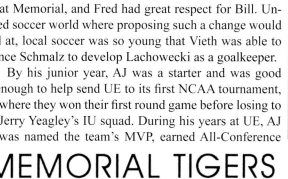

MEMORIAL TIGERS

honors and, most importantly, met a lovely young lady named Kay who had played tennis for her high school in Nashville.

After graduation, AJ was drafted by the Pittsburgh Spirit of the MISL (Major Indoor Soccer League), a team owned by the DeBartolos who owned the NFL's 49ers and the NHL's Penguins. AJ was also the starting goalkeeper for the United States National Futbol team, the country's first indoor national team that played in the first FIFA Indoor World Cup in the Netherlands in 1989. During that time, he became the first American goalkeeper to score a goal in an FIFA-sanctioned event. He then spent two years with the LA Lasers, staying in touch with Kay each off-season. The couple married in 1989, and after two years with the Atlanta Attack, AJ realized that it was time to get a 'real job' and settle down with a family.

In 1992, AJ and Kay welcomed Maxwell Anthony into the world, and the diminutive dynamo would thrive in the advanced environment of the area's soccer culture. Still playing soccer as a club sport under the auspices of the IHSSA (Indiana High School Soccer Association), Memorial had captured five state titles ('79, '80, '81, '83, '84) before Bill Vieth Jr. took over the program in 1986. Vieth Jr. then led the Tigers to four more IHSSA championships ('88, '89, '90, '92) before soccer was finally adopted as an IHSAA sport. The Tigers won the first IHSAA championship in 1994, and by the time Max arrived, the school had already produced seven high school All Americans: Bill Vieth ('80&'81); Jack Mitchell ('82); Mike Traylor ('84); Scott Cannon ('85); Tim Vieth ('87&'88); Paul Barton ('91); and Mitch Day ('07).

In his early years, Max kept busy with several sports, playing little league baseball, football through the 7th grade and basketball through his freshman year. But with his size limitations (5'9, 150 pounds as a senior) and his exposure to soccer through his father, it was a given that the sport was his ticket to a college education and possibly a professional career. With those goals in mind, Max played soccer virtually year-round, and after his high school season, he would begin training with his club team in hopes of catching the eye of college coaches.

"You could see he had the ability to do something in college," said his father from the family's home on Evansville east side. Because of the potential, Max took every opportunity to showcase his talents, working with Olympic development teams and national teams, like the U-15 team that played in Argentina. He also won two state championships with his Futbol Club of Evansville teams in 2009 and 2010 with teammates like Drew Schall, Tyler Vieth, Eric Teppen and Mitch McCord.

Max entered Memorial in 2007 and promptly won two IHSAA State titles ('07&'08) with teammates that included Mitch Day, Kyle Kessler, Trev Wilgus and Austin King. The '07 team was arguably the finest in school history, finishing the season undefeated (23-0-2), winning the school's first IHSAA State title and earning a #1 national ranking. The Tigers did not capture the State crown again, however, falling to Columbus North in the semi-state in '09 and to Lake Central in the Final Four in 2010. A four-year starter, Max piled up the accolades as a three-time first team All-Stater and two-time *Courier* Metro Player of the Year. To top it off, Lachowecki was named an All-American by the National Soccer Coaches Association of America. Max led his team in scoring his final three seasons, and he scored 195 points for his career (79 goals and 37 assists), the third-highest point total in school history. His talents did not go unappreciated by his coach, a man who has seen his share of All-Americans. "Max was a tremendous high school player," said Bill Vieth. "He had great athletic ability and great instincts, and neither of those can be taught. What separated him from the rest was that he had those things plus he worked incredibly hard."

"It's sure a nice way to get sent off to the next level," Max told *Courier* journalist Steve Ford, and the 'next level' he spoke of was his college choice. After building a strong resumé by leading his four Memorial teams to a composite record of 81-8-7, Max had no shortage of college offers. As a 5.5 student (on a 6.0 scale), Lachowecki considered a number of fine schools and visited Butler, Tulsa, Northwestern, Kentucky and Notre Dame, and when the dust settled, the Irish won the prize.

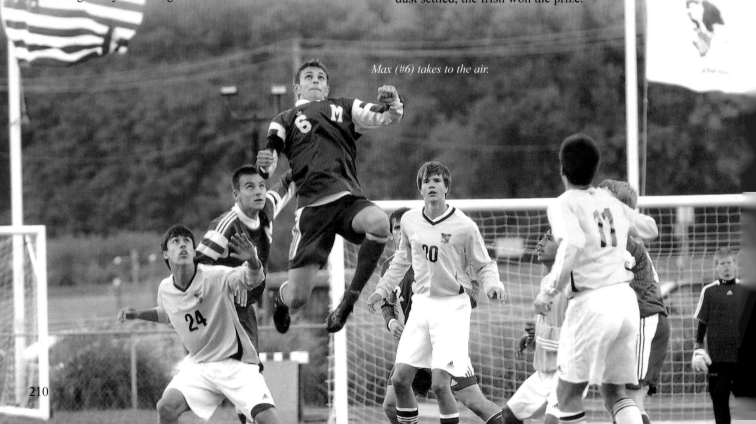

Max (#6) takes to the air.

While Max was pounding the pitch and learning the game as a youngster, his pretty little sister was watching his every move, and as she grew, she staked her own claim to a spot in the annals of Memorial's soccer history. Mary Gracen Lachowecki was named for Kay Lachowecki's Aunt Gracen, and the precocious girl began kicking the ball in the backyard at age three. One of her early club teams, the U-8 Orange Crush, featured several future classmates at Memorial, including Maddie Riedford, Claire Ehrensbeck and Claire Church, and as she was approaching her teens, Gracie was facing some serious competition.

Gracie's SWISA (Southwestern Indiana Soccer Association) teams finished as the state runner-up three consecutive years, losing to Carmel each year, and as she looked forward to high school, the girls program at Memorial was making some noise of its own on the state level. While Gracie was in the 8th grade, the Lady Tigers captured the State championship, and her freshman year, she teamed with Sarah Stone, Haley Meyer, Emily Hayden, Courtney Deem, Katie Loehr and others to begin building a legacy of their own.

Gracie admits that when she was young, she lacked eye-hand coordination, but she found her comfort level by using her feet. "She's just a good goal scorer," said her father. "She is a good finisher with both feet." Those feet have been instrumental in the young lady's incredible success, and on a Region II team that traveled to Holland representing 14 midwestern states, Gracie was the only Hoosier on the 18-player team. Some may argue that the youngest Lachowecki is not the best player in Indiana, but don't try to sell that to those who have watched her develop. Although her Memorial teams have yet to duplicate the State title of 2008, they have come close. In '09, the Lady Tigers finished 23-3 and advanced to the State Finals before falling 1-0 to Ft. Wayne Snider. Her sophomore year, Gracie joined fellow All-Metro first teamers Alex Kixmiller and Sarah Stone in leading Memorial to a 15-1-2 season that ended with a disappointing loss to Castle in the sectional. That was followed by a 16-1-4 junior season that saw the Tigers fall 3-2 in the semi-state to their nemesis Carmel. But who knows how it may have turned out if not for a serious injury Gracie suffered in 2011.

At a Friday night game in Zionsville, Gracie went down hard. "I was taking a shot but slid to get there because someone was coming from the side," Gracie explained. "Somehow my foot got caught. They thought I broke my fibula (a bone in the lower leg)." X-rays revealed no break and no torn ligaments, but the high ankle sprain and stretched ligaments required extensive work with therapist Pat Wempe. For five weeks, Pat worked with Gracie, and after missing seven games, Gracie returned to play with her ankle heavily-taped and enveloped in a heavy-duty ankle brace.

Gracie has one more chance in 2012 to raise the State champion trophy, and without question, that will be a primary goal for the season. But regardless how the season turns out, Gracie's career will have been a success. Despite her injury, she was again named the *Courier*'s Metro Player of the Year, joining teammates Lisa Murphy, Mackenzie Reynolds and Meghan Day on the All-Metro team with Memorial's Angie Lensing named the Coach of the Year.

Playing from the forward position, Gracie led the city in scoring all three years, scoring 22 goals and 15 assists her freshman year, 24 and 14 her sophomore year and 26 and 8 as a junior in spite of the seven games missed. To the best of our knowledge, her 181 points (2 per goal and 1 per assist) is already a Memorial career record, and when she leaves the program after the 2012 season, the record book will have her name all over it.

Gracie had great concentration even at age 10.

"Gracie Lachowecki is a very special and unique athlete, and it makes me smile thinking of her because I can remember her at our youth camp as a second grader," said Coach Lensing. "She is more than a talented technical soccer player. Gracie has a gift for creating offensive opportunities out of very little. She has the ability to make everyone around her better. She works extremely hard on the field and will willingly do whatever it takes to help her team. Her commitment, discipline and attitude are a direct reflection of the young lady she is on and off the field."

As one could imagine, Gracie was courted by several college programs and eventually chose the University of Miami over Dayton and several others, including Notre Dame where Max went. With her 5.9 GPA (out of six), she should have little problem pursuing a degree in Nursing, and if all goes as planned, she will make a dramatic impact on the Hurricane's soccer program.

When Gracie graduates in 2013, the Lachowecki era at Memorial will be over, and the local soccer landscape will have been greatly enhanced by the family's presence. Although their sport is still relatively new, the local athletes who toil on the pitch have represented our area well, and while southwestern Indiana has seen its share of super siblings, very few brother-sister combinations can match the achievements of Memorial's Max and Gracie Lachowecki.

THE MCINTOSH BOYS:
ALL THE CLICHÉS AND MORE

A few minutes spent with Tim and Lori McIntosh is all it takes to find out that the McIntosh family is just as thrilled to be part of the Reitz football program as the program is to have the McIntosh boys as part of the Reitz football family. And in the storied history of the proud program, it could be argued that no family has had a greater impact on Reitz football than the McIntosh brothers, Paul, Ryan and Matt.

The signs of athleticism were evident very early in the McIntosh home, and much of their growth took place literally in the family's backyard. Paul, the oldest, showed skills and a fearless attitude on the mini-trampoline, while Ryan, a year younger, was a natural at hitting and throwing a baseball and Matt, the youngest by two years, rode a bicycle the very first time he tried.

As the boys grew, many an hour was spent playing games in the yard, either with dad or just the three of them, and strong bonds were formed between the brothers. Tim McIntosh recalled days when he would smack tennis balls into the stratosphere with a racquet and watch each boy track it down and catch it. Then there were days when the three boys would run patterns while alternating as the quarterback, receiver and defensive back.

Like many of our local legends, the boys' abilities came naturally, but their roots stretch northward and to the west. Tim was an athlete from Inver Grove, Minnesota who played junior college football for Randy Rodgers, and when Rodgers took the job at U of E, Tim followed him to Evansville. After his graduation, he attended grad school in Wyoming and served as a grad assistant in football. While there, he met a lovely young lady working for the athletic department, and the two hit it off and eventually married.

Lori was a fine athlete herself as a star in three sports in Pine Bluff, Wyoming. With a graduating class of only thirty, Lori led her school to two state titles in volleyball and one in basketball as she averaged 18 points. In track, she was even more impressive winning 5 championships in the hurdles, long jump and 200-meter dash and setting state records in the long jump (17'5) and 75-meter hurdles (11.6).

After grad school, the couple lived in Minnesota for a year and Florida for a year and a half where Tim coached and taught and Lori was a dental assistant. In 1988, Tim worked in Tell City for Pat Malone, who later became the A.D. at Harrison, and from 1990 through 1993, he was the head football coach at Gibson Southern followed by six years at South Spencer. In 2000, he was hired as the athletic director at Reitz, and although he has since become the principal at Helfrich Park Middle School, the entire family has become immersed in the culture of the Reitz Football Nation.

Tim credits much of the boys' success to the early training they received from coaches at the west side junior football league. "The little league (football) program here is tremendous," Tim said, "with Randy Babb, Chuck Brunson, Brock Babb (now deceased), the Weinzapfels, Kelly and Dane Maurer and lots of others." Paul went on to explain how the program is mostly a feeder league for Reitz and Mater Dei but that folks also come from the east side, Gibson County and even southern Illinois.

Paul McIntosh entered Reitz in 2004, followed a year later by Ryan. Paul started as a varsity cornerback as a freshman and then took over the quarterback duties as a sophomore for coach John Hart. Hart had replaced Bob Gaddis in 2001 and immediately led the Panthers to solid seasons of 10-4, 10-2 and 12-1. In 2005, Paul's first season under center, the Panthers finished 11-2 and won City, SIAC and sectional titles, and in '06, Reitz won the

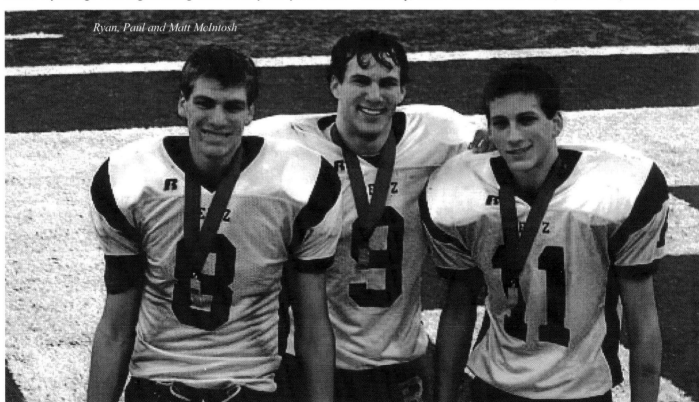

Ryan, Paul and Matt McIntosh

212

All three boys showed great talent as youngsters.

sectional before finishing 9-4. But Paul's final year was the one that would add to the Reitz legacy in a big way and provide a lasting memory for Tim and Lori McIntosh.

The 2007 Panthers weren't as dominant as many Reitz teams of the past, but what they lacked in physical qualities, they made up for with determination and grit. With an offensive line anchored by Josh Winegar, Moose Campbell, Tyler Mattingly, Josh Lefler, Adam Hermann, Cameron Kolb and Josh Oglesby, the Panthers posted easy wins over Jeffersonville (38-12), Owensboro Catholic (40-6) and Memorial (42-3) to open the season.

The Reitz backfield featured Tyler Julian and Chris Deig, and Paul threw to a talented crew of receivers that included Ryan, Jeff Hudson, David Sturdivant and Slade Gander. The defensive unit included Craig Austin, Marquell Snoddy and Tony Ewers on the line, linebackers Lucas White, Mason Stroud and Chris Fischer and DBs Houston Hobbs and Zach Kissel, and the boys finished a perfect regular season at 9-0.

The Panthers then dominated their sectional with convincing wins over Owen Valley (48-13), Boonville (47-0) and Jasper (34-8) before facing a two-game odyssey the likes of which the program had never seen. Paul led Reitz to a thrilling 61-60 win over Columbus East with a final drive that featured three clutch passes, two to his brother Ryan and one to Tyler Julian. After an offsides penalty by Columbus on the extra point attempt, the Panthers executed a two-point conversion for the win. As one would imagine, the highlight reel was full after the shootout, including a 75-yard fumble return for a TD by Tony Ewers, an acrobatic over-the-shoulder catch by Slade Gander, a beautiful catch by David Sturdivant over the middle and Paul's interception to end the game.

The semi-state was just as exciting as Paul hit Ryan on a fade just before the half for a touchdown. The boys in blue and gray overcame double digit deficits twice for a 35-34 win, and once again there were monumental contributions, like Chris Deig's hit that caused a fumble recovery by Zach Kissel after Cathedral gained momentum with an interception. Tyler Julian was stellar on the ground with over 100 yards and also caught a 'Waggle' pass from Paul to give Reitz the lead with under a minute to play.

After the two barnburners, the State Final was anticlimactic as the Panthers made easy work of Lowell in a 33-14 win, giving the program another State title. Paul finished the year with 2,467 passing yards for 23 TDs with another 1,603 on the ground for another 33 scores and reaped the benefits of the remarkable season. In addition to making the *Courier*'s All-City and All-Conference teams, Paul was named the Indiana Gatorade Player of the Year, but most importantly, he became the first area player to be named Indiana's Mr. Football, the state's highest award.

At 6'1 and 197 pounds, Paul was excited when he learned that Army had proclaimed him their #1 recruit in the nation, and with his abilities and excellent grades (Magna cum Laude honor roll), he thought it would be a perfect match. But as the opportunity unfolded, Paul became disillusioned and decided to leave for the University of Southern Illinois. Because of their character, Paul and his family choose not to elaborate on the circumstances surrounding his departure from Army out of respect for the institution and the men and women who study there.

Instead, they focus on his education and his football experiences at Southern Illinois. After sitting out in 2008, Paul played as a redshirt freshman in '09 and wasted no time assaulting the school's record book. After some mop-up duty behind junior starter Chris Dieker, Paul got his chance in the eighth game when Dieker left with a broken collarbone. On Paul's very first pass as the team's top gun, he threw for an 86-yard touchdown, the second longest completion in school history. He then went on to post a 5-1 record and lead the Salukis to their second straight MVFC title, the program's seventh straight playoff appearance and a #1 national ranking. In doing so, Paul set a school record for rushing by a quarterback (588 yards) while passing for 888 yards with 8 TDs and a 67.7 completion percentage, second in school history.

Unfortunately, Paul wasn't able to build on his solid premiere with the return of the 6'5, 232-pound Dieker for his senior season. Paul, however, did play in nine games with one start, a 15-30 performance against San Diego State for 231 yards and 3 touchdowns.

In 2011, Paul was poised for his breakout season, starting four games as a captain before suffering a season-ending shoulder

213

injury against Western Illinois. For his four starts, Paul threw for 649 yards and ran for 218, and as the 2012 season approached, he was in position to take control of the offense once again.

After Paul graduated, popular Reitz coach John Hart departed for Indianapolis and was replaced by Tony Lewis. With a glaring void to fill after Paul's graduation, Lewis pulled Ryan aside to pop the question, and Ryan's response was a prime example of the type of player he was. When asked if he wanted to follow in Paul's footsteps as a QB, Ryan said, "Go ahead and let Matt play because he'll have three years."

By all accounts, Ryan was as unselfish as they come, and yet he was also a superior athlete. "Ryno (Ryan's nickname) is the ultimate team player," Tim McIntosh told me. "He is probably the best athlete of the three, but he has no flash. As a quarterback (as a freshman and as Paul's backup), he was an extremely accurate passer. I mean incredibly accurate."

Tim went on to explain how Ryan had quarterbacked his youth football teams to undefeated seasons and yet how selfless he was when it came to working with his brothers. Tim spoke of the long hours Ryan would spend running patterns for Paul and Matt in sweltering heat and how he would never complain as he kept coming back for more.

Ryan finished his senior year as an All-City receiver and then attended USI to get a degree. While there, he quarterbacked his intramural football team and was named the school's Intramural Athlete of the Year.

Ryan's final season at Reitz was Matt's first as the pilot of the ship for coach Tony Lewis. By any other school's standards, it was an excellent year, but to Reitz fans, it was only business as usual. The Panthers finished 9-2, losing only to Owensboro in the second game and to Jasper in the sectional final, 38-35. Matt had a solid debut season as he shared the running responsibilities with Alordo Bell (1,233 yards, 14 TDs) by gaining 831 yards on 135 carries (6.2 per carry) with 11 touchdowns, while passing for 1,081 yards and another 10 TDs.

With a season under his belt, the youngest of the McIntosh boys and his talented teammates were poised to add to the Reitz mystique, and they would do so in impressive fashion in 2009. The defensive front featured Ewers, Mo McCray, Jeff Fentress and Shane Woodget with linebackers Cody Dimmett, Brandon Kemp and Damion James backing them up. The DBs were Eric Bryant and Hamilton Carr, among others, and the defense was virtually impenetrable all year. Matt's offensive weapons were many, with Bell as his feature back and great receivers like Carr, Jeff Hudson, Morgan Jones and Cuda Dimmett. All were protected by a talented front line that included Mike Clem, Steven Mullen, Zach Wimpleberg, Josh Balbach and Corey Smith.

The Panthers opened with a 27-0 win over Henderson County followed by a 14-2 victory at Daviess County. From there, they pummeled their Indiana opponents with only Memorial coming within two touchdowns (28-14). Reitz made light work of some typically tough opponents, with wins over Castle (42-7), Central (55-7), North (35-6) and their archrivals Mater Dei (59-0).

In the tournament, they were just as effective, with easy wins over Seymour (35-0), Central (35-7) and Jasper (42-6) in the sectional and a 52-28 slugfest over East Central in the regional. Their foes in the final two games were identical to 2007, but no late-game heroics were needed. Against nemesis Cathedral, DB Cuda Dimmett came up with picks on Cathedral's first two drives, and Reitz opened on offense with some flash when they ran a flea

flicker on their first play from scrimmage. The defense did its part with three consecutive sacks in the fourth quarter, and a key offensive play was a 4th and 25 pass from Matt to Hamilton Carr for a TD.

As always, the Reitz fans tailgated and had the time of their lives at Reitz Bowl, and after the 31-10 victory, they were making plans once again for the State championship game. Just as they did in '07, the boys came through with another victory over Lowell (23-9), and Matt McIntosh had another State title to call his own.

Matt finished his high school career in 2009, and the six-year McIntosh era was over. Matt capped off his career with another perfect regular season and sectional and regional championships before a bruising loss to Cathedral, but just prior to that loss was a school record 28-game winning streak. He also just missed becoming our area's second Mr. Football, finishing second behind Lawrence Central QB and IU recruit Tré Roberson.

As a senior, Matt completed 131 of 208 throws (63%) for 2,202 yards for 29 TDs with only 8 interceptions. In addition, he rushed for 1,183 yards (a 7.9 average) for another 14 touchdowns. Like his brother, he was named the Indiana Gatorade Player of the Year, and as of 2012 was competing for the starting job at Northern Illinois.

It is only natural that the oldest and youngest brothers be compared as quarterbacks, but it is virtually impossible to draw a clearcut conclusion. Both were extraordinary leaders who were equally adept on the ground and in the air, and both led teams to State championships with exemplary records, including undefeated seasons. Some fans say that Paul was heavier and more physical and a better runner, while Matt was a more accurate passer. Still others, like long-time TV sportscaster Lance Wilkerson, proclaim Paul to be the better pocket passer and Matt the better athlete.

And ex-Panther coach John Hart has yet another take on all three McIntosh brothers. "Paul may be the best leader I ever had," Hart revealed. "His leadership qualities were unbelievable. I remember a kid being in trouble and you could tell the kid was ready to quit. Paul understood about leadership and went out after practice and told this kid, who was a gifted kid, 'You're not going to quit. I'm not going to let you,' and he ran those disciplines (punishments) with him, about three weeks of them. This kid was in trouble! By the end of the three weeks, Paul and all the seniors were out there running with him without ever saying a word or having expectations of getting any credit.

"Matt and Paul had a lot in common in terms of athleticism and toughness," Coach Hart continued, "I'd probably give a slight edge to Paul in leadership and maybe Matt in athleticism. And Ryan is what made everything work. You have to have those kind in a family. His touchdown catch (in the '07 semi-final against Cathedral) was one of the greatest I've seen. It was a goalline fade, and he went up with one hand."

Coach Hart and anyone from the Panther Nation know that the McIntosh story runs deeper than what the boys did on the field. Much of the tale involved the reverence that the Reitz faithful feel as part of the culture. One of Tim McIntosh's first comments to me was a memory of the time he met Reitz icon Don Hansen. Hansen was the star of the famous 1961 team that finished the season unscored on, and he was back for a reunion. Tim, the school's AD at the time, felt Hansen's huge paw and noticed how the 60-something Hansen looked like he could still play.

Tim and Lori both reminisced about the tailgate parties at 3:00 in the afternoon with smoke from grills filling the air and visiting

The Panthers made sure to include Zach Harris (in wheelchair) in the festivities.

Fans were emotional when Jonathan Johan led the 'death walk' onto the field for the State championship game.

team busses having to take a specific route to avoid a stalemate from the parked cars of the Reitz faithful. Tim also mentioned the Wednesday night gatherings the team would have to watch film. The event would rotate between parents' homes, and no coaches were present. At one such meeting at Tyler Julian's house, the boys were in the basement on a huge sectional, and Tim remembers it well. "I was sitting with Mr. Julian," Tim recalled, "and we looked back and there were about twelve guys and they looked like they were ten-year-old cousins, just giggling and enjoying themselves."

There were also some very emotional moments created by the special atmosphere, like the story of Jonathan Johann. Johann suffered a stroke as a sophomore in 2009, and Coach Hart designated him as a player/coach so that he could be on the field. In a special moment that will never be forgotten, the fans watched through tears as Johann led the Panthers onto the field at Lucas Oil Stadium as they did the 'Death Walk', a slow stroll around the field, to the delight of the Reitz crowd. Tim also mentioned the heartwarming story of Zach Harris, a student confined to a wheelchair who inspired the team for four years as the team manager.

Tim's eyes teared up as he spoke of Cam Kolb, a player who blew out his ACL and could have had surgery but played through the pain his entire senior year. Both parents spoke of the number of boys who were excellent students, including their three sons, and how one season, 15 seniors on the team were all taking Calculus.

The McIntoshes, like most Reitz football families, have a deep respect and appreciation for the program that touched their sons' lives. "They're team players, and they loved Reitz football and their teammates," said Tim McIntosh. "They appreciate walking out on that field for a big game. If you don't play Division I

athletics, you won't play in front of crowds like they have. Reitz football on a Friday night is the place to be. It's hard to describe. There are a lot of people over 50 that come hell or high water are going to climb those hills and go up and down those 30-inch steps. Like the Reitz Rowdies; it's a happening."

"We were very blessed to have been part of it," said Tim. "People always say, 'you must be proud of your kids,' then I'd say, 'The happy meter is off the charts.' I'm proud that they gave great effort and hopefully helped the younger ones."

"I would call us blessed because they were part of such great teams," added Lori. "They got to experience something special that a lot of kids never get to experience."

No one can argue that the McIntosh brothers were not great players, but they are also fine people. Each of them was a superior student, and they all gave back to the community through organizations like the West Side Nut Club's Special Needs Buddy program. "I can't remember being around a better family than those three boys," John Hart told me. "Anything and everything they've gotten they've earned. Mom and dad created such a competitive atmosphere at home, and I think it really helped them scholastically and on the football field."

Each of the boys, along with the baby of the family, Sarah, an excellent volleyball player herself, has been nurtured in a home environment and athletic environment that have enabled them to excel, and their impact has been substantial. During the six 'McIntosh years', Reitz won 62 and lost 9 (87%) with two perfect seasons and two State championships. But more importantly, the boys set a standard of leadership that reflects the program's storied past and also stands as an example for future generations, as well.

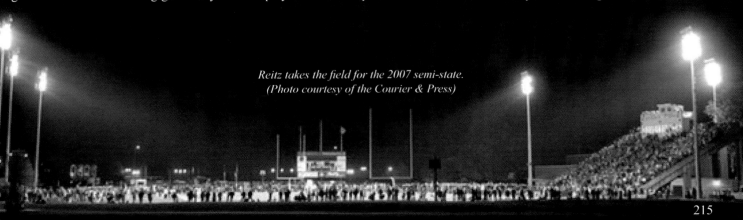

Reitz takes the field for the 2007 semi-state.
(Photo courtesy of the Courier & Press)

THE RISINGERS: TREE-MENDOUS FAMILY

JOE RISINGER

RICK

CLAY

COURTNEY

JOE

MEGAN

JAY

JOHN

There is no question that Evansville Harrison High School has produced a significant number of Division I athletes, perhaps more than any area school based on the schools' ages. One of Harrison's best was John Risinger, and although his roots aren't entirely local, the family tree is impressive and there are plenty of local ties.

John's grandfather, Joe Risinger, played at Hartford City before becoming a three-year starter at Ball State ('36, '37 & '38). Joe and his wife, Mary, later moved to Richmond where his two sons, Jim and Rick, starred for the Spiders under legendary coach Dick Baumgartner. Jim was All-Conference as a senior and earned a scholarship to North Carolina State, where he lettered three years ('69, '70 & '71) and helped the Wolfpack capture the ACC tournament his junior year. After a bye, NC State was eliminated by Bob Lanier's St. Bonaventure team that coincidentally lost in the Final Four to Jacksonville, a team that featured Evansville Harrison's Vaughn Wedeking, and Greg Nelson. Rick Risinger was an Indiana All-Star for Richmond and then played for Purdue with local legend Bob Ford from Evansville North.

Rick had three children: Clay, Courtney, and Megan. Clay was a star swimmer while Courtney starred in basketball at Terre Haute South. She was named an Indiana All-Star in 1998. Megan was a standout in basketball, as well, playing on the 2002 State champions. Rick took over the Heritage Christian girls program in 2005 and promptly led the 2A school to four consecutive State titles ('06, '07, '08 & '09), making him the only coach in Indiana history to accomplish the feat. (Ft. Wayne Bishop Luers won four from '99-'02 but not under the same coach.)

Jim Risinger moved to Evansville and eventually became the president and CEO at Old National Bank. His two sons, Jay and John, then became stars at Harrison. Jay was a 1993 grad who played for the school's first sectional champion in 1992, a team that featured local legend Walter McCarty. Jay then attended UK where he played on the JV team in '95-'96, the same year Coach Rick Pitino guided the Wildcats to the NCAA title with a team led by McCarty, Derek Anderson, Ron Mercer, Antoine Walker and Tony Delk.

John Risinger

Younger brother John made some history as a youngster and then finished his high school career as one of the school's best. As a ten-year-old, John played Biddy Basketball for his father on the Lakeview Optimist all-star team and captured the 1989 World Championship in Puerto Rico. John was named the team's MVP and joined teammates A.J. Bost and J.R. Edwards on the All-Tournament World Biddy Team. In 1995, John led Harrison to its first regional title and its first 20-win season since 1966. That team, which also included A.J. Bost, Scott Evernham, Jeremy Redd and Brad Harris, is still the only Harrison team to complete a season without losing to an SIAC opponent. John was named the *Courier*'s Metro Player of the Year and is still the only male in history to earn that honor as a junior. John was named All-City and All-State as a senior and is still (as of 2012) Harrison's all-time leader in games played (84) and scoring (1,219 career points), passing such greats as McCarty, Reggie Hayes, Rick Atkinson and Calbert Cheaney. After a year and a half with the Evansville Aces, John transferred to UNC-Asheville where he finished his impressive career as a two-year starter and team captain.

From Hartford City in the 1930s to the new millennium, the Risingers have won State championships and excelled at the Division I level. With basketball in their blood, it will come as no surprise if the family tree grows even stronger in the years to come.

THE EMMONS SISTERS:
A RECIPE FOR SUCCESS

No one would argue that the gold standard for softball programs in this part of the state has been that of the Boonville Pioneers, and the teams have been a source of pride for the community for over 25 years. Many outstanding athletes have taken the field in the program's history, and two of the best wore the black and gold as the new millennium arrived.

There are many paths to stardom and many recipes for success, and for a very close family on Walnut Street, the recipe worked like a charm. To begin, you find two young ladies with natural ability who are anxious to learn and add a loving father with maniacal tendencies. To finish the masterpiece, sprinkle on a pinch of a role model and then marinate for seven years in the guidance of a hall of fame coach.

As I arrived at the family home to meet the subjects of this story, I was greeted by the man whose extreme passion for the sport was the inspiration for the success that would follow. Dave Emmons had donned his Boonville softball cap and T-shirt for the occasion, and to set the tone, he immediately ushered me into a room that his daughters refer to as "the shrine." The walls of the room were covered with photos and plaques, and what seemed like hundreds of trophies adorned the shelves. Every item had a story, and Dave Emmons could remember the details of every one.

As I joined the family at the kitchen table, several photo albums were laid out and the family was gracious and warm as we began to reminisce about some of the finest years in the history of Boonville softball. The sisters, Rachel and Shannon, were born eleven months apart but started school together, causing many to assume they were twins. From the time they were small, the girls watched their father

Shannon (left) and Rachel Emmons

play slow-pitch softball and heard stories about his younger days as an athlete.

Dave is a native of Boonville, and, with the exception of his college years, has lived there all his life. In fact, he is not only a small town guy but he actually married the girl next door, his wife Theresa who literally lived in the house adjacent to where he grew up. Theresa would have loved to compete in sports, but like many of her generation, she revealed that "they didn't have girls sports when I was in school."

Dave, on the other hand, excelled at Boonville, playing just behind Dan Labhart, one of Boonville's finest, and sharing pitching duties with Scott McCain as they led the first Boonville team in any sport to the State Finals in 1972, Dave's junior year. The Pioneers finished 13-1 Dave's senior year, and he finished the season with a 0.00 ERA.

At only 5'9 and 145 pounds, Emmons' strength was his curveball, and there were rumors that he would be drafted out of high school. Instead, he attended the College of Central Florida. After a career there, where he led all Florida junior college pitchers in strikeouts, Dave returned home to start a family.

In the mid-'70s, Dave competed locally against some very strong slow-pitch athletes, like Jeff King (who starred for Quentin Merkel at Memorial), Curt Welch, Kevin Oxley, Tom Kopatich, Jimmy Williams, Billy Scales and Donnie Miles, to name a few. For several years, his family had fun following Dave as he played, but by the early '90s, he hung up his cleats to focus on working with his daughters.

Dave knew that pitching a softball was far different from throwing a baseball, so he learned along with the girls. When they were nine, he sought the services of men like Ron Bacon, Jimmy Ray Wilson, whose daughters had played at Boonville, and also Bob Canada, an excellent hurler in men's fast-pitch.

As he always did, Dave poured himself into learning the game, and as the girls progressed, they caught the eye of legendary Pioneers coach Mike Wilson. Knowing how hard the girls were working, Wilson allowed them to travel with the high school team during the days when players like Wendy Wood and Amy Anderson were leading the way at Boonville.

Dave looks back fondly on those days and remembers a situation when Mike Wilson reached into his bag of tricks to create a defining moment for Rachel. "At twelve, we went down to watch a game with Lakeview one summer," Dave informed me. "This is how Mike works. Boonville's getting beat bad, and Mindy Bacon (who starred at Boonville) is playing for Lakeview. The pitcher is Heather Hook, a very good pitcher. The bases are loaded, and Wilson says, 'Rachel, go warm up.' We weren't even on the team; Rachel's only twelve and this is an 18 & under team.

"She had to borrow a pair of cleats," Dave continued. "Mindy Bacon is up with the bases loaded and a 3 & 0 count, and Wilson says, 'Rachel, you're in!' She was twelve years old against Mindy, who was first team All-State that year. Rachel struck her out on three pitches. Think about the confidence that gave Rachel. That's how Mike does it."

As the girls matured, the workouts grew more intense, but Rachel and Shannon enjoyed the challenges. "Once I got the softball bug and learned how to do it, we started going to the gym in the winter," Dave explained. "We would find an open school and go pitch on Sundays. Their freshman year, after practice, I'd come after work and we'd practice for another hour after practice. We learned that from Wendy Wood (a four-time first team All-State pitcher). Wendy was Rachel's mentor; we just loved her and her dad (Arel). He was really smart about pitching, and we figured if the workouts were good enough for Wendy, they were good enough for us."

The girls admit to spending countless hours in the backyard throwing against a fence with a strike zone painted by Dad, and many holidays included practice time, with only the month of August being softball-free. On more than one occasion after a poor outing away from home, Dave and the girls would head to the lighted field for more work.

But to the girls, this was life, and they always respected what their father was trying to do. Nothing irritated him (or any coach, for that matter) more than giving up walks, and it wasn't unusual to spend some late evenings throwing after a bad outing. But some of the tutelage Dave offered was special. "I remember laying in bed with Dad," Shannon revealed. "We had this piece of cardboard with a basketball court on one side and softball on the other. He would quiz me on different situations."

Rachel and Shannon look back fondly on those days and admit that sports, especially softball, were their primary focus. When asked about grades, both were open and honest. Shannon admitted that "I got by to play softball," and Rachel disclosed that "I didn't become a good student until I was in college. I was an athlete at Boonville, and that's how everybody knew me."

As for other sports, Shannon played basketball until her junior year, while Rachel showed the lighter side of her personality when she proclaimed, "I played another sport, it's called boy chasing."

Throughout their high school careers, the girls led the program to some of its finest years. Rachel was a fantastic pitcher with a wicked drop ball who shared the duties as a freshman with Mindy Bacon. Later she shared the circle with her sister, her cousin, Brandi Bates, a hard thrower who was All-State as a senior, and Tiffany Hall, who had an excellent change-up.

Typically, Rachel and Shannon would alternate playing first base and pitching, and their teams were undefeated in the conference all four years and were four-time sectional and regional champions. But with all the talent, including Lacey Haynes in center field and Mandy Schmitt at third, among others, the girls could not capture a State title. As sophomores, the Lady Pioneers fell 1-0 in the semi-state to eventual champ Center Grove, and as juniors and seniors, they fell in the semi-finals by identical scores of 5-3 in extra innings. Shannon in particular is still frustrated by their final loss as high school players. On a day when she was 4 for 4 at the plate, she came up with the team down 5-3, the bases loaded and two out only to ground out to short to end the game.

For their four-year career, the Emmons sisters and their teammates compiled a record of 116-11, a 91% winning percentage, and with the success came the recognition. Both girls were four-time All-Conference and All-Area selections, with Rachel named first team All-State twice and Shannon three times. Both were also named to the North-South All-Star game as seniors and left school with their names all over the record book. Though neither matched the no-hitter totals of their role model Wendy Wood (10) or Mindi Wilson (8), Rachel recorded 3 and Shannon 1. Shannon was second to Wood with 340 strikeouts, and the girls left the program #1 and #2 in ERA with Rachel at 0.632 and Shannon at 0.65. (Virtually every pitching record has since been broken by Erica Taylor.)

As a hitter, Shannon cracked the top five in several categories, ranking first in career hits (167) with Rachel third (124). Shannon also left as the program's career home run leader (13) and RBI leader (132). A career .434 hitter, her most impressive record was her total of 70 extra base hits, nearly double those of #2 Jenny Tuley.

Both Rachel and Shannon took their considerable talents to nearby Wabash Valley Junior College before accepting full rides to Oakland City College (Rachel) and USI (Shannon).

Rachel was the pioneers' ace.
(Photo by Janet Metzger.)

Shannon was an outstanding fielder and hitter.
(Photo by Janet Metzger.)

With their careers behind them, the girls went their separate ways but remain close. Rachel is a teacher at Newburgh Elementary. Shannon tried her hand at coaching and resurrected the program at Lincoln Trail, turning the perennial conference doormat into a qualifier for nationals after landing two prized local recruits, Jennifer Bartley of Jasper and Casey DeWeese of Memorial. After earning conference Coach of the Year honors, breaking a long streak by Wabash Valley's Paul Schnarre, Shannon joined the business world and now works at Toyota.

Looking back, the Emmons sisters appreciate the discipline they learned from their father, and they both agree that Mike Wilson is the type of coach who isn't appreciated as he should be until his athletes leave. "You see other coaches," said Shannon, "and you think, 'I had it really good.'"

Both Dave Emmons and Mike Wilson pushed the girls hard, and even Dave was amazed at how much his daughters endured. "I'd go down there and Mike Wilson was on Shannon like a dog," Dave explained. "I thought, 'Oh, my gosh! I don't know how Shannon takes that?' She would cry. He knew how good she could be."

When asked about the methods used years ago, Shannon smiled and assured me that "nothing left scars," and Rachel confirmed the feeling. "I remember when (Coach) Wilson told me, 'If I ever stop yelling at you, you should be concerned because it means I don't care anymore.'"

For four years, Mike Wilson reaped the benefits of the Emmons girls' talents, but opponents respected them as well. "They were great competitors," said Pat Lockyear, the coach of arch-rival Castle. "They were hard to dislike. You couldn't help but like them even though they were beating you like a drum. They're the kind you want on your team. They had the right approach to the game and were so humble about it."

In their four years, from 1997 to 2000, the Emmons sisters and their teammates put together the finest four seasons in school history, and when asked to recall their fondest memories, neither hesitated. "Softball was the pride of the school," Shannon answered, "and that made us so proud to be part of that. We wanted to win not just for the team, but for the town and for Coach Wilson."

"What stands out for me" said Rachel, "was Leisa Winchester's diving catch." The play Rachel mentioned was made in the semi-state championship game at Turkey Run with Boonville leading 3-1 with runners on and two outs. "To this day, I still don't know how she caught the ball," Rachel continued. "She laid out (down the left field line), and it was like magic."

Though the girls are nostalgic, no one has stronger emotions than dear old dad. "I really miss it," Dave told me. "We practiced year-round. I remember in 1997 when Shannon pitched a no-hitter in the JV game and then Rachel pitched a (varsity) no-hitter against Reitz and Shannon played shortstop. I could go on and on because I had so much fun. I miss it. I put out a big garden, but it ain't the same thing. We lived for it."

It's hard to imagine how many softballs the girls wore out over the years, and by all accounts, they were two of the toughest competitors in local history. By combining the right ingredients, Coach Wilson, Dave and Theresa Emmons, and the Boonville fans had the privilege of enjoying the sweet taste of success as they witnessed the careers of Rachel and Shannon Emmons, two of the most celebrated players in local softball history.

PETE AND CHAD RUPP:
LIKE FATHER, LIKE SON

Memorial High School has had its fair share of father and son combos who have starred as athletes at the east side school, and the Rupp family is no exception. Both father and son excelled in multiple sports, and each left his mark as part of Memorial's storied sports legacy.

Pete Rupp

Though he probably didn't realize it at the time, Pete Rupp was surrounded by some of the great names in Evansville's athletic history as he honed his skills on local fields and courts. When Pete first played competitive sports, his little league, League 5 at East Side Park across from the Armory, was run by local sports icon Arad McCutchan, and his coach was Wally Southwood, the father of two boys, Gene and Jerry, who would fashion amazing careers at Central and Bosse, respectively.

As a player at the East Side Pony League, his team came one run short of playing in the World Series with fellow 14-year-old Connie Garnett and a talented group of 13-year-olds. The younger boys, including standouts like Vaughn Wedeking, Terry Wedgewood, Donnie Collins, Gordon Slade and many more, actually won the World Series the following year.

Pete was also fortunate to have the influence of the strong Catholic youth sports programs in basketball and football. His first football coach at Christ the King was none other than Bob Hargrave, a local legend who starred with Billy Hillenbrand at Memorial in the 1930s and also at Notre Dame. Hargrave's assistant was Bob Meeks who played at Arkansas. Rupp joined players like Don Crane, P.R. Deters and Robbie Kent to pull off a feat that made headlines in the *Courier*. The article explained how the powerful 1961 Reitz Panthers, led by All-American local legend Don Hansen, finished the season undefeated and unscored on and how the Christ the King CYO team duplicated that rare distinction.

Pete's elementary school basketball teams were nearly perfect, as well, finishing 34-1 as seventh graders and a perfect 35-0 the following year. Rupp starred on those teams with support from an impressive nucleus of future stars, like Kent, Dave Dant, Tom Hargrave and the Scheller brothers, Bill and Jim.

Rupp grew up during an era that many consider the best in local history, and he watched amazing performers like Dave Schellhase, Mickey Martin and Steve Schroer at North and Bob Griese at Rex Mundi, to name a few. Pete particularly remembers the battles with their east side rival Harrison, pointing out that "talent-wise, we shouldn't have been on the same court with them." In fact, Pete has stated many times that his proudest moment was winning the basketball sectional by beating three teams that had beaten Memorial during the season, Central, Rex Mundi and Harrison. Harrison had beaten the Tigers by three during the regular season, and when both teams advanced to the final, no one gave Memorial a chance over the powerful Warriors. Coach Frank Schwitz's Harrison team was one of the strongest in Evansville history, with five starters who played big-time ball in college: Rick Atkinson, Pete Helmbach, Ned Schnacke, Vaughn Wedeking and Greg Nelson. That lineup also had strong support from the likes of Randy Lutterman, Terry Wedgewood and Mike Shoulders. But on this night, the gutsy Tigers, under coach Ron Wannemueller, overcame a 17-point deficit in the third quarter to pull out a 3-point victory, with Pete connecting on 7 of 8 free throws in the fourth quarter. The team went on to capture the regional before ending their season with a loss to North Vernon in the Evansville Semi-state.

Pete ran into some serious competition on the football field also and was quick to mention Abe Krause and Dean Volkman from North as well as Bosse's Oscar Mulvey and Bob Rogers and Steve Vessels and Keith Krietenstein from Reitz. As a 5'11, 175-pound running back for the Tigers, Rupp recalled Reitz's Bill Hape, saying that, "he was probably the hardest hitter I ever faced," and as a defensive back, he has nightmares about a big fullback from North. "The hardest runner I ever tried to tackle was Ken Bargo," Rupp pointed out. "That SOB would run over you. He was a beast!"

Proving that things haven't changed much over the years, a school's football season back then was judged by how your team did against Reitz, and Pete counts a

Chad Rupp during his record-breaking career at Franklin College.
(Photo courtesy of the Rupp family)

win against the Panthers in 1965 as one of his fondest memories. The Tigers took Reitz to school on the cold fall night, and Saturday's *Courier* headline proclaimed "Reitz takes worst beating in 50 years 32-0"

Under football coach Gene Logel, the Tigers captured the City and SIAC during Pete's sophomore year with players like Kenny Mills and Donnie Crane, and they repeated those feats Pete's senior year with players like Robbie Kent, Bill Muller, Gerald Seib and quarterback Mike Hobgood. Looking back on his football career at Memorial, Rupp has a strong grasp of what he and his teammates accomplished, and anyone who has played in Evansville will appreciate his perspective. "No matter how your season went, if you beat Reitz, you had a successful year," he stated. "During my four years, we never lost to Mater Dei or Reitz. How many can say that?"

Rupp finished his career in 1966 and was one of the city's best in all three sports. In baseball, he pitched and played right field for local legend Quentin Merkel for a year while Merkel was still a student at Evansville College and then for Ralph Weinzapfel. On the basketball court, he was a smooth-shooting left-hander who averaged 18 points his senior season, and on the gridiron, he was All-City for three years and All-State as a senior.

After entertaining football offers from IU, Illinois, Western Kentucky and others, Pete chose to play football and basketball for Florida State. At the time, freshmen could not play varsity, and Pete played all three sports at the freshman level. On the basketball court, he was the team's sixth man and played alongside a 6'9 fiery redhead named Dave Cowens from Newport, Kentucky, who became an NBA star with the Boston Celtics.

During spring football, Pete was working as a second string defensive back for the Seminoles when a problem developed. Having gotten married, he was looking for student housing and discovered that married housing for athletes could only be offered to seniors. This prompted a change of plans, and when Evansville College coach Jim Byers found out, he welcomed Rupp home with open arms.

Pete finished his athletic career with the Purple Aces, and after sitting out a season because of the transfer, he enjoyed his years under Coach Byers. Pete played wide receiver for the Aces and caught passes from Craig Blackford. He also joined some local stars at E.C., including Memorial's Gerald Seib and Paul Gerhardt, North's Doug Atherton, Rex Mundi's Randy Mattingly and linebacker Mike Forche (pronounced FOR • kee), who was called 'The Animal' by his teammates.

After his graduation in 1971, Pete entered the business world, joining the family business, Royal Foods, that was founded by his grandfather in 1940. With his career behind him, Pete and his wife Tina went about the business of raising a family, and his youngest would make some noise of his own as a record-breaking athlete at Memorial.

As Chad Rupp grew up, there were many similarities between his athletic experiences and those of his father's, and some of the key differences may have been due to their generations. Chad played his little league baseball at Golfmoor, his youth basketball at LVO and West Terrace, and even wrestled until fifth grade.

His junior league football coaches were Chuck Brunson and Randy Babb, two ex-Reitz Panthers who coached Chad's Lions team. Chad wanted to play wide receiver, as his father did for Evansville College, but Babb and Brunson used him at quarterback.

The starting seniors at Memorial. Front row (L-R): Paul Gerhardt, Keith Austin, Gerald Seib. Second row: Jerry Cambron, Pete Rupp, Robbie Kent. (Photo courtesy of the Rupp family)

As a near mirror image to his father, 6 feet tall, 180 pounds but right-handed, Chad flourished in a system that reflected the times in which he grew up. According to Pete, his son was a late bloomer physically, but he made up for it with his deadly accuracy as a thrower.

At the turn of the new millennium, run-and-gun offenses were sweeping the nation, offering teams that were less imposing physically a fighting chance. Memorial head coach Larry Mattingly and offensive coordinator John Hurley loved the rapid-fire system and attended college camps to learn the various nuances of different systems. They took a particular liking to the style of Franklin College coach Mike Leonard and invited him down to Memorial to work with the boys during the summer prior to Chad's sophomore season.

That very important summer launched Chad to heights he never could have imagined and gave him the vehicle for a high school and college career that few Evansville quarterbacks have achieved. Rupp earned the starting quarterback spot as a sophomore and played during an era that may have produced the greatest aerial shows in local football history. Week after week, Chad matched passing numbers with the likes of Nick Hart (Reitz), Joey Elliott (Harrison), Dustin Slaton (Mater Dei) and Chris Owen (Central), and fans got whiplash while trying to follow the action.

Chad grew into a fine quarterback and finished his three-year career as one of Memorial's finest. Though his team suffered his sophomore season with the new spread offense, the Tigers posted a winning season in 2003 and 2004 and won the City and tied Castle for the conference Chad's senior year. Memorial's only downfall was the inability to get past powerful Mater Dei and Heritage Hills in the sectional.

Chad graduated with virtually all the school's passing records, including career completions (505), yards (6,698) and touchdowns (50), and as he examined his future possibilities, his choice turned out to be a no-brainer.

As a small quarterback by Division I standards, Chad considered offers from Butler, Hanover and Kentucky Wesleyan, but

Pete puts on the brakes against Topcat Tyler (left) and the Central Bears. (Photo courtesy of the Rupp family)

in his heart, the match was made years earlier. Chad was a natural for the Franklin College offense and had formed a bond with Coach Leonard, so Rupp headed north in 2005.

As a freshman, Chad watched and learned as senior quarterback Mike Fritz ran the offense, and the highlight of the season was a win over rival Hanover, a team the Grizzlies had not beaten in seven years. Chad was inserted early in the game to add a wrinkle by running the option, and his performance was a sign of great things to come. He ran for 80 yards and passed for over 100 with 3 TD passes.

For his final three seasons, Rupp was at the controls, and his career earned him recognition as one of the best quarterbacks in Franklin College history. Chad's three-year record was 32-5 as a starter as his teams finished 9-1 in 2006, 10-2 in '07 and 11-2 in '08. The Grizzlies made the NCAA Division III playoffs his final two seasons and suffered a disappointing loss his senior year to Wheaton College on a snowy, bone-chilling afternoon to end his career. The 2008 season is considered one of the finest in Franklin College history, and Chad left the school with most of the program's passing records.

Rupp won Conference Player of the Week honors nine times, and in 2007, he finished #1 in Division III passing efficiency. Among Chad's many records, were single game marks for total offense and passing yards (576), completions (41) and TD passes (7), and his senior season, he set standards for total offense (4,625), completions (313) and touchdown passes (45). He also left the program as its career leader in total offense (10,446 yards), completions (717), completion percentage (.662), passing yards (9,806) and TD passes (103).

After graduation, Chad played for a year in Germany in a league started by U.S. servicemen. Only four Americans (wearing an 'A' on their helmets) were allowed on a team, and only two could be on the field at once. Chad led the league in passing and almost returned for a second season, but instead chose to become a grad assistant at the University of Indianapolis. After witnessing the long hours the coaches spent working, he decided to leave the game he loved to join the workforce like his father.

Pete and Chad Rupp were similar in many ways, and both excelled as undersized players in a big man's game. They were also representative of their generations. Pete played in an era of low-tech football equipment with grind-it-out offenses, and the basketball venues could hardly be tolerated by today's players. In fact, Memorial's gym was not even built until 1969, meaning that players of his era withstood some antiquated but historic arenas, like the Agoga Tabernacle, for example.

"The showers (at Agoga) were awful with nothing but cold water," Pete recalled. "The floor had dark spots and shadows. Opponents hated playing there. They hardly ever turned on the heat; we loved it."

Though neither was physically imposing, Pete and Chad Rupp demonstrated natural talent and the ability to compete. There are many bloodlines locally that have produced fine athletes, and the Rupps can be numbered among them. Pete Rupp earned the respect of all who played with and against him in the '60s, and forty years later, Chad showed similar traits and built a career that made Pete Rupp one proud papa.

AREA PLAYERS TO SCORE 40 OR MORE POINTS IN THE IHSAA BOYS BASKETBALL TOURNAMENT

Roy Burris, Washington – 58 (1921 sectional)
Scott Rolen, Jasper – 49 (1993 sectional)
Michael Lewis, Jasper – 45 (1996 regional)
Toby Madison, Wash. Catholic – 43 (1993 regional)
Tyler Zeller, Washington – 43 (2008 State championship)
Andy Benes, Central – 42 (1985 sectional)
Kyle Despain, Tell City (1996 sectional)

THE ZELLER FAMILY: A FOUNDATION FOR SUCCESS

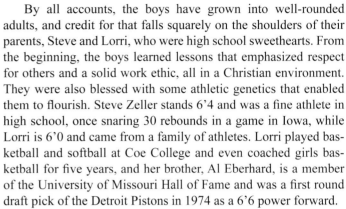

In the 100 years that high school sports have been played in earnest, it is doubtful that any local family has dominated one sport more than the Zeller boys from Washington. With an upbringing that stressed faith and family values, Luke, Tyler and Cody Zeller grew up before our eyes and became giants in more ways than one.

Luke Zeller
(Photo courtesy of the University of
Notre Dame Media Relations)

By all accounts, the boys have grown into well-rounded adults, and credit for that falls squarely on the shoulders of their parents, Steve and Lorri, who were high school sweethearts. From the beginning, the boys learned lessons that emphasized respect for others and a solid work ethic, all in a Christian environment. They were also blessed with some athletic genetics that enabled them to flourish. Steve Zeller stands 6'4 and was a fine athlete in high school, once snaring 30 rebounds in a game in Iowa, while Lorri is 6'0 and came from a family of athletes. Lorri played basketball and softball at Coe College and even coached girls basketball for five years, and her brother, Al Eberhard, is a member of the University of Missouri Hall of Fame and was a first round draft pick of the Detroit Pistons in 1974 as a 6'6 power forward.

The family moved to Washington from Winona, Wisconsin in 1993, just as Luke was preparing to enter kindergarten, and Steve and Lorri chose a home that had a basketball goal in the driveway, not knowing, of course, that they would eventually be raising three 7-footers. As the boys grew, the two-on-two games became more physical and often ended up with Steve having broken glasses or a black eye, so alternative methods were developed. Because of Lorri's position as secretary to the athletic director, who also happened to be the basketball coach, she had access to the gym, and many long hours were spent with Steve using a football blocking shield to toughen the boys up.

Steve's purpose was to expose the boys to physical play without them losing their cool, and the method would prove invaluable as the boys faced defenses designed to frustrate them. The boys grew up on the AAU circuit, and Luke's experiences made things better for Tyler and Cody as Steve Zeller learned from his mistakes. Stories were revealed in magazine articles about long car rides where Luke would get an earful from his father before asking, "Did I do anything right?" Steve admitted that he learned from the experience and tried to offer mostly positive comments after that.

Luke was 6'5 as an eighth grader and occasionally worked out with the varsity under head coach Dave Omer, who had come to Washington from Barr-Reeve in 1995. "I saw his potential before he got to high school," Coach Omer said. "He was a hard worker. He played every day and was serious about everything. He'd want to stay after practice and do more. He made himself a tremendous shooter. He was one of the best three-point shooters around, and he was an excellent passer."

As a freshman, Luke made the All-Big Eight team after averaging 15.3 points and 8 rebounds on a 14-7 team that was led by seniors Nick Clauss (11.4 per game) and Tony Goble (10.7). The team fell to Jasper in overtime in the sectional to end their season, and the following year, Washington improved to 18-4 with a team that featured Drew Streicher, Bart Young and Justin Smith.

The team lost to Vincennes Lincoln in the sectional (55-51), just as they would do the following year after an 18-5 season. But with the arrival of a big sophomore for the '04-'05 season, Washington fans had high hopes.

Cody Zeller (Photo courtesy of Mark's Gallery)

Coach Omer welcomed an experienced crew of seniors in 2004 along with super soph Bryan Bouchie, and the Hatchets battled through a tough schedule, losing only to Carmel (54-37) and Bellmont (59-54) in a mid-season tournament. In the sectional, the boys eliminated Gibson Southern and then knocked out their nemesis Vincennes Lincoln before capturing the 3A regional with wins over Edgewood (72-33) and Scottsburg (88-68). Luke was brilliant throughout, and after a 51-46 victory over Roncalli, the Hatchets were headed to State.

In front of a capacity crowd of 18,345 at Conseco Fieldhouse, the first sellout since the class system began in 1998, Washington squared off with Plymouth for the title. The 22-4 Pilgrims were on fire in the first half and torched the nets on 10 of 23 shooting from behind the arc as they trailed 36-34 after two periods. Washington came out after halftime in a man-to-man defense to try to cool Plymouth off and led 57-47 with a quarter to go. As the Hatchets tried to milk the clock, the Pilgrims chipped away at the lead and eventually tied the game at 64 to force overtime.

The teams gave each other all they had in OT, and with Washington clinging to a 71-70 advantage, Plymouth called timeout with 9.8 seconds left. According to Plymouth coach Jack Edison, who had won the 1982 State championship on a desperation heave by Scott Skiles, the first two options on the play were Kyle Benge, who had 22 points on the night, and the team's leading scorer Geoff Scheetz. As the play developed, neither could find daylight and freshman Randy Davis slithered his way to a scoop shot past Washington's Bryan Bouchie for a one-point lead with only 1.8 showing on the clock. On most days, that effort would have been enough to place Davis in the Indiana legend category, but on this day, that title was reserved for someone else.

Like many Hoosier hot shots who spend hours alone in driveways or parks while they dream of making the last-second shot to win the big game, Luke Zeller had played out this scenario many times in his head. Luke told reporters after the game that he knew what had to be done as soon as the timeout was called. "It was a situation where I didn't want anybody else on the team to have it on their shoulders," Luke explained to the journalists. "Win or lose, I wanted to have it. I wanted it on me."

The fact that the discussion on the bench took place at all was a total surprise to Dave Omer, because when Davis hit the shot, Washington had no timeouts left. For some reason, Plymouth called timeout, and what happened next was eerily similar to the famous scene in the movie *Hoosiers*. But the hero wasn't Jimmy Chitwood; it was Luke Zeller.

"He said, 'If you get me the ball, I'll score,'" Dave Omer recalled. "So that's what we did." Omer knows that the Hatchets were fortunate that Edison called time and still doesn't understand why he did. But the break did give Omer time to set up a play. "Maybe he didn't know we were out of timeouts," Omer hypothesized. "Had he not called timeout, I don't know what we would have done. We tried to set up the old Christian Laettner play. We ran a down screen for (6'8 sophomore) Bryan Bouchie and got Luke open. Justin Smith was a soccer player and knew how to throw the two-handed overhead pass. Luke had time to catch it, make one dribble and square up and shoot. It wasn't a throw. He was strong. He could shoot jump shots from half-court easily."

What followed was a shot that was a thing of beauty, and as despair turned to jubilation, Luke Zeller's name became destined to be emblazoned in the annals of Indiana State tournament lore forever. For 24 hours or so, the shot was the top play shown on ESPN, and Luke searched for ways to describe the feeling. "I still can't put it into words," Zeller told Ted Kluck of Sports Spectrum. "After playing for four years and working so hard and taking that shot so many times in my backyard, it was a pretty awesome way for it all to play out."

The Hatchets finished the 2004-2005 season 27-2 with the leadership of six seniors: Luke (19.6 per game), Isaac Stoll (11.1), Justin Smith (11.0), Joel McDonald (5.3), Bart Young (2.9) and Brett Matteson (2.6). Luke led the team in the final game with 28 points, 11 assists and 9 rebounds, and because of his character and 4.0 grade point average, he was named the Trester Award winner.

Luke was a four-year starter and All-Big Eight each year and was the only player from a school smaller than 4A to be named first team All-State. In addition, he was honored as both a McDonald's and Street & Smith All-American. Perhaps the honor he will treasure most, however, is being named Indiana's Mr. Basketball. Luke received 101 of 247 votes, beating out Richmond's Dominic James (63 votes) and Carmel's Josh McRoberts (41) and joining Washington's Steve Bouchie (Bryan's father) as the only Hatchets to be so honored. Called "the best player I ever coached" by Dave Omer, Zeller finished his career with 1,727 points (18.4/game) and 820 rebounds (8.7), and needless to say, he had several options available to him at the next level.

IN GOOD COMPANY

When their high school careers were over, Luke, Tyler and Cody Zeller had become only the third set of three or more brothers to score 1,000 points each in Indiana history. The brothers before them were Larry, Howard ('Bugsy'), Willie and Junior ('June Bug') Humes of Madison and Matthew, Andrew and A.J. Graves of White River Valley.

Steve and Lorri Zeller were as new to the recruiting process as Luke, and Steve admitted later that Luke's was a learning process that benefitted the younger brothers years later. The family eventually narrowed the choices to IU, Purdue, Notre Dame, Kansas, Stanford and Missouri, and West Lafayette looked to be his destination early. "Purdue was a real option," Luke told the *News Sentinel.* "I really liked Coach (Gene) Keady. He's like my high school coach. They're like twins. I liked the way his teams got after it."

But Keady announced his impending retirement and Purdue slid down the list. The eventual winner was Mike Brey and his Fighting Irish, and though Luke's career at Notre Dame wasn't spectacular, he contributed for four years and was working in the NBA Developmental League as of 2012.

As Luke's shot sailed through the net in 2005, one of the fans in the stands was his brother Tyler. A year prior, Tyler was a 5'10 eighth grader, but he sat in Conseco Fieldhouse in '05 as a 6'6 freshman. 2005 marked the end of Luke's career and also the end of Coach Omer's, as he retired after the season. So as Tyler Zeller made his debut in 2006, so did Gene Miiller, the highly successful coach who had spent thirty years at Kankakee Valley ('76-'81), Vincennes Lincoln ('82-'98, replacing local legend 'Gunner' Wyman) and Lafayette Jeff ('99-'05).

Miiller had followed the Zellers from afar and learned more when he returned to the area in 2006. "Tyler was a late developer," Miiller said from his office just off the gym. "He really didn't have a lot of success until his sophomore year (after his growth spurt). It was only then that he started to really want to play. Luke had been a good young player, and Cody was a good young player. In fact, after my first game here (Tyler's first as a varsity player), a lady came up to Lorri and said, 'I didn't even know you had a middle son.' Between his freshman and sophomore year, he just blossomed."

As a 6'8 sophomore, Tyler averaged 14.9 points, second on the team to Bryan Bouchie's 15.3. Zeller and Bouchie were named to the All-Conference team, and the team finished 18-6, losing 64-61 to Madison in the regional.

By his junior year, Tyler was nearly full-grown, nearing 7'0 and wearing a size 19 shoe. Once again, the Hatchets went 20-4 and won the sectional before falling in the regional to Bosse 71-47. Tyler earned All-Conference honors again and led the team in scoring with his 18.3 average, followed by four seniors: Bouchie (15.5), Ross Wade (5.6), John Sturgeon (5.3) and Andrew Obaseki (5.0).

DID YOU KNOW?
The Zeller brothers were encouraged to pursue other interests. In fact, Tyler Zeller took piano lessons until his freshman year and played for three years on the school's tennis team.

Tyler Zeller (Photo courtesy of Mark's Gallery)

Tyler had watched his brother grab the brass ring only three years earlier, and only one more chance remained for the late bloomer of the family. As the 2007-'08 season played out, not only did Tyler earn another trophy for the mantle but he put together one of the finest individual seasons in the storied history of Washington basketball.

After an opening win over Barr-Reeve, the Hatchets fell 61-57 to Central and then lost 66-64 to Edgewood in the fourth game despite Tyler's 42 points. From there, Tyler went on a tear and his team never felt the sting of defeat again. In the next game, Zeller lit up Bosse for 47 points on 20 of 23 shooting and a perfect 7 for 7 at the line. He would match that 47 later against Sullivan as Washington rolled into the tournament at 17-2.

Tyler opened the sectional with 34 points as his team pulverized Pike Central 81-29, and then he torched Vincennes Lincoln for 31 in a 76-49 victory. In the regional, it was déjà vu all over again for Edgewood as they fell 70-63 and watched Tyler put up 32. To finish up the regional, Tyler tallied 38 points in the championship game against Evansville Memorial, and with two teams between him and the title, fans would soon see that he was saving the best for last.

In the semi-state, Batesville gave Washington all they could handle but couldn't tame Tyler as he dominated from the outset with 38 points in the 73-69 win. With all eyes upon him, Tyler stepped onto the floor at Conseco just as Luke had done three years earlier, but this game wouldn't require any last-second heroics.

With the fieldhouse draped in a sea of black and gold, Ft. Wayne Harding tried its best to batter Washington's big man, but Zeller was not to be denied. Hitting 14 of 22 from the field and 15 of 18 from the line, Tyler made the 84-60 win look easy with his 43 points that broke a State championship game record that had stood since 1970.

Tyler finished his career as the school's #2 all-time scoring leader with 1,624 points (22.2/game) to go with 696 rebounds (9.5). He also recorded the best three field goal percentage seasons in Hatchets history with his .686 ('08), .680 ('07) and .675 ('06) for a career percentage of .682. Even more remarkable was his senior season when he scored 30 or more points 17 times in 25 games and 38 or more 12 times.

With the help of a strong supporting cast, including 6'11 senior Seth Coy (13.6/game), senior Kyle Price (8.4), junior Cody Osman (6.5), sophomore Sam Gines (3.3), sophomore Ethan Hunsinger (2.7) and a 6'2 freshman named Cody Zeller, Washington had recorded the school's fifth State title. Along with Seth

Coy, Tyler was honored on the All-Big Eight team, but his accolades extended far beyond southwestern Indiana.

Tyler had attracted a lot of attention with his remarkable season, and one man who observed with great interest was retired coach Dave Omer. "I've seen them all," Omer proclaimed when asked to assess the talents of Tyler Zeller. "I've seen Bob Ford (Evansville North, 1967), George McGinnis, all of them, and Tyler Zeller was as good a big man as I've seen. He had all the tools. He's a wonderful shooter, he has great post moves, he's an excellent rebounder, and he has phenomenal hands. You couldn't keep him from scoring."

Like Luke, Tyler was named a McDonald's All-American and was handed the #1 Indiana All-Star jersey, making he and Luke only the third set of brothers to be named Mr. Basketball, joining twins Tom and Dick Van Arsdale (1961) and Billy and Dave Shepherd ('67 & '70).

With college coaches hovering like flies, Steve and Lorri Zeller had become more savvy about the recruiting process and learned to spend the majority of their efforts on true contenders. Another advisor was Coach Miiller, who did his best to help when he could. "We would sit right here in this room and talk about it," Gene said as he gestured toward the walls of his office. "In fact, we were right here when Tyler decided he was going to North Carolina. He had it narrowed down to IU, Purdue and North Carolina."

Miiller went on to say that Tyler had doubts that he could play in Chapel Hill, but head coach Roy Williams and his staff convinced him and the marriage turned out to be a successful one. Zeller started the first two games of his freshman season in place of the previous season's national Player of the Year, Tyler Hansbrough, who was out with a leg injury. Tyler scored 18 points in the opener over Penn and then played well in a 77-58 win over Kentucky before suffering an injury of his own. With less than two minutes to go, Tyler broke away for a dunk but then fell awkwardly after a foul by Ramon Harris. The fall broke both forearm bones, and Zeller didn't return until late in the season. He did make it back in time, however, to play one minute of the team's 89-72 victory over Michigan State for the NCAA championship in 2009.

As a sophomore, Tyler averaged 9.3 points and 4.6 rebounds, and in his junior year, his minutes jumped from 17 to 28 as he averaged 15.7 points on 54.7% shooting to go with 7.2 rebounds per game. The highlight of the year occurred on December 8, 2010 when Tyler returned to southwestern Indiana to earn MVP honors with 27 points in a 76-49 win over the Evansville Aces in front of the first full house at Roberts Stadium since 2004.

When his senior season rolled around in 2011, Tyler was a fully matured specimen whose solid play had drawn praise from many of the sport's gurus, and his stock as a potential pro rose significantly. In the second game of the year, he rang up UNC-Asheville for 27, and in February, he tallied 22, 23 and 25 points against Maryland, Duke and Virginia, respectively. He also popped for 30 in a rematch with Maryland.

North Carolina advanced to the regional final for the second straight year before losing to Kansas on March 25, 2012. As a result of his fine season, the 7-foot, 250-pound Zeller was named the ACC Player of the Year, becoming the first Tarheel to be so honored as a senior since Phil Ford in 1978. Known for his cerebral approach to the game, Zeller averaged 16.3 points as a senior and also excelled in the classroom, earning Academic All-ACC honors all four years.

With his career far from over, Tyler drew high praise from many who were looking toward the NBA draft, including one man who knew him as well as anyone. "I think he is the finest running big man in the country," said UNC coach Roy Williams, "and he has a tremendous shooting touch to go with that ability to run the floor."

Apparently there were some who agreed with Coach Williams' assessment, and verification of Tyler's worth showed itself in the 2012 NBA draft. Expected to go mid-first round, Zeller was selected 17th by the Dallas Mavericks and then promptly traded to Cleveland for the 24th, 33rd and 34th picks. Although Tyler downplayed that he could be as valuable as three players, the Cavaliers certainly thought so, and time will tell as we watch the three he was traded for, Jared Cunningham (#24 from Oregon), Bernard James (#33 from Florida State) and Jae Crowder (#34 from Marquette) take their shots as professional players.

With Tyler on his way to an NBA career, the baby of the family was making some history of his own in Bloomington, and just like his older brothers, it all began at the Hatchet House. As a freshman, Cody had watched his brother put together one of the best seasons in Indiana history, and as a young boy, his eyes followed Luke's miracle shot as it found the net and brought him legendary status. With this kind of family history, what can a young man do to live up to the expectations?

During the 2008 championship season, Cody had seen limited action and averaged 2.4 points and 2.1 rebounds on the varsity, but as a sophomore, he began to assert himself, using his 6'9 frame to establish himself as a post player. The team finished 21-3 before losing to Salem 58-51 in the regional, and with some nice players around him, Cody was ready to write his own chapter in the Hatchet history book.

The 2009-'10 season started better than any in recent history with Cody and his pals winning the first twelve games before a two-point loss to Princeton. Shortly thereafter, the Hatchets fell to Vincennes Lincoln by two and then ended the regular season with a 56-44 loss to Memorial. In the sectional opener, Washington avenged the loss to Vincennes with a 54-35 spanking and then captured the title with a 43-30 win over Jasper.

The boys then defeated Corydon Central (52-45) and Boonville (55-47) to take the regional and Danville (57-38) in the semistate to punch their ticket to Conseco. The Hatchets used balanced scoring and cool heads to stay close with Gary Wallace in a game marred by controversial calls and a steady parade to the foul line. Neither team could separate from the other, and with 36 seconds left, Wallace's Latroy Taylor canned a three-pointer to knot the game at 56-56. After a missed three by Washington's Sam Gines, the contest went to OT. Gines sank two free throws with 53 seconds remaining to put the Hatchets up 65-61, and all the Hornets could muster was a single point, giving Washington its third State title in six years.

Cody led the team with 20 points and a State Finals record 26 rebounds, and he was supported with balanced scoring, led by Kurtis Anthony's 17. The other starters were solid as well, with Sam Gines and Dylan Ervin scoring 8, Robert Pittman with 6 and Ethan Hunsinger playing 29 minutes off the bench and scoring 6 points.

Cody and Sam Gines played the entire 36 minutes, and Cody stepped to the podium for the second time. Although he had one-upped his brothers by leading the Hatchets to a title in his junior season, his body of work was far from over.

With several players returning, Washington fans had visions for the 2010-'11 version of the Hatchets, but the boys struggled early, losing four of their first eleven games to Evansville Central (54-53), Forest Park (70-65) and to Center Grove (68-64) and Warsaw (46-44) in the holiday tournament. After that, they righted the ship and dominated from there, eventually earning the state's #1 ranking in 3A.

In the sectional, the Hatchets claimed the title with wins over Vincennes (56-36) and Southridge (47-36), and then they defeated Bosse (71-49) and Corydon Central (68-41) to capture the regional. Then, after a surprisingly easy 66-48 win over Batesville in the semi-state, they were off to Conseco once again.

This trip was not as traumatic, as Coach Miiller's boys played like the veterans they were. After falling behind Culver Academies 18-15 with 35 seconds left in the first, the Hatchets took control with a 20-4 run and never looked back. During the spurt, Robert Pittman scored 6 and Dylan Ervin played his usual solid defense and scored 6 as well. Once again, Cody led the way with 20 points and 18 rebounds, but he was amply supported by Ervin's 18 points and 6 rebounds and Kurtis Anthony's 10 points and 4 assists in the 61-46 victory.

The Hatchets had won their final 17 games to finish 24-4 and had beaten every tournament opponent by double digit scores. More importantly, Cody and his teammates had equaled a feat accomplished by the great Washington teams of 1941 and 1942 by winning back-to-back State titles.

Cody finished his career with 1,539 points, placing him third on the school's all-time list behind Tyler's 1,624 and Luke's 1,727. Just like his brothers, Cody was also selected as a McDonald's All-American and became the third Zeller brother to be named Indiana's Mr. Basketball, a feat that will almost certainly never be achieved again.

It wouldn't be much of a stretch to say that no Indiana high school player faced more scrutiny and hype than Cody Zeller, and with his laid-back, intelligent approach, he delivered in a big way. As a summer AAU player, it was common to see Purdue's Matt Painter, Butler's Brad Stevens, Tom Izzo of Michigan State plus other big names like Pitino and Krzyzewski only a few feet away, and with the 6'11, 215-pounder ranked in the top 20 recruits nationally, the Zellers had a lot to consider.

After some serious discussions with his mom and dad, Cody politely said no to Butler and North Carolina and gave a highly anticipated YES to Coach Tom Crean at IU. Both his brothers looked hard at Indiana, but the time just wasn't right. Luke would have committed to a shaky situation when Mike Davis was at the controls, and Tyler wasn't comfortable with the feeling he got during the Kelvin Sampson regime that proved to be a low point for the program.

But Coach Crean had revived the pride in IU basketball and inspired Indiana fans of the past to return, and Cody was a key factor in the revival. Cody has proven that he can handle extreme pressure. In high school, he was expected to be a McDonald's All-American and Mr. Basketball, and he was, and as an IU Hoosier, he has drawn comparisons to Damon Bailey, the knight in shining armor who was pre-ordained to lift the program to new heights.

Cody called the choice "a tough process" when speaking to the *Courier*, and in the same story, Coach Crean summed up his feelings by saying, "When you use the phrase 'the sky's the limit,' you can put Cody Zeller's name next to it. I see no ceiling for that young man."

Zeller was greeted by a standing ovation at his first open scrimmage at Assembly Hall, and if his freshman year is any indication, he will go down as one of IU's all-time greats. He averaged 15.6 points and 6.6 rebounds with a 62.3% field goal percentage (4th in the country) and opened the season with a double-double (16 points, 10 rebounds) to the delight of the crowd. He earned Freshman of the Year honors in the Big Ten and was named a Freshman All-American by *Sporting News* and others. Most importantly, he and a strong contingent of teammates returned IU to the NCAA tournament with Cody appropriately scoring the team's first points on a jumper from the free throw line.

Cody was picked as a pre-season All-American for 2012-'13 and has done at IU what he did at Washington, worked hard to get better and lived up to expectations. Like his brothers, the upbringing provided by his parents has enabled him to keep life in perspective and to thrive as a competitor. All three brothers excelled in the classroom, with Luke honored as Washington's valedictorian with a 4.0 GPA and Tyler and Cody right behind at 3.976.

"Their parents raised them in a very Christian home," Coach Miiller explained. "You could count on each one of them doing the right thing, in practice or in the classroom. They just made the right decisions. I'm sure there are people out there waiting for them to stumble."

With all their similarities, there are also differences, and Coach Miiller knew the boys well. "Luke is the most out-going," Miiller pointed out. "He's very social. Tyler is more reserved and probably the most outwardly competitive. Cody is a little bit of a prankster, and he has a very dry sense of humor. He's competitive in a different way. We called him 'ESPN Cody' because he could tell you everybody's averages. Tyler didn't pay much attention."

As for their games, all are impressive, but most agree that the younger boys are more physical. "Luke liked to step out on the perimeter, even though he was seven-feet," Coach Miiller revealed. "Tyler was more of an inside player and was happy being inside. He could shoot from outside; he just didn't do it much. He was a scoring machine. Cody was a nice mix of both. He's probably the most versatile of the three."

Steve and Lorri Zeller were the guiding force behind their sons' successes and were two people I really wanted to meet, but, citing concern over NCAA eligibility and plans to write a book of their own, they politely requested not to be interviewed. Their wishes were respected, but the family story was a necessity as a local legend.

Steve and Lorri are respected by everyone I met, and their methods obviously produce results. Lorri once explained to a reporter the challenge of having three star athletes to keep track of, saying, "I'm the travel agent. We have a calendar on our refrigerator that is color-coded, red for IU, blue for Carolina with Luke's (professional schedule) in purple. It's a juggling act."

Steve and Lorri have always been there for their sons, and the family is working together to spread the message of their faith and success principles to youngsters through their DistinXion basketball camps. Their central message explains how to build a foundation for a successful life.

Luke, Tyler and Cody Zeller are living examples of that code, and their basketball careers have reflected their parents' values. With this foundation, they have done their school proud, recording a record of 182-36 (83%) during the nine-year Zeller Era at Washington. They also led their teams to four State championships in their last seven seasons, and, most significantly, became the only family in Indiana history to produce three Mr. Basketballs.

THE WINSETT SISTERS:
UNPARALLELED SUCCESS

As I traveled the backroads of Warrick County in June of 2011, I was preparing myself for a full day of interviews, but what happened next was one of the most enjoyable of all my Local Legends experiences. I realized that I had missed a turn when the dirt road ended at a logging site, so I backtracked to my destination. After I climbed the sloped driveway of the secluded home, I gathered my gear, knocked at the back door and was greeted by a family that captured my heart the second I met them.

As we walked inside, the kitchen was filled with the aroma of a delicious lunch simmering on the stove, and as I looked around, there were no obvious signs of the magnificent athletic careers of the lovely ladies who were there to share their story with me. As a group, we proceeded into the room that I'm sure was the primary gathering place over the years for their family of seven. Although there were no shrines to the sisters displayed in the house, the long dining room table was packed with photos and mementos that I assume had been pulled from storage for our meeting.

At the opposite end from where I sat were George and Ruth Winsett, two of the most genuine people I have ever met, and on each side of the table were three of the four sisters who were as skilled as any female athletes in local history. As I set up my photo scanner and tape recorder, as I had done hundreds of times before, little did I know that what I had expected to be just another interview with great athletes would turn into a story that encompassed so much more.

The process was a bit more complicated than normal because there were actually several interviews going on at once, and the girls quickly caught on to the fact that the recorder doesn't know who is speaking. Consequently, they learned to say their names before they spoke, a system that evoked plenty of laughter with its redundancy throughout the late morning.

Becky, the oldest of the sisters, sat to my left. Beth, the second oldest, could not make the meeting, and the two youngest, Barb and the baby of the family, Billie, were to my right. Although not a subject of this story, I should also mention Brett Winsett, who ran track and played football at Boonville High School. As we talked about Brett, Ruth was sure to point out that her son was the only state champion in the family, as a turkey caller and in archery, once as an amateur and once as a professional.

As we got to the crux of the story, I soon realized how close the sisters were as a pattern developed of finishing each other's sentences. For the most part, George and Ruth sat quietly as the girls chatted, and at one point, I looked across and saw Ruth smile at me as if to say, "What a beautiful family we have."

George Winsett is originally from Richland, Indiana, near Rockport, and lettered in football, basketball, baseball and track at Luce Township High School. He was the first in his family to earn All-Conference honors and played two years of football at Evansville College (U of E) in the '50s as well as a little basketball during the era of Hugh Ahlering, Jerry Clayton and Boonville's John David Brimm.

Ruth was a Reitz graduate, and although there were no sports for her to play, she enjoyed watching her brother, Mark Helfrich, as he played football for the Panthers and then at Evansville College. She was introduced to George because a classmate of

The Winsett sisters (L-R), Barb, Becky, Beth and Billie.

Beth (left) and Barb played together at BHS.

The Winsetts at home on the farm, (L-R) Brett, Barb, Billie, George, Ruth, Becky, Beth.

George's thought they would be perfect for each other, and his intuition was right on the money.

The couple settled into the farming life in Warrick County and originally planned to have four boys, but when the little ladies began to arrive, they had to come up with girls' names. For whatever reason, B's became the theme, and after Billie arrived and her birth was announced in church, the story goes that someone acknowledged all the B's and George proclaimed, "We've got a whole hive of them!"

The first of the B's was Becky, and her athletic talents seemed to serve as inspiration to the others as they followed in her footsteps by competing in volleyball, basketball and track. In track, Becky ran the 100 hurdles, the 800, 400 and relays, and she boasted that her relay team held the 1600 school record before revealing with a chuckle that it was the first year for the sport.

When the subject of basketball came up, I mentioned that I had done a story in the first book about the great Reitz team of 1981 that starred Shelly Brand and Barb Dykstra and won the State championship under Coach Louise Owen. But Becky wasn't thrilled with the topic. She had played for Boonville at the time, and as she began to tell the story, her sisters laughed out loud, knowing that I was about to hear a story they had sat through many times over the years.

The story revealed Becky's competitive nature, and knowing the importance placed on basketball in our part of the world, her blood warms up a few degrees when reminded of the '80-'81 season. Becky's teammates in 1981 were Karen Cornell, Mona Callis, Monica Dimmett and Dana Cummings, and the team had high hopes when tournament time rolled around. Apparently, a crucial referee's call (or non-call) could very well have cost Boonville the game against Reitz in the regional, leaving Becky and her teammates to wonder, 'Oh, what might have been?!'

Becky was in middle school when the Boonville volleyball program began, and she started under Coach Marlene Day when IHSAA volleyball was played under the one-class system. The Pioneers went 14-2 and 13-3 the first two years as Becky grew into a six-foot-tall powerful outside hitter. Her junior year, 1979, the team improved to 19-3, and in 1980, Boonville almost ran the table, recording the best record in school history at 26-1, losing only in the State Finals. Becky's four teams in high school amassed a record of 72-9 (89%), making her class the winningest in the program's history in terms of winning percentage.

Becky was the recipient of the Mental Attitude Award at State and was talented enough to get scholarship offers in all three sports. Because of her perfect grades and status as Boonville's valedictorian, her options were diverse, and she eventually accepted a volleyball scholarship to Purdue, a program consistently ranked in the top 15 nationally. During her years in West Lafayette, Becky was a busy lady as she played volleyball, served with Athletes in Action in Japan, Hong Kong and China, and earned

numerous academic honors before graduating magna cum laude with a Bachelors degree in Elementary Education. Becky had set the standards in every facet of her life, and the steady stream of talented sisters followed one after the other.

Beth Winsett entered Boonville High School as Becky was leaving and led the Pioneers to an 81-29 record (74%) for four seasons under new coach Mary Cox, including three sectional titles and a semi-state championship her senior year (1984). At the State Finals, Beth became the second Winsett to receive the Mental Attitude Award, and in addition to her excellence at the net as a 5'11" outside hitter, she also set the school 800-meter record on the track. Yet another achievement was one Beth didn't discover until years after she'd left. In the mid-'90s, a girl was about to set the school scoring record in basketball and when they researched the books, they found that Beth Winsett held the record. The only reason Beth knows that it was over 1,000 points is that she was hoping for a basketball scholarship and had kept her stats.

The hoops dream didn't work out, but Beth did play volleyball at Southern Illinois and became an Academic All-American. She then earned a Masters, Doctorate and Post-Doctorate and now is a chemist in Houston working for Exxon Mobil.

The oldest Winsett girls had led the way for their sisters and had done their part to elevate Boonville volleyball to elite status in our area, and a woman who watched first hand was Mary Cox, as an assistant during Becky's years and as a head coach for Beth. "Becky was a great competitor, and she has become an even better friend," Mary said. "She has given back to the sport by coaching ten years in Jasper. We had some great matches (with Jasper) and it was tough competing against a Winsett. Beth was a very intelligent player who worked very hard to learn a skill. She would practice and ask questions until she got it right."

For the only time in the Winsett era at Boonville, the coach was blessed with two sisters on the same team when Barb Winsett joined Beth in 1983 and '84. Those teams finished 19-6 and 29-2 respectively, and the '84 team won sectional and regional crowns before losing to Plymouth in the State semi-finals. Barb finished at Boonville in 1987 after earning All-Big Eight honors each year in all three sports and All-State two years in volleyball in addition to being president of the student council and valedictorian. Her four teams at BHS finished a combined 101-16 (86%), and with college on her mind, she traveled to many high-level camps and clinics.

Anytime the girls were going through the recruiting process, George and Ruth would keep a low profile but offer advice when asked. In Barb's case, though, some astuteness on her mother's part became a key component of the decision. A few years earlier, while watching Becky play in the Big Ten tournament, Ruth noticed that although Illinois was the conference whipping boy, their new coach, Mike Hebert, was turning things around. Consequently, they watched closely and saw the potential, and in 1987, Barb signed with the Fighting Illini.

Earlier in the interview, Ruth had told me that none of the girls had wanted to follow an older sister to college, but in Barb's case, she never really had the opportunity because of a situation that the girls still laugh about today. When the recruiting process was over in '87, Barb noticed that the only Big Ten school that hadn't contacted her was Purdue, Becky's alma mater, and when Barb brought up the subject, Beth and Billie looked at each other and wondered.

The comedy played out during Becky's first year at Purdue when the team was playing in a spring tournament. At an event at the University of Kentucky, the family came to watch and the Purdue coach asked Beth and Barb if they would stand next to the video camera to protect it from errant volleyballs. As a freshman, Becky didn't play much and spent a good deal of time on the bench.

At this point in the narration, Barb interrupted to tell me that she knew nothing about this until after she had graduated from college, and as she continued the story, Billie laughed hysterically. "She (Becky) didn't play much," Barb explained, "and we thought the coach was wrong; we KNEW the coach was wrong. We kept saying, 'I don't understand why Becky's not playing.' The coach's name was Dewey, and Beth and I were cutting up and saying, 'Phooey on youey, Miss Dewey.' THE WHOLE MATCH!"

According to Barb, it wasn't until the last game that they realized an important fact. Gasping, Barb looked at her sister and pointed to the camera, saying, 'Beth, do you think this thing picks up sound?'"

Obviously it did, and the recorded shenanigans may have been the reason that Purdue was the only Big Ten school to ignore Barb during the recruiting process. Though she was shunned by the Boilermakers, however, she became a standout at Illinois as her first two teams there ('87 and '88) advanced to the NCAA Final Four with her as the starting setter. Her final two years, Barb was named All-Big Ten before graduating with honors with a B.S. in Accounting.

After Barb's graduation, area schools were able to breathe easy for a year with no Winsett donning the black and gold. The last in line would enroll at BHS in 1988, and Mary Cox was nearing the end of a great ride. Mary was fond of Barb and had kept an eye on Billie since she played in elementary school.

"It was a great thrill for me as a coach to see Barb play in the NCAA Finals at Market Square Arena in Indy," Mary said. "It really was a 'WOW moment'. Billie was long-legged and very skinny. She moved like a newborn colt. She developed her strength and coordination at BHS in the pool, which she didn't like too much.

"She started out very young coming to camp with her sisters," Mary continued. "She told coaches who were there recruiting that she would be talking to them some day because she was going to be the best one yet."

Whether Billie was the best is probably a matter for debate, but her success is undeniable. As a freshman at Boonville, her team finished 27-7, and the next year Boonville finished 30-6 and advanced to the semi-state before losing to Muncie Burris, the most dominant program by far in Indiana history. In 1990, the Lady Pioneers finished at 22-8, and Billie's team her senior year was 30-5 with a runner-up finish at the semi-state.

The youngest Winsett had finished her career with a combined four-year record of 109-26 (81%) and was a four-year letter winner in volleyball, basketball and track. On the track, she long jumped and ran the 400, and she and teammates still hold the school record in the 1600 relay. In volleyball, Billie earned All-State honors her last three years and played for the USA junior national team in the summers of 1990 and 1991.

With serious interest from many schools, Billie opted for one of the best in the country, Nebraska. According to Coach Cox, Billie continued to work on her strength and coordination at Nebraska by taking a ballet class, and the work paid off. Billie starred for the Cornhuskers, earning Academic All-Big Eight honors from '93-'95 and making the All-Tournament Team in 1995 as Nebraska won the NCAA national championship. During her years in Lincoln, Billie also played for the USA Olympic Festival team for three years, and in 1996, she was honored as the NCAA Woman of the Year.

With her college career over, Billie was invited to practice with the U.S. Olympic team, but her husband, 'Fletch', was going to medical school, so drawing from the values of her upbringing, she went about the business of building a family. Today, Billie Fletcher runs Fletch's medical practice and lives on the property that touches her parents' land. On the other side of the property are Barb and her family, while Becky lives in Jasper with her kids and husband, who pilots jets internationally.

As we sat at the table, the sisters seemed to enjoy reminiscing about the good old days, but each has moved on to a new life. Though it was been over twenty years since Billie graduated, those years were significant for Boonville High School and southwestern Indiana. During the Winsett Era, from 1977 to 1991, Boonville won every sectional, and the sisters' combined record was 243-66 (79%), placing them among the most successful sibling athletes, male or female, in area history.

Obviously, there was some exceptional athletic talent involved, but the girls were anything but one-dimensional. George, who had excused himself earlier to bale hay and then returned, spoke up at one point when the girls were giggling, probably during the telling of the 'Videogate' scandal story when Beth and Barb recorded the Purdue game. "I want to mention one thing that has nothing to do with sports," George said. "Contrary to what it may sound like (with all the joking around), they were all valedictorians." George went on to say that in all their years at BHS, no Winsett sister ever received a grade lower than an 'A', a testament to their resolve and work ethic.

That environment for success was created in the home, and each of the sisters is highly aware of how fortunate they were. "We worked hard. It was just in our genes," said Beth Winsett on the phone from her home in Houston. "They would help us stay balanced, because we tended to go overboard sometimes."

"They both provided the work ethic example," Becky added. "Dad used to coach me in running in the yard and down behind the lake. He made a basketball court for us."

Billie referred the time when she proclaimed that she should be playing more on the basketball team, only to be reminded by George and Ruth that she needed to take responsibility for herself and work harder. "I never, ever heard them, even once, say anything ill about a coach or another player," Billie revealed. "They always taught us to do our best, and if we don't play, we need to get better."

Barb had a similar experience, saying: "I remember the drive to Illinois (to play college volleyball). Mom told me, 'This is a different environment; you are not going to get to play right away. You've always been the best and started every game. This is your time to sit and watch and learn as much as you can.'"

As usual, mom was right, and the girls did plenty of watching and learning as they saw the work ethic of their father on the farm and their mother, who was constantly busy and willing to learn something new. Ruth works for Billie at her husband's medical practice and "does the work of three employees without complaining." In addition, Ruth tends a huge garden, cans everything and gets up early and sews before going to work. Through all this, George and Ruth instilled in their girls values that ensured success.

"They provided us not with material things but good family-oriented things," said Billie, "like a Christian education and work ethic. There was no mental or emotional baggage, so anytime there was free time, we could play."

As they spoke of their parents, the girls seemed proud of what many kids today would be embarrassed about, like the fact that none of them owned a vehicle until they were a sophomore in college. The girls were always responsible for chores, like tending the garden, cleaning the pig pen and, in fact, putting up 10,000 bales of hay one summer – all without pay.

George told of the time that Becky wanted a job in the pharmacy but couldn't do it because of her work schedule. "I'll tell you what I'll do," George told the girls. "I have two acres of tobacco, and if you girls want to put it out, I'll furnish the equipment and you furnish the work." According to George, the girls planted, hoed and housed two acres for two years, and even Billie, who

was six at the time, still brags to this day about the "brand new Commodore 64 computer and leather volleyball" she bought with her money.

Over the years, Ruth Winsett worked as an RN at a hospital and nursing home but always found a way to be home for her children, and it should come as no surprise that the girls look to her as a model. Beth is a single working mother in Houston, and Barb worked at Mead Johnson but is now a stay-at-home mom. Becky has coached volleyball in Jasper for ten years and is home with the kids, and Billie taught the sciences in high school but now manages her husband's medical practice from home as she watches the kids.

"I saw how important it was and how nice our home life was," Billie explained when asked why she and her sisters were stay-at-home moms. "I wanted to provide what mom and dad provided for us."

Barb echoed Billie's feelings, saying, "I loved to work, but there came a time when I said, 'God didn't give me three healthy children for someone else to take care of.'"

The Winsett sisters are now raising a new generation, with 15 grandkids for George and Ruth to watch over, and perhaps someone will write about them one day. The story I was there to research on that June morning turned out to be so much more than a tale about four superb athletes, and I realized that one of the perks of writing a book like this is that it offers the opportunity to meet some great folks.

What was intended to be a 45-minute fact-finding meeting turned out to be two hours of pure enjoyment, and as I drove down the hill to the dirt road that would take me back to so-called civilization, I couldn't help but think about the family I had just met. These girls who achieved so much in the athletic arena had just spent the majority of our time together praising their parents. So as I watched the fields roll by outside my window, I marveled at what I had just experienced, and I thought to myself how much nicer the world would be if we all could have been raised with the values and guidance of George and Ruth Winsett.

THE SCHIFF BROTHERS:
AN ERA OF SUPREMACY

In nearly 100 years of football, southwestern Indiana has seen some great players, and many have played the quarterback position. The last fifty years alone have produced such greats as North's Dean Volkman, Rex Mundi's Bob Griese and Gordon Slade of Bosse, and more recently local fans have watched great passing performances by Jay Cutler, Curtis Painter, Chris Owen, Joey Elliott, Paul and Matt McIntosh and many, many more. But no one could light up a scoreboard and put up numbers like Adam and Jake Schiff of Mater Dei.

The boys' father, Mark Schiff, played for the Wildcats under Joe Gossman and Frank Will and was good enough to earn a partial scholarship to U of E but decided to go to work instead. Judy Schiff, the boys' mother, was a 1975 Reitz grad whose allegiance has shifted from one powerhouse west side football program to another. Mark and Judy took a low-key approach to the development of the boys athletically, and based on the results, their philosophy paid off. Mark did coach Adam and Jake in football, basketball and baseball in the early years, with an emphasis on fundamentals and having fun, but he soon turned his sons over to other coaches and stayed in the background as they developed.

Both boys were self-motivated and blessed with a strong work ethic as they became all-stars in each sport, and as Adam and his teammates reached their teen years, Mater Dei fans were hopeful that the football program was about to turn a corner after a long dry spell. Adam would become the starter in 2006, and in the ten years prior, the Wildcats were 58-56. More importantly, they were only 4-6 against archrival Reitz and only 2-5 against the Panthers since 1989.

"When Adam's eighth grade cub team won City, it was the first time the cub team even won a game, let alone the city," Judy Schiff explained. "So that was a big deal, and everyone was so excited to have a good group of boys who were really good athletes. And then you could see it from Adam to Jake."

Though the talent was there, results were not immediate, and Adam had some tough times ahead when he assumed control of the offense in 1996. Like many small schools, Mater Dei couldn't match up physically with larger schools year in and year out, and coach Mike Goebel (pronounced GAY•buhl) opted to re-vamp the offense. Using Hanover College as a model, Goebel went to a spread offense, and Adam bore the brunt of the punishment by opposing defenses as the Wildcats struggled to learn the system.

"He suffered a lot," said little brother Jake, who watched the mauling from the stands. "They hadn't learned how to pick up a blitz, and he got pounded." The result was a painful 5-5 season that included an ugly 48-7 loss to Castle and a 42-14 shellacking by Memorial in the sectional.

Despite the challenges, Adam persevered and had a good season by ordinary standards, completing 164 of 284 passes (57.1%) for 1,917 yards and 13 touchdowns. With the '96 season behind him, Adam and his teammates worked to hone the intricacies of the run-and-gun offense, and things soon improved for the Wildcats.

Coach Goebel's new scheme proved to be a perfect match for the Schiff brothers, and Jake waited in the wings as he watched his older brother immerse himself in the system with his cerebral approach to the game. From studying countless hours of game

Adam (on one knee) and Jake Schiff

film, Adam learned to detect defensive tendencies of upcoming opponents, and as he studied the system, he became proficient at calling audibles to change a play at the line of scrimmage.

As a junior, Adam's production nearly doubled as he led Mater Dei to a 9-4 record behind a much-improved line that included Dustin Macke, Dave Hisch and Brian Eickhoff, among many others. The Wildcats fell to Central, Harrison and Owensboro Apollo but defeated both Castle (32-24) and Reitz (14-6) before capturing the sectional and then losing to Western Boone in the regional to end their season. Adam finished the year with 3,456 yards and 27 TD passes, the second best passing season in school history.

In 1998, Adam's senior year, the Cats finished 10-3, losing only to Harrison (19-14) and Castle (27-24) during the regular season and to Western Boone once again (28-21) in the regional. Adam had become totally comfortable in the new system and had another fine year, completing 248 of 366 passes (67.8%) for 3,370 yards and 29 TDs, pulling him ahead of Jeff George and others on the all-time Indiana career passing list.

During his years at the helm of the new offense, Adam was fortunate to throw to some very talented receivers who penetrated opponents' defenses from all angles, and four of them recorded seasons that rank among the top 15 in Mater Dei history: Brandon

Adam was an excellent multi-sport athlete who went on to star on the diamond at USI.

Jake Schiff passed for nearly seven miles of yardage while at Mater Dei.

Boots (1997 – 80 catches, 1,208 yards, 9 TDs); Ike Miller (1998 – 84, 1,094, 11); Andy Woehler (1998 – 62, 880, 7); and Nathan Schiff (1998 – 49, 840, 9).

Adam finished his career with 8,743 career passing yards, 56 TD passes and a completion percentage of 62.6%, all school records. He was also recognized on the All-City, All-Conference and All-State first teams and was a finalist for Indiana's Mr. Football award. At 5'11, he was courted by smaller football schools, but his options were increased by his skill as a multi-sport athlete. On the basketball court, he was a two-year starter and Kiwanis Award winner, and on the baseball field, he was even better. Earning *Courier* All-Metro Player of the Year and All-State honors, he was a member of Mater Dei's 2A State runner-up in 1998 and the State champion Wildcat team in '99. Adam opted to stay near home at USI and became a four-year starter, earning All-GLVC honors as a second baseman and becoming a lifetime member of the .300+ batting average club.

While Adam was helping Coach Goebel work the kinks out of the new offensive system, Jake was preparing himself as the heir apparent. His cub team finished 7-0, and his freshman team 8-0, and as he watched Adam complete his career, Jake looked forward to wearing Adam's familiar #13 varsity jersey.

In his very first game as the starter, Jake and his talented teammates created quite a stir with a 28-0 win over perennial juggernaut Indianapolis Cathedral, and they followed that with wins over Central (35-14), Memorial (35-32), North (48-16) and Bosse (48-7). The team's only blemish during the regular season was a 44-35 slugfest in a losing effort against a talented Harrison team

that featured Andre Thomas, Quentin Jackson, Billy Strother and Jelani McGee. Mater Dei then finished the regular season with victories over Owensboro Catholic (42-3), Castle (35-28) and Reitz (27-24 in overtime).

After the regular season, the Wildcats breezed through the sectional and regional before falling to Danville 54-47 in the semi-state at Reitz Bowl. The '99 Wildcats lit up the scoreboards for 556 points as Jake shattered Adam's school records with 3,947 yards and 42 touchdown passes, and the semi-state loss to Danville would turn out to be the last Jake and his gang would experience for a long time.

Mater Dei opened the 2000 season with a 38-20 win at the Bowl over Indianapolis Broad Ripple, and that was as close as anyone would come for the next six weeks. The Wildcats finished the regular season with victories over their two greatest adversaries, Castle (19-7) and Reitz (42-21), before skating through the sectional with laughers over Paoli (70-6), Mitchell (70-28) and Tell City (40-6). After taking the regional 24-7 over Brownstown Central and the semistate 42-28 over Danville, the Wildcats then prepared for the 2A State championship at the RCA Dome.

From the opening kickoff, #2-ranked Mater Dei made a mockery of the ranking system as they annihilated #1 Ft. Wayne Bishop Luers. On the first play from scrimmage, Wildcat running back Nathan Wildeman split the Knights' defense for 65 yards, and as the game progressed, the line dominated as Wildeman rambled for 169 yards on the day. Jake was his usual remarkable self, leading Mater Dei to touchdowns on their first six possessions for a 42-3 halftime lead and an eventual 56-10 victory over the ten-time State champs.

"We played a solid game all-around," Jake answered when asked about the game. "The offense and defense were both great. Our receivers, especially Albert Schmitt and Jared Schiff, came up with huge catches. The atmosphere was incredible in the RCA Dome, and the Mater Dei fan base was very loud. My emotions were in check, and I felt focused the whole week, and the coaching staff did a great job of keeping us on track."

Jake let up on the throttle in the second half but still torched Luers for 218 yards (206 in the first half) on 16 for 23 passing with three touchdowns to help make Mater Dei the first Evansville team to win a football State title in the 28-year history of the tournament

For his efforts, Jake was named first team All-State and the S&L Publishing Class 2A Offensive Player of the Year as well as every local honor imaginable. Jake and his teammates put up staggering numbers once again, prompting fans and pundits to search the Indiana record books to find out how Jake stacked up with a season still ahead of him. In 2000, he threw for 275 yards or more seven times and had four TD passes against Broad Ripple, Harrison, Reitz and Mitchell. In the Reitz game, balls were flying all over the field as Patrick Mallory caught 9 passes for 4 touchdowns and Jared Schiff snagged 6 for 2 TDs while Reitz receivers Chris Brunson and Andy Kissel grabbed 8 apiece.

When Jake's senior season rolled around, the defending State champions had a target on their backs, and Jake continued to put in the effort to stay on top of his game. Unlike Adam, Jake abandoned basketball and baseball after his freshman year, and he took great pride in his mental preparation. "He would take a legal pad and watch game tapes, and that thing would be full," Judy Schiff explained. "Then he'd talk to the coaches the next day."

Mark Schiff agreed and mentioned the fact that Adam was living at home as he worked on his degree at USI. "Jake was a film rat," Mark disclosed. "He would get a film of the next opponent and break it down through the week. Adam had an understanding of the offense, and they would watch it together."

Jake's knowledge afforded him a great deal of freedom in the offensive scheme, and it was not unusual for him to design a play that Coach Goebel would add to the playbook. When Jake explained his routine and how he would audible maybe 70% of the time, his eyes reflected his competitive intensity. "I always wanted to outwork the next team," Jake informed me. "With our style of offense, you needed that preparation because a lot of things were changed at the line of scrimmage. It was a blast!"

Jake's work paid off his senior year as the Wildcats bullied their opponents, with only Castle (28-21) and Reitz (38-31) coming within a touchdown during the regular season. In the sectional opener, Jake and Tell City's all-time greatest Marksman put on a show for the crowd as they threw for 904 combined yards. Jake completed 28 of 38 for 556 yards and 4 TDs and Tell City's Phillip Johnson threw for 348 in Mater Dei's 63-28 victory with Wildcat receivers Nick Lain (12 catches) and Blake Kollker (9 catches) also having huge games.

Mater Dei followed the shootout with comfortable wins over South Spencer (49-7), Southridge (45-22), Brownstown Central (55-39) and Speedway (49-20) to punch their ticket once again for the RCA Dome. In the championship game, the Wildcats faced Ft. Wayne Bishop Luers once again and matched the Knights punch for punch for 45 minutes. Trailing by eight points with under three minutes to go, the stage seemed to be set for a Hollywood ending that would cap off a fantastic career for Schiff. But the 'happily ever after' was not to be as interceptions turned into touchdowns that inflated the final score to 57-29 when the smoke cleared.

Though the season ended in disappointment, Jake Schiff had competed to the very end, and his final numbers were a reflection of the hard work he had put into his career. In his three seasons as Mater Dei's top gun, Jake was a model of consistency as he recorded the three best passing seasons in school history. As a sophomore, he completed 260 of 406 passes (64%) for 3,947 yards and 42 touchdowns. He then went 217 of 349 (62.2%) for 3,780 yards and 43 TDs as a junior and capped off his career with the finest season for a quarterback in Indiana history as he connected on 279 of 415 passes for 4,468 yards and another 45 touchdown passes.

Even more important than his individual stats were his team numbers. As a leader, Jake's teams from his cub football season on won 56 games and lost only 3, and his record as a varsity quarterback was 41-3, including a remarkable 29 consecutive wins in 2000 and 2001.

When the season ended, the accolades flowed as Jake was named Indiana's runner-up for Mr. Football, was named first team All-State and was selected as the Gatorade Indiana Player of the Year, among many other honors. As a 3.776 student (out of 4.0) and eventual magna cum laude grad, Jake had several colleges interested in his talents, including Purdue, Northwestern, IU, Harvard, Yale and Princeton, but as discussions progressed, the options dwindled. He was very excited about the potential of directing the wide open offense of Joe Tiller at Purdue, but even though Jake was about the same size as Boilermaker great Drew Brees, he was told by Tiller that he was too small. Schiff eventually opted for Indiana State and was building a fine career when a persistent collarbone injury forced him to retire.

Jake looks back at his high school years as some of the best in his life, and he knows how fortunate he was to have had talented teammates around him to keep him safe. He mentioned his running backs, like Ryan Dewig and Sam and Nate Wildeman, pointing out how Nate "saved me many times by picking up blitzing linebackers."

Jake did his best to recall his linemen during the three years who allowed only about one sack per game in the pass-oriented offense, citing Tim Unfried, Jake Boehman, Don Faraone, Ben Verkamp and Jason Lewis as his protectors in 1999. As a junior, Jake lined up behind Verkamp, Faraone, Bob Schmitt, Brett Devault, Matt Hoon and Justin Greubel, and his senior year he was protected by Greubel, Devault, Schmitt, Dustin Beal, Brent Schmitt and Kenny Miller.

Jake also admits that he was blessed with some sure-handed receivers at Mater Dei, as was Adam. Patrick Mallory and Jared Schiff caught Jake's passes and stand first and second on the school's all time list in career receptions with 169 and 138, respectively. Right behind are two of Adam's receivers, Brandon Boots (154) and Ike Miller (151). Joining these in the school record book are other fine receivers like Dan Alcorn and Justin Elpers (Jake) and Andy Woehler and Nathan Schiff (Adam) among others.

Mater Dei's Patrick Mallory is #4 in the state in single season receiving yardage with 1,795 in 2001. Fellow Mater Dei receivers Brett McDurmon (17th, 1,397 yards) and Jared Schiff (21st, 1,397) are the only other area receivers to be ranked in the top 25.

"The success I was able to achieve individually was the result of a lot of hard work from the other great football players who played along with me," Jake said. "The guys around me worked just as hard as I did, and Coach Goebel did a fantastic job leading us and keeping us grounded. That hard work resulted in many wins and a whole lot of fun for everybody."

Part of the "fun" Jake alluded to was the bond formed between him and Mike Goebel, and one memory in particular brought a smile to his face. The moment took place against Brownstown Central in the 2000 regional at Reitz Bowl. According to Jake, BC ran a 3-4 defense with linebackers moving in and out and he was having trouble adjusting and had already thrown two early interceptions. "I was rolling out to the right toward our sideline and I threw a pick right in front of our bench," Schiff recalled. "It was a bad pick; I just threw it right to a linebacker. My momentum carried me right into Mike (Goebel), and he yelled 'Are you trying to lose this $@#&% game?' He was hot!" Jake did recover from the debacle however, and according to Lance Wilkerson, Mater Dei scored so many points that Brownstown Central would kickoff with onside kicks because they thought they had a better chance of recovering than stopping Jake.

Though the moment wasn't funny at the time, Mater Dei did go on to win the game and eventually the State title, and that season and Jake's whole career were memorable for many local fans. One particular incident took place in a crowded Reitz Bowl against nemesis Castle, and those who witnessed it could not believe Jake's toughness and resilience. "The Castle-Mater Dei game was one of the neatest experiences and memories I have of going to the Bowl," recalled Jon Carl, a Reitz teacher and coach and a local historian. "I wish Reitz played more afternoon games. It felt like a college game. It was as crowded as I've ever seen it. Jake got drilled and laid out by Castle defensive end Andrew Burk and another player, and they carried him off the field. I thought, 'there's no way he's coming back. His head snapped back and they drove him into the ground."

Jake remembers the hit well and seriously thought that his leg was broken. On the sideline, teammates gave Jake some privacy by surrounding him as Reitz team doctor, Dr. Rohleder, peeled off Jake's pants to examine and treat him. Like a script from a movie, Jake returned to replace backup Kyle Hartz after one series, and the spectacle is one TV sportscaster Lance Wilkerson will always remember, saying, "Of all the times I covered games at Reitz Bowl, when he came out, it was the loudest ovation I ever heard."

When asked to re-live some of his favorite moments, the memories came flooding back for Jake. He mentioned the Mater Dei-Reitz game his sophomore year (1999) when the two undefeated teams squared off for the last time in the millennium and the Wildcats prevailed 27-24 in overtime with Justin Elpers catching the ball on a post route and stretching with the ball over the goalline as he hit the turf. Jake also mentioned the loyalty of the Mater Dei alumni and the volunteer coaches who give so much for the program.

Mark Schiff informed me that both his sons had considered coaching at one point but instead opted for the business world, Adam in manufacturing and Jake in finance. As of 2012, Jake had fallen in love with golf and was becoming a force on the local scene, finding it somewhat of a catharsis, saying, "It gets those juices flowing. The only thing similar to it (golf) was on the football field." He has also stayed close to his favorite sport as a color man on Channel 14 football broadcasts with Mike Blake.

LIFE AIN'T FAIR

The knock against Adam and Jake Schiff as potential Division I quarterbacks was their lack of height at 5'11. As it turned out, both threw to cousins in high school, Adam to Nate Schiff and Jake to Jared Schiff. Both cousins stood 6'2 or 6'3. Mark Schiff, Adam's and Jake's dad stands 6'3 while the cousins' father, Bob, stands only 5'11. Go figure!

As the years pass, Jake and Adam will forever be remembered as two of the finest quarterbacks in local and state history, and they and their family were well thought of for more than just football. "You could walk the earth and meet as many people as you could but you'll never meet nicer people than Mark and Judy Schiff," said Lance Wilkerson, who has become a close friend of the Schiffs.

And as far as the boys' reputations, no one knew them better than Mike Goebel. "When we had the Schiffs, we had a great chance of success," Goebel explained. "They were two of the finest young men I've ever been around. Adam kind of paved the way for Jake. He took a beating when we put in the new offense. It wasn't the players' fault; we just didn't have things worked out. They both had the intelligence and will to win, and I think both could have played at a much higher (collegiate) level than they did."

By all accounts, Adam and Jake were extreme competitors and excellent students who loved the mental aspect of the game. The 'Schiff Era' was one of the finest in Mater Dei history, and the results bear it out. For five straight years, from 1997 to 2001, the Wildcats took home the West Side Nut Club trophy with victories over Reitz, and Jake and his teammates have the distinction of going 3-0 against both Reitz and Castle.

In the Mater Dei record books, Jake and Adam stand #1 and #2 in career passing yards at 12,195 and 8,743 respectively just ahead of Dustin Slaton (8,322, '01-'04) and Eric Goebel (7,314, '89-'91), and Jake and Adam recorded 5 of the top 6 seasons in passing yardage.

Adam Schiff withstood some tough challenges and had a remarkable football career, ranking seventh on Indiana's top ten career passing list while also excelling in basketball and baseball. Jake Schiff focused entirely on the gridiron and was touted by Coach Goebel with the following: "In my 27 years as a high school football coach, I have never encountered a player with more intelligence, work ethic and athletic ability than Jake Schiff possesses."

As for his place in local history, there are only a few athletes whose achievements on a statewide level have withstood the test of time. Castle's Lanae Renschler was the first player, male or female, to capture four State tennis titles, and Blake Maurer of Mater Dei is one of only a handful to win four State wrestling championships. Mt. Vernon's Ron Jones still holds the State high jump record (7'1 ¼" in 1980) after 32 years, and Memorial's Tom Martin (1977) was the record holder in the 880-yd./800-meter run for 34 years until Austin Mudd of Center Grove surpassed him in 2011.

Jake Schiff deserves to be included with this group and perhaps should top the list. As of 2012, he had outperformed such greats as Earl Haniford, Jeff George and many more to capture state records for completions in a season (279) and career (756), TD passes in a season (45) and career (130) and yardage in a season (4,468) and career (12,195). To add to his achievements, Jake's 12,195 career yards make him the #9 career passer on a national level. Jake accomplished all this as part of a successful system at Mater Dei with teammates who shared his passion for the sport. He was far more than a man with a missile launcher for an arm; he was also a student of the game who used his talents to become the most prolific passer in Indiana history.

THE NAME GAME

The Mater Dei football program has become a rite of passage for many west side families. According to the Mater Dei football website, the most common surname in the history of the program is Goebel, and here are the first names of those 26 players with the years they played there.

Adam ('97-'99)
Andy ('62-'64)
Andy ('86-'88)
Brian ('85-'87)
Charles ('65)
Chris ('82-'84)
Corey ('02-'03)
Dan ('93-'95)
Eric ('89-'91)
Gary ('70-'71)
Glen ('73)
Jeff ('94)
Jeremy ('03)
Jim ('84-'85)
John ('83-'85)
Lucas ('93-'95)
Matt ('87-'89)
Mike ('67-'69)
Nathan ('91-'93)
Nick ('97-'98)
Raymond ('01-'03)
Rick ('75-'77)
Steve ('67)
Tim ('03)
Tom ('83-'85)
Woody ('85-'87)

In case you're curious, there have been 8 Schiffs who played Mater Dei football as of 2012, and here are their names:
Adam ('96-'98)
Jake ('99-'01)
Jared ('98-'00)
Jim Sr. ('66-'68)
Jim Jr. ('93-'95)
Logan ('03)
Mark ('74-'75)
Nathan ('96-'98)

The following are the other most common names (as of 2012) found on Wildcat rosters over the last 63 years.

22 – Weinzapfel
14 – Martin
13 – Folz
11 – Wildeman
11 – Hermann
11 – Schenk
11 – Niemeier
10 – Moore

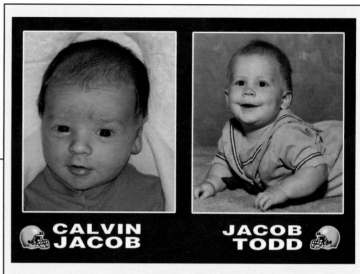

CALVIN JACOB   JACOB TODD

NAMESAKE

Lance Wilkerson always wanted his son (four years old in 2012) to be a quarterback. After getting to know and respect Jake Schiff, he named his son after the record-breaking Mater Dei quarterback. Shown here together are Jake (right) and Lance's son: Cal (after Cal Ripken Jr.) Jacob Wilkerson.

CAREER PASSING LEADERS

Evansville's own Jake Schiff is the state's leader in career passing yards, but other area QBs have been outstanding as well. Below are the area leaders with their state rankings and totals.

1st – Jake Schiff (Mater Dei) – 12,195
7th – Adam Schiff (Mater Dei) – 8,743
8th – Grant Gribbons (Memorial) – 8,715
9th – Dustin Slaton (Mater Dei) – 8,322
13th – Chris Owen (Central) – 8.102
18th – Joey Elliott (Harrison) – 7,797
23rd – Eric Goebel (Mater Dei) – 7,314
(Source: IHSAA Website)

DID YOU KNOW?

Patrick Mallory of Mater Dei is the area's career receiving leader with 3,412 yards. Tyler Schlaf of Castle is second with 2,557 yards.

CHAPTER EIGHT

DIAPER DANDIES

For over 100 years, local fans have enjoyed watching their favorite players, coaches and teams on the fields of battle, and as the competitions played out, legends were made. Our final chapter is dedicated to young athletes whose careers are just beginning but have shown signs of brilliance. So to give the younger generation their due, we now pay tribute to our Diaper Dandies.

MACIE ELLIOTT:
FIERCE AND FEARLESS

When I met Macie Elliott in August of 2011, the first thing that stood out was her obvious fitness. She had just returned from a workout with her coach, Stephanie Hazlett, and when the pretty brunette sat down, she and her parents were ready to talk tennis. Macie was preparing to begin her junior year at Memorial, but not before we took a quick peak back at a fabulous year she had just completed that laid the groundwork for her to be counted among our area's finest players.

Like many of the subjects in this book, Ms. Elliott blossomed at a young age. She started at age four, and she and her mom, Kathy, hit together until age ten when Macie started to win. Then, after a year at Advantage Fitness with Stephanie, she rose in the age-group junior ranks and became a force on the circuit.

"After she had been with Stephanie for a year, it was very noticeable how she'd progressed beyond other girls she had been playing with," said Rick Elliott, Macie's father. "She started beating girls who had drummed her two years earlier in these tournaments."

Her most recent season (2011) was Macie's coming out party of sorts, as she won the Central Indiana Tennis Association girls 18 championships in the summer and reached the quarterfinals of the Midwest Closed Girls 18s as well. She also placed second in the girls 16 nationals in Alabama and reached the round of 16 at the Clay Court National Championships in Virginia, finishing the year ranked #49 in the country among girls in her class.

Prior to the sensational summer, Elliott joined Memorial's Margo Stevenson as an individual IHSAA State champion with a 6-3, 6-2 win over Chelsea Carter of Indianapolis North Central. Using the State title as a springboard, Macie not only finished well in the summer's prestigious tournaments but her confidence soared with some big wins over notable opponents. Among her victories were wins over Kelsey Dieters, who was ranked #5 in the Midwest and is now playing for Ohio State; Stephanie Fox, who earned a full-ride to UK; and Ellen Silver, now playing at Iowa.

By all accounts, Macie's strength lies in her toughness, and that was never more evident than at the 2011 National Hardcourts in San Diego. With numerous college coaches looking on, Ms. Elliott displayed one of the intangibles that coaches search for in an athlete. After falling to the court and writhing in pain from a separated shoulder, Macie responded like a gladiator.

"My shoulder popped out," Macie explained matter-of-factly, "and I popped it back in place. It hurt really bad, but I still had to play with practically no serve." Playing through the pain, Macie hung tough, won the match and finished the tournament with two wins and two losses.

Macie's style is all power with a relentless tenacity that wears opponents down. "She just keeps coming at you and coming at you," Kathy Elliott pointed out. "She is never going to give up."

Coach Hazlett agrees and is working to give Elliott's game more diversity. "Macie is a power player," Hazlett explained. "She likes to hit the ball hard, with a big serve, but she can get overly aggressive at times. She's developing the skills of playing

longer points and rallying at a harder, higher-level pace, which has made her successful at the national level."

Much of Macie's attack mentality comes from her mindset, but much of her power comes from her training with Stephanie, an extreme competitor herself who can be very demanding. "She's a very, very good coach." Macie disclosed shortly after returning from a practice where Stephanie had not been in the best of moods. "Most of the time, we get along very well on and off the court. We have similar personalities in the way we like to play. She can read my mind when I'm out on the court because she's been there."

Stephanie understands the sometimes-testy relationship and has seen how Macie's physical and mental makeups have made her a winner. "She works with me three days a week," Hazlett divulged. "We do footwork, plyometrics (lunge and squat jumps that develop powerful bursts and explosion) and sprints a couple days a week, and then we do a day of lifting, bench presses and squats. But her will and competitiveness are what get her through a ton of matches. She's not going to give up."

In the past, Macie had been a well-rounded athlete, playing T-ball, volleyball, basketball, soccer and even taking dance classes, but as she grew, tennis became her passion. As with any athlete who can compete on the national level, sacrifices have to be made to reach their goals.

"Many are home-schooled," Rick Elliott informed me about the culture of junior tennis. "They can't be in a traditional school environment. There's too much of a time commitment."

"Sometimes you're torn," Kathy admitted, "because you see that she could be THIS good, but you see how few really make it."

As Macie listened to her parents, she joined in by describing a situation that illustrated the lifestyle perfectly. She had taken a friend to a tournament in Michigan during the holidays because her parents and coach couldn't go. "This is my first Thanksgiving dinner since I was six and the first pumpkin pie ever," Macie recalled her friend saying.

When asked about her personal goals, Macie doesn't obsess with becoming the next Serena Williams or Steffi Graf. Instead, she looks at her situation pragmatically. "I want to go to a high-level, D-I school and be able to play on the team," she revealed. "I don't necessarily have to play #1 or #2; I would be fine playing 3 or 4. It's more important to me to be a part of a better team."

As a 5.97 student (on a 6.0 scale), thanks to a 'B' in geometry her freshman year, Macie's options are many, but the college process isn't as easy as it is for some other sports. She has received emails from Princeton, Yale and Florida State and has had more personal contact from Minnesota and Penn State, and the Elliotts are doing their part to make the process work. Macie has been playing up at the 18 & under level to catch the eye of college coaches, and her junior and senior seasons are critical.

To Macie, just being the #1-ranked player in her class in Indiana isn't enough. She has an impressive resumé, with championships at the Ann Arbor Junior Open ('08), the Midwest Open ('10), and the CITA Midwest Qualifier ('08 and '11) among other achievements, but there is much to be accomplished.

At Memorial, the future looks bright for girls tennis, with Macie leading the way joined by Jasmine Lee (a sophomore in 2012), a fellow first team All-Stater with Macie, and Brenna Wu (junior in '12) and senior Liz Wilm, who both made the 2011 All-State second team.

Macie seems focused on what needs to be done, and her goals are well within reach. She has proven that she is willing to continue to attack and that she is not afraid to go for broke, and those traits have already placed her in elite company when she joined local stars Lanae Renschler (Castle – '83-'86), Elissa Kim (North – '91-'92), Stephanie Hazlett (Heritage Hills – '91) and Margo Stevenson (Memorial – '95) as IHSAA State champions.

Only time will tell if Macie will join Lanae and Elissa as multiple winners and I certainly wouldn't bet against her. "I guess I always want to surprise people and go past what their expectations are of me," Macie proclaimed in 2011. "I like to make people proud." Regardless of what may come for Macie Elliott, based on those words, she has already achieved success.

Macie was a swinger at an early age.

IHSAA STATE CHAMPIONS UPDATE

TENNIS

School	Year	Record	Coach
Memorial	2012	25-0	Ray Trapp

Individual	School	Year	Record
Macie Elliott	Memorial	2011	31-1

JASMINE LEE:
A PRODUCT OF DESIRE

At any other area school, Jasmine Lee would be an undisputed #1 singles player on the tennis team. But at Memorial, she plays behind Macie Elliott, giving the Lady Tigers the best 1-2 punch in the state.

Jasmine began playing at age five and started competing at ten, but her parents weren't terribly impressed. "We didn't see any potential," Jeana Lee, Jasmine's mom, confessed. "Her dad and I used to joke about how she had no athleticism. She didn't have any innate talent. Like Lukas Greif, he's pedigreed. Jasmine is one of those people who is a product of desire and a lot of hard work."

But eyes were opened when ten-year-old Jasmine competed at a Midwest qualifier. "It was clear from the beginning that she really liked competition," Jeana explained. "She was out there for 4 ½ hours in 100-degree heat because she just wasn't going to give in. There was no way she was going to lose."

Jasmine also realized when a light came on that lit her competitive fire. "It was probably at eleven or twelve," she recalled. "I got second in a pretty big tournament, and I started wanting to improve my ranking and travel more outside of Indiana."

Most of that improvement occurred when Jasmine got some serious coaching from two outstanding instructors. One is Peter Moore, the pro at Tri-State Athletic Club; the other is Stephanie Hazlett, and according to Jeana, they each play a significant role.

"They both identify what needs to be focused on," Jeana Lee revealed. "It's incredible that we have Peter Moore in Evansville. He used to coach Gigi Fernandez, the #1 doubles player in the world. He's amazing.

"At 12, 13, 14, the hormones start to kick in in tennis," Jeana continued. "You see girls who flourished in the 10s and 11s and their hormones take over and their negative attitude takes over. We felt that it would be better if she had a female presence, and Stephanie was really great with her. For Jasmine, Stephanie is her mental coach, staying strong and not letting one point color the rest of the match. Technique-wise, it's been Peter Moore."

No one knows Jasmine's game better than Ms. Hazlett, and she has a perspective on the youngster's talent and how her game compares to Macie Elliott's. "Jasmine is a tenacious girl," Stephanie informed me. "She is willing to stay out there all day long and make her opponents hit tons of balls. You have to beat her."

Stephanie also teaches Memorial's #1, Macie Elliott, and the two girls illustrate how different styles can be effective. Elliott is very aggressive, and Jasmine, not so much. "Jasmine will step up and hit the ball and come to the net more, but under pressure, she's the one who's going to grind it out," Stephanie pointed out. "They could each use a touch of the other's qualities. Jasmine had one of her biggest wins of her career this past summer (2011) against the #2 seed, a girl named Keisha Clousing in a national tournament. She's a top 50 player in the country, consistently ranked higher than Macie. It was a turning point in Jasmine's confidence against higher-level players. It proved to her that she was capable of not only playing with them but beating them."

Jasmine has a clear grasp of her game and areas where improvements are needed. "Especially in the 12s and 14s. Sometimes I would throw the match away or yell or hit my racket on the ground and not compete as hard," Jasmine noted. "Stephanie always got mad at me when I had a bad attitude."

When asked what her plans are for the future, Jasmine answers as if she had decided some time ago. "I want to keep on playing after college," she answered. As for college, with her 6.0 average (out of 6.0), the Ivy League is within reach, and the tennis is strong at some Ivy League schools.

As for her plans after college, only time will tell for the human return machine that drives opponents crazy. In 2011, the Memorial freshman was named All-State and was rated #12 in the Midwest 16 & under age group and #1 in the USTA Central Indiana girls 16s, among many other accomplishments.

Whether it was good fortune or a bad break, Jasmine will be banging balls with Macie Elliott for two more years, and they will continue to be two of the fiercest competitors our area has produced. Her natural talents may have been questioned by some, but one thing is certain: Those who stand across the net from this dynamo will always have their hands full, because Jasmine Lee gives in to no one, and that fire and determination cannot and will not be denied.

Memorial tennis coach Ray Trapp once said that the best match he has ever seen was at practice when Jasmine Lee battled with Macie Elliott. He tried his best not to cheer at the great shots and thought to himself how strange it was to see this caliber of tennis with no crowd to enjoy it.

MCKINLEY WARREN

A freshman running back on the varsity level in the SIAC is a rarity indeed, but in 2011, the Memorial Tigers featured a back who more than held his own against local competition. Named for his paternal grandfather, McKinley Warren was somewhat surprised when Memorial coach John Hurley called on him to take practice reps with the varsity, but the fact was, his breakaway speed was an asset the team sorely needed, and it was something he was just blessed with.

"The thing I noticed first was his speed," recalled Lisa Warren, McKinley's mother. "Steve (the boy's father) had it, and McKinley has it, and I see it in Isaiah (McKinley's younger brother). It's just natural." Steve Warren played his high school sports in East Stroudsburg, Pennsylvania and was on his way to a scholarship in basketball when he was diagnosed with Hodgkins Disease. As a four-year starter, he was approaching 1,000 points, averaging over 25 as a senior, when the disease struck.

Fortunately, doctors caught it early and he is doing fine, and he also sees potential in his oldest son. Coming from a football state, Steve pointed out that James Mungro, an alumnus of East Stroudsburg High, was a phenomenal player. Mungro was a high school All-American who set the state rushing record with 8,432 yards then starred at Syracuse and played five seasons backing up Edgerrin James with the Indianapolis Colts. "I see a lot of that in him," Steve said about McKinley. "I probably saw it in the seventh grade that he had it."

Obviously, comparisons to Mungro are premature, but the young Warren did show promise. After the family moved to Newburgh from Pennsylvania McKinley competed in track and football at St. John's and played on Memorial's feeder basketball team, but ironically, if not for a gentle prod from a coach, this story may never have been written. After taking a beating on the field as a seventh grader, Warren had decided not to play football the following year, but Coach Scott Stratman convinced him to give it one more try.

As the story played out, McKinley found himself playing on Friday nights, and his 4.6-4.7 speed (in the 40-yard dash) proved to be a perfect complement to another fine runner for the Tigers. McKinley was used on 'bubble routes' and sweeps while the bulk of the inside runs were the responsibility of senior Sam Curtis. "I always looked up to him," McKinley said of Curtis. "He could run up the gut and carry people on his back. I liked to get outside. He was like my older brother on the field. He accepted me for who I was."

McKinley is very aware that with Curtis' departure, he will have to expand his game, and to do that, there is plenty of work ahead. "I have to get a lot stronger," Warren said. "I know now that if you want to be the best, you have to work like the best."

According to Max Preps, McKinley led all Indiana freshman in 2011 in kickoff return yardage with 618 (an average of 22) and was second in the state to Whiting's Ethan Young in rushing yardage with 764 yards in 13 games. His plans are to run the sprints for the track team and hopefully play basketball, but he is well aware of what needs to be done if he wants to reach his lofty goals.

"Next year," McKinley said, "I want to rush for 1,000 yards, and (eventually) I want to play for the Florida Gators."

Whether those aspirations are in the cards or not remains to be seen, and Warren knows he has to get stronger to withstand the punishment a featured back must endure. As we all look on, it will be fun to see what the young man can achieve, and no one is more invested than Tigers head football coach John Hurley. "It is not often that freshmen come in and step into a varsity role," Coach Hurley answered when asked about his young back. "McKinley has the gift of natural ability that so many kids don't have. He added excitement as a freshman, and as he gains strength, he will become an even more physical runner. Memorial has produced numerous great student-athletes, and I look forward to seeing him mature to continue the tradition."

BOSSE'S SUPER SOPHS

It is rare indeed for a high school basketball team to have four Division I prospects, but Evansville Bosse coach Shane Burkhart was blessed with such good fortune in 2011. One of the four was a senior leader who offered stability and leadership while three thoroughbred sophomores matured and fine-tuned their games. Though such talent is great to have for a coach, there are inherent problems that come with this scenario, because as the scrutiny heightens, college programs descend like a pack of wolves and new challenges arise.

Coach Burkhart grew up and played in one of Indiana's basketball Meccas and understood the fanaticism that surrounds Hoosier Hysteria. He earned twelve varsity letters, four each in football, basketball and baseball at Marion, a school with seven State basketball titles, tied with Washington and only one behind Muncie Central's eight.

When Burkhart accepted the job at Bosse in 2008, he inherited a program with a rich history, including two recent teams that experienced success. Bosse had captured three State championships, the back-to-back champs of 1944 and '45 led by Broc Jerrel and Bud Ritter and the '62 team led by Gary Grieger and Jerry Southwood. Even as recently as '06 and '07, Bosse had remarkable seasons. In 2006, Coach Jeff Hein's boys finished the regular season undefeated before a shocking upset to Mater Dei when the Wildcats' Kelly Muensterman buried a shot near the buzzer in the sectional, and in '07, the Bulldogs advanced to the final game at State before falling to Plymouth.

Burkhart had served as an assistant coach at Marion for five years, and when Hein left for Vincennes Lincoln, Shane was offered the job at Bosse. When he made the trek south, Burkhart brought one of the eventual super sophs with him, his son Bo, but he wasn't aware of the strong class Bo would be a part of. He became aware of his other future stars when he watched Bo team with JaQuan Lyle at Washington Middle School as they played Perry Fairrow's team at Glenwood.

Burkhart's son may lack some of the size and physical traits of his classmates, but it should come as no surprise that he makes up for his shortcomings with basketball savvy. "Bo has been around basketball all his life," Shane said from his office at Bosse. "He's traveled to numerous AAU tournaments as a fan and a player."

One of Shane's fondest (and scariest) moments occurred while on a trip to Disneyworld. While enjoying the park, Bo was suddenly nowhere to be found, and after a frantic search, they found him sitting with a team from Minnesota talking basketball. Bo admits that he has been a gym rat all his life, but he is also a well-rounded athlete. As a freshman, he kicked for the football team, and as a sophomore, he earned All-City and All-Conference honors in soccer, setting a school record with 20 goals. On the gridiron, he was a multiple threat as a sophomore, playing backup QB, punting, kicking and finishing as the team's second-leading tackler as a strong safety.

Shane is well aware of the added pressure Bo feels. "It's difficult because he's the coach's son," Coach Burkhart confided, "but he puts in a lot of time. As a father, I'm extremely impressed and proud. He maintains a 3.5 GPA (Shane says that Bo gets his brains from his mother), and he could have a lot of letters when all is said and done." On the basketball floor, Bo averaged 8.5 points as a sophomore, and his dad says that college scouts are waiting to see if he'll grow. As of 2012, Bo had been contacted by Western Kentucky, Loyola, Gardner-Webb and Oklahoma State, among others, and he's trying to stay focused. "I try not to let it go to my head," Bo said, "because that's usually when problems happen."

Being surrounded by great talent, Bo realizes that his role is to "play defense, rebound and shoot when I get the chance." But Bo has also shown that he can stroke it when the opportunity is there. "He had a great year defensively for us," Shane pointed out. "I don't think I've ever told another kid that I don't need him to score. I think that hurt him a little in confidence. But he

Bo Burkhart

Perry Fairrow

JaQuan Lyle

really stood out in our defensive scheme. There are a lot of talented kids in our conference, and we always put Bo on their best player. The young man at Harrison (Ernie Duncan), Bo held to single digits twice this year ('11-'12), and the young man at Memorial (Alphonso Baitty), Bo held him to one basket in the second game. I think next year, he'll showcase a little bit more of his talent. He can shoot it with the best of them." With great support from Shane, his mother Stacy, and a grandfather (Steve Burkhart) who has been a huge influence, Bo plans to enjoy every sport as he waits to see where his future takes him.

Another talented member of the class of 2014 is Perry Fairrow, and as his skills continue to develop, he could become a big-time prospect. Perry has spent a lot of time over the years at the YMCA and was influenced by his cousin, Jeremy Fairrow, who starred in basketball and football at Central. The hours he has spent at the 'Y' doing drills, shooting and lifting weights have helped him draw the attention of schools like Indiana Purdue-Ft. Wayne, Murray State, Buffalo and Western Kentucky.

As I sat with Fairrow in Coach Burkhart's office, we discussed the influences on his life and the pressures young athletes face today. When asked about the temptations to make bad decisions, the quiet young man hesitated and Coach Burkhart spoke up, showing his vigilance about protecting his boys. "There are a lot of people around them who want to see them fail," he pointed out, "but it's their choice to stay on the path we're trying to put them on."

Perry was more responsive when asked about those who have supported him through the years, especially one. "My grandmother (Jacquilla), she's a big deal in my life. I love her to death. She's the one that guides me on the right path and keeps my head on straight."

According to Coach Burkhart, Perry is a light-hearted kid and somewhat of a practical joker, and Perry smiled at the comment and put his attitude toward basketball in perspective. "I like to joke around," Fairrow admitted, "but when it's serious time, I get serious. I'm still just 15. I'm trying to stay humble and work toward my goals."

Shane Burkhart has watched Perry mature and sees great potential. "Perry is a young man that shoots the ball unbelievably," Burkhart said. "He is so fast and long and athletic. He's grown probably four or five inches over the summer (2011). He was our leading scorer (15.4 per game) on the JV as a freshman. We couldn't put him on the varsity because we had so many talented guards."

Though he couldn't play as a freshman, Fairrow quickly established himself as a sophomore. "Perry really came out of his shell offensively," said Coach Burkhart. "He was the team's third-leading scorer with over 350 points. He had an amazing sectional. If he's not there for the sectional, we don't win it. He also hit a huge shot in the regional to tie the game, 26 feet. To put that kind of pressure on yourself as a kid that just turned 16 years old, that's fantastic. He's grown by leaps and bounds. He has a lot more growing to do. He's just going to flourish as a junior and senior."

The final Diaper Dandy in Coach Burkhart's stable is one of the most celebrated and publicized players in local history and is a reflection of the new world we live in. In the vein of what Damon Bailey experienced as an eighth grader when Bob Knight sang his praises publicly, the hype surrounding JaQuan Lyle has been in overdrive. In the atmosphere of cyberspace, news travels at the speed of light and the world knows instantly if an athlete catches a cold. Lyle has had to deal with the avalanche of attention in his early teens, and according to Shane Burkhart, he has handled it relatively well.

As JaQuan traveled playing AAU ball with Eric Gordon's Elite teams, it wasn't unusual to find Magic Johnson in the stands, not as a scout but as the best friend of JaQuan's grandfather. With that kind of fan base, it's no wonder that the young man attracted some serious attention. In fact, Lyle was offered a college scholarship before he ever played a high school game.

"I got a phone call (in 2010) from Coach Buckley (an assistant at IU)," Shane Burkhart recalled. "He said he had heard that we had some freshmen here and that he wanted to come down and see them play. He watched 25 minutes of open gym and walked into the hallway. We had no idea what to do because, to be honest, that was the first time a college coach came to one of my practices when I was the head guy. In two or three minutes, he came back in and then left. Within five minutes, (IU head coach) Tom Crean called me and said he was coming in two days later. Coach Crean sat here in the office and offered him a scholarship on the spot."

Burkhart quickly became accustomed to the madness of handling a rare talent. After JaQuan's first game as a freshman, Xavier chimed in, and after the third and fifth games, Illinois and Purdue, respectively, joined the fracas. In September of 2011, Michigan State made an offer, followed later by such schools as Kansas, Tennessee, Kentucky, North Carolina, Georgetown and UCLA.

The attention can be maddening for a coach and his team, but it also has residual benefits for Lyle's teammates. "The reason we have a lot of coaches in our gym right now is because of JaQuan Lyle. He's the reason these other kids are getting looks. Coaches come in and see the other ones, and if they're maybe not good enough to play at the highest level, they call somebody they know at another school and it snowballs from there."

And as for JaQuan, Burkhart sees unlimited potential. "He is a young sophomore," Shane said in 2011. "He will not be 16 until February. He's projected to play 1 through 4 (point guard though power forward) in college, depending on how much he grows. A lot of people like him as a combo guard. He's been compared to some pros already, like Jalen Rose and Steve Smith. His court presence is amazing, and the way he sees the play develop before it actually happens is uncanny."

Burkhart also believes in Lyle as a person. "I love having him," he said. "He's a very soft-hearted young man. He's been through a lot, and his grandmother's done a fantastic job raising him. He remembers Father's Day, and even though I'm not his father, he calls me. The first day of school this year, he played basketball with two learning disabled kids and never batted an eye."

Burkhart knows the challenges that lie ahead and is very candid about JaQuan's life under the microscope. "He is very misunderstood because of his body language," Burkhart explained. "At his age, he doesn't know how to control it. There are a lot of people who think he has a bad attitude and who want to look at the negative things. The rumors that are thrown around by people who want to judge him are not true. I'm sure it takes a toll on a 14- or 15-year-old kid. JaQuan will be successful if he doesn't get in his own way."

JaQuan is 6'5, and after bulking up from playing football as a sophomore, he is a strong 205. He averaged 15.4 points in 2011-'12 with 9 rebounds and 8 assists as a leader on the school's sectional championship team, and he has been rated by Rivals.com as the #8 guard in the country and a top 25 prospect overall.

Like any young athlete, JaQuan Lyle still has hurdles to clear and landmines to avoid, but one thing is certain: The dandiest of Coach Burkhart's Diaper Dandies has phenomenal potential, and as we watch his career unfold, the world will be watching with us.

LUKAS GREIF:
EXTRAORDINARY TALENT

When visiting with 'Diaper Dandy' Lukas Greif, the first thing that comes to mind is that the apple doesn't fall too far from the tree. Although young Lukas (age 11 in 2011) has shown promise in other sports, he has a strong resemblance to his father when it comes to tennis talent.

John Greif, a local periodontist, played basketball at Memorial but was a true standout as a tennis player, going undefeated throughout his high school career. During his era, there were no individual State tournaments, but his team reached the semi-state level three times before losing to Indianapolis Brebeuf. So, unfortunately, although John never lost, even in the team State tournament, he was never able to call himself an IHSAA State champion.

After graduating in 1979, John accepted a tennis scholarship to Southern Illinois University, where he played #2 singles, #1 doubles and was named the team's MVP twice. Lukas' mom, Joanie, learned the game after she and John were married, and each of their children has been blessed with natural talent.

Daughter Abby Greif partnered with Catherine Hofmann to win the State doubles title in 2005 while also lettering in volleyball and swimming at Memorial. Her talents earned her a full-ride tennis scholarship to the Florida Institute of Technology.

Lukas' two brothers were also athletes for the Tigers. Oldest brother Grant played on the golf team for four years, while Charlie is competing now (2012) as a quarterback and receiver in football and as a shortstop on the baseball team.

The youngest of the family has tried several sports in recent years, but the time is approaching when multiple activities won't be practical. He played basketball and baseball for Holy Rosary and played select soccer and football as well, but when conflicts occurred, tennis always took precedence.

Lukas showed potential early on, and his father recognized the degree of his talent before anyone else. "At around six you could tell," John Greif explained from the family home in Newburgh. "He was really quick and tenacious for that age. He could beat older kids."

Grant and Charlie eventually lost serious interest in tennis, but little Lukas was just getting started. Almost from the beginning, Lukas played up a level against older boys, and he was ranked #7 nationally as an 11-year old and 26th in the age group above, 12 and under.

Each year, Lukas competes in four national competitions, and the schedule can get grueling. "Oh, we travel," Joanie Greif disclosed. "In 2010, we went to Tucson, West Palm Beach, North Carolina, Kalamazoo, Arkansas." The tournaments require a great deal of sacrifice and dedication, because if a kid is good, they can be at a tournament for a week. In fact, several times a year, Lukas will miss school on Friday and Monday just for a weekend tournament.

Like virtually all of the area's top players, Lukas trains under Stephanie Hazlett, a local legend herself who was a State champ at Heritage Hills and went on to become a college and professional player. "Stephanie is very tough," said John Greif, "but they respond well. She makes these kids so much better."

Lukas also trains with Peter Moore at the Tri-State Athletic Club one day a week. While Stephanie works on Lukas' overall game, Peter works on techniques for certain shots and makes Lukas use them as they play points against each other.

Obviously, the boy is very early in his development process, but when I asked where he wanted tennis to take him, the response was instant. "I want to play professionally," he answered, and he is already making the sacrifices necessary to merit such a lofty goal.

Lukas had just turned 12 in early 2012 and was meeting with Stephanie and his parents to plan out the itinerary for the year. Stephanie has seen Lukas develop and agrees that the sky is the limit, but his talent brings with it some inherent problems. For one, in a year or two, there may not be enough local players of any age powerful enough to hit with him. In addition, the ever-present threat of injuries is always lurking. But Stephanie believes that Lucas has what it takes to do great things.

"I have never met a kid who is more focused and detailed about what he does on the court at such a young age," Ms. Hazlett said. "He is very aware, very in control of himself. It's like he has a 40-year-old mind out there, very good with his emotions on the court, and that's what puts him above most kids his age and even older players. He has the hands and speed, too. We're still waiting on the size, but both his parents were athletic. It was just something he has been born with."

Lukas started playing tennis at age 3 and played in his first tournament at age 6. He won his first tournament at age 7 (10 & under) and was on the Indiana Junior Davis Cup team for two years. In addition, he has been invited to the Midwest USTA Training Center and is invited to the USTA National Training Center in Boca Raton, Florida. In total, he has played over 375 matches before the age of 12 and, as of 2012, was ranked #1 in Indiana, #5 in the Midwest, and 6th among America's 6th graders. In the summer of 2012, Lukas and his doubles partner, Danny Thomas of Canal Winchester, Ohio, captured the USTA Clay Court Boys 12s national doubles championship.

As sports fans, we can look forward to watching this young man as he matures, and we hope things work out to keep him here as his game develops. Our area has seen some great tennis players over the years, and it is obviously too soon to place Lukas among them now. But more than one tennis aficionado, including Anna Hazlett, Stephanie's mother, has stated that if his health holds up and he stays humble and dedicated, Lukas Greif has the potential to become the best tennis player our area has ever seen.

TRAVIS WANNEMUEHLER:
LITTLE MAN, BIG LEG

Photo by Darren Dedman

Since the most popular sport in the world was first played in earnest here in our area, Memorial High School has dominated local competition. So when a star appears that doesn't wear blue and white, it's big news in the world of Indiana soccer. This was the case when Mater Dei's Travis Wannemuehler emerged and then stood out on the gridiron as well.

Travis and his brother came by their talents naturally. Their father, Brian Wannemuehler, was a teammate in youth soccer of Bill Vieth Jr., an All-American at Memorial and now the Tigers' head coach. Bill Vieth Sr., the man who was largely responsible for the sport's development locally, was Brian's first coach. Brian grew up in Melody Hills and was the starting center fielder for Mickey Martin at North. He also starred in the early years of the soccer boom, graduating in 1981 and becoming the first local player to earn a soccer scholarship to U of E. While there, Brian was a member of the 1985 Aces team that was ranked #1 in the nation and advanced to the NCAA Final Four.

Travis' older brother Bradley was a 2010 Mater Dei grad who teamed with Hank Larue on the basketball court, starred as a center fielder in baseball and was also an All-City and second team All-State performer in soccer. Brad was named the *Courier* Metro Player of the Year, and with his explosive speed, could have played soccer in college but instead chose to play baseball at USI, where he started as a freshman and hit .305.

Unlike many of his teammates at Mater Dei, Travis was heavily committed to soccer over the years, and only some friendly prodding from friends could get him to try something new. As an eighth grader at Resurrection School, he was one of 34 players chosen to represent America on the U-14 team that spent a week in Guadalajara, Mexico. Although he was an excellent baseball player, with high school approaching, he had to choose between baseball and travel soccer, and his desire to play college soccer made that decision easy. But when he was approached about joining Mike Goebel's football team, he became curious. At 5'8 and 145 pounds, he was certainly not going to risk injury by banging heads with the likes of physical specimens like Bernie Boots (6'5, 290) or Cody Hess (5'8, 195) in practice, but he knew he could be a contributor with his powerful leg.

With the kicking position opening up in 2011, Travis was approached in class by football assistant Jeff Jewell, the son of hall of fame Gibson Southern coach Jack Jewell. "Some of my friends played football," Travis said, "like Cody Hess, Blake Schoettlin and Hunter Owen, and they kind of joked about it."

Travis decided to give it a try as a junior in 2011 and spoke with Coach Goebel. It was agreed upon that soccer would take preference if any conflicts occurred, so Travis went to work to become a kicker. The early days were challenging, with two-a-day practices in each sport. He would practice soccer from 6:00 a.m. until 8:00 and then go straight to football before doing the same in the afternoon and evening. Although he wouldn't participate in contact drills for football, he did do all the running, no easy task after full soccer practices.

"I felt like I was part of the team, so there was no reason not to," Travis confided, showing an attitude that earned him the respect of his teammates.

As the dual-sport scenario played out, there were only two conflicts during the season, but he only missed one football game and part of another. One involved a 5:30 soccer game and then a quick ride from the Double Cola soccer fields near Roberts Stadium to Reitz Bowl for a game against Memorial. After changing uniforms in the car, Travis was dropped off at the Bowl, and before he could even warm up, he was pressed into service just in time to connect on a field goal late in the first quarter.

One of his highlights during the season was a pressure-packed situation against Castle. Down by three, speedy Mater Dei receiver Hunter Owen gathered in a pass from Dane Maurer at Castle's 28-yard line with four seconds left on the clock. Although he was used to pressure on the soccer field and had worked hard on the skill set needed to put the ball through the football uprights, he had never experienced the challenge of delivering with thousands of fans looking on and the game on the line. Fortunately, some encouraging words were delivered from a good friend. "Cody (Hess) told me, 'I've seen you make 55-yarders in practice,' Travis explained. 'If we lose, it's not because of our kicker.'" Travis' kick from the left hash mark was pure, and although the Wildcats lost in overtime, Travis came through and proved that he belonged.

For the season, Wannemuehler connected on 54 of 57 extra point attempts and 10 of 12 field goals, and his leg played a role in the team's success. Mater Dei finished another fine season by advancing to the State Finals, and although they fell short by losing to Ft. Wayne Bishop Luers, his nine points (2 field goals and 3 extra points) in the semi-state were the difference in an 8-point victory.

Travis is also proud of the two tackles he contributed on kickoffs, and when asked if he'd felt the sting of a brutal hit, he smiled before he answered. "One time!" he revealed. "This kid just clobbered me," he said of a vicious hit courtesy of Adam Ricketts of Reitz.

While he was getting his first taste of the gridiron, Travis was also enjoying a fine season on the pitch, and his coach at Mater Dei saw his potential very early. "It was pretty amazing how fast he separated himself," said Matt Settles in a *Courier* article by Steve Ford. "I've never welcomed a freshman in with his talent, polish and experience." His finest performance took place in the soccer semi-state when he recorded one of the greatest performances in Indiana history. A hat trick (3 goals in a game) is rare for a soccer player, and Travis did it in back-to-back games against Sullivan and Lawrenceburg before the Wildcats lost to Ft. Wayne Canterbury (3-0) in the State Finals.

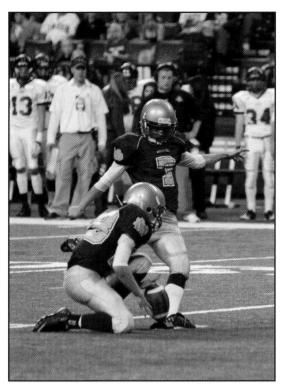

Travis, #7, starred on Friday nights for Coach Mike Goebel's Wildcats.

Another memorable moment involved some heroics against Castle, a team the Wildcats traditionally had trouble with. In a hard-fought game, Travis assisted on a goal by Joe Hayden in the 47th minute and then found the net himself from a tight angle on the right side of the penalty box with 2:55 left to deliver a 2-1 victory.

With teammates Josh Weinzapfel, Andy Hamilton, Kyle Wilson and others, Coach Settles' 2011 crew finished the season ranked #2 in 2A with a 17-6 record, and Travis was the straw that stirred the drink. He tallied 21 goals and 14 assists for 56 points, despite missing several games with an ankle injury, and his play had college coaches courting in bunches. Over 40 schools came calling, including Mike Jacobs from Evansville, and Travis quickly narrowed his options to UE, Indiana, Butler and North Carolina State. At the time of our meeting, the decision hadn't been made, but it came soon after.

Travis eventually committed to Coach Keith Findley, who had been in touch as the head coach at Butler before taking over the program at NC State. According to his father, Travis said that he could see himself going there and had a great rapport with the coaches. He also felt that he would have a chance to play and have an impact as a freshman."

The fact that Wannemuehler will be playing in the Atlantic Coast Conference is a testament to his talent. The ACC is undeniably the most powerful soccer conference in the country, winning ten NCAA titles in the last 21 years.

In March of 2012, Travis received a letter inviting him to participate in the training camp for the U.S. Under-18 Men's National Team in Carson, California. The letter indicated that the camp will "play a vital role in his continuing development as one of the most talented soccer players in the United States." One downside to the opportunity is the increased time commitment required by the U.S. Soccer Federation to make American soccer more competitive. Because of this, Travis was required to make a decision and had to tell his high school coaches and teammates that he will not be available in either soccer or football as a senior.

The news came as a shock to everyone, but Travis can hardly be blamed for the choice he made. When his college days are over, Travis hopes to play the game professionally one day, and the time spent with the development team will only help in that quest. Although fans won't get to see how his senior campaigns would have turned out, they will remember him as an excellent two sport athlete, and regardless of what the future holds, one fact cannot be denied: Travis Wannemuehler accomplished a rare feat indeed as one of the few Indiana athletes to earn first team All-State honors in two sports in the same season.

THE DUNCANS:
A TRUE FAMILY AFFAIR

Beginning in 2010, the Duncan name began to grace the local sports pages on a regular basis, and based on recent performances (2012), the name will be a fixture for many years to come. The publicity is and will be based on five brothers, and to say their story is unusual would be an understatement.

The tale begins with the patriarch of the family, Stan Duncan. Stan played some ball in the '70s as a 6'6 front line player under Bob Walker on Evansville North's JV team. He loved the game but admits that lack of guidance de-railed his dream much too soon.

As the father of the five boys, Stan has chosen an unorthodox path, and he makes no apologies for his methods. His daughter Mary had no interest in athletics and progressed through the public school system in a normal fashion, winning spelling bees and excelling in the classroom. But where the boys were concerned, Stan took a different approach.

All the boys were intentionally placed a grade behind most other students their age to allow their bodies to mature an extra year, and for a few years, they were pulled from school to get their education at home. With his wife, Melinda, working, Stan handled the home-schooling and believes the curriculum and schedule met the boys needs as students and as basketball players.

To begin the process, Stan analyzed what the area high schools had to offer, and although the family lives in Bosse's district, he didn't like the "fit." They also considered Evansville Day School but weren't comfortable with it because of the school's Class A athletic status and limited gym time. So after careful analysis, Stan opted for Harrison. All the boys attended Fairlawn Elementary for four or five years before beginning the home-school regimen, and this is where the line between education and athletics becomes blurred for some who disagree with Stan's methods.

"I decided a few years ago that in basketball you need time to develop," Stan explained from the family's home near Dexter school. "I saw that Ernie had the ability, but I wanted to give him some time. My wife works and I'm a house-husband right now. We have an EBA (Evansville Basketball Academy) membership, so we hit the books for three or four hours in the morning and then go to the gym for three or four hours and work on basketball."

Mr. Duncan purchases text books from local bookstores for all the core material, like English, math and science, but admits that a good portion of the day has been spent at the gym or in front of the TV watching NBA games that were recorded from the night before. With the two younger boys, Brandon (born in 1997) and Robin (born in 1998), listening to our discussion, it was interesting to see the boys' demeanor as their father spoke. While many youngsters would fidget and appear bored, the boys hung on their dad's every word and were polite and articulate when they spoke.

In the summers, all five of the Duncan boys head to the EBA for 'two-a-days', morning and afternoon sessions where they work on different skill sets, and those who watched were impressed at their focus and dedication. They all also compete in AAU tournaments in their age groups or above and have drawn attention with their talents. Ernie has competed with an Indiana Elite team out of Bloomington South, and the twins, Everett and Stanley (born in '95), played on the Indiana Elite Jazz out of Indianapolis that was the best in Indiana. Brandon and Robin played the 2011-'12 season with Harrison's seventh grade feeder team, with Robin averaging 15 points and 7 assists and Brandon averaging 14 points, 4 assists and 6 rebounds.

During the school year, the youngest boys play in two different leagues, and on Saturdays and Sundays, they're gone all day playing. The traveling and meals away from home have become a way of life for the Duncans, and Stan believes that spending the small family budget on basketball as their family vacations will pay big dividends in the future. He also appreciates Melinda. "I couldn't do it without her," he confessed. "That's all we do. I guess I'm living my life through my kids, to be honest with you. I get enjoyment watching them develop and be successful at something that I wish I could've."

When asked if the boys had ever tried other sports, Stan's answer was quick and definitive. "No," he answered. "Sports have become year-round now. To be prepared and keep up, you have to be playing all the time. They could have played other sports, but I encouraged them not to. When Ernie was about seven, I noticed he had a love for basketball, and the others just followed along."

Ernie (born in 1994) has developed into a superstar for coach Bryan Speer at Harrison

The older Duncan brothers
(L-R): Stanley, Ernie and Everett

and caught the eye of college coaches across the nation at a young age. As an eighth grader at McGary, he was listed by ESPN as one of the top 100 players in the country in his class and was receiving letters before his freshman year.

Stan enrolled Ernie and the twins back into the public school system in 2009 with Ernie as an eighth grader and the twins a year behind. The three boys promptly led McGary to the city championship game where they lost to JaQuan Lyle's Washington team. (As a side note, whether the twins' impact as seventh graders played a role or not, the following year, the rules were changed so that seventh graders could not play on an eighth grade team.)

Before he had ever played a high school game, Ernie was fielding contacts from several colleges, and after his freshman season, the attention got serious. In 2011, he visited Coach Tom Crean at IU and Matt Painter at Purdue and was approached by Xavier, Butler, Indiana State, Michigan and Ohio State, to name a few.

Ernie averaged 17.3 points and 4 rebounds as a freshman for the 13-7 Warriors, and in January of 2012, midway through his sophomore season, Ernie made a verbal commitment to Coach Marty Simmons' Evansville Aces, and Bryan Speer thinks Simmons landed a winner. "Hey, Ernie's a basketball player," Coach Speer said from his office as Harrison's AD. "He can handle the ball; he's a great passer; he can shoot; and he sees the court very well on offense and defense. You know, Ernie's not lightning quick, but he led us in steals as a freshman because of his basketball IQ and positioning on defense."

Coach Speer went on to rave about Ernie's maturity and how he has handled situations like Tom Crean visiting the gym when Ernie was a freshman. He also spoke of the twins, who have made their own mark already. Everett, a 6'5 freshman, led the varsity with a 16-point average as a starter and has proved to be deadly from the three-point line, and Stanley averaged 20 points on the JV team before moving up to become the varsity's sixth man.

When asked his impression of the Duncan boys and the controversial approach to education used by Stan Duncan, Bryan Speer has strong opinions. "There's no reason to criticize," Speer replied. "They're great kids. They've been held back a year, which is what a ton of kids have been, but no one ever says anything about it. It's not a secret. They're very good students; they're extremely coachable; and they have a great work ethic."

As I sat with Stan Duncan in 2011, the youngest boys were entering the last few months of home-schooling, and Stan looked realistically at where they've been and what lay ahead. "They're looking forward to entering school (Brandon as an eighth grader and Robin in the seventh at McGary)," Stan pointed out. "They're burnt out with me, and I'm kind of burnt out with home-schooling. I'll get a job. It's been a sacrifice."

In 2012, Stan saw the first fruits of his labor when Ernie committed to U of E, and at some point, the grumbles of criticism will cease. When asked if he would proceed differently if he could do it again, Stan was honest and to the point. "I don't think so," he replied. "I think it gives them a focus in life. I mean, all your lessons in life are there. You know, we're not rich people, middle-class at best. I could have been out there in the dog-eat-dog world and give them all the material things.

"I think a lot of people misunderstand me. I've heard comments that said, 'He's denied those boys a childhood or kept them from having a balanced life.' It's what you want to put into something. I thought basketball would open up doors for them, and it has. We have a calendar here (in the fall of 2011), and I've got it marked until our scrimmage with Memorial and the number of days until Everett and Stan begin their high school careers. I know people think I'm nuts."

Nuts or not, Stan Duncan has devoted several years of his life to developing his sons, and to this point, it's hard to argue with the results. The boys seem well-adjusted and are flourishing academically, and if basketball provides a college education, then all the better.

In a world where many young athletes, especially tennis players, golfers and swimmers, are home-schooled to maximize their potential through specialization, Stan Duncan's methods may not seem so far-fetched. He makes no excuses and offers no apologies. What he has done is enabled the Duncan boys to shine, giving local fans an opportunity to witness their talents on the courts of southern Indiana.

THE FUTURE IS NOW

In preparation for their careers at Harrison High School, Brandon and Robin Duncan and their teammates captured the 2012 7th grade IBA (Indiana Basketball Academy) state championship, finishing the season with a 51-6 record and defeating teams from Evansville, Bloomington, Indianapolis, Ft. Wayne and South Bend on the way to the title. Front row (L-R): Heath Seaton (head coach), Robin Duncan, Kiano Brodi, Cameron Seaton, Brandon Duncan, Brian Owen (asst. coach). Second row: Aaron King, Michael Rogers II, De'Ante Booker, Adam Shoulders, Eric King.

TORI SCHICKEL:
POWER IN THE PAINT

Photo courtesy of Mary Ellen Muensterman

In addition to her impressive skills, Victoria (or Tori) Schickel is fortunate to be blessed with assets that can't be coached – great size and long limbs. These gifts and a solid work ethic enabled the pretty brunette to crack Mater Dei's starting lineup as a freshman, and what a debut season it turned out to be.

As a 6'1" 14-year-old, Tori entered Mater Dei with high expectations and was battle-tested. Some of the experience came from years spent playing AAU ball, and some came from long hours in the driveway with family members. Tori's parents, Tim, who is 6'3, and Theresa (5'6") admit that sports were not their forte, but there was plenty of family influence elsewhere.

"I played a lot in the driveway with Uncle Jeff, Uncle Mark, Uncle Tim and Uncle Danny," Tori said. Apparently the Elpers brothers (her uncles) banged the youngster around pretty good on the court in order to prepare Tori for what would become a life in the paint.

Theresa also feels that her daughter's height and skills came partially from another uncle, Ralph Schickel, who was a solid player at Reitz. "She was always off the chart in height," Theresa informed me. "There weren't any big spurts; it just happened gradually."

Like her brothers, Tori showed promise early. Her older brother, Tyler, graduated in 2012 and was a State qualifier in both cross country and track (1600 & 3200) who shattered Mater Dei running legend Jim Kaiser's conference 1600 mark with a time of 4:13.58. As a senior, Tyler finished sixth at State in the 3200 (9:09.28) and seventh in the 1600 (4:12.92). 11-year-old Tanner Schickel is just getting started and is currently trying several sports. Tori experimented with several as well, and her height and talent caught the eyes of youth coaches at an early age. In most cases, she played with older girls, which accelerated the learning curve.

Terry Muensterman, a multi-sport star at Mater Dei and father of sophomore (in 2012) star Maura Muensterman has watched Tori develop before his very eyes. "I remember when Maura was a first grader and Tori was in kindergarten," Terry recalled. "They played Biddy Ball against each other. I knew Tori's parents, and I thought it would be neat if they could play ball together, and here we are.

"Tori's very coachable, she'll work hard, and she's long and athletic. She knows the game, she works all summer, and she has a big, big upside."

In elementary school, Tori teamed with Laura Greenwell and Ashlynn Spahn at St. Wendel, losing only to Maura's team at Corpus Christi. After the school season, Tori would then join the older girls for AAU tournaments. As a sixth grader, she played up two levels, and after that, she played up one level as she learned from coaches like Terry, Ed Saiko and Phil Kessler.

Like many athletes at Mater Dei, Ms. Schickel represents her school in multiple sports. As a middle hitter in volleyball, she moved up to varsity early in the season and shared time with Erin Wildeman.

As she grows and matures, local fans will enjoy the fruits of Tori's labor. She already seems well-grounded and comfortable with her size, which is not always the case for teenage girls who tower over most of their classmates. When asked if she ever feels uncomfortable, her answer is that of a typical teen, "There are times," she disclosed, "like shopping. You can't find pants."

But as for her comfort level on the court, there is no question. "I'm comfortable inside," she told me. "but I need to work on my outside shot and my ballhandling."

For a young athlete, Tori seems very aware of where she is and where she wants to go, and those around her can see her potential. "She's always gotten compliments on being coachable," said Theresa Schickel, "and ever since she was little, her defense has been excellent."

"She's a great player and has been for a long time," added Maura Muensterman. "I love having her on my team. When teams focus on her, she knows when to shoot and when to pass. She's not only tall but she has the fundamentals. Looking inside and seeing somebody who's 6'1, that's always nice."

And no one has watched Tori more than Coach Steve Goans. "She's very coachable," Goans mentioned, "and she has nice inside moves and can go to her left or right. She's also hard to block out because she moves so well. She can run the court."

Coach Goans and Terry Muensterman, Steve's assistant, are also very aware of the areas in which Tori needs to improve, like increasing her shooting range and building strength. But even with those deficiencies, Schickel has done fairly well for herself in her inaugural high school season. After starting every game, Tori joined Maura on the *Courier* All-City first team with a scoring average of 15.3 while hauling in 7.6 rebounds and blocking 2.5 shots per contest. In addition, she and Maura teamed with a very strong supporting cast to deliver the program's first State championship.

Although only a freshman, Schickel has already attracted looks from college programs, including U of E, Butler, Rutgers, Marquette, Xavier and many more. She admits that the attention is flattering but is mature enough to know that she still has three years to develop her game and assess her college prospects.

As an observer and fan, it has been a pleasure to watch Tori Schickel make such a splash at such a young age. In addition to her amazing attitude and abundant skills, she also showed a delightful exuberance and charm. She was every bit the lady, with her quirky superstitions, like wearing a green rubber band in her hair or eating a peanut butter and jelly or bologna sandwich before every game. But at the same time, she hung tough against some stiff competition under the boards.

We as fans are fortunate to have three more years to follow Tori and her talented teammates and watch her reach her potential. She is a perfect example of what can be accomplished when natural ability meets a tremendous work ethic, and if she can stay healthy and grounded, Tori Schickel should be a part of the greatest wave of Division I talent our area has ever seen.

THOSE WERE THE DAYS

Before the wheels of 'progress' created the era of consolidation, nearly every small town had its own school around which the community rallied in support of the school's athletic teams. Those tiny institutions are now long gone, but they are not forgotten. Below are the schools from our area with their nicknames and the school that absorbed them through consolidation.

Birdseye Yellow Jackets (Forest Park)
Chandler Panthers (Castle/Boonville)
Chrisney Wildcats (Heritage Hills)
Cynthiana Annas (North Posey)
Dale Golden Aces (Heritage Hills)
Decker Aces (South Knox)
Decker Chapel Panthers (South Knox)
Elberfeld Hornets (Tecumseh)
Evansville Lincoln Lions (various schools)
Evansville Rex Mundi Monarchs (Mater Dei/Memorial)
Ferdinand Crusaders (Forest Park)
Folsomville Eagles (Boonville)
Ft. Branch Twigs (Gibson Southern)
Fortville Demons (Mt. Vernon)
Francisco Owls (Wood Memorial)
Frichton Eagles (South Knox)
Gentryville Pirates (Heritage Hills)
Glendale Indians (Washington)
Grandview Greyhounds/Yellow Jackets (South Spencer)
Griffin Tornadoes (North Posey)
Haubstadt Elites (Gibson Southern)
Hazelton Lions (Princeton)
Holland Dutchmen (Southridge)
Huntingburg Happy Hunters (Southridge)

Ireland Spuds (Jasper)
Luce Township Red Devils (South Spencer)
Lynnville Lindys (Tecumseh)
Mackey Aces (Wood Memorial)
Millersburg Wildcats (Castle)
Monroe City Blue Jeans (South Knox)
Mt. Comfort Buccaneers (Mt. Vernon)
Mt. Olympus Mountaineers (Princeton)
Newburgh Wildcats (Castle)
Oakland City Acorns (Wood Memorial)
Owensville Kickapoos (Gibson Southern)
Patoka Wrens (Princeton)
Poseyville Posies/Panthers (North Posey)
Princeton Lincoln Lions (Princeton)
Rockport Zebras (South Spencer)
Selvin Wildcats (Tecumseh)
Stewartsville Owls (North Posey)
Tennyson Tigers (Boonville)
Troy Trojans (Tell City)
Union Eagles (Princeton)
Vernon Township Vikings (Mt. Vernon)
Wadesville Red Devils (North Posey)
White River Rapids (Princeton)
Yankeetown Yanks (Castle)

MAURA MUENSTERMAN:
THE BEST OF THE BUNCH

An argument could be made that no family has had a greater impact on the Mater Dei athletic program than the Muensterman family, and the youngest of the clan has developed herself into, perhaps, the best of the bunch. Maura Muensterman, a sophomore in 2012, has taken inspiration from family role models to mold herself into a physical presence that should place her among the finest female athletes in local history.

Maura's skills come naturally, and she didn't have to look far for guidance. In fact, she only had to look around the dinner table to find all the motivation she would need. Maura's mother, Mary Ellen (Greaney) was a 1978 Mater Dei grad who ran track for a year, played tennis for three years and played basketball for two years at Mater Dei when the sport was played in the school for the first time. But it was on the volleyball court where she became dominant.

Mary Ellen was so good, in fact, that she was honored as an All-American volleyball player in high school with enough talent to attract attention from some of the premier college programs. She was planning on attending UCLA but got cold feet after her visit. She was born in California and had sent the Bruins' coach a tape but didn't care for the campus. Instead, she stayed home and played at U of E, where she became a four-year starter and earned All-American honors again as a senior. She was a good enough athlete that she also started for four years on the Aces softball team even though she had never played fast pitch before.

The father of the family, Terry Muensterman, graduated from Mater Dei in 1973 and was a three-sport athlete as well. Terry played baseball for two years and basketball and football for four. He played his football under legendary coaches Joe Gossman and Frank Will and his basketball under Tom Gore and Don Sheridan. Playing with teammates like Mark Fehr, Charlie Boberg and Dave Schenk, Terry broke the school's basketball scoring record held previously by local legend Paul Gries.

Maura's siblings were also athletes, with sister Kaitlin earning three letters in track and the oldest child, brother Kelly Muensterman, excelling on the gridiron and the basketball court. At 6'2 and 170 pounds, Kelly started as a receiver for Mike Goebel and teamed with Matt Halbig, Wacey Hall, Drew Alcorn and Craig Maier as starters in basketball under John Goebel.

As a sophomore, Kelly averaged 8 points as part of the 21-6 Wildcat team that won the 2004 State championship, and as a junior, he averaged over 17 points per game for Mater Dei's sectional champs. His senior year, Mater Dei knocked off the (class 3-A) #1 Bosse Bulldog team that featured Cardell McFarland, Matt Lander and Courtney Johnson and then advanced to the semi-state, where they were ousted by New Castle. Kelly earned All-City and All-SIAC honors and was named the *Courier*'s Metro Player of the Year and 3A Player of the Year in the state. He finished his high school career as the school's all-time leading scorer, breaking records held by Matt Kiefer for points in a game (42 vs. Memorial), season (695) and career (1,270).

According to Kelly, there was no secret to his success, just tons of effort. Kelly's father ran Mater Dei's feeder league, so there was plenty of access. "I probably hit more shots at Mater Dei's gym than anybody else had taken," he said. And with a great work ethic came great results.

Photo by David Hicks Photography.

So Maura had plenty to live up to as she learned the fundamentals as a youngster. When she was very young, her parents nicknamed her 'Klutzy', but as her skills caught up with her body, heads began to turn. In the third grade, she was moved up to play with the fourth graders, and from her fourth grade season through the eighth, her teams at Corpus Christi went undefeated with the help of teammates like Taylor Anderson, Caroline Scales and Maddie Schneider. Until her sixth grade season, her girls team competed at the EBA against the boys, facing such athletes as the Duncan brothers, Ernie, Everett and Stanley.

In 2010-2011, Maura had possibly the greatest year for a freshman in Evansville history, earning All-City and All-SIAC first team honors in three sports, something that had never been done. In softball, the 5'11 Muensterman played center field, batted cleanup and finished the year with a .333 average, two home runs, 19 RBIs and 12 stolen bases.

On the basketball court, Maura set single-game (40) and season (554) scoring records at Mater Dei and began to zero in on the career Wildcats record of 1,470 held by Missy Glaser. She averaged 25.2 as a freshman to go with her 5.6 rebounds and 5.1 assists per game. She finished the season in 2011 as the #2 scorer in all of

Mary Ellen (Greaney) Muensterman was a high school and college All-American volleyball player. (Photo courtesy of the University of Evansville, Sports Information)

Indiana and earned honorable mention All-State in the process.

Maura continued her success as a sophomore, once again earning Player of the Year honors in volleyball and basketball. With a solid supporting cast, she not only dominated on the basketball court as an individual but she and her teammates earned the state's #1 ranking and captured the State title with a thrilling 56-52 win over powerhouse Bishop Luers. Though Maura was stymied somewhat by the triangle & two defense designed for her and freshman post player Tori Schickel, she still managed 14 points and a wonderful floor game. Showing her poise and leadership, Maura delivered like the champion she is. With five seconds remaining in overtime and everyone in the Hulman Center knowing Maura was getting the ball, she looked baseline, then spun to her left off the dribble and drilled a 12-foot jumper to give the girls program its first basketball title.

Muensterman finished her second year with a 22-point average (third in the state) to go with 7 rebounds and nearly 5 steals per game and a state-leading 8 assists per contest. There are some who expect someone with her skills to record numbers like Pete Maravich, but those who know her best understand that putting up numbers aren't what Maura is all about. "I've had many people comment on how she passes too much," said Terry Muensterman. "There were a lot of games where she would have 20 points at halftime and we're ahead comfortably, and she would get the ball to her teammates."

Head coach Steve Goans totally agrees. "I can't say enough about her," he said. "It amazes me. She's had every defense thrown at her, her uniform torn. She's been called every name in the book, but you would never know it by watching her on the floor. She enjoys making a pass just as much or more than scoring. She could easily average 35 to 37, but she knows she doesn't need to.

"Her basketball knowledge at this level (as a sophomore) is surprising, although her dad has a lot to do with that. She's kind of a gym rat, and he was too. Her game is very advanced for her age. She's quick, and she jumps better than any female I've seen. At times, she's been too unselfish. There were games where she scored 40 and could have had 70. She wants to get other people involved, and that shows a lot of character. That kind of player doesn't come along very often. She's very special."

As fans, it is amazing that with all Muensterman has accomplished, she still has half her career remaining. With her great size and athleticism, one can only imagine what her future may hold. No one knows better than Maura what areas of her game need

Kelly Muensterman left Mater Dei as the school's all-time scoring leader. (Photo courtesy of the Evansville Courier)

improvement, and with her will to succeed, she is a sure bet to enhance her game, a very scary thought for opponents. Her talents have already drawn attention from schools as far away as New Mexico, and she has been contacted by every Big Ten school except Nebraska and others like Indiana State, Butler and U of E.

One day after her amazing finish in the State Finals, it was announced that Maura was nominated as a Gatorade National Player of the Year candidate, and as her career continues, there is no telling how many more honors will come her way. One thing is certain, however, and that is the legacy she will leave when she graduates in 2014.

If the past is any indication, there is much more to be written for the Maura Muensterman story. She is already the youngest player in school history to reach 1,000 points, and she was the undisputed star on Mater Dei's greatest team ever. Maura will never accept mediocrity, and her work ethic and core values as a true team player assure a very bright future.

Although her place in local history won't be cemented for several years, no one can argue that the 15-year-old phenom from Mater Dei may very well become our area's greatest ever as an individual and as a leader on some of the finest basketball teams in local history.

TYRA BUSS: LITTLE SURE SHOT

When word reached me in 2010 about a blonde dynamo from Mt. Carmel named Tyra Buss who was turning the world of local girls basketball on its ear, I just had to expand the *Local Legends* landscape by three miles to include Ms. Buss. After doing research and interviews, I was then able to discover two additional stories *(see Don Liddle on page 53 and Mt. Carmel football on page 17)* from the small town in southeastern Illinois. Although Tyra is a splendid multi-sport athlete, it is on the hardwood where she most excels, and if any young woman deserves to share the nickname 'Little Sure Shot' with Wild West sharpshooter Annie Oakley, it's the 5'7" Tyra Buss.

A self-professed gym rat, Tyra was destined to be an athlete because of the pedigree and environment created by her parents. Tim and Kelly Buss met at the University of Wisconsin-La Crosse, where Tim played basketball and Kelly was a cheerleader. As a high school athlete, Tim earned induction into his school's hall of fame as an All-State player in football, basketball and baseball. Kelly Buss was an All-State track athlete in Wautoma, Wisconsin and has mentored her daughter as Mt. Carmel's track coach.

Tyra's brothers were exceptional athletes also. Oldest brother Tyler was a fullback and linebacker for the Golden Aces teams that reached the 4-A State Finals in 2001 and '02 and currently coaches three sports at Mt. Carmel. Tyra's older brother Kyle was an All-State quarterback and also starred on the basketball court.

So with such athletic genes running through her veins and an atmosphere of athletic success, little Tyra began to develop her skills as a toddler. When asked how early he saw his daughter's potential, Tim Buss never hesitated with his answer. "When she could walk," he said. "The two older boys took her everywhere. If they went to play football, she went with them. I am a firm believer that girls have success when there are older siblings who have been successful."

Another influence on Tyra as a youngster was John Hart, the very successful former coach at Mt. Carmel, Evansville Reitz and Warren Central. Coach Hart is Tyra's godfather and is very close to the Buss family. "When our boys (Nick and Derek) stayed at the Buss's house, Tyra would be downstairs playing basement basketball," Hart recalled. "She came up crying one night and her dad told her, 'Hey, if you're going to be a cry baby, then don't go down there and play!' She learned how to play like a boy without ever knowing that there was any other way of playing."

To verify John Hart's point, when Tyra was young, she passed on playing softball and instead played little league baseball with the boys, where she pitched, played shortstop and was the leadoff hitter. She also followed her brothers into the NFL Pepsi Punt, Pass & Kick competition and set records along the way. She was the national runner-up in the 12-13-year-old division in 2009-'10 and set records for the most state championships (3) and overall score in two different age groups. In 2006, she received the sixth-highest score in the nation, and in 2005, scored in the top four.

As a youngster, Ms. Buss was no stranger to success in other sports as well. In the Elk's Hoop Shoot, a free throw contest for the state of Illinois, Tyra was a four-time state champ and a national finalist in 2010, hitting 25 of 25 to become the regional champion.

When Tyra entered high school in 2010, the school with 600 students and the town of Mt. Carmel, population 8,000, were anxious to see if she could live up to the hype. Her achievements as a young athlete had been well-chronicled by local media, and those close to her knew it wouldn't always be smooth sailing for the gifted freshman to be accepted by teammates and parents.

The first decision made was for Tyra to forgo her AAU basketball season after her eighth grade year to stay with her future high school teammates. Although this would cost Tyra exposure to college coaches, the family felt it was important to allow her to form bonds with older girls in the Mt. Carmel program.

Tyra's approach to the situation was to continue with the same mindset she had learned early on. She focused on the job at hand. She began her freshman year with the cross country and tennis teams, where she finished 43rd out of 168 in the State cross country meet and joined the 18-Minute Club. On the tennis court, Tyra was voted the Southern Illinois Player of the Year and made honorable mention All-State in singles. She was also the sectional champion and finished the season with a 28-2 record.

As a track athlete in the spring, Ms. Buss has excelled for several years. In junior high, she was the 2010 State champion in

the 400 meters, was part of her school's State champion 1600-meter relay team, with teammates Karina Speth, Alex Rosignol and Callie Dunkel, and finished 3rd with the same teammates in the 400-meter relay, setting sectional, conference and school records in every event. A year earlier, Tyra was the State champion in the mile run and State runner-up in the 800. Her first high school season resulted in a 5th place finish in the State in the 300-meter low hurdles and a school record performance in the 800-meter run (2:22.07).

But it is the season between fall and spring where Tyra's talents really shine as she lights up the scoreboard on the basketball court. When I saw her for the first time, her father had shown me to the gym where she was helping her coach with a clinic for younger girls. As she sauntered across the court to meet me, her athleticism was obvious in her movement. Her body, though slim, was toned, and seeing her at 5'6" and 100 pounds, it was easy to imagine how three more years of growth and strength training would make her an even greater threat to opponents.

Tyra had just begun to lift weights, under her mother's supervision, and she also heeded her mom's advice when it came to conditioning. Those who know her have seen the hours she's put in honing her skills, and a testament to that dedication was clear when she broke the record in practice for consecutive free throws made with 138. Her dad also explained how Tyra would end every workout with the same ritual, shooting until she makes one from half-court, the volleyball line and the three-point line followed by a free throw, a right- and left-handed layup and an alley-oop for fun.

Coming into high school, her situation was not easy, being so talented at such a young age, but Ms. Buss has handled it well. Her competitive nature has brought a winning mindset, and in her very first year, the Lady Golden Aces finished 27-5, the best season in school history. When asked how she has done it, Tyra's answer was simple and to the point. "I just love the game," she said as she looked out at the young girls in the clinic. "I have two older brothers, so they taught me a lot of things I needed to know. I'm a hard worker, and I like to be the best I can be."

Tim Buss echoed that philosophy. "Her attitude is that she is going to be the best," he explained, "and to be the best you have to out-work and out-practice everybody. That's the only way she knows. She doesn't ever want to finish second — EVER! She carries that into the classroom too. She's #1 in her class right now, and she wants to be valedictorian."

Tyra's coach, Tim Willis, knows the challenges of a young phenom entering a program with older girls, and he marvels at the way she has performed as a player and teammate. "We had such an outstanding senior class last year (2010-'11)," he said. "They really embraced her and the whole freshman group. That senior class knew she was going to be a big part of what they did.

"The good thing about Tyra is her outstanding personality. She always mentions her teammates in interviews. A lot of people don't give her credit for some of the little things she does. They don't look at her defense and leadership skills, and she is one the most competitive we've ever had."

Coach Willis has also looked on while opponents have plotted strategies to stop Buss. "What haven't they tried," he responded when asked about the tactics. "You see every junk defense out there. She's a good enough talent that when you get the ball in her hands, she can make a play for her or one of her teammates. Her talent is just unbelievable."

Though still very young, Tyra has already drawn interest from major college programs. She has been invited to the camp of Tennessee's legendary coach Pat Summitt and has been approached through her coaches by numerous Division I schools, including every Big Ten school except Nebraska.

As Tyra continues to develop, there will be many more offers and too many highlights to count for the young lady with the smooth shooting stroke and endless energy. Her freshman season was one for the history books, as she amassed 1,025 points, a school record for a season and the fifth best season in Illinois history. If she can avoid serious injury, the state record is in reach. The mark of 4,031 is held by Brittany Johnson from up the road in Olney, who played four years at Ohio State.

Tyra's freshman season also included school records for points in a game (52 against Evansville Reitz) and season records for free throws made (283), three-pointers (96) and steals (137). In 32 games, she also compiled 111 assists (3.5/game) and 121 rebounds (3.8) while setting an Illinois prep scoring record for freshmen.

Her sophomore year was more of the same. On a national level, she was recognized for the second time. As a freshman, she had appeared in the "Faces in the Crowd" section of *Sports Illustrated*, and in 2012, she was honored as the National High School Coaches Association/GTM Sportswear Athlete of the Month for February. Listed an inch taller at 5'7 her sophomore year, Tyra was the only unanimous choice for the Class 2A All-State first team, making the team for the second time, and she became the fastest player in Illinois history to reach 2,000 points (2,146). She broke or re-broke numerous school records, and her two seasons now rank third (1,121 points as a sophomore) and sixth (1,025 as a freshman) on the state's all-time list. Maxpreps.com ranked her as the third highest scorer in the nation, and her 2,146 points make her Mt. Carmel's all-time scoring leader, male or female, eclipsing the previous mark held by IU legend Archie Dees.

And she still has two seasons left!

Much of Tyra's success can be attributed to the dedication and supervision of her parents, and their philosophy has paid dividends

Tyra is also a standout in tennis and track.

for all their children. Tim Buss admits that he and Kelly have put their own interests on hold to help their kids. "I always said that if there's something I could do to help, I'm going to give them whatever they need," he confided. "It's what parents do to make kids successful. We made a pact that we're going to push everything aside for our recreation until our kids are done doing what they do. When they're done, then we'll have our time together."

One thing is certain: that Tim and Kelly Buss's daughter is not done yet. By the time I saw Tyra next, at a game on January 2, 2012 at North's new gym, she had already become Mt. Carmel's career scoring leader. That night, North did their best to slow Tyra down with a "triangle and one with an attack chaser" (according to a *Courier* article), but Tyra and her teammates would have none of it. With great team support, the young Ms. Buss rang up North for 47 points and six three-pointers in a Mt. Carmel victory.

What I saw that night was a ferocious competitor who stroked at least three shots from at least 25 feet and was deft at penetrating and drawing fouls (she went a "disappointing" 21-28 from the line). I also witnessed an athlete whose mental approach seemed well advanced of her years as she never flinched at a referee's call and remained focused.

Most importantly, I saw the impact an athlete of her caliber can have on a program and sport. According to Coach Willis, for the first time in history, the girls program has sold reserve seats for their home games, and another official stated that at least half of the very nice crowd at North's gym was there to see Tyra play.

The road won't be easy for Tyra and her family as she continues to dominate at the high school level, but as a fan, her skills are exhilarating to watch. Although her story is not fully written, her achievements thus far are impressive indeed. It is possible that area fans may be witnessing the most prolific scorer in Illinois and local history, but at the very least, we've seen a dedicated athlete pursuing and attaining benchmarks that very few will ever attain.

IHSAA STATE CHAMPIONS UPDATE
GIRL'S TRACK

Individual	School	Year	Event	Distance/Time
Cassie Wertman	Southridge	2011	discus	143-4
Cassie Wertman	Southridge	2012	shot put	50-1¼
Taylor Wiley	Central	2012	800-meter run	2:11.85

IN THE PRESENCE OF GREATNESS

Ed Claybourne, the long-time coach at Harrison and Central, once coached legendary sprinter Wilma Rudolph.

AMAZING BUT TRUE

When Lauretta Wells went to State in 1977, she and teammate Cassandra Lander each won their events (Lauretta in the long jump and Cassandra in the high jump). Their 20 combined points were good enough to place Bosse second in the team competition, only 14 points behind winner Jeffersonville.

YAMANI HUNTER:
CHASING HISTORY

There is no question that the athletic talent coursing through Yamani Hunter's body comes from a family tree that sports several impressive branches. The most immediate branch is that of Yamani's mother, Jennifer Martin. Jennifer and twin sister Larissa starred at Bosse in the early '90s. Larissa played basketball and track while Jennifer was a four-year starter in basketball and an All-SIAC performer in the shot put.

Yamani's uncle, Mark Wells, was once a heavyweight boxer who was ranked #10 in the world and fought against Greg Page and 'Terrible Tim' Witherspoon. Mark also spent several years traveling with Mike Tyson as a sparring partner, but perhaps the most talented of the family was Yamani's Aunt Lauretta. Lauretta (Wells) Tyler was a two-time State champion in track at Bosse, winning the long jump in 1977 with a jump of 19'0 after losing the same event by half an inch in '76. She also ran the third leg on the winning 4x100 relay team in 1975 with teammates Krista Fentress, Natasha Sutton and Lynnie Williams in a time of 50.4.

To add yet another offshoot of the tree, Lauretta's daughter, Ashleigh Tramill, played hoops and won the track sectional and regional for Bosse in the hurdles. Kennedy Madison, Yamani's cousin, is also in the process of building what could become an outstanding track career at Bosse. In addition, Kennedy's older sister Khryssnee was an excellent track athlete at Bosse and was a leader on the best volleyball team in school history. She is so strong in fact, that she will attend Alabama State in 2012 on a full ride volleyball scholarship.

Yamani, whom I met with her mother and Aunt Lauretta in 2011, was in the middle of her freshman year at Bosse and had already begun to make a name for herself. In volleyball, the 5'6" middle hitter earned second team All-Metro honors, and on the track, she would begin her assault on the record books.

While Yamani learns and grows as an athlete, she will draw from the wealth of resources at her disposal. Her mother worked with her in both sports when she was younger, and both Jennifer and Lauretta are track assistants at Bosse under head coach Cathy Ferris. Yamani first caught the public's eye in a *Courier* article following the 2011 middle school track meet. Her performance was worthy of a story, but what made it special was the record she will begin chasing in 2012.

In the middle school varsity meet, Yamani leaped 17'7, shattering the 16'-8 ½" record set by Dana Perkins in 2006. In the story, Jennifer stated that it was in the fifth or sixth grade when they discovered that Yamani and Kennedy had special talent, so Lauretta came into the picture to offer help. The irony is that the coaching she is providing may contribute to her name being erased from the record books, but she approaches the situation philosophically.

Her 18'-2 ½" city record has stood for 35 years, and her niece was six inches shy of it in the eighth grade. "I'm definitely excited," Lauretta told me. "I've been around track, and I go to the City meet every year and make sure nobody breaks my record. I always said if somebody in my family breaks it, I would like to be the one to put the medal around their neck. It would be an honor, because Yamani is truly a good athlete."

Yamani has proven already to be exceptional. As a youngster, she excelled in gymnastics, winning the state title in the vault while competing for Acros. In the middle school sprints, she finished second in both to Plaza's Brianye Copeland, and on the volleyball court she is a natural.

When asked what college may entail, Jennifer sees potential in both for her daughter. "I can see either/or," she told me. "She (Yamani) will probably tell you volleyball, but I can see people wanting her for either. Yamani is very self-driven. She's always looking for what else she can do to get her where she wants to be."

The youngest of the clan (at present) is Millai Madison, George and Larissa Madison's daughter, and the Lodge fourth grader (in 2012) is reported to have good size and great talent. She is known as 'Little Wilma' to family members, in reference to track icon Wilma Rudolph, and perhaps she will be chasing Yamani's record in a few years.

In 2012, Yamani began what should be a very productive track career as a jumper and as part of a relay team that is a true family affair. At her very first City meet, Yamani teamed with Khryssnee and Madison (and also Jasmine Washington) and ran 4:03.96 to break the 1600-meter relay record set by the Bosse quartet of Asia Brimm, Ayriane Millender, Deatris Cheaney and Latoya Jagoe.

In the 2012 SIAC meet a week later, the same foursome won the conference and Yamani captured the long jump with a leap of 16'-11". The young relay team also qualified for their first State meet, finishing 24th in 4:08.97. As for Yamani, she saved her best jump of the season for last, leaping 17'5 ¾" at State for the 9th place medal.

For now, we will sit and watch as Yamani chases her own piece of history. Her idol is Megan Hodge, the great volleyball player from Penn State, but she also has big plans on the track as well. "I want to win State in the long jump," she informed me, "and I want to go D-1 for college."

Yamani is bright and talented and packed with potential, and if she remains healthy, there are a multitude of honors coming her way. One that will be a joy to watch, should it come to pass, is the day she bends down to accept the medal from Aunt Lauretta, the lady who mentored her niece as she broke one of the longest-lasting records in local track history.

Photo courtesy of the Evansville Courier

PRINCETON'S JACKIE YOUNG: THE SKY'S THE LIMIT

It is fair to say that 35 years ago, circa 1977, girls basketball in our area was in its infancy stage and not very exciting for the die-hard fan. But, oh, how times have changed! The '80s heated up with stars like Shelly Brand and Barb Dykstra from Reitz and Bosse's Cheryl Dowell and the Lander sisters (Vicki and Cassandra). Then the '90s soared with Eileen Weber of Washington Catholic, Washington's Julie Helm, Haley Harris (Wood Memorial) and Stacie Mueller (Harrison), to name a few.

The turn of the century brought even more excitement as the ladies' skills began to approach those of their male counterparts, with the likes of Harrison's Khristian Hart, Castle's Maria Olsthoorn, Leah Phillips and Jasmine Ussery and Bruce Dockery's Memorial stars, Jill Hartman, Kate Endress, FahKara Malone, Mallory Ladd, and Natalie Cohlmeyer, among many others.

But the current crop of stars of the 2010s has taken the evolution to a whole new level. The class of 2014 alone features the phenomenal talents of Tyra Buss of Mt. Carmel and Mater Dei's Maura Muensterman, and Mater Dei's Tori Schickel's dominance as a post player shows great potential for the class of 2015. But perhaps the greatest star on the horizon is a 5'11 point guard from Princeton named Jackie Young, a member of the class of 2016.

Jackie is blessed with incredible natural talent, and she has the bloodlines to justify it. Her mother, Linda, was a good athlete for Princeton, and her older brother, Terrance, was a member of the 2009 undefeated Tigers who brought home a State title. Another member of that team was Jordan Simmons, Jackie's cousin. Still another branch of the family tree features two of the most talented athletes in Princeton history: Justin Lynch, a tremendous football player who also scored 1,381 points on the court, and his brother Travis Trice, who score 1,222.

Jackie's pedigree showed itself early on, according to her middle school coach, Jeffrey Wilkerson. "She started playing at the age of five," he said, "and even at that age, you could tell that she was a special player."

As one might expect, Ms. Young excels in other sports as well, especially softball as a shortstop, and track, where she does the sprints and has high jumped 5'2 as a seventh grader. But it's on the court where her true beauty as an athlete is revealed.

As I pulled into the family's driveway for our interview, a portable basketball goal showed signs of countless hours of use, and on the steps by the door were a pair of basketball shoes, also heavily worn, that symbolized the young lady's love for the game. "She works hard at it," Linda Young revealed when I asked about Jackie's work habits. "She's the last one out of the gym, and if they don't have practice, she'll find a gym to work on her own or she'll shoot in the driveway."

To complement her work ethic, Jackie has been blessed with tremendous physical tools. Her chiropractor has said that she should grow another two inches or so, and by year's end (2012), she should be grabbing the rim. Coach Wilkerson is so high on Jackie's potential that he plans to develop a program over the

This group of Princeton Middle School 8th graders has been undefeated since the 4th grade. First row (L-R): Kaylan Huff, Reghan Jones, Katie Christy, Kiana Hardiman, Lacy Elliott. Back row (L-R): Jeffrey Wilkerson (head coach), Alyssa Muckerheide, Ashleigh Chestnut, Jackie Young, Hannah Brewer, Samantha Hyneman, Caitlin Huff, Kristin King (asst. coach).

summer where a goal will be lowered to allow her to experience various dunks in preparation for the day when he believes she will become the first female Hoosier to dunk in a game.

Though Jackie has sometimes had to adjust her game slightly while her teammates catch up to her skills, her court vision and ability to fire no-look passes have forced those around her to up their games, and the results thus far have been impressive. In fact, she and her classmates have never lost from their fifth grade through eighth grade seasons.

As an eighth grader, Young averaged 27 points, with a high of 55 against Boonville, and although stats are not accurate at the middle school level, Coach Wilkerson is certain that her rebound and assist averages are at least eight per game. On January 19, I sat in the stands myself and found that the hype I had heard was not exaggerated. Jackie jumped center to open the game at Castle North and then took over the game. On the first possession, she sank a silky smooth jumper from twelve feet, followed by a steal and a crossover dribble for a layup. By the end of the half, Jackie had 23 of her team's 29 points, including a 22-footer with perfect form. Her evening was virtually over at the half, as Coach Wilkerson played her only three minutes in the second half of the blowout.

To say that the sky is the limit for Jackie is an understatement, and although there are obstacles to avoid, she seems to have the proper mindset and a solid support group to help her. Coach Wilkerson knows her game as well as anyone and believes her talent can take her as far as she wants to go. "Jackie Young is a winner, and she is the best female basketball player I've ever watched or

coached," he proclaimed. "I've been coaching now for five years (as of 2012), and she has been one of the hardest-working kids I've had the privilege to coach. She's one who leads by example, and she is working on being a verbal leader as well. Her work ethic is going to earn her respect from the upperclassmen. She's already talking about voluntary workouts in the spring."

Ed Saiko, Jackie's coach with the Evansville Basketball Association's Indiana Elite AAU team has watched her progress as she has played up a level and still excelled and has watched other local stars like Mater Dei's Maura Muensterman and the Duncan brothers from Harrison while at the EBA. "She has it all," Coach Saiko said. "She's made herself a good shooter over the last two years. I don't see any holes (in her game). She's the first girl I've seen who could play at (the University of) Tennessee."

When asked to put her game in perspective, Jeffrey Wilkerson explained that he likes to use NBA players as points of reference. "She has the vision of LeBron James and Magic Johnson," he said. "She seems to see the next play coming. She can go left or right, she has a nice post-up game and she's a lockdown defender with the wingspan and quickness she has. And as beautiful as her shot is, she's committing herself to 200 shots a day in the summer to improve. She has goals, and that's something you don't see in young adults. And her work ethic is through the roof."

Needless to say, Jackie's future is bright indeed, and her talent has already caught the eye of colleges around the country. Purdue sent an assistant to watch a game and in February of 2012, offered the eighth grader a full-ride scholarship. Jackie didn't accept and is keeping her options open, and when I asked about others who've shown interest, her brother pulled out a box to show me. In it were letters from Michigan State, Penn State, Dartmouth, Ball State, Xavier and many others. She has dreamed of playing for Coach Pat Summitt at Tennessee and says she hasn't ruled out IU because she loves Indiana basketball. But when pressed about which way she was leaning, Jackie smiled and would not give in to the good-natured pressure and tip her hand.

"You have to be dedicated to get to where you want to be," Jackie said softly as we talked in her living room, and after hearing her story and seeing her gifts in action, I have no doubt about her potential. Thanks to her mother's guidance, her grades are solid, and under the leadership of good coaches, she should stay humble and flourish.

Jackie says that her idols are Candace Parker, the Tennessee and LA Sparks star, and Skyler Diggins, the Notre Dame point guard, and she aspires to one day play in the WNBA. In the meantime, she will continue to work and we will get to watch as she pursues her dreams. She knows where she wants to be, and if she can stay healthy and focused, she has the potential to receive the highest basketball honor our state offers each year. If she stays grounded and continues to work hard, it is my belief that Jackie Young has the potential to be the greatest our area has ever witnessed.

These young people represent the latest generation of impressive athletes from our neck of the woods, and as they mature, another group will soon follow to continue the legacy. So, just as I did in *Local Legends I*, I will end with another optimistic look to the future at another possible Legend in the Making, our grandson Hayden. You never know!

INDEX

AUTOGRAPHS